THE

ASSASSINATION

OF

ABRAHAM LINCOLN,

LATE PRESIDENT OF THE UNITED STATES OF AMERICA,

AND THE

ATTEMPTED ASSASSINATION

OF

WILLIAM H. SEWARD,

SECRETARY OF STATE,

AND

FREDERICK W. SEWARD,

ASSISTANT SECRETARY,

ON THE EVENING OF THE 14TH OF APRIL, 1865.

EXPRESSIONS OF CONDOLENCE AND SYMPATHY INSPIRED BY THESE EVENTS.

KONECKY&KONECKY

Konecky & Konecky
72 Ayers Point Rd.
Old Saybrook, CT 06475

10 digit ISBN: 1-56852-749-7
13 digit ISBN: 978-1-56852-749-9

Printed and bound in China

Note from the Publisher

News of the terrible events of April 14, 1865, quickly spread across the globe and resulting in an unparalleled outpouring of condolences. In the words of the citizens of the French city of Caen: "There are crimes which shock and distress not one nation only, but the conscience of mankind." Hundreds of letters expressing this universal sympathy were directed to American ambassadors and envoys, the United States Congress, the newly inaugurated president, Andrew Johnson, and to the American people.

On March 2, 1867, the U.S. Senate and House of Representatives passed a joint resolution instructing that this correspondence be collected and there be "printed for distribution by the Department of State, on fine paper, with wide margin, a sufficient number of copies to supply one copy to each senator and each representative of the Thirty-ninth Congress and to each foreign government, and one copy to each corporation, association, or public body, whose expressions of condolence or sympathy are published in said volume; one hundred of these copies to be bound in full Turkey morocco, full gilt, and the remaining copies to be bound in half Turkey morocco, marble edged."

The totality of the correspondence that arrived from beyond the borders of the United States is reproduced in this volume for the first time since its original publication. It was considered at the time and remains an extraordinary tribute to the character and achievements of the sixteenth president of the United States, Abraham Lincoln.

※　　※　　※

The publishers would like to thank Joyce and John Raymond whose love of history first brought this book to our attention.

UNITED STATES OF AMERICA.

IN THE SENATE OF THE UNITED STATES,
December 18, 1865.

Whereas the melancholy event of the violent and tragic death of ABRAHAM LINCOLN, late President of the United States, having occurred during the recess of Congress, and the two houses sharing in the general grief, and desiring to manifest their sensibility upon the occasion of the public bereavement: Therefore,

Be it resolved by the Senate, (the House of Representatives concurring,) That the two houses of Congress will assemble in the hall of the House of Representatives on Monday, the 12th day of February next, that being his anniversary birth day, at the hour of 12 meridian; and that in the presence of the two houses then assembled an address upon the life and character of ABRAHAM LINCOLN, late President of the United States, be pronounced by the honorable Edwin M. Stanton, and that the President of the Senate *pro tempore* and the Speaker of the House of Representatives be requested to invite the President of the United States, the heads of the several departments, the judges of the Supreme Court, the representatives of foreign governments near this government, and such officers of the army and navy as have received the thanks of Congress, who may then be at the seat of government, to be present on the occasion.

And be it further resolved, That the President of the United States be requested to transmit a copy of these resolutions to Mrs. Lincoln, and to assure her of the profound sympathy of the two houses of Congress for her deep personal affliction, and of their sincere condolence for the late national bereavement.

Attest: J. W. FORNEY, *Secretary.*

IN THE HOUSE OF REPRESENTATIVES UNITED STATES,
December 18, 1865.

Resolved, That the House concur in the foregoing resolution that the two houses of Congress will assemble in the hall of Representatives on Monday, the 12th day of February next, being the anniversary of the birthday of the late President, to hear an address upon his life and character, and participate in such other commemorative exercises as may be proper on that occasion, recited in said resolution.

Attest: EDWARD McPHERSON, *Clerk.*

EXPRESSIONS OF CONDOLENCE AND SYMPATHY.

Official arrangements at Washington for the funeral solemnities of the late Abraham Lincoln, President of the United States, who died at the seat of government on Saturday, the 15th day of April, 1865.

WAR DEPARTMENT, ADJUTANT GENERAL'S OFFICE,
Washington, April 17, 1865.

The following order of arrangement is directed:

ORDER OF THE PRCESSION.

FUNERAL ESCORT, IN COLUMN OF MARCH.

One Regiment of Cavalry.
Two Batteries of Artillery.
Battalion of Marines.
Two regiments of Infantry.
Commander of Escort and Staff.
Dismounted officers of Marine Corps, Navy, and Army, in the order named.
Mounted Officers of Marine Corps, Navy, and Army, in the order named.
All military officers to be in uniform, with side-arms.

CIVIC PROCESSION.

Marshal.·
Clergy in attendance.
The Surgeon General of the United States army and physicians to the deceased.

PALL-BEARERS.   HEARSE.   PALL-BEARERS.

On the part of the Sénate.	*On the part of the House.*
Mr. FOSTER, of Connecticut.	Mr. DAWES, of Massachusetts.
Mr. MORGAN, of New York.	Mr. COFFROTH, of Pennsylvania.
Mr. JOHNSON, of Maryland.	Mr. SMITH, of Kentucky.
Mr. YATES, of Illinois.	Mr. COLFAX, of Indiana.
Mr. WADE, of Ohio.	Mr. WORTHINGTON, of Nevada.
Mr. CONNESS, of California.	Mr. WASHBURN, of Illinois.

Army.	*Navy.*
Lieutenant General U. S. GRANT.	Vice-Admiral D. G. FARRAGUT
Major General H. W. HALLECK.	Rear-Admiral W. B. SHUBRICK.
Brevet Brigadier General W. A. NICHOLS.	Colonel JACOB ZEILIN, Marine Corps.

Civilians.

O. H. BROWNING.	THOMAS CORWIN.
GEORGE ASHMUN.	SIMON CAMERON.

Family.
Relatives.
The Delegations of the States of Illinois and Kentucky, as mourners.
The President.
The Cabinet Ministers.
The Diplomatic Corps.
Ex-Presidents.
The Chief Justice,
And Associate Justices of the Supreme Court.
The Senate of the United States, preceded by their officers.
Members of the House of Representatives of the United States.
Governors of the several States and Territories.
Legislatures of the several States and Territories.
The Federal Judiciary,
And the Judiciary of the several States and Territories.
The Assistant Secretaries of State, Treasury, War, Navy, Interior, and the
Assistant Postmasters General, and the
Assistant Attorney General.
Officers of the Smithsonian Institution.
The members and officers of the Sanitary and Christian Commissions.
Corporate Authorities of Washington, Georgetown, and other cities.
Delegations of the several States.
The Reverend the Clergy of the various denominations.
The clerks and employés of the several departments and bureaus,
Preceded by the heads of such bureaus and their respective chief clerks.
Such societies as may wish to join the procession.
Citizens and strangers.

The troops designated to form the escort will assemble in the avenue, north of the President's house, and form line precisely at 11 o'clock a. m., on Wednesday, the 19th instant, with the left resting on Fifteenth street. The procession will move precisely at 2 o'clock p. m., on the conclusion of the religious services at the Executive Mansion, (appointed to commence at 12 o'clock, meridian,) when minute guns will be fired by detachments of artillery, stationed at St. John's church, the City Hall, and at the Capitol. At the same hour the bells of the several churches in Washington, Georgetown, and Alexandria will be tolled.

At sunrise on Wednesday, the 19th instant, a federal salute will be fired from the military stations in the vicinity of Washington, minute-guns between the hours of twelve and three o'clock, and a national salute at the setting of the sun.

The usual badge of mourning will be worn on the left arm and on the hilt of the sword.

By order of the Secretary of War:

W. A. NICHOLS,
Assistant Adjutant General.

CORRESPONDENCE

THE ASSASSINATION OF ABRAHAM LINCOLN.

AUSTRIA.

[Translation.]

Count Meysenbug to Mr. Motley.

VIENNA, *April* 28, 1865.

The undersigned has the honor to acknowledge the receipt from the honorable J. Lothrop Motley, envoy extraordinary and minister plenipotentiary of the United States of America, of the esteemed note concerning the frightful act perpetrated against the President, Mr. ABRAHAM LINCOLN, and to state that he at once laid the said note before his most gracious master, the Emperor.

The imperial government could not receive the news of this horrible event without the deepest indignation, which has made upon it the more painful impression as shortly before it had seen reason to instruct its minister at Washington to express to the government there its sincere congratulations upon the brilliant results which promised a speedy end to the bloody contests in the States of the Union.

The horrid crime of which Mr. LINCOLN was the victim could not but inspire the government of his Majesty the Emperor with the more sincere grief as at no time have the relations between Austria and the United States borne a more friendly character than during the official term of Mr. LINCOLN.

The imperial government cannot but cherish the liveliest desire that the hopes of a happy future for the United States, which in this country it was believed might be confidently based on the distinguished characteristics, the wisdom, and moderation of the lamented President, may be fulfilled under his successor, and the peaceful relations between the United States and foreign powers be preserved undisturbed.

In conclusion, the undersigned feels it his duty to give expression to the sincere wish of the imperial government that it may please Providence to preserve to the country still further the eminent Secretary of State, whose life has also been in danger from murderous hands.

The undersigned avails himself of this occasion to renew to the honorable minister the assurance of his distinguished consideration.

In the absence of the minister of foreign affairs, the under secretary of state,

MEYSENBUG.

His Excellency J. LOTHROP MOTLEY,
Envoy Extraordinary and Minister Plenipotentiary

[Translation.]

SESSION OF THE HOUSE OF DEPUTIES.

APRIL 29, 1865.

The session opened at 10.40.

Deputy Dr. BERGER spoke as follows:

GENTLEMEN: The news of the tragical fate which has befallen the President of the United States, ABRAHAM LINCOLN, through a murderous hand, at the very moment in which the cause of the northern States, and with it the cause of freedom and civilization and humanity, was victorious, has—I believe I may announce—deeply moved all circles and all classes of society in our fatherland also.

From the very beginning of that eventful and bloody struggle, which has lasted several years, Austria was always on the side of the North; and on the day on which the news of the last victory of the northern States reached Washington, the man who now stands at the head of the United States declared that the sovereign of the state to which we belong, from the beginning an enemy of every rebellion, had always stood on the side of the North.

I think that it becomes this house, which represents the population of Austria, to express its sympathy for the cause of the northern States, its sympathy for the tragic fate of ABRAHAM LINCOLN, the plain, simple man who has risen out of the people to be placed at the head of the greatest state, and I move that the president should summon the house to signify, by rising from their places, this its double sentiment—sympathy for the tragic fate of President LINCOLN—sympathy for the cause of the northern States.

The PRESIDENT. I doubt not that the house shares the views and feelings which the deputy Berger has expressed, and will be ready to give proper evidence thereof by rising from their seats.

The assembly rises. During this ceremony the ministers are in their places as deputies.

[Translation.]

VIENNA, *April* 27, 1865.

BARON: It is with the deepest indignation that the imperial government has heard the news of the horrible crime which has put an end to the days of President LINCOLN, and also that of the attempted assassination of the Secretary of State, Mr. Seward.

The more the success obtained by the northern States in the bloody strife with the South caused us to experience satisfaction, from seeing therein the security for the early re-establishment of peace over the vast territory of the republic, the more must we deplore this day the tranquil end of the eminent statesman whose energy, combined with wise moderation, has so powerfully contributed to these brilliant results, and caused the hope for his country of a future of peace and prosperity. We love, at any rate, to think that the sad event which has happened will not bring about any change in the conciliatory interests of the American government, and that its enlightened efforts will continue to tend towards an early pacification of countries so long ravaged by civil war, as well as towards the maintenance of friendly relations with foreign powers.

I invite you, baron, to express yourself in these terms to the Secretary of State, by rendering you the eventual interpreter of the wishes we form for the preservation of the life of Mr Seward.

Receive, baron, the assurance of my distinguished consideration.

MEYSENBUG,
The Under Secretary of State, for the Minister of Foreign Affairs
The BARON DE WYDENBRUCK, *Washington*

[Translation]

NEW YORK, *June* 14, 1865.

SIR: I have received by the European mail of yesterday a despatch from my government, dated 18th May, which charges me to express to his Excellency President Johnson the felicitations of my august court on the occasion of his advent to the presidency of the United States.

Finding myself still not in condition, in consequence of the breaking of my arm, to go to Washington to acquit myself of these orders of my court, I take the liberty to send to you, Mr. Secretary of State, the above-mentioned despatch, in the original, begging you to place it before his Excellency the President. Let me be allowed to add, that I participate in the most lively manner in the sentiments of which I am charged by Count de Mensdorff to be the interpreter in respect to yourself, and that I offer the most sincere wishes for the complete restoration of that health so precious in so many respects.

Begging you, Mr. Secretary of State, to return to me, after using it, the aforesaid despatch, I seize this occasion to reiterate to you the assurance of my most distinguished consideration.

WYDENBRUCK.

Hon WILLIAM H. SEWARD, *Secretary of State.*

[Translation.]

VIENNA, *May* 18, 1865.

BARON: I have received the despatches you have done me the honor to address to me up to the 2d instant.

By one of these despatches you transmit a copy of the note of the Acting Secretary of State, Mr. William Hunter, enclosing the official announcements of the tragic events of the 14th April, and of the advent of Mr. Andrew Johnson to the presidency of the United States, as well as the answer you made to that communication.

Having already previously had occasion to request you, baron, to signify to the government of the United States the deep share we have taken in the calamity which has plunged the American people in sorrow, it remains now that I should ask you to express to Mr. Andrew Johnson our felicitations on the occasion of his accession, which we hope will not bring about any change in the relations, so satisfactory, which subsisted between the two countries during the presidency of Mr. LINCOLN.

Please, baron, to say to Mr. Seward, when occasion may offer, how happy we are to hear of the progress of his cure, and accept the assurance of my distinguished consideration.

MENSDORFF.

BARON DE WYDENBRUCK, *Washington.*

[Translation.]

IMPERIAL LEGATION OF AUSTRIA,
Washington, April 18, 1865.

Mr. SECRETARY: I can scarcely find words to express my consternation at the news of the tragic event, the subject of your respected missive of this day, which deprived President LINCOLN of his life.

No one participates more sincerely than I do in lamenting the sad catastrophe that has filled the American nation with mourning; for, though but recently arrived in this country, I had learned to appreciate the rare and eminent qualities of him whose loss we deplore this day.

It is my painful duty to announce the sad news to my august court. It will certainly be received with a feeling of affliction; and I think I may add that the entire Austrian nation will sympathize deeply with the American people in their distress for the great calamity that has overwhelmed them.

The abominable attempt upon the lives of the Secretary of State and his son has also filled me with horror. I thank Heaven the crime was not accomplished; and I sincerely desire the speedy and perfect recovery of the intended victims.

I will also hasten to inform my august court of the inauguration of Mr. Andrew Johnson as President of the United States.

Have the kindness to accept the expression of my most distinguished consideration.

WYDENBRUCK.

Hon. WILLIAM HUNTER,
Acting Secretary of State.

[Translation.]

BIELITZ, AUSTRIA, *April* 29, 1865.

Mr. PRESIDENT: We, the undersigned, members of associations of the several branches of commerce and industry in the contiguous cities of Bielitz and Biala, in the interior of the Austrian dominions, who have always followed with the liveliest interest and the sincerest sympathy all the events that affected the country and the people of the United States, take the liberty to beg of you, Mr. President, to receive the expression of our most heartfelt sympathy for the terrible loss the Union has sustained in the death of President LINCOLN. Amidst our rejoicings over the triumph of the Union we received the intelligence of this great calamity.

Sorrow and deep affliction followed our exultation, and the deepest abhorrence for the terrible crimes to which this great and wise man fell a sacrifice, and which brought his faithful co-laborer in the difficult undertaking, the Secretary of State, Mr. Seward, to the brink of the grave, fills every heart.

With terrible violence the noble leader was deprived of the happiness to enjoy with his self-sacrificing and devoted people, after the most tremendous struggle, the fruits of a long-hoped-for peace.

May the final complete victory of the good cause, and the great work of re-establishing the Union to its former greatness, be reserved for you, Mr. President.

That reverence for law and justice, as well as love for liberty, which the people of the United States have ever manifested during this great war, will support you.

With feelings of the inmost sympathy we beg to assure you of our most distinguished consideration.

LUDWIG BRÜLL, and 26 others.

Hon. ANDREW JOHNSON,
    President United States, North America.

Mr. Motley to Mr. Seward.

No 101.]   LEGATION OF THE UNITED STATES,
Vienna, April 30, 1865.

SIR: The news of the great tragedy which has brought desolation upon our country, in the very moment of our highest joy, reached this place on the 26th. This is the first post which leaves Vienna since the receipt of the intelligence.

I shall not even attempt to picture the consternation which the event has caused throughout the civilized world, nor to describe the anguish which it has excited in my own heart, as in that of every loyal American, whether at home or abroad.

The European public spontaneously expresses in every public way its admiration for the character of the murdered President, and its horror at the vile assassin who has taken his life. And if the inhabitants of foreign and distant lands are giving expressions to such deep and unaffected sentiments, what must be the emotions now sweeping over our own country? I confess that I shudder at the thought of the despatches and journals now on their way to Europe. As yet we have nothing but the brief telegraphic tale of horror published by the Secretary of War to Mr. Adams, in London, and by him transmitted to the United States legations on the continent.

Not often in human history has a great nation been subjected to such a sudden conflict of passions.

In the midst, not of triumph nor vulgar exultation, but of deep, religious, grateful joy at the final suppression of a wicked rebellion, the redemption of the land from the perils of death and the certainty of its purification from the great curse of slavery, blessings brought about under God by the genius of our great generals, the courage of our armies, and the sagacity of our statesmen, the American people have seen their beloved and venerated Chief Magistrate murdered before their eyes.

The eminent statesman who with such surpassing ability has guided our foreign relations during the most critical and dangerous period of our history seems, thank God, to have escaped death—if we may trust the more recent telegrams received last night; but we must await with intense anxiety the arrival of more than one post before we can feel confidence that the cowardly and murderous assault upon him in his sick-bed has not, after all, been successful. May God grant that his invaluable life may be spared, and that the country may long have the benefit of his wise and faithful counsels May the life of that excellent son, who has so nearly perished in the attempt to defend his father, also be preserved.

What may be the effect of this sudden revulsion in the national feeling I hardly dare to contemplate.

The benignant heart of the late President was filled, as we have reason to believe, with thoughts of peace and reconciliation and reunion—with feelings of compassion for the criminals, mingled with detestation of the crime, becoming the chief of a great, free, and magnanimous nation in the hour of its victory—when the assassin took his life. And the country itself, conscious of its strength, seemed fully to respond to these sentiments of the President.

Will not these gentler feelings give way to a desire for vengeance, to a conviction of the necessity of terrible severity, now that the great treason has just accomplished its darkest crime, now that the most illustrious of all the innumerable victims of the slaveholders' rebellion has been so basely and wantonly sacrificed?

I should apologize for giving expression to these thoughts, not suitable to a formal despatch; but in such days as these, and in the midst of such a national sorrow, it is difficult to be formal and impossible to be calm.

Nor can I resist the impulse to add my humble contribution to the universal eulogy which I know is pouring forth at this moment from so many more eloquent tongues than mine, and out of many millions of sorrowing and affectionate hearts, now that the most virtuous of chief magistrates is no more.

I know that one should avoid the language of exaggeration, of over-excited enthusiasm, so natural when a man eminent in station, mental abilities, and lofty characteristics is suddenly taken away; yet I am not afraid to express the opinion that the name of ABRAHAM LINCOLN will be cherished, so long as we have a history, as one of the wisest, purest, and noblest magistrates, as one of the greatest benefactors to the human race, that have ever lived.

I believe that the foundation of his whole character was a devotion to duty. To borrow a phrase from his brief and simple but most eloquent inaugural address of this year, it was "his firmness in the right as God gave him to see the right" which enabled him to discharge the functions of his great office, in one of the most terrible periods of the world's history, with such rare sagacity, patience, cheerfulness, and courage. And God, indeed, gave him to see the right, and he needs no nobler epitaph than those simple words from his own lips.

So much firmness with such gentleness of heart, so much logical acuteness with such almost childlike simplicity and ingenuousness of nature, so much candor to weigh the wisdom of others, with so much tenacity to retain his own judgment, were rarely before united in one individual.

Never was such vast political power placed in purer hands; never did a heart remain more humble and more unsophisticated after the highest prizes of earthly ambition had been obtained.

Certainly "government of the people, by the people, for the people"—to quote again his own words—shall never perish from the earth so long as the American people can embody itself in a character so worthy to represent the best qualities of humanity—its courage, generosity, patience, sagacity, and integrity—as these have been personified in him who has been one of the best of rulers, and is now one of the noblest of martyrs.

If it seems superfluous and almost presumptuous that I, a comparative stranger to Mr. LINCOLN, although honored with his commission, should speak of him thus at length to those who shared his counsels and enjoyed his intimacy, I can only reply that the grief which, in common with every loyal American, I most profoundly feel at his death, demands an expression, and that at this distance from my country it is a consolation for me to speak of his virtues to those who knew him best.

I have followed his career, and have studied every public act and utterance of his with an ever-increasing veneration for a character and an intellect which seemed to expand and to grow more vigorous the greater the demand that was made upon their strength.

And this feeling, I believe, is shared not only by all Americans worthy of the name, but by all the inhabitants of foreign lands who have given themselves the trouble to study our history in this its most eventful period.

I wish to conclude this despatch by requesting you to convey my most respectful compliments to President Johnson, together with my prayers for his success in administering the affairs of his great office.

That he is animated with the warmest patriotism, and by a determination to meet wisely and manfully the great responsibility which has devolved upon him, we are all convinced, and I am sure that the best wishes of every patriotic heart and the counsels of the wisest minds will be ever ready to support him in the great task of reconstructing that blessed Union which traitor hands have failed, with all their efforts, to destroy.

I have the honor to remain, respectfully, your obedient servant,

J. LOTHROP MOTLEY.

Hon. WILLIAM H. SEWARD,
          Secretary of State, Washington.

Mr. Motley to Mr. Seward.

No. 102.]   LEGATION OF THE UNITED STATES,
                                   Vienna, April 30, 1865.

SIR: The impression created in this capital by the horrible murder and attempts to murder just committed in Washington has been intense.

The whole diplomatic corps, with scarcely an exception, have called upon me as representative of the United States, and their warm and sincere expressions of sympathy at our national loss, of cordial good-will for the Union, and, more important than all, of decided respect and admiration for the character of our lamented President, have been most grateful to my heart.

The journals of the capital—all of them, as I have often had occasion to remark, conducted with great ability—have vied with each other in eloquent tributes to the virtues of Mr. LINCOLN, in expressions of unaffected sympathy for the great cause of which he was the impersonation, and of horror at the accursed crime by which one of the best of men has been taken from the world.

  *   *   *   ·   *   *   *   *

I send a translation of the report taken from the journals of the day of the action taken on the subject in the Reichsrath.

Dr. Berger, the member who pronounced the brief but feeling eulogy upon Mr. LINCOLN, is one of the most distinguished and eloquent members of the house.

I have the honor to remain, sir, your obedient servant,
                                   J. LOTHROP MOTLEY.

Hon. WILLIAM H. SEWARD,
       Secretary of State.

ARGENTINE REPUBLIC.

[Translation.]

MINISTRY OF FOREIGN AFFAIRS,
       Buenos Ayres, May 27, 1865.

SIR: I have the honor to enclose your excellency a copy of the resolutions issued by the government, ordering all flags of the republic to be put at half-mast, as sign of mourning for the death of the illustrious citizen President of the United States of America.

The Argentine government laments with the most profound sorrow the irreparable loss that deprives the United States of their noble President, ABRAHAM LINCOLN, whose persevering efforts were just being crowned by victory in favor of the cause of the Union.

In communicating this resolution to your excellency, I take pleasure in offering my most distinguished regards.

RUFINO DE ELIZALDE,
Minister of Foreign Affairs.

Hon. ROBERT C. KIRK,
  Minister Resident of the United States of America.

[Translation.]

DEPARTMENT OF THE INTERIOR,
Buenos Ayres, May 27, 1865.

Resolved: The illustrious President of the United States of America, ABRAHAM LINCOLN, having been assassinated just as the cause so nobly sustained by the American people was being crowned by the most splendid triumph, the Argentine government and people, sorrow-stricken by the loss that deprives that great republic of the distinguished and important services of so illustrious a citizen, resolve, that in testimony of their deep regret for so irreparable a loss, the offices and other public establishments on which the national flag flies, as also the national vessels of war in port, keep, during the day of to-morrow, the 28th instant, their respective flags at half-mast. The present resolution to be communicated to whom it may concern for its accomplishment.

WILLIAM RAWSON.
RUFINO DE ELIZALDE.
LUCAS GONZALES.
EDWARD COSTA
JOHN A GELLY Y OBES.

A correct copy:
  EDWARD T. BARBAL.

[Translation.]

LEGISLATIVE CONGRESS OF THE ARGENTINE NATION,
Buenos Ayres, June 3, 1865.

Marcos Paz, president of the Congress of the Argentine nation, to the president of the Congress of the United States of America, greeting:

Conscious of the loss that liberty and democracy have suffered by the death of ABRAHAM LINCOLN, the great republican, the Argentine congress joins the people of the United States in their mourning, by a resolution that its members shall wear mourning for three days, as you will see by the accompanying authentic copy of the resolution, which you will please transmit to the Congress of the Union.

MARCOS PAZ

Hon. PRESIDENT *of the Congress of the United States of America.*

[Translation.]

The senate and chamber of deputies of the Argentine nation, in general assembly convened, resolve:

ARTICLE 1. The senators and deputies of the Argentine people shall wear mourning for ABRAHAM LINCOLN for three days after the adoption of this resolution.

ART. 2. The national banner shall remain at half-mast over the house of sessions for the three days.

ART. 3. The president of the Argentine congress shall address a letter of condolence, with a copy of this resolution, to the president of the Congress of the United States.

ART. 4. Let this be promulgated, &c.

Given in the hall of congress, in Buenos Ayres, on the second day of June, the year of our Lord one thousand eight hundred and sixty-five.

JOSÉ E. URIBURU.
MARCOS PAZ.
CARLOS MARIA SARAVIA,
Secretary of the Senate.

BERNABÉ QUINTANA,
Secretary of the House of Deputies.

A true copy:
[L. S.]

BERNABÉ QUINTANA,
Secretary of the House of Deputies.

CARLOS MARIA SARAVIA,
Secretary of the Senate.

[Translation.]

BUENOS AYRES, May 28, 1865.

SIR: The assassination of the illustrious republican, ABRAHAM LINCOLN, President of the United States, has caused in Buenos Ayres the most profound regret.

The governor of this province, the same as all his countrymen, moved by this execrable crime, sympathizes most heartily with your excellency for the misfortune that casts into mourning that joy caused by the recent victories obtained, that would secure the union and liberty of the great republic you so nobly represent.

May it please your excellency to accept the sympathy of this province, and the respect that I have always had for the eminent citizen that the country of your excellency has just lost.

I salute your excellency with most distinguished esteem.

MARIANO SAAVEDRA,
Governor of the Province of Buenos Ayres.

His Excellency Hon. ROBERT C. KIRK,
    Minister Resident of the United States of America.

Mr. Kirk to Mr. Seward.

[Extract.]

No. 115.]   LEGATION OF THE UNITED STATES,
Buenos Ayres, May 30, 1865.

SIR : The awful report of the assassination of President LINCOLN and the attempted assassination of yourself reached here on the 27th instant. I will not attempt to describe the intense excitement, indignation, and heartfelt sorrow it has produced throughout this part of South America. During Saturday and Sunday I had continual calls from ministers and citizens giving expression to words of condolence. On the same day the news arrived here I received a letter from the minister for foreign affairs, with a resolution passed by his government.   *   *   *   *   *   *

Agreeably to that resolution, on Sunday the national and provincial flags were at half-mast, and the flags of foreign consuls followed the example.

All the newspapers of this city appeared in mourning.   *   *   * The native press is filled with glowing editorials on President LINCOLN.

It has never been my lot to witness such intense sorrow as this sad event has produced, and the universal prayer is that you may speedily be restored to health. The same mail which brought the sad news brought the news of the surrender of Lee's army.

The provincial legislature has passed a decree authorizing the next town started in this province to be named "Lincoln."

Hoping sincerely that you may soon recover from your injuries, I am, sir, your obedient servant,

ROBERT C. KIRK.

Hon. WILLIAM H. SEWARD,
    Secretary of State.

SPANISH DEMOCRATIC COMMITTEE OF BUENOS AYRES.

[Translation.]

BUENOS AYRES, *June* 4, 1865.

The Spanish democratic committee in this city would fail in one of its most sacred duties did it not manifest to the superior government of the United States, which you represent, the sad impression caused by the news of the assassination of the illustrious citizen President, ABRAHAM LINCOLN, the minister of foreign affairs, Mr. Seward, and all the other victims of that drama of murder and consternation.

The committee earnestly wishes that the tomb of those great men may inspire their successors with fortitude and firmness, so that along with the triumph of the United States of America, republican principles may triumph wherever the want of liberty is felt.

Please, then, citizen minister, to lay this manifestation before the superior government of the United States, which you so worthily represent near this republic, and rely on the assurances of the most distinguished consideration and respect of the committee.

By order of the committee:

THE DIRECTOR.

Mr. Tomas Guido to Mr. Kirk.

[Translation.]

BUENOS AYRES, *May* 30, 1865.

DEAR SIR: I do not fear to renew your sorrow by uniting mine to the unutterable grief that the American people and all friends of liberty feel at the sight of ABRAHAM LINCOLN'S grave.

That great republican, torn from his country, family, and friends at a time when his sacred patriotism had gained its end, has sealed his work with his blood. That blood, though a stain on his murderer's hand, will cherish yet the seed of liberty in all generations.

Peace to the memory of that great and just man, worthy brother of Washington, with whom he is now in a better world to come.

You, dear sir, who so honorably represent your country, let it mitigate your sorrow to find sympathy among Argentines for this great misfortune, and I as one of them feel most deeply affected.

I am your most obedient servant,

TOMAS GUIDO·

ROBERT C. KIRK, Esq.,
United States Minister Resident.

Resolutions adopted at a meeting of American citizens resident in Buenos Ayres,
held May 31, 1865.

Whereas the sad tidings have reached us of the death of ABRAHAM LINCOLN, President of the United States, by the hand of a vile assassin—

Resolved, First, that as loyal and ever faithful citizens of the United States of America, now resident in Buenos Ayres, we have been severely shocked, and at the same time filled with indignation and sorrow, on the receipt here, on Saturday last, the 27th instant, of intelligence of the dastardly murder of the late eminently distinguished President of our country, ABRAHAM LINCOLN, in whom we have always recognized inflexible honesty and pure patriotism, and to whom we now assign in our memories a place among the very ablest and best statesmen of America.

Resolved, Second, that to the grief-stricken family of the illustrious deceased we tender our most unfeigned and profound condolence.

Resolved, Third, that in celebration of the obsequies of our late beloved President, ABRAHAM LINCOLN, whom we would proclaim and consecrate to posterity as the second Father of his Country, the Reverend William Goodfellow, the American clergyman resident in this city, be invited to deliver, at an early day, an appropriate discourse, commemorative of the distinguised virtues of the deceased.

Resolved, Fourth, that as a measure emblematic of our sincere distress at this most deplorable occurrence, we will wear a badge of black crape around the left arm for the space of thirty days.

Resolved, Fifth, that we gratefully accept, as a compliment to our country and to ourselves, the voluntary and considerate action of the authorities here on Sunday last, the 28th instant, in causing all the national and provincial flags to be hoisted at half-mast, as a token of grief at the untimely loss of the honored and lamented subject of these resolutions. And we feel thankful that amid the unparalleled trials of the most gigantic rebellion ever organized among rational and misguided men, our leaders and defenders have acted with such moderation and justice as to secure the sympathies of such enlightened and progressive statesmen as those whom we have the honor to know in the persons of President Mitre and his cabinet.

Resolved, Sixth, that Governor Saavedra and the legislature of the province of Buenos Ayres are equally entitled to our thanks for their complimentary resolutions of last evening, declaring that the next new town or city which shall be organized within the province shall be designated "Lincoln."

Resolved, Seventh, that in a corresponding vein of thankfulness and gratitude, we make our acknowledgments to the press of Buenos Ayres for appearing in mourning on Sunday last, and for their numerous and well-expressed eulogiums of our own martyred President, and also to the whole body of the Argentine congress, for their sympathetic resolutions of yesterday, among which was one to signify their sad and painful recognition of this solemn occasion by wearing the badge of mourning for the space of three days; and to the Argentine people, whose sympathies with us have been so unreservedly shown during the long and severe trials of our country, and particularly in this last and saddest event.

Resolved, Eighth, that to our fellow-citizens in the United States we renew our pledge of continued and unfaltering fidelity to the Union and to the federal government as constitutionally organized in Washington.

Resolved, Ninth, that four copies of these resolutions be presented to our minister resident in this city, the honorable Robert C. Kirk, with the request that he will transmit one of them to the bereaved family of our late President, one to the Department of State in Washington, one to the government in the Argentine republic, and the other to the government of the province of Buenos Ayres.

Also resolved, That in the attempted assassination of William Henry Seward, Secretary of State, part of the same dastardly conspiracy which resulted in the death of ABRAHAM LINCOLN, we recognize the fitting close of a rebellion begun in robbery and perjury, and ending in cowardly and cold-blooded murder, and we extend to him our warmest sympathies, and offer at the same time our best hopes and wishes for his speedy recovery.

ROBERT C. KIRK, Chairman.

GARDNER B. PERRY, *Secretary*

BELGIUM.

[Translation.]

BRUSSELS, April 29, 1865.

MY DEAR MINISTER: While I transmit to Washington the expression of the sentiments of the government of the King, on account of the horrid crime perpetrated upon your venerable President, I must inform you of our astonishment at the sad news that has resounded through the entire country, and beg you to be the medium of our sentiments to your government.

I also take the liberty of asking you to have the kindness to be my interpreter with the family of Mr. Seward, for whom I have always professed a particular regard. The news given by the papers leave some hope for the recovery of the eminent statesman, and it is my dearest wish that he may be restored to perfect health, and give peace to a country so long desolated by the calamities of a war greatly to be deplored by all friends of liberty.

Accept, my dear minister, the new assurance of my very high and affectionate consideration.

CH. ROGIER,
Minister of Foreign Affairs.

H. S. SANFORD, Esq.,
Minister of the United States.

[Translation.]

LEGATION OF BELGIUM TO THE UNITED STATES,
Washington, April 16, 1865.

Mr. SECRETARY: It is with real grief that I have the honor of acknowledging the reception of your communication of the 15th, announcing the horrid crime that has deprived the United States of its Chief Magistrate.

The government of the King, my august sovereign, will sympathize sincerely with the American nation.

The sentiments of respect and affection which I personally entertain for the honorable Secretary of State and Mr. Frederick Seward, induce me to hope their injuries will have no serious consequences.

Wishing them a speedy recovery, I beg you, Mr. Secretary, to accept the assurance of my most distinguished consideration.

A. BERGHMANS.

Hon. WILLIAM HUNTER,
Acting Secretary of State.

[Translation.]

MOTION IN ORDER.

Mr. LE HARDY DE BEAULIEU. Gentlemen, you were all horrified three days ago on hearing of the assassination of the President of the United States. You all felt that it was not only the chief of a free nation that was struck down, but at the same time it was law, the safeguard of all, and I may say civilization itself, for there is no longer any personal security when political passion substitutes brutal action for the protective power of law. I have thought it becoming, gentlemen, for us not to let this occasion pass without the expression of our painful sentiments.

I will not give you the history of the eminent man who is no more; he sprung from the humblest ranks of society, and elevated himself by labor and industry; when the American nation, with that acumen that rarely fails an intelligent people in important emergencies, chose him as a guide to direct it through a dangerous situation, where a formidable insurrection had placed it.

You all know, gentlemen, what difficulties Mr. LINCOLN had to overcome. Confronted by a portion of the nation that rebelled against the laws they themselves had made, he did not falter once in his patriotic duty. In the most perilous circumstances, in face of all kinds of dangers, external and internal, he was always calm, and, I may even say, benevolent to his bitterest enemies.

After gigantic efforts, after a struggle of four years, Mr. LINCOLN at last reached the close of that most bloody contest on American soil, and the greatest troubles of his life seemed over. He had already expressed the sentiments of conciliation that animated him—it was in his last message, his political testament—when the assassin's bullet struck him in the back of the head, and laid him low.

I cannot foretell the consequences of that crime, so horrid that no terms are strong enough to condemn it; all I can say is, that the parliament of a free nation like Belgium would fail in its duties of international confraternity, if it did not express its feelings of horror and regret at a crime that has robbed a great and generous nation of its eminent Chief Magistrate.

In expressing these sentiments we confirm the unanimous wishes that the deplorable loss may not deprive the American nation of that calmness which is necessary to finish the great work of conciliation and pacification which Mr. LINCOLN has so nobly begun. I am done.

Mr. DE HAERNE. I agree with my honorable colleague in the sentiments he has expressed, and I am persuaded that the feeling of horror produced by this sad news from America is felt not only in this house, but in every quarter of the globe. Yes, gentlemen, we feel the greatest indignation at this political crime that has plunged a great people in the deepest mourning, but has not discouraged it, we must hope; for the great President who was the victim of the barbarous and cowardly act has set an example which his successors should follow, for the good of the nation they represent and the enlightenment of a free people.

The dreadful catastrophe that has thrown America into the greatest consternation, and has appalled the world, contains a great lesson for the people, particularly when contrasted with the victories that had rejoiced the American Union only a few days before.

On Palm Sunday the news of General Lee's capitulation was announced in most of the cities of the United States—on that day, consecrated to the Prince of Peace, as an American paper expresses it; and on Good Friday, Mr. LINCOLN and Mr. Seward were attacked by barbarous assassins. And this recalls a profound remark of the august and holy pontiff Pius IX, who, speaking of the many vicissitudes of his reign, said, "Truly Good Friday is very near to Palm Sunday!"

The people of the Union, who were identified with their chief, particularly after the last presidential election, were morally immolated with him, after enjoying the national triumph, to which Mr. LINCOLN added glory by his moderation.

The nation is plunged in grief; but hope will resurrect her from the gloom, like the Prince of Peace and Glory. This grand and terrible lesson of misfortune to the people and their government will prove a valuable instruction by the spirit of conciliation bequeathed them by their worthy President, as a mysterious pledge of future prosperity, the secret of which is hidden in their past glory.

If there is a nation that ought to sympathize with America in its grief on this occasion, that nation is Belgium; for we are the only nation that has remained faithful in spirit to traditional rights, and followed America from the foundation of her political establishment and her liberal institutions. Yes, gentlemen, we looked upon England, on the one hand, as worthy of imitation in the march of progress in the path of true and practical liberty; but, at the same time, we were conscious that there were certain customs in the institutions of that country we could not adopt, and we cast our eyes beyond the Atlantic, where we found a great people worthy of entire imitation, and it is the institutions of that people we have chiefly inscribed upon our organic charter. We have followed their example in all that regards public liberty, the distribution of power, the election of representatives and decentralization of rule. For that reason, I say that Belgium ought to sympathize with America by expressions of horror and indignation, such as all civilized nations feel, and protest against the act of barbarism that has stained the soil of America with the last mournful trace of expiring slavery, which has now vanished before the vivifying breath of modern civilization.

The sentiments manifested in this house are felt throughout all Europe. England has protested through Parliament; France has spoken by the mouth of her Emperor; Prussia by her legislative assembly, where all the members arose to declare that the infamy of the horrid act deserved the condemnation of all civilized nations. We must also do homage to the man who was the victim of that atrocious crime, to the man who, as the honorable Mr. De Beaulieu has truly said, sprung from the people to adorn a nation, and like certain popes, come from the lowest ranks of society to be the greatest honor to the church.

LINCOLN was a self-made man; he drank from the spring of liberty; he was guided by the light of a democratic nation, and merit elevated him to the highest dignities of the country.

He has set a worthy example, which his successor ought to follow, relying on the support of public opinion, which should be his constant guide, never to be abandoned or opposed.

That, gentlemen, should be his greatest honor, which, united with his firmness and wise impartiality, will mark him a place in history.

In joining other civilized nations in our protest against this political crime, we do a good deed ; by our participation in the sentiment of universal indignation, we help to arrest the contagion of an abominable example that might attack other nations.

By outlawing monsters guilty of such crimes, we terrify those who might be tempted to commit them.

Mr. ROGIER, minister of foreign affairs. It is useless for me to say, gentlemen, that the government participates in the sentiments so eloquently expressed by the two honorable members of this assembly entertaining different political opinions. Our government sympathizes with the bereaved nation, and has transmitted the expression of its sorrow to the government of the United States and their honorable representative in Brussels.

The motion just made is new to Belgium ; but it has been made elsewhere, and the importance of the event justifies it. I consider the sympathy expressed in the speeches of the honorable Mr. De Beaulieu and Mr. l'Abbe De Hearne as the unanimous opinion of the house ; and thus the legislative assembly joins the government in the regrets felt and expressed on the occasion of a crime that has filled Belgium and the rest of the world with dismay.

We must also express our wishes for the recovery of the eminent statesman who was attacked at the same time with the venerable President of the republic. His life must be preserved to insure the final pacification of a splendid country, too long desolated by the calamities of a war afflicting to all friends of true liberty.

May that great statesman, now burdened with a heavy duty, persevere in the sentiments of moderation he has always shown through the excitement of the great struggle, and may we soon hear of the restoration of his health, and the return of peace between the factions of a great people whom we admire, who have always had our sympathies, and who will soon resume their exalted station in the world.

THE PRESIDENT OF THE HOUSE. Gentlemen, as no objection is offered, it is now decided that this house is unanimous in its approval of the sentiments just expressed by the two honorable members whose speeches you have just heard.

[Translation.]

(Note from the Moniteur of the 30th April, 1865.)

The King ordered one of his aides-de-camp to go to Mr. Sanford's and express to him the sorrow his Majesty felt at the news of the attacks on the President and Secretary of State of the United States of America.

His highness the Count of Flanders also sent one of his aids to the minister, on the same mission.

The minister of foreign affairs and other members of the cabinet, on their part, hastened to call on Mr. Sanford, and instructions were sent to the Belgian legation in Washington to express to the American government the sentiments of regret and condemnation excited by such odious acts.

In the house, session of yesterday, Mr. Hardy De Beaulieu spoke in the most moving terms of the emotions produced in Belgium by the news of the tragic event which has just occurred in the United States. He called general attention to all the eminent virtues of President LINCOLN.

Mr. De Haerne joined Mr. De Beaulieu in a eulogy of much beauty upon the character of the late lamented President.

The minister of foreign affairs added, that the government sympathized sincerely in the sentiments just expressed by the honorable members, and that he had already despatched a communication of that effect to the government of the United States, and to their honorable representative in Brussels. He expressed the most fervent wishes for the recovery of the distinguished statesman, Mr. Seward, whose life was necessary to the final pacification of a country that had been so long ravaged by the desolation of war, and the prosperity of which was greatly desired by all friends of liberty.

Mr. Sanford to Mr. Seward.

No. 257.]   LEGATION OF THE UNITED STATES,
                                           Brussels, April 28, 1865.

SIR: The tragic tidings from Washington of the assassination of the President and murderous assault upon the Secretary of State has caused a deep impression here of horror and indignation at the cowardice and cruelty of the confederate plotters.

Following so rapidly upon the excitement created by our late victories, and the public demonstrations on account of them, the announcement has aroused unusual agitation in this city and through the country. The King from his sick-bed sent to me one of his aides-de-camp, Major General Bormann, to express in his name his deep feeling at this tragic event, and for the great loss we have sustained.

The minister of foreign affairs and the other members of the cabinet, the president of the house of representatives, the high dignitaries of the court, and most of the foreign legations, and a very large number of persons of every rank and station, have come personally to offer their condolence and to express their horror at this crowning atrocity of the rebellion.

M. Rogier informed me he had sent a despatch to the Belgian chargé d'affaires at Washington, to offer directly to the government the expression of their sympathy at the sad event.

Immediately on receipt of Mr. Adams's telegram, I addressed a circular to our consuls.

The shock caused by this news is too great to permit me to appreciate calmly its influence on public sentiment touching our affairs abroad. It cannot fail, I think, to cause a far-reaching reaction in the sympathies heretofore entertained by the so-called "better classes" in Europe for the rebels and their cause, and to stimulate, on the other hand, a more friendly feeling toward us and the cause of the Union.

The fact that the confederate loan at the London exchange yesterday rose three per cent. upon the news, is a significant indication of the effect which the instigators of this dreadful crime imagined it would have upon their cause.

The calm transition of the executive power to other hands, at Washington, contrasted with what would be likely to occur on a similar occasion in most European states, cannot but help to strengthen the conviction, already becoming general by the influence of the success which has crowned this trial, under the strain of the rebellion, of the power, fitness, and durability of our system of government.

I have the honor to be, with great respect, your most obedient servant,

H. S. SANFORD.

Hon. WILLIAM H. SEWARD,
Secretary of State.

Mr. Sanford to Mr. Seward.

[Extract.]

No. 261.] LEGATION OF THE UNITED STATES,
Brussels, April 30, 1865.

SIR: His royal highness the Count de Flanders sent to me yesterday one of his officers of "ordnance" to express in his name his condolence on the untimely death of the President.

I also received in the afternoon a private note from M. Rogier, expressive of his sentiments, of which, as he refers to it in public debate, I venture to enclose a copy, "A." I replied to it by a few lines of thanks.

In the house of representatives this afternoon, M. Hardy De Beaulieu, a member of the extreme left, moved, in accordance with previous notice, for an expression of feeling at the late tragic events at Washington. He was followed and warmly seconded by the late Canon De Hearne, of the "conservative" party, who is the author of a widely disseminated pamphlet on our war, and is an ardent friend of the cause of the Union, and by M. Rogier, who announced that he adopted on the part of the government the views just expressed, and that he hoped the house would join in the expression of his desire for the recovery of the eminent statesman, Mr. Seward, to whose existence was attached, in so great a degree, the definitive pacification of the country, for too long a time desolated by war; and after rendering homage to the moderation which he had displayed, the minister expressed the hope "that they might one day rejoice over the restoration of his health, at the same time with the re-establishment of peace between the factions of a great people whom they admired, and which has always had their sympathies, and which he hoped would take again in the world the great part which is assigned to it."

All which, interrupted by frequent marks of approval by the members, was declared by the president to be the unanimous sentiment of the house.

*　　*　　*　　*　　*　　*　　*　　*　　*　　*

I have the honor to be, with great respect, your most obedient servant,

H. S. SANFORD.

Hon. William H. Seward,
　　Secretary of State, &c., &c., &c.

[Translation.]

Ghent, *May* 20, 1865.

Mr. Minister: The Septentrion Masonic Lodge of Ghent could not remain indifferent in presence of the crime which has spread consternation through the civilized world.   During the strife, our sympathies and our prayers accompanied the heroic efforts and unshakable perseverance of the defenders of justice and humanity.   We are associated with the triumphs of the Americans of the northern States, whose noble persistence has saved the federal Union from a fearful disruption, and caused to issue from the social tempest a new corroboration of the indissoluble power of the United States; and inasmuch as the news of the monstrous crime, which has brought mourning into the midst of joy, has reached us, we feel stricken as yourselves; for Lincoln personified the cause of liberty and human fraternity, and this cause, which unites nations in a common aspiration, honors and mourns in him one of its most illustrious martyrs.

The Septentrion Lodge at its solemn meeting on the 16th of this month unanimously decided to address through you a tribute of regret and of sympathy to the republic of the United States.

Receive, Mr. Minister, the assurance of our sentiments of high consideration.

R. MADRENNIGER, *President.*

Alph. Buisman, *Secretary.*

BAVARIA.

Mr. Hagedorn to Mr. Hunter.

BAVARIAN CONSULATE,
Philadelphia, May, 1865.

SIR: I have the honor to enclose the very eloquent instructions sent me by the minister for foreign affairs at Munich, with a translation attached to it, dated Munich, April 29, 1865, (which translation falls short of the original in regard to beauty and feeling expressed in the original,) in which his excellency Baron Von der Pfordten directs me, in the name of his Majesty, Louis the Second of Bavaria, whom I have the honor to represent in this country, to express to your excellency, and through you to the President of the United States, the regret and deepfelt sympathy of the King and of the people of Bavaria, which the news of this most cruel and dastardly murder of the late President, ABRAHAM LINCOLN, has spread over all Germany. Being physically unable to hand this in person to his Excellency Andrew Johnson, I beg of you to do so, and to add that I hope and trust that this cruel and most grievous trial may not delay the onward progress of the American nation, so nobly and victoriously commenced by the noble martyr, President LINCOLN.

Receive, sir, the assurance of my very distinguished consideration.

Your very obedient servant,

C. F. HAGEDORN,
Consul General of Bavaria.

Hon. WILLIAM HUNTER,
Acting Secretary of State, Washington, D. C.

BAVARIAN CONSULATE,
Philadelphia, May 19, 1865.

SIR: I have been directed by his Majesty the King of Bavaria, whom I have the honor of representing, through his minister, to express to your excellency the sympathy and regret which his Majesty and the Bavarian nation in general feel at the unforeseen calamity which has befallen this country, in the assassination of the beloved President of the United States of America, at a moment when the success of the arms of the Union and the prospect of an early peace had filled every heart with joy.

At the same time I have the honor of transmitting to your excellency the letter of condolence addressed to me by the prime minister, by order of his Majesty the King of Bavaria.

Having resided for more than forty years in this country, having witnessed its growth and prosperity during that period of time, my feelings have become identified with the same, and I cannot allow this opportunity to pass by without expressing my personal regret and deep feelings of sorrow at the bereavement under which this country is at present suffering. At the same time I pray that, under your Excellency's wise administration, the work which your late lamented predecessor has so nobly and successfully commenced will be fully accomplished, and that unity and peace may again bless the whole of this once happy land.

I have the honor to remain, with the highest respect, your Excellency's most obedient, humble servant,

C. F. HAGEDORN
Consul General of Bavaria.

His Excellency ANDREW JOHNSON,
President of the United States of America.

[Translation.]

MUNICH, *April* 29, 1865.

ESTEEMED SIR: By order of his Majesty the King, I beg leave to send you the following communication:

The dreadful, accursed deed, the news of which came to Europe across the ocean but a few days ago, has also filled with deep abhorrence the land of Bavaria.

The President of the United States of North America, ABRAHAM LINCOLN, has fallen by the hand of an assassin at the moment when he was on the point of terminating a bloody civil war—a struggle in which he had upheld the banner of the Union against secession with undaunted courage for the period of four years.

It is true that the quiet transition of the highest political power in that immense empire is a guarantee that by the death of ABRAHAM LINCOLN the grand victorious success which crowned his persevering efforts will not be jeoparded. By firmness and moderation the new President of the United States will be no less successful in soothing the irritated passions and reconciling and reuniting the different parties. But this fortunate circumstance does in no way lessen the just and deep feeling among all classes of people which is called forth by the tragic end of this celebrated statesman, and I hereby request you, as consul general, to tender to the government of the United States the expression of heartfelt sympathy and sorrow which we, and particularly our most gracious lord the King, feel at the death of their President, wishing, at the same time, that the noble work of renewed unity and restored peace may soon be accomplished, as much for the welfare of the United States of North

America as for that of all the countries which entertain peaceful relations with the same.

Please to accept also, on the present occasion, the assurance of my respect.

VON DER PFORDTEN.

C. F. HAGEDORN, Esq.,
Consul General at Philadelphia.

BRUNSWICK.

NEW YORK, June 5, 1865.

SIR: The undersigned, consul general of the government of his serene highness the Duke of Brunswick, has been specially instructed to convey to you the sentiments aroused in the minds of the authorities, and of all classes of the people of the duchy, by the atrocious murder of your illustrious predecessor, the lamented ABRAHAM LINCOLN, and by the deep loss thus entailed upon the United States. The inestimable qualities uniting in the character of the deceased—his pervading humanity and his lofty sense of right--the indomitable energy with which he sustained all the vicissitudes of a sanguinary civil war, outlived all sacrifices, and eventually triumphed over all obstacles in the restoration of the blessings of civil order to his distracted country, as well as the mild and conciliatory disposition so nobly manifested at the approaching close of the struggle, have gained him the warm regard and esteem of the civilized world, and will embalm his memory in the affectionate reverence of coming generations.

May the peace now vouchsafed to your republic be as lasting, and the prosperity which now dawns upon its future as unbroken, as even the great heart of the departed patriot could have desired.

I have the honor to be, sir, most respectfully, your obedient servant,

G. J. BECHTEL.

ANDREW JOHNSON,
President of the United States.

DUCHY OF BADEN.

Mr. Schmidt to Mr. Hunter.

CONSULATE GENERAL OF BADEN,
New York, May 23, 1865.

SIR: I have the honor to herewith transmit to you a translated copy of a letter received by me from the Baron Von Roggenbach, minister of foreign affairs of his royal highness the Grand Duke of Baden, expressing the feelings of his royal highness and the people of Baden at the assassination of the late President of the United States.

Requesting you to lay the same before his Excellency the President, I have the honor to remain,

Your most obedient servant,

LEOPOLD SCHMIDT,
Vice-Consul and Acting Consul General.

Hon. WILLIAM HUNTER,
Acting Secretary of State, Washington.

[Translation.]

CARLSRUHE, *April* 28, 1865.

HIGHLY HONORED SIR: The atrocious deed which, at the most critical turning-point in the destinies of the United States, has deprived them of the steadfast and glorious guidance of the great citizen who, with firm hand, had led the gigantic contest of the past four years to a victorious end, has called forth universal indignation equally felt by all classes throughout Germany.

What people, indeed, could more deeply and painfully sympathize with the loss sustained by the American commonwealth than the German people, who have watched every turn in the contest now so gloriously ended by the triumph of the Union arms, with an interest as though the issue were their own. Above all, however, all free hearts and all minds solicitous for the future of our civilization, followed with ever-increasing sympathy the constant and never-failing courage of the man who continued the same, unchanged in good as in evil days, and whose name will ever be inseparably linked in history with the merit of the final successful issue. He it was who valued the true friendship of the German people as highly as the more enlightened among ourselves are accustomed to value that of the American people.

His royal highness the grand duke has shared these feelings to the full, and the grand ducal government but fulfils a duty imposed by the universal desire of the hearts of all in desiring to make known to the government of the United States that in this its hour of trial all our wishes have been alive for the welfare and unshaken prosperity of the mighty and free commonwealth to which we are united by so many ties—above all, by that of a common aim, the advancement of civilization, which this war has furthered, and to which President LINCOLN devoted his powers to the very last.

I charge you to communicate to the Acting Secretary of State these sentiments of the grand ducal government in such manner as you may deem proper.

With distinguished consideration,

ROGGENBACH.

[Translation.]

CARLSRUHE, *April* 30, 1865.

Mr. EDITOR: We send you our most hearty thanks for giving us Swiss people the opportunity of expressing our sympathy for the victory of the American Union.

We, the undersigned, Swiss polytechnists, residing in Carlsruhe, have watched the course of American affairs with intense interest, believing that the republic beyond the ocean was undergoing a trial by fire, not only for the principles of civilization, but for the good of the American States and of the whole world.

The news of the late Union victories gave us great pleasure, as that of the death of your first and greatest citizen caused us extreme sorrow.

The address and supplement, in Nos. 115 and 116 of the Bund, expresses our exact sentiments, and we hereby request you to add our names to it, with our most cordial approbation.

Very respectfully, your obedient servants,

J. GLAUSER, *of Berne.*

H. HANHART, *of Winterthur.*

E. BRUNNEN, *of Küsnach.*

CARL MULLER, *of Zurich.*

EUGENE SCHMIDT, *of Lausanne.*

The EDITOR of the Bund, *Berne, Switzerland.*

[Translation—in substance.]

KAPPEL RHEIN, *May* 1, 1865.

To the President of the United States:

The Turners' Society, of Kappel Rhein, in the grand duchy of Baden, express their sorrow and horror at the murder of President LINCOLN—refer to his exalted character as conservator of the Union, and asserter of the equal rights of man by doing away with slavery

In the Turners' Society:

BERTHOLD RICHTER, *Leader*.
FRANZ RICHTER.
ADAM LOSSEL.
AUGUST LOSSEL.
SANDELIN ARMBRASTER.
MELCHIOR BAUMANN.
F. HENNISGAR.

BRAZIL.

[Translation.]

MINISTRY OF FOREIGN AFFAIRS,
Rio de Janeiro, May 19, 1865.

At the conference I had yesterday with J. Watson Webb, envoy extraordinary and minister plenipotentiary from the United States of America, I manifested to him the great sorrow caused by the information of the dreadful crime perpetrated in Washington, on the 14th of last month, on the person of his Excellency the Honorable ABRAHAM LINCOLN, President of the United States.

It is my painful duty now to tender to General Webb, in the name of the government of his Imperial Majesty, the expressions of the feelings with which it finds itself overwhelmed. The imperial government, with the highest severity, condemns an act so criminal as the one which has for its victim the Chief Magistrate of the Union; and it comprehends the infinite pain thus inflicted upon American citizens, with whom ours so sincerely sympathize, in consequence of the close relations of the two countries.

With the hope that General Webb will be pleased to convey this sincere manifestation to the knowledge of his government, I have the honor to reiterate the assurances of my perfect esteem and distinct consideration.

JOSÉ ANTONIO SARAIVA.

J. WATSON WEBB, Esq., *Minister of the United States.*

[Translation.]

IMPERIAL LEGATION OF BRAZIL,
Washington, July 19, 1865.

The undersigned, chargé d'affaires *ad interim* of his Majesty the Emperor, has the honor to communicate to the honorable William H. Seward, the Secretary of State of the United States, that the chambers of senators and deputies of Brazil, uniting in the manifestation of sympathy which has been caused in the empire by the loss which the American Union has suffered in the person of the illustrious President, ABRAHAM LINCOLN—above all, for the atrocious manner in which his existence was terminated, have resolved to cause the unanimous expression of their sorrow to be presented to the Congress of the United States, and have recurred for that purpose to the government of his Majesty the Emperor.

The imperial government, in obedience to the commission thus received from both of the branches of the legislative power, has ordered the undersigned to transmit to the honorable William H. Seward that manifestation of sympathy, requesting him to be pleased to bring it to the knowledge of the Congress.

While complying with the orders of the imperial government, the undersigned avails himself of the occasion to reiterate to the honorable William H. Seward the assurances of his highest esteem and consideration.

IGNACIO DE AVELLAR BARBOZA DA SILVA.

Hon. WILLIAM H. SEWARD, &c., &c., &c.

The Marquis d' Abrantes to General Webb.

[Translation.]

BOTAFOGO, *May* 21, 1865.

MY DEAR GENERAL: Allow me to fulfil the painful duty to manifest to you my deep personal sorrow on the deplorable event which has deprived your country of her so highly distinguished President, Mr. LINCOLN.

But it may be said that the horrible act which has brought to a close his existence has heightened him still more in the esteem of the thankful citizens of the United States, and insures him a still more renowned name in history.

In wishing to your great and fair country every prosperity, I remain, with the most perfect esteem and consideration, my dear general, your friend,

ABRANTES.

J. WATSON WEBB, Esq., *Minister of the United States.*

Mr. Webb to Mr. Seward.

[Extract.]

No. 118.]   LEGATION OF THE UNITED STATES,
                                 Rio de Janeiro, May 23, 1865.

SIR : I have no heart to dwell upon the horrible and distressing news brought by an arrival from the West Indies and confirmed on the following day·by telegraphic despatches received at Lisbon on the 29th of April, and which were brought to this city by the French steamer from Bordeaux on the 24th.

I was at Petropolis. The Emperor kindly telegraphed the distressing intelligence to the Duke of Saxe, who at once sent his secretary and principal chamberlain to impart it to me, and on the following morning I came to town.

I will not attempt any description of the universal horror and dismay which this melancholy news caused among all classes in this city.

Every member of the diplomatic corps has made a visit of condolence, and the ministers of Peru and the Argentine republic have addressed to me letters expressive of their sorrow and sympathy.   *   *   *

I have received a very friendly letter from the government, to which I shall reply to-day, and forward by the next steamer. Also a letter of a similar character from the Marquis d'Abrantes, late minister of foreign affairs, whose friendship for our country and personal feelings towards myself are known to the department.

The Rev. Mr. Simonton, a missionary of the Presbyterian church in the United States, preached, at my request, on Sunday, the 21st, an appropriate sermon, and nearly every United States citizen resident in Rio, except a few well-known traitors, were present. At the close of the services, Mr. Simonton announced that the government officials would wear crape on the left arm for the space of thirty days, and that all our citizens were requested to do the same. Also, that the legation and consulate flags would be at half-mast during the same period; and that American vessels in port during the next thirty days would be expected to exhibit the same manifestation of mourning.

I have the honor to be, very respectfully, your obedient servant,
                                         J. WATSON WEBB.
Hon. WILLIAM H. SEWARD,
        Secretary of State.

[Translation.]

                                 RIO DE JANEIRO, *May* 18, 1865.

The Peruvian minister at Brazil has the honor to address himself to his excellency General Webb, minister plenipotentiary of the United States, in order to express to him the great sorrow with which he has received the news of the tragic death of the very excellent ABRAHAM LINCOLN, that powerful nation's President.

Wounded to death by a fanatic's weapon, when he finished to surround himself with the purest glory, at a final victory of the redemption war which he conducted as far as his arm reached, the pain of his martyrdom, the feeling of his loss, and the mourning of the North American people will reach every Christian soul, every freeman, every civilized people, and especially the Peruvians and their government, who, closely connected with the Union's people and their government, and sympathizing with that great upholder of human dignity, will lament his death more perhaps than they applauded his victories.

The undersigned is persuaded that in expressing these feelings to his excellency General Webb he is a faithful translator of those of the nation and government represented by him, and he begs his excellency to accept them at the same time with his protest of his high esteem and especial consideration.

B. SEVANE.

J. WATSON WEBB, Esq.,
Minister of the United States.

[Translation.]

RIO DE JANEIRO, *May* 18. 1865.

The undersigned, envoy extraordinary and minister plenipotentiary of the Argentine republic, hastens to present to his excellency General Webb, envoy extraordinary and minister plenipotentiary of the United States of America, the testimony of his profound grief caused by the sad incident that has put all the citizens of the United States in deep mourning—the undersigned being on this occasion, in the feelings that he transmits to his excellency, the true exponent of the sincere sorrow that will be felt by the Argentine people and government when they hear of the unfortunate event which happened on the 14th of April in the country of their greatest sympathies.

The Divine Providence which has protected the destiny of the United States in this the most trying epoch of its history will know how to make of his martyrdom a new encouragement for the faith and heroism of the American citizens in the holy war in which they defend, along with the institutions of their country, the highest principles of human dignity.

The funeral of that great citizen will be morally accompanied by all the free countries of the universe. And be it allowed to the undersigned to assure his excellency General Webb that no country will more sincerely and spontaneously regret this event than the citizens of the Argentine republic. And again presenting his excellency the plenipotentiary of the United States the expression of his profound sorrow, the undersigned begs, at the same time, your excellency to accept the expressions of his highest esteem.

J. MARMOL.

J. WATSON WEBB, Esq.,
Minister of the United States.

BOLIVIA.

Mr. Hall to Mr. Hunter.

No. 41.]   LEGATION OF THE UNITED STATES,
Cochabamba, Bolivia, June 24, 1865.

SIR: I have had the honor to receive your circular, No. 29, apprising me of the horrible assassination of the late President LINCOLN. The news of that deplorable event was received here a fortnight ago, through the Panama papers, and produced a sensation of universal and deep regret. From the inhabitants of this city I have received many expressions of sympathy and condolence. The instructions accompanying the circular, "that all officers and others subject to the orders of the Secretary of State wear crape upon the left arm for the period of six months," will be carefully regarded by me.

I have the honor to be, very respectfully, your obedient servant,
ALLEN A. HALL.

Hon. W. HUNTER,
Acting Secretary of State.

CHILI.

[Translation.]

DEPARTMENT OF FOREIGN RELATIONS,
Republic of Chili, Santiago, May 30, 1865.

SIR: The government of the republic has been penetrated by grief as sincere as profound in receiving the melancholy intelligence of the crime which has just snatched from the United States their Chief Magistrate and one of their most illustrious sons.

This sad occurrence is a just motive of grief, not only for the country which that eminent citizen governed liberally and wisely, but also for all those nations which, like Chili, accompanied him with their prayers and sympathies in the

EXPRESSIONS OF CONDOLENCE AND SYMPATHY.

cause of liberty and civilization, which he has not expired without leaving triumphant, and which he sustained for more than four years with incomparable wisdom and perseverance.

President LINCOLN is no more; but the beneficent results of the victory obtained under his glorious government will be sufficiently imperishable to immortalize his name Beautiful privilege of free nations, whose works are not chained to the life of one man, be he ever so great !

As a free and republican people, as a sincere friend of the United States, Chili has a double right to consider as her own, and to fraternally share, the grief which bows down the generous nation of which your excellency is the worthy representative.

My government believes itself the faithful interpreter of the sentiments of the country in expressing its own, and in offering, through the medium of your excellency, to the government and people of the United States its most profound sympathy and sorrow for the grave calamity with which God, in his inscrutable designs, has permitted the resignation and energy of that great republic to be put to proof.

As far as regards myself personally, I sympathize with my heart with the grief which oppresses the mind of your excellency, and avail myself of this sad opportunity to reiterate to you the testimony of my most distinguished consideration and regard.

Your excellency's most obedient servant,

ALVARO COVARRUBIAS.

The ENVOY EXTRAORDINARY AND MINISTER PLENIPOTENTIARY
of the United States of North America.

His Excellency José Joaquin Perez, President of the republic of Chili, in his annual message to the congress of 1865, thus alludes to the assassination of Mr. LINCOLN:

[Translation.]

" Nor have we been indifferent to the mourning in which the United States of America have been plunged by the death of their illustrious ruler, ABRAHAM LINCOLN. This melancholy event has awakened throughout the country and in the government manifestations of grief and sympathy as just as sincere."

[Translation.]

LEGATION OF CHILI IN THE UNITED STATES OF AMERICA,
Washington, April 15, 1865.

Mr. SECRETARY: I have been honored with the reception of your note of to-day, informing me of the treacherous assassination perpetrated last night upon the person of Mr. ABRAHAM LINCOLN, President of the United States, and of the no less horrid attempt on the life of Mr. Seward, Secretary of State, and Mr. F. W. Seward, Assistant Secretary, who were dangerously wounded. You also inform me that Mr. Andrew Johnson, the Vice-President, assumes the exercise of the functions of President from this date, in conformity with the provisions of the Constitution of the country, and authorizes you to discharge the duties of Secretary of State *ad interim*

These most extraordinary and unexpected events have caused me the most intense sorrow and surprise, and I assure you that the grief felt by the government and people of Chili at the news of this public calamity, that justly covers your great nation with mourning, will be as profound and sincere as mine. In the name, therefore, of the government and people that I represent, I offer, through your intervention, to your government and nation, due sympathy and condolence on account of the unfortunate event that has just overwhelmed them with the tragic death of their illustrious and patriotic President, and for the serious injury to the worthy Secretary of State; and at the same time our sincere wishes for the prosperity and happiness of the sister republic, under the administration of its new Magistrate, whose promotion to the dignity of President I will be pleased to communicate to my government.

Be pleased to accept the sentiments of my very distinguished consideration and esteem.

F. S. ASTA BURUAGA.

Hon. WILLIAM HUNTER,
Acting Secretary of State, &c., &c., &c.

[Translation.]

DEPARTMENTAL GOVERNMENT OF THE ANDES,
June 3, 1865.

SIR: The illustrious municipality of this department, over which I have the honor to preside, has resolved to address to your excellency the following note: The death of ABRAHAM LINCOLN, the great republican and President of the United States of North America, by the hand of an infamous and daring assassin, has produced in the hearts of this corporation bitter grief. They also participate in the profound sorrow which, in consequence of this sad event, has been manifested by all those who live beneath the protection of republican institutions, and who now lament the loss of LINCOLN, the venerated apostle of American democracy.

I have the honor to transcribe the foregoing to your excellency, in compliance with the resolutions of the illustrious municipality.

God guard your excellency.

J. RUFINO DEL CANTO.

Hon. ENVOY EXTRAORDINARY AND MINISTER PLENIPOTENTIARY
of the United States of North America.

[Translation.]

MUNICIPALITY OF THE DEPARTMENT OF CARELMAPU,
Calbuco, June 22, 1865.

SIR: This corporation, feeling the most lively and profound pain for the grief which you have been caused by the catastrophe which has befallen one of those prominent men, the immortal President LINCOLN, who has rendered services so important to the country of the free, the republic of the United States of America, has the honor to address itself to your excellency, accompanying you in your just sorrow for so immeasurable a misfortune.

But this corporation feels that it would be a consolation to your excellency in this irreparable loss, so justly wept over by every republican country, that he should have won the glory of preserving intact and unsullied the rights of his country, the natural consequence of which will be, as your excellency cannot doubt, the enjoyment by that magnanimous people of a perpetual peace.

Be pleased, your excellency, with the protest of our most earnest sincerity and sympathy, to accept the condolence of this corporation.

We remain, very respectfully, your excellency's most obedient servants,

R. N NUNEZ VILLALON.
FERNANDO ANDRADE.
GREGNIO GONSALEZ.
FRAN'CO S. NAVARRO.
JUAN MA. PEREZ.
CARPTANO ALVARADO.
SANTIAGO MARTINEZ.
J. MA. BUSTAMANTE.

NICOLAS BARRIENTOS,
Secretary.
THOMAS H. NELSON, Esq.,
Minister of the United States.

[Translation.]

COPIAPO, *June* 5, 1865.

SIR: The people of Copiapo, in a reunion held yesterday in this city for the purpose of paying a just tribute of grief to the memory of the illustrious President of the United States, ABRAHAM LINCOLN, wantonly assassinated in Washington on the 14th of April last, have commissioned us to address ourselves to you, as the representative in Chili of that great nation, for the purpose of manifesting to you how profound has been their grief for this melancholy event, and how sincerely they accompany the North American people in their mourning for the loss of the great man whose political genius saved the Union from the formidable designs of its enemies, and emancipated millions of men who had groaned in slavery.

If there be anything which can mitigate the bitter sorrow for a loss so immense, it is the consideration that the cause defended by ABRAHAM LINCOLN has been definitely consolidated; and that the hand that dealt the fatal blow to the elect of the people, while it severed, it is true, a precious existence, inscribed from that moment the name of the victim in the book of immortality, wounding to the death the inhuman principle of slavery, in whose name was perpetrated the execrable crime which has caused abundant tears to be shed by the republicans of the whole world.

In complying with the commission, at once grateful and painful, of communicating to you the resolutions of this community, we have the honor to express to you our own especial sorrow at this bereavement, and to subscribe ourselves, with every consideration, your most obedient servants,

RAFAEL VALDEZ.
EMILIO G. BEECHE.
CARLOS GONSALEZ UGALDE.
MANUEL CONCHA, R.
EMILIO ESCOBAR.
PEDRO L. GALLO.
JAVIER VERGARA.
JOSÉ R. ROJAS, 2D.
JOSÉ RAMON CORBALAN.
RAMON FRITIS.
J. EDWARDS.

THOMAS H. NELSON, Esq,
  Minister of the United States.

Mr. Nelson to Mr. Seward.

[Extract.]

No. 196.]   LEGATION OF THE UNITED STATES,
Santiago de Chili, June 1, 1865.

SIR: I know not in what terms to give utterance to the feelings of grief and dismay which overpowered me upon learning of the brutal assassination of our great and good President and of the dastardly attempt upon your own life. It is still difficult for me to realize that crimes so awful have been committed.

The effect upon the residents of Santiago and Valparaiso was sad beyond description. Strong men wandered about the streets weeping like children, and foreigners, unable even to speak our language, manifested a grief almost as deep as our own.

Being temporarily in Valparaiso, I invited our countrymen to meet me at the American consulate at four o'clock upon the 29th ultimo, (the steamer having arrived that morning,) to take such action as might be proper in the premises. At that hour, the rooms, the hall, the staircase, and even the street fronting the building, were crowded, and upon my addressing the assemblage, the exhibition of profound grief was such as I have never seen equalled. Several, overcome by their emotion, sat down upon the very ground and wept; and men whose stoicism had never been affected, gave violent course to their grief. Prayer having been offered by the Reverend Dr. Trumbull, a series of appropriate resolutions were proposed and adopted.   *   *   *   *

Upon the same day the intendente called upon me and stated that he had been instructed by the President to tender his earnest sympathy in this awful calamity, and to inquire in what way the government of Chili could most acceptably manifest how sincerely it mourned with the people and government of the United States. Thanking him cordially for the kind attention, I informed him that, while I should be deeply grateful for every mark of respect shown to the memory of the late President, it was not for me to indicate the form of such demonstration.

Instructions were then issued that the American and Chilian flags should be drooped at half-mast from all the native vessels in the harbor, during eight days; and as I left for Santiago on the following day, minute guns were being fired from the sloop-of-war Esmeralda The flags upon the public buildings, those of the foreign consuls, and of many private residences, were also hoisted at half-mast. Similar evidences of sympathy were also shown by the government and diplomatic corps in Santiago; and I have been informed that the government proposes, as a further tribute of respect, to order a parade of all the military organizations in Santiago, to file past the legation with arms reversed and flags shrouded in mourning.

I have also received letters of condolence from the secretary of foreign relations; from the Spanish minister; the Society of Primary Instruction; the Workingmen's Union, and others, to all of which I have endeavored to reply appropriately. All the members of the diplomatic corps have called to express their sympathy, as well as a large number of citizens and strangers.

The President in his message, delivered this afternoon, alluded feelingly to the great loss sustained by the United States, and congress, in an informal meeting held prior to the delivery of the message, ordered the flag of the capital to be placed at half-mast.

Mournful and depressing as is this sad bereavement, it behooves us not to forget, in our sorrow, that the Divine Ruler has preserved to us a life whose importance at this crisis of our country's regeneration cannot be too highly estimated Permit me, therefore, to offer you my most earnest and sincere congratulations upon your own almost miraculous escape from the hands of the assassin, and to express the hope that you may be spared for many years to receive the grateful thanks of the country for which you have so nobly labored, and to which your very life came so near being made a sacrifice.

The steadfast and self-denying ·devotion manifested throughout the whole of our great struggle with treason by the eminent patriot who has succeeded to the presidency, gives cheering assurance to the hearts of our countrymen that the great purpose of Mr. LINCOLN will be ably, firmly, and conscientiously carried out.

   *   *   *   *   *   *   *

I have the honor to remain, very respectfully, your obedient servant,

THOMAS H. NELSON.

Hon. WILLIAM H. SEWARD,
        Secretary of State.

Mr. Nelson to Mr. Seward.

[Extract.]

No. 197.]   LEGATION OF THE UNITED STATES,
                          Santiago de Chili, June 1, 1865.

SIR: At one o'clock to-day the congress of Chili was convened for the purpose of opening its regular sessions, and to listen to the annual message of the President.

Upon my entering the senate chamber, where both houses were assembled, manifestations of enthusiasm were made, while the members rose to their feet and remained standing until I had taken my seat.

The message was read by his Excellency in person. Alluding to the United States, he said:

"In the relations of cordial friendship which we cultivate with the United States of America, it has been impossible for us to view without lively and sincere satisfaction the intelligence which insures the complete re-establishment of peace.

" The happy termination of the sanguinary struggle which has afflicted them will permit them to return again to the prolific labors of arts and manufactures, cleansed from a social plague which Chili banished from the earliest days of her emancipation. and which conflicted with the character and free institutions of that great republic.

"Nor have we been indifferent to the mourning in which they have been plunged by the death of their illustrious ruler, ABRAHAM LINCOLN. This melancholy event has awakened throughout the country and in the government manifestations of grief and sympathy as just as sincere"

* * * * * * * * *

I have the honor to remain, very respectfully, your obedient servant,

THOMAS H. NELSON.

Hon WILLIAM H. SEWARD,
    Secretary of State.

Mr. Nelson to Mr. Seward.

[Extract.]

No. 201.]   LEGATION OF THE UNITED STATES,
                        Santiago de Chili, June 15, 1865.

SIR: In my despatches Nos. 196 and 197, of the first instant, I had the honor to transmit to you numerous evidences of the very deep sympathy manifested in Valparaiso and Santiago in our great national bereavement From that date until the present these manifestations of kind feeling have continued almost uninterruptedly.

On the fourth instant, at noon, by order of the navy department and that of war, a national salute was fired, in honor of the late President of the United States, from the fort at Valparaiso, at the conclusion of which twenty-one guns were fired from the Chilian sloop-of-war Esmeralda, at intervals of two minutes, and a like salute from the fortress of Hidalgo, in Santiago.

An hour later a procession was formed, consisting of the fire department, with flags and apparatus draped in mourning, the Society of the American Union, bearing the flags of the different American republics, also shrouded in crape, and citizens, most of them dressed in mourning, with crape upon the left arm. As the procession passed the legation, which was appropriately draped, I observed tears falling from the eyes of many, and the absolute silence and decorum of the thousands of spectators who filled the streets for squares was in itself a tribute to the memory of the illustrious dead

In Copiapo on the same day, the fourth instant, a very earnest demonstration of respect took place. Pursuant to a call signed by the principal citizens, the residents met at noon and proceeded, escorted by the military forming the garrison, to the *alameda* or public walk, where, upon the uncovering of the portrait of Mr. LINCOLN, a national salute was fired and appropriate discourses delivered. The national flag was hoisted upon the public and private edifices at half-mast, and salutes were fired at sunrise, noon, and sunset. Half-hour guns were also fired during the day.

Additional letters of condolence have also been addressed to me by the Society of the Union Americana, by the Anglo-Saxon Workingmen's Society of Valparaiso, and by the municipality of the department of Los Andres. *   *

In addition to these public demonstrations, I have received very marked and numerous evidences of sympathy from private citizens, and have endeavored in return to evince my grateful sense of the universal and profound respect shown in Chili to the memory of the late President.

I have the honor to remain, very respectfully, your obedient servant,

THOMAS H. NELSON.

Hon. WILLIAM H. SEWARD,
  Secretary of State.

Minister Resident of Spain to Mr. Nelson.

[Translation.]

LEGATION OF SPAIN TO CHILI,
Santiago de Chili, May 29, 1865.

MY DEAR SIR : Through the newspapers which I have just received, I learn with the deepest pain of the brutal assassination and horrible crime perpetrated in Washington against the most worthy President of your excellency's nation, ABRAHAM LINCOLN, and his minister, William H. Seward.

As an evidence of the sincere sorrow which will be felt by my august Sovereign and her government when they shall be informed of it, as well as of that experienced by myself, I immediately hoisted my flag in position of mourning.

I hasten to inform your excellency of this, with the earnest assurance of distinguished consideration and regard with which I am your excellency's most obedient servant,

SALVADOR DE TAVIRA.

THOMAS H. NELSON, ESQ., &c.

Society of Primary Instruction

[Translation.]

SANTIAGO, *May* 30, 1865.

The board of directors of the Society of Primary Instruction, over which I have the honor to preside, resolved, upon the motion of one of its members, to address a note of condolence to the envoy extraordinary and minister plenipotentiary of the United States for the death of the President of that republic, Mr. ABRAHAM LINCOLN.

I comply with so sad a duty as the organ of the said board, manifesting to the minister how intense has been the grief experienced by its members in learning of the horrid and brutal crime of which the illustrious Mr. LINCOLN has been the victim.

Will the minister be pleased to receive this sincere expression of sympathy and the personal consideration of regard with which I subscribe myself your most obedient servant,

RAFAEL MINVIELLE.

ROBUSTIANO VERA, *Secretary.*
Mr. THOMAS H. NELSON, *&c.*

Union Club of Santiago.

[Translation.]

SANTIAGO, *May* 30, 1865.

The Santiago Union Club has received with profound sorrow the news of the assassination perpetrated upon the person of the illustrious President of the United States, ABRAHAM LINCOLN, and has authorized me to transmit you the expression of its grief.

LINCOLN was the incarnation of modern democracy, and perishing a victim to the partisans of slavery, has been elevated to the category of the martyrs of humanity.

In communicating to you the sentiments of the members of this club, I deem it my duty to express my own, and to subscribe myself your most obedient servant,

MANUEL ALCALDE.

Hon. THOMAS H. NELSON, *Santiago.*

Workingmen of Santiago.

[Translation.]

SANTIAGO, *May* 30, 1865.

SIR: The profound sorrow caused among the working classes of Santiago by the sad news of the crime committed upon the person of LINCOLN the honest, by the hand of an assassin, has impelled the council of the artisans' society, called the "union," to spontaneously unite last night in a session for the purpose of manifesting to your excellency the deep grief which it feels for so tragic an event.

Since this society was the first to congratulate you upon the approaching termination of the war which has afflicted the great republic, it cannot view unmoved one of the most execrable crimes which have been committed in modern times by the apostles of evil. Upon me has devolved the duty, in the name of the council of the society and in that of the working classes, to manifest to you the grief experienced by them for the loss of one of the most devoted defenders of the rights of humanity, one whom with justice your fellow-citizens have called the *father of his country.*

So tragic an occurrence will awaken the indignation of honorable men, and even the sorrow of the advocates of slavery, for a deed as brutal as it was infamous. From this day forward future generations will be unable to peruse without an abundant tribute of tears the page of mourning which closes the period of blood through which the greatest and most powerful nation governed by democratic principles has just passed.

The memory of ABRAHAM LINCOLN will live in the heart of humanity so long as the current of the Potomac flows or the Andes endure. This reflection may, perhaps, in some degree mitigate your own grief, and that of your fellow-countrymen.

With sentiments of the most profound respect, I have the honor to offer myself as your humble servant, who prays to the Supreme Dispenser of All Good to avert from your country the evils consequent upon crimes such as astound the world.

JOSÉ SANTOS VALENZUELA,
First Vice-President.

Hon. THOMAS H. NELSON,
Envoy Extraordinary and Minister Plenipotentiary
of the United States.

From the Union Americana, of Santiago.

[Translation.]

SANTIAGO, *June* 1, 1865.

SIR: The atrocious crime which has plunged your noble country in the most profound and just affliction cannot fail to draw forth expressions of grief from all who learn the mournful news, and such we come to utter to you in the name of the Union Americana of Santiago.

We, who have rejoiced in the triumphs obtained by the soldiers of the law and the apostles of humanity in the titanic war against slavery, uniting our hopes and prayers to those of the people and government of the United States—we, who were preparing to join in their songs of victory and to applaud, as heretofore, their heroism in battle, their clemency in the hour of triumph—to-day accompany in their grief that people and government, who have lost in Mr. LINCOLN one of their best and most illustrious representatives.

The deplorable system which during four years has been aiming at the life of your country, and which had for its base and object the most horrible and unjustifiable iniquity, slavery, has concluded by summing up and declaring itself in the most iniquitous and inexcusable of crimes, the assassination of President LINCOLN, thus confirming, as a sentence without appeal, the anathema which all free men and free nations have launched against it.

Those of your fellow-citizens who, misled, have allowed themselves to be dragged by party passions or by interests of caste into a fratricidal war, may read to-day, in the ashes of their cities, how powerless and direful, and, in the death of Mr. LINCOLN, how sterile and perverse, were the designs and instruments which have served the most odious of causes; and may God grant that, horrified by results so lamentable, they may turn to the aggrandizement of the country all the means and all the abilities employed during four years to destroy it. The blood of the President martyr thus counsels them, and thus also the hand of the assassin, from an ignominious solidarity with whom they ought to justify themselves, protesting by deeds, not of a blind party, but such as are worthy a great and enlightened people.

Amid the painful emotions excited by this atrocious deed, it is at the same time a consolation and a lesson to perceive that the victim and the slayer were each faithful to the principles and the flag which each defended—in the name of which one dies, noble and magnanimous, as he had lived, serving his country and humanity; and the other, a brutal assassin, *strikes,* serving the monstrous requirements of an oligarchy or the instigations of a shameful speculation.

The death of the honored and patriotic President is, for your country, and even for the entire world, a just cause for immense grief; but it is not and cannot be a motive for doubting the triumph and final consolidation of the work begun a hundred years ago by Washington, Jefferson, and Franklin, converting three millions of weak colonists into as many proud citizens, and which, to-day is crowned by Lincoln, Grant, and Seward, converting four millions of poor slaves into as many freemen, who will consolidate with their efforts the most just and prolific of governments.

Amid the bitter grief which the death of Mr. Lincoln has caused us, and which has crowned with the aureola of martyrdom the defender of the Union, and has placed the stigma of infamy upon the brow of the dying rebellion, we do not cease to feel the most abiding confidence that the situation of your country must continue developing itself in the most prosperous and secure manner; that the bloody hand of an assassin will not be permitted to retard the chariot of civilization, nor to impede the triumphantly progressive march of democracy.

The atrocious deed of the parricide Booth has proven that the cause of law, of Union, and of true republican government is not bound to the inspiration and energy of a single individual, even though that individual be great of soul as LINCOLN, but to the decision, the prudence, the self-denial of a nation, which, after teaching to the world that the practice of liberty is the most fruitful condition of prosperity, has taught it that in that practice are to be found the elements of war and victory, and will yet teach it that therein alone are rooted and flourishing the germs of concord and true fraternity.

And thus will be belied one by one the doleful auguries which badly informed or evil-intended statesmen have not ceased to utter ever since the shadows of civil war came to eclipse the splendor of the stars of your country, which, by its course in defeat and victory, in peace or war, has once again proved that the only and indispensable conditions for the stability of a government are liberty in all its forms and justice in all its applications.

In expressing to you, sir, our grief for the death of President LINCOLN, and also our confidence in the proximate and lasting re-establishment of the Union, we believe ourselves to be not only the organ of our society, but that of our entire country, which has always found in the events of your prosperity motives for cordial rejoicing, and in those of your adversity even more powerful ones to sympathize, as to-day, in a grief the most profound and just.

Be pleased, sir, to receive the considerations of high esteem with which we have the honor to subscribe ourselves your obedient servants,

MANUEL BLANCO ENCALADA.
M. A. MATTA.
PEDRO MONCAYO.
JUAN AUGUSTIN PALAZUELOS.
DEMETRIO RODRIGUES PEÑA.

Hon. THOS. H. NELSON, &c., &c., &c.

Anglo-Saxon Workingmen's Association of Valparaiso.

VALPARAISO, *June* 5, 1865.

SIR: The Anglo-Saxon Workingmen's Mutual Benefit Association of Valparaiso, being animated by the same deep sense of grief which has been felt by all classes of society at the untimely and violent death of the illustrious personage who filled the high and important position of President of the United States, beg you to accept the expression of their sincere regret at the manner in which his valuable life and services have been brought to an end.

The body which we represent, and the class of society to which we belong, will be an excuse for the want of proper language or flowing rhetoric in which some addresses may have been sent to you; but at the same time, dear sir, we can assure you that what is wanting in language to express our sentiments will be found deeply engraved in the hearts of those whose feelings and sense of right would by none be more highly appreciated than by him whose lamented death has called forth our just and truest sympathies.

Having, as is well known, risen to eminence from the humblest walks of life, his example gives an impulse, especially to men in our station, teaching us that through uprightness, perseverance, and a strict adherence to the principles of society, there is no limit to the degrees of excellence and dignity which may be attained by him who, like ABRAHAM LINCOLN, proves himself throughout life an honest and hard-working man.

We remain, sir, most respectfully and truly yours,

GEORGE LEBERT,
H. B. GREENSTREET,
WILLIAM H. BROWN,
Committee.

RICHARD GROVES, JR.,
Secretary.

Hon. THOMAS H. NELSON,
United States Minister, Santiago de Chili.

Resolutions adopted at a meeting of American residents at Valparaiso, May 29,
1865.

Deeply impressed and appalled by the intelligence this day received, that ABRAHAM LINCOLN, the President of the United States of America, has been assassinated in a manner unsurpassed for treachery and cowardice, we adopt the following resolutions:

Resolved, That our beloved country has in this event suffered the loss of one of her purest and noblest sons, one of her best and most self-sacrificing citizens, one of her most upright and sagacious statesmen.

Resolved, That we blend our sympathies with those of our fellow-citizens at home and abroad in the sorrow irrepressibly awakened by this occurrence, the atrocity of which, in the view of all honorable men, can be measured only by the distress it produces in the bosoms of patriots.

Resolved, That we cherish in highest honor the private virtues and the public career of the late President, who in his lifetime patriotically sought, with animosity towards none, with charity towards all, to save the nation's life and heal its wounds; while his death, investing his counsels with new value, cannot fail to endear him more than ever to his friends, as well as to disabuse the prejudices and assuage the animosity of his opponents.

Resolved, That while we bow with the humility appropriate to our limited vision before the wisdom of God, who has permitted this wild outbreak of the wrath of man to succeed, we do still acknowledge His merciful intervention that had spared so long a life on which such interests hung through the earlier periods of greater confusion and greater peril; and we do yet cherish profoundly the hope, and offer reverently the prayer, that the nation's life may still be dear in His all-embracing eye; that its institutions may be maintained unimpaired, and its banner ever wave, an emblem of justice and freedom on earth.

Resolved, That while the depths of grief are unutterably stirred within us. we still yield to no despondency in view of the machinations of men of criminal intent, confident that other patriots, true, wise, and brave, will arise from among the popular ranks, to serve the cause of our country, to maintain under God her liberties, and to guide her destiny to the wisest and noblest ends.

These resolutions were at once adopted with entire unanimity and emotion.

The following resolution was also proposed by the committee, in relation. to the attack on the life of Secretary Seward:

Resolved, That this meeting rejoices to learn that the dastardly attack on the honorable William H. Seward, Secretary of State of the United States, at the time an invalid in his bed, failed utterly; while we hope that, yet living to witness that honorable and permanent peace for which so assiduously he has labored, restored throughout the land, he may long be spared to serve his country, and to have her do him the honor his patriotic devotion to her interests and suffering on her behalf have deserved.

Mr. Caldwell recommended that the citizens of the United States, in conformity with the custom at home, should wear some token of mourning on the arm or chest for the term of fifteen days. This was seconded by Paul Delano, esq., and adopted.

HENRY M. CALDWELL, *Secretary.*

Resolution of the municipality of Quillota.

[Translation.]

No. 1615.]   INTENDENCY OF VALPARAISO,
                              Valparaiso, June 28, 1865.

The following resolution has been approved by the municipality of the department of Quillota in its session of the 20th instant:

The illustrious municipality over which I preside, in its session of the 20th instant, has approved the following draught of a resolution:

The melancholy news which has plunged an entire continent in the deepest mourning could not be received in this city without filling its inhabitants with grief and consternation. This news was no less than the extinction of an existence precious to humanity, that of an apostle of the truths of democracy—an untiring laborer for the greatness and prosperity of America, and a loyal and sincere friend of our country. Such was the President, ABRAHAM LINCOLN, sacrificed on the fatal night of the 14th of April by the infamous hand of an assassin.

In the privileged brain of the immortal LINCOLN were meditated the gravest interests of the human race, under the impulses of the tendencies of a noble soul, and of a genius predestined to do good. From the lofty position achieved by his virtues, he watched with the utmost solicitude over the destinies of America, exhibiting with notable brilliancy a policy of justice in his relations with weak nations, and manifesting, especially towards our own republic, sincere sympathy and regard.

He co-operated earnestly in the crusade against the ominous oligarchy, protector of the most horrible of all social inequalities. He showed a constant zeal for the preservation of the integrity of the great republic which-intrusted its direction to him, thus insuring the stability of the most perfect form of political existence, and demonstrated that policy of justice by his course towards the Brazilian nation, weak in material power, while powerful in the right of her claims; and, finally, by his course towards Chili, which can only be interpreted as an evidence of the spirit of the most perfect cordiality.

While mourning over the blow which has wounded every American heart in its innermost depths, our satisfaction has been great to see the great republic pass unharmed through so fiery a trial. This is the privilege of governments resting not upon the shifting basis of force, but upon the solid foundations of principles—principles that study the means of elevating the august sovereignty of man to the position for which nature designed him, and not of strengthening dynasties by the legacy of millions of men to be converted into slaves and puppets.

Mankind may weep, but it gazes upon his great work finished; while the human race exists will it remain. Although this result, the necessary consequence of the propagation of democratic ideas, is for us a just motive for rejoicing, it is not sufficient to do away with the painful impression which the news of this great calamity has caused us. The family of redeemers is few ? Washington left, for his part, political personality. LINCOLN added social personality. The former made colonists into citizens ; the latter made citizens from slaves Washington gave a country to those he redeemed; LINCOLN, to those he liberated, gave one also, saying to them, "Be ye men." Both made great conquests for mankind, giving back to man that which prejudice and egotism had usurped. From the time of Washington to that of LINCOLN, America has completed her first era in the mission of redemption.

As Chilenos, as Americans, as men, we have a just right to join with the republic of the north in celebrating the prosperous events of its existence, as well as in accompanying it in our sympathy in the hours of misfortune; and in order to attest in some external manner the grief of the residents of this city for the death of the illustrious LINCOLN, we address ourselves to you as their immediate representative, soliciting your suffrages in favor of the following draught of a resolution :

The people of Quillota, profoundly moved by the unexpected event of the death of ABRAHAM LINCOLN, sixteenth President of the United States, approach their representative in Chili in order to offer to that nation the most earnest expression of condolence for so painful an event.

A copy of this resolution will be transmitted, together with the requisite note of enclosure, to the Hon. Thomas Henry Nelson, minister plenipotentiary of the United States of North America

QUILLOTA, *June* 12, 1865.

In transcribing to your excellency the foregoing resolution of the municipality of Quillota, I take pleasure in manifesting to your excellency identical sentiments on the part of this intendency.

God guard your excellency.

J. RAMON LIRA.

THOMAS H. NELSON, Esq.,
Envoy Extraordinary and Minister Plenipotentiary
of the United States of North America.

COSTA RICA.

[Translation.]

PALACIO NATIONAL, SAN JOSÉ, *May* 30, 1865.

The President of the republic has, with profound grief, in the despatch you were pleased to send me from Punta Arenas, found the confirmation of the sad intelligence of the murder committed on the person of the President of the United States, ABRAHAM LINCOLN, which occurred on the 14th of last month, at Ford's theatre, in the city of Washington.

You have also been pleased to inform me of the criminal attempt to assassinate in their own house the Messrs. Seward, Secretary and Assistant Secretary of State, an attempt which, though fortunately frustrated, caused to these gentlemen several wounds and blows endangering their lives.

My government would wish, in honor of humanity, that this savage act should appear isolated, and solely chargeable to the wretched assassin who attacked the life of the unfortunate President. And it must be so. Whatever ferocity may be ascribed to the anti-national party, it is inconceivable how, even in a state of desperation, it should go to the extreme of defiling its cause with the most horrible of all crimes, without any other political result but that of calling down upon it the indignation of the whole world.

Costa Rica deplores as her own the loss sustained by the United States in the death of the eminent man who for four years governed, with such justice, firmness, and loyalty, the great republic of the north, in the midst of the troubles and anxieties of an intestine war. She laments the violence of passions called into existence by political fanaticism, and condemns, now more than ever, the cause of those who attempted to destroy the American Union.

In mark of mourning the President ordered the national flag on all public buildings to be raised half-mast during the 14th instant.

Rejoicing in the restoration of the momentous health of the honorable Mr. Seward, and in the inauguration of Mr Andrew Johnson in his character as President,

I have the honor to reiterate, &c.,

J. VOLIO.

Hon Señor C. N. RIOTTE, *&c., &c., &c.*

[Translation.]

PALACIO NATIONAL, SAN JOSÉ, *May* 30, 1865.

I have the honor, in reply to your esteemed note of the 26th instant, to communicate to you that the government and the people of Costa Rica join, with the greatest spontaneity and alacrity, in the public demonstration of mourning and grief which the republic of the north, our sister and ally, is making in memory of the good man that left the earth.

Proper orders have been issued that on the 1st of June next the national flag will be hoisted half-mast.

Repeating, &c.,

J. VOLIO.

Hon. Señor CARLOS N. RIOTTE, &c., &c., &c.

[Translation.]

NATIONAL PALACE, SAN JOSÉ, *May* 25, 1865.

SIR: The assassination perpetrated in the person of ABRAHAM LINCOLN, President of the United States, and the criminal attempt made against the Secretary of State, Mr. Seward, which you communicated in your despatch No. 186, has caused the profoundest regret to the members of this government, and generally to the Costa Rican people, who understand and appreciate the merit of the illustrious victims of such a horrible event.

This government has read with esteem the communications, copies of which you enclosed, exchanged between the secretaryship of state and that legation, in relation to said events, and it is highly pleased that it fell to you the honor to be one of the commission charged with the manifestation to the family of the ill-fated Mr. LINCOLN of the share of the diplomatic body in the general mourning, and with the expression to Mr. Seward and his family of its sympathies and prayers for their recovery.

As soon as the dismal intelligence reached this capital, his excellency the President directed the national flag to be hoisted at half-mast on all the public buildings.

I am also informed of the inauguration of the new President, Mr. Andrew Johnson, and of the speeches on that solemn occasion.

While the enormities to which political fanaticism may lead are lamented, it is a source of consolation that the attitude preserved at so very critical moments by the nation so cruelly wounded, remaining immovably true to its institutions, and exhibiting sentiments of horror and bereavement, is equally worthy of a great and generous people as of the illustrious personages to whom they were devoted.

Hailing the miraculous preservation of the Hon. Mr. Seward, and offering prayers for the restoration of himself, his worthy son, and all other persons of his estimable family, I close this, recommending you to communicate its contents in the usual form, which might be more acceptable.

I am, sir, your obedient servant,

JULIAN VOLIO.

His Excellency Don Luis Molina,
Envoy Extraordinary and Minister Plenipotentiary
from Costa Rica, Washington, D. C.

[Translation.]

LEGATIONS OF COSTA RICA, NICARAGUA, AND HONDURAS,
Washington, April 15, 1865.

SIR : Sincerely sharing in the feelings of the people of the United States, the persons connected with the government, and yourself, on the occasion of the melancholy events which you communicate to me in your note of this date, I do not venture anything in at once assuring you that the governments and the peoples I have the honor to represent near the United States will receive with due appreciation the sad intelligence of the national calamity referred to, fully sympathizing with the national sorrow.

At the same time you have the kindness to inform me that, according to the Constitution of the United States, the Vice-President has formally assumed the functions of President, and that you have been by him authorized to perform the duties of Secretary of State.

The uninterrupted existence of the constitutional government of the United States will doubtless be looked upon in the republics of Costa Rica, Nicaragua, and Honduras as the surest guarantee of the friendly relations they so much desire to cultivate with this country, and will now be a relief accompanied with the hope that the administration of President Johnson may advance those relations as well as that of his lamented predecessor.

Let me offer my personal condolence with the family of the late President in their bereavement, and my earnest wishes for the recovery of Mr. Seward, his son, and family.

I have the honor to offer to you the assurances of my high consideration.

LUIS MOLINA.

Hon. WILLIAM HUNTER,
Acting Secretary of State of the United States, Washington, D. C.

Mr. Riotte to Mr. Hunter.

[Extract.]

No. 123.]   LEGATION OF THE UNITED STATES,
                                                San José, May 22, 1865.

SIR : I had the honor of receiving on the 13th instant at Punta Arenas, whither I had gone for the purposes indicated in my despatch No. 122, your despatches Nos. 100 and 101 and your order of 17th April last.

The terrible tragedy recited in your despatch No. 100 has created a degree of painful sensation in this country altogether unexpected and heretofore evinced on no occasion. The President, immediately upon the arrival of the mail, raised the flag on his mansion half-mast, and the same was done by his order on all public buildings. The foreign diplomatic and consular representatives followed, and most of them wrote me letters or paid me visits of condolence. And the grief was not merely an official one, as to my sincere satisfaction I had abundant proof to convince myself. A real gloom was spread over the whole community.

It would not be proper in this place to speak of my personal feelings, but I hope I will be pardoned for saying that the great debt of gratitude I owed Mr. LINCOLN made me feel his loss like that of a brother. In the miraculous salvation of the venerable chief of our department I rejoice most heartily, with every true friend of the great cause of our country, which I am persuaded, in the hands of Mr. Johnson, will be sustained ably and energetically..

   *   *   *   *   *   *   *   *   *

I have the honor, sir, to be your obedient servant,

                                                            C. N. RIOTTE.

Hon. WILLIAM HUNTER,
        Acting Secretary of State

Mr. Riotte to Mr. Hunter.

[Extract.]

No. 125.]   LEGATION OF THE UNITED STATES,
                                                San José, June 4, 1865.

SIR : I have the honor to acknowledge the receipt of despatches Nos. 102 and 103, and enclose a copy of a note addressed to this government, and a copy and translation of the reply thereto ; also a copy of the circular note directed by me to the diplomatic and consular representatives of foreign nations, calling upon them to join in the celebration of the day set aside by the President as a day of mourning in memory of our lamented late President.

On that mournful day I was made the recipient of a number of letters of condolence and of visits from many distinguished citizens and the chargés of Peru and Spain. Without one single exception all flags in this capital were at half-mast, some draped in crape. The legation and its flagstaff I had draped in black and white, while long black streamers hung down from the flag.

Most Americans wore black, and two of them volunteered to put up the drapery on the legation.

    *   *   *   *   *   *   *   *

I have the honor, sir, to be your obedient servant,

C. N. RIOTTE.

Hon. WILLIAM HUNTER,
    Acting Secretary of State.

CHINA.

Prince Kung to Mr. Williams.

[Translation.]

JULY 8, 1865, *(Tungchi, 4th year intercalary, 5th moon, 17th day.)*

Prince Kung, chief secretary of state for foreign affairs, herewith sends, in reply:

I had the honor yesterday to receive your excellency's communication informing me that the President of the United States had been removed by death, an announcement that inexpressibly shocked and startled me. But, as you add that on the same day the Vice-President succeeded to the position without any disturbance, and the assassin had been arrested, so that the affairs of government were going on quietly as usual, I hope that these considerations will alleviate your grief at the event, and you will be able to attend to public business.

I shall be pleased to embody the particulars connected with this event in a memorial to his Majesty, and thereby evince the cordial relations which now exist between our countries, which is the purpose of sending the present reply.

His Excellency S. W. WILLIAMS,
    Chargé d'Affaires of the United States, in China.

Mr. Williams to Mr. Seward.

[Extract.]

No. 4.]   LEGATION OF THE UNITED STATES,
                                        Peking, July 11, 1865.

*   *   *   *   *   *   *   *   *

Since my last the mail has brought full accounts of the lamentable assassination of our beloved President, and I have taken the telegraphic despatch of the Secretary of War, of April 16, to Mr. C. F. Adams, at London, which appeared in the English papers, as containing the principal facts, and have notified the Chinese government of this sad event. Prince Kung responded in a friendly spirit. Previous to this I had informed the Chinese officials of all the details then known respecting the occurrence.

The telegraph brought the first notice to Peking *via* Russia in forty days, but nearly a fortnight elapsed before further news arrived to induce us to believe that such a horrid deed could have been committed in the United States.

The contentment and joy caused by the previous news of the fall of Richmond and the surrender of Lee's army, foretokening the cessation of arms and final suppression of the rebellion and restoration of the Union, were turned into grief and indignation at learning that the President had been thus removed. All the Americans in Peking alike mourned his death, and all we could do was to pray that God, who had brought the nation to see the triumph of its arms against treason, would strengthen the national cause by leading to the adoption of those plans which would best uphold justice and best promote union.

The limits of a despatch will hardly allow me more than to add my tribute of admiration of the character of Mr. LINCOLN. His firm and consistent maintenance of the national cause, his clear understanding of the great questions at issue, and his unwearied efforts while enforcing the laws to deprive the conflict of all bitterness, were all so happily blended with a reliance on Divine guidance as to elevate him to a high rank among successful statesmen. His name is hereafter identified with the cause of emancipation, while his patriotism, integrity, and other virtues, and his untimely death, render him not unworthy of mention with William of Orange and Washington.

I have the honor to be, sir, your obedient servant,

                                        S. WELLS WILLIAMS.

Hon. WILLIAM H. SEWARD,
     Secretary of State, Washington.

DENMARK.

Mr. Raaslöff to Mr. Hunter.

[Translation.]

DANISH LEGATION,
Washington, April 17, 1865.

SIR: I have the honor to acknowledge the receipt of your note of the 15th instant, by which you inform me of the death of President LINCOLN, and of the attempted assassination of the Secretary of State and of his son, the Assistant Secretary of State.

I need not assure you of the deep and sincere grief with which I have received that information, but I may be allowed to add, that the feelings of my Sovereign and of the people of Denmark will, when the news of those sad and terrible events shall reach them, be those of the warmest sympathy, not only with the immediate victims, but with the whole deeply afflicted people of the United States.

Having been informed by this same note that, pursuant to the provision of the Constitution of the United States, Andrew Johnson, the Vice-President, has formally assumed the functions of President, and that the President has authorized you to perform the duties of Secretary of State, I beg you to accept the assurance of the high and distinguished consideration with which I have the honor to be, sir, your obedient, humble servant,

W. RAASLÖFF.

Hon. WILLIAM HUNTER,
Acting Secretary of State of the United States, Washington.

[Translation.]

DANISH LEGATION,
New York, May 20, 1865.

PRESIDENT: I have the honor, in conformity with instructions from my government which have just reached me, to tender you, in the name and on behalf of his Majesty the King, my august Sovereign, the assurance of profound grief with which his Majesty has learned the death of the late lamented President LINCOLN by the hand of an assassin, and the murderous attempt made to take the life of the honorable Secretary of State.

His Majesty the King, as well as the whole people of Denmark, sincerely and earnestly sympathize with the people of the United States in their affliction and their mourning over the loss of a ruler whose great qualities and many virtues were fully appreciated by my countrymen.

Be pleased to accept the expression of the warm and earnest wishes for your prosperity, and for the welfare of the United States, which it is my pleasant duty to offer to you in the name of my sovereign, who will have learned with sincere gratification that the great trial through which this country has had to pass in consequence of the sad events to which I have alluded, has served to prove once more the strength of its institutions and the patriotism of its people; and that the prospects of this great nation were never more promising or inspiring greater or more general confidence than at this present moment, when peace and concord are rapidly being restored under the auspices of a wise and magnanimous Chief Magistrate.

I have the honor to be, President, with the highest respect, your obedient, humble servant,

W. RAASLÖFF.

Mr. Wood to Mr. Seward.

[Extract.]

No. 194.]   LEGATION OF THE UNITED STATES,
                                                  Copenhagen, May 1, 1865.

SIR: There was but one feeling of horror here on learning the assassination of President LINCOLN and the attempt on your life.   As soon as it was authoritatively known, the diplomatic corps and the ministers of state called to express their sympathy, and the King, in a note from Mr. Blumhe, the foreign minister, (who is still confined to his house from illness,) feelingly expressed his; and this on the day of the funeral services for the deceased Czarowitz, his intended son-in-law, and at which all the foreign ministers assisted.   I congratulate you on your narrow escape.   I hope I can on your son's, but the news is contradictory, and I fear the worst.

This terrible tragedy at Washington is a natural sequence of this rebellion, and in keeping with the murder of Union prisoners by starvation.   It is a consequence of slavery.   Well if the nation now rouse to the conviction (as I long since have, as you well know) that there is a class at the south, (of whom Booth was one,) the plotters of this rebellion, and their brigands, who must, as a political necessity, be expatriated, or in some way annihilated from our soil, if the freedmen and the northern emigrant are to dwell in peace and safety at the south.   The future of the South demands this.   *   *   *

I remain, very truly, your obedient servant,

BRADFORD R. WOOD.

Hon. WILLIAM H. SEWARD,
        Secretary of State.

Governor Birch to Mr. Perkins.

GOVERNMENT HOUSE,
St. Croix, June 14, 1865.

SIR : I have the honor to acknowledge the receipt of your communication of the 3d instant, in which you have informed me of the assassination of the President of the United States.

President LINCOLN'S sudden death has everywhere in the civilized world called forth a profound sympathy, and the nefarious act—a deed in foul atrocity scarcely ever equalled—to which he fell a victim, has awakened a vivid horror and indignation.

I am aware that these sentiments have been fully participated in in Denmark; and here in his Majesty's West India colonies, connected as they are with the United States by many and near interests, the tidings of the abhorrent crime must necessarily seize all minds.

I beg, sir, to express to you the sincere sorrow I have felt at the great calamity that has befallen the American nation.

About the same time we had received the sad intelligence of the murder of President LINCOLN, we also received the account of those achievements that finally terminated that disunion which for more than four years has split the United States ; and it has given me great joy, through every new information which has reached us from America, to find expressed an unshaken faith in the future, and a full confidence in the new President, Mr. Johnson. I can therefore, to the expression of my deep concern at President LINCOLN'S tragic fate, fully add the expression of my best and heartfelt wishes for the United States and President Johnson's prosperity and welfare, which I beg you in behalf of your government and your country to accept.

It gives me much pleasure to know that the Hon. William H. Seward, the Secretary of State, and his son, Mr. F. W. Seward. the Assistant Secretary, will soon have completely recovered from the wounds inflicted upon them by a murderous hand, extended from the same villanous plot that destroyed the President's life.

I have the honor to be, sir, with the highest consideration,

W. L. BIRCH.

E. H. PERKINS, Esq.,
Consul of the United States of America.

ECUADOR.

Mr. Herrera to Mr. Hassaurek.

[Translation.]

QUITO, *May* 22, 1865.

The undersigned, minister of exterior relations of the republic of Ecuador, has received and communicated to his Excellency the President your excellency's note of the 15th instant, in which your excellency informs the undersigned of the death of his Excellency ABRAHAM LINCOLN, President of the United States, who was assassinated in the city of Washington on the 14th of April, and that in consequence of this deplorable event his Excellency Andrew Johnson, Vice-President of the United States, has succeeded to the presidency.

Such a lamentable and painful event has filled the Ecuadorian people and government with the deepest grief, because of the cordial and sincere sympathies which they have entertained and do entertain for the powerful republic of the Union; and to manifest their condolence, the government of the undersigned has ordered that all the officers and employés of the republic shall wear mourning for three days, during which time the flag of the republic shall be displayed at half-mast.

The undersigned avails himself of this opportunity, &c., &c.

PABLO HERRERA.

His Excellency the MINISTER RESIDENT
    Of the United States of America.

Mr. Herrera to Mr. Hassaurek.

[Translation.]

QUITO, *May* 22, 1865.

The government of the undersigned has received with deep regret the communication of your excellency, dated Guayaquil, May 15, informing the undersigned that on the fatal night of the 14th of April, and almost at the same hour when the President of the United States was assassinated, an attempt was made by an unknown individual to assassinate his excellency William H. Seward, Secretary of State of the United States, but that fortunately, by the protection of Divine Providence, his life was saved, and that, though wounded by the assassin, he was already considered out of danger; also that for the time being the honorable William Hunter has taken charge of the department of foreign relations.

The undersigned entertains the most fervent wishes for the recovery of his excellency William H. Seward, and for the preservation of order and peace in the powerful republic of the United States.

Availing himself of this opportunity, &c., &c.

PABLO HERRERA.

His Excellency the MINISTER RESIDENT
   Of the United States of America.

President Moreno to Mr. Hassaurek.

[Translation.]

QUITO, *May* 22, 1865.

The fatal news which arrived by yesterday's mail has produced a profound and painful impression on me. Never should I have thought that the noble country of Washington would be humiliated by such a black and horrible crime; nor should I ever have thought that Mr. LINCOLN would come to such a horrible end, after having served his country with such wisdom and glory under so critical circumstances.

Although the minister has already written to you officially to manifest to you the grief which we all feel for the lamentable loss the great republic has sustained, I wanted to write to you individually, as a friend and as an American, to unite my regret with yours and that of all righteous and honorable men.

I am your affectionate friend and obedient servant,

G. GARCIA MORENO.

His Excellency F. HASSAUREK,
   United States Minister Resident, &c., &c., &c.

Mr. Hassaurek to Mr. Seward.

[Extract.]

No. 155.]   LEGATION OF THE UNITED STATES,
          Guayaquil, May 21, 1865.

SIR: The shocking news of the assassination of President LINCOLN and the murderous assault on you has produced the greatest consternation here. * *

Enclosed you will find the proceedings of a meeting of American citizens held at this place on the 17th instant, to give expression to their grief and indignation. At the request of the secretary, I enclose one copy of the proceedings directed to you, and another to the widow of our lamented late President.

But these feelings of grief and sorrow are not confined to the American residents. The native population sympathizes with us ,most tenderly in our great affliction. Numerous were the visits and expressions of condolence I received from the authorities and prominent citizens; and I may say that, for many years, no other announcement has produced such sadness here as the death of President LINCOLN. For him a whole continent is in mourning, and his loss will be lamented all over the world.

I have the honor to remain your most obedient servant,

F. HASSAUREK.

Hon. WILLIAM H. SEWARD,
   Secretary of State.

Mr. Hassaurek to Mr. Seward.

[Extract.]

No. 160.]   LEGATION OF THE UNITED STATES,
            Guayaquil, May 29, 1865.

SIR: Besides ordering that all the officers and employés of the republic of Ecuador shall wear mourning for three days, during which time the Ecuadorian flag shall be displayed at half-mast from all the public buildings, President Garcia Moreno, immediately after the arrival of the horrible news of President LINCOLN's death at Quito, wrote me a letter of condolence. * * *

I also received letters of condolence from the minister for foreign affairs, and other prominent citizens of Quito. These and other manifestations will enable you to judge what a sensation of amazement and regret Mr. LINCOLN's lamentable death has produced in Spanish America. Even those who were but lukewarm friends of the Union, or open sympathizers with the rebellion, are now loud in their condemnation of the South.

With expressions of profound respect and consideration, I have the honor to remain your most obedient servant,

F. HASSAUREK.

Hon. WILLIAM H. SEWARD,
   Secretary of State.

EGYPT.

Mr. Hale to Mr. Hunter.

No. 25.]

AGENCY AND CONSULATE GENERAL

OF THE UNITED STATES OF AMERICA,

Alexandria, Egypt, May 5, 1865.

SIR: I have the honor to report that his highness the Pacha of Egypt has seized the earliest opportunity to express to me the pain with which he has heard the sad tidings of the assassination of the President of the United States, his detestation of the abominable crime, and his sympathy for our country in the grievous loss we have sustained.

I have the honor to be, sir, most respectfully, your obedient servant,

CHARLES HALE.

Hon. WILLIAM H. SEWARD,
    Secretary of State.

Mr. Hale to Mr. Hunter.

No. 26.]

AGENCY AND CONSULATE GENERAL

OF THE UNITED STATES OF AMERICA,

Alexandria, May 13, 1865

SIR: I have the honor to acknowledge the receipt of your instructions under date of the 17th of April, with official intelligence of the foul assassination of the President and of the dastardly attempt, happily unsuccessful, to take the lives of the Secretary of State and the Assistant Secretary.

I have already, in my despatch No. 25, reported the cordial expression of sympathy which his highness the Pacha of Egypt hastened to make me, in an official interview, immediately after the sad news was known here.

I have since received and am daily receiving other expressions of the public feelings of all nationalities represented here, in respect for the memory of the late President and of confidence in the administration of the government by his successor.

A special religious ceremony has been ordered by the Greek community at the Greek church, and one will be held at this consulate general, conducted by the American missionaries, on the day appointed.for the purpose in the President's proclamation.

I have the honor to be, sir, very respectfully, your obedient servant,

CHARLES HALE.

Hon. WILLIAM HUNTER,
    Acting Secretary of State.

FRANCE.

Mr. Drouyn de Lhuys to Mr. Bigelow.

[Translation.]

PARIS, *April* 26, 1865

SIR : The telegrams published in the evening papers inform me of the horrible crime of which Messieurs LINCOLN and Seward have been the victims. I would not delay a moment longer to express to you our profound sympathy.

Yours, very sincerely,

DROUYN DE LHUYS.

JOHN BIGELOW, Esq.,
   United States Minister, Paris.

COMMUNICATION FROM THE GOVERNMENT.

[Translated from the Moniteur of May 2, 1865.]

The PRESIDENT. M. the minister president of the council of state has the floor, for the purpose of presenting a communication from the government. [The house becomes attentive.]

His excellency M. VUITRY, minister president of the council of state. Gentlemen of the senate : In pursuance of the orders of the Emperor, I have the honor to communicate to the senate the despatch* addressed on the 28th of April last by M. the minister of foreign affairs to M. the chargé d'affaires of France at Washington on the occasion of the death of President LINCOLN.

I do not think, gentlemen of the senate, that this communication needs any commentary; it explains itself. I trust the senate will share the feelings of which the despatch which I have had the honor of reading contains the ready expression. In uniting together to brand with reprobation a horrible crime, the Emperor, the great bodies of the state, and France in its totality will give to the republic of the United States a fresh testimony of their sincere sympathy. [Loud approbation.]

The PRESIDENT. Gentlemen : In acknowledging the communication just made by M. the minister, I beg the senate will permit me to express, in its name, a sentiment which, in its unanimity and energy, is equally felt by all The senate felt a deep emotion at the news of the crime committed against the illustrious head of an allied nation. Mr. LINCOLN, placed since 1861 at the

---

*See despatch from M. Drouyn de Lhuys to M. de Geofroy.

head of the American nation, had passed through the most afflicting trials that could befall a government founded on liberty. It was at the moment when victory presented itself, not as a signal of conquests, but as the means of recon- ciliation, that a crime, still obscure in its causes, destroyed the existence of that citizen, placed so high by the choice of his countrymen. Mr. LINCOLN fell at the moment when he thought he was at the point of arriving at the term of the misfortunes by which his country was afflicted, and when he indulged in the hope of seeing it soon reconstituted and flourishing. The senate, which has always deplored the civil war, detests still more that implacable hatred which is its fruit, and which disgraces politics by assassination. There can therefore be but one voice in this body, to join in the ideas expressed by order of the Emperor, in the name of a generous policy and of humanity. [Approbation.]

I propose to the senate to decree that a copy of the minutes of the present sitting be officially transmitted to the minister of state. [Loud and prolonged approbation.]

CORPS LEGISLATIF—SITTING OF MONDAY, MAY 1.

[Translated from the Moniteur of May 2, 1865.]

President SCHNEIDER. M. the minister of state has the floor to transmit a communication from the government. [The assembly becomes very attentive and silent]

His excellency M. ROUHER, minister of state. Gentlemen: An odious crime has plunged in mourning a people composed of our allies and friends. The news of that odious act has produced throughout the civilized world a sentiment of indignation and horror. [Assent.]

Mr. ABRAHAM LINCOLN has displayed in the afflicting struggle which con- vulses his country that calm firmness and that invincible energy which belong to strong minds, and are a necessary condition for the accomplishment of great duties. [Repeated assent.]

After the victory, he had shown himself generous, moderate, and conciliatory. [Hear, hear.] He was anxious to at once terminate the civil war and restore to America, by means of peace, her splendor and prosperity. [Hear, hear.]

The first chastisement that Providence inflicts on crime is to render it powerless to retard the march of good. [Repeated assent.] The deep emotion and elevated sympathies which are being displayed in Europe will be received by the American people as a consolation and an encouragement. The work of appeasement commenced by a great citizen will be completed by the national will. [Hear, hear.] The Emperor's government has sent to Washington the expression of a legitimate homage to the memory of an illustrious statesman torn from the government of the States by an execrable assassination.

By his Majesty's order I have the honor to communicate to the legislative body the despatch addressed by the minister of foreign affairs to our representative at Washington. It is thus worded : [For the despatch see note from Mr. Drouyn de Lhuys to Mr. de Geofroy. The reading was frequently interrupted by expressions of approbation and by applause.]

This despatch, gentlemen, does not call for any comment. The Emperor, the public bodies, and France, from one end to the other, are unanimous in their sentiments of reprobation for a detestable crime, in their homage to a great political character, victim of the most criminal passions, and in their ardent wishes for the re-establishment of harmony and concord among the great and patriotic American nation. [Unanimous assent.]

President SCHNEIDER. Gentlemen : I wish to be the interpreter of your thought in publicly expressing the grief and indignation which we have all felt on learning the news of the bloody death of President LINCOLN. That execrable crime has revolted all that is noble in the heart of France. Nowhere has more profound or more universal emotion been felt than in our country. We therefore heartily join in the sentiments and sympathies which have been manifested by the government. [Yes, yes.]

Having been called to the direction of public affairs at an ever-memorable crisis, Mr. ABRAHAM LINCOLN has always proved himself fully equal to his difficult mission. After having shown his immovable firmness in the struggle, he seemed by the wisdom of his language and of his views destined to bring about a fruitful and durable reconciliation between the sons of America. [Hear, hear.]

His last acts worthily crown the life of an honest man and a good citizen. Let us hope that his spirit and his sentiments may survive him, and inspire the American people with pacific and generous resolutions. [Approbation]

France has deplored the bloody struggles which have afflicted humanity and civilization. She ardently desires the re-establishment of peace in the midst of that great nation, her ally and her friend. [Hear, hear.]

May our prayers be heard, and may Providence put an end to these painful trials. [Unanimous approbation.]

The legislative body acknowledges the receipt of the communication just made to it by the government, and demands that an extract of the minutes of the sitting shall be officially addressed to the minister of state. [General marks of assent]

[Translation.]

After the meeting of the deputies of the opposition, which took place April 30, the following letter was addressed to Mr. Schneider, vice-president of the legislative chambers:

Mr. PRESIDENT : In presence of the misfortune which has just fallen upon the American republic, and seeing the demonstrations of foreign parliaments which have taken place, we cannot conceal our astonishment that we have not been called together in a public sitting, and we beg of you, sir, to satisfy the legitimate sentiment which we express to you.

Be pleased to accept, Mr. President, the expression of our high consideration.

JULES FAVRE.	JULES SIMON.
CARNOT.	PELLETAN.
ERNEST PICARD.	GARNIER PAGES.
HERRON.	JOSEPH MAGUIN.
GUEROULT.	LANJUINAIS.
BETHMONT	GLAIS BIZOIN.
DORIAN.	

Address of the deputies of the left to Mr. Bigelow, minister of the United States at Paris.

[Translation.]

United from the bottom of our hearts with the American citizens, we desire to express to them our admiration of the great people who have destroyed the last vestiges of slavery, and for LINCOLN, the glorious martyr to duty.

JULES FAVRE.	JULES SIMON.
CARNOT.	PELLETAN.
GARNIER PAGES.	GLAIS BIZOIN.
LANJUINAIS.	JOSEPH MAGUIN.
BETHMONT.	DORIAN.
ERNEST PICARD.	HERRON.
GUEROULT.	A. MALESPINE.
ALEX. BONNEAU.	C. SAUVESTRE.
J. LABBE.	A. MERAY.
H. MALOT.	ARNAUD.
JOUSSENEL.	J. J. BLANC.
ED. POMPERY.	E. GUERIN.

FOURAY.

LOUIS NOIR.

COUTANT.

DR. MONTANIER.

AZEVEDO.

J. VINET.

CAUCHOT.

PFLUGER, PÈRE.

E. CLARAC.

F. BARBADIE.

H. PERRA.

J. BACHEREAU.

G. BOTH, (of Strasbourg.)

SOISSONS.

C. MAZANDIER.

A. A. MADINIER.

DINET.

A. ROUSSEAU.

A. BACHEREAU.

E. MARTINET.

J. LEROUX.

J. E. GRAND.

J. LEELEREG.

H. PFEIFFER.

HEROLD.

FERRARI.

J. M. CAYLA.

PAUGIN.

VICTOR MEUNIER.

FRANCISQUE SARCEY.

MAN.

FOLLENFAUT.

E. HUET.

DAVEZAC.

V. B. VIGNIER.

BARAGUET.

L. TISON.

A. SIMOUNIN.

H. BARCLAY.

LEGRAND, (Hub.)

CH. BONNEAU.

CH. PIGUENOT.

L. LAZARE.

OLIVE.

A. GILLOT.

A. COGUERET.

G. PERRIN.

H. GAUTER.

DREO.

EMMANUEL ARAGO.

M. de Lhuys to M. de Geofroy.

[Translation.—Communicated by the French legation.]

DEPARTMENT OF FOREIGN AFFAIRS,
Paris, April 28, 1865.

SIR: The news of the crime of which President LINCOLN has recently become the victim has caused to the imperial government a profound sentiment of indignation.

His Majesty immediately charged one of his aides-de-camp to repair to the residence of the minister of the United States, to ask him to transmit at once the expression of his indignation to Mr. Johnson, who is now invested with the presidency. I also desired, myself, by the despatch which I addressed to you of yesterday's date, to apprise you, without delay, of the sorrowful emotion we have felt, and I have to-day, in conformity with the will of the Emperor, to render merited homage to the great citizen whose loss the United States deplore.

Elevated to the chief magistration of the republic by the suffrage of his countrymen, ABRAHAM LINCOLN had brought to the exercise of the powers placed in his hands the most substantial qualifications. Force of character was allied in him with loftiness of principle. Therefore, his vigorous spirit never quailed before the terrible trials reserved for his government. At the moment when an atrocious crime snatched him from the mission which he filled with the sense of religious duty, he enjoyed the consciousness that the triumph of his policy was definitively assured.

His recent proclamations are traces of the thoughts of prudence which inspired him in undertaking resolutely the task of reorganizing the Union and of consolidating peace. The supreme satisfaction of accomplishing this work has not been accorded to him. But, in gathering up these last testimonials of his high wisdom, as well as the examples of good sense, of courage, and of patriotism which he has given, history will not hesitate to place him in the rank of citizens who have done most honor to their country.

By order of the Emperor, I transmit this despatch to the minister of state, who is charged to communicate it to the senate and legislative body. France will unanimously take share in this thought of the Emperor.

Receive, &c.

DROUYN DE LHUYS.

Mr. L. DE GEOFROY,
  Chargé d'Affaires of France, Washington.

P. S.—You will please remit a copy of this despatch to the Secretary of State of the United States.

Mr. Geofroy to Mr. Hunter.

[Translation.]

LEGATION OF FRANCE TO THE UNITED STATES,
  Washington, April 16, 1865

SIR: I have received the note by which you announce to me the sad events which now afflict the people of the United States.

You please to inform me at the same time that the Vice-President, Andrew Johnson, has, under the Constitution, officially entered into possession of the presidency, and has authorized you, sir, to fill, until further order, the functions of Secretary of State.

I only anticipate the instructions of my government in assuring you of the deep and painful regret with which it will learn the death of President LINCOLN, and other outrages which accompanied that great crime.   That it will take very lively interest in your calamities you cannot doubt.   Please, therefore, receive all the condolences which I this day offer to you in its name, to which I add at the same time the very sincere expression of my personal feelings.

I renew to you on this occasion the assurance of my most distinguished consideration.

L. DE GEOFROY.

Hon. WILLIAM HUNTER,
    Acting Secretary of State.

[Translation.]

BOYAN-ON-THE-SEA, *May* 5, 1865.

To the United States Minister in Paris:

Frenchmen living upon the shores of the Atlantic have but to glance over the ocean, and thus feel as if they were in immediate communication with your country.

The undersigned inhabitants of Boyan, for this reason, have felt more seriously the awful event which occurred at Washington on the 14th of April last.   They now meet to express their profound grief and deep indignation to the minister, the government, and the country.

We cannot help admiring the honest and much respected ABRAHAM LINCOLN, who resisted the attacks of southern fanatics, and thus created four millions of new men.   We admired his calmness in the struggle, his lenity in victory, taught him in his civil education, by his religious observance of the law.   And now the miserable, depraved slaveholders, capable of all crimes, have cowardly deprived him of his life, and attempted that of two noble souls, Mr. Seward and his son, worthy colleagues and fellow-countrymen of the newly elected citizen President.

With firm hopes that this horrid event will serve to strengthen the Union, we ask you to receive our condolence and our cordial sympathy.

V. JOUAIN, AND FORTY OTHERS.

[Translation.]

LODGE OF LA FRANCHE UNION, AT CHOISY-LE-ROI,
    DEPARTMENT OF THE SEINE, *the* 17*th of May*, 1865.

SIR: All honest hearts were filled with indignation at the news of Mr. LINCOLN'S death, and earnestly execrated the fratricidal hand that felled the great citizen of the United States.   Tell your fellow-countrymen that during this mortal duel between freedom and slavery we never ceased to offer up our prayers for the good cause. Tell our brothers of the great republic we mourn with them the loss of a brother whose memory will be ever dear to patriots and Freemasons. He honored masonry, and we ought to feel more sensibly than others the loss caused by the assassin's dagger, hid under the cloak of liberty. His death reminds us masons, living in the shadow of Rouget de l'Isle's tomb, that in times of great convulsions it is from the field and workshop that great men spring with a bound to save their countries; and the history of our two nations furnishes many such examples. Honor also to Mr. LINCOLN for the simplicity he brought from his home to the palace where he exercised the great trust confided to him, and proved the most perfect model of a chief magistrate. This lodge in its last session decided by acclamation to make known to the brethren in the United States that it wears with them mourning for the hero and martyr whose patriotism has made him the fellow-citizen of all friends of justice and liberty.

From this date the name of ABRAHAM LINCOLN is inscribed on the list of our members, and at each session for three months a brother will rise at the call of his name, and answer: ABRAHAM LINCOLN died like a mason, to elevate humanity, outraged by slavery. At the expiration of three months we will celebrate a masonic funeral to his memory. inviting the brethren of all the other lodges.

BOURGEON, JR.,
President of the Franche Union.
AND TWENTY-FOUR OTHER MEMBERS OF THE LODGE.

The UNITED STATES MINISTER.

[Translation.]

CHAVANIAC, May 2, 1865.

SIR: I hope you will excuse me for addressing you this little note; but you will certainly think it natural that a member of the Lafayette family should wish to join the citizens of the United States in their mourning. At the time the odious crime was committed I was absent from Paris, and was sick; so it was impossible to unite with some of my countrymen in their public expressions of sorrow for the death of the eminent American statesman.

I now express all my regrets, and ask you to accept my personal esteem.

Your obedient servant,

OSCAR DE LAFAYETTE.

The UNITED STATES MINISTER, *in Paris.*

[Translation.]

PERFECT UNION LODGE,
Charente, June 1, 1865.

SIR: The Perfect Union Masonic Lodge, Orient of Confolens, grievously felt the assassination of ABRAHAM LINCOLN. We were regarding in admiration, with great interest, the gradual development of a policy which had for its object the abolition of slavery, for human liberty is one of the fundamental principles of masonic doctrine, when we were struck with stupor by the horrid news of the crime that deprived the world of one of its most honest men and most illustrious citizens.

But we are consoled when we think of the strength and vitality of your institutions, that will not leave Mr. LINCOLN's great work unfinished, and we have unanimously decided that the testimony of our sorrow, admiration, and respect should be written in the golden lodge book, and transmitted to the American nation through its representative in Paris.

Accept, sir, the assurance of our most distinguished sentiments.

The Venerable A. DUCLOU.
E. DUCHIRON, *Watchmaker.*
ULKEVETIER.
RABAUD-LARIBIÈRE.
AUDOIN, *Secretary.*

Sealed by—
E. GIBOUIN, *Keeper of the Seals.*
The UNITED STATES MINISTER, *in Paris.*

Mr. Talbot to Mr. Bigelow.

[Translation.]

CAEN, CALVADOS, *October* 20, 1865.

SIR: At the first news of the assassination of President LINCOLN we had circulated the address which we send you so late to-day.

This address was covered with the signatures of the most prominent persons of our city, and names collected from all classes of society.

Wishing to add to the number, one of our friends took the address and caused it to pass from hand to hand, and finally it was mislaid for several months.

It was impossible to think of asking for so many signatures over again, but happily we succeeded in finding the paper, and now hasten to send it to you.

We think indeed that it is never too late to testify once more the sympathy of the French people for the American people, and to add our felicitations to your President Johnson upon the re-establishment of the Union in a manner at once so conciliating and so energetic, so firm and so lawful.

Thus America gives to the Old World a grand and noble lesson. Among us, a powerful general, commanding nearly a million soldiers, would have profited by that crime to proclaim that it was necessary to save the republic by a dicta- torship, and he would at last have destroyed it for the profit of personal ambition.

With you the Constitution has been respected with a sublime simplicity. Grant, Sherman, and all your generals remain simple citizens, but great citizens.

We thank them, we thank your President and your noble American people, for giving to us at this day the spectacle of the manly virtues of the bright days of the Roman republic—to us people of the Latin race, who have now before our eyes only Octaviuses, without vigor, tottering in their buskins while trying to play the part of worn-out Cæsars, amid the suppressed jeers of Europe.

Hail, then, to Johnson, to Grant, to Sherman! Hail to all your citizens, and Heaven grant that they may send back to France with the winds of the ocean—with its tempests if need be—those powerful blasts of liberty which it sent to them a century ago, at its first awaking.

We salute you fraternally.

EDWARD TALBOT, *Proprietor.*

SETE, *Retired Merchant.*

Mr. BIGELOW, *Minister Plenipotentiary*
of the Republic of the United States, at Paris.

The inhabitants of the city of Caen to the honorable Mr. Johnson, President of the United States.

[Translation.]

SIR: There are crimes which shock and distress not one nation only, but the conscience of mankind. At the first rumors of the assassination of Mr. LINCOLN all Europe shudders with indignation and grief. Impelled by this emotion, spontaneous, universal, irresistible, the public authorities themselves bow with respect before that new-made grave.

Why these unanimous regrets? It was not only because, springing from the ranks of the people, Mr. LINCOLN, by force of will, of toil, of energy, had reached the highest dignity of his land; it was not only because, in the face of immense difficulties, he had arranged all, smoothed all, surmounted all; but it was, above all, because he had accomplished that enormous task without veiling the statue of liberty; it was because he had become a great man by respecting the laws, and remaining an honest man.

This is why your sorrow is the sorrow of all good men.

But at the same time they have confidence in your institutions, and they know that the crime which has been committed will but confirm anew their vitality and power.

They intended to slay the future of a people; they have only smitten slavery. A great man is dead; a great people remains.

It is to them that we send across the ocean our deep regrets, our fraternal sympathies. Say to them that we love them; tell them that we have suffered with their sufferings; that we have followed with anguish the changing aspects of their implacable strife, and applauded their victory with the enthusiasm of hope, and ask them also to love us, and to love our France.

Tell them to weep for their great citizen departed, but not to pity him. LINCOLN had prevented the dismemberment of his country; he had abolished slavery; he had lived enough; he could die. *Dulce et decorum est pro patriâ mori.*

Tell them, in fine, that humanity has never given birth but in sorrow ; that to just and holy causes there is need of noble martyrs, and that for the ages the only true crowns are the crowns of thorns, shining over Calvaries.

CAEN, CALVADOS, *May* 10, 1865.

An address sent to Mr. Bigelow by M. Ed. Laboulaye, on the part of the inhabitants of the town of Guingamp

[Translation.]

MONSIEUR LE MINISTRE: ABRAHAM LINCOLN has just fallen a martyr to liberty. He dies in the full blaze of triumph, struck down by an assassin at the moment when the great republic of the United States had passed through the most grievous trials, thanks to the civic virtues and the energy of their illustrious President. The undersigned, citizens resident at Guingamp, hasten, sir, to testify to you the feeling of affliction and indignation in which this cruel event has plunged them. They are not uneasy about the future of your great nation, because they know that with a free people the fate of their institutions does not depend upon the life of one man, however illustrious he may be, but they do not the less consider it a duty to deplore with you the death of the excellent man whose name will be inscribed in history by the side of that of Washington.

H. LEMASSON,	LEMASSON, PÈRE.
P. LEMASSON, FILS	S. JERET.
ED. GUYOMARD	G. ARGUINT.
J. M. THOMAS	HILARY.
G. LECORNEE.	O. DONIELL.
LE GUOYOT.	P. LE COY.
A. BERNARD	H. LEBENAFF.

AND OTHERS.

[Translation.]

SIR: At the terrible news now resounding throughout the whole world, the hearts of all French Masons are filled with sorrow. They have shed tears of sympathy for the glorious death of one who, after having used the hammer, square, and compass, those living implements of our immortal society, raised himself by his genius, his virtues, and spotless life to be the great chief of the American people.

The most holy causes, by a necessary consecration, have always had their martyrs; and ABRAHAM LINCOLN will be reckoned as one of them, the noblest victim of duty.

The New Friendship Lodge of Grasse lends its voice to the echo of universal regret of French Freemasonry.

It does not forget that if all men are brothers, France and America are still closer united by this sublime bond, and trusts that a supreme consolation will reach the soul of ABRAHAM LINCOLN.

No! the grand villain's crime cannot destroy the great work of the immortal citizen. A final peace and the abolition of slavery are the just fruits of his glorious conduct, and these rewards of his martyrdom will show the world what the devotion of a noble heart can do against the prejudices of ignorance.

Receive, sir, the assurance of our most respectful consideration.

[Signed by all the officers of the lodge; names cannot be deciphered.]

A similar letter is addressed by this lodge to the Grand Lodge of New York, and a sealed letter to Mrs. Lincoln.

To all the Freemasons of the Grand Lodge of New York, by their brothers the United Benefactors of Gentilly.

[Translation.]

MOST ILLUSTRIOUS BROTHERS: The holy cause of liberty has one martyr more. The secular work of emancipation of the human race began the day when tyranny took the place of fraternity between the strong and the weak; was continued in the Parthenon and on Calvary; then by reform and revolution has finally gained a new victory in the United States, where again the blood of the just has been shed. It is one of the laws of human development that no change can be effected in the social or political order without terrible convulsions, and at the sacrifice of the most precious lives. A victim of his devotion to the eternal principles of justice and truth, the very illustrious brother, ABRAHAM LINCOLN, has given his life for the love of his country and his fellow-creatures, thus setting the most noble example a masonic brother can give to his brethren—*transiit benefaciendo!*

The horrid crime that felled him in the hour of victory has carried pain and consternation into every heart. Let us mourn! Freemasonry has suffered an irreparable loss. Let us mourn! For persecuted virtue only triumphs after long and frightful struggles, and after most cruel sacrifices.

But let us hope that the blood of ABRAHAM LINCOLN has not been shed in vain. The redeemer of the black race will hereafter be numbered among the benefactors of the human race.

Brothers, you will complete the work of the great and generous citizen, whose name will shine in history by the side of that of Washington; the founder and restorer of the American Union will go down to posterity together. Courage, brothers, courage! Slavery of the body is conquered; but slavery of the soul, the worst kind of servitude, yet remains. Let us face it boldly; we in the old continent, you in the new. Let us struggle to destroy the ignorance and prejudices that yet enslave the human mind.

Our zeal in effecting the complete emancipation of the human race is the greatest and most worthy homage we can render to the memory of the eminent man whose premature and tragic end is now deplored by all Freemasonry.

Brethren of the Grand Lodge of New York, receive the sincere expression of our ardent sympathy. Let our hearts form a chain of union. Fraternity knows no distance; let us stretch our hands across the Atlantic. Our thought is in you, as yours is in us.

Your devoted brothers of the United Benefactors,

Honorary Venerable, LECAILLIER.
. Venerable, CAMPAGNE.
First W., DEGONY, *Orator*.
Second W., V. FREQUDRE, *Simors*.
Secretary, E. PERRECHAY.
Almoner, BOURNIR.
Treasurer, GUENDIN.

AND MANY OTHERS.

[Translation.]

The abominable crime of Wilkes Booth has thrown into your hands all the duties and all the powers of the great republic of the United States. ·

The Freemasons who assemble at the Orient of Gaillac (Tarn) in the Lodge of St. John, under the distinctive title of *Orion*, wish to express to you their sentiments of admiration, gratitude, and regret for LINCOLN, and their profound sympathy for the government of which you are the head.

The blood of your martyred magistrate becomes a fecundating dew to give to liberty a new baptism throughout the entire universe.

Sound democracy laments LINCOLN in blessing his memory. God has received him into glory, and his wisdom inspires you. We, the members of this lodge, salute you in the name of the true children of light.

GARY.

P. NIGAL.

DEMURE.

CASSAGNES.

PANTHE.

AND MANY OTHERS.

Mr. ANDREW JOHNSON,
President of the United States of America.

[Translation.]

To the senators and representatives of the American Congress :

GENTLEMEN: We, creoles of Guadeloupe, of African descent, wish to express the profound sorrow we feel at the loss your great republic has suffered in the person of its illustrious President, ABRAHAM LINCOLN.

This event, which has shocked the civilized world and all the true friends of the northern cause—the cause of the freedom of an oppressed race—cannot find us indifferent. Therefore we hasten to lay before you the solemn testimony of our sincere grief and cordial sympathy on this occasion of the ever to be regretted loss of the eminent statesman to whom you had intrusted the destinies of the Union, and to take part in the mourning of the land of Washington and Jefferson, those glorious heroes whose virtue will ever be the eulogy of posterity for one who will henceforward be placed by their side in the history of humanity, ABRAHAM LINCOLN.

Accept, gentlemen, with our regrets, the wishes we express for the prosperity of the American republic, and for the triumph of the great principles of liberty and equality.

A. GABRIEL.

P. GIRAUD.

CELESTIN NICOLAS.

F. BLANC.

SYL. BORY.

O. ST. JULIEN

DL. DAGUIN.

C. DUMAS.

AND MANY OTHERS.

[Translation.]

LYONS, FRANCE, *May* 30, 1865.

CITIZEN PRESIDENT: The republicans of Lyons were profoundly moved on hearing the news of the crime committed upon your illustrious predecessor, and a fraternal feeling inspires them with the sacred duty of sending their sad regrets to the free country of which you have the honor of being the Chief Magistrate. We have witnessed all the phases of the gigantic struggle sustained with so much energy by the much lamented ABRAHAM LINCOLN. We participated in all the emotions of republicans faithful to the Union, and we meet them with our sympathies.

Our city, by its manufactures, is more closely united to the republic of the United States than any other in France, and in our feelings for your losses we have still closer ties. The war has injured us by paralyzing our industry; but, like you, we preferred conquest to compromise, because it insured the true principles of universal freedom.

We wish these expressions of our sympathy to be communicated to your Congress, and desire them to be made known to all the citizens of America who have been so brave in their duty, so invincible in their liberty. Let them know that in France they have brothers who appreciate their patriotic efforts, and, like them, love liberty, and understand the power of institutions that resist assassinations and oppose conspiracies.

Honor to Mr. LINCOLN! eternal regrets to his venerated memory; and may his glorious name become the pledge of alliance between the American republic and the democracy of Europe.

Members of the committee:

THIVOLLET, *President.*

AND MANY OTHERS.

The PRESIDENT.

P. S.—The republicans of Lyons hope soon to send an honorary banner* dedicated to the memory of Mr. LINCOLN.

THIVOLLET.

---

* The silk weavers of Lyons subsequently presented the United States government with the banner above referred to, woven without seam, and on which the following inscription is beautifully embroidered in gold:

SOUSCRIPTION POPULAIRE.

A LA REPUBLIQUE DES ETATS UNIS OFFERT EN MEMOIRE

D'ABRAHAM LINCOLN.

LYONS, 1865.

[Translation.]

LYONS, *April* 28, 1865.

Permit us, the undersigned, to offer to the American people, through you, Mr. President, the expression of our poignant grief caused by the cowardly and odious crime that has plunged all friends of the Union into mourning. Strangers to politics, we, members of the Evangelical Alliance of Lyons, who have many friends in your country, feel as Christians the necessity of telling you how much we rejoice in the triumph of your holy cause, the abolition of slavery; but this triumph was crowned by martyrdom; for it we shed tears, but feel it is a great stain on the garments of iniquity, though it is one more pledge of victory. Already, during the course of your long struggle, the Christians of France have taken the occasion to send to their brothers in America words of cordial sympathy. Our prayers were united with yours. We sighed at the thought of so much bloodshed, and prayed for the end of the fratricidal war. To-day our prayers are heard. Millions of human beings have felt their fetters fall. We thank God for it. We will continue to ask aid from on high to heal so many wounds, to comfort so many widows and orphans, and to raise from LINCOLN's tomb such spirits as may bless the world. The gospel makes it our duty to pray for princes—for those in high power—for rulers of a people, and we fulfil this duty towards the President of the United States. May the Lord, the author of all grace, endow him with many benedictions.

Accept, Mr. President, the homage of our most profound respect.

Members of the committee of the Evangelical Alliance of Lyons:

S. DESCOMBAZ,
Pastor and President.

E. MILSAM.
DARDIER.
FELIX FOY.
Rev. C. A. CORDES.
J. WALTHER.
Rev. J. KIRCHOFFER.

The PRESIDENT OF THE UNITED STATES.

[Translation.]

To the glory of the Great Architect of the Universe. The Lodge of Toleration and Progress, 24th day of the month, in the year of light 5865. Wisdom, strength, union.

SIR: The honest people of all countries are struck with horror at the crime to which the illustrious ABRAHAM LINCOLN has fallen a victim, and in the masonic lodges especially, devoted to benevolence and the relief, human suffering, the death of the glorious martyr has filled all hearts with profound sorrow. This respectable Lodge of Toleration and Progress, in the Orient of Lure, (Upper Saone,) at its session the 10th of May instant, requested me to forward to you this testimony of their sympathy for the memory of Brother LINCOLN.

Receive the homage of my high consideration.

The Venerable COUTHERAT,

Notary at Lure.

The MINISTER OF THE UNITED STATES.

[Translation.]

L'ESCOLE DE LA MORALE LODGE OF LIBOURNE,

16*th day of the 3d month, in the year of light* 5865.

Our emotions were deep on hearing the news of the crime committed upon the person of your President, Mr. LINCOLN, our illustrious brother. The lodge unanimously resolved, at a called session, to wear mourning for three months, in token of the deep affliction caused by the loss of him who was among the greatest benefactors of the human race.

Have the goodness to accept this decision, and regard it as a proof of our deep attachment to and our feeling for the noble cause you so worthily defend.

We have the honor to be your very humble and very devoted servants,

AUDRIER.
J. GALLET, JR.
J. MORIA, *M.*
CASTANET.
PUJO.
KREMP.

His Excellency the MINISTER
of the United States of America, at Paris

[Translation.]

MACON, *May* 16, 1865.

The R. L. of Combined Arts at Macon to the President of the United States:

The masonic lodge, known by the distinctive name of Les Art Reunis Orient de Macon, wishing to associate itself with the universal mourning caused by the horrible crime committed by a wretch on the respected person of President LINCOLN, begs you to please to become to your countrymen the interpreter of its deep sorrow and its sympathies.

It is for us, Freemasons, who know no distinction of race or color—who receive without distinction in our temples the prosperous of this world in the same manner as the disinherited, and who believe sincerely in human brotherhood—it is for us, to express aloud to your brave nation all the sorrow that masonry has felt in learning that the worthy man twice called by the suffrages of his countrymen to preside over the destinies of your great republic, had been cowardly assassinated at the moment when his task seemed done.

After such a misfortune we can only say to you, courage, brave defenders of the oppressed against oppression, of the wretched slave against the unpitying master—courage, your cause is gained !

The death of the glorious martyr of equality and fraternity that we mourn to-day will not hinder the accomplishment of his work of redemption ; as the genius of Voltaire has survived his profaned remains, the spirit of LINCOLN will survive his mutilated body.

As for yourself, Mr. President, may you be his worthy continuation—finish breaking the chains of the poor slave—this new brother you have to protect, to instruct, and to love.

Please to receive, Mr. President, the assurance of our sympathies.

The Venerable (in function) F. MARTINELLE,

The Second (18) Supervisor.

The First Supervisor VINCAUX, M.

The Venerable *ad vitam* Leger 18, CORFFARD, Fils.

The Orator, FRAUEN GUERIN.

[SEAL OF THE SOCIETY.]   The Keeper of Seals and Stamp, BERTHELON.

N. L. GRUND.

By order of the lodge :

DAVID.

The Secretary, BERTRANT.

VICTOR JAMES, *G.* 1 *Exp.*	VICTOR, M.
LAMBERT.	JANVIER.
MAUDELEIN MOULET.	GAMBER,
LAURENT.	E. LOISOT, *Sergeant Major.*
BREMONT.	G. BORGIA.

[Translation.]

To the glory of the Great Architect of the Universe. Under the auspices of the Grand Order of France, Order of Metz, (this 10th May, 1865, of the vulgar era,) and St, John's Lodge, all under the title of The Friends of Truth.

To the Ambassador of the United States :

RESPECTED SIR : At a time when exclamations of condemnation arise in all parts of the world against the horrid crime of which President LINCOLN has been the victim, Freemasonry would be derelict to its duty if it did not raise its voice in expression of profound grief for his death, sympathy with the adversaries of slavery, and its esteem and admiration for the great and good man, so great a loss to the American Union.

The members of the lodge of The Friends of Truth, in Metz, decided, in their session of the eighth of this month, that the banner of their lodge should be draped in black for a month, as mourning for and in honor of the memory of President LINCOLN, who, by his death, the result of his devotion to a holy cause, has gained a glorious placé in history, and that an address, signed by the five dignitaries, should be sent to you in expression of the participation of the Metz lodge in the universal mourning for the loss of the good man, who, by his uprightness, his loyalty, his public and private virtues, his devotion, and his benevolence, carries to his grave the great regrets and profound esteem of all good people.

Hoping the address may be favorably received, we beg you will accept the most respectful homage of the members of the Metz lodge.

> THIERY, *W. M.*
> P. MESSE, *S. Warden.*
> JANON, *J. Warden.*
> CARRERE, *Orator.*
> INCIENSUY, *Secretary.*

[Translation.]

MONTAUBAN AND TOULOUSE, *May* 3, 1865.

SIR: We appear in our two-fold capacity, as members of the French Protestant church and as correspondents of the London Society for the Abolition of Slavery, to express to you our profound and painful sympathy, felt on hearing of the atrocious crime committed on the person of your honorable President, Mr. ABRAHAM LINCOLN.

In him the United States has lost the most upright and the best of citizens; the blacks, a wise and firm supporter of their emancipation; and humanity a strong defender of order, justice, and liberty. The death of none of our contemporaries could have caused more regret, or produced a more universal mourning; and this homage has been well deserved, for ABRAHAM LINCOLN, next to Washington, will leave to history a name the most worthy of respect. He knew how to reconcile moderation with the maintenance of right, and the sentiments of a faithful Christian with the highest virtues of the citizen.

We bow to the mysterious ways of Providence, and we hope that this event, sad as it is, may tend, in the hands of Him who can bring good from evil, to hasten the re-establishment of the great American Union, and to remove the last remaining obstacles to the complete emancipation of the slaves.

The conscientious portion of humanity had already declared for the North, because it upheld a just and holy cause, and it will become bolder advocates after this horrid crime that has soiled southern partisans; and we are happy in thinking that the greater part of the rebels themselves will wash their hands of this stain, and hasten to recognize the legitimate authority of their country and its proper laws.

Have the kindness, sir, to be the interpreter of our sympathies to Mrs. Lincoln and to the American nation, and accept for yourself the expression of our respectful and devoted sentiments.

G. DE FELÍCE, D. D.,
Professor of Theology at Montauban.
FRANK COURTOIS,
Banker in Toulouse.
ARMAN COURTOIS,
Banker in Toulouse.

Although I do not belong to the committee for slave emancipation, I am happy to join in the sentiments expressed by my friends in the preceding letter, and take pleasure in embracing this occasion to manifest my profound affection for the American people.

LAFORGUE,
President of the Toulouse Consistory.

The UNITED STATES MINISTER, *Paris.*

[Translation.]

Lodge of St. John of Jerusalem to the United States Minister at Paris.

NANCY, *May* 24, 1865.

SIR: If the savage crime perpetrated upon your illustrious President has excited the indignation of all civilized nations, much more sensibly has it been felt by the great masonic association that gloried in calling Mr LINCOLN one of its children.

Sprung from the people, he won the highest position in his country by his industry, merit, and intelligence, and honored it by his deeds. Unwavering in the terrible struggle, in his gentleness he forgot and pardoned in the hour of victory; and, like a truly great man, by his persevering energy united a nation dismembered by egotism and ambition; and by severing the chains of slavery, had the honor of restoring to the human race one branch of the family too long neglected. His glory is now united to that of George Washington and Benjamin Franklin, his immortal countrymen.   The Freemasons belonging to the Lodge of St. John of Jerusalem, at Nancy, join in the universal mourning, and request you to assure the brethren in America their regrets are shared, and that we feel in all its bitterness the grief of the heroic citizens of the Union.   They bow with profound respect before the sorrow of Mrs. Lincoln.

Accept the expression of our most respectful sentiments.

LA FLIZE, *the Venerable.*
B. TISSERAND, *S. W.*
G. THIEBAULT, *J. W.*
ED. LAUMANC, *Orator.*

By order of the secretary :

L. FRANK.

[Translation.]

NIMES, *May* 3, 1865.

To the United States Minister in Paris:

We have the honor of transmitting to you in this envelope the address of our house, on the occasion of the death of the great American citizen, whom we and the whole world lament.

We join in this universal manifestation of sorrow, and ask you to send our homage to its address.

Receive the respectful greeting of your very humble servants,

LOUIS & CASIMIR DIDETT.
FATHER AND SON, *Hat Manufacturers in Nimes*

[Translation.]

MADAM LINCOLN : Will you have the goodness, madam, to receive the expression of our sincere regret, and permit us to lament with you the immense loss which you have just experienced in the person of the greatest and most honest citizen in the universe.

Yes, we deeply lament the loss of the man who, sprung from the laboring class, has, by his intelligence, energy, and virtue, earned the glory of creating equality in his country by the abolition of slavery.

Let all America accept the wishes which we sincerely feel for the prosperity of her noble country ; and let the family of that great man believe in our affectionate sentiments, with which we have the honor to be your devoted servants.

[Here follow thirty-three signatures.]

NICE, FRANCE, *May* 1, 1865.

To his Excellency Andrew Johnson, President of the United States:

The undersigned, Americans residing at Nice, desire to express to you the profound sorrow they feel in hearing of the abominable crime which has deprived the United States of the pure and noble-hearted ABRAHAM LINCOLN.

Their faith remains unshaken, however, that under God's protection the republic, already victorious over a wicked rebellion, will come out of its trials purer and stronger than it ever has been, and they earnestly pray that God may bless and sustain you to complete the great work so faithfully carried on by your lamented predecessor.

Mr. JOHN WURTS, *New York.*

Mrs. JAMES LESLEY, *Philadelphia.*

Mrs. JAMES LESLEY, Jr, *Philadelphia.*

R. M. DEL CASTILLO, *Louisiana.*

Mrs. ISAAC R. ELWOOD, *New York.*

FRANK W. ELWOOD, *New York.*

Mrs. E. C. KINNEY.

ALBERT DABADIE, *Philadelphia.*

Mrs. F. A. DEPAU, *Philadelphia.*

COUNTESS BOUXHOWDEN, *Bordentown, N. J.*

JULIA P. PILATTE, *Virginia.*

CHARLES O. HALL, *Massachusetts.*

Mrs. CHARLES O. HALL, *Massachusetts.*

Mr. Bigelow to Mr. Seward.

No. 86.]   LEGATION OF THE UNITED STATES, ·
Paris, April 28, 1865.

SIR: An aide-de-camp of the Emperor called early yesterday morning at the legation, officially to testify the horror and sorrow which his Majesty experienced on learning the crime which had just deprived the United States of its President. On the receipt of the first report his Majesty had refused to credit it, but a second despatch, later in the evening, left no room to doubt its correctness. It was then too late to send to the legation, but the aide-de-camp was instructed to come at an early hour the next morning to express the sentiments of his Majesty, and to request, on behalf of the Emperor, that I would transmit an expression of them to the Vice-President.

It is my duty to add my conviction that his Majesty, in the communication which he has requested me to make, is but a faithful interpreter of the sentiments of his subjects, who have received the intelligence with a unanimous expression of horror for the crime and of sympathy for its victims.

You will find some of the evidence of this in the journals which I send you.

I have been occupied most of the afternoon in receiving deputations from students and others, who have called to testify their sorrow and sympathy. Unfortunately, their feelings were so demonstrative in some instances as to provoke the intervention of the police, who would only allow them in very limited numbers through the streets. One of the delegations told me that there were three thousand of them who would have wished to have united in a formal expression of their feelings, if the police had not stopped them. I am sorry to hear that some have been sent to prison in consequence of an intemperate expression of their feelings. I can now count sixteen policemen from my window patrolling about in the neighborhood, who occasionally stop persons calling to see me, and in some instances, I am told, send them away.

I had no idea that Mr. LINCOLN had such a hold upon the heart of the young gentlemen of France, or that his loss would be so properly appreciated.

I have received many letters of condolence already from distinguished citizens, of which I send copies of two; the first from his excellency Drouyn de Lhuys, and the second from his Imperial Highness Prince Pierre Napoleon Bonaparte.

I must reserve for another mail the expression of my own feelings under a dispensation which has almost paralyzed me, and which yet seems to me like the revelation of a troubled dream. I hope this may find you recovering from your wounds, and mercifully sustained under the great trials with which God has been pleased to visit you and yours.

I am, sir, with great respect, your very obedient servant,

JOHN BIGELOW.

Hon. WILLIAM H. SEWARD,
  Secretary of State, &c., &c., &c.

Mr. Bigelow to Mr. Seward.

[Extract.]

No. 87.]   LEGATION OF THE UNITED STATES,
            Paris, May 3, 1865.

SIR: His excellency the minister of foreign affairs was kind enough, on Saturday last, the 29th of April, to read, and at the same time to hand me, a copy of a communication which he had made, by order of the Emperor, to the French minister at Washington in reference to our recent national bereavement. His excellency also informed me that it would be communicated to both of the legislative branches of the government on the Monday following. It would have been communicated on the day it was shown to me if the corps legislatif had been in session.

As I had been notified, his excellency Mr. Vuitry, minister president of the council of state, at the opening of the senate yesterday, and by order of the Emperor, read the despatch to which I have referred, and added that he hoped the members of the senate would unite in the sentiments which the Emperor had charged him to testify to them.

The president of the senate, M. Troplong, replying in the name of the assembly to the commissioner of the government, declared that the senate shared entirely the views of the Emperor; that it had been struck with the same sorrow, and even indignation, when it heard of the attempt made upon the person of a citizen borne to the supreme power by the free choice of his country; that this sorrow could only be increased by the recollection of the noble sentiments of moderation and of conciliation manifested in the recent proclamation of President LINCOLN.

The president, Troplong, then proposed, and the senate unanimously voted, its adhesion to the sentiments of the despatch to the French minister at Washington, in the usual form.

The same communication was simultaneously submitted to the corps legislatif by his excellency Monsieur Rouher, minister of state, with a few impressive remarks. The vice-president, Schneider, interpreting the feelings of the assembly, expressed its horror at the crime which had been thus brought to their notice, and announced that the corps legislatif shared completely the sentiments of the government.   *   *   *   *   *   *   *

I am, sir, with great respect, your very obedient servant,

JOHN BIGELOW.

Hon. WILLIAM H. SEWARD,
    Secretary of State, &c., &c., &c.

Mr. Bigelow to Mr. Seward.

[Extract.]

No. 90.]   LEGATION OF THE UNITED STATES,
             Paris, May 10, 1865.

SIR: At my suggestion a meeting was held at this legation on Tuesday, the 2d instant, which appointed a committee of nine to prepare an address that should express the feelings inspired among them by the horrible crimes perpetrated at the seat of government on the night of the 14th of April.

On Tuesday, the 9th instant, the committee, at the legation and in the presence of a large concourse of our country people, presented me the address, which they had prepared in compliance with their instructions, and which was signed by several hundred Americans.   *   *   *   *

You will find also that the address and reply have been deemed worthy of the hospitality of the Moniteur of this morning, a grace which will probably insure their general circulation throughout France.

It would have been more satisfactory to our colony here, because more in accordance with our national usages, to have held a public meeting, in the exercises of which there could have been a more general participation; but, in view of the profound excitement produced throughout France by the events which would constitute the pretext for holding such a meeting, I did not think proper to give to such a demonstration any encouragement. A funeral service, conducted by the respective pastors, was held in both the American chapels here on different days, and both had an overflowing attendance.

The expressions of sympathy which reach me daily from every quarter are to me, as an American, of the most gratifying, I might indeed say of the most flattering character. The press of the metropolis shows sufficiently how overwhelming is the public sentiment. Among innumerable written testimonials of sympathy, I have received some from public bodies and from groups of people, which I propose to send you as soon as I have enough copying force liberated to prepare them.

I am, sir, with great respect, your very obedient servant,

JOHN BIGELOW.

Hon. WILLIAM H. SEWARD,
  Secretary of State, Washington, D. C.

Mr. Bigelow to Mr. Seward.

No. 109.]   LEGATION OF THE UNITED STATES,
              Paris, May 31, 1865.

SIR: Among the manifold testimonials of sympathy elicited by the assassination of our late President, some have seemed worthy of being transmitted to Washington to be read, and, perhaps, placed among the archives of the government; others have other destinations, for reaching which the facilities of the State Department are more or less requisite. I transmit them in a body, trusting that you will give them, respectively, their proper direction.

I have divided them into three categories: the first category consists of eleven letters addressed to Mrs. Lincoln; the second category consists of twenty-nine communications from masonic lodges, three addressed to President Johnson, eighteen to the United States minister at Paris, and eight to American lodges; the third category consists of four letters and addresses to heads of the government, and of twenty-eight to the United States minister at Paris—making in all seventy-two enclosures.

Though these form but a small proportion, numerically, of the testimonials of sympathy which have been already addressed to me by the people of France, and a still smaller proportion of those yet to be expected, they will suffice to show not only how profoundly the nation was shocked by the dreadful crime which terminated President LINCOLN's earthly career, but how deep a hold he had taken upon the respect and affections of the French people. It is difficult to exaggerate the enthusiasm which his name inspires among the masses of Europe at this moment—an enthusiasm before which the ruling classes, however little disposed to waste compliments upon anything tainted with republicanism, are obliged to incline. I think it is generally conceded that the death of no man has ever occurred that awakened such prompt and universal sympathy at once among his own country people and among foreign nations. There can be no better evidence that the world is advancing in civilization than this unprecedented and spontaneous homage to the virtues of Mr. LINCOLN. It shows that the moral standard of nations has been greatly exalted within the memory of living men. It does not deserve to be reckoned among the secondary achievements of our people during the last four years to have furnished the world with such a striking demonstration of this gratifying truth.

I am, sir, with great respect, your very obedient servant,

JOHN BIGELOW.

Hon. WILLIAM H. SEWARD,
    Secretary of State.

Mr. Bigelow to Mr. Seward.

LEGATION OF THE UNITED STATES,
Paris, December 7, 1866.

MY DEAR SIR: I have been requested by a committee of some of the most eminent republicans of France to transmit the accompanying medal and letter to the widow of our late President LINCOLN. No opportunity presenting itself immediately of sending directly to Mrs. Lincoln, I have thought best to send it by the despatch bag directly to the State Department, and to rely upon your finding or providing suitable means for its delivery to Mrs. Lincoln. I was the less disinclined to give the State Department this trouble as I realize the importance of having Mrs. Lincoln seasonably and well advised in regard to the reply which it becomes her to make to the letter which is addressed to her.

I remain, dear sir, very faithfully yours,

JOHN BIGELOW.

Hon. WILLIAM H. SEWARD.

Eminent citizens of France transmits a gold medal to Mrs. Lincoln

[Translation.]

PARIS, *October* 13, 1866.

MADAM: On behalf of more than forty thousand French citizens, anxious to manifest their sympathies for the American Union, in the person of one of its most illustrious and purest representatives, we are instructed to offer you the medal* which has been coined in honor of the great and good man whose name you bear.

If France had the freedom enjoyed by republican America, not thousands, but millions among us would have been counted as admirers of LINCOLN, and believers in the opinions for which he devoted his life, and which his death has consecrated.

Deign to accept, madam, the homage of our profound respect

Members of the committee:

ETIENNE ARAGO.	CH. L. CHAROIN.
EUG. DESPOIS.	ALBERT.
J. MICHELET.	V. CHAUFFOUR.
E. LITTRE.	VICTOR MAUGIN.
EUGENE PELLETAN.	L. GREPPO.
L. KNEIP.	LAURENT PICHAT.
C. THOMAS.	JULES BARNI.
J. DELORD.	V. JOIGNAUX.
V. SCHOELCHER.	LOUIS BLANC.
EDGAR QUINET.	VICTOR HUGO.

Mrs. MARY LINCOLN.

CHICAGO, *January* 3, 1867.

GENTLEMEN: I have received the medal you have sent me. I cannot express the emotion with which this proof of the sentiments of so many thousands of your countrymen fills me. So marked a testimony to the memory of my husband, given in honor of his services in the cause of liberty, by those who in another land worked for the same great end, touches me profoundly, and I beg you to accept, for yourselves and those whom you represent, my most grateful thanks.

I am, with the profoundest respect, your most obedient servant,

MARY LINCOLN.

---

* The medal above mentioned is inscribed as follows :

LINCOLN, *an honest man ; abolished slavery, saved the republic, and was assassinated the* 14th *of April,* 1865.

On the reverse :

Dedicated by the French democracy to LINCOLN, *twice elected President of the United States.*

LIBERTY ! EQUALITY ! FRATERNITY !

[Translation.]

PARIS, *April* 26, 1865.

SIR: I believe I am fulfilling a duty, but a very painful one, in begging you to accept the expression of the profound affliction I feel in hearing of the death of President LINCOLN. The sympathy with which that great man has honored my father's memory increases my profound regret. This regret shall be shared by all noble hearts in all countries; and the glorious name of LINCOLN, standing by the side of Washington's, shall be the everlasting honor of your great republic.

With great respect and cordial fraternity, I have the honor to be, sir, your very obedient servant,

PIERRE NAPOLEON BONAPARTE.

Mr. BIGELOW,
United States Minister, Paris.

[Translation.]

PARIS, *May* 1, 1865.

CITIZEN MINISTER: President LINCOLN has fallen by the assassin's pistol; the representative of a democracy of noble and consistent virtues has fallen in the hour of his triumph—has fallen at a happy time, after a hundred battles, as calm in victory as he was firm in defeat, and, like a new Washington, has saved the great republic.

A glorious and enviable death! LINCOLN died a victim of his great idea, that of safety to his country and liberty for all. He belonged to the race of strong men; he is now numbered among the martyrs.

Let America know that all enthusiasm is not extinct in the youth of France; the blow that destroyed LINCOLN still agitates their hearts

American democracy has lost only one of its greatest citizens; in that land of liberty, if a hero falls, whether he be named Washington or LINCOLN, the country is not lost; its destinies depend not on a single man; the living virtue of democracy is in itself.

We must not be concerned; we are sure, in spite of what has happened—in spite of traitor Davis, whose malign influence has been exorcised by the great and good man—that the patriotic idea of a country in peril —the idea of Grant, Sheridan, and Sherman—supported by liberty, will finish the work begun by ABRAHAM LINCOLN.

Be assured that the bloody drama of which America has just been the scene, awakens the warmest sympathies of the youth of France.

May the double crime that has just laid President LINCOLN in the tomb, and Mr. Seward upon a painful bed of sickness, be soon avenged by the complete establishment of the American Union.

In the name of the young men of France, the selected reporters,

ETIENNE HANAU,

No. 28 *Prince Street.*

V. MARCHAI.

Mr. BIGELOW,
    United States Minister, Paris.

[Translation.]

CLEMENT FRIENDSHIP LODGE,

Paris, May 14, 1865.

SIR: Impressed with profound grief for the death of ABRAHAM LINCOLN, this lodge has unanimously decided to assume mourning for the space of three months.

Pursuant to this vote, taken at the session on the 4th of May, instant, it was decreed as follows :

The banner shall remain draped in mourning three months ;

The officers shall wear crape on their insignia ;

A mortuary salvo shall be fired at each session.

Please remit to your countrymen this expression of our regret for the immense loss we have all sustained.

We Masons mourn him, not only as a brother, but as a friend of the whole human race. His name will live, not only as the symbol of the abolition of slavery, but it will remain as the highest expression of that spirit of justice which is the foundation of every social edifice.

Four years of rude experience and terrible vicissitudes could not stagger his faith in the progress of human liberty and in the justice of the principle of the equality of races.

As right and victory coincided, not an unjust act tarnished the holy cause during his patriotic life. LINCOLN's first thought was the Mason's motto: fraternity. His last act was pardon, forgetfulness.

People of the American Union, may his generous blood be the last to flow in the saintly cause of liberty! Be assured the great soul of him who was your chief will rejoice if, using his clemency after victory, you will cause the spirit of integrity, of which he has set the example, to prevail throughout the entire land.

Please, sir, make known our sentiments of condolence to the bereaved widow and family of the great citizen whom we all regret.

Accept the assurance of our high consideration.

BÉRINGER,
Master of the Clement Friendship Lodge.

By order of the lodge :

CHOTARD, *Chief Secretary.*

Mr. BIGELOW,
United States Minister, Paris.

[Translation.]

ORIENTAL LODGE OF PARIS,
May 8, 1865, *(common era.)*

SIR : The lodge éntitled Triumphant Friends, truly interpreting the fraternal feelings which should animate all Freemasons, requests you to transmit to the American people the expression of profound sorrow at the horrible assassination of Mr. ABRAHAM LINCOLN.

As a worthy expression of regret, the lodge has decided to drape its banner in mourning for three months. It sincerely desires the prosperity of your country, the abolition of slavery, and the reign of liberty.

Please accept, sir, for yourself and your fellow-citizens, the expression of our profound sympathy.

For the Lodge of Triumphant Friends,

MOTARD, *W. M.,*
No. 15 *Avenue Clignancourt.)*

The UNITED STATES MINISTER, *Paris.*

[Translation.]

To the glory of the Great Architect of the Universe. In the name and under the auspices of the Grand Order of France. Chapter of Mars and the Arts. Union, strength, wisdom.

ORIENT OF PARIS,
May 11, 1865, *(common era.)*

To the Minister of the United States of America, greeting :

SIR : The sad misfortune which has recently happened to the great American republic has vividly impressed us, and we meet, for the first time since the horrid crime of the 14th of April, to protest most sincerely against the flagitious tendencies of that monstrous moral aberration, suggested by some sinister doctrine, which would made an act of heroism and devotion out of a political assassination. But, for the honor of humanity, we behold with pride that energetic expressions of condemnation have arisen from all quarters against this insane act, this revolting doctrine.

And now, sir, suffer us to express the profound sympathy we feel for a people that have destroyed slavery, the great social evil, and for the illustrious citizen who, amidst the hardest trials, has ever been true to the regenerative mission he accepted.

Happy the country that gives birth to such men, and glory to the institutions in which such powerful individualities can be developed without danger to the nation. They are the true representatives of God upon the earth, who have such a comprehension of his justice; and of them it may be said, they are sent by Providence, the messiahs of civilization and progress. The work which they accomplish exalts them so high that they cannot be termed citizens of any particular country, for they are citizens of all; and though one single nation may claim them, their name belongs to all humanity and their death becomes a universal mourning. For this reason every lover of liberty has the right to weep with you over the premature death of ABRAHAM LINCOLN. But a stronger bond, a more intimate union, than the common tie united us particularly to his great heart.

ABRAHAM LINCOLN was our brother. Let us not be astonished, then, that he persevered so courageously in that moral work, the emancipation of the blacks, in the name of the grand principle of human dignity, which he understood so well. Like us, he knew that all men are equal, all brothers, whatever their race; and that there is nothing true but liberty, equality, fraternity, and justice.

Be, then, dear sir, our interpreter with the people of the Union. Tell them that we share their grief, that we participate in their hopes, and that we pray for peace over the entire land of America.

Bear our condolence to the bereaved family that has purchased the freedom of your beautiful and great country with the blood of such a mighty sacrifice. May the testimony of respect and sincere sympathy which reaches her from so many alleviate the heaviness of her incomparable sorrow.

The Lodge of Mars and the Arts, in solemn meditation, fired a funeral salute in honor of the illustrious dead, and decreed that the lodge banner should be draped in mourning of crape for the space of three months.

Accept the assurance of our distinguished sentiments.

LEON RICHER.

Adopted in solemn session, the 11th of May, 1865.

FELIX GUILLON, Secretary.

[Translation.]

Union, solidity, strength, fraternity. Scotch Lodge, No. 146, the Right Line. Extract from the minutes of the session of April 29, 1865, of the lodge called The Straight Line.

The Freemasons of this lodge, in the Orient of Paris, unanimously decide to send an address to the citizen Vice-President of the United States, in expression of the profound indignation of all true friends of liberty and human merit at the odious crime that has deprived a great nation of one of her most noble sons.

The name of ABRAHAM LINCOLN is indelibly impressed in the memory of all men; and the Freemasons of the Right Line express a wish that his blood, in flowing for the human race, may give life to the germ of liberty—that liberty to which ABRAHAM LINCOLN devoted his life, and for which he died.

The brethren of the Right Line, moreover, give expression to the confidence they have in the prosperity of the great republic that has fought so bravely for the abolition of slavery.

This is an authentic extract. NENE, *Secretary.*

[Translation.]

SOVEREIGN CHAPTER OF THE FRIENDS OF THE COUNTRY,

Paris, May 24, 1865.

SIR: The Sovereign Chapter of the Friends of the Country, in the Valley of Paris, expresses its cordial sympathy with the American people, and participates in the numerous manifestations of sorrow which have come from all parts of the world on account of the event that deprived them of their Chief Magistrate.

Immortal homage to the large heart that has inscribed the principles of human liberty upon the Constitution of the country by the abolition of slavery. Glory to our brother, LINCOLN, who practiced the virtues inculcated by our order, and whom masonry is proud to number among the number of her children.

Please send our tribute of respectful sorrow to the President of the American Union and to the family of the illustrious deceased.

Accept the assurance of our most distinguished consideration.

A. H. MORIN,
For the Sovereign Chapter.

By order:

GREHAN, *Secretary.*

The MINISTER OF THE U. S. OF AMERICA, *Paris.*

From the Lodge called L'Avenir to the ambassador of the United States.

[Translation.]

PARIS, *May* 25, 1865.

SIR : We fulfil a painful duty in expressing to you the profound emotion we feel and the bitter regret we have for the death of brother ABRAHAM LINCOLN. Though born in an humble and modest condition, he raised himself to the highest rank in the republic by his perseverance in good, by the superiority of his character, and by the excellence of his principles. By the votes of the North he was twice elected President. To him was reserved the glory of substantiating the dogma of human liberty upon the ruins of expiring slavery, and of effacing the shame that veiled the face of society for so many centuries. During the war that has been rending America, we admired the unwavering firmness of his design, the loftiness of his views, the disinterestedness of his spirit, his prudence in danger, his moderation in victory; and when the Atlantic's waves cast the astounding news upon our shores, we uttered a deep cry of desolation and despair.

Rest in thy tomb, sublime and immortal dead! Posterity will proclaim that you overcame the hydra of servitude, and crowned the triumph of liberty with the martyrdom of your life.

Receive, sir, the assurance of our most distinguished sentiments.

GUILLET, *the Venerable.*
A. FAUZAIS, *First Warden.*
ANTOINE BLATU, *Secretary.*
PAUL MARITAIN, *Speaker.*
CHARLES DORIOT, *Keeper of the Seals.*

Scotch Masonic Lodge La Prévoyance, No. 88, *Orient of Paris.*

[Translation.]

To the United States Minister at Paris.

SIR : The guilty hand that struck Mr. ABRAHAM LINCOLN to glut the vengeance of an unrelenting fanaticism, selected the noblest and most glorious defender of the three principles all humanity is endeavoring to realize, namely, liberty, equality, and fraternity. The Masonic Lodge La Prévoyance, in obedience to the Supreme Council of Paris, asks you to transmit to the people of the United States the expression of sorrow and indignation felt by all its members on the reception of the news of the horrible crime.

We hope the blood of the great citizen who willed and proclaimed equality of races in his country will be the last spilled in such a glorious cause, and that the crime will have the effect of fecundating the germ of liberty and fraternity already planted in the soil.

President LINCOLN died for his country and for humanity; and our lodge would be pleased to see all nations join in the erection of a monument to his memory in one of the public squares of New York.

Accept the assurance of our sympathy with the great nation you represent.

J. A. HUET, *the Venerable.*
H. CHANDELIER, *First Warden.*
REBIERRE, *Second Warden.*
D. PARENT, *Secretary.*
L. QUANQUIN, *Orator.*

By order:
DESGARDINS, *Keeper of the Seals.*

Saint John's Lodge, No. 147. *The heroes of humanity.—Extract from the minutes of the working-book.*

[Translation.]

ORIENT OF PARIS, *May* 20, 1865.

SIR: All Freemasonry mourns the death of the President, ABRAHAM LINCOLN, and this lodge also regrets the loss of a man who was not only an honor to our order, but the firmest support of your young republic.

We lament the death of the great citizen, the chosen spirit who trampled the prejudices of ancient routine under his feet and undertook the defence of the oppressed, devoting his entire life to the abolition of slavery. An indefatigable worker, impressed with the greatness of his cause, he spared no sacrifice to accomplish his mission. He was struck down at the moment of victory, and his blood confirms the work of freedom. A true martyr to liberty, he could yet pardon his murderer.

Assure his widow, his children, and all your citizens, of our whole sympathy; time only can assuage their grief, and his spirit will be their protection.

Accept the assurance of our affectionate sentiments.

A. BAILLEUX.

By order of the lodge:
JULES GONJAT.

Mr. BIGELOW,
United States Minister, Paris.

The Ancient Accepted Scotch Rite.   Universi terrarum orbis summi architectoris gloria ab ingeniis.   Ordo ab chao.

[Translation.]

PARIS, *May* 17, 1865

To the Minister of the United States:

SIR : As interpreter of the sentiments of Scotch masonry in France, I must express to you the just indignation and profound sorrow felt by all our lodges on hearing of the odious crime which has deprived North America of her illustrious President, Mr. LINCOLN, whom we had the honor to count among our brothers. He had done his duty, hard and difficult as it was, and all that remained for him to accomplish was easy and agreeable. The world saw in him the repairer of all the evils produced by the most sanguinary of civil wars. His words of clemency and benevolence, coming spontaneously from his heart, were eagerly accepted by the world; and the Scotch Masons, whose thoughts and acts are directed by the spirit of charity, join in the same hope of all generous souls. The blow that felled one man has wounded a whole nation and deprived it of its greatest glory ; and though it has disturbed our happy predictions, we still hope his spirit will rule in the councils of his successor.

Have the kindness to convey to your new President the expression of our fraternal sorrow, and to make known to the unhappy widow our participation in her misfortune. May she find some consolation in the expressions of sympathy that reach her from all quarters of the globe.

We thank you in advance for the favors expected, and ask you to accept the expression of the sentiments with which we have the honor to be, &c.

VIENNET,
Grand Commander of the Scotch-Rite, and Member of the French Academy.

[Translation.]

LODGE OF HENRY THE FOURTH,
Paris, May 15, 1865.

SIR: It is with feelings of profound grief that this lodge heard of the crime that strikes all Europe with consternation. At their first meeting, after paying a just tribute of regret for the martyr of a holy cause, they unanimously resolved to address a testimonial of their sympathy to you, the representative of a great nation, the most generous and free on the globe, and which has been so cruelly tried.

While we express horror at the assassination, we confess admiration for your institutions, which sustain you in this terrible catastrophe. God will not suffer the blood of the just to be spilled in vain. ABRAHAM LINCOLN's work will not perish with him; the total abolition of slavery was his·inspiration, and it will ever be a venerable crown of glory to his memory. It is the only thing that affords consolation for the irreparable loss; and you will finish the good work, worthy of a people who are determined to maintain the highest rank by acts of civilization and humanity. Progress is your motto, your supreme law, and the assassin's dagger cannot arrest it; you understand it, and your magnanimous nation will take a noble revenge for the death of ABRAHAM LINCOLN by fulfilling the dream of his life.

With this token of mourning saddening our hearts, accept the sentiments of respectful esteem we have for you and the nation you represent.

J. POULAIN,
ACOVEY,
P. DUBOE,
J. LAVERRIERE,
BERTIN,
Delegates to the Lodge of Henry the Fourth.

Mr. J. BIGELOW

[Translation.]

PERSEVERANCE LODGE, ORIENT OF PARIS, *May* 15, 1865.

SIR : The members of this lodge rejoice in the restoration of the American Union, while they lament the loss of the great man who gave so many proofs of his devotion to progress.

His cowardly assassination has filled us with sorrow, for he was dear to us for more than one reason. Has any living man practiced so well the humane principles inculcated by Freemasonry? And who is more deserving of the regrets of his brethren?

We ask you to be our interpreter to the President of the Union in the expression of our regrets and sympathies, and of the hope that the great nation of the United States will prosper, in spite of traitors and assassins; for principles outlive men.

In its session of the 6th instant this lodge ordered a triple mourning salute in memory of brother LINCOLN, and resolved to drape their banner in mourning for the space of three months. The resolution was unanimous

Receive the expression of our most distinguished consideration.

The Venerable, A. H. MOZIRY,
For Perseverance Lodge.

Mr. BIGELOW,
United States Minister, Paris.

[Translation.]

SIR: The respectable lodge, Admirers of the Universe, Orient of Paris, joining in the sentiments expressed by the whole fraternity in France, begs you to receive their regrets at the horrible crime that has taken from a great nation its first citizen, and added to the martyr list of humanity the pure and glorious name of ABRAHAM LINCOLN.

The respectable lodge has decided that a salute shall be given in sign of mourning, for ten years, on the anniversary of the mournful event.

This first tribute paid to the memory of brother ABRAHAM LINCOLN, the lodge expresses its confidence in the eminent qualities of his successor, Mr. Johnson, and is pleased to see in his love of justice the qualities of heart that augur a peaceable administration.

The lodge requests you to be the interpreter of its sentiments to the great American nation.

LEBARE

Mr. BIGELOW,
    United States Minister, Paris.

[Translation.]

THE SCOTCH HIVE, *Paris, May* 26, 1865.

SIR : Freemasonry is moved with just indignation at the atrocious crime that has deprived it of one of its most illustrious representatives, and has already expressed its reprobation of the act ; nor can the Scotch Hive remain mute on such an occasion : it met expressly to protest against political assassination, and to transmit to brethren beyond the sea, as well as to the inconsolable widow, their condolence for the loss of the eminent American citizen and the zealous Mason who has proclaimed the great masonic principles of liberty, equality, and fraternity.

It was therefore decided unanimously that the lodge banner should be draped in mourning for three months, and that at each session a salvo should be given in honor and to the memory of the very illustrious brother, ABRAHAM LINCOLN.

Accept the assurance of the distinguished and fraternal sentiments of all the members of the Scotch Hive.

Venerable, T. ELIOT,   H. RAFIN,
        G. LECREUX,   BISSON,
        BOSSUS,   G. DUEER,
        CHENEVAUX,   H. BAUVIER,
        CAUX,   ARCHAMBAUD,

Delegates.

UNITED STATES MINISTER, *Paris.*

The Lodge of St. John of Jerusalem to the Grand Lodge of New York.

[Translation.]

EXCELLENT AND ILLUSTRIOUS BROTHERS: At the sound of the sad news that has filled the world, the hearts of all French Masons were filled with grief. They shed tears of sympathy for the glorious death of one who had handled the hammer, square, and compass, the living insignia of our immortal society, and then arose to the head of the American people by his genius, his virtues, and his spotless life. The holiest causes have always had their martyrs, as a necessary kind of consecration; and ABRAHAM LINCOLN is one of these, the noblest victim of his duty.

This lodge mingles its regrets with the other lodges of French Freemasonry. It does not forget that if all people are brothers, those of France and America are more so than any others; and we hope this will give supreme consolation to the soul of ABRAHAM LINCOLN.

No; a villain's crime cannot destroy the immortal work of the great citizen. A final peace and the abolishment of slavery—the just fruits of his glorious acts, a worthy recompense of his martyrdom—will show the world once more what the devotion of a noble heart can do against the fanaticism of ignorance.

We are, &c.,

Z NURSE.
E. CHIRI.
LANTRIN

AGRULLY, *Keeper of the Seals.*

Homage rendered to the remains of Mr. Lincoln by Harmony Lodge.

[Translation.]

To their Brethren in America:

LINCOLN is dead! The body of the victim of a mad assassin has disappeared from the surface of the earth, but his spirit is immortal. This spirit soars above the tomb where rest the mortal remains of one who was—

———— "a man, a ruler, and a sage;
A truly worthy model of the age."

While angry discussions are disturbing a continent, a simple, unknown man, who earns his daily bread by the honest labor of his hands, is studying to improve his mind in the silent hours while others are reposing; suddenly he springs into light, and LINCOLN is raised to the supreme rank.

He owns the virtues of a philosopher; the love of humanity is his strength; his sharpest weapon is persuasion.

A love for his country was a crown for which he gave his life, which he offered as a sacrifice to his people.

Now wondering Europe knows his name. Low jesters deride him no more; pride-corrupted individuals taunt him no more with poverty; infamous enemies of progress bend before the Titan, to whom nature gave the figure of a giant, and God the spirit of a hero, who became the regenerator of his people.

His blood spilt in America by the base assassin's hand will fertilize the continent of Europe. The assassin was the representative of the enemies of progress.

Lincoln's name is now defended by all nations, and the example of his virtues is sealed by his blood upon the frontispiece of the temple of nations.

Venerable, LE HALLE.

ARMENAULT.

LEBORGNE.

And many others.

By the unanimous authority of Harmony Lodge:

Lebesque, *Keeper of the Seals.*

Letter addressed to the editor of Temps.

[Translation.]

Mr. Editor: The indescribable act which has just torn from us F** Abraham Lincoln, member of the Grand Lodge of New York and President of the republic of the United States of America, has profoundly afflicted all Frenchmen.

Thus the members of the Lodge Saint Pierre des Acacias, at their sitting on Thursday, the 27th of April last, testified the profound grief they felt by a peculiar demonstration (*en tirant une triple batterie de deuil*) in memory of that noble victim. Every one thought that the blood of Lincoln would be the consecration of the principles of liberalism, so courageously and so nobly explained and upheld by that great citizen.

The members of the Lodge Saint Pierre des Acacias will wear mourning for three months for the death of their brother, Abraham Lincoln.

Have the goodness to accept, &c.

J. HAART, *Ven.** d'Honneur.*

HIMET, *Ven.** Titulaire.*

LOUIS REDEN, *Orateur.*

RICHARD, *First Surveillant.*

PAULOMIER, *Second Surveillant.*

E. BRAS, *Secretaire.*

Address of the Lodge of the Fraternity of the People, in the east of Paris, to the American Freemasons, on the occasion of the death of Mr. Lincoln.

[Translation.]

The Loge la Fraternité des Peuples has profoundly felt the great grief which has agitated the world on the receipt of the news of the horrible outrage to which F** LINCOLN has fallen a victim. F** of America, the Masons of France lament the irreparable loss of the virtuous citizen, of the great politician; but they know that with them and by them slavery will be annihilated, and that the sacred cause of liberty will shine forth in a great triumph which is at hand, a glorious compensation for the deep grief of this sad period.

E. DENISE, *Ven.* **.

[Translation.]

SCOTCH LODGE, No. 146, THE RIGHT LINE,
Paris, May 13, 1865.

CITIZEN PRESIDENT: The crime by which ABRAHAM LINCOLN has perished deprives humanity of a glorious example, the United States of an eminent magistrate, and masonry of a brother.

The fratricidal war which has made thousands of victims was deplored by the entire world with indignation; the murder of one man strikes the moral universe with stupor, but it is a sign that illuminates the abyss. Religious sentiments, social and political principles, unite in producing a deep emotion in every human heart; it is at first a feeling of grief, but becomes by time and reflection a source of great instruction.

Glory to the man whose death joins religions, nations, and individuals in one common mourning. Glory to the nation whose trials are admired by the universe, whose destiny is beyond the reach of human passions

Citizen President, you have united the national strength in one patriotic bond All good men, all upright souls, are with you. The United States are aiding you, and the universe is looking on.

GAUTRIN, *Venerable*
DR. HENRY RUELLE.
G. RAMIER.

By order of the Secretary:
MENOT.

[Translation.]

PARIS, *June* 12, 1865.

SIR: In remitting through your hands the eulogies and funeral orations which the superior grand honorary conservator and the grand president of the masonic order of Misraim have dedicated to the memory of President LINCOLN, the sovereign grand council general is happy, through me, to express their feelings of sympathy for a great people, of admiration for a great citizen, of attachment to an admirable principle.

President LINCOLN'S death was a calamity, the cessation of war is a blessing, and President Johnson's administration may be of great service to humanity.

Let national law have its course, and teach wicked men that they cannot shed innocent blood in vain. Let them be condemned if justice demands it, and let Europe learn, let the civilized world know, that with strength and right there may be magnanimity and clemency to pardon, where there has only been injury and hatred.

Such are the feelings of this lodge for their worthy brethren in America.

With great respect and high consideration, I am your humble servant,

GIRAULT, *Grand President.*

The UNITED STATES MINISTER.

The allocution delivered by M. Massol, president of the Loge Renaissance.

[Translation.]

MM * * F. F. * *: I propose to you a manifestation of regret for the late Mr. LINCOLN. I have nothing to say about his death; it is well known to you all, as well as his life. Let it suffice for me to remind you that it was after having gone through all the graduations of labor that he attained to the most eminent post to which a man can aspire, that of President of a great nation of freemen.

LINCOLN will be hereafter a great type of humanity, of honor, of courage, and loyalty. He is one of the purest and most faithful expressions of democracy. History, indeed, will tell with what good sense, what firmness, what moderation he has known how to direct the affairs of the Union under the most difficult circumstances, without exceptional laws, without having recourse to dictatorial power, preserving the preponderance of the civil power, aided in so doing, it must be said, by the republican virtue of such generals as Grant, Sherman, and Sheridan.

LINCOLN is the veritable emulation of Washington, if he has not surpassed him. However that may be, they are two names inseparable in the memory not only of Americans, but of men in all countries.

If Washington founded the Union, LINCOLN firmly maintained it.

If Washington assured the liberty of his fellow-citizens, LINCOLN has endowed a portion of the human family with that liberty. He has forever closed the hideous sore of slavery.

If Washington laid the foundation of the true form of democracy, LINCOLN has made it possible throughout the world. He made the ideal for all.

To Washington and LINCOLN—one sprung from the ranks of the aristocracy, the other of the humblest extraction—is owing the firm settlement of that universal confederation of which Freemasonry has long been the model according to philosophical views.

All the virtues possessed by LINCOLN are masonic virtues, symbolized in our degrees of initiation.

When an apprentice, he purged his mind of all the subversive passions, which was an indispensable preparation for the good conduct of life.

As a companion, he had learned to live orderly by labor, and a scrupulous observance of right and justice, a course which was marked out by rule, square, and compasses.

Finally, like Hiram, he succumbed to the blows of an outrageous pride for having remained inflexible in the discharge of his duties He is the moral man *par excellence.*

Is that all? No, M * * F * *; that sample of honesty, above all temptation; that loyalty, courage, moderation, sense of justice; that inflexibility of persistence in the right road—all these qualities were enhanced in him by an admirable simplicity and goodness, and that was his characteristic trait.

Indeed, his public life was terminated by an appeal to fraternity, concord, and peace, addressed to the conquered rebels, and in proclaiming the political rights of the men of color whom he had freed. This is, in my view, his highest honor. A working man himself, he showed what the government ought to do for men of that class: abolish all servitude, and modify the institutions after the requirements of justice, while liberty never failed to be respected.

And now, M * * F * *, however painful may be this death, it will alter nothing in the destinies of the United States. The people who have the happiness to govern themselves are not at the mercy of events like these, even though the most distinguished and useful among them fall. They experienced no humiliating fears. Moreover, if the slave owners were already conquered, the blow of the 14th of April ruined them forever in public opinion, and in the conscience of the people.

Confidence, then, and hope. Only let the memory of LINCOLN, of that citizen of the world, remain in each of us as an incentive to emulation, as a model and a guide. This grandeur in simplicity must not die. Let it always therefore be present to our minds, and may it become fruitful.

Lodge of St. Augustus, the Beneficent, to the Grand Lodge of New York.

[Translation.]

In a solemn session on the 21st of April last, our lodge expressed its sympathies for the United States. It decreed to wear mourning for three months in Mr. LINCOLN's memory, and to send funds to purchase tools and clothing for the colored freedmen.

We have always been for your cause, dear brethren, because it is that of humanity. The curse of excommunication is now taken from the blacks. LINCOLN has followed Washington.

No threatening cloud now hangs over that glorious country, justly called the Republic of the United States. Its coat of arms has now no bar sinister to disfigure it. We mourn over the heroic victim of the struggle that has ended so gloriously. Mothers are shedding their last tears; entire families are ruined; widows are deranged with grief; orphans seek with haggard eyes those whom they called their parents; all are mourning.

Terrible hate has separated provinces, families, and citizens. Men who used to give their hands, turned to take each other's hearts, and hundreds of thousands of their pale bodies repose under the earth that has been fecundated with their generous blood. Let us mourn.

This dividing gulf has at last been filled up by the body of a great man. Alas! you had to make the greatest sacrifice. ABRAHAM LINCOLN was struck by a madman; a master-piece of nature has been destroyed by a horrid being, the vilest piece of nature's work.

Your sublime cause has had the sublimest martyr. Let us lament him. But he who came into the world, like Jesus of Bethlehem, to take away its sins, has not given his life in vain for the good of his countrymen. Slavery is dead as well as LINCOLN, and is now reposing in its final tomb. With its mortal memory human dignity is raised to immortality. The ancient institution may leave its traces here and there in savage lands, but slavery will soon disappear from the face of the earth, and the spirit of the great martyr will aid in its destruction.

And you, dear brothers, will imitate the example of the model man that has been left for the good of the world. His head and heart were perfect. First the son of a laboring man, he was an apprentice; then he became a journeyman, and last a master, thus realizing our masonic symbols He learned, he loved, he worked, he suffered, he persevered. Glory be to his memory forever!

In the work of emancipation, his intelligence has been shown in traits of fire; his heart is protected by the halo of martyrdom. One can do good by imitating LINCOLN, and more good by circulating his biography, which is a second gospel. It began in America, and will spread abroad in the world. Accept, dear brethren, the expression of our most fraternal sentiments.

DELABY, *Venerable.*
JACQUIN, *First Warden.*
BEAUGRAND, *Second Warden.*
JOBLOT, *Keeper of the Seals.*
A. CARETTE, *Orator.*
L. DZIEDZIC, *Secretary.*

Address of the French Committee of Emancipation to the President of the United States, May, 1865.

[Translation.]

PARIS, *May* 1, 1865.

A committee is formed in Paris under the title of the French Committee of Emancipation, for the purpose of corresponding with the societies founded in America, England, and other countries, to aid the entire abolition of slavery, the education and assistance of the freed families, and the publication of all facts connected with that great cause of humanity.

The committee is provisionally composed of the Duke de Broglie, former president of the committee of 1843 for the abolition of slavery; Guizot, of the French Academy, honorary president; Laboulaye, of the institute, president; Augustin Cochin, of the institute, secretary; Audley, Prince de Broglie, of the French Academy; Leopold de Gaillard; Charles Gaumont, former member of the committee of 1848; Leon Lavedan, Henry Martin, Guillaume Monod, Count de Montalembert, of the French Academy; Henry Moreau, E. de Pressensé, H. Wallon, of the institute; Cornelis de Witt.

The first act of this committee was the presentation of the following address:

To Andrew Johnson, President of the United States:

Mr. PRESIDENT: The undersigned, faithful friends of the United States, sons of the French nation who fought for the independence of your nation, permit themselves to address to you the expression of the sentiments produced in their soul by the horrid crime which has placed in your hands the functions of ABRAHAM LINCOLN and the care of his memory.

He did not die in battle among the soldiers of the Union; he perished by the hand of an assassin. He is dead, but his country still lives, and his death may be beneficial to it if the United States, suppressing the horrors of the first emotion, will lament their President, imitate him, and listen to him still, instead of avenging him.

We French have also experienced civil war; more than once have we seen the most noble and innocent victims sink under unexpected blows in the midst of sanguinary struggles. The hand of a murderer has always perpetrated these acts. Crimes are isolated, glories are national. The guilty man seals his own fate as well as that of his victim. Leaving the assassin in the shade of his ignominy, let us think only of the dead, and let us repeat the sentence that must have been the supreme wish of his soul, "May my blood be the last that is shed."

Punish the guilty, punish those monsters, hateful alike to all parties, who murder men by the side of their wives and attack the sick in their beds, but do not suffer indignation to seek revenge afar.

The only vengeance worthy of ABRAHAM LINCOLN is the purification of conscience, the return of opinion, the melancholy glory shed upon his name, and especially the energetic union of his successor with his ministers, his generals, and the representatives of the people to finish the work that he began so nobly.

History will perform its part. We will show his soul in no pompous language, but in the simple praise of his life and his words, or rather by his acts and by his language.

A simple smile pervaded Europe in the autumn of 1860, when it was heard that an obscure lawyer from the little town of Springfield, in the State of Illinois, was seated in the place of the great Washington, and that he had left his modest mansion to advocate three causes: the integrity of the national territory, the supremacy of the Constitution, the limitation and perhaps the suppression of slavery. The smile was broader when we learned that this President, once a carpenter, a boatman, and a clerk, had to carry on war, to triumph over the evil designs of Europe, to quell domestic dissensions, and to contend with military, financial, and political difficulties all at the same time.

In fact, he was neither financier, nor general, nor director, nor diplomatist, nor seaman; he was only a man of the people, honest, religious, modest, and determined; who had read nothing but the Bible and the Life of Washington before he was twenty-five years of age; who had known no other school than that of life; had no instructor but labor, no protector but liberty.

It is hard to comprehend in Europe, in spite of our love of equality, how a man can reach the highest rank without protection, and how he can sustain himself without pride. We cannot see the power an honest man finds in the two great weapons, conscience and patience. These qualities formed the whole strength of Mr. LINCOLN. It was his secret.

On the morning of the 11th of February, 1861, a few friends attended him to the railway station in Springfield. He started after his election, alone and without an escort, to be inaugurated as President.

"My friends," said he, "no one not in my position can appreciate the sadness I feel at this parting. To this people I owe all that I am. Here I have lived more than a quarter of a century. Here my children were born, and here one of them lies buried. A duty devolves upon me which is greater perhaps than that which has devolved upon any other man since the days of Washington. He never would have succeeded except for the aid of Divine Providence, upon which he at all times relied. I feel that I cannot succeed without the same Divine aid which sustained him, and on the same Almighty Being I place my reliance for support; and I hope you, my friends, will pray that I may receive that Divine assistance without which I cannot succeed, but with which success is certain."

He who pronounced this touching farewell had not yet been inaugurated, and the South was already in arms.

Federal electors were chosen on the 6th of November, 1860, and the majority (180 out of 303) were favorable to LINCOLN. South Carolina raised the standard of revolt on the 20th of December. On the 11th of January, 1861, the governor of that State ordered the commander of Fort Sumter, near Charleston, to surrender. Major Anderson, commander of the fort, consulted the new President on the 6th of February, and answered, "If you besiege me, if you begin the civil war, *the responsibility will rest upon you.*"

Calm and firm, in spite of these provocations, the President in his first message (4th of March, 1861) addressed to the insurgents these words, which clearly show the origin and true causes of the war:

"In your hands, my dissatisfied fellow-countrymen, and not in mine, is the momentous issue of civil war. The government will not assail you; you can have no conflict without being yourselves the aggressors. You have no oath registered in heaven to destroy the government; while I shall have the most solemn one to preserve, protect, and defend it.

"One section of our country believes slavery is right and ought to be extended, while the other believes it is wrong and ought not to be extended; and this is the only substantial dispute.

"Physically speaking, we cannot separate; we cannot remove our respective sections from each other, nor build an impassable wall between them. If the minority will not acquiesce, the majority must; there must be submission on the one side or the other. If a minority secede, another minority will secede from them, and thus cause ruin. Plainly the central idea of secession is the essence of anarchy."

These words were uttered on the 4th of March, and on the 12th of April, at four o'clock in the morning, the first cannon was fired by the South. President LINCOLN believed so little in the long continuation of the war, that on the

15th of April he only called out seventy-five thousand men to arms; but he was so firmly resolved to maintain the Constitution, and to interpret it in favor of human liberty, that in passing through Philadelphia a short time before his inauguration, even in the hall where the Declaration of Independence was signed in 1776, he said:

"I have often inquired what great principle or idea it was that kept this confederacy so long together. It was not the mere matter of the separation of the colonies from the motherland, but that sentiment in the Declaration of Independence, which gave liberty, not alone to the people of this country, but I hope to the world for all future time. It was that which gave promise that in due time the weight would be lifted from the shoulders of all men. Can the country be saved on this basis? If it can, I will consider myself one of the happiest men in the world if I can help to save it; but if it cannot be saved without giving up that principle, I would rather be assassinated on this spot than surrender it. I am ready to live for this principle, or, if God so ordains it, to die for it."

He was assassinated; but the war is over, the Union exists, slavery is destroyed; and before he fell, Mr. LINCOLN entered the rebel capital, and on the morning of his death he publicly eulogized the brave adversary, Robert Lee, whom his brave generals had just conquered, thus honoring him who had surrendered his arms.

He lived to raise the national Union colors in Richmond just four years from the day when, invited to raise the national standard on Independence Hall, he said:

" Besides this, our friends had provided a magnificent flag. I had to raise it; and when it went up, I was pleased that it went to its place by the strength of my own feeble arm; when the cord was pulled and it flaunted in the bright glowing sunshine of the morning, I hoped it was a propitious omen. I was the humble instrument in its elevation; the people had made it, and arranged the machinery for its hoisting; and if I can have the same generous co-operation of the people of the nation, I think the flag of our country may yet be kept flaunting gloriously."

After having laid aside the emblems of his power, in the midst of war and in the face of calumny, to submit to a new election, at the moment of his second inauguration on the 4th of March, 1865, he pronounced these memorable words, which have become a solemn testament:

" Fondly do we hope, fervently do we pray, that this mighty scourge of war may soon pass away; yet if God wills that it continue until all the wealth piled by the bondman's two hundred and fifty years of unrequited toil shall be sunk, and until every drop of blood drawn with the lash shall be paid with another drawn by the sword, as was said three thousand years ago, so still it must be said, ' The judgments of the Lord are true and righteous altogether.'

"With malice toward none, with charity for all, with firmness in the right, as God gives us to see the right, let us strive on to finish the work we are in, to bind up the nation's wounds, to care for him who shall have borne the battle, and for his widow and orphans, to do all which may achieve and cherish a just and lasting peace among ourselves and with all nations."

Admirable words, and well worthy of him who wrote again, at the end of his message of the 1st of December, 1862, in which, after delaying, waiting, suffering for two years, he finally resolved to propose the abolition of slavery:

"Fellow-citizens, we cannot avoid history; the severe trial we are now undergoing will stamp us with honor or dishonor to the latest generation."

Upon you, Mr. President, has the guardianship of that honor and the heritage of that great man devolved. Like him, you were a working man; like him, you have gained bread, knowledge, esteem, and power, by the sweat of your brow; like him, you bravely defended the Union in the Senate; like him, you hate slavery; like him, you are surrounded by great ministers, great generals, that hate would have laid with him in death. It is your duty to enter into the sentiments of ABRAHAM LINCOLN, and to finish the work of force by conciliation.

Peace, amnesty, union, liberty, new posterity! These were certainly the designs of Mr. LINCOLN. Such are the vows of the civilized world. Be generous in victory, after having been inflexible in contest.

Europe did not expect to see a commercial people become warlike, without the military spirit lapsing into despotism. Europe did not expect to see four millions of poor slaves resist the temptation to revolt, and twice save a country that persecuted them, by furnishing it brave soldiers, and exciting an external interest, an emotion of opinion, which probably prevented intended interventions. Europe did not expect to see the North, caught unprepared, conquer the South, so brave and well provided.

But spare us more surprises, and console us for the length and the calamities of the war by a prompt, solid and generous peace among all the citizens of that nation to which has been given the beautiful name of The Union. The future will say that Washington founded it, that LINCOLN and you rebuilt it. May his blood be the last shed!

[Translation.]

CITIZEN AMBASSADOR: At the news of the horrid death of one whom two worlds admired yesterday, and lament to-day, the young men of the schools extend the expression of their grief to the United States representative. We openly proclaim our sympathy for the brave defender of that great cause of justice called, in America, emancipation of slaves—in Europe, liberation of the oppressed.

In President'LINCOLN we weep for a fellow-citizen, for no country is shut up now; and our country is that where there are neither masters nor slaves; where every man is free, or is fighting to become free.

We are the fellow-citizens of John Brown, of ABRAHAM LINCOLN, and of Mr. Seward. We young people, to whom the future belongs, must have the courage to found a true democracy; and we will have to look beyond the ocean to learn how a people who have made themselves free can preserve their freedom.

He who died was a citizen of that republic where the great men are not conquerors who violate the rights and privileges of the people, but the founders and guardians of their independence, like Washington and LINCOLN.

Honesty and simplicity, energy in their struggles, moderation in victory, respect for liberty, always and everywhere: these are the admirable qualities of LINCOLN, of all of the elect of the American people. How magnificent compared with the meanness of those *elect of God* whom ignorant or servile historians adduce as worthy examples in our old Europe.

To murder such men is to kill the law itself. In a republic, where laws are made by a free people, all those who are intrusted with the administration of the laws, and those who take a solemn oath to obey them, and never violate them, these men are sacred; to kill them is to commit the most detestable of crimes, and such murderers are termed assassins, as their victims, like LINCOLN and Seward, are called martyrs of justice and liberty.

The President of the great republic is dead, but the republic itself shall live forever.

In the name of those who composed the meeting

A. REY,
Student of Medicine.

[Translation.]

Permit us to present to your excellency, as members of the international committee of the Darien Canal Company, the expression of our warmest sympathy and profound sentiments of sadness on account of President LINCOLN's death. Many of us have lived in the great republic; they know the country and are devoted to your cause. They lament the great man who is no more.

We must also say, on this sad occasion, that we will never forget the marks of benevolence we have always had from your government, and particularly from Mr. Dayton, your lamented predecessor, up to the last moments of his existence

Accept the expression of our respectful sentiments.

Members of the company for the obtaining of the American canal through the isthmus of Darien.

MOUGEL BEY,
President, Aumale Street, No. 10.
CROCHARD.
F. FORTIN.
CH. DU BREIL,
Marquis of Rays.

CH. DU BREIL,
Marquis of Rays, for { COUNT AMPHERNET,
{ EMILE DE SOLMINIHAC.

N. CORDIER.
B. DE CASTRO.

His Excellency Mr. BIGELOW,
   Minister of the United States of America, Paris.

[Translation.]

PARIS, *May* 1, 1865.

In its session of the 28th of April last, the general committee of the National Union for Commerce and Manufactures, passed, by acclamation, the following resolution, moved by its president:

"The general committee, interpreting the sentiments of the society it represents, before proceeding to regular work, express their profound sympathy for the American people, and join in their regrets for the assassination of Mr. LINCOLN, President of the United States. We feel a horror at the odious crime of which the illustrious man has been a victim."

We have the honor of transmitting to you our annual circular, which shows our association to have among its members forty-two mayors and about four thousand merchants.

Accept the assurance of the high consideration with which we have the honor to be your very humble servants,

ALLAIN NIQUET,
President of the General Committee of the Union.
PASCAL BONNIN,
Director.

The UNITED STATES MINISTER.

[Translation.]

PARIS, *May* 2, 1865.

SIR: Instruments as we are to works of reconciliation and peace, we cannot remain silent at this event that has excited the indignation and sorrow of all civilized nations.

We now come in our turn to pay a tribute of admiration to the memory of that great and good man, who has so nobly served the cause of humanity, and to express the profound regret we feel at the death of ABRAHAM LINCOLN, the noble martyr of duty. As his existence was an honor to our age, so every contemporary laments his exit from this world.

Honor to the country that produces such paragons for modern society. They are the glory of labor and religion in their most liberal forms, of all virtues that are the bases of liberty and public prosperity.

With such citizens it is not astonishing that America pursues the realization of the principles contained in its immortal Declaration of Independence: " We hold these truths to be self-evident: that all men are created equal; that they are endowed by their Creator with certain inalienable rights; that among these are life, liberty, and the pursuit of happiness."

Accept the expression of our sentiments of high consideration and cordial sympathy.

HENRY CARLE, (46 School street,)

WITH TEN OTHERS,

In the name of the Universal Religious Alliance.

Mr. BIGELOW,
  United States Minister, Paris.

Copy of an extract of the proceedings of a conference of the pastors, ministers, and elders of the national churches of France.

[Translation.]

PARIS, *May* 9, 1865.

The pastors, ministers, and elders of the two national churches of France, (Reformed Church and Church of the Confession of Augsburg,) united in conference on the occasion of the annual religious meeting, and justly moved at the catastrophe which has taken away from the United States their pious and wise President, experience the need of expressing to their brethren of the United States their profound horror at the assassination of their glorious President, and at the attempt on the life of his eminent minister, Mr. Seward, and their hopes that the great citizen who presided over the destinies of America may have, in his successor, a worthy follower of his generous and Christian enterprise.

This expression of their sincere sympathy will be presented to his excellency the minister of the United States at Paris by the president, the vice-president, and the secretaries of the conference.

PARIS, *April* 27, 1865.

A true copy :

H. BLANC,
One of the Secretaries.

His Excellency the MINISTER *of the United States of America.*

Letter addressed to madam, the widow of the late President of the United States, and sent to the care of the United States minister at Paris

[Translation.]

PARIS, *April* 27, 1865.

MADAM : We learn with stupor the horrible crime which has plunged in mourning your family and all the people of the United States, and which has changed rudely into lamentations the song of triumph and thanksgivings.   The name of ABRAHAM LINCOLN embodied, in our estimation, one of the greatest causes with which heart can be inspired, and it is just at the moment when that cause is crowned with victory, after a cruel struggle, that he to whom the triumph is mainly due perishes, the victim of an unaccountable fanaticism. Only this was wanting to complete the horrors of slavery, the consecration of victory, and the glory of the defender of liberty.   Madam, we do not seek to console you with the idea of the glory henceforth attached to the name of your husband, whom future ages will rank, as we do now, among the benefactors of the human race.   But directing your attention, as well as our own, to something higher, let us adore the mysterious will of God who has deigned to make of ABRAHAM LINCOLN one of those powerful workers that he employs in the accomplishment of his designs, and who has allowed him to be taken away from this world after the gloom and labor of the combat.   We associate ourselves from the bottom of the heart in your grief, which is not only a national mourning but extends throughout humanity.

We pray God to console you as He alone can do, and show you, by faith, him whom we mourn in that eternal glory of the kingdom of heaven, where God gathers all his children, illustrious or obscure, around Jesus Christ, who gave his life to save the world.   We pray that the indignation excited by the horrible act may not change the thoughts of charity which ought to crown the work of empacipation.   May God now finish that work, and confer his benedictions on the people of the United States, who have been so cruelly tried, and on you, madam, whose grief we share, and on the many thousand souls who have each borne their tribute of suffering in this violent intestine commotion of the country.

In the name of the conference of pastors, ministers of the Holy Evangel, and the members of the consistories of the two national churches of France, (Reformed Church and Church of the Confession of Augsburg.)

L. VALLETTE, *Pastor,*
President of the Conference.
DE CONNUICK, *Vice-President.*
CAHOUS, *Pastor, Secretary.*
H. BLANC, *Minister,*
H. E. Secretary.

His Excellency the MINISTER *of the United States.*

[Translation.]

Mr. PRESIDENT : The Constitution of your country has forever put American democracy beyond the possibility of being affected by the violence done to persons. Where liberty reigns, where the law alone governs, the first magistrates may perish without shaking or even threatening the institutions. Regret and indignation may agitate the people, they cannot be seized with fear. We know that these are the holy conditions enjoyed by the people of the United States by reason of their institutions.

Permit us, however, to express the grief we feel at the death of the citizen who has just fallen a victim to assassination. ABRAHAM LINCOLN will be lamented as he has been admired by the French democracy. What finer model, indeed, can we have than that great man of the people—that laborious man, sprung from the humblest ranks, and coming to be the first magistrate of his country, and remaining the faithful servant of the laws?

Tell the people of the Union, Mr. President, that we associate ourselves with their sorrows as we participate in their hopes. Slavery is dead; liberty will never die; and the triumph of the great republic is assured.

(Here follow the names of the editors of the four papers : the editor in chief of the Temps, being A. Nefftzer ; of the Opinion Nationale, R. de Guerault ; the Avenir National, A. Peyrant ; and the Siecle, L. Havin.)

PRESIDENT JOHNSON.

[Translation.]

PARIS, *June* 9, 1865.

SIR : I was struck with horror when I heard the news of Mr. LINCOLN'S death. The illustrious genius and worthy magistrate did not live to enjoy the glory of his great deeds. The abominable crime of his death ought to be avenged. Justice will be done; but, unfortunately, the most guilty will not receive it, but they will wither like the weeds in barren fields. His memory will be venerated by all nations living; and generations to be born will yield him homage. Rash assassins have spilled a precious blood; but it will cry aloud from earth for vengeance, and its voice will be heard afar.

Horrid slavery is no more. Europe rejoices at it; let the world rejoice. A new order of events will rise, and men will be blessed whose hopes had almost vanished. The black has a right to enjoy liberty as well as life; and now he has it in America.

May the successor of the deceased be worthy of his place, and finish the labor to be done; then the world will chant a chorus of *gloria in excelsis, in populo supremo.* Amen.

Accept the expression of my highest consideration.

IMBERT, *Ex-Professor, &c.*

Mr. JOHNSON,
    President of the United States.

J. C. Lusine to Messrs. Seward.

[Translation.]

PARIS, *May* 25, 1865.

GENTLEMEN : There are names which explain the condition of a country, and Mr. LINCOLN's is one of them. The illustrious citizen who protested against slavery and assassination has fallen a victim to fanaticism.

In dedicating this day a *sprig of anemone* to the memory of your glorious martyr, thus joining in the prayers of thousands, be assured that my heart also protests against assassination, whatever may be its motive, and particularly against that of which you yourselves, together with your friends, came near being the victims.

Mr. LINCOLN placed entire confidence in you, gentlemen, and you may believe that a poor French workingman feels intense satisfaction in your speedy recovery, because he sees in it a determination on your part to finish the task begun by President LINCOLN, and to attend more devotedly to the cause of the slaves liberated by your blood and his.

May peace hereafter preside over your noble efforts.

J. C. LUSINE,
    No. 26 *Bernard Street, Paris.*

(Enclosed is a printed sonnet taken from the Phare de la Loire, May 2, 1865, entitled: *Un Rameau d'Immortelle.*)

[Extrait du Phare de la Loire du 2 Mai, 1865.]

UN RAMEAU D'IMMORTELLE.

LINCOLN, grand citoyen, fils de la liberté,
Intègre magistrat, vertu digne d'Homère;
Toi qui n'oublias point ton berceau ni ta mère,
Gloire de l'Amérique et de l'humanité!

Ton devoir est rempli: Ton ombre avec fierté
Voir l'esclavage en vain quêter un victimaire,
Il n'a pris que ton corps; le crime est éphémère.
Ton œuvre à toi s'envole à l'immortalité!

Aussi, comme une femme au fruit de ses entrailles,
Le Sud au Nord uni pleure à tes funérailles:
Ton sang dicté la paix au peuple fier géant!

Reçois donc, ô martyr de la liberté sainte,
Des travailleurs Français dans le deuil et la plainte:
Un rameau d'immortelle à travers l'océan!

J. C. LUSINE,
Employé, ancien ouvrier relieur.

28 AVRIL, 1865.

Alfred Monod, lawyer at the council of state.

[Translation.]

PARIS, *April* 27, 1865.

I will express to you without delay the very sincere and profound sorrow at the news of the horrid catastrophe that reached us to-day.

The loss of a man like LINCOLN is a cause of mourning for all in the world who have at heart the triumph of liberty and democracy.

Mr. Seward's death is a blow almost as terrible.

Allow me to inform you of a fact you will certainly be glad to learn. The different religious Protestant societies are now holding their public annual conferences. The Evangelic Society assembled yesterday evening. The Reverend William Monad announced the horrid news to the astounded assembly in these terms:

"The terrible manifestation of wickedness of which we have heard to-day has struck us all with consternation.

"President LINCOLN has been assassinated.

"We cannot give full expression to our feelings at such a loss. We are not discouraged; it is even the abolition of slavery that God has sealed with LINCOLN's purest blood.

"Let it be known to our brethren in the United States that we mourn with them their greatest citizen.

"John Brown, ABRAHAM LINCOLN! both were martyrs to a holy cause.

"John Brown was the first; God grant that LINCOLN may be the last!"

Accept the homage of my very sincere and respectful devotion.

A. MONOD

The UNITED STATES MINISTER.

[Translation.]

PARIS, May 3, 1865.

ABRAHAM LINCOLN fell a victim to the most execrable crime known, at the very moment the Union was saved by his firmness, patriotic energy, and moderation.

The Sunday Courier boasts of being the first among French newspapers to embrace the American cause from its beginning, and to advocate the ideas to which Mr. LINCOLN made himself a martyr; and to-day we express the profound grief his unexpected death has caused us.

This great citizen belonged not only to America, but to the entire human family; and his death is felt by all those of old Europe who believe in liberty, law, and justice.

When the northern armies entered Richmond, we felt that the last rampart of slavery had fallen, and we rejoiced in the victory; now we ask the right to participate in your mourning.

If America wants this good man's memory to be handed down to future generations in a monument of marble, we will be the first to contribute our humble aid, as we were the first to help the glorious cause in our journal.

Accept the assurance of our respectful and devoted sentiments.

PH. TARGET,
E. VILLETARD,
Responsible Editors of the Sunday Courier.

The UNITED STATES MINISTER.

TO THE MEMORY OF MR. ABRAHAM LINCOLN,

President of the republic of the United States of America—May, 1865.

[Translation.]

The works of Satan fill the earth with pain;
The world is now mourning one of his wicked deeds,
Who has not heard of his last exploit?
The news is carried by the tolling of a bell.
Public welfare now demands that we be all united;
Let feelings of jealousy be laid aside;
We only think of saving our country.

Free and noble children of America!
The hero of the great republic is no more;
He who, when in danger, saved its flag!
Washington will receive him as a brother,
But the world will mourn him more than Washington.
The universe will sing a hymn,
And say he went down as a martyr to the tomb.

When the madman in his fury struck the sage,
The human race was shocked with horror and remorse.
Why should just men tolerate such fiends among them?
If such men were less common now, in France,
We would ne'er regret so many crimes.

God cries in his anger, vengeance;
Justice wants another bloody sacrifice,
And LINCOLN fell, the victim of innocence.
Like Christ, like Brown, he was a martyr.
He died to save his country and to free the blacks.
Now his holy reign is over,
Forget him not, ye generous sons of Ham.

Let us now look up to heaven,
And ask his immortal soul,
Freed from the trammels of the flesh,
If his work was not perfect.
The world moves on, and men rejoice
That freedom is restored to all.
Some may not bless him now;
But ere they die they'll see the good he did,
And praise him.

AUGUSTE L'ALLOUX,
Former interpreter of Du Petti Thouars, Bruat and Hamlin,
Bachelor of Arts, professor of English, first primary
free teacher, 38 Chaussée du Maine, Paris.

[Translation.]

34 TAITBOUT STREET, *April* 29, 1865.

DEAR SIR : I should have written to you sooner in expression of my feelings at the horrid news, but I was sick when I first received it ; yet sick as I was, I lectured last Thursday, on Franklin, at the Conservatory of Arts and Trades, and spoke of President LINCOLN. Never in my life, as a professor, have I found so much sympathy. The audience applauded three times with great enthusiasm, not for the speaker, but for the noble victim of a base assassination. You should see how general the excitement is in Paris; it is much greater than I expected. Cochin, Broglie, and myself are drawing up an address, which I am sure will be signed by the most important men in France.

What more can we do ? If I can be of any service to you, dispose of me, and consider me one of your best friends.

Do not take the trouble to answer this unless you have some important communication to make, for you must have many letters to write ; but when you write to Washington, assure Mr. Seward how much I am interested in his situation, and that I wish his speedy recovery. Mr. Seward is now more necessary to America and to the whole world. Adieu.

Your very devoted,

ED. LABOULAYE.

The UNITED STATES MINISTER.

[Translation.]

PARIS, *May* 20, 1865.

SIR : I have the honor of sending you with this letter several copies of an ode I have composed in honor of ABRAHAM LINCOLN, and two letters, one for the widow of the great man, and the other for Mr. Johnson, now President of the United States.

I shall be infinitely obliged to you if you will send them to their destinations in the shortest possible time.

You will also do me the favor to fix a day when I can have a brief interview with you.

Accept my sympathy for your glorious country, and the assurance of my most distinguished consideration.

PAUL THOUZERY.

Mr. BIGELOW,
  Minister Plenipotentiary of the United States of America.

[Translation.]

PARIS, *May* 20, 1865.

Mr. PRESIDENT : To one whom ABRAHAM LINCOLN loved and associated with him in his great work I send an ode addressed to the memory of that great man.

May my verses find an echo in every American heart! May your worthy citizens aid you in the labor you have undertaken! You only were worthy to succeed LINCOLN.

The ode I send you to-day will prove, I hope, that the sympathy of the world is with you.

To eulogize the dead in presence of the living is honoring the latter, by showing them that we confide in their genius and in their impartiality.

I am, with respect, Mr. President, your humble admirer,

PAUL THOUZERY.

Mr. JOHNSON,
    President of the United States of America

À ABRAHAM LINCOLN.

ODE.

I.

Oui, ce n'est que trop vrai, la fatale nouvelle,
Dont eût voulu douter notre raison rebelle,
S'est confirmée, et tous nous peint son affreux sort;
Et les peuples tremblants, dans l'un et l'autre monde
Sentant leur cœur saisi d'une douleur profonde
    Disent en pleurs: LINCOLN EST MORT!

Il est mort, ce héros digne des temps antiques
Que ne puis-je aujourd'hui, dans des chants homériques
Apprendre à l'univers quels furent ses bienfaits,
Rappeler ses vertus, parler de sa sagesse;
Il vous a surpassés, vieux Nestors de la Grèce!
    J'en veux pour preuve ses hauts faits.

Il est mort, mais du moins son œuvre est immortelle;
Sa glorie, désomais, rayonnera plus belle,
Comme le Christ, il a gravi son Golgotha,
Et son sang répandu sur un nouveau Calvaire,
Pollen délicieux, fera germer sur terre,
    Les rêves d'or, qu'il enfanta.

Il est mort, avec lui périra l'esclavage,
Son martyre à nos yeux en est un divin gage,
Son vœu le plus ardent ainsi s'accomplira :
Des bords de l'Orénoque, au rivage du Tibre
Et du Tage à l'Indus, tout homme sera libre ;
    Au grand livre chacun lira !

Il est mort, mais du moins sa tâche fut complète,
Il est mort sur la brèche, ainsi qu'un noble athlète ;
Quand on a bien vécu, qu'importe le trépas ?
Pour le penseur, mourir, n'est-ce donc pas renaître ?
C'est se transfigurer, devenir un autre être,
    Puisque l'âme ne périt pas !

II.

O toi dont l'aveugle furie,
A semé la terre de deuil,
Wilkes Booth, traître à la patrie,
A genoux, devant ce cercueil.
Héros d'un drame épouvantable,
Maudissant ta haine exécrable,
Viens courber ta tête coupable,
Devant ces restes adorés,
Viens écouter la plainte amère
Qui, de tous les points de la terre,
Monte vers la céleste sphère,
Sortant de nos cœurs atterrés.
Ton audace égala ta rage,
Mais ton projet avortera.
Et l'Amérique, avec courage,
Toujours vers son but marchera.
En vain, tu frappas ta victime,
Sache-le bien, jamais le crime
Ne pourra rendre légitime
Le plus odieux des desseins ;
Et ton nom, maudit d'âge en âge,
Par l'humanité qu'il outrage
Sera cloué sur une page,
Au pilori des assassins.

III.

Et toi noble martyr que le monde révère,
Toi, qui des opprimés voulais être le père,
En vain tu succombas sous le plomb meurtrier,
Ton nom, le plus grand nom, de toute république,
Rayonnera toujours au front de l'Amérique
    Comme un splendide bouclier.

Quelle étoile jamais fut pareille à la tienne?
Comme Franklin, issu de race plébéienne,
Parti des derniers rangs, fils de ta volonté,
Tu montas, tu montas jusques au rang suprême,
Puis JUSTICE ET DEVOIR furent ton diadème,
          Et ton sceptre, la LIBERTÉ.

Comme John Brown, ce Christ de l'humanité noire,
Tu brilleras sans cesse, au zénith de l'histoire,
Les siècles à venir encor te béniront,
Et, plus vil fut celui qui t'arracha la vie,
Plus belles, désormais, malgré l'infâme envie,
          Tes œuvres étincelleront.

Dors en paix, dors en paix dans tes langes funèbres,
La raison, chaque jour, dissipe les tennèbres
Que répandaient sur nous l'ignorance et l'orgueil;
De ces rudes fléaux nous chasserons la race,
Et nos fils heureux, en marchant sur ta trace,
          Ne rencontreront nul écueil.

                    ————

Salut, salut à vous, martyrs de la pensée,
Chacun de vous travaille à l'œuvre commencée,
Et de la même foi vous dressez les autels;
Depuis celui qui prit, sans trembler, la ciguë,
Chacun de vous ressent quelque douleur aigue,
          Salut, vous êtes immortels!

Oui par vous notre terre où tout se renouvelle
Verra régner un jour la paix universelle,
L'amour entre ses fils mettra l'égalité!
Et l'homme comprenant enfin le grand dictame,
Sentira tressaillir et résonner son âme
          Au grand nom de fraternité!

PAUL THOUZERY.

AVRIL, 1865.

────────────

[Translation.]

9 VILLA ST. MICHEL, (BATIGNOLLES,)
Paris, May 17, 1865.

The triumph of the federal cause, or rather of justice, in America, made every heart friendly to liberty palpitate with joy. Why should sorrow come in such a tragic manner to change the sentiments of harmony and concord that seemed to surround this generous successor of Washington at a time when his moderation and tranquil virtues promised a perpetuity of peace? What a grand and noble duty he had to perform after what he had done already with such calm energy. In sacrificing such a man, blind passion, we have no doubt, consecrated his memory while it conquered and killed forever the worst of causes. Such are the sentiments I have endeavored to express in the language of my adopted country in honor of that beautiful American republic of which I would like to have the glory of being a citizen, and to the eminent magistrate for whom the world now mourns.

You will honor me much, sir, by accepting the dedication of this ode, and bestowing upon its author a benevolent regard.

I have the honor to be, with the most profound respect, your very humble and obedient servant,

F. CAMPADELLI,
Ex-Lieutenant of Italian Volunteers.

Hon. Mr. BIGELOW,
> *United States Minister at Paris.*

ODE.

Abraham Lincoln, ou le triomphe de l'Union Américaine: dédié a l'honorable Monsieur Bigelow, Ministre des Etats Unis.

Le monde gémissait de cette lutte immense
Où s'exaltait l'orgueil et l'insigne démence
D'olygarques brisant le pacte d'Union,
Pacte sacré, portant en sa puissante séve
Des destins que n'ont pas les conquètes du glaive
Pour conduire à son but la grande nation.

De Washington pour eux l'œuvre serait chimère—
Quand ce héros vengea la liberté, sa mère,
Contre les oppresseurs d'un monde en son berceau,
Afin de lui donner sa base légitime,
Il groupa sans effort, par un lien intime,
Des Etats fraternels sous un même drapeau.

Et ce labeur, scellé du sang de tant de braves,
Fondé par la vertu, pure de ces entraves
Que l'ambition forge au profit des tyrans,
A constamment fleuri près d'un siècle prospère,
Donnant à l'Univers l'exemple salutaire
Du saint respect des lois qui fait les peuples grands.

Si l'Europe se plaît à se faire une idole
De tout usurpateur sans frein qui les immole,
Dictant pour toute loi sa seule volonté,
Sur ce sol généreux, immense champ d'asile.
Conviant l'homme fort à le rendre fertile,
Le premier fruit vital est dans la liberté.

Là, ce n'est pas en vain que tout mortel l'implore:
Du faible elle est le droit, et le puissant s'honore
De toujours maintenir son niveau respecté.
Alors, chez lui, talents, génie, honneur, fortune,
Au lieu d'être un danger pour la cause commune,
Sont les gages certains de sa prospérité.

Aussi, quelle grandeur au vieux monde inconnue
L'Amérique atteignait, depuis la bienvenue
De l'ère où Washington vînt affirmer ses droits!
La Maison-Blanche a vu sans garde prétorienne,
Sans licteurs, sans l'éclat de la pompe ancienne,
Des magistrats plus grande et plus fiers que des rois.

Droit moderne, salut! Et voila ton prodige!
Palais de la vertu, salut! car ton prestige
Ne vient pas d'un pouvoir par la force usurpé:
Quiconque en tes lambris pense, agit ou repire,
N'est grand qu'en subissant et maintenant l'empire
Des lois qui font l'honneur d'un peuple émancipé.

Eh quoi! des héritiers de ce plan magnifique
Où se développait la grande République
Ont ose le briser, sous le prétexte vain
De cette liberté qui serait leur victime,
Si, triomphant avec l'esclavage, leur crime!
Ils lui faisaient subir un affront souverain!

'Mais le droit s'est levé dans sa virile force:
Tout un peuple a flétri cet infâme divorce
Que pour eux seuls rêvaient d'orgueilleux citoyens;
Et, saisissant le fer contre la ligue impie,
Il a vaincu—laissant toute haine assoupie
Quand ont mis l'arme bas ses aveugles soutiens.

Gloire, honneur à LINCOLN! homme d'une foi pure,
Qui porta le fardeau si grand, sans dictature,
Sans violation du temple saint des lois;
Honneur à ces guerriers loyaux, vaillants et fermes,
Qui des rébellions ont pu franchir les termes,
Sans jamais imprimer de tache à leurs exploits!

Ils atteignaient déjà l'heure de la concorde—
Amérique! c'était un éloquent exorde
Pour la démocratie en marche d'avenir—
Que peuvent désormais les sophismes néfastes
Dont se parent encor les tyrans et les castes,
Quand devant eux surgit l'ombre de ton martyr!

O crime! ô trahison! dans ton revers suprème
Tu glisses dans le sang et l'ignoble blasphème—
En vouant pour jamais à l'immortalité
Un champion du droit clément, dont la grande âme
Est l'auguste rachat de ce tribut infâme
Qu'une race payait à la fatalité!

F. CAMPADELLI,
Ex-Lieutenant des Volontaires Italiens

PARIS, *ce 1er Mai,* 1865.

[Translation.]

PARIS, *June* 7, 1865.

MOST ILLUSTRIOUS EXCELLENCY : I have the honor of sending you a copy of my letter to Mrs. Lincoln and the illustrious nation whose destinies are intrusted to your hands. You will see in it the faithful expression of my sentiments for the great statesman, ABRAHAM LINCOLN. You will find, at the same time, an antidote to the plague which threatens America by the crime of Dr. Blackburn.

I do not doubt but the papers will make known this remedy by publication, and thus snatch from certain death thousands of victims, if the dreadful plague should break out.

May God give you the light to lead the great nation of the United States to its highest destiny, is my most cordial wish for you, whom Providence has called to the eminent post of President.

Deign to accept the humble homage of the distinguished sentiments with which I have the honor to be your excellency's very humble and most obedient servant,

J. H. VRIES

The PRESIDENT.

[Translation.—Extract.]

Letter from J. H. Vries, surnamed the Black Doctor, to Mrs. Lincoln and the illustrious nation of the United States of America.

PARIS, *May* 24, 1865.

The sanguinary and fratricidal war that caused the generous blood of your country's children to flow like water has fortunately found a termination amid the plaudits of the entire world. God has made the cause of right, justice, and civilization to triumph ; victory has been given to the North, that hideous slavery might no longer pollute that land marked by the seal of the cross of Christ.

Every heart was given up to transports of joy caused by those decisive victories, when a new disaster occurred to plunge us into mourning. Hell sought another victim to pay the ransom of the liberty of more than four millions of slaves.

ABRAHAM LINCOLN was struck down in the midst of the triumph for the cause of which he was the glorious personification. Alas ! it was ever so. History has never shown us a single step in the progress of humanity that was not paid for by the sacrifice of those who contributed most to its advance.

Permit me to address you, madam, the illustrious widow of the great man whose loss we deplore with so much bitterness and tears. We all know that your magnanimous heart would willingly have suffered a thousand deaths to redeem the life of your worthy spouse and consort. Such was not the will of God ; but you can seek consolation in your great and lawful sorrow.

While Mr. LINCOLN lived, no one paid him greater homage than myself. At the beginning of the war I prophesied the triumph of the cause that he defended. I foretold his re-election to the presidency long before it occurred, and in 1863 I published a letter in which I openly declared that he would obtain the victory.

But if Mr. LINCOLN was so much applauded in his glorious mission for the abolition of slavery and the maintenance of the Union, it is now our holy duty to glorify him in the death he received at the hands of an infamous and satanic murderer, in the midst of his triumph.

We may truly say that no other man, since the coming of Christ among us, has held a more exalted mission in his hands than ABRAHAM LINCOLN. History only gives us the pictures of great men waging sanguinary wars for territorial extension and the subjugation of neighboring nations to their insatiable ambition; but LINCOLN battled for the liberty of four millions of men, whom the blind prejudices of race and color separated from the whites, who are their brothers in every sense of the word.

The cause of which he was the great representative was pre-eminent; it is the most glorious that could arm the cohorts of a generous people, and it will mark the greatest epoch in the progress of humanity that could be caused by the irresistible advance of destiny towards true civilization.

With this brilliant setting, it is certain, madam, that the name of ABRAHAM LINCOLN will shine in the annals of history with a radiant and immortal splendor. The martyr's halo that now crowns him, so far from lessening the grandeur of his name, will only serve to place the seal of glory on it. He will hold the first rank among the great men that ages and generations have exalted, and he will even rise above them all, for the cause that he served and which has triumphed, is the purest and most noble in the progress of humanity.

Therefore, in the midst of our profound regrets, we must learn to temper our sorrow and to dry up our tears. The judgments of God are just and righteous ; martyrdom has placed the sublime victim upon a pedestal of glory, before which the many races and generations of men, like his contemporaries, will offer the splendid homage of their admiration and their love.

We published three letters in the papers of 1863, which duty prompted us to write. The first, addressed to the Queen of England, implored her gracious Majesty to remember that most of the American people were descendants of persons born upon the soil of Great Britain.

*   *   *   *   *   *   *   *   *

In our letter to Mr. LINCOLN, we advised him to arm the colored slaves as soldiers, and thus insure an infallible victory to the North. That letter plainly shows how well founded were all our presentiments, and how certainly they have been realized by the Almighty.

In a letter addressed to Mr. Jefferson Davis, we implored him to cease a strife that had no just cause; for the maintenance of the black race in slavery was essentially and palpably wrong. We begged him, while it was yet time, to spare the effusion of more blood, but he persisted in his detestable and criminal design, and he was overcome as we predicted.

And now a price is put upon his head. His condition is worse than that of his slaves whose emancipation he sought to prevent by force of arms. He is wandering, a fugitive and vagabond, without an asylum or sanctuary for the preservation of his life.

In him, too, we now see exemplified that terrible *lex talionis* laid down by God in His holy scriptures, and repeated by Mr. LINCOLN in his admirable inaugural address at the beginning of his second presidential term. He is now treated in the same manner that he once treated his brothers; may God have mercy upon him, for he may expect no pity from his fellow-men.

* * * * * * * * *

I have labored all my life for the abolishment of slavery, and therefore I have a twofold right to exult at the glorious dawn of universal emancipation which has been given us through the courage, fortitude, and magnanimity of the incomparable ABRAHAM LINCOLN.

And so I have put on mourning for that great man, as an illustrious brother, whom it was becoming to honor by a public homage.

In the intimate conviction of my soul, I believe that God intends a glorious destiny for the United States of America, and all my prayers are that the generous nation may consummate the great designs of God for the triumph of civilization and the progress of humanity.

Condescend to accept, madam, and my countrymen, the sincere protests of my high regards.

J. H. VRIES.

[Translation.]

MAY 3, 1865.

MONSIEUR LE MINISTRE: ABRAHAM LINCOLN has fallen a victim to the most execrable outrage at the moment when the re-establishment of the Union was assured, thanks to his own firmness, energetic patriotism, and moderation.

The Courrier du Demanche, among all the French journals, may boast of the honor of having been from the first day of the struggle, and without hesitation, the defender of the views for which LINCOLN has lost his life ; and we come to-day to express to you the profound grief which all my brother editors feel at the death of this great citizen.

It was not only to America but to the whole of humanity that he belonged. The blow which fell upon LINCOLN has been felt by all those who in our old Europe believe in liberty, in law, and justice. It was but a few days ago, when the armies of the north entered Richmond, we felt, on thinking that the last rampart of slavery had fallen, all the joys of victory. We now ask of you, to-day, the right of taking part in your mourning.

Does America desire that marble shall transmit to future generations the memory of that good man, who steadfastly remained, in spite of the most fearful trials to which the head of a government could be exposed, the faithful servant of the laws ? If your country will consecrate his glorious memory by a monument worthy of it, we should claim the honor of being foremost in this act of gratitude, as we have been the first to welcome the double election of this ever illustrious victim.

Receive, sir, the assurance of our profound respect.

P. TARGET

E. VILLETARD.

[Translation.]

The editor in chief of the journal, The Europe, has addressed the following letter to MM. Havin, Peyrat, Guerault, and Nefftzer, editors in chief of the Siècle, the Avenir Nationale, and the Opinion Nationale:

MAY 2.

" GENTLEMEN AND DEAR CONFRÈRES: By the side of that experience— those lessons and examples which have been left to the world by the life and death of ABRAHAM LINCOLN—must be placed that great feeling which is alone capable of presiding over the universal renovation, the feeling of joint responsibility.

" Yes, before the death of the great republican citizen the hearts of all free men have been united in the same sadness, the same convictions, the same hopes.

" I will, therefore, dear confrères, send you, in the name of the editors and printers of the republican journal, The Europe, the most sympathetic in your address, to citizen-President Johnson.

" It is not so much the feeling of regret which unites us around the tomb of ABRAHAM LINCOLN as the joy of placing there the cable which will henceforth connect European democracy with American institutions.

" Sincerely yours,

"GREGORY GANESCO."

[Translation.]

PARIS, *April* 27, 1865.

General Count Faubert, former minister plenipotentiary from Hayti to Rome, and his son, Fenelon Faubert, secretary of the Haytian legation to Madrid, present to the United States minister plenipotentiary in Paris the expression of their sincere sympathy, and the horror they felt on hearing the news of the double assassination of President LINCOLN and Mr. Seward, Secretary of State.

The UNITED STATES MINISTER PLENIPOTENTIARY,
Near the Court of the Tuilleries.

An address from French West Indian colonists in Paris to citizen John Bigelow, envoy extraordinary and minister plenipotentiary of the United States of America at Paris.

[Translation.]

CITIZEN: Only a few days ago the glorious news of the final triumph of emancipation reached us, and we, children of the Franco-American colonies, devoted to your cause, were in the midst of our rejoicing when the terrible news of President LINCOLN's death came to trouble our mirth.

ABRAHAM LINCOLN, the illustrious President of the great republic, the benefactor of humanity, is no more. He has fallen a victim of his devotion to liberty, pierced by a slaveholder's dagger.

If we rejoice with you in your victories, we must also mourn with you the immense loss to the republic and to humanity. But we fear not for the cause of the Union and the universal abolition of slavery. An odious crime has been committed in vain; it has failed in its aim. ABRAHAM LINCOLN died a martyr to liberty, with a halo of glory purer than any that ever crowned a statesman, and his works shall live after him.

The providential mission of the United States fortunately does not depend upon the life of a single man, and the liberty begun by ABRAHAM LINCOLN, we are sure, will produce worthy successors of him who was brave in war, magnanimous in victory, and who will ever live to be the first in the hearts of the whole world.

We have the honor to be your very humble and devoted servants,

A. MICHELY, *Guyana.*
E. GUERIN, *Guadeloupe.*
E. LACOUNIÉ, *Martinique.*
AND SEVENTEEN OTHERS, *from Guyana and the French Antilles.*

From the legation of his imperial majesty the Shah of Persia, at Paris, to the United States minister.

[Translation.]

PARIS, *May* 9, 1865.

I have just received a telegram from Teheran, expressive of the horror felt by the government of his imperial Majesty the Shah of Persia at the news of the assassination of Mr. LINCOLN.

I am requested by him to express to you his great regrets on this occasion, and to ask you to transmit them to your new President.

Accept the assurance of my very high consideration.

SULEIMAN KHAN,
Persian Chargé d'Affaires.

His Excellency Mr. BIGELOW,
United States Envoy and Minister Plenipotentiary, &c,

To his Excellency John Bigelow, Envoy Extraordinary :

SIR: We have learned with the most profound emotions that our beloved late Chief Magistrate is no more ; that at the height of his fame and usefulness he has been stricken down by an assassin's hand. Our joy over the nation's deliverance from the horrors of civil war is turned into mourning, by an event shocking to humanity, and lamented by every friend of liberty and law.

Separated as we are, temporarily, from our native land, and standing amid the hospitable altars of a people associated with our most cherished traditions, our hearts impel us to give some expression, through you, of our sorrow and our sympathy.

We beg to assure you that we share the grief that fills the hearts of our countrymen at home, and mourn with them the loss of the illustrious citizen, the wise magistrate, the just, pure, and good man.

Yet, while we mourn this incalculable loss, we would gratefully remember that Providence which spared him to his country until he had successfully guided us so near the end of the strife.

His firmness, his justice, ever tempered with mercy, his faith in the dignity and rights of man, and his absorbing patriotism, were the inspirations of his official life, and, under God, have afforded us the happy vision of approaching peace and a restored Union.

Four years ago he was wholly unknown to the world at large, and, except in his own State, had yet to win the confidence of his fellow-citizens. To-day, after an ordeal as severe as ever tested ability and character, he is universally accepted as one of the few born to shape the best destinies of States, and to make the most powerful impress for good upon the fortunes of the human race.

If it was not reserved for him to create a nation, he was called most conspicuously to aid in preserving one against the most formidable armed conspiracy ever aimed at the life of a state

If, in the completeness of our institutions, it was not his office to add to the safeguards of liberty for his own race, it will be his undying glory to have lifted four millions of a feeble and long unbefriended people from bondage to the dignity of personal freedom.

The rights of humanity at last are vindicated, and our country is relieved of its great reproach.

Already the world is claiming for itself this last martyr to the cause of freedom, and ABRAHAM LINCOLN has taken his place among the moral constellations which shall impart light and life to all coming generations.

We would here gratefully remember the words of sympathy for our country, and of respect for the fallen, uttered with united voice by the rulers and people of Europe. We believe this event, which all humanity mourns, will strengthen the tie of friendship which should ever unite the brotherhood of states.

We would not in this address say more of the assassin than express our abhorrence of his dreadful crime, but we lovingly remember that the last utterances of him we mourn were words of clemency toward the defeated enemies of his country: "With charity to all, and malice for none," he was superior to revenge. "Peace and union!" These secured, there was little place in his heart for the severities of justice.

It was this gentleness, united to an integrity and unselfishness of character never surpassed, that won the hearts of his countrymen. We mourn not only the magistrate we revered, but the friend we loved.

It is not for us to scrutinize the dealings of a just God; we bow before his dispensations when least intelligible to human wisdom. But in sealing with his blood the work to which he was called, Mr. LINCOLN has, we believe, been the means of placing upon more imperishable foundations the unity, the glory, and the beneficent power of our beloved country. And if there be inspiration in high example, we know that his wise and upright policy in all our domestic and foreign relations will be an additional guarantee for peace, charity, and justice throughout the civilized world.

We beg to assure you, and through you Mrs. Lincoln and her family, of our deep sympathy in this their hour of affliction. We know how inadequate is all human consolation, but it is grateful to us to assure the bereaved that we mourn with them their irreparable loss.

To the honored Secretary of State, Mr. Seward, whose death was also purposed, and the Assistant Secretary, Mr. Frederick W. Seward, and their families, we wish also to express our sympathies, in view of their great perils and sufferings.

We deem it fitting to express to our distinguished fellow-citizen who succeeds to the chief magistracy our sense of the trying circumstances under which he is called to his new trust. We find in the record of his long and useful public career the basis of the most perfect confidence in his ability, his justice, and his patriotism.

We beg you, sir, to assure our fellow-countrymen, and the more immediate sufferers by the terrible tragedy, and the President, of these our most heartfelt sentiments.

We have the honor, sir, to be, very respectfully, your obedient servants,

N. M. BECKWITH,
JAMES O. PUTNAM,
JAMES PHALEN,
WILLIAM C. EMMET,
THOMAS W. EVANS, M. D..
ROBERT M. MASON,.
RICHARD M. HOE,
JOHNSTON LIVINGSTONE,
Committee.

PARIS, *May* 4, 1865.   AND SOME TWO HUNDRED OTHERS.

Reply of Mr. Bigelow.

GENTLEMEN : I respect and share the emotions which have inspired this address. I shall have a melancholy satisfaction in communicating it to those whose stricken hearts have the first claim to its consolations.

The crime which has provoked this impressive demonstration from the loyal Americans in Paris is one which unites all the elements of human depravity in their largest proportions. Its victims are among those whose loss at the present moment the whole civilized world would most unanimously deplore. Upon us, his compatriots, who knew best what a rare collection of public and private virtues went down into the grave with ABRAHAM LINCOLN, this blow has fallen with peculiar severity, and I thank you for the faithful eloquence with which you have interpreted our common sorrow.

But no crime was ever committed that was not an involuntary homage to virtue. The war between the principles of good and evil is always waging ; and if the Lamb that took away the sins of the world had to bear his testimony upon the cross, why should he who proclaimed deliverance to a race of bondmen be safe from the treacherous hand of the assassin ? How more appropriately could our great national reproach ultimate itself ? Was it more than historic justice to mark the grave of chattel slavery in the United States by a crime that was never perpetrated, whatever the pretence, except in the interests of slavery ?

Those who, like myself, are accustomed to search for the hand of God in the phenomena of human life, cannot but feel, as, after much reflection, I am led to feel, that our people were never nearer to Him than at the dreadful moment when we seemed, humanly speaking, most deserted. What revelations that crime has made; what lessons it has taught, and will teach; what prejudices it has corrected; what hostilities it has suspended; what sympathies it has awakened! They are in every one's mind; they are on every one's tongue. Even here in a foreign land, and where what we most cherish in our political institutions may be supposed to be but imperfectly comprehended, what American has not been surprised and comforted by the spontaneous and universal demonstrations of sympathy which our national bereavement has elicited from all parties, and from every class, from the humblest and from the most exalted? Such a tribute was never paid to our country before; such homage was never paid to any other American. And why to Mr. LINCOLN? Because his death, and the time and manner of it, seem to have rendered his whole public career luminous, and to make it clear to the most distant observers that our late President, inspired by a love which made all men his brothers, had been building wiser than they knew; that he had been fighting the fight of humanity, of justice, and of civilization; and, finally, that he had been summoned hence to receive a crown of triumph more enduring than that which was preparing for him here.

It is not too much to say that during the long four years of our bloody struggle with this rebellion the world made less progress in comprehending its baleful origin and purposes, and the common interest of humanity in resisting it, than has been made during the brief interval which has elapsed since this dreadful tragedy. By the hand of an assassin that simple-hearted and single-minded patriot has been transfigured, and has taken his place in history as the impersonation of a cause which henceforth it will be blasphemy to assail.

I was never so proud of being an American as when I learned with what comparative unanimity my countrymen put the seal of their approbation upon all the sacrifices he had invited them to make by re-electing him to the presidency. Nor was I ever more proud of being a man than since I have learned by his death how, during all his troubled administration, his public and private virtues have been secretly but steadily graving themselves upon the hearts of mankind. My heart goes out more than ever to our brothers in foreign lands who have shown such readiness to lessen the burden of our great affliction by sharing it with us.

I desire to join with all my heart in your expression of sympathy for those whose grief is yet too poignant to be assuaged by such considerations as these. May God sustain them, and in His own good time reveal to them the silver lining which always lies concealed in the folds of the darkest clouds.

And, while weeping with those that weep, you do well to rejoice with those who rejoice that God in his mercy shortened the arm that was lifted against our venerable and illustrious Secretary of State and his noble sons. Had they, too, been swept into a martyr's grave, then, indeed, had assassination triumphed. But thanks be to God, they still live, and in them lives on our lamented President. In their trials, in their disappointments, in their plans, in their hopes, in their triumphs, the late President and Mr. Seward were one.

In Mr. Seward's escape the murderer of the President is deprived of every advantage that could possibly have tempered the remorse by which, for the remaining hours of his wretched life, he must have been tormented. Swift justice has already overtaken him, and he is now where we have no occasion to follow him, either with our wrath or with our commiseration.

I had occasion, some three years ago, to warn Mr. Seward of plots maturing then against the lives of leading loyal statesmen in different cities of our republic, intelligence of which had reached me here. His reply has acquired, from recent events, such a painful interest that I feel justified by the present occasion in reading it to you:

" DEPARTMENT OF STATE,
" *Washington, July* 15, 1862.

*   *   *   *   *   *   *   *   *

" There is no doubt that from a period anterior to the breaking out of the insurrection, plots and conspiracies for purposes of assassination have been frequently formed and organized. And it is not unlikely that such an one as has been reported to you is now in agitation among the insurgents. If it be so, it need furnish no ground for anxiety. Assassination is not an American practice or habit, and one so vicious and so desperate cannot be engrafted into our political system.

" This conviction of mine has steadily gained strength since the civil war began. Every day's experience confirms it. The President, during the heated season, occupies a country house near the Soldiers' Home, two or three miles from the city. He goes to and from that place on horseback, night and morning, unguarded. I go there, unattended, at all hours, by daylight and moonlight, by starlight and without any light."

*   *   *   *   *   *   *   *

You will remark in these lines that same hopeful, confiding nature that thinketh no evil; that inextinguishable reliance on the good sense and manly instincts of his country-people, which has sustained him, and through him, in a great degree, the nation, during four long years of trial which required, if any ever did, statesmen that walked by faith and not by sight.

Among the many marvellous results of this great tragedy there is still one to which, I am sure, you will pardon an allusion.

The fatal ball that raised ABRAHAM LINCOLN to the glory of a martyr, discharged a debt of gratitude to Andrew Johnson, for which nothing short of the highest national honors would suffice. Among the statesmen now living it would be difficult to name one who, according to his opportunity, has placed his country under greater obligations than the constitutional successor of President LINCOLN. With some experience of almost every condition of social life, he has passed through every grade of public distinction in the United States, from the lowest to the very highest, and he never quitted any public trust except for one of greater honor and responsibility. That could never be said of an ordinary man. Mr. Johnson has now entered upon new and unprecedented trials. I share fully your confidence in his ability to meet them all. It should be a matter of congratulation with us, in this hour of national affliction, that the mantle of our lamented President should have fallen upon the ample shoulders of a statesman so experienced, so upright, and so meritorious as Andrew Johnson.

A∴ L∴ G∴ D∴ G∴ A∴ D∴ L∴ U∴

[Translation.]

ORDER OF PAU, *May* 18, 1865.

To His Excellency, Ambassador of the United States:

The regrets of the whole world accompanied ABRAHAM LINCOLN when he fell, triumphant, from the murderer's bullet. His admirable good sense, his inviolable respect for the laws, his regard for the liberty and dignity of the people who had trusted their destiny to him, his unwavering faith in justice and truth, have made him one of the most noble characters of modern times. In the first rank of great men, history will point him out as one of those rare modern examples of true patriotism, placing its strength in the practice of civil virtues. By this murder the assassin has not gained his end. He has taken a precious life, but he has not destroyed the existence of the American people; they, by their institutions and the practice of liberty, are beyond the reach of such human events.

This lodge, the cradle of Henry the Fourth, at Pau, under the sad circumstances, regrets the great citizen, and has the greatest confidence in the great republic of the United States.

A. LACOSTE.
FELIX ARRIA.
A. BIVOT.
A. DUMOULON.
A. VERRIN.
E. GENERSE.
P. ETCHEBARTER.

To his Excellency the Minister of the United States at Paris :

Sir : The undersigned, residents and visitors at Pau, forgetting their political dissensions before such a national calamity as the dastardly murder of the late President, ABRAHAM LINCOLN, beg leave most respectfully to convey to your excellency the expression of their horror and indignation at so criminal an act.

They earnestly wish, moreover, through the medium of your excellency, to add the testimony of their sympathy, in common with their own countrymen and all the civilized world.

They have the honor to be, most respectfully, your obedient servants,

E. RORRUN GRAVES.
A. G. VAN ZANDT.
P. McCARTY.
THOS. McCARTY.
PRESCOTT HALL WARD.
JNO. A. POST.
EUGENE CRUGER.
AUSTIN L. S. MAIN.
MUSGRAVE HENRY, *N. S. V. C.*
CHAS. RUSH, *Vice-Admiral, B. M. S.*
W. H. BEYTU, *R. A., B. M. S.*
ARTHUR NUGENT, *R. J. A.*
FRANCIS P. BLAIR RIGGS.
WILLIAM CORCORAN RIGGS.
A. S. DANIELL.
J. D. OGDEN.
J. M WRIGHT.
GEORGE TALBOT BAGOT.
C. O. SHEATFIELD, *Major General.*

[Translation.]

REFORMED CHURCH OF FRANCE, CONSISTORY OF PONS,
Pons, May 2, 1865.

I propose to sign the address which my colleagues, now in conference at Paris, have had the honor to send to you for Mrs. Lincoln.

I join in the sympathetic regrets of that missive, from the bottom of my heart, with good wishes to Mrs. Lincoln, and to the people of the United States, in the great cause of liberty that Mr. LINCOLN has carried through so victoriously.

Our souls were chilled when the fatal news reached us; our hearts sank to hear of a man who was extending the olive branch to the conquered, from the soldier to the commander-in-chief, being shot by a miserable fanatic.

We regret to see your great nation lose that halo of glory—respect for the elect of the people. Your former Presidents could mingle among crowds of people without a shade of danger; now, as with us in Europe, you must protect them by a hedge of bayonets. Let us hope that it may not be so; that this political crime will remain solitary and alone in the history of your republic; so that in the future, as in the past, you may teach Europe due respect for the representative of sovereign power.

We have the firm conviction that the death of your President will not prevent you from liberating the last of your slaves; yet with that respect for the conquered, and that great charity of which Mr. LINCOLN has given you such a good example, may God help you to finish the work, and shed his benedictions upon the people of the United States.

I have the honor to be your very humble and most devoted servant,

BARTHE,
Pastor and President of the Consistory of Pons.

Mr. BIGELOW,
Minister Plenipotentiary of the United States to France.

The Friends of Perfect Union Lodge to the United States ambassador in Paris.

[Translation.]

PERPIGNAN, *May* 31, 1865.

SIR: At its session on the 12th instant the Friends of Perfect Union Lodge fired a triple battery of mourning to the memory of ABRAHAM LINCOLN, the late illustrious President of the United States.

We have the honor of sending you, with this, an extract of the minutes of the session on the 12th, and a cantata composed for the occasion by two members of the lodge.

We respectfully request you to have the kindness to transmit these documents to Mrs Lincoln through the Grand Lodge of New York

With great respect, your very humble and obedient servants,

Officers of the lodge:

BOURGUET, *the Venerable.*
RAYNAL, *Senior Warden.*
ROLLAND, *Junior Warden.*
HERNCOE, *Orator.*
MERIE, *G. de Seals.*
C. THOUBERT, *Secretary.*

Extract from the working book of the Lodge of the Friends of Perfect Union, session of the 12th of May, 1865.

[Translation.]

The members being called to order, the Master speaks :

" DEAR BROTHERS : An illustrious Mason, a great citizen, the very dear brother ABRAHAM LINCOLN, President of the United States, fell by the pistol of an assassin on the 14th of April last.

" A keeper of flocks, a laborer, a woodman, a lawyer, Brother LINCOLN grew up to work, a self-made man.

" He abolished slavery. Honor to the memory of that good man who has been of such signal service to the cause of humanity.

" Let us give, then, a triple battery of mourning to the memory of our very illustrious brother ABRAHAM LINCOLN."

Brother Vallarino then sang an anthem, composed by Brother Mercadier, and set to music by Brother Coll, a member of the lodge.

Brother Mercadier then speaks :

" May the song you have just heard bear beyond the ocean the expression of our profound regrets. May our affliction, mingled with that of the world, temper the sorrow of the widow and children of the great citizen who has given his life for liberty.

" In destroying the last vestiges of slavery, he finished the task begun more than eighteen hundred years ago by the Just Man, who was crucified for wishing to free the human race.

" LINCOLN'S was a great mission upon this earth, and he has most nobly fulfilled it. May he live forever in all hearts ! May his noble figure beam in the future and serve as a beacon to all friends of humanity.

" Let us then, my brethren, give a triple salute of joy, in honor of the great, firm, glorious, and immortal ABRAHAM LINCOLN !"

It was unanimously decided that the banner of the lodge should be veiled in a mourning of crape for seven days ; and that an extract of the minutes of this session should be sent to the Grand Lodge of the State of New York, with the request to have it sent to the widow of the very illustrious brother, ABRAHAM LINCOLN.

> BOURGUET, *the Venerable.*
> D. RAYNAL.
> J. MERIE.
> A. ROLLAND.
> C. THOUBERT, *Secretary.*

Lodge of the Friends of Perfect Union to Mrs. Lincoln.

[Translation.]

MADAM: Some misfortunes are irreparable, and for which there is no consolation; these have fallen to your lot, and the world deplores it.

These are not, then, vain efforts of comfort we extend to you, but simply the humble tribute of the profound regrets that weigh down our hearts. If the pure and holy life of your great husband made him the favorite of a great nation, his death has rendered him immortal.

The liberator of slaves had to be a martyr! Was not the Nazarene crucified?

LINCOLN is now surrounded by a halo of glory that ages can never efface; his name will be forever blessed.

Be resigned, madam, to the inscrutable decrees of Providence, who needed a great soul to accomplish its designs, and fixed upon the man most suited to its purpose.

We remain, madam, with the most profound respect, your very devoted servants.

Officers of the lodge:

BOURGUET, *the Venerable.*
D. RAYNAL, *First Warden.*
A. ROLLAND, *Second Warden.*
A. THERODÉE, *Orator.*
C. THOUBERT, *Secretary.*
J. MERIE, *Keeper of the Seals.*

Lodge of the Friends of Perfect Union to the Grand Lodge of the State of New York.

[Translation.]

PERPIGNAN, FRANCE, *May* 31, 1865.

VERY DEAR BRETHREN: All friends of humanity shuddered with horror when they heard of the death of the illustrious LINCOLN; and the world sympathizes with the great nation that trusted him with their destinies.

Our lodge takes part in your affliction, and that of the family of the lamented President.

We ask you, brothers, to be the interpreters of our regrets to the inconsolable widow, by transmitting to her the enclosed pieces to her husband's memory.

Accept our fraternal salutations.

BOURGUET, *the Venerable.*
D. RAYNAL.
A. ROLLAND.
C. THOUBERT, *Secretary.*
J. MERIE, *Keeper of the Seals.*

IN TOKEN OF RESPECT.

[Translation from Latin verses.]

From humble parentage and low degree
    LINCOLN ascended to the highest rank;
None ever had a harder task than he.
    It was perfected—him alone we thank.

Did the assassin think to kill a name,
    Or hand his own down to posterity?
One will wear the laurel wreath of fame,
    The other be condemned to infamy.

Cæsar was killed by Brutus,
    Yet Rome did not cease to be;
LINCOLN by Booth, and yet the slaves
    In all America are free!

RIETI, *May,* 1865.   F. B.

Royal Scotch Lodge the Elect of St. Stephen.   Courage, charity, discretion.

[Translation.]

SIR: The Lodge of the Elect, at St. Stephen's on the Loir, has unanimously decreed to wear full mourning in memory of the death of ABRAHAM LINCOLN, the American patriot and martyr of human emancipation; and to make known to you the deep sorrow it felt at the news of the crime of which the illustrious President of your free America has been the unfortunate victim

The five officers of this lodge are glad to communicate these facts, so consonant to their own feelings.

Accept this evidence of our regrets and sympathy, and of our respectful good wishes.

G. L. MARÉCHAL, *Venerable.*
FREYNET, *Warden.*
E. BESSY, *Keeper of the Seals.*
AYMARD, *Orator.*
M. LIART, *Secretary.*

[Translation.]

LODGE OF GOOD FAITH,

St. Germain-en-Laye, May 15, 1865, *(common era.)*

The Masonic Lodge of Good Faith, on hearing of the odious crime that deprived the United States government of its illustrious President, ABRAHAM LINCOLN, experienced the same sorrow felt by the whole world. French Freemasonry does not meddle with political passions; but as a body of enlightened men it professes those great principles of humanity that your regretted President practiced with so much skill and success.

The abolishment of slavery, the great work so long desired by civilized nations, the sacred design of the wisdom and justice of all governments, was prosecuted with tact and ingenuity by your predecessor, for which he has a right to not only the gratitude of his own nation, but to the homage of everybody who recognized in him the honorable representative of the liberal ideas adopted by the human race in this age of progress. This spirit recoils before no obstacle, but in its onward march crushes tyranny, intolerance, and prejudice.

No, this assassination cannot destroy the great fundamental principles of universal morality. Martyrs may fall under the cruel blows of blind fanaticism, but truth will rise more radiant and triumphant out of the darkness where ignorance and obstinacy sought to bury it. As ardent propagandists of masonic faith, which is one day to unite all men, we will escape all future imminent dangers.

In completing the noble task of your predecessor you will be sustained in the sacred duty by our good wishes and our prayers in the accomplishment of this humane labor.

Under these unexpected circumstances the Lodge of Good Faith adopts your ideas of universal happiness, and is proud to say it joins you, heart and soul, in the sympathetic bonds of love for the public good.

Our wishes will be satisfied if you deign to receive, at this solemn moment, the respectful homage of our fraternal sentiments, and the assurance of our profound and sincere affection.

PERROT, *Venerable.*
P. FONTAINE.
MAYER.
BAMBRINE.
AND MANY OTHERS.

The PRESIDENT OF THE UNITED STATES.

Address sent to Madam Lincoln by a great majority of the students of the Faculty of Protestant Theology at Strasbourg.

[Translation.]

STRASBOURG, *May* 5, 1865.

MADAM: The undersigned, students of the Faculty of Protestant Theology at Strasbourg, identify themselves with the great sorrow caused by the crime of which President LINCOLN has been the victim for having re-established the Union and destroyed slavery.

They know that even should the powers of evil triumph momentarily in the world, Christ will reign in the end, and with him justice and liberty.

Receive, &c., in the name of the subscribers.

E. L. PRUVOT.

[Translation.]

STRASBOURG, *May* 9, 1865.

ABRAHAM LINCOLN's life was a long homage paid by that honest man to the rights and liberties of the people who elected him. His death is a public calamity, deplored by all those who believe in the providential mission of the republic of the United States. But they are comforted in remembering that no private misfortune, however great it may be, can prevail against a' cause founded on justice, or against institutions based upon liberty.

The inhabitants of Strasbourg, signing this address, have the honor of asking you to accept the expression of their sentiments of profound condolence for the death of ABRAHAM LINCOLN.

A. SCHMIDT, *Prof. of Theology.*
CH. GEROLDE.
A. SCHALLER, *Minister.*
BOUVARD, *Proprietor.*
V. GEISTOD.
C. F. SCHMIDT.
AND MANY OTHERS.

Mr. BIGELOW,
United States Minister, Paris.

Address of the working classes of Tarare.

[Translation.]

TARARE, *May* 4, 1865.

The working classes of Tarare, profoundly moved by the death of the illustrious citizen LINCOLN, President of the great American republic, the equal of Washington, associate themselves, heart and soul, with the addresses of the students and the four journals of Paris—addresses so conformable with the true sentiments of liberty, justice, and hope, and stamped with so grievous a sympathy.

LAGANTE.
DEMANGÉ.
BOST.
GAY.
FAUXANT.
V. JAY.
AND SOME THIRTY OTHERS.

[Translation.]

TOURS, *May* 17, 1865.

SIR: I hope the address of the democrats of Tours will have a favorable reception from you.

It was hard to obtain 208 signatures in a city where there is only one newspaper, where the press only speaks the official language of the prefecture, where liberty is limited by policemen and public functionaries, and where democracy's warmest partisans are among the common people.

Our document will reach you after passing through the soiled hands of our hardy workmen, who cannot leave the sheet of paper spotless whereon they have put their hearts with the signature of their hands, to express their sympathy for your great republic.

It is not you, a representative of a country where labor leads to the highest dignities of a nation, that will disdain our address because it carries the visible impress of hands devoted to work.

These are the hands that will break, in this country, all the bonds and fetters that are put on liberty under the specious pretext of measuring and regulating its gait; these are the hands that will shake most cordially those of your citizens.

Accept the assurance of our sympathetic sentiments for you and your country.

ARMAND RIVIERE,
Chevre Street, No. 12.

Mr. BIGELOW,
Minister Plenipotentiary of the United States to France.

[Translation.]

The democrats of the city of Tours applauded the victories gained by the Union over the partisans of slavery. They always hailed with joy the triumph of the great cause of humanity, so bravely sustained by your LINCOLNS, GRANTS, Sheridans, Shermans, and Sewards. But joy gave place to grief when they heard that a madman had murdered the President of your republic, the great citizen, who, like Washington, had no other ambition than the good of his country and of humanity, who sought to make no pedestal but of his civil virtues and the respect for the laws of his country.

As precious as were the lives of ABRAHAM LINCOLN and of Seward, treacherously assassinated by the fanaticism of slavery at bay, your republic is fixed upon such a solid basis that neither the poniards nor revolvers of monsters, though they deprive it of the best citizens, can destroy it or arrest the progress of its glorious humanitary conquests.

Tell your valiant and true citizens that wherever true democrats are found, their hearts have felt the blow given to your country, and those of Tours will be happy to transmit beyond the sea their fraternal salutation to the great people who have severed the last chains of slavery, and have held so high and so firmly the banner of liberty.

A. RIVIERE, *Lawyer.*	PIMBERT.
AL. BOUDROD.	L. DESMOULINS, *M. D.*
MALERAT, *Merchant.*	DESTOUR, *Retired Captain.*
GROGNARD.	BREAU.

AND TWO HUNDRED MORE.

To the United States minister at Paris.

[Translation.]

The undersigned join in the same sentiment to reprove and condemn with all their might and deplore with all their soul the nameless crime that has taken from the world and from great America the greatest of men and the most honest of citizens.

Tell the people you have the honor to represent, that from this central part of France, the country of Lafayette and Mirabeau, hearts beat full of hope, though oppressed by the weight of deep grief, and confidence in the future of your country, made great and imperishable by liberty.

ARMAND BAZILL.	L. PENOTT.
LOUIS GRENOUILLER.	COLIN.
A. THIOR.	GOLS.

AND ONE HUNDRED AND FIFTY OTHERS.

VIERZON, *April* 27, 1865.

EXTRACTS FROM THE PRESS OF PARIS.

[Translations.]

[From the Avenir National, April 27, 1865.]

The telegraph brings us disastrous news, and which will certainly give cause for mourning throughout the whole of Europe. President LINCOLN has been assassinated. The great citizen has fallen a martyr to his cause, but to a triumphant cause. The death of a citizen, however great and illustrious he may be, can in no way compromise the destinies of a people surrounded with democratic and free institutions.

But if it can be safely said that the triumph of the people of the United States cannot possibly become a question owing to the death of ABRAHAM LINCOLN, one cannot help feeling a certain degree of apprehension from the disappearance from the arena of politics of him who, with the prestige and authority of spotless patriotism, might have served as moderator among his fellow-citizens, carried away by the exultation of victory.

[From the Avenir National, April 28, 1865.]

ABRAHAM LINCOLN receives his reward—the only one doubtless which he would be ambitious to obtain, if any ambition whatever could have entered the heart of that great citizen. The Old and the New Worlds are mourning for his death.

What is particularly striking in the effect produced here by this unexpected intelligence, and which it is important to note, is the conviction universally entertained that the death of a man, however great he may be, can neither disturb public affairs nor shake the institutions of the American republic. Among a people really free there are no men who are indispensable, nor men providentially raised up. There are citizens; so much the better for that people if these citizens are great, devoted, and honest like LINCOLN; but, as there it is the institutions which make the men, the grandeur of a citizen has never anything detrimental in it to the happiness of the nation.

With the theory of providential men we begin with Washington, but we never know with whom we shall end; with the theory which designates men for the institutions, and which makes especially the greatest of them the pillars of the land, a commencement is made with Washington to end with LINCOLN, or rather not to end thus. The list goes on from one honest man to another; from one good citizen to another good citizen. We see Andrew Johnson installed President twelve hours after the death of LINCOLN, bowing to the national representatives, speaking not of his rights, but of his duties, and declaring that he will faithfully perform them.

The government of the United States is the freest, the mildest, and at the same time the strongest on the face of the earth; and what especially distinguishes the United States is not so much the courage with which they achieved their independence, as the wisdom with which they have constituted their liberty. That a people driven to extremities should overturn their oppressors is the most common thing in history; what is more rare is to see a people sufficiently energetic to assert their rights, vigilant and firm enough to preserve them. To conquer liberty, to lose it, to possess it and not know how to enjoy it—that is to say, to be ignorant of the way to be free—such has been the spectacle afforded more than once by European democracy.

But to consolidate liberty after having acquired it, to seek the guarantee of liberty in vigorous institutions, to form around it the impenetrable rampart of good laws, preserving it in this way from its own erratic courses, that is a secret which antiquity never learnt, which Europe knows but little, and which the New World has revealed to the Old.

It is in fidelity to principles that the guarantee of liberty is found; they are the light which in great political crises is a guide to men who preside over the destinies of nations, and it is because he has been devoted to liberty, even to martyrdom, that LINCOLN is lamented in the two worlds, and that he has, as we said three days ago, his appointed place by the side of Washington.

We acknowledge that he was not what is called a man of genius; and, far from regretting it, we must rejoice at it, for it proves what can be done, even without great talents, by loftiness and firmness of character, political honesty, and devotedness to the cause of justice and liberty.

A. PEYRAT.

[From the Avenir National, April 29, 1865.]

Many of our friends, faithful interpreters of liberal and democratic opinion, call upon us to open a subscription to erect a monument to ABRAHAM LINCOLN.

Men like LINCOLN, of whatever country they may be, are the glory of their time, and it is befitting, for the interests and the honor of democracy, that a monument should bear witness to posterity of the admiration and gratitude of their contemporaries. Reverence for those to whom liberty was dear, and by whom its interests have been promoted, is a proof of the maturity and morality of nations.

We join, then, without reserve, in the wishes of our friends; and if we consulted only our feelings, we would immediately open the subscription. But unless better advised, we believe that the initiative in this case ought to be left to the United States. They will take it beyond all doubt, and the whole of democratic France will associate herself with the homage rendered by his fellow-citizens to the upright man, who in a crisis where so many passions were let loose, and liberty was menaced with so many dangers, gave to the world a rare example of moderation and respect for the laws.

The Avenir National will then open a subscription at its offices, and will inscribe its name at the head of the first list.

A. PEYRAT.

[From the Avenir National, May 1, 1865.]

The northern cause is a cause doubly French; it is French by the traditions of our international policy ; it is especially so by the identity of our principles and interests. Thus, France, who sees all the parliaments spontaneously addressing to the United States an evidence of their sympathy, is astonished at the silence of the legislative chambers. This astonishment is well expressed in the letter addressed to Mr. Schneider, and will be approved without reserve.

As for the address, there is much reason to fear that it will not obtain the same approbation. Under circumstances like these, an address signed by the deputies of the left must be a political act. Now a simple testimony of grief and sympathy is not a political act

LINCOLN represented the cause of democracy in the largest and most universal acceptation of the word. That cause is our cause, as much as it is that of the United States. This is what the address of the deputies ought to have said, or said nothing at all. It should have expressed the sentiments which M. Pelletan expressed, when he spoke at the close of the discussion on the address. That which the chamber, agitated and fatigued, was unwilling to listen to, is precisely that which ought to have been embodied in their address. Such as it is, this address may be signed by everybody without distinction of opinion, for the excellent reason that no opinion is either expressed or implied in it.

It is a manifestation without meaning, an act without character; and we believe that the address of the deputies on this occasion ought not to have been destitute of these qualities.

A. PEYRAT.

[From the Avenir National, May 3, 1865.]

The speech of M. Rouher and the despatch of M. Drouyn de Lhuys, which we published yesterday, the speech of M. Troplong, and the address of the journals which we publish to-day, are a striking and unmistakable testimony of the sympathy of France with the United States. The address of the four journals adds nothing to what they have already said, each one individually, since the day when they learned the assassination of ABRAHAM LINCOLN. We might, therefore, appear to be useless as well as to have come late; but our confrères thought that a collective manifestation would give more force to the expression of our common sentiments, and we have not hesitated to identify ourselves with it. Under circumstances so solemn, it cannot be too often repeated, in every variety of tone, that the triumph of the North is the triumph of democracy; and we cannot express in too strong a manner to the United States the gratitude we owe them for the examples and lessons they have given us.

The United States have performed two great services, one to liberty, the other to human dignity.

It was a very old axiom of a very old school of publicists, that the durable establishment of a democratic government was not possible in a country of great extent and with a numerous population.

The United States extend over a territory thirteen or fourteen times as large as France; they have a population of thirty-five millions, and from the most moderate calculations, and without taking into account the constantly increasing immigration, North America, before the end of the present century, will contain from seventy to eighty millions, united by everything that can make a people great and strong—commerce, industry, the form of government, and the configuration of the territory.

What dominates in this country, to which so great a past promises so brilliant a future, is not only the republic, it is the greatest democracy and the most absolute which ever existed. And not only has this democracy endured from 1787, but it has not ceased a single day to enlarge itself and to gather strength. "I know nothing so annoying," said Joseph de Maistre, "as the praises lavished on this infant in swaddling cloths; let it grow." The infant has grown; it is now the most powerful republic that has ever appeared, a people with which Europe has for a long time had extensive dealings, and who shares with her the empire of the seas

Democracy, in its conception and affiliation, in the most radical spirit, is, therefore, not incompatible with great extent of territory, or the power and duration of a great government. This has been demonstrated on the other side of the Atlantic, and that is the service which the United States have rendered to liberty.

They have rendered another, equally important, to human dignity, in showing that the citizen has become among them great and powerful, precisely because he has been little governed; they have proved that the real grandeur of the state depends upon the high personal qualities of the individuals. In our old societies power put the man in tutelage, or rather the man put himself in that position in the hands of the government, whom he looked to for everything he wanted in life, and for solutions which no government, whether monarchical or republican, could give.

The United States, on the contrary, have granted to public power just what it is fit that that power should possess, neither more nor less.   There the government meddles neither with religion nor education, nor with morals.   It does not, under the pretence of protection, hinder anything, impose restraints upon any one, or cause destruction of any kind.   In demanding of governments what it is not in their power to confer, we have multiplied problems and rendered the solutions impossible.   The United States have solved almost everything, because they have simplified everything.

The fundamental principle of society in the United States is, that each draws his own conclusions and acts in an independent manner.   The citizen has entire liberty of action ; but this liberty is granted to him at his own risk and peril.   " Go ahead; depend only upon yourself."   Such is the motto of the American ; and this motto, applied as well to political as to private life, has made a great people and great citizens.   This is the service that the United States have rendered to human dignity.

We should look in vain elsewhere for such examples, such lessons, for so valuable a subject of political observation ; we cannot borrow everything from a people, and there are many things in America which are unsuitable to Europe ; but that which we should avail ourselves of everywhere is experience, because experience, being applicable to things in general as well as to fundamental matters of policy, is independent of the latitude and divergences of institutions, and teaches us to distinguish what forms the essence of a free government from that which is purely French, English, or American.

Now what in all countries constitutes the essence of a free government is the feeling of dignity and personal valor which urges the man to make his way in the world without direction and assistance—to struggle alone, with the help of his intelligence and labor, against the trials of public and private life.   Consequently, whoever desires not only to be free, but worthy of freedom, must act upon the American motto—" *Go ahead ; depend upon yourself.*"

A. PEYRAT.

[From the Avenir National, May 4, 1865.]

*   *   *   *   *   *   *   *   *   *

The telegraphic despatches, the journals, and our private correspondence speak only of the demonstrations in all parts of Europe to express the grief caused by the death of President LINCOLN.

These demonstrations acquire, by their imposing unanimity great, political significancy ; they show how extremely popular the ideas of liberty and equality have become, as they are represented by the United States. Over the ashes of the President of the American republic the whole of Europe has come to confess her democratic faith.

This movement has been so general, so active, and so spontaneous, that governments have joined with the people in the expression of their sympathies for the United States and their horror at the assassination. The court of Rome alone has remained silent.   *   *   *   *   *   *

A. GAIFFE.

[From the Constitutionnel, April 29, 1865.]

The horrible outrages committed in the United States have excited in France and throughout Europe a unanimous feeling of sorrow and indignation. All differences of political opinion vanish before assassination, and all honorable people, however they may be divided upon the questions of the day, feel the same horror. The death of Mr. LINCOLN is a cause of mourning for all civilization.

Mr. LINCOLN owed solely to himself, to his labor and his merit, his gradual elevation to political honors, and to the highest post in the country, that of Chief Magistrate. Whatever opinion may be entertained as to the conduct of the federal government, people are generally agreed, in America and in Europe, to render homage to the excellent and distinguished qualities of the President. Everybody recognized in him an upright character, honest intentions, and practical shrewdness, which was often his safest guide in that crisis in the midst of which he had been called to power, and which was one of the most terrible crises that a nation had ever had to go through.

But what will reflect most honor, perhaps, upon the memory of Mr. LINCOLN is moderation. Such were the kindly dispositions, the equitable and conciliatory views, which he manifested at the moment when victory declared itself in favor of the federal cause, and a few days before the commission of the crime which so suddenly and so cruelly terminated his career, Mr. LINCOLN was evidently inclined to treat the confederates less as a conquered people than as brothers and fellow-citizens whom it was necessary by all means to appease and bring back into the Union. He was wiser in that respect than certain sections of the Unionist party, whose impetuosities he had some difficulty in restraining.

The last speech of Mr. LINCOLN is a summary of these generous sentiments; and his last thoughts were probably more patriotic and humane than any that he has expressed. Mr. LINCOLN believed conciliation to be possible, and he indulged "the hope of a just peace." A just peace! That expression, which embodies an entire policy, might be engraved upon his tomb.

PAULIN LIMAYRAC.

[From the Constitutionnel, May 2, 1865.]

An important communication was made yesterday to the senate and legislative chambers.

The report of the sitting of the legislative chambers is now before our readers; that of the senate we will publish to-morrow.

The communication refers to a despatch addressed by the minister of foreign affairs to our representative at Washington, to apprise him of the sentiments of the imperial government on learning of the horrible crime committed in the United States.

France is a country of noble feelings and generous thoughts; in this direction no nation goes before it; here all countries follow France; everybody knows that on the first news of the assassination of President LINCOLN and of the Secretary of State, Mr. Seward, the Emperor charged one of his aides-de-camp to express to the minister of the United States the affliction and horror which these abominable outrages occasioned him.

To-day his excellency M. Rouher, in the admirable language of a statesman and an honest man, stamped with infamy, and in the most indelible manner, the crime that has been committed, and showed that its first punishment was its impotency. The reading of the despatch of M. Drouyn de Lhuys did not make a less powerful impression. It was impossible that a noble policy should meet with more faithful and more eloquent interpreters. Thus the observations of the minister of state and the despatch of the minister of foreign affairs have obtained the unanimous approbation of the legislative chamber. The language of Mr. President Schneider is not less noteworthy, and it may be said that this sitting will send across the Atlantic the thoughts of the Emperor and the voice of France.

PAULIN LIMAYRAC.

[From the Epoque, April 28, 1865.]

ABRAHAM LINCOLN.

Yesterday, in the first moment of stupor, we would almost doubt the news; to-day there is no possible room for doubt. The President of the United States has been assassinated, and ABRAHAM LINCOLN is dead. After five years of constant and persevering efforts in the cause of the Union, he has fallen at the very moment of his triumph. The restorer of the American country—the destroyer of slavery—has paid for his victory with his blood. His life revealed the virtues of the citizen—virtues claimed by the government of a republic—and his death makes him one of the greatest men of his time.

(Here follows an account of the life and public services of Mr. LINCOLN.)

This is not the moment to revert to the severance which followed his election—to that four years' struggle from which, thanks to the perseverance of LINCOLN, the North has just come out a conqueror—and which is a signal proof that patience and integrity, united to a firm and settled conviction, are, in a free country, the three instruments of victory. The North was convinced of it, for it re-elected LINCOLN President, and the first year of this new presidency was signalized by the final triumph of the federation.

The honor of LINCOLN is not only that he conquered, but that he conquered without ever departing from the republican forms, without one single infraction of the laws of his country. When every temptation was offered to him—when certain violent measures even were demanded by the situation—he still thought he could do without them, and, in fact, he did know how to dispense with every measure of a dictatorial character. He took his stand upon legality, and never lent himself to an exceptional or arbitrary act.

In a word, ABRAHAM LINCOLN was a lawyer—he was the living law. To say this of a man who has ruled over a republic, and who has governed it in the midst of a crisis such as that which has just passed over the United States, is to give him the highest praise that can be accorded to a powerful citizen in a free country.

Such is the man who has just perished. Just and firm in his government, simple and almost patriarchal in his private life, always moderate and loyal, he has been struck down at the moment when, having re-established the Union by his energy, he was cementing it by his clemency. He will be admired and recorded in history as the restorer of the Union, and will be likened to that great man by whom it was founded.

When his assassin took flight he is said to have exclaimed " *Sic semper tyrannis!*" God grant that the American government may never have any other but such tyrants as he.

A. CLAVEAU.

[From the Epoque, April 29, 1865.]

From despatches received to-day we see that hopes are still entertained that Mr. Seward will survive the wounds which he has received. That would be the most fortunate circumstance that could happen to the Union. The most eminent man in the republican party—the friend and habitual counsellor of Mr. LINCOLN—retaining his position as the most influential member of the cabinet, would there maintain the traditions which constituted the power of the American government during the four critical years through which it has just passed, and which are still alone capable of averting the new dangers with which it is threatened.

JOSEPH PERRIN.

[From the Epoque, May 3, 1865.]

When we regretted a few days ago the indifference (not to say more) shown by the legislative chamber towards the United States in the discussion on the address, we were far from foreseeing that this indifference would so quickly give place to an expansive and enthusiastic sympathy. Whatever may be the feeling of indignation excited in everybody by the crime which has just been perpetrated in Washington, that crime changes nothing in the way of policy; and the partisans of the South, while deploring the kind of stain which has been impressed upon their cause, appear to have no reason to abandon it.

Now, we cannot help observing that in the sitting which took place yesterday in the legislative chamber, the government, the majority, and the opposition agreed not only to execrate an odious crime, not only to deplore the death of an excellent man, but to evince their sympathies for the American republic, and to express their wishes for the durable re-establishment of the Union.

We can give no other interpretation to the language of the minister of state, in the name of the government, and that of Mr. Schneider, in the name of the chamber. We point out especially to our readers in the speech of M. Rouher two passages significant in themselves, and the purport of which is made still more emphatic by the accent in which the minister delivered them:

" The first punishment which God inflicts on crime is to render it powerless to retard the *progress of good.*

" The profound emotion and high sympathy which are manifested in Europe will be received by the American people as a consolation and an *encouragement.* The work of appeasing the passions, commenced by a great citizen, will be finished by the will of the nation.   *   *   *   *   *

" The Emperor, the public authorities, and the whole of France are unanimous in the reprobation of a detestable outrage, in their homage to a great political illustration, the victim to the most criminal passions, in their ardent wishes for the re-establishment of harmony and concord in the bosom of the great and patriotic American nation."

Mr. Schneider was not less explicit.

The applause of the chamber proved to the minister of state and the president that their sentiments were now universally shared   The same deputies who exclaimed *So much the worse!* when Mr. Pelletan announced the taking of Richmond, cried "Very good!" when Mr. Rouher expressed his wishes in behalf of the American Union, which could not be accomplished without the fall of that city.

For the rest, the Americans are receiving at this moment, on all sides, marks of sympathy as lively as they were unexpected; and it is known that the two English houses of Parliament occasion them a surprise analogous to that which has just come from the French legislative chambers.

It remains to ascertain how the Americans will receive the marks of sympathy which are now lavished upon them, and whether they will not have some recollection of somewhat different sentiments, which were lately exhibited towards them—we will not exactly say by the two governments of France and England, but at least by the principal organs, in which one is accustomed to look for the views and feelings of the government.

JOSEPH PERRIN.

[From La France, April 28, 1865.]

THE ASSASSINATION OF MR. LINCOLN.

The news of the odious outrage to which the President of the United States has just fallen a victim has caused a profound sensation throughout Europe. A conspiracy was evidently organized to assassinate the supreme heads and principal functionaries of North America. Mr. Seward has been struck in his bed. General Grant and Mr. Stanton were marked for the hand of the assassin, and accident alone has saved them.

Public opinion will everywhere protest with equal indignation against the fanatics who would dishonor, if it were possible, the party to which they belong, and the cause they pretend to defend.

But it would be unreasonable to throw upon the entire South the responsibility of these abominable crimes. It cannot be that an act of fanaticism should serve as a pretext for rigorous reprisals against the innocent. Nothing can diminish the horror inspired by this crime; but nothing should be suffered to exaggerate resentment to such a point as to lead to useless vengeance.

[From La France, April 30, 1865.]

All the European governments have hastened to manifest the indignation with which they have heard of the assassination of Mr. LINCOLN, and to send to Washington the expression of their grief and sympathy.

This horrible outrage has provoked similar manifestations in all the parliaments of Europe now sitting at Turin, London, and Berlin.

We have reason to believe that the French chambers will not fail to take part publicly in the expression of that feeling with which the whole country is animated.

[From La France, May 1, 1865.]

The legislative chambers will assemble to-morrow at a public sitting. The Moniteur announces that a communication from the government will then be presented to them.

It is thought that the government intends to communicate to the chambers the letter addressed by the Emperor to the government of Washington, on the occasion of the death of Mr. LINCOLN, and that thus the legislative body will have an opportunity of expressing their feelings of sympathy for the government and the American people.

A. RENAULD.

Mr. Drouyn de Lhuys, minister of foreign affairs, wrote to the minister of the United States, on the same day when the news of the assassination reached Paris, a letter expressive of the liveliest sympathy and of the deepest grief.

Mr. Bigelow, on his return from Brest, where he had been to be present at the inauguration of the railway, hastened to go in person and thank the minister for this demonstration, as cordial as it was spontaneous.

*   *   *   *   *   *   *   *

No light whatever has yet been thrown upon the odious outrage to which Mr. LINCOLN has fallen a victim. The assassins have not been arrested, and it is impossible to say what motives led to the crime, or with what party it is identified. It is certain, that among the southerners, as among the northerners, the same feeling of indignation has arisen against the authors of this abominable crime. The letters of Mr. Mason, in London, and Mr. Slidell, in Paris, are certainly the true expression of every sensible and honest man among the confederates.

We said, in announcing the death of Mr. LINCOLN, that it was necessary carefully to prevent a feeling of vengeance against the South becoming the result of the legitimate emotion everywhere caused by the assassination of the President of the United States. The cause of the confederates has nothing to do with these savage acts, and justice will not confound in this way the innocent with the guilty.

Well, we say it with regret, many Paris journals appear desirous of including in the same anathemas the assassins of Mr. LINCOLN and the valiant defenders of the independence of the South ; and American despatches speak of the excitement of the northern populations, who utter the unjust cry of "Vengeance against the South."

Not vengeance, but justice ; not passion, but reason ; not fanaticism, but moderation and equity !

This is what the French press ought to say to the American people if it would preserve the traditions of generosity and civilized grandeur which everywhere characterize the policy of France.

A. PAULIN.

[From La France, May 3, 1865.]

MODERATION IN VICTORY.

The great bodies of the state have nobly associated themselves with the profound emotion with which the views of the tragic death of Mr. LINCOLN has been everywhere received. Everybody will applaud the eloquent language in which the minister of state yesterday branded with infamy the political assassin, and glorified the eminent man whom North America has just lost.

President Troplong, in the senate, and Vice-President Schneider, in the legislative chamber, expressed in the best manner what were the unanimous sentiments of the two chambers; in the same way M. Drouyn de Lhuys, in the important despatch addressed by him to our chargé d'affaires at Washington, represented with great fidelity the sympathetic regrets of the Emperor and the feeling of the public mind.

These official manifestations will convey to the American people the loyal expression of our sympathy for the friendly nation whose independence the arms of France assisted to achieve, and whose grandeur is dear to us; but these manifestations carry with them at the same time advice, and hopes and wishes of a just and legitimate character.

In the universal emotion which the assassination of Mr LINCOLN gives rise to, there is no doubt a natural feeling at an act of savage fanaticism which excites the indignation of every honest conscience; but there is also much grief at the disappearance from the scene of events, at a moment when his presence appeared to be most needed, of the man who could best maintain the policy of the United States in the line of moderation and justice, which is much more desirable after victory than when hostilities are pending.

Mr. LINCOLN showed himself sincerely animated, during the last few days of his life, with a spirit of wise conciliation, which was the best augury for the definitive pacification of the Union.

Well, the words of condolence which the representatives of France are sending at this moment to the United States are a special encouragement to persevere in the policy of peace and clemency upon which President LINCOLN had so visibly entered.

That language tells the American people that the best way to honor the memory of him whom they now lament is, to immolate upon the altar of the common country hatred, passion, and useless revenge, and to hold out to the beaten South a fraternal hand.

Will this appeal be heard? Everything urges it upon the good sense and patriotism of the United States. Four years of civil war have left sufficient ruin to repair, sufficient disasters to make good, sufficient wounds to heal—that all good citizens should courageously apply themselves to the work, in order to return to the American republic the material prosperity and moral greatness which she formerly possessed.

That is a policy worthy of a great nation; it is the only one that can be advised by the generous and civilized voice of France.

We could have wished that, on the part of the friends of the North, as among the friends of the South, this advice of concord and humanity should come in every variety of form from beyond the Atlantic.

Up to the present time, let us say it with regret, we have not found the expression of it in the addresses which the organs of advanced democracy, and even many Paris journals, have signed and sent to Washington.

Certainly, we approve the sentiments which the members and journals of the opposition manifest with so much warmth; but if they join with us in urging moderation in victory, forgetfulness of the past, and the re-establishment of peace on the basis of justice and right, would they not do something worthy of the civilization of the nineteenth century, and of the great policy of our time?

J. COHEN.

[From the Gazette de France, April 28, 1865.]

Another political assassination! The horrible doctrine which found in the Old World pupils and adepts has crossed the sea. The New World has nothing to envy in the Old in this respect. There are in Washington, on that ground of liberty, men who, imbued with examples drawn from our saddest annals, take the poniard or revolver and assassinate the heads of a government, simply because they detest it, using words formulated after the fashion of a regular judgment. It is related that the assassin of Mr. LINCOLN exclaimed *Sic semper tyrannis!* This pretentious phrase, and which indicates a preconceived intention to produce effect, is itself a revelation.

An American, of the North or of the South, who had made up his mind to commit so horrible a crime, would never have thought of displaying this theatrical exhibition, and parading a Latin quotation under circumstances so terrible. One sees there a fanatical adept from that school which has made the assassin a political medium, which proclaims the holiness of insurrection, and makes a man the judge of the head of the state, and the executioner under the warrant which he has delivered against him.

These assassins would recoil from a crime against one in their own station of life; but they have no hesitation in attempting the life of a sovereign—of a man who is the representative of a policy. *Sic semper tyrannis!* exclaimed Booth over the body of his victim. On reading this kind of sentence, which would be ridiculous if it were not odious by the act which it seemed to have inspired, it is easy to understand that in his own mind he thought he was performing the part of a great citizen. It is like an echo of the homage done by Garibaldi at Naples, on the day when he decreed to Agesilas Milano the title of "The Country's Martyr." Booth had to speak Latin to make himself recognized in the land of liberty, where he accomplished his crime. He had to speak the language of Brutus to reveal his origin, and to show plainly that he belonged, by the nature of the deed, to the Old World. There is only one feeling throughout all France against this odious assassination, which counts three victims; unfortunately the public conscience is too often moved by events of this nature.

What will be the consequences of the death of Mr. LINCOLN, and of that of Mr. Seward? It is necessary to know, first of all, how the Americans interpret this odious act. If, in their anger and excitement, they desire that the responsibility of the abominable deeds of the assassins should, in the general opinion, weigh upon the whole of a valorous and chivalric nation, incalculable evils may be the result. If, on the contrary, taking a more just view of things, they consider that the heinousness of the crime should fall only on the heads of the guilty parties, the death of Mr. LINCOLN will not plunge the country into a new civil war, which would not be long before it degenerated into complete anarchy. But will the friends of Mr. LINCOLN have sufficient wisdom to render this last homage to the political idea of the President of the United States? They ought to have, out of respect to the memory even of him whom they so properly lament.

GUSTAVE JANICOT.

ASSASSINATION OF PRESIDENT LINCOLN.

This crime, as may be supposed, has produced unutterable emotion and profound indignation in the United States. It is the first outrage committed against the federal authorities since the American republic was founded. America had not been previously dishonored by a political assassination.

Mr. LINCOLN died a martyr for the cause of the Union, and it is impossible to foresee what will be the consequences of his death, under the present circumstances, as critical as they are solemn. By his firmness, by his good sense, and also, let us say, by the moderation with which he showed himself to be animated, especially since the decisive victory gained over the confederates, it is probable that Mr. LINCOLN would have succeeded in mastering the situation, in calming excited passions, in pacifying the South, and in reconstituting the Union on conditions honorable to all. The task before him was full of difficulties, but everything encouraged the hope that he would solve that which stood in the way of pacification as successfully as he had surmounted the obstacles and dangers of war. The workman was more than ever necessary for the work which had to be carried out to a successful issue. He alone, perhaps, was able to inspire the southern States with sufficient confidence to treat of their submission with a feeling of security, for he had determined to hold out to them a friendly hand. He had so determined because he proposed to himself no other object than to restore the federal edifice on the basis of perfect equality, such as had been founded by Washington and Jefferson, the fathers of the American republic, and he renewed the engagement to do so three days before he fell from the ball of an assassin. It is certain that at that hour he alone had sufficient authority and influence to restrain the party to whom he owed his elevation to the presidency, and to bring it back to less hostile feelings towards the South, which that party desired to punish for its rebellion by treating it as a conquered country. Therefore, it is to be feared that in him the United States have lost more than an honest and able President. It is to be feared that the passions, instead of being calmed, will be excited afresh; that hatreds will be still more embittered; and that the South, seeing that it has henceforth to do with pitiless conquerors, will be guided only by despair, and renew the struggle. The worst solution that could be arrived at would be that which imposed on the South dishonorable conditions, and placed it in a state of inferiority and subjection to the North. The South might now, in consequence of exhaustion, bear the weight of these two chains, but it would not submit to them without impatience and anger, with the firm resolution to break them asunder as soon as they recovered their strength. The shadow of the Union thus built up again would be constantly threatened with dissolution. The United States would exhaust their strength in the efforts to maintain it, without being able to succeed.

To establish a durable and advantageous reconciliation, an appeal must be made to concord: the North must make up its mind to offer to the South, not the hand of revenge, but a fraternal hand. It is necessary that the treaty of peace should be ratified by unmistakable evidence of a peaceful and forgiving disposition. That was Mr. LINCOLN's ambition; and Mr. LINCOLN was equal to that patriotic task.

A. ESCANDE.

[From the Gazette de France, April 30, 1865.]

POLITICAL LETTER TO THE DIRECTOR OF THE GAZETTE DE FRANCE,
APRIL 29, 1865.

My DEAR FRIEND: What frightful news this is about the assassinations in America. If the chief victim was not the worthiest of Washington's successors, we should have to ask ourselves whether the horrible event of the night of the 14th of April really took place on the other side of the Atlantic. What! in an open theatre, by the side of his wife ; in the midst of an enthusiastic and grateful population ; on the morrow of the greatest success which the Union has ever obtained since its foundation, this excellent man—this great and honest citizen, ABRAHAM LINCOLN—killed by a shot from the revolver of a fanatic. The assassin, a comedian, jumping on to the stage, and brandishing the classic dagger, exclaiming to the affrighted public the stupid phrase, *Sic semper tyrannis !* No, really—and you are right in saying so—that is not American. I remember but one assassination adorned with a Latin quotation, but it took place in Florence, and in the sixteenth century. Lorenzino treacherously killed his cousin, Alexandre de Medicis, who was in reality a tyrant, and left in writing near the body the line of Virgil on Brutus : *Vincet amor patriæ laudisque immensa cupido !* To tell you what I really think, the great want of fame, of which the poet speaks, has been, I believe, the real incentive to these savage deeds. In this way the public is found to be an involuntary accomplice. Perhaps it is our duty to remind the public of it on the occasion of every fresh attempt to acquire favor by the perpetration of a crime. At all events, John Wilkes Booth, the assassin of the President, and the accomplice who at the same time stabbed the Prime Minister, Mr. Seward, may be sure that they will never find apologists, although they may take their place in the gallery of historical assassins. Like Ravaillac, they killed in the bud the hope of an entire people, and perhaps destroyed the peace of a whole continent. Like Louvel, Fieschi, and Orsini, they have, besides shedding innocent blood, sacrificed the life and honor of the cause they desired to save. Who, I ask, will dare to undertake their defence ? If the whole of Europe condemned them—if the North rises up in indignation— what will not the South do, more cruelly afflicted by the crime committed, in spite of her, in her name, than by the taking of Richmond and the capitulation of Lee ?

Moreover, it would be just—it would be providential—if the tragic *denouement* served at least to bring back to a greater sense of equity—I do not say of favor—the feeling of our country respecting the quarrel which for four years has stained America with blood. How far we are removed from the period when the young *noblesse* of France, represented by the Lafayettes, the Rochambeaus, the Castries, the Noailles, the Broglies, the Segurs, the Chastellaxes, and so many others, crossed the seas to defend, against the attacks of England, the independence of some millions of Quakers and Methodists. At the present day, on the contrary, the prejudices against America proceed from the English journals, and are accepted, without dispute, by the public of France. Because certain agents of the United States (all of the south, be it said, by the way) were able, before the presidency of Mr. LINCOLN, to alienate themselves from the cabinets to which they were accredited; because numerous piratical expeditions—all southern—had gone to brave Spain at Cuba, and England at Canada because the evident interest of these same southern States, which has already taken Texas from Mexico, would be immediately to oppose their intervention to ours in that unfortunate country; because President Monroe (a southerner, and appointed by the South) determined, forty-five years ago, that America should remain to the Americans, and that Europe should never be permitted to interfere in any way whatever with her affairs; because, in short, the people of Washington are too apt to assume the airs of the New World, claiming a right to disdain the Old, is that any reason to forget all principles of policy, and to labor with England for the dismemberment of that great republic which we have contributed so greatly to create—of that great navy, which would be for us so natural and so powerful an ally? The worst of it would be, that the Americans would discern, under this systematic hostility to the maintenance of the Union, a vague fear, unavowed and unavoidable, of witnessing the success of the experiment of liberty without anarchy, and of democracy without Cæsarism, of which the United States has afforded us, up to the present time, the seductive spectacle.

We must have the courage to acknowledge that, in this direction, as well as many others, public opinion has gone back. Drawn towards the United States by the lingering idea of her monarchy, and the first bound of her revolution, she has seen herself led on to an imitation of ancient Rome by the splendors and despotism of the first empire. Washington and Napoleon belonged to history within a few years of each other. I defy any one to admire, at one and the same time, the simple grandeur of the liberator of America and the theatrical genius of the dominator of Europe.

However that may be, the foundation of the American republic is a part of our history and national policy—not less gloriously so than the crusades, or the struggle between the house of France and that of Austria. It should remain for us a monarchical tradition, and of the brightest epoch, since it dates from Louis XVI, and from '89. On this ground I venture to say that no journal has been more directly identified with the republic than the Gazette de France.

But, I shall be asked, cannot America be respected without sacrificing the South to the North? Ought we to forget Louisiana was French up to the epoch when the First Consul sold that beautiful province for eighty millions? Do we not know that slavery was the pretext and not the cause of the war which has just been brought to a close?

You will doubtless recollect that admirable passage in Tocqueville's book, where he describes, from the quarter-deck of his steamer, the two banks of the Ohio, one of them belonging to the slave States, the other to the free States. On the left bank there are few habitations, and but little going on; some negroes going and coming, carrying on the work of cultivation indolently and disinterestedly; many forests not yet turned to account, and the activity of nature substituted for that of man. On the right bank, on the contrary, are farms, villages, magazines in great numbers, a variety of crops—everywhere life and industry, and the willing application of manual labor. Well, up to within late years, the government of the Union was on the left bank of the Ohio, and it was because the elections of 1860 made it pass to the right bank that civil war broke out. The cause of the South, as we have often said, is that of the feeble and oppressed, and that, we feel sure, is the reason that has procured the South so many partisans. Let us be understood It has never been denied that the southern confederation was inferior to its rival, not certainly in bravery, but in the numerical strength of its armies and resources. The northern States reckon from thirteen to fourteen millions of inhabitants; the seceded States only between six and seven millions, not taking into account the slave population. It is not less true, that out of eighteen Presidents who have succeeded Washington, twelve were chosen from among the southerners—slave owners. It is equally true, too, that nearly all the Secretaries of State, charged with the foreign relations, of the Presidents of the Senate, of the Speakers in the Chamber, and the Attorneys General, of the foreign ministers, were also slave owners.*

How is this apparent anomaly to be explained? In two ways, as it seems to me: one, a general reason, the other special. The first is, because the rich planters of the slave States formed in the republic a kind of aristocracy of men of leisure and study, whose aptitude made them writers, orators, statesmen; and the military profession developed itself with more facility among them than among the busy and laborious populations of the North. The second is, that the maintaining inviolable what they called their "peculiar institution," was confounded by them with the defence of their own existence, while to declare war upon them would only be to the people of the other States an affair of pure reform in a day of an abuse of many ages' duration; but he was one of those Christians who see in the negro a brother more oppressed and despised than any other, and that was sufficient for the South to discern immediately that it had no other resource than an appeal to force. Far from feeling themselves sufficiently strong to resist the North, the slave States were obliged to gain over, one by one, all the States to their "peculiar institution," either by substituting slave labor for free labor in the newly formed States, or by making

---

* For full details on this subject, see the practical and instructive book of M. Cochin, on the "Abolition of Slavery."

themselves recognized over the whole territory of the Union, by establishing the right of pursuit of the fugitive negro doctrine, about which they were far from coming to an agreement among themselves. Thus slavery, vigorously upheld on one side, was feebly contested on the other. Only this odious interest was a matter of life and death for a part of the Union, and whenever the abolitionists exclaimed against slavery in the Congress, they were answered with the threats of immediate separation; and scarcely had Mr. Lincoln been elected President, when the South drove out the federal garrison from Fort Sumter, and fired the first shot of the civil war.

Lincoln, however, was not like General Frémont, who was one of those enemies to slavery who think to give an account of the progress of this propagandism. It is sufficient to state that when the war broke out there were fifteen States where slavery was established, and seventeen free States, and that the negro population, which only numbered from 300,000 to 400,000 when Washington, dying, pronounced the manumission of those of Mount Vernon, now reckons from three to four millions. It will be seen whether it is the North which threatened the South, and if it was not time to stop this gangrene of slavery, which by degrees would have gained over all the wholesome members of the great American republic.

Abraham Lincoln was the worthy instrument chosen by Providence to commence this great work. God grant that it may be continued in the same spirit of moderation and justice! God grant that in that country blood may not be answered with blood, and that a private crime may not be invoked as an excuse for public crimes. "Yet, if God wills," said Lincoln on the 4th of March last, when he took possession of the presidency for the second time, which was so soon to terminate in his martyrdom, "that it continue until all the wealth piled by the bondman's two hundred and fifty years of unrequited toil shall be sunk, and until every drop of blood drawn with the lash shall be paid by another drawn with the sword, as was said three thousand years ago, so still it must be said, 'The judgments of the Lord are true and righteous altogether.'

"With malice towards none; with charity for all; with firmness in the right, as God gives us to see the right, let us strive on to finish the work we are in; to bind up the nation's wounds; to care for him who shall have borne the battle, and for his widow and his orphan—to do all which may achieve and cherish a just and lasting peace among ourselves, and with all nations."

Do you know any government in Europe who can speak such language as this, and a people who are worthy of listening to it? That, however, is the language of real power and true liberty. No funeral oration can attain to the simple and religious eloquence of these words, which will remain as the political bequest of Abraham Lincoln. Who among us would think of pitying him? A public man, he enters, by the death which he has received in the full work of pacification after victory, into that body of the *elite* of the historic army which M. Guizot once called the battalion of Plutarch. A Christian, he has just ascended before the throne of the final Judge, accompanied by the souls of four millions of slaves created, like ours, in the image of God, and who have been endowed with freedom by a word from him.

LEOPOLD DE GAILLARD.

[From the Gazette de France, May 5, 1865.]

The lodges of Freemasonry are at work ; with the symbolical mallet and trowel they make manifestations in honor of LINCOLN, for ABRAHAM LINCOLN was a member of the Grand Lodge of New York. Whether they are produced in the form of harangues uttered in the workshop, or as addresses sent to RR** FF** of America, these manifestations are all preceded by a special formality peculiar to these mournful occasions, a " *batterie de deuil*," followed by a " *batterie allegresse.*" The lodges thereby declare that F** LINCOLN has fallen, like Hiram, from the blows of the enemies to duty, and they proclaim him forever honorable, because he has forever consolidated, by his life and death, the foundation laid by Washington, " of that universal confederation of peoples of which Freemasonry has for a long time been the model in the order of philosophy."

They also celebrate F** LINCOLN ; and this is better, because he has known how to direct the affairs of the Union in the most difficult circumstances, without exceptional laws, without having recourse to dictatorial power, and being able to preserve the preponderance of the civil power.   *   *

AUBRY FOUCAULT.

[From the Journal des Debats, April 28, 1865.]

Fresh details have been received of the horrible crime of which Mr. LINCOLN, Mr. Seward, and his son have just fallen victims. This triple assassination, it is asserted, is connected with a vast conspiracy against the principal heads of the government of the United States. We must needs hope that there is some exaggeration in this news, and that the abominable deed which has excited one universal feeling of horror is the work of some isolated fanatic. If it were otherwise, all humanity would be immediately afflicted. The United States have sustained an irreparable loss, and we must go back to Washington to find a citizen who has done the great American republic so much service as the noble and unfortunate President who has just fallen by the hand of a miserable assassin.

Mr. LINCOLN was born in 1809. He was not an old man, and yet it can be affirmed that no career of a statesman was ever better fulfilled. In him were found, if not the brilliant qualities which are perhaps thought too much of in Europe, those solid virtues of a citizen, and that strong good sense, which seem to be peculiar to the American race. History, in fact, will tell with what firmness, and, at the same time, with what moderation, he knew how to direct the policy of the Union in circumstances of the greatest difficulty; and without having recourse to exceptional laws, without arming himself with dictatorial power, he passed victoriously through a crisis in which his country might have been destroyed; and it was at the very moment when, at last, he was effecting the great object of his patriotic exertions, when he was about to witness the reconstruction of the American country in all its integrity, that this great citizen was carried off by a premature and bloody death. Fate sometimes deals those blind and cruel blows which fill with consternation and grief all those for whom patriotism and virtue are not mere idle words. America will revere the memory of LINCOLN equally with that of Washington; these two names will be written together in her gratitude; for if the one founded the Union, the other saved it from destruction.

Men ask themselves now what will be the political consequences of the death of the President of the United States? We do not think the situation of affairs will be sensibly modified by this catastrophe. Certainly it is far from our intention to make the cause of the South responsible for the crime of a few fanatics, but it is not the less true that the horror inspired by an act so atrocious can have no other effect than to lessen the sympathies which the secessionists have met with in Europe. Already materially overcome, or very nearly so, they are made to sustain a moral defeat. What is most to be feared is lest the North in its exasperation should allow itself to be drawn into a system of reprisals, or at least that the sentiments of conciliation, of which it began to give the secessionists proofs, would give place to feelings of an opposite nature, and that it would take advantage of its victory to impose hard conditions upon the South However, we have too much confidence in the good sense of the North to entertain any serious apprehensions on this head. Its legitimate indignation will not make it deviate from the line of moderation and prudence which it has pursued up to the present time. It will understand that the best way to do honor to the memory of Mr. LINCOLN is not to wander away from the political traditions of this great statesman.

Like the French press, the press of England is unanimous in the expression of horror which is felt at the assassination of the President of the United States An address of condolence has been presented to the American minister by the members of the House of Commons.—*Leading article.*

[From the Journal des Debats, April 29, 1865.]

The Index, of London, publishes a letter addressed to the Times by Mr. Mason, representative of the southern States in England. This letter is a reply to the despatch of Mr. Stanton, Secretary of War, to Mr. Adams, on the subject of the assassination of the President of the United States. We can easily understand that Mr. Mason should desire to exculpate his party from all complicity in so abominable a crime; but we cannot help lamenting the violent tone of his letter. This was not the moment to give himself up to bitter recriminations; and every one will be of opinion that the observations by which Mr. Mason endeavors to invalidate certain assertions made by Mr. Stanton, would have had much more weight had they been of a more moderate character. The sad impression produced upon all minds by the murder of Mr. LINCOLN will put the language of the representative of the South in a light all the more unfavorable.—*Editorial.*

On learning the terrible calamity which has just snatched from the republic of the United States its best citizen, our mind was immediately carried back beyond the last four years to that sad moment when the news of the election of Mr. LINCOLN and the outbreak of the civil war came across the Atlantic almost simultaneously. Then every one among us took sides—each of us enrolled himself morally in one of the two armies, according to his habits of thought and the bent of his inclination. A great many Frenchmen have, in the midst of our barren revolutions, and after numberless deceptions, contracted a kind of general aversion to democracy, and in the eyes of those Frenchmen, who are now in a frame of mind exactly the reverse to that of their forefathers rushing to the help of the American republic, the probable fall of that same republic was not an unwelcome event. Others again, the friends of democracy, but of a democracy disciplined, guided by a single master, or rather personified in one head, saw with not less pleasure the approach of a dissolution which would confirm their theories, and demonstrate once more that democracy can only exist at the price of liberty. Fashion, the spirit of imitation, our supposed interest in the Mexican enterprise, came in aid of these sentiments, and the South was so little wanting in partisans among us, that hardly a fortnight ago the news of the taking of Richmond was received with an exclamation of regret in the midst even of the legislative chambers.

[NOTE.—See the last sitting, on the discussion of the address, and the cry of "So much the worse," reported in the Moniteur of the 16th of April.]

On the other hand, the political instinct which made enlightened Frenchmen interested in the maintenance of the American power, more and more necessary to the equilibrium of the world—the desire to see a great democratic state surmount the terrible trials, and continue to give an example of the most perfect liberty, united with the most absolute equality—the need, in short, of lodging somewhere a sympathy, an admiration, and a hope which were but little stimulated in the Old World, assured the cause of the North a number of friends, jealous of maintaining the political traditions of France, and the liberal spirit of our country.   We ourselves were of that number, and we still remember the uneasiness with which we awaited the first words of that President, then unknown, upon whom a heavy task had fallen, and from whose advent to power might be dated the ruin or regeneration of his country.   All we knew was, that he had sprung from the humblest walks of life ; that his youth had been spent in manual labor ; that he had been shepherd, carpenter, farmer, rail-layer ; that he was self-taught, then raised by degrees in his town, his county, and his State, until he became the candidate of a great party, and was elected by the majority of his fellow-citizens.   What, however, was this favorite of democracy ?   Might not his elevation have been due even to his imperfections ?   Was it not to be feared that this election was one of those errors in the choice of men to which democratic societies are so liable, and which are so fatal to them?   But as soon as Mr. LINCOLN arrived at Washington, having encountered many dangers, and been already threatened with the knife of the assassin, as soon as he spoke, all our doubts and fears were dissipated ; and it seemed to us that fate itself had pronounced in favor of the good cause, since, in such an emergency, it had given to the country an honest man.

He was in fact an honest man, giving to the word its fullest meaning, or rather the sublime sense which belongs to it, when honesty has to contend with the severest trials which can agitate states, and with events which have an influence on the fate of the world.   Very different in this respect from most of the great men whom it is agreed at the present day to admire.   Mr. LINCOLN had but one object in view from the day of his election to that of his death, namely, the fulfilment of his duty, and his imagination never carried him beyond it.   The idea of doing more or anything else than his duty never entered his plain and upright mind.   It is a common error on this side of the Atlantic to praise or blame Mr. LINCOLN for having undertaken spontaneously the abolition of slavery, and having plunged his country into war to abolish it.   It was to know him very little to attribute such conduct to him, or even such designs Undoubtedly Mr. LINCOLN loudly condemned the injustice of slavery; and while deploring not long ago the duration of the great struggle, he said that it was, perhaps, in the order of Providence that civil war should cause as much blood to flow by the sword as had been shed by the lash, and that it should destroy as much wealth as had been produced by the labor extorted from man by the iniquitous violence of man.   But Mr. LINCOLN never confounded his feelings with his duty, nor looked upon that duty in any other light than as tending to the well-being of the republic whose destinies had been committed to his hands.   There is no doubt that he felt a lively joy the day when the necessities of the war commanded him, rather than permitted him, to decree the abolition of slavery, and he thanked God for being the instrument of such an act. But he did not hasten on that event by a day or an hour; and this noble desire was only second to another ardent wish, because the performance of his duty—that is to say, the welfare of the United States—was foremost in all the aspirations of his heart.

Such was this plain and great, good man; and if it is desired to estimate the value of a man of this kind to a nation in danger, only conceive that the United States, instead of finding at their head a resolute servant, devoted to duty, had fallen into other hands. Let us suppose that, instead of consulting only the clear and strong voice of conscience and honor, Mr. LINCOLN had asked himself, like a profound philosopher, on which side preponderates the chances of this civil war; if the American Union was not in fact too large to hold together; if geography and the philosophy of history did not decree its dissolution; if Jefferson Davis were not, after all, the instrument of this great change, and the man expressly sent to accomplish it—such reasonings, supported by a few defeats, (and defeats were not wanting,) would very quickly have persuaded Mr. LINCOLN that in resigning himself to peace and the dissolution of the republic, he was simply acting in obedience to destiny. These are the roads in which a man may travel when he looks for rules of conduct elsewhere than in his conscience. But Mr. LINCOLN was as far removed from these subtleties as light is from darkness. He had the good fortune to be religious: but his religion ranged itself by the side of his duty. He did not think that God could hold another language to him than that of his conscience; and if he regarded the reverses of honest men as trials, it was because he always believed that God was with them.

So that nothing could shake him. He supported, both patiently and ably, the ill-will of Europe; he saw without alarm the armies of the republic losing courage or dispersing; he saw without fear and anger his capital filled with traitors; he carried on recruiting in the middle of New York when the city was on fire. He repelled all idea of a dictatorship; submitted himself, at the period fixed by law, to the popular election, and taking his burden willingly upon him, set out on his road, and took no account of obstacles. A sense of duty has this extraordinary advantage in it, that the chances of life cannot affect it.

He approached at last the termination of so many trials. Guided by the instinct of an upright heart, and seconded by the able counsels of that minister who had the honor of being attacked at the same time with himself, and whose death appeared to be equally necessary to the enemies of his country, Mr. LINCOLN had eventually thwarted by victory the blind and lamentable enterprise undertaken by the authors of the civil war, and of which his generous moderation was about to be employed in effacing the recollection. He could display with some degree of pride aloft and triumphant that Union flag which had been twice intrusted to him, and which he had preserved through so many perils. It is at the moment that he is struck that the unforeseen blow resounds so grievously in the hearts of all honest men in the Old as in the New World. The Romans have held in pious reverence the memory of a certain Fabius Dorso, who, during the siege of Rome by the Gauls, passed slowly through the enemy's lines, carrying with him respectfully the necessary offerings for a sacrifice, which was to be offered in a day and at a place fixed. It is in a very similar manner that this honest man has pursued his course for more than four years, holding religiously in his hands as a sacred deposit the threatened existence of his country. Less fortunate than Fabius Dorso, he has fallen at the very foot of the altar, and covered it with his blood. But his work was done, and the spectacle of a rescued republic was what he could look upon with consolation when his eyes were closing in death. Moreover, he has not lived alone for his country, since he leaves to every one in the world to whom liberty and justice are dear a great remembrance and a pure example.

PREVOST PARADOL.

[From the Journal des Debats, May 3, 1865.]

We cannot but identify ourselves with the sentiments so warmly expressed by M. Rouher, in the speech delivered by him yesterday in the legislative chamber, and with those of M. Drouyn de Lhuys and Messieurs Rouher and Vuitry, one to the legislative chamber, the other to the senate. We feel only one regret, which is that the French government has been so tardy in publicly proclaiming that honest ABRAHAM LINCOLN had devoted his life to the defence of a just cause, and that he served it with as much moderation as patriotic zeal. The acclamation with which the legislative chamber welcomed the words of M. Rouher says plainly enough what is the opinion of France on this subject.

The crime to which Mr. LINCOLN has fallen a victim has put an end to the hesitations of England as well as those of France. The House of Lords unanimously adopted the address to the Queen proposed by Earl Russell. In the House of Commons, Sir George Grey and Mr. Disraeli did full justice to the patient heroism which the North displayed, and still displays, in the midst of such cruel trials. Sir George Grey, speaking in the name of the Crown, said in substance that "if the sympathies of the English people were at first divided, they were ranged on the side of the North as soon as the news was received of the horrible atrocities committed at Washington."

F. CAMUS.

[From the Journal des Debats, May 4, 1865.]

It is well to die; that is a reflection we cannot help making on reading the funeral oration of ABRAHAM LINCOLN, such as was pronounced on the 1st of May by Earl Russell in the House of Lords. If the good citizen and the honest, excellent man whom America laments has waited a long time for a little justice at the hands of the English ministers, the justice now due to him is so much the more striking as it has been slow.

No fear appears to be entertained in North America about the consequences of the murder of LINCOLN. Certainly, some alarm and perturbation were felt at first; here the northern soldiers wanted to massacre the prisoners of the south; there old soldiers of the south, enrolled under northern banners, attempted to revolt; elsewhere the mob desired to burn the offices of the journals of the democratic party. All these movements were very quickly and very easily put down. The taking of Mobile, moreover, was another blow dealt to the cause of the South. The murder of LINCOLN has aggravated the difficulty of treating with the South, and done nothing to embarras the victory of the North.

F. CAMUS.

[From the Journal des Debats, May 8, 1865.]

The grief and horror caused by the murder of LINCOLN cannot but be more deeply felt when we think of the touching and truly religious language in which, a month before his death, this good man thanked his fellow-citizens for his re-election. LINCOLN felt nothing of the intoxication of triumph; victory inspired him with no other feeling than the satisfaction arising from the consciousness of duty having been performed and justice satisfied. On taking possession for the second time of the supreme magistracy of the republic he said: " Neither party expected for the war the magnitude or the duration which it has already attained. Neither anticipated that the *cause* of the conflict might cease with, or even before, the conflict itself should cease. Each looked for an easier triumph, and a result less fundamental and astounding. Both read the same Bible and pray to the same God, and each invoke His aid against the other. It may seem strange that any men should dare to ask a just God's assistance in wringing their bread from the sweat of other men's faces; but let us judge not, that we be not judged. The prayers of both could not be answered; that of neither has been answered fully. The Almighty has His own purposes. ' Woe unto the world because of offences! for it must needs be that offences come; but woe to that man by whom the offence cometh.' If we shall suppose that American slavery is one of those offences which, in the providence of God, must needs come, but which, having continued through His appointed time, He now wills to remove, and that He gives to both North and South this terrible war as the woe due to those by whom the offence came, shall we discern therein any departure from those divine attributes which the believers in a living God always ascribe to him? Fondly do we hope—fervently do we pray—that this mighty scourge of war may speedily pass away. Yet, if God wills that it continue until all the wealth piled by the bondman's two hundred and fifty years of unrequited toil shall be sunk, and until every drop of blood drawn with the lash shall be paid by another drawn with the sword, as was said three thousand years ago, so still it must be said, 'The judgments of the Lord are true and righteous altogether.'" These were nearly the last words—the *novissima verba* of ABRAHAM LINCOLN—and man may meet his God with calmness when a violent death snatches him from this world with sentiments like these.

*   *   *   *   *   *   *   *

JOHN LEMOINE.

[From The Monde, April 27, 1865.]

We have no desire to pronounce a precipitate judgment; what is to be wished for the sake of honor and humanity is, that this odious outrage may have been the work of some isolated fanatic. It would be too sad a spectacle to see a lost cause replying by assassination to the magnanimity of its conquerors.

It may be affirmed, moreover, that this odious deed is also a useless crime. Mr. LINCOLN dies surrounded with the purest glory that ever crowned a statesman; but his work will survive him, and the greatest victory of liberty will not have been won in vain. The mission designed by Providence for the United States does not depend upon the life of one man, and that liberty which created Mr. LINCOLN, and which he has served so well, will infallibly raise up worthy successors to him.

GUSTAVE ISAMBERT.

[From the Opinion Nationale, April 28, 1865.]

It is with profound grief that we yesterday received the news of the abominable crime which has so suddenly extinguished in the United States a noble and precious life.

President LINCOLN was one of those men who do honor to their country, to the age in which they live, and to all humanity. The American republic never produced a better, a greater citizen.

Mr. LINCOLN was the embodiment of duty. He knew but one road—the right line—and to admirable perseverance he joined a loftiness of view, a correctness of judgment, a moderation, a generosity of sentiment which inspired respect, commanded admiration, and elicited sympathy.

Mr. Seward, whose life we still hope will be preserved, is himself a man of integrity—a remarkable politician—a diplomatist of skill and tact, altogether unexceptionable, which he has proved under circumstances peculiarly difficult, in warding off from his country the constantly threatening danger of foreign complications.

One thing only can console us in this heavy misfortune: the crime will remain an abortive one. The Union, re-established by President LINCOLN, will be free from all attacks after the last and decisive victories of Grant and his generals. We will say more. It is in the nature of these frightful outrages against moral and social order to recall men to the wholesome appreciation of things, to the necessity of concord, and the importance of fraternity; and the assassination of Mr. LINCOLN will lead to the more speedy return to the Union of the defenders of the secessionists' cause, who are in a state of alarm and consternation at a crime of which they are innocent, but which was none the less committed in the name of their cause.

It is true that on the 6th of April Mr. Jefferson Davis published a proclamation in which he declared his intention to carry on war; but this manifest was previous to the surrender of Lee and his army, and the valiant general who laid down his arms in order to avoid a perfectly useless shedding of blood, morally obliged Mr. Davis to give up a struggle which henceforward could hold out no possible hope of success.

If he persisted it would prove that passion had the mastery of his reason, and that pride goes for much in that ill-understood patriotism which has done nothing but heap disasters upon disasters and ruin upon ruin.

If, besides, the conduct of General Lee had not enlightened Mr. Jefferson Davis, the blood which has just flowed at Washington under the steel of assassins, would, no doubt, bring him to his senses, if it were only to ward off an accusation which would not fail to be made, that of having seen in the crime of the assassins an unexpected piece of good fortune, and having sought to turn it to account in resuscitating a ruined cause.

In another column will be found some circumstantial details of the great assassination, and we devote a special article to the policy of President LINCOLN.

The emotion caused by the death of Mr. LINCOLN has been immense in England, and the London journals manifest with energy the horror with which this frightful outrage has inspired them.

An address of condolence has been presented to the American minister by the members of the House of Commons. Business has been suspended at the Exchange and in the markets; and the most enthusiastic partisans of the secessionist cause have themselves expressed the most intense indignation.—
Editorial.

MR. LINCOLN.

The odious crime of which the President of the United States has just become the victim will be felt as a public misfortune throughout the whole of the civilized world. Mr. LINCOLN had had that rare good fortune, for a statesman, to attain to power by the idea of which he had become the personification, and of having been able to bring to a close the immense task which events, much more than his own will, had imposed upon him; an abolitionist by conviction, but, above all, a practical and experienced man, he would not, perhaps, have taken the initiative in the formidable question of slavery, if the precipitation of the South had not found in the elevation of Mr. LINCOLN to the presidential chair a cause or a pretext for an insurrection which had been long premeditated. Provoked by an open revolt, which permitted him neither to fall back nor to think of a compromise, Mr. LINCOLN accepted without hesitation the heavy responsibility which had fallen upon him. Without allowing himself to be discouraged by the first reverses, he applied himself with invincible tenacity to create, to organize everything that he wanted—men, generals, an army. The immensity of the pecuniary sacrifices, the mediocrity of the first generals whom he found at hand, the brilliant successes of his adversaries, the threatening sympathies of Europe, nothing stopped him, nothing made him go on faster than his own wisdom counselled him to do. It is to be remarked, too, that, abolitionist as he was, he decided to proclaim the abolition of slavery with a sort of hesitation peculiar to resolute characters, who do not easily make up their minds to go forward, precisely because they know that they will not recede.

At length, after four years' exertions, victory crowned his policy; his fellow-citizens, full of confidence in him, conferred upon him a second time the power of the presidency. Skilful generals, whom the war had brought to the surface, reduced and disarmed the insurrection. Then this firm and intractable man, who could never be brought to negotiate with insurrection, appeared in a fresh light, and showed himself as though he were disarmed by victory. The most noble sentiments of conciliation, a kind of chivalric delicacy which disguises from the conquered the bitterness of defeat, an anxious solicitude to reconstruct the Union, with the help even of those who had broken away from it, burst forth spontaneously in the language of the conqueror of a new type, and impressed upon him a character of modest grandeur and superior morality which is refreshing to the mind, and makes one feel proud and honored to belong to human nature. The attitude of Mr. LINCOLN during the last days of his life, and his language with regard to the southern States, form, with the correspondence so heroically simple exchanged between Grant and Lee, a characteristic picture of which the New World has a right to be proud.

The intention which guided the arm of the assassin of LINCOLN appears also to have inspired the outrage of which Mr. Seward and his son have been the victims; it appears even, if reliance can be placed upon the summary details which comprise all the information that has at present come to hand on this melancholy subject, that it is only by a fortunate accident that Grant and the Minister of War, Mr. Stanton, have escaped an attempt of the same kind.

So painful an experience of the furious passions left upon the mind after the defeat of the South, will urge upon the principal civil and military heads of the Union a system of personal precautions, the necessity for which is only too grievously demonstrated. Let us hope that it will occasion no other modification of the generous policy inaugurated by LINCOLN, and which will be for his fellow-citizens the best and most prolific portion of their inheritance.

As for Europe, it will feel acutely the premature death of the great and good man whom America has just lost. His firmness, moderation, and patriotism, sincere and without ostentation, were a pledge that, entirely absorbed with the desire of healing the deep wounds inflicted by civil war, he would not divert attention with foreign broils so as to render the American people careless of their internal reorganization.

The death of LINCOLN puts everything in a state of uncertainty. Until now, Vice-President Johnson, whom this melancholy accident has invested with power, was the object of certain prejudices, which it is asserted have no foundation. Do not let us be in a hurry to judge the matter. Responsibility carries along with it much deliberation and caution; and, then, the force of public opinion, the power of democracy, that sound collective sense which comes from the midst of a free population, always well informed upon public affairs, and watched over by an unshackled press, and accustomed to decide upon their own interests—all this assures us that the fate of the great American republic cannot be endangered by the death of its Chief Magistrate, however superior or great a man. There are, in the depths of democracy, valuable reserves of character and unknown talents, which necessity will raise to the surface. We are afflicted with the death of President LINCOLN, but it throws us into no uneasiness. And, again, why should we grieve? Since we are all born to die, who could dream of so desirable a death!

Have not the duties of LINCOLN's career been fulfilled? Is not his work finished? And does not his triumphant death lend a tragic brilliancy to the sober and masculine virtues of this worthy successor of Washington?

R. DE GUERAULT.

The slave rebellion has closed, with a triple assassination, the terrible conflict which it has sustained for four years with the Washington government. It was not sufficient for it to have caused rivers of blood to flow on the fields of battle. It demanded, even after the war, still more victims. It has immolated

Mr. LINCOLN, the great citizen; a man as conciliatory as he was energetic; the head of the state, who, finding himself confronted with the most terrible civil war related in history, has shown how, at one and the same time, to save his country and solve the most difficult social problem of modern times.

The crime was not, unfortunately, the act of a madman, but the result of a conspiracy, plotted by the envenomed partisans of slavery. At the moment when one of the assassins, Wilkes Booth, struck down Mr. LINCOLN at the theatre, another stabbed the Secretary of State, Mr. William H. Seward, and his son, Frederick Seward, at their own residence. This is the intelligence sent by the Secretary of War, Mr. Stanton, and communicated yesterday to the London journals by Mr. Francis Adams.

ABRAHAM LINCOLN, William Henry Seward, and Frederick Seward have been assassinated.

In the presence of these corpses, which will long dwell in our thoughts, before these tombs, which have scarcely closed over them, it is well that democracy should utter a word of fraternity.

Great reforms have not been accomplished but at the price of the lives of the reformers.

The freedom of the blacks has been prefaced with the execution of John Brown, and the epilogue is the assassination of LINCOLN. That is the order. Conquered reactions protest by the use of hemlock, the dagger, the funeral pile, and the gibbet.

It will always be thus so long as the dogma of the inviolability of human life shall not have penetrated all consciences.

After John Brown, the scaffold ceased to appear to be a ligitimate resort. After LINCOLN, political assassination, the old Spartan doctrine of the *sic semper tyrannis*, remains irredeemably condemned. Who will profit by the abominable act? Will the South? Certainly not! The South was only conquered; now it is dishonored. But it is the great republic now consecrated by martyrdom. It is the black race redeemed by the blood of the just, and it is especially the inviolability of human life that will be benefited by the deed.

No more scaffolds! No more tyrannicide! It is time that the eastern doctrine of the redemption of blood should cease to receive the consecration of history.

J. LABBE.

[From the Opinion Nationale, April 30, 1865.]

The funeral service, which we yesterday announced at the end of our bulletin, took place to-day, at 12 o'clock, in the Episcopal chapel, in Rue Bayard, being celebrated by the Rev. M. Lamson.

The chapel was hung with black, and ornamented with flags and escutcheons, with the colors of the United States.

The attendance was numerous, and were impressed with a deep sense of the solemnity of the occasion. Among the French persons present were the following deputies: MM. Berryer, Jules Favre, Eugene Pelletan, Jules Simon, Garnier Pages, Ernest Picard, General Franconniere, aide-de-camp of Prince Napoleon, and a great many lawyers, writers, and journalists, among whom were MM. Henri Martin, Cremieux, A. de la Forge, Floquet, Degauve, Denucques Andre Pasquet, Dreo. &c.

This mournful ceremony had nothing in it of a political or official character and was exclusively religious.

[From the Opinion Nationale, May 1, 1865.]

*　　*　　*　　*　　*　　*　　*　　*　　*

We are assured that Mr. W. H. Seward is out of danger, and America may still reckon upon the services of this skilful diplomatist, who is at the same time an honest man.

It has been remarked that the federal securities have experienced no depreciation in the different markets of the United States. Such is the power of democratic institutions, when they are founded upon ripe judgments, and upon the energy of religious sentiment, which no incident, how lamentable soever, is able to shake by compromising the national credit and the public wealth.

[From the Presse, April 28, 1865.]

A DISHONORED CAUSE.

How blind are those assassins who take up arms at the instigation of political hatred! They think they strike the cause which they detest, but it is their own cause which they injure and which they dishonor—the idiots!

What has been accomplished by the fatal shot by which President LINCOLN lost his life? It has abridged by some years, by some months, by some weeks, perhaps by some days only, the existence of ABRAHAM LINCOLN, who might have been carried off by an illness, or an accident, as a few days before Mr. Seward was nearly killed by a fall from a carriage; but the blow which has deprived Mr. LINCOLN of life has assured him immortality.

Some hours less in a lifetime! What are they? Can they be put in the balance with succeeding ages in posterity?

The history of the republic of the United States counts fourteen Presidents. The names of the greater part of them are already forgotten, but there are three names which will never die—those of Washington, Jefferson, and LINCOLN. That of Washington, personifying the lofty disinterestedness which refused the crown; of Jefferson, personifying power made illustrious by respect for liberty; of LINCOLN, personifying the devotedness of a man who dies for having given freedom to millions of men.

The assassination of ABRAHAM LINCOLN will have a withering effect upon Jefferson Davis, if, with the impulse of indignation, shame, and grief, the first act of the president of the Confederate States be not to protest, in the name of the cause which he defended, against this new appendage to war, which, if it became general, would descend from collective to individual murder—to the usurping executioner, constituting himself an avenger of faithless victory. War was wanting in the process by which this boasted crime might become a qualified one; so that, after having commenced war on the field of battle, it might be ended in the assize court!

Perhaps this termination was necessary in order that the eyes might cease to be blinded by the smoke of gunpowder, and that persons dazzled with glory should ask themselves what difference there was between the ball which might have struck General Grant in the theatre of war and that which in another theatre struck President LINCOLN.

This is no commonplace suggestion. Let it not be said that the soldier who aimed at General Grant would have risked his life, and that it was not so with the assassin who fired the fatal shot at President LINCOLN. Let the first continue to be called brave, but let not the second be called a coward. That would be neither true nor just. Wilkes Booth and his accomplices were quite aware that they risked their lives, and when those lives come to be taken by the executioner, the greatest dishonor will not rest upon the men personally, but on their cause, if every connection between them and it be not, we repeat, spontaneously and solemnly repudiated by president Davis, basing his submission upon the horror with which this outrage inspired him, and, as a pledge of the sincerity of this submission, consigning himself to voluntary banishment.

For president Davis and those of his generals who have not laid down their arms there is no other honorable course to pursue. If they hesitate, they are not only lost but dishonored, and it will be upon them that the responsibility will justly fall of all the excesses which an angry populace and an irritated and desperate army might, but we hope would not, commit in the excitement of anger and indignation.

If president Jefferson Davis does not hasten to furnish this example of political candor and honesty, let him reckon no longer upon the sympathies of Europe, which were attached to his person and his cause. In the eyes of all whose conscience is not perverted by passion there will be only one malefactor fallen still lower than his accomplices, the assassins of ABRAHAM LINCOLN and Frederick Seward, and his precursor, the executioner of John Brown.

What a sorry cause was that which commenced in November, 1859, with the destruction of John Brown, that glorious martyr, whose firmness never forsook him a single moment; and which finished in April, 1865, by the assassination of ABRAHAM LINCOLN, that imperturbable President, who demonstrated that democracy had only to spread open its wings to soar from the lowest regions to the grandest and loftiest elevations.

Oh! let us be believed when we say that the first who will go into mourning for the illustrious victim of the stupid Wilkes Booth will not be the Americans who have the honor to belong to the North, for the woodman LINCOLN has his successor naturally designated in the tanner Grant; it is those who have the misfortune to belong to the South, since the assassination has changed into opprobrium the prestige which at one time attached to their cause.

EMILE DE GIRARDIN.

[From the Presse, May 1, 1865.]

Let us note to the honor of our old Europe, that it has been grievously wounded by the blow that has fallen upon LINCOLN. The Emperor has sent one of his aides-de-camp to Mr. Bigelow, requesting the minister to transmit to Washington the expression of his sympathy for the deceased President, and the horror he feels at the crime which has been committed. The English Parliament will to-morrow vote an address to the government and people of America. The Italian Parliament has already voted an address, proposed by M. Crispi, and the flagstaff which bore the Italian colors on the Carignan palace was draped with crape; at Brussels an immense meeting was held, to send across the Atlantic the sympathies of the Belgian people. Finally, at Berlin, the Chamber of Deputies had a solemn manifestation, and M. de Bismarck wrote a letter to the new President, expressive of the sentiments of the people and government of Prussia.

Thus, across the Atlantic, the Old and New Worlds extend the hand to each other over the coffin of ABRAHAM LINCOLN. Extreme views and the most divergent opinions meet around this tomb—it is because LINCOLN was the personification of energy in the struggle, and wisdom in power; moderation in view of defeat, and conscience in the face of liberty.

GEORGES JAUBERT.

[From Le Pays, April 28, 1865.]

MR. LINCOLN.

President LINCOLN has fallen under the ball of an assassin, at the moment when the rare honor of re-election crowned with eclat his political life—at the moment when victory pronounced definitively for the arms of the North.

We are not among those who have approved of everything that has been done in Mr. LINCOLN's administration. We have never hesitated to speak the truth about him, however severe it may appear to have been. Upon points to which a portion of the French press gave a blind admiration, we ourselves, with candor and firmness under the loyal impulse of our conscience, observed a necessary reserve.

More than once we have had occasion to censure an unfortunate choice—more than once to regret imprudent or illegitimate acts. Having never been the flatterers of Mr. LINCOLN, we are, on that account, more at liberty now to declare that we lament from the bottom of our heart this most cruel death, and that we condemn in the strongest possible manner this detestable crime.

Mr. LINCOLN was an excellent man, and united in himself everything which can constitute the character of a great citizen.

In the terrible crisis during which Providence put into his hands the destinies of America, he showed an unalterable firmness, and a confidence beyond all praise in the rightfulness of his mission, and in the future of his cause.

Assuredly, the American people reckon among the glorious list of her Presidents men who were, in intelligence, superior to Mr. LINCOLN, but there were none who were above him in largeness of heart; in the vigor of patriotism; in tenacity of will; in the energy of the active faculties. Thus these masculine and simple characteristics, with the truly democratic stamp of roughness and primitive austerity, will not fail to occupy an honorable place in the history of our time.

What will be the consequences, in a political point of view, of this bloody event? That, however, is what we shall soon learn; moreover it would seem to us to be impious, at this early hour of grief and sorrow, when so much and such mournful news is constantly reaching us from the other side of the Atlantic.

All that we have at heart to-day is to render sorrowful homage to the memory of an honest man, struck down by an assassin in the midst of a renewed career and a triumphant achievement, and to address to the American nation, so cruelly deprived of their chief, the expression of our sympathy and fraternal grief.

[From La Patrie, April 28, 1865.]

THE DEATH OF MR. LINCOLN.

The violent death of Mr. LINCOLN has thrown the mind of every one into profound stupefaction.   Nobody knows what to think of this assassination, which invests the American question with new complications.   We dare not venture to think that this crime is the work of a political party, and one hesitates to admit that private revenge can have thus encompassed in its fury two states-men—the two veritable heads of the government of the North.

Fatality weighs upon this unhappy country, which for four years has been devastated by an unjust war, and which, in the day when peace appeared to be possible, saw itself suddenly plunged into the most terrible eventualities.

The first feeling inspired by such a catastrophe can be nothing but one of horror.   Whatever may have been the motive of these assassins, there is in this act too much baseness not to fill the whole of Europe with indignation.   But there is another feeling, arising from the thought of the troubles which the murder of Mr. LINCOLN and his minister may give rise to, as well in the north as in the south, and that feeling is one of mingled apprehension and sorrow.

*   *   *   *   *   *   *   *   *

ERNEST DREOLLE.

[From La Patrie, May 3, 1865.]

Were we right in saying that not one of the manifestations on the occasion of the death of Mr. LINCOLN, by persons ever desirous to thrust themselves forward, was equivalent to a single one of these simple and dignified measures taken by the government ?

The sittings held yesterday in the senate and the legislative chamber will answer for us.

In the first place, there is a letter addressed by M. Drouyn de Lhuys to our chargé d'affaires at Washington, which is as remarkable for its mode of expression as for the depth of feeling evinced in it.   Its language responds to public opinion, outraged as it is by the assassination of the 14th of April; it is also the kind of language which should be held by the minister of a government remaining neutral in the struggle by which America was divided.

In the legislative chamber it was M. Rouher who did homage to the memory of Mr. LINCOLN, and in the senate M. Vuitry discharged that office. Then the presidents of the two chambers became in eloquent terms the inter-preters of the sentiments of their colleagues.

The manifestation, therefore, was complete and truly national.   MM. Rouher, Vuitry, Schneider, and Troplong vibrate in America with the force they deserve.   M. Rouher desires to see in North Americans "an allied and friendly people;" M. Schneider desires peace; M. Troplong acknowledges, with truth, that "America has passed through more grievous trials than ever fell to the lot of a country founded on liberty!"

May the future justify the confidence of the minister of state! May it satisfy the desires of M. Schneider, and may the trials spoken of by M. Troplong as having been endured in North America speedily cease! That is the wish which we also entertain from the bottom of our hearts.

ERNEST DREOLLE.

[From the Revue des Deux Mondes, May 1, 1865.]

During the last fortnight the news from the United States has brought us the greatest political consolation which liberal opinion has received for the last fifteen years, and at the same time one of the most poignant griefs which could be felt by the afflicted spectators of the most tragical of human events.

Sorrow has come at last.   Mr. LINCOLN, who for four years had sustained in the midst of difficulties and the most cruel trials that a nation could pass through, the fortunes, imperilled on every side, of the democratic and liberal republic of the United States; Mr. LINCOLN, who had with so much tranquil firmness of mind saved his country from the calamity of internal dissolution; Mr. LINCOLN, who helped to achieve the late victories by which the integrity of the American republic has been assured; Mr. LINCOLN, who now caught a glimpse of the blessings of peace, and already applied his honest and scrupulous mind to the work of the reconciliation of parties and the reorganization of the great American party; Mr. LINCOLN has suddenly fallen beneath the hand of an assassin, having been shot with a pistol.   An atrocious conspiracy, designed to annihilate at once the genius and the arm of the American government, which was to have been brought to bear at the same time against General Grant, Mr. Seward, and Mr. Lincoln, has not missed the most eminent of the victims contemplated by it, and has horribly succeeded in killing the President of the republic.

One universal feeling of stupor, indignation, and affliction has followed upon the announcement of this atrocity.   Europe, as the United States well know, has not been less sensibly affected than themselves by the crime under which their chief has fallen.   Feelings and pre-occupations of many kinds mingle with our first emotions of painful surprise.   We have been, as it were, thunderstruck by the sudden contrast which places such a catastrophe on the morrow of the great and decisive victories obtained by the American government.   Men anxiously ask one another how far the work of American reconciliation will be embarrassed and obstructed by this loss; to what hands the supreme power is about to pass; what violence and what reprisals the detestable provocation of political assassination may probably lead to. But this astonishment, these doubts and fears, have been subordinate, in the conscience of European communities, to the deep-felt sympathy for the noble and generous victim. The general grief is spontaneously assuaged, so to speak, by the endeavors to do justice to the merits and virtues of Mr. LINCOLN. Assuredly, in some of the great nations, and in several government departments of Europe, there has been little disposition during the last four years to be just to Mr. LINCOLN and his most devoted colleagues. Death seems to have revealed to all eyes the real worth of this honest man; it has taught the indifferent and the inattentive themselves the loss which the cause of political probity and humanity has sustained in him. Opinion has done Mr. LINCOLN wrong while living. We may say that it is now making solemn efforts to repair that wrong when he is no more.

This is a spectacle of high morality. What was the last President when the election carried him to supreme power, and when the civil war broke out which threatened the destruction of the United States? The biography of Mr. LINCOLN was then already known; but it was not such as surrounds their heroes with the admiration of Europe, or the exclusive sympathies of refined circles. There was nothing brilliant in the career of the man; none of that prestige which attaches to tried talent. The only extraordinary thing in the life of Mr. LINCOLN was his elevation to the highest office in the state; and that promotion, even, was a cause of surprise and distrust. With the prejudices which we, in our old Europe, entertain, how few of us can understand how he, who began life as an illiterate workman, should become the enlightened head of a nation of thirty-five millions of souls! We are familiar only, in Europe, in political matters, with the slow process of education acquired by traditional classes, administrative supernumeraries, and by long literary culture. Old classical politicians, we doubt not that the most rapid and the most solid of educations, how little elegant and gracious it may be in form, is under a government freed from the shackles of social conventionalisms—that acquired in a private, laborious, and struggling life, united with the political life exercised in the midst of liberal institutions. Mr. LINCOLN, then, was formerly a workman, a rail-splitter, self-taught, had become attorney's clerk, then an attorney, and had passed over the various gradations of political functions more easily than he had risen by manual labor to the exercise of a liberal profession. He came from the rude West, unpolished, absolutely destitute of self-sufficiency, of the elegant manners and the shining qualities which accompany the practiced politician, the fortunate speculator in commercial cities, the gentleman planter of the southern States. He and his friends succeeded for the first time to the direction of affairs. Power had long been monopolized by the southern and democratic coalition, over whom they triumphed; and it seemed that there were no statesmen known in America but those who had been chiefs of this coalition. His own principles were not sufficiently defined and settled to enlighten public opinion as to his future policy. It seemed that he was to carry into the government that kind of hesitation and awkwardness which were observed in him personally. It was even because there was in him something of indistinctness and confusion that he was preferred to candidates better known in the republican party, to the brilliant and adventurous General Frémont, and to the eloquent and skilful Mr. Seward. In a word, Mr. LINCOLN was not one of those men who bring to the power with which they are invested a force and brilliancy acquired beforehand; he belonged to that class, on the contrary, who borrow their grandeur and prestige from the task with which they are charged, the duties which it imposes upon them, and from the manner in which they fulfil those duties. He did not, thank God, belong to that family of great men in the Old World, of whom it has been said, " It is fortunate that Heaven has spared a number of them to the human race; for one man to be exalted above the human family, it would cost too dear to all the others." But from the first words and first acts of Mr. LINCOLN, it was easily foreseen that he would fulfil his mission, and would not be found unequal to the situation.

Mr. LINCOLN appeared to take as the rule of his conduct the principle of a law whose observance elevates the simple and strengthens the humble. He sought the path which simple duty pointed out to him, that which is readily perceived and immediately adopted, and which is not created, so to speak, by an effort and a caprice of philosophical induction. Mr. LINCOLN undertook the government, determined, according to a common expression, the beauty of which his life and death will make us thoroughly understand, to be the slave of duty. The circumstances amidst which he arrived at Washington in 1861 to take the presidency will not fail to be remembered. He narrowly escaped an attempt at assassination. The integrity of the United States was a cause which had then but feeble defenders; and the commander-in-chief, at that time old General Scott, considered he had gained a great victory when he succeeded in maintaining sufficient order in the capital to make it possible for the ceremony of the inauguration of the new President to take place. Mr. LINCOLN showed immediately that, in his eyes, simple duty, direct and close at hand, was the mainstay of the Union and the honest performance of his duty. He drew the line indicated by this sense of duty as tight as possible. It was necessary to do away with every pretext put forward by those who prepared and proclaimed the separation of the southern States. The pretext alleged by the secessionists was the design they attributed to the republican party, now in power, to impose upon the southern States the forcible abolition of slavery. Undoubtedly, Mr. LINCOLN felt the repugnance of every enlightened mind and clear conscience against this institution of slavery which the fanatics of the south were not afraid, for so many years, to erect into an institution of divine right; but the simple duty, the direct and consequently superior duty of the President of the United

States, was the preservation of the Union before laboring for abolition—to be an unionist before an abolitionist. Mr. LINCOLN showed himself ready, if the Union were preserved, to give his adversaries every chance of an honorable compromise on the question of slavery. How much he was reproached for this moderation at the time! Some looked upon it as a weakening of the cause of the North—the disavowal of the generous sympathies of the world, acquired by a government which undertook to carry out boldly the work of abolition; in the eyes of others, it was a one-sided and perfidious policy, which concealed its real object by mere manœuvres of routine. The war broke out—the impetuous South Carolinians drove from Fort Sumter the small federal garrison, and insulted the stars and stripes of the national flag. This insult was deeply felt by the mass of the American people; the southern States proclaimed the separation, and the struggle was commenced. Mr. LINCOLN still resisted the strong tendencies of so violent a situation; for many months he maintained the cause of the Union as superior to that of abolition, being anxious, as long as possible, to leave a door open to conciliation. It was more than a year afterwards, and when the fortunes of war were most unfavorable to the cause of the United States, that Mr. LINCOLN resolved to decree the abolition as a war measure and a means of legitimate defence, but still not by way of a sovereign right which his government had arrogated to itself against the private rights of the southern States. In thus confining himself to the accomplishment of his duty within the narrowest limits, Mr. LINCOLN (and it is not less honorable to his sagacity than his integrity) was satisfied that he stood upon the most national, and consequently most unassailable, ground. The persistent carrying out of this line of conduct, however, has displayed at once the wisdom and successful policy involved in it. Sectarian dissensions have disappeared in this large and simple policy, and nothing has been lost to the collateral advantages resulting from the triumph of the Union; on the contrary, they have gained by remaining subordinate to the clearest and most considerable of the national interests. It is evident that Mr. LINCOLN found his mind strengthened and his conscience tranquillized by this close observance of the line of duty. It is proved by the course of events. He suffered himself to be cast down by no reverse, nor to be unduly elevated by any amount of success. The calmness of his mind was manifested in the familiarity of his bearing and language, in that good humor which was peculiar to him, in those proverbs and those innocent witticisms which often teemed in his conversation, and which the popular good sense understood so correctly. A thousand anecdotes are told of him, and a thousand phrases, which displayed extraordinary self-possession in the midst of a crisis unparalleled, and a mind which always saw its way clear in the midst of the most confused and perilous circumstances. To a serene and simple firmness was added a moderation to which his contemners and enemies of former times now hasten to do justice. He was never seen to be rash and inflated in his predictions; irritated or regretful against such of his agents as had been unfortunate, endeavoring to amuse or lead away popular sentiment by attacks directed against persons, or against the foreign governments of whom America had a right to complain. By his circumspection and care he avoided the risk of augmenting the number of the enemies, or aggravating the dangers which might threaten his country. After the last decisive military successes of the North, his first thoughts and first words, like those of the man whom political hatred designed to send out of the world with him, Mr. Seward, were in favor of clemency and peace at home and abroad. In a very short time, in the space of four years, this man, whose mind and character were an enigma to all at the beginning of 1861, had acquired an immense ascendancy over his countrymen, and gained their confidence. A striking proof of this is furnished by the last presidential election, and it is confirmed by the deep and heartfelt grief which seized upon the people of the United States at the news of his tragical end.

Keen sorrow must have its way in the imposing and touching manifestations which surround the memory of that statesman who was faithful to his duty until death. All Europe has been deeply affected. The despotic governments of the continent have joined in official expressions of profound regret addressed to the representatives of the United States. The free people of England and Italy participate in the movement by the demonstrations of their parliaments and their municipal corporations. Such a spontaneous burst of human feeling is not only an imposing homage rendered to a noble victim; it is a pledge of sympathy given by the world to the United States; it marks with indelible characters in the conscience of humanity the signification and extent of the internecine struggle which the republic has sustained; it is a weighty piece of advice given to the American government to persevere in the road of humanity, conciliation, and indulgence on which Mr. LINCOLN had entered; it is in this sense of itself a great event. When we consider the degree of sensation every-where excited by the murder of Mr. LINCOLN, it seems that we have a right to hope that this sad catastrophe will not be attended by those politically disastrous consequences which were at first apprehended. Destinies like that of Mr LINCOLN, crowned by a sort of martyrdom, inculcate clemency. The United States can do no better honor to this great victim than by remaining faithful to the spirit of his policy. The American people will not convert into a feeling of vengeance against the South, which is at their feet, the just horror with which so infamous a crime has inspired them. Misplaced controversies have arisen as to what were the political opinions of the assassin of Mr. LINCOLN If this assassin is really the man he has been taken for, namely, the comedian Wilkes Booth, it is hardly possible to doubt that he was a violent secessionist It is asserted, in fact, that this Booth, at the time of the attempt of the aboli-tionist, John Brown, which excited in Virginia some years ago an alarm so cruel in its consequences, enrolled himself in the troop which took Brown, and that he was one in the cortege of inexorable fanatics who conducted the unfortunate (Kansas) farmer to the gibbet. There would be a sort of ferocious fatality in the coincidence which made one of the executioners of Brown the pitiless murderer of Mr. LINCOLN; but whatever may have been the fanaticism with which the assassin was animated, it would be an odious injustice to treat as accomplices in the murder the populations who furnished Stonewall Jackson and Robert Lee the heroic soldiers under their command. The American people will not commit this injustice.   *   *   *   *   *

[From the Siècle, April 28, 1865.]

The American republic had triumphed over the rebellion of the slave States; nothing more was required than to subdue the difficulties of peace itself. The man who had accomplished the first of these tasks, and was on the point of effecting the second, ABRAHAM LINCOLN, has just fallen beneath the blow of a secessionist. Slavery, therefore, has its fanatics !

What was LINCOLN before the suffrages of his fellow-citizens placed him at the head of the republic ? A carpenter. Then a grocer, taking advantage of his brief intervals of leisure to study the law. Charged with the government of one of the greatest nations in the world, in a crisis the most terrible in its history, the ex-carpenter showed himself equal to the situation. It will be the same with him who succeeds Mr. LINCOLN in so unexpected a manner, and who, like his predecessor, attained to the rank he occupies by the various gradations of labor. The great republic will pursue the course of her glorious career. As for the man who has just paid with his life for the place which history reserves for him, by the side of Washington, he goes down to the grave followed by the regret of the whole world. We should utter our own feelings of sorrow with greater emotion if the calm and simple figure which we have just employed did not arrest our pen, and impose upon us a degree of tranquillity and simplicity.

While one of the assassins killed Mr. LINCOLN, another penetrated into the room of Mr. Seward, who was in bed suffering from an accident reported in all the journals, and stabbed him repeatedly with a dagger. The son of Mr. Seward lost his life in endeavoring to defend his father. It was only by an accident that General Grant himself escaped death. On the departure of the mail, Mr. Seward was still living. May his life be spared to find in the esteem and respect of every friend of liberty some compensation for the loss which he has just sustained as a father and a citizen. A distinguished writer, an eloquent speaker, Mr. Seward has been able to show what he was worth, as a statesman, under the most difficult and delicate circumstances. Thanks to him that northern America has been able to preserve an attitude at once calm and firm in the face of foreign powers, which have been nearly all either ill-disposed or hostile.

TAXILE DELORE.

A GREAT DEMOCRATIC MARTYR.

Slavery, before expiring, has summoned up what remained to it of power and rage, in order to strike, from behind, the man by whom it was to be overthrown.

The satanic pride of this perverted society could not be resigned to defeat. It would not fall with honor, like other causes, destined to rise again. It expired, as it had lived, by violating every law, human and divine.

There is the spirit and probably the work of the famous secret association of the Golden Circle, which, after having for twenty years made preparations for the great rebellion, spread its accomplices thoughout the west and the north, and around the chair of the President gave the signal for that impious war on the day when public conscience at last snatched from the slaveholders the government of the United States.

On the day when the good man of whom they have just made a martyr was raised to power, they endeavored to carry into effect what had been concocted by treason.

But they failed; not succeeding in overthrowing LINCOLN by the force of war, they felled him by assassination.

The conspiracy appeared to have been a most desperate one. In assailing with the President his two principal ministers, on one of whom an attempt was made, and the commander-in-chief, who was saved by an unforeseen circumstance, the murderers reckoned upon disorganizing the government of the republic, and imagined that they were resuscitating the rebellion.

Their expectations will be disappointed. These sanguinary fanatics, whose cause is much less damaged by material superiority than by the moral power of the democracy, had become incapable of comprehending the nature and the results of the free institutions which their fathers had gloriously contributed to establish. We shall see a fresh example of what these institutions are able to effect.

The indignation of the people will not be exhausted in a passing explosion; it will become consecrated; it will be resumed in the unanimous action, persevering and invincible, of the universal will. Whoever are to be the agents, the instruments of this work, we may rest assured that it will be accomplished. The event will show that it was not dependent upon the life of one man, or upon several men. It will be accomplished after LINCOLN, as well as it was accomplished by him, but LINCOLN will remain the austere and sacred personification of a great epoch, the most faithful exponent of democracy.

This man, simple and upright, strong and prudent, raised by degrees to the command of a great people, and always equal to the situation, executing quietly and without precipitation, and with excellent good sense, the most colossal undertaking, giving to the world an example of civil power in a republic, directing a gigantic war without for a moment compromising free institutions, or threatening them with military usurpation, dying at last at the moment when, having conquered, he was about to pacify the country—(and God grant that the atrocious madman who killed him may not have destroyed with him the feeling of clemency, and determined upon pacification by force, instead of the peace which he desired!)—this man will live in the traditions of his country and of the world, in some sort the embodiment of the people, modern democracy itself. It was necessary, then, that the blood of the just should seal the great work of emancipation, which the blood of the just had inaugurated! The tragic history of the abolition of slavery, opened with the gibbet of John Brown, will close with the assassination of LINCOLN.

And now let him repose by the side of Washington, as the second founder of the great republic! The whole of the democracy in Europe is present in spirit at his funeral obsequies, in the same way that it heartily voted for his re-election, and applauded the victory in the arms of which he has fallen. Democracy will identify itself wholly and directly with the monument which America will raise to him in the capital in which he cast down slavery.

HENRI MARTIN.

[From the Siècle, April 30, 1865.]

I pause to pay a tribute of homage to the memory of that great and good man, ABRAHAM LINCOLN; he will have been the apostle and the martyr of freedom. The cause of slavery could only be put an end to by assassination It dies as it had lived, the dagger in hand. What a lost cause! What a dishonored cause! The frightful drama of Golgotha is the purchase of the disinherited. The blood of the just is invariably the ransom of slaves.

EDMUND TEXIER.

[From the Siècle, May 2, 1865.]

We yesterday expressed our opinion that the legislative chambers had a great duty to perform; we are able to state to-day that that duty has been nobly accomplished. The words uttered by M. Rouher, minister of state, respond to the feelings of the whole of France.

The despatch of the minister of foreign affairs is written in the same spirit, and these two declarations corroborate each other, and perfectly agree with the national feeling.

The American republic is partly the work of France. Our most eminent fellow-citizens watched over it in its infancy. In troublous times it has served as a counterpoise to the omnipotence at sea which England pretended to exercise, who was then our rival, but now our ally.

When all the European parliaments had testified their sympathy with the United States, it would have been an anomaly if the legislative body of France failed to honor the martyr to progress, the firm and devoted virtuous man, who, in the midst of the horrors of a protracted civil war, never for a moment despaired of the future of the great cause of civilization, and who vigorously upheld the great principles of the American Constitution. Let us observe that the president of the legislative body, in carrying out the wishes of the government with respect to these communications, gave expression to noble sentiments, with which the chamber identified itself; and this unanimous concurrence is not the least significant symptom of the power of public opinion in our democratic France.

*   *   *   *   *   *   *   *   *

EMILE DE LA BEDOLLIERE.

[From the Temps, April 27, 1865.]

Frightful news reaches us at the moment of going to press. President LINCOLN has been assassinated; and an attempt has been made upon the life of Mr. Seward, but he survives. We wish we could doubt the correctness of these particulars, which, unfortunately, come to us in a form altogether affirmative.

We are not at all uneasy about the grandeur of the Union, nor in respect of American liberty. A ruined cause can never be sustained by crime, but every one will readily understand that the whole Union, in the south as in the north, is deeply wounded by the ball which has just carried off this great citizen in the midst of such critical circumstances.

[From the Temps, April 28, 1865]

The fresh and grievous details which we receive of the lamentable tragedy at Washington leaves scarcely any room for the doubt we expressed yesterday. The assassination perpetrated on President LINCOLN, on Mr. Seward, and intended for Mr. Stanton, Minister of War, and probably also for General Grant, is indeed the result of a political plot. American despatches confirm it, and it is the unanimous impression of the English press. We cannot help remembering, besides, that the passions which have just struck down Mr. LINCOLN conspired against him at the time of his first election, and that on going from Springfield to Washington to be installed he was nearly being assassinated at Baltimore, in February, 1861.

Let us take care, however, not to fall into a too common error, and charge the whole of the southern people with the execrable crime which completes the downfall of their cause. No doubt there are many in the rebel States, many who do not repudiate with horror the atrocity of this vengeance, and many politicians who do not look upon the evil as irremediable.

How are we to understand, for example, that a man like General Lee, if he were not bound by his word of honor given to General Grant, if he still believed the struggle to be possible, would consent to resume his sword and place it again in the service of a cause dishonored by assassination? The wretches who killed Mr. LINCOLN have at the same time destroyed the South.

It is probable that they meditated more than a simple act of vengeance. In their eyes, perhaps, the chief crime of Mr. LINCOLN and Mr. Seward was not that they had triumphed over the South, but rather that they had proclaimed a policy of moderation and conciliation which would assure to the restored Union peace with foreign nations, and the respect of the world. To create irreconcilable hatred between the two sections of the Union; to exasperate the North; to replace temperate chiefs of the States by men of an opposite character; to substitute passion for wisdom, and to hurl the United States into the dangerous hazard peculiar to violence and anarchy—this was no doubt what they desired to effect, but in which they have not succeeded. They have misunderstood human nature, in taking no account of the horror which would be excited by their act, even in the south, and they have not the less misconceived the imperishable destiny of the United States. We associate ourselves with the general grief, but we share in no way whatever the apprehensions which we perceive are attached to it. The United States will not fail in any of the duties prescribed to them by the situation of affairs. The policy which Mr. LINCOLN and Mr. Seward have had the honor of sealing with their blood will be the policy of their successors; for the latter cannot deviate from it without making themselves the dupes and the accomplices of assassins.

A. NEFFTZER.

[From the Temps, May 1, 1865.]

After having registered the prompt and spontaneous manifestations which have taken place in the English, Italian, and Prussian parliaments, we at last hear something of the legislative chambers of France.

Nobody will have any difficulty in identifying himself with the sentiment manifested in this address; but we confess that we have no very clear notion as to what is meant by it. Do the deputies who signed it propose, as may be inferred from the letter which they sent at the same time to the President, to submit it to the chamber? It is certainly conceived in a manner not at all calculated to awaken susceptibilities of any kind; but besides that, one cannot discover how the chamber can be affected in this way; there is no explanation of the extra parliamentary signatures which are attached to the address, and which would furnish a reason for its non-reception. Will they, on the contrary, after having made this manifestation on their own account, and simply in the quality of citizens, provoke a parliamentary manifestation in which they are prepared to join? In that case we do not understand the double purpose to be served; for what has just been read is assuredly the least that the legislative chambers could say; and, to express our thoughts fully on this matter, we trust that if this assembly is called upon to pronounce, in any way, upon the event referred to, something more precise, emphatic, and appropriate to the circumstances will result from the deliberation in the chamber.

A. NEFFTZER.

<hr>

[From the Temps, May 2, 1865.]

The succession of LINCOLN has been settled without a moment's uncertainty, by the application, pure and simple, of the Constitution, the wisdom of which once more displays itself on the present occasion. It may be easily imagined, on the day after the commission of a political crime, in the midst of the difficulties of internal pacification, what confusion and perturbation might be occasioned by general elections, of which nobody could foresee the consequences. On this point there can be no doubt: the presidential chair had scarcely been vacant a few hours, when Andrew Johnson was installed at the White House.

The horror of a crime which the excitement of the struggle could in no way palliate, the painful feelings occasioned by the extinction of a pure glory in all its lustre, would at first produce a kind of stupor. No one can manifest too much grief for the murder of an eminent patriot, which has nothing of the effect of the heroes of Franconi; but the highest praise that can be bestowed on LINCOLN is just this, that having arrived at the period of great trouble, he did nothing to make himself indispensable, and that his disappearance has nothing in it threatening to stability, which is a condition too often attached to the existence of one man. It would be, then, to misconceive the real grandeur of the character of LINCOLN to dwell upon the commonplaces of funeral orations, instead of giving ourselves up without faltering to the examination of the questions which the succession gives rise to.

[From the Temps, May 4, 1865.]

PARIS, *May* 1, 1865.

TO THE EDITOR: The government and the great bodies of the state have solemnly testified the grief and indignation they felt at the assassination of President LINCOLN.

The press, it may be said, of all shades of political opinion, has gone before the public authorities in the spontaneous expressions of horror and regret.

Some citizens, necessarily in small numbers, will be able to add their signatures to those of the deputies and writers who have taken the initiative in an address of condolence to the United States.

But will not the people of Paris, whose sympathies and liberal instincts have been so deeply wounded by this crime, have an opportunity afforded them of publicly lamenting the fate of the former workman—almost one of themselves—who was the greatest and the purest minded among the successors of Washington ? The mass of the people cannot sign addresses. Would it not be a great satisfaction to them to find some easy mode of expressing their sentiments, such as the wearing some sign of mourning—for example, a piece of crape, or a simple black ribbon—on the arm ? This mourning might last a day or two, and commence, suppose, on Monday next.

Nobody, it seems to me, would think of doing any party act, much less committing himself to any seditious proceeding, in a manifestation common to all, the result of official manifestations, whose great moral effect would be completed by this demonstration.

If you coincide with these views, sir, will you have the goodness to submit them to your confrères, and also to your readers ? They will be well received, if I am not mistaken, and religiously carried out.

Accept, &c.,

RENE DUBAIL,
34 *Rue du Chateau d'Eau.*

GREAT BRITAIN AND DEPENDENCIES.

Earl Russell to Mr. Adams.

FOREIGN OFFICE, *May* 1, 1865.

SIR: I have had the honor to receive your note of this day's date officially communicating to me the melancholy intelligence of the death by the hand of an assassin of the late President of the United States.

When the first intelligence of this sad calamity reached this country I conveyed to you by letter and in person the deep impression of horror and indig-nation which so atrocious a crime on the President of the United States had made upon me and on the several members of her Majesty's government, and it only remains for me now, in acknowledging your letter, to acquaint you that, by the command of the Queen, I have directed her Majesty's minister at Washington to convey to the government of the United States the assurance that her Majesty sincerely condoles with the family of the late President, and that her Majesty's government and the British Parliament and the British nation are affected by a unanimous feeling of abhorrence of the criminal guilty of this cowardly and atrocious assassination, and their sympathy with the government and people of the United States under the great calamity which has befallen them.

I have the honor to be, with the highest consideration, sir, your most obedient, humble servant,

RUSSELL.

CHARLES FRANCIS ADAMS, Esq., &c., &c., &c.

Earl Russell to Sir Frederick Bruce.

FOREIGN OFFICE, *April* 28, 1865.

SIR: It is impossible to describe the sentiments of horror and indignation which have been inspired by the sad intelligence from Washington.

Her Majesty has directed me to express her sincere condolence with the families of the late President, and of Mr. Seward, under their present afflictions.

It is my duty to request that you will convey to the government of the United States the assurance that the government, the Parliament, and the nation are affected by a unanimous feeling of abhorrence of the criminals guilty of these cowardly and atrocious crimes, and sympathy for the government and people of the United States, thus deprived of those to whom they looked for authority in administration and wisdom in council.

Notice has been given in both houses of addresses, to be moved by ministers of the Crown, expressing in a formal shape the sentiments of sorrow and indignation felt by Parliament on this sad occasion.

I am, &c.,

RUSSELL.

Hon. SIR FREDERICK BRUCE, G. C. B., &c., &c., &c.

Earl Russell to Sir Frederick Bruce.

FOREIGN OFFICE, *May* 6, 1865.

SIR: In pursuance of the notice which, as I informed you in my despatch of the 28th ultimo, had been given by her Majesty's ministers in both houses of Parliament, I moved in the House of Lords, on Monday last, the address of the Queen, of which I send you a copy. The motion was seconded by Lord Derby and agreed to, *nemine dissentiente*. In the absence of Viscount Palmerston, who, to his great regret, was prevented by illness from being present on the occasion, Sir G. Grey, her Majesty's principal secretary of state for the home department, moved a similar address to the House of Commons, which motion was seconded by Mr. Disraeli, and was likewise unanimously agreed to.

The Queen has been pleased to return to both houses the most gracious answer of which I enclose a copy.

In giving a copy of this despatch and of its enclosures to the Acting Secretary of the United States, you will say to him that these addresses of the two houses of Parliament express the sentiments of the whole British nation on the deplorable assassination of the late President of the United States.

I am, &c.,

RUSSELL.

Hon. SIR F. BRUCE, G. C. B., &c., &c., &c.

ASSASSINATION OF THE PRESIDENT OF THE UNITED STATES.

Resolved, nemine contradicente, That an humble address be presented to her Majesty, to convey to her Majesty the expression of the deep sorrow and indignation with which this house has learned the assassination of the President of the United States of America, and to pray her Majesty that, in communicating her own sentiments on this deplorable event to the government of the United States, her Majesty will also be graciously pleased to express on the part of her faithful Commons their abhorrence of the crime, and their sympathy with the government and people of the United States.

To be presented by privy councillors.

The Queen's answer to address respecting the assassination of President LINCOLN:

I entirely participate in the sentiments which you have expressed to me in the address which I have received from you on the assassination of the President of the United States, and I have given directions that my minister at Washington shall make known to the government of that country the feelings which you entertain, in common with myself and my whole people, with regard to this deplorable event.

[From the London Times, May 2, 1865.]

HOUSE OF LORDS—MONDAY, *May* 1.

ASSASSINATION OF PRESIDENT LINCOLN.

EARL RUSSELL (who was very indistinctly heard) said: My lords, I rise to ask your lordships to address her Majesty, praying that in any communications

which her Majesty may make to the government of the United States, expressing her abhorrence and regret at the great crime which has been committed in
the murder of the President of that country, her Majesty will at the same time
express the sorrow and indignation felt by this House at that atrocious deed.
In this case I am sure your lordships will feel entire sympathy with her Majesty,
who has instructed me already to express to the government of the United
States the shock which she felt at the intelligence of the great crime which has
been committed. [Hear, hear.] Her Majesty has also been pleased to write a
private letter to Mrs. Lincoln [cheers] expressive of sympathy with that lady
in her misfortune. [Cheers.] I think that your lordships will agree with me
that in modern times there has hardly been a crime committed so abhorrent to
the feelings of every civilized person as the one I am now alluding to. [Hear,
hear.] After the first election of Mr. LINCOLN as President of the United
States, he was re-elected to the same high position by the large majority of the
people remaining faithful to the government of the United States, and he was
in the discharge of the duties of his office, having borne his faculties meekly, at
the moment when an assassin attacked him at the theatre. There are circumstances connected with this crime which, I think, aggravate its atrocity President LINCOLN was a man who, though not conspicuous before his election, had
since displayed a character of so much integrity, so much sincerity and straightforwardness, and at the same time of so much kindness, that if any one was able
to alleviate the pain and animosities which prevailed during the period of civil
war, I believe that ABRAHAM LINCOLN was that person. It was remarked of
President LINCOLN that he always felt disinclined to adopt harsh measures, and I
am told that the commanders of his armies often complained that when they had
passed a sentence which they thought no more than just, the President was always
disposed to temper its severity. Such a man this particular epoch requires
The conduct of the armies of the United States was intrusted to other hands,
and on the commanders fell the responsibility of leading the armies in the field
to victory They had been successful against those they had to contend with,
and the moment had come when, undoubtedly, the responsibilities of President
LINCOLN were greatly increased by their success. But, though it was not for
him to lead the armies, it would have been his to temper the pride of victory,
to assuage the misfortunes which his adversaries had experienced, and especially
to show, as he was well qualified to show, that high respect for valor on the
opposite side which has been so conspicuously displayed. It was to be hoped
that by such qualities, when the conflict of arms was over, the task of conciliation might have been begun, and President LINCOLN would have an authority
which no one else could have had to temper that exasperation which always
arises in the course of civil strife. [Hear, hear.] Upon another question the
United States and the confederates will have a most difficult task to perform. I
allude to the question of slavery, which some have always maintained to have

been the cause of the civil war. At the beginning the House will remember that President LINCOLN declared that he had no right by the Constitution to interfere with slavery. At a later period he made a communication to the commander-in-chief of the United States forces, in which he proposed that in certain States the slaves should be entirely free; but at a later period he proposed, what he had a constitutional qualification to propose, that there should be an alteration in the Constitution of the United States, by which compulsory labor should hereafter be forbidden. I remember that Lord Macaulay once declared that it would have been a great blessing if the penal laws against the Catholics had been abolished from the time of Sir R. Walpole, though Sir R. Walpole would have been mad to propose a measure for that purpose. So the same may be said of slavery, though I believe that the United States were justified in delaying the time when that great alteration of the United States law should take place. But, whatever we may think on these subjects, we must all deeply deplore that the death of President LINCOLN has deprived the United States of a man, a leader on this subject, who by his temper was qualified to propose such a measure as might have made this great change acceptable to those before opposed to it, and might have preserved the peace of the great republic of America while undergoing that entire new organization which would be necessary under such circumstances. [Hear.] I think we must all feel both sympathy with the United States in this great affliction, and also a hope that he who is now, according to the American Constitution, intrusted with the power of the late President, may be able, both on the one subject and on the other—both in respect to mercy and leniency towards the conquered, and also with regard to the measures to be adopted for the new organization which the abolition of slavery will render requisite—to overcome all difficulties. I had some time ago, at the commencement of this contest, occasion to say that I did not believe that the great republic of America would perish in this war, and the noble lord at the head of the government had lately occasion to disclaim on the part of the government of this country any feeling of envy at the greatness and prosperity of the United States. The course which her Majesty's government have had to pursue during this civil war has been one of great anxiety. Difficulties have occurred to us, and difficulties have also occurred to the government of the United States, in maintaining the peaceful relations between the two countries; but those difficulties have always been treated with temper and moderation, both on this side and the other side of the Atlantic. I trust that that temper and moderation may continue, and I can assure this House that, as we have always been guided by the wish that the American government and the American people should settle for themselves the conflict of arms without any interference of ours, so likewise, during the attempt that has to be made to restore peace and tranquillity to America, we shall equally refrain from any kind of interference or intervention, though we trust that the efforts to be made for restoring peace will be successful, and that the great republic of America will always flourish and enjoy the freedom it has hitherto enjoyed. [Hear, hear.] I have nothing to say with regard to the successor of Mr. LINCOLN. Time must show how far he is able to conduct the difficult matters which will come under his consideration with the requisite wisdom. All I can say is that, in the presence of the great crime which has just been committed, and of the great calamity which has fallen on the American nation, the Crown, the Parliament, and the people of this country do feel the deepest interest for the government and people of the United States; for, owing to the nature of the relations between the two nations, the misfortunes of the United States affect us more than the misfortunes of any other country on the face of the globe. [Hear, hear.] The noble earl concluded by moving an humble address to her Majesty to express the sorrow and indignation of this House at the assassination of the President of the United States, and to pray her Majesty to communicate these sentiments on the part of this House to the government of the United States.

The EARL OF DERBY. My lords, when, upon the last occasion of our meeting, the noble earl opposite announced his intention of bringing forward the motion he has now submitted to the House, I ventured to express my hope that the government had well considered the form of the motion they were going to make, so that there might be nothing in the form which would in the slightest degree interfere with the unanimity desirable on such an occasion. It would have been more satisfactory to me if the noble earl had entered somewhat upon the consideration of the question, and had informed your lordships upon what grounds he proposed so unusual a course—though arising, I admit, out of unusual, if not unprecedented, circumstances—as that of addressing the Crown, and praying her Majesty to convey to a foreign government the sentiments of Parliament with regard to the event which has taken place. For myself, I confess that I am rather of the opinion that the more convenient, and, I will not say the more usual, but the more regular course would have been to have simply moved a resolution of this, in conjunction with the other house of Parliament, expressing those feelings which it is proposed by the motion to place in the form of an address to the Crown. [Hear.] But I am so extremely desirous that there should not appear to be the slightest difference of opinion at this moment [hear] that I cannot hesitate to give my assent to the form proposed by the government, whatever doubt I may entertain that the form is the most convenient which might have been adopted. In joining in this address— that is to say, in expressing our sorrow and indignation at the atrocious crime by which the United States have been deprived of their Chief Magistrate— your lordships will only follow, though the event has been known so short a time, the universal feeling of sympathy which has been expressed from one end of this kingdom to the other. [Hear, hear.] And if there be in the United States any persons who, misled by our having abstained from expressing any opinion as to the conflict now going on, or even from expressing the opinion we may have formed upon the merits of the two great contending parties—if there be any persons who believe that there is a generally unfriendly feeling in this country toward the citizens of the United States—I think they could hardly have had a more complete refutation of that opinion, [cheers,] conveyed in what I hope will be the unanimous declaration of Parliament, following the declarations which her Majesty has been pleased to make, both publicly and privately, to the American minister, as well as to the widow of President LINCOLN, and again following the voluntary and spontaneous expression of opinion which has already proceeded from almost all the great towns and communities of this country. [Hear, hear.]   Whatever other misfortunes may have attended this atrocious crime, I hope that, at least, one good effect may have resulted from it, namely, that the manner in which the news has been received in this country will satisfy the people of the United States that her Majesty's subjects, one and all, deeply condemn the crime which has been committed, and deeply sympathize with the people of the United States in their feelings of horror at the assassination of their Chief Magistrate.   [Hear, hear]   For the crime itself there is no palliation whatever to be offered.   There may be differences of opinion as to the merits of the two parties who are contending, the one for empire and the other for independence, in the United States—I follow the words of the noble earl opposite; but there is, there can be, no difference of opinion upon this point: that the holiest and the purest of all causes is desecrated and disgraced when an attempt is made to promote it by measures so infamous as this.   [Hear, hear.]   If it were possible to believe that the confederate authorities encouraged, sympathized with, or even did not express their abhorrence of this crime, I should say they had committed that, which was worse than a crime—a gross blunder; because, in the face of the civilized world, a cause which required or submitted to be promoted by the crime of assassination would lose all sympathy and kindly feeling on the part of those who might otherwise be well disposed toward it.   But I am perfectly satisfied—I am as well satisfied as I can be of anything—that this detestable act of assassination is so entirely alien to the whole spirit in which the South have conducted this war, [cheers,] is so alien to the courageous, manly, and, at the same time, forbearing course which they have adopted in the struggle for everything that is dear to them, that I am convinced that, apart from the error of judgment which would be involved in sanctioning such a crime, they cannot have been guilty of so great a blunder, and cannot fail to express for it their detestation, and to feel at the same time that no step could have been taken which could have inflicted so great an injury on their own cause.   [Hear, hear.]   I will not venture to follow the noble earl even into the slight discussion which he has originated with regard to the internal politics of the United States.   I will not discuss the difficulty which at the present moment is felt in the United States—the difficulty caused by slavery. I will not express any opinion as to the question whether the late defeats, serious as they are, and apparently fatal to the cause of the South, have produced, or are likely to lead to, an early termination of the war. In whatever way the war may be terminated, it must be the desire of every friend of humanity that it should be terminated soon, and without further and unnecessary effusion of blood But I join entirely with the noble earl in lamenting the loss of a man who had conducted the affairs of a great nation, under circumstances of great difficulty, with singular moderation and prudence, and who, I believe, was bent upon trying to the utmost a system as conciliatory as was consistent with the prosecution of the war in which the country was engaged. I agree that the death of such a man, in such a manner, and at such a time, is a subject not only for deep regret and for abhorrence of the crime by which he was deprived of life, but that it is also a serious misfortune, in the present condition of affairs, for the state over which he exercised authority, and for the prospects of an amicable settlement. [Hear, hear.] I can only hope that, notwithstanding some ominous expressions which have already fallen from him, the successor who has so unexpectedly been elevated to the high position filled by Mr. LINCOLN may be disposed and enabled to follow the wise and conciliatory course which, I believe, in the prospect of success, Mr. LINCOLN had decided upon adopting. [Hear.] I am not insensible to the danger that public exasperation arising out of this act may force upon the government a less conciliatory and more violent course than that which Mr. LINCOLN seemed to have marked out for himself; but I am satisfied that the adoption of such a course can only further protract the horrors of this civil war, adding to the other motives of the South the most powerful of all motives—the motive of despair—leading the South to fight out this question to the bitter end, so that while the one side is exasperated into the desire to exterminate its opponents, they, in their despair, will be ready to submit to extermination, rather than accept the unreasonable terms of the North. [Hear, hear.] Thus in the act itself, in the circumstances under which this crime has been committed, and in the fatal influences which it may exercise upon the returning prospects of peace in the United States, we must find reasons for deeply lamenting the occurrence which has taken place and I am quite sure that, independently of all political motives, but not saying that political motives do not enter into our views, I am expressing the universal feeling of this House and of the country when I say that we view with horror, with detestation, and with indignation the atrocious crime by which the life of the President of the United States has been ended. [Cheers.]

LORD STRATFORD DE REDCLIFFE. My lords: In consideration of my residence in the United States of America—at a somewhat distant period, it is true, but nevertheless in the character of a British representative—I hope I may be allowed to offer a few words in addition to those which have been so ably and justly expressed on both sides of the House. I cannot pretend to make any addition of real importance to what has been said already with so much effect, and it is therefore only for the gratification of a private feeling, and for the discharge, as it were, of a personal debt, that I venture to claim your lordships' indulgence for a few moments.   The crime of assassination is so utterly revolting to the hearts and feelings of Englishmen, that we cannot wonder at the cry of horror and indignation with which the death of President LINCOLN has been received in this country, throughout the breadth and length of the land   The circumstances under which that atrocious crime was perpetrated could not but heighten the abhorrence with which the act itself is to be viewed   Whether we look to the private affliction caused by its commission, or to the public consequences which may flow from the catastrophe, our compassion on the one side, and our anxiety on the other, is naturally roused to the highest degree.   It is not in my province to pronounce any kind of judgment on the qualities, the conduct, or the intentions of the late President of the United States.   It would be unkind and unworthy not to give him credit for the best claims on our esteem and regret.   But when I figure to myself the Chief Magistrate, the temporary sovereign of a great nation, struck down by a sudden and dastardly blow in the presence of his astounded family, in the first moments of relaxation from the toils and severe anxieties of a great civil contest, and in the midst of those who gave him their admiring acclamations, every thought is lost in one overpowering sentiment of horror and disgust   [Hear, hear.]   At the time of my personal acquaintance with America the relations between the different portions of the Union were such as to promise a long series of peaceful and prosperous years. The dreadful rupture which took place on the election of the late lamented President could hardly have been foreseen by the most sagacious and far-sighted politician.   This country, as we all know, was seized with unfeigned astonishment and deep concern at the unexpected event; and I must do her Majesty's government the justice to say that during the whole course of the war the balance of a strict neutrality has been maintained with the most even-handed and resolute sense of duty.   I am slow to believe that the people of the United States entertain towards this country the sentiments of mistrust and animosity which have been sometimes attributed to them.   Of this I feel sure, that no such hostile sentiments are entertained by the people of this country towards them; and, were it otherwise, I am persuaded that while on this side every unpleasant feeling unaffectedly merges in sympathy for the late bereavement at Washington, so, on the other, the expression of that sympathy, pure and deep as it is, cannot fail to obliterate any impressions unfavorable to us which may have arisen in any portion of the American population.   The expression of our sympathy is not confined to numerous associations in every part of the country. It now assumes the more solemn character of a parliamentary condolence, confirmed by the unanimous consent of both houses, and crowned by the gracious participation of a sovereign whose sad acquaintance with sorrow is the strongest pledge of her sincerity.   It is not for me to hazard any conjecture as to the cause of that atrocious crime which we all concur in lamenting, or the quarter whence it proceeded   But it is next to impossible that the gallant and high-minded leaders of the one conflicting party could have descended so low as to support their imperilled cause by an assassination as base as it is execrable, and equally hard to conceive that those of the triumphant Union should entertain a suspicion at once so improbable and so unlike the magnanimity they are called upon to display.   It is rather to be hoped and expected that the terrible calamity which has occurred, with such awful suddenness, will sober the agitated passions on both sides, and render acceptable to all the expressions of sympathy about to be transmitted from this country to our kindred beyond the Atlantic. [Hear, hear.]

The motion, having been put by the lord chancellor, was carried *nemine contradicente.*

HOUSE OF COMMONS—Monday, *May* 1, 1865.

THE ASSASSINATION OF PRESIDENT LINCOLN.

Sir G. GREY said: I very much regret the unavoidable absence of my noble friend at the head of the government, in whose name the notice was given of the motion which it now devolves upon me to ask the House to agree to.   I feel, however, that it is comparatively unimportant by whom the motion is proposed, because I am confident that the address to the Crown which I am about to ask the House to agree to is one which will meet with the cordial and unanimous assent of all.   [Cheers.]   When the news a few days ago of the assassination of the President of the United States, and the attempted assassination—for I hope that we may now confidently expect that it will not be a successful attempt—of Mr. Seward reached this country, the first impression in the mind of every one was that the intelligence could not be true.   [Cheers.]   It was hoped by every one that persons could not be found capable of committing a crime so atrocious.   [Hear, hear.]   When the truth was forced upon us, when we could no longer entertain any doubt as to the correctness of the intelligence, the feeling which succeeded was one of universal sorrow, horror, and indignation. [Cheers.]   It was felt as if some great calamity had befallen ourselves, [renewed cheering,] for in the civil war, the existence and the long continuance of which we have so sincerely deplored, it is well known that the government of this country, acting, as I believe, in accordance with the almost unanimous, or perhaps I may say, in accordance with the unanimous feeling of this country, had maintained a strict and impartial neutrality.   But it is notorious, and it could not in a great country like this be otherwise, that different opinions have been entertained by different persons with regard to the questions at issue between the northern and southern States of America, but still I believe that the sympathies of the majority of the people of this country have been with the North. [Cries of "No, no," "Hear, hear," and "Question, question."] I am desirous on this occasion of avoiding everything which may excite any difference of opinion. I may say, therefore, that in this free country different opinions have been entertained and different sympathies felt, and that in this free country the freest expression has been given, as should be the case, to those differences of opinion. [Hear, hear.] I am sure I shall raise no controversy when I say in the presence of that great crime which has sent a thrill of horror through every one who heard of it, all difference of opinion, all conflicting sympathies, for a moment entirely vanished. [Loud cheers.] I am anxious to say at once, and I desire to proclaim that belief with the strongest confidence, that this atrocious crime was regarded by every man of influence and power in the southern States with the same degree of horror which it excited in every other part of the world. [Loud cheers.] We may, therefore—and this is all I wish to say upon this subject—whatever our opinions with regard to the past, and whatever our sympathies may have been—we shall all cordially unite in expressing our abhorrence of that crime, and in rendering our sympathy to that nation which is now mourning the loss of its chosen and trustful chief, struck to the ground by the hand of an assassin, and that, too, at the most critical period of its history. [Cheers.] While lamenting that war and the loss of life which it has inevitably occasioned, it is impossible, whatever our opinions or our sympathies may have been, to withhold our admiration from the many gallant deeds performed and acts of heroism displayed by both parties in the contest, and it is a matter for bitter reflection that the page of history, recording such gallant achievements and such heroic deeds by men who so freely shed their blood on the battle-field in a cause which each considered right, should also be stained with the record of a crime such as we are now deploring. [Cheers.] At length a new era appeared to be dawning on the contest between the North and the South. The time had come when there was every reason to hope that that war would speedily be brought to a close. Victory had crowned the efforts of the statesmen and the armies of the federals, and most of us—all I hope—had turned with a feeling of some relief and hope for the future from the record of sanguinary conflicts to that correspondence which has but recently passed between the generals commanding the hostile armies. [Cheers.] And when we turned to Mr. President LINCOLN, I should have been prepared to express a hope, indeed an expectation—and I have reason to believe that that expectation would not have been disappointed—that in the hour of victory and in the use of victory he would have shown a wise forbearance, a generous consideration, which would have added tenfold lustre to the fame and reputation which he has acquired throughout the misfortunes of this war. [Hear, hear.] Unhappily the foul deed which has taken place has deprived Mr. LINCOLN of the opportunity of thus adding to his well-earned fame and reputation; but let us hope, what, indeed, we may repeat, that the good sense and right feeling of those upon whom will devolve the most arduous and difficult duties in this conjuncture will lead them to respect the wishes and the memory of him whom we are all mourning, [cheers,] and will lead them to act in the same spirit and to follow the same counsels by which we have good reason to believe the conduct of Mr. LINCOLN would have been marked had he survived to complete the work that was intrusted to him. [Cheers.] I am only speaking the general opinion when I say that nothing could give greater satisfaction to this country than by means of forbearance, it may be of temperate conciliation, to see the union of the North and South again accomplished, especially if it can be accomplished by common consent, freed from what hitherto constituted the weakness of that union—the curse and disgrace of slavery. [Cheers.] I wish it were possible for us to convey to the people of the United States an adequate idea of the depth and universality of the feeling which this sad event has occasioned in this country, that from the highest to the lowest there has been but one feeling entertained. Her Majesty's minister at Washington will, in obedience to the Queen's command, convey to the government of the United States the expression of the feelings of her Majesty and of her government upon the deplorable event; and her Majesty, with that tender consideration which she has always evinced for sorrow and suffering in others, of whatever rank, [cheers,] has with her own hand written a letter to Mrs. Lincoln, [loud cheers] conveying the heartfelt sympathy of a widow to a widow [renewed cheers,] suffering under the calamity of having lost one suddenly cut off. [Cheers.] From every part of this country, from every class, but one voice has been heard, one of abhorrence of the crime, and of sympathy for and interest in the country which has this great loss to mourn. The British residents in the United States, as of course was to be expected, lost not an hour in expressing their sympathy with the government of the United States. The people of our North American colonies are vying with each other in expressing the same sentiments. [Cheers.] And it is not only among men of the same race, who are connected with the people of the United States by origin, language, and blood, that these feelings prevail, but I believe that every country in Europe is giving expression to the same sentiments, and is sending the same message to the government of the United States. I am sure, therefore, that I am not wrong in anticipating that this House will, in the name of the people of England, of Scotland, and of Ireland, be anxious to record their expression of the same sentiment, and to have it conveyed to the government of the United States. [Cheers.] Of this I am confident, that this House could never more fully and more adequately represent the feelings of the whole of the inhabitants of the United Kingdom than by agreeing to the address which it is now my duty to move, expressing to her Majesty our sorrow and indignation at the assassination of the President of the United States, and praying her

Majesty that, in communicating her own sentiments to the government of that country upon the deplorable event, she will express at the same time, on the part of this House, their abhorrence of the crime, and their sympathy with the government and the people of the United States in the deep affliction into which they have been thrown. [Loud cheers.]

Mr. DISRAELI said: There are rare instances when the sympathy of a nation approaches those tenderer feelings which are generally supposed to be peculiar to the individual, and to be the happy privilege of private life, and this is one. Under any circumstances we should have bewailed the catastrophe at Washington; under any circumstances we should have shuddered at the means by which it was accomplished. But in the character of the victim, and even in the accessories of his last moments, there is something so homely and innocent, that it takes the question, as it were, out of all the pomp of history and the ceremonial of diplomacy; it touches the heart of nations, and appeals to the domestic sentiment of mankind. [Cheers.] Whatever the various and varying opinions in this House, and in the country generally, on the policy of the late President of the United States, all must agree that in one of the severest trials which ever tested the moral qualities of man he fulfilled his duty with simplicity and strength. [Cheers.] Nor is it possible for the people of England at such a moment to forget that he sprung from the same fatherland, and spoke the same mother tongue. [Cheers.] When such crimes are perpetrated the public mind is apt to fall into gloom and perplexity, for it is ignorant alike of the causes and the consequences of such deeds. But it is one of our duties to reassure them under unreasoning panic and despondency. Assassination has never changed the history of the world. I will not refer to the remote past, though an accident has made the most memorable instance of antiquity at this moment fresh in the minds and memory of all around me. But even the costly sacrifice of a Cæsar did not propitiate the inexorable destiny of his country. If we look to modern times, to times at least with the feelings of which we are familiar, and the people of which were animated and influenced by the same interests as ourselves, the violent deaths of two heroic men, Henry IV, of France, and the Prince of Orange, are conspicuous illustrations of this truth. In expressing our unaffected and profound sympathy with the citizens of the United States on this untimely end of their elected chief, let us not, therefore, sanction any feeling of depression, but rather let us express a fervent hope that from out of the awful trials of the last four years, of which the least is not this violent demise, the various populations of North America may issue elevated and chastened, rich with the accumulated wisdom and strong in the disciplined energy which a young nation can only acquire in a protracted and perilous struggle; then they will be enabled not merely to renew their career of power and prosperity, but they will renew it to contribute to the general happiness of mankind. [Cheers.] It is with these feelings that I second the address to the Crown [Loud cheers.]

The motion was then put and adopted unanimously, the announcement of which fact by the speaker was received with cheers.

Mr. Burnley to Mr. Hunter.

WASHINGTON, *April* 17, 1865.

SIR: I have the honor to acknowledge the receipt of note of the 15th instant, announcing to me the lamented death of the President of the United States on the night of the 14th instant, from the effects of a pistol-shot received at the hands of an assassin, while attending the performances at the theatre, and the dastardly attempt to assassinate, in like manner, the Secretary of State and his son, Mr. Frederick Seward.

It is with feelings of the deepest regret that I have heard of these crimes— a regret which will be shared by my government on reception of the sad news. I sincerely trust that Mr. Seward and his son may recover from the wounds inflicted on them and be restored to health.

I take this opportunity of acknowledging the announcement of the formal assumption of the functions of President by the late Vice-President, Andrew Johnson, and of your appointment to perform, temporarily, the duties of Secretary of State.

I have the honor to be, with high consideration, sir, your most obedient, humble servant,

J. HUME BURNLEY.

Hon. W. HUNTER, Esq., &c., &c., &c.

Resolutions by the convener court of the seven incorporated trades of the city of Aberdeen, North Britain.

At Aberdeen, and within the Trinity Hall there, the ninth day of May, eighteen hundred and sixty-five.

At a meeting of the convener court representing the seven incorporated trades of the city of Aberdeen, North Britain, the following resolutions were unanimously adopted :

1. That this court expresses its sorrow and indignation at the act of atrocity lately committed on President LINCOLN, of the United States of America, and its sympathy with the government and people of those States in their peculiar circumstances, and its hope that, under Providence, the establishment of peace there, and harmony between them and the whole world, will soon be promoted.

This court cannot separate without expressing its liveliest feeling and sympathy with Mrs. Lincoln and family, and prays that the worthy example of her husband will prove that a straight-forward and honest course is alike honorable and worthy of imitation.

Signed in name and by appointment of the meeting, and the seal of the court appended hereto by me, convener of said court.

[SEAL.]   ROBERT THOMSON.

At Aberdeen, the first day of May, in the year 1865, in presence of the lord provost, magistrates, and council of the city of Aberdeen.

Which day the lord provost stated that, before proceeding to the ordinary business, he would propose " that the council enter on their minutes an expression of the sorrow and indignation which pervaded this city on receiving the intelligence that the President of the United States of America had been murdered, and the life of one of their most distinguished statesmen (Mr. Seward) endangered by the hands of assassins; and also of the earnest sympathy of the council and community with the government and people of the United States." Which proposal was unanimously agreed to; and the council directed a copy of this resolution, under the common seal of the city, to be signed by the lord provost, and transmitted to the minister in this country of the United States.

[SEAL.]   ALEXANDER,
                                                Lord Provost of Aberdeen.

The mayor, aldermen, and common council of the borough of Axbridge to Mr.
Adams.

SIR: We, the mayor, aldermen, and common council of the borough of Axbridge, in the county of Somerset, beg through you, sir, to express our deep sympathy with Mrs. Lincoln and the American nation generally under the heavy and distressing bereavement which she and they have been called on to sustain in the brutal and cowardly assassination of Mr. President LINCOLN.

We earnestly pray, however, that the all-wise disposer of events may not only support Mrs. Lincoln in this the hour of her grief, but that He may, according to the purposes of His own gracious will, overrule for good the dire calamity which has thus befallen the American nation.

Given under our corporate seal at the Town Hall, in Axbridge aforesaid, this sixth day of May, one thousand eight hundred and sixty-five.

[SEAL.]

His Excellency Hon. CHARLES FRANCIS ADAMS,
    Envoy Extraordinary and Minister Plenipotentiary
        United States of America, London.

Excerpt from minutes of meeting of the town council of the royal burgh of Anstruther-Easter, in the county of Fife, North Britain, May 5, 1865.

Inter alia, on the motion of the provost, the council unanimously agreed to record their abhorrence and detestation of the assassination of the President of the United States, and their sympathy and condolence with the Americans under the great loss which they have sustained, and requested the provost to forward an excerpt from this minute to Mr. Adams, the American minister in London.

Extracted by—

MAB. F. CONOLLY, *Clerk.*

To his excellency the honorable Charles Francis Adams, envoy extraordinary and minister plenipotentiary for the United States of America :

We, the provost, magistrates, and town council of the royal burgh of Ayr, in council assembled, beg to express to you, as the representative in this country of the government and people of the United States of America, our utter abhorrence of the atrocity whereby that great people have been deprived of the services of their Chief Magistrate, who, after years of a most terrific struggle, approved himself to his countrymen by his patriotism, honesty of purpose, and great integrity, who had the fullest confidence of that great nation during the most critical period of its history, whose unwearied patience and perseverance under circumstances of trial, of difficulty, and of defeat, were only matched by his moderation evinced in the hour of success, and whose magnanimity and forbearance made an impression here that ABRAHAM LINCOLN was a great and good man.

We also desire to express our heartfelt sympathy and condolence with the government and people of the United States, who have been so suddenly deprived of their Chief Magistrate at a momentous crisis in the history of their country.

Signed in name and by authority of the magistrates and council by me, provost of Ayr.

J. MAC NEILLE.

To his excellency the honorable Charles Francis Adams, envoy extraordinary and minister plenipotentiary for the United States of America :

We, the provost, magistrates, and town council of the royal burgh of Arbroath, beg to convey to you, as the representative in this country of the government and people of the United States of America, that expression of the feelings of profound sorrow and indignation with which we received the melancholy intelligence of the assassination of the President of the United States. We deeply sympathize with the government and people of the United States in the loss they have sustained by the death, so much to be deplored, of their late President, who was so well fitted by his character and the confidence reposed in him to heal those divisions by which his country had been torn asunder.

We join in expressing our best wishes for the welfare of the United States, and the hope that the termination of the war will enable them to make that rapid progress for which their country presents so great advantages.

Signed in name and by appointment of the magistrates and town council of Arbroath, and the common seal of the said burgh affixed hereto, on Thursday, the 25th day of May, eighteen hundred and sixty-five.

[SEAL.]   JOHN LUMGAN,
                              Provost and Chief Magistrate of Arbroath.

At a meeting of the town council of the borough of Ashton-under-Lyne, in the county of Lancaster, held on Wednesday, the 10th day of May, 1865, John Galt, esquire, mayor, in the chair, it was moved by Mr. Alderman Mason, seconded by Mr. Councillor Wood, and resolved as follows :

The mayor, aldermen, and burgesses of the borough of Ashton-under-Lyne, in council assembled, having heard with profound grief of the brutal and cowardly assassination of Mr. ABRAHAM LINCOLN, the President of the United States of America, hereby record their feelings of horror and detestation at the malignity and treachery of the act which has deprived that great country of its Chief Magistrate ; and express their heartfelt sympathy with the people of that country in their time of all-absorbing sorrow.

This council beg to offer their tribute of reverence for the memory of a great American whose ripened experience and humane nature pre-eminently fitted him to reconcile the animosities of a divided people, and heal the wounds of a distracted nation.

This council fervently trust that the magnanimous policy of the late President may continue to guide the American people, that war and bloodshed may come to a speedy end, and that peace, prosperity, and happiness may again prevail.

This council also respectfully offer to Mrs. Lincoln their genuine affection and sympathy for her irreparable loss, and trust she may find sweet consolation in witnessing the grand results of the wise, unselfish, and patriotic career of her martyred husband.

The corporate seal was affixed in the presence of—

[SEAL.]   JOHN GALT, *Mayor.*
                        WILLIAM MARSHALL, *Town Clerk*

Resolutions passed at a meeting held by the Temperance Society of Ashton-under-Lyne.

ASHTON-UNDER-LYNE, *May* 10, 1865.

The president, vice-president, officers, and members of the Ashton-under-Lyne Temperance Society, in meeting assembled, have heard with profound grief of the brutal and cowardly assassination of Mr. ABRAHAM LINCOLN, the President of the United States of America, and hereby record their feelings of horror and detestation at the malignity and treachery of the act which has deprived that great country of its Chief Magistrate, and express their heartfelt sympathy with the people of that country in their time of all-absorbing sorrow.

This meeting beg to offer their tribute of reverence for the memory of a great ruler, whose ripened experience and humanity pre-eminently fitted him to reconcile the animosities of a divided people and heal the wounds of a distracted nation. This meeting feels all the more earnest in their attachment to Mr. ABRAHAM LINCOLN because he had for more than fifty years adopted and carried out those great principles of temperance and total abstinence (from all intoxicating drinks) for which we are contending; that, whether he enjoyed the privacy of home, or sustained the dignities of a palace; that, whether he performed the duties of a citizen, or the more difficult duties of governing a great nation, he had the wisdom to see, and the moral courage to adopt, the great principles of temperance, truth, and progress.

This meeting also respectfully offer to Mrs. Lincoln and family their genuine affection and sympathy for their irreparable loss, and trust they may find sweet consolation in witnessing the grand results of the wise, unselfish, and patriotic career of their martyred husband and father.

Signed on behalf of the committee and society by—

MARTIN PARKINSON, *President.*

EDWIN WILLIAMSON, *Vice-President.*

His Excellency ANDREW JOHNSON,
President of the United States of America,
and through him to Mrs. Lincoln.

Address of the Union and Emancipation Society of Ashton-under-Lyne to Mrs. Lincoln.

ASHTON-UNDER-LYNE UNION AND EMANCIPATION SOCIETY,
May 26, 1865.

The sorrowful intelligence which has been recently transmitted to us, announcing the death of your much-beloved husband, ABRAHAM LINCOLN, has filled our hearts with pain and sadness. We little expected that his valuable life would have been so suddenly destroyed by the treacherous hand of a cowardly assassin, and cannot but lament the irreparable loss which has deprived you of a faithful protector, your children of an affectionate father, and the American people of a thoughtful and sagacious statesman.

We consider the death of the late President a world-wide calamity, because the impression made by it seems to be the strongest and most general that has ever appeared upon the death of a fellow-man; and it is for this reason that we desire to convey to you our united expressions of grief in this severe trial of your affliction and bereavement, and also to declare our abhorrence of the brutal and horrible crime by which his life was sacrificed.

In contemplating his character we have often felt a just admiration which his many virtues command; but to dwell upon them here, in any particular, is unnecessary, and, upon this occasion, would perhaps be improper. That his loss has been generally lamented cannot be wondered at, for certainly there never was a more just cause for universal sorrow. To lose such a man at such a critical time, so unexpectedly and so barbarously, must add to every feeling of regret, and make the sense of bereavement more severe and acute to all thinking minds. He was snatched away in the midst of a crisis when America could spare him least; at a time when the people hoped to be especially benefited by his energy, his benevolence, and his wisdom. His ardent desire to promote the welfare of his fellow-men was conspicuously the animating motive of his active life. His indefatigable labors to strike off the fetters which have so long bound the down-trodden negro have at length been rewarded by a glorious and triumphant victory. Millions of them are already free—free as the very breath of heaven; and the accursed slave-stain, which has ever soiled the American banner, will now be eradicated, and the fate of the accursed system forever sealed with the martyred blood of a holy Christian man. Never was he known to shirk the onerous duties of his responsible office; in every instance we have found him true to his sacred oath; even in the latest hours of his life, kindness to his enemies was the uppermost sentiment of his generous heart, prompting the most considerate arrangements for the happiness and comfort of a great and mighty people.

In conclusion, permit us to hope that the humble and genuine affection so widely entertained towards him will tend to mitigate in some degree the heavy bereavement of his afflicted family, consoling them with the knowledge that the labors of the departed are truly appreciated by thousands of earnest hearts in far distant lands.

Signed on behalf of the members of the Ashton-under-Lyne Union and Emancipation Society.

> JAMES BROADBENT, *President.*
> JOHN HAGUE, *Vice-President.*
> JOHN GLAZEBROOK, *Treasurer.*
> JOB ARUNDALE, *Secretary.*

Mrs. LINCOLN.

Resolution of the Anglesey Baptist Association of Beaumaris.

HOLYHEAD, *June* 14, 1865.

At the above association, held at the county town Beaumaris, on the 30th and 31st ultimo, it was

Unanimously resolved, That this association desires to express the deepest regret at the irreparable loss which has befallen the people of the United States by the untimely death of President LINCOLN ; and its sincere condolence with Mrs. Lincoln on the sad event; also to congratulate our Christian brethren in America on the triumph of negro emancipation.

JOHN LEWIS,
Chairman of the Association.
JOHN PALMER,
Secretary of the Association.

His Excellency Mr. ADAMS,
Ambassador of the United States, London.

Motion of a meeting held in Bolton on 27*th April,* 1865.

Moved by Alderman Furguson, seconded by Mr. Rigby, and carried unanimously—

That this meeting do hereby express their strongest feelings of abhorrence and grief at the atrocious assassination of the President of the United States, and the dastardly attempt upon the life of Mr. Seward.

Also their deep sorrow and heartfelt sympathy with Mrs. Lincoln and family.

That the chairman be requested to forward the same to the American minister.

BOROUGH OF BOLTON, COUNTY OF LANCASTER, ENGLAND.

Copy of resolution of the council of the said borough, unanimously passed at a meeting thereof held on the 10*th day of May,* 1865.

Resolved, That this council regards with intense horror and detestation the diabolical assassination of President LINCOLN, the twice elected Chief Magistrate of the United States ; and hereby records its heartfelt sympathy with his widow and countrymen, in their mourning for his loss and untimely end, hoping that their sorrow may speedily be assuaged by the return of national peace and prosperity.

Resolution of the council of Brechin.

At Brechin, and within the council chambers there, on the tenth day of May, eighteen hundred and sixty-five.

In a meeting of the council of said city, the following resolution, moved by Alexander Guthrie, esquire, provost, was unanimously agreed to:

The magistrates and councillors of the city of Brechin, in the county of Forfar, Scotland, having heard with feelings of sorrow and indignation of the cowardly assassination of President LINCOLN, resolved to express their abhorrence and detestation of the cold-blooded and murderous deed, and their cordial sympathy with the people of the United States, on being thus deprived of one who, by his honesty of purpose and patriotism, as well as steadfast adherence to what he considered the principles of right and justice, has left behind him a name that will long be remembered; and the council further resolve, that a copy of this resolution, signed by the provost, and having the seal of the city affixed, be transmitted to his excellency Mr. Adams, the United States minister in London.

[SEAL.]   ALEXANDER GUTHRIE,
                                                     Provost.

We, the mayor, aldermen, and burgesses of the borough of Berwick-upon-Tweed, in council assembled, in unison with all classes of her Majesty's subjects, beg to add our expression of horror and indignation at the unparalleled crime which has deprived the United States of America of their admirable President, and of our deep and sincere sympathy with the sorrow of that great people, caused by an act of such atrocity.

Given under the common seal of the borough, at our quarterly meeting, on the 3d day of May, 1865.

[SEAL.]   Sealed in open council this 3d day of May, 1865.

At a meeting of the town council of the borough of Burnley, held at the council room, Burnley, on the 3d day of May, 1865—the mayor presiding—

Resolved unanimously, (on motion of Mr. Alderman Coultate, seconded by Mr. Alderman Massey,) That this meeting, as representing the inhabitants of Burnley, desires to express its profound sympathy with the people of the United States of America at the irreparable loss sustained by them through death, by assassination, of their President, ABRAHAM LINCOLN; and to record its abhorrence of the infamous crime which has excited so much horror, as well in this country as throughout the United States; and that a copy of this resolution, signed by the town clerk, be forwarded to Mr. Adams, the American minister in London.

I certify the above to be a true copy.

[SEAL.]

A. B. CREEKE,
Town Clerk.

At a meeting of the town council of the royal burgh of Burntisland, Scotland, held on the 2d day of May, 1865, the following resolution was unanimously agreed to, and the provost was requested to forward a copy of the same to his excellency the honorable Charles Francis Adams, United States minister:

The provost magistrates and town council of the royal burgh of Burntisland, in their own name, and in that of the community whose interests they represent, beg, most respectfully, to offer to the people of America their expressions of deep sympathy and condolence on the occasion of the lamented death of the late able, high-minded, and enlightened President of the United States, and desire at the same time to record their strong feelings of abhorrence and detestation of the crime by means of which the death of the President of the United States was accomplished.

[SEAL.]

C. K. SWAIRIGHT,
Provost of Burntisland.

BOROUGH OF BARNSTAPLE, *in the county of Devon, to wit:*

At a quarterly meeting of the town council of this borough, held on the 10th day of May, 1865, it was

Unanimously resolved, That this council, in its corporate capacity, desires to express its sorrow and indignation at the assassination of the President of the United States, and to convey the expression of its sympathy and condolence at the loss which his widow and the American nation have sustained.

That a copy of this resolution, with the corporate seal attached, be forwarded to the representative of the United States in this country.

[SEAL.]

THOMAS LAMBE WILLSHIRE,
Mayor.

BOROUGH OF BRECON:

At a meeting of the town council of the chartered borough of Brecon, held at the Guildhall of the same borough, on Thursday, the 11th day of May, 1865, Geo. Cansick, esquire, mayor, in the chair, it was

Unanimously resolved, (on motion of Mr. Alderman Thomas, seconded by Mr. Councillor Davis,) That this meeting desires to express its unqualified abhorrence of the crime by which the United States of America have lost their President, ABRAHAM LINCOLN, and to record its sincerest sympathy with his widow and family, as well as with the government and people, on their irretrievable loss.

Resolved, also, (on the motion of Mr. Councillor Bright, seconded by Mr. Councillor Prothero,) That the above resolution of sympathy be signed by the mayor on behalf of the meeting, and the common seal of the borough be affixed, and that the member for the borough, Colonel Watkins, be respectfully requested to forward the same to the American minister in London for transmission.

[SEAL.]   GEO. CANSICK, *Mayor.*

At a special meeting of the town council of the borough of Banbury, in the county of Oxford, held on Friday, the 5th day of May, 1865, the mayor in the chair, it was

Unanimously resolved, That this council has heard with the deepest sorrow and indignation of the assassination of President LINCOLN, and sincerely sympathize with the parliament and people of the United States in the great loss they have sustained, by the death of so able and so good a man, and this council cannot thus express its feeling without adding its heartfelt sympathy with Mrs. Lincoln.

That Sir Charles Douglas, member of Parliament for the borough, be requested to forward a copy of the above resolution to the American minister.

[SEAL.]   RICH. EDMUNDS, *Mayor.*

Address of the mayor, aldermen, and burgesses of the borough of Bridport, Dorset county.

We, the mayor, aldermen, and burgesses of the borough of Bridport, in the county of Dorset, in council assembled, entertaining, in common with the whole British people, feelings of just indignation at the unnatural and cowardly crime recently perpetrated, beg to offer to our American brethren our deep sympathy at the great loss they have sustained by the untimely death of President LINCOLN, at a moment when his steadfast energies were apparently devoted to the pacification of your powerful country. We would also express our satisfaction at the escape of Mr. Secretary Seward from the attempt made upon his life, and our hopes that before long he may be restored to his friends and the American nation in perfect health and vigor.

At the same time we would desire to unite in the common expression from this country of respectful sympathy with Mrs. Lincoln on this occasion of her deep and awful bereavement.

Given under our common seal the ninth day of May, one thousand eight hundred and sixty-five.

[SEAL.]   HERBERT E. HOUNSELL, *Mayor*

Hon. CHARLES FRANCIS ADAMS,
   Minister of the United States of America.

GUILDHALL, *Bath, May* 2, 1865.

SIR: We, the mayor, aldermen, and burgesses of the city and borough of Bath, in council assembled, beg to join our fellow-countrymen of all classes in expressing our profound indignation and sorrow at the assassination of the President of the United States.

At any moment, and under any circumstances, the English nation would have been filled with horror on hearing that a powerful ruler, trusted and beloved by millions, had been struck down by the hand of violence, but that this act of odious wickedness had been committed now, when Mr. LINCOLN's, life was so precious to himself, to his country, and to the world, is an event far more than commonly distressing.

We feel, sir, that we should very imperfectly discharge our duty if we merely offered you our sympathy, earnest and heartfelt as it is. We are anxious, also, to assure you that no words of wisdom and gentleness, conciliation and peace, uttered by your late lamented President will be forgotten in England, or fail to secure our affectionate gratitude; and while we mourn deeply with all and for all who suffer from the event, especially for her to whom he was bound by the tenderest ties, we yet trust that even this awful bereavement will be overruled for good, and that your statesmen and warriors may be filled with stronger desire and greater power to overcome the difficulties in the way of peace; and, not least, that between America and England there will always be the harmony and the confidence so natural in their near relationship, and so essential to their mutual prosperity.

Signed on behalf of the town council of the city and borough of Bath.

JEROM MURCH, *Mayor.*

His Excellency the MINISTER
   of the United States of America.

*Extract from the minutes of a meeting of the town council of the borough of
Buckingham, held on Monday, the first day of May, 1865.*

That this council desires to express its deep feeling of abhorrence at the
dreadful crime committed in America by the assassination of the President of
the United States, and its sympathy with the people of America in the sad and
mournful event; and, at the same time, to indulge the hope that the establishment of a lasting peace throughout the entire republic may not be jeoparded
or delayed by the awful calamity.

GEORGE NELSON,
Town Clerk.

---

*Address of condolence from the corporation of Bedford to the government and
people of the United States of America.*

The mayor, aldermen, and burgesses of the ancient borough of Bedford, in
quarterly meeting assembled, desire to convey to the government of the United
States of America an expression of the horror and grief with which they
received the intelligence of the atrocious assassination of President LINCOLN,
and the murderous attack upon Mr. Seward, his Secretary of State. Shocking
and revolting as is the crime of murder at any time and under any circumstances, it is the more especially to be deplored in this instance, where the
ruler of a great nation was suddenly cut off from the people at a moment when
his untiring energies, calm judgment, and conciliating disposition were most
needed for the advantage of his countrymen, and, indeed, for the interests of the
civilized world.

Under these appalling circumstances the municipal body of this ancient
borough offer to the government and citizens of the United States their sincere
and heartfelt condolence, and while sympathizing with them in this their great
hour of difficulty, they beg to express their earnest wishes and ardent hopes
that the spirit of conciliation and desire for peace which so eminently distinguished the late excellent President may now influence the councils of the
American nation, that a secure and lasting peace may be insured, and that a
prosperous and glorious future may be in store for the people who have lately
passed through so sad and grievous an ordeal.

To the widow and family of the murdered President the municipal body
desire to offer their sincere condolence, and to express their deepest sympathy.
They would rejoice to be able to give words of comfort to them in this great
affliction.

Grievous and irreparable as is the bereavement under which the widow
and family are now suffering, it is consoling to reflect that the best exertions

and talents, and finally the life of the lamented President, were spent in the service of his country.

Given under the common seal of the mayor, aldermen, and burgesses of the borough of Bedford, the 11th day of May, 1865.

[SEAL.]   JAMES HOWARD, *Mayor.*

At a meeting of the council of the borough of Bridgenorth, in the county of Salop, held at the Town Hall on the 12th day of May, in the year 1865,

Resolved unanimously, That this council desires to express to the President of the United States its abhorrence of the atrocious crime which has deprived the States of the life of their late President, and at the same time sincerely to record its deep and earnest sympathy with the government and people of the United States in this great calamity.

Resolved, That the seal of the council be attached, and that the same be transmitted without delay to the honorable C. F. Adams, ambassador for the United States, resident in London.

[SEAL.]   JOHN PERRY, *Mayor.*

At a meeting of the town conncil of the city of Bristol, held on the 28th day of April, 1865, on the motion of the mayor, it was

Unanimously resolved, That the following address be signed by the mayor and transmitted to the American minister in London:

We, the mayor, aldermen, and members of the town council of the city of Bristol, have heard with feelings of the deepest indignation and horror that the President of the United States of America has been cruelly murdered, and we express our heartfelt sympathy with the American minister, and through him with the American people, in this their time of national sorrow.

We desire also to offer our respectful condolence to Mrs. Lincoln, under the overwhelming bereavement which she has sustained, and we earnestly hope that the sad event which has happened may be overruled by Providence to the welfare of America, and that the future of that great country may be one of peace, progress, and prosperity.

WM. NAISH, *Mayor.*

COUNCIL HOUSE, *Bristol, May* 4, 1865.

SIR: I have the honor of informing your excellency that at a largely attended meeting of the citizens of Bristol, over which I presided, the following resolutions were unanimously adopted; and the duty having devolved upon me of forwarding them to your excellency, I take leave to express my heartfelt concurrence in the sentiments they convey

I have the honor to be, sir,

WM. NAISH, *Mayor of Bristol.*

His Excellency CHARLES FRANCIS ADAMS,
United States Minister, London.

Resolution 1. That this meeting desires to record its utter abhorrence of the diabolical crime by which the life of Mr. LINCOLN, President of the United States of America, has been taken away, and to express its sincere condolence with Mrs. Lincoln, and deepest sympathy with the American nation in their present time of national sorrow.

Resolution 2. That this meeting would convey to the American people its sincere desire that the disastrous war which has so long afflicted their country may speedily terminate, that the system of slavery may cease, and that their affairs may be so guided by Providence as to insure the permanent issue of peace, concord, and prosperity in their great country.

Resolution 3. That the right worshipful the mayor be requested, as chairman of this meeting, to forward a copy of these resolutions, now passed, to the American minister.

BRISTOL, *May* 1, 1865.

HONORED SIR : We, the undersigned, teachers connected with the Bristol ragged schools, beg permission to express through you our unqualified indignation at the brutal act which has deprived America of one of its best Presidents, and of the man especially adapted to the requirements of the time.

We venture to ask that you will kindly forward our condolence to Mrs. Lincoln, who has been so barbarously bereaved of her illustrious husband.

We earnestly pray that God will speedily restore peace to your united and great country, and rescue it from the effects of a most wanton and wicked rebellion.

JAMES SHIPPERLY, *Master.*
MARTHA JANE HORWOOD,
Infant Mistress.
JOHN ALLEN.
ELIZA OXBURGH.
LOUISA COX.
RICHARD WEYMAN, *Tailor.*
ELIZA PALMER.
JOSEPH PALMER.

Hon. C. F. ADAMS,
United States Minister.

2 GREAT GEORGE STREET,
Bristol, April 29, 1865.

SIR: At a meeting of the members of the Bristol Workingmen's Club and Institute and others, held last evening in the hall of the club premises, to propose a resolution of condolence with Mrs. Lincoln and the American people upon the great loss which they have sustained, the following resolution was unanimously adopted:

"That this meeting, consisting of members of the Bristol Workingmen's Club and Institute and others, have heard with grief and indignation the sad intelligence of the assassination of President LINCOLN; that it desires to express its deep sympathy with Mrs. Lincoln in her bereavement, earnestly praying that the Almighty Disposer of events may support her in this her hour of trial, and in His own good time overrule for good the terrible calamity which has befallen the American nation."

I am instructed to have it forwarded to Mr. Adams, at the legation of the United States in London, for presentation through him to Mrs. Lincoln and the American people. Will you do me the favor to get this done, at the same time expressing to him the mingled feelings of indignation and sorrow which filled the hearts of those present, and which led them to take this early opportunity for the expression of their sympathy.

I have the honor to be, sir, yours, very respectfully,

HERBERT THOMAS,
President of the Club, Chairman.

ZEBINA EASTMAN, Esq.,
United States Consul, Bristol.

Resolution passed at a meeting held by the Bristol Reform Union.

SIR: We, members of the Bristol Reform Union, in meeting assembled, believing it to be the duty of all public bodies to put on record an expression of the feelings of horror and indignation excited in every right-minded person by the atrocious murder of a wise, honest, and patriotic President of a great republic, and regarding with equal detestation the cowardly assault on the chief Secretary of State, desire to convey to the President and people of the United States, to the bereaved widow and family of ABRAHAM LINCOLN, and to the honorable Mr. Seward and his family, the assurance of our heartfelt sorrow and sincere sympathy in their profound affliction and abhorrence of the treacherous and cold-blooded murder of their noble and illustrious President by a ruthless assassin, the tool of a foul conspiracy.

Associated for the purpose of obtaining political rights for the unenfranchised millions of our own country, we feel the sudden removal of such a man as a loss not only to you, but to ourselves and the world at large.   Sprung from the people, and raised by the force of his native genius and industry to be the Chief Magistrate of a great and free people, he has endeared himself to all lovers of liberty by his devotion to the great cause of negro emancipation, and by his earnest desire to confer the blessings of equal rights and privileges on all, without distinction of party, creed, or color.

While thus deeply sharing your grief and sorrow that just as the great work he had set himself to was approaching its consummation, his death has turned the hour of triumph into one of mourning, we fervently trust that his successor may adhere to the policy he inaugurated and tread in his footsteps, by tempering justice with mercy, and by advancing those glorious principles of freedom and progress to which he had devoted himself; and we sincerely hope that whatever differences of opinion, imaginary grievances, or animosities may exist on either side, they may not disturb the cordial amity and good feeling which ought to prevail between two nations so like in race, language, and religion, but that the common interests of humanity, the mutual dependence of the two countries, and the sympathy evoked by this sad catastrophe from all classes of Englishmen, may knit more closely the bonds of Union and brotherhood between England and America.

Signed on behalf of the meeting:

CHARLES MORRIS, *Chairman.*

His Excellency the MINISTER
of the *United States.*

Address of the inhabitants of the borough of Brighton.

To the people of the *United States of America :*

The address of the inhabitants of the borough of Brighton, in the county of Sussex, in public meeting assembled, on the 2d of May, 1865 :

We, the inhabitants of Brighton, in public meeting assembled, desire to express our utter abhorrence and indignation at the atrocious murder of Mr. ABRAHAM LINCOLN, the President of the United States, by the hand of a ruthless assassin, and the profound sympathy of our hearts towards those who are our brethren in origin, at the awful calamity which has thus befallen their great nation and stricken us with amazement and terror

While we recognize an overruling Providence in all things, it is beyond human power to fathom the depths of this mysterious dispensation at so eventful a crisis in your history.

It is our confident hope and earnest prayer that America may speedily emerge from this sad sorrow, and all her troubles, and continue with our nation the happy relations of peaceful commerce for generations to come.·

Signed on behalf of the meeting:

JOHN LEONHANDT BRIGDEN,

Mayor of Brighton.

BOROUGH OF BRIGHTON, *May* 2, 1865.

At a public meeting of the inhabitants of the borough of Brighton, held at the Town Hall on Tuesday, the 2d May, 1865, for the purpose of expressing the sentiments of the town on the diabolical assassination of the American President, and of sympathy with the American nation under this fearful calamity, and to adopt such resolutions thereon as to the said meeting may appear expedient, the worshipful the mayor, J. L. Brigden, esq., in the chair, it was

Resolved, That this meeting regards with feelings of utter abhorrence and indignation the atrocious murder of Mr. ABRAHAM LINCOLN, the President of the United States, by the hand of a ruthless assassin, and desires to express its profound sympathy toward those who are our brethren in origin at the awful calamity which has thus befallen their great nation and stricken us with amazement and terror.

Resolved, That the deepest sympathy of this meeting be presented to Mrs. Lincoln on this most calamitous event, which, while it has deprived the nation of the United States of its President, has rendered her a sorrowing widow under circumstances so. cruel, lamentable, and distressing.

JOHN LEONHANDT BRIGDEN,

Mayor of Brighton.

At a public meeting of the trading and working classes of Brighton, held at the Town Hall on Friday evening, the 5th of May, 1865, on the assassination of the President of the United States—J. L. Brigden, esq., mayor, in the chair—it was unanimously resolved as follows :

That this meeting regards with feelings of utter abhorrence and indignation the atrocious murder of ABRAHAM LINCOLN, the President of the United States, by the hand of a ruthless assassin, and desires to express its profound sympathy with those who are our brethren in origin at the awful calamity which has thus befallen their great nation, and stricken us with amazement and horror; and that this meeting of working men sympathize the more deeply with the untimely death of ABRAHAM LINCOLN, as he was the first President elected from the working classes to the high position of ruler of one of the mightiest nations of the globe; that he carried successfully the struggle of free against slave labor, and we confidently hope and believe that his successor, Andrew Johnson, who also sprang from the same class, may complete the work so nobly begun.

That the deepest sympathy of this meeting be presented to Mrs. Lincoln on this most calamitous event, which, while it has deprived the nation of the United States of its President, has rendered her a sorrowing widow, under circumstances so cruel, lamentable, and distressing.

That the address adopted at this meeting, as well as the foregoing resolutions, be presented to his excellency Charles Francis Adams, minister of the United States, by the mayor of Brighton, in conjunction with the members for the borough, who are hereby respectfully requested to join him therein.

Signed on behalf of the meeting:

JOHN LEONHANDT BRIGDEN,
Mayor of Brighton, Sussex, Chairman.

BRIGHTON, *May* 5, 1865.

To the people of the United States of America :

We, the working men of Brighton, in public meeting assembled, desire to express our utter abhorrence and indignation at the atrocious murder of Mr. ABRAHAM LINCOLN, President of the United States, by the hand of a ruthless assassin and the profound sympathy of our hearts towards those who are brethren in origin at the awful calamity which has befallen their great nation, and stricken us with amazement and horror. While we recognize an overruling Providence in all things, it is beyond human power to fathom the depths of this mysterious dispensation at so eventful a crisis in your history.

It is our confident hope and earnest prayer, that America may speedily emerge from this sad sorrow, and all her troubles, and continue with our nation the happy relations of peaceful commerce for generations to come.

Signed on behalf of the meeting:

JOHN LEONHANDT BRIGDEN,
Mayor of Brighton, Sussex, Chairman.

Resolution passed at a meeting held by the Local Board of Health of Balsall Heath.

At a meeting of the Local Board of Health for the district of Balsall Heath, near Birmingham, in the county of Warwick, held at their offices in Vincent street, Balsall Heath, aforesaid, on Wednesday, the 3d day of May, 1865, it was

Unanimously resolved, That this board desires to express its deepest sympathy with the government of the United States of America, and Mrs. Lincoln, in the bereavement which both have sustained by the lamented death of the late President, and to record its horror and detestation of the crime which has caused so great a national loss.

SAMUEL BRIGGS, *Chairman.*

BOURNEMOUTH, *April* 28, 1865.

We, the undersigned, inhabitants of Bournemouth, have learned with the deepest horror and regret that the President of the United States of America has been deprived of life by an act of violence, and we desire to express our sympathy on the sad event with the American minister in London, as well as to declare our hope and confidence in the future of that great country, which, we trust, will continue to be associated with enlightened freedom, and peaceful relations with this and every other country.

A. MORDEN BENNETT, *Perpetual Curate.*
R. S. McDOWELL, M. A.,
Assistant Curate of St. Peters
ALEX. B. ARMOUR.
WILLOUGHBY M. BURSLEM, M. D.
L. UPPLEBY.
GEORGE J. BARTON, *Banker.*
CHRIST'R C. CREEKES.
FRED. W. COATES, M. D.
WM. STEWART FALH, M. D.
ROBT. CANN LIPPINCOTT.
AND OVER ONE HUNDRED OTHER NAMES.
His Excellency the Hon. CHARLES FRANCIS ADAMS,
Minister of the United States of North America, at London.

To the President of the United States of America:

SIR: At a public meeting of the inhabitants of the township of Bilston, it was

Unanimously resolved, That this meeting desires to express its feelings of grief and abhorrence at the assassination of President LINCOLN, and at the horrible attempt to murder Mr. Secretary Seward; also to convey to the government and people of the United States, and to Mrs. Lincoln, the expression of their profound sympathy and condolence under the awful and lamentable bereavement which has befallen them.

GEORGE BEARD, *Chairman.*

This address was adopted at a banquet held to congratulate the American government on the suppression of the slaveholders' rebellion.

BARRHEAD, RENFREWSHIRE, *May* 4, 1865.

DEAR SIR: We cannot express the grief and horror which filled our hearts at the tidings of President LINCOLN's death. But who shall say that a crime less atrocious than the murder of that great and good man, who, in the eyes of the world, stood, by character and position, the most prominent representative and champion in the history of this or any other age of the cause of personal and national freedom, would have befitted the death desperation of southern slavery? In the light of this, its last and culminating sin, which has at length revealed its infamous depths as a treason against all that is sacred to humanity, and shocked the world, we bless God for the men and the measures which have swept that accursed institution away forever.

We congratulate your government and people on the suppression of this gigantic rebellion, and the successful assertion of your indissoluble unity as a nation—results fraught with incalculably blissful interest to every other nation, and especially to the sons of toil everywhere throughout the whole earth.

And while we would turn with tenderest sympathy to the sad, bereaved ones in your midst, from the home first desolated by this fearful struggle to that of your lamented President, and would seek to mingle our sorrow with theirs, and while we would weep for the innocent sufferers whose natural protectors have fallen in a bad cause, we cannot but hail the dawning of a future for your country infinitely more glorious than its past, and rejoice in it, not for your sake alone, but for our own, and for the cause of liberty and labor in all time coming.

Signed at a social meeting assembled for the purpose.

RICHARD LIVINGSTON, JR.
JOSEPH McNAB.
ALEXANDER JOHNSTON.
ROBERT PATRICK.
JOHN McDERMOTT.
THOMAS PATRICK.
WILLIAM PATRICK.
MATTHEW CRAIG.
WILLIAM CRAIG.
ANDREW CRAIG.
JAMES BAILEY.
AND FIFTY OTHER NAMES.

Hon. CHARLES FRANCIS ADAMS.

At a public meeting of the inhabitants of Bridlington and the Quay, held in the Town Hall, on Monday, the 15th of May, 1865, convened by the chief lord of the manor, in compliance with a requisition, numerously and respectably signed, the following resolutions were unanimously adopted:

1st. That this meeting desires to express *emphatically* its feelings of horror and indignation at the atrocious crime by which the life of Mr. LINCOLN has been sacrificed, and that of Mr Seward endangered, and its warm sympathy with the American people in the loss they have sustained in the untimely death of their distinguished President.

Moved by the Rev. J. Dickinson, Independent minister; seconded by Mr. John Reed.

2d. That this meeting desires to convey to Mrs. Lincoln its sincere and earnest expression of sympathy and condolence in the heavy bereavement she has sustained by the sudden and untimely death of her distinguished husband.

Moved by the Rev. J. Hodgson, Primitive Methodist minister; seconded by Mr. P. Mackley.

3d. That the aforesaid resolutions be forwarded by Thomas Cape, esq., chief lord, the chairman of this meeting, to the honorable C. F. Adams, the American minister, to be by him sent to the American government and to Mrs. Lincoln.

Moved by the Rev. Thomas Barnes, United Methodist church; seconded by George Baron, esq., West Huntow House.

THOMAS CAPE, *Chairman.*

Resolution adopted at a meeting held by the inhabitants of the borough of Blackburn, in the county of Lancaster.

At a public meeting of the inhabitants of this borough, held in the Town Hall, on Tuesday, the 2d day of May, 1865, the following was adopted: That this meeting desires to express the feelings of horror and indignation with which they have heard of the assassination of ABRAHAM LINCOLN, President of the United States of America, and of the murderous attack made upon Mr. Seward, Secretary of State.

This meeting further expresses its cordial sympathy with Mrs. Lincoln, and the relatives of the late President, believing that her husband's name will remain embalmed in the future as a martyr; and prays that an all-wise Providence may protect and cheer the widow, who has thus lost her affectionate partner in life, in the service of his country.

[SEAL.]   WILLIAM STINES,
Mayor and Chairman of the Meeting.

BOROUGH OF BLACKBURN, IN THE COUNTY OF LANCASTER.

At a public meeting of the inhabitants of this borough, held in the Town Hall, on Tuesday, the 2d day of May, 1865, the following address was adopted :

To Mrs Lincoln and family, Mr. Seward and family, and the American people generally: We, the inhabitants of Blackburn, in public meeting assembled, desire to convey the deep sympathy we feel for the unfortunate position in which you were placed, through the assassination of President LINCOLN and the attack on the life of Mr. Seward.

We deeply lament the existence of the civil war which has for four years devastated your country and stopped your progress in the paths of peace, but in our regret we recognize the future greatness and prosperity of your nation; in all your troubles and afflictions, whether as governors, families, or people, we have sympathized.

It has been wisely said, that the exigency of a nation demands an able leader, and that God, in his providence, always sends the man for the time.

We believe that ABRAHAM LINCOLN was the man raised up for the special work, and lament his horrible death by the hand of the assassin.

We read with pleasure, that in the cabinet council, on the night the assassination took place, the flush of victory in the fall of Richmond and the surrender of General Lee did not inspire your lamented President with revengeful feelings, but that his last words were for the reconstruction of the Union on conciliatory principles, in which mercy for his opponents was the leading feature.

To the American people we send loving words, and trust that these great afflictions will work out an abundant harvest of liberty, whereby free institutions may be consolidated, and labor, by whomsoever performed, dignified.

[SEAL]   WILLIAM STINES,
                                 Mayor and Chairman of the Meeting.

Resolution passed at a meeting held at Burnham, Somersetshire.

HONORED SIR : The underneath resolution was unanimously passed on Wednesday last, by a crowded meeting in the Union Chapel, Edith Meod, Burnham, Somersetshire, at the close of a lecture delivered by the Reverend J. S. Balmer, of Bridgewater, on " the late President LINCOLN and his assassination," and I have now the honor, as chairman of the meeting, to forward the same to your excellency.

                                           RICHARD WILLIAMS.

Hon. C. F. ADAMS.

"That this meeting desires to express its horror and indignation at the assassination of ABRAHAM LINCOLN, the late distinguished President of America, and to assure the bereaved widow, and the American people, of its deepest sympathy with them in their hour of great. trial. It would further express the ardent prayer that America may yet come out of this struggle, trusting in God, who has hitherto been its helper, and that, guided by Him, it may be led to permanent peace, great prosperity and entire national freedom."

SIR: We have heard with profound sorrow of the death of your late distinguished President, and that he has fallen by the hand of an assassin, and that other citizens of the United States have narrowly escaped a like fate, and are still suffering from their wounds. We believe there is not a Christian community who will not, by deep and heartfelt sympathy, participate with you, and with your country, in an expression of grief and sorrow at this event, as well also of horror and execration of the murderers.

The inhabitants of the village of Broomfield, in the county of Essex, in England, have been reminded of this terrible crime when assembled for divine worship; and having prayed with especial reference to the calamities of the war now devastating your land, that Almighty God would mercifully grant peace and concord to all nations, they desire to express to your excellency their sincere condolence; and they further desire their church wardens will cause this document to be forwarded to Mr. Adams, the American minister, for transmission to the United States.

J. B. WHITING, *Vicar.*

G. MAUNSELL, *Curate*

HENRY C. WELLS,
Church Warden.

THOMAS B. DAY,
Church Warden.

AND THIRTY-THREE OTHERS.

His Excellency ANDREW JOHNSON,
President of the United States of America.

At a public meeting on Tuesday evening, called by the mayor, at the request of a large number of the citizens of this town, for the purpose of expressing their feelings of condolence in regard to the assassination of the late President of the United States, the mayor was called to the chair, and Mr. D. Wylie appointed secretary.

The Rev. Mr. Poole opened the meeting with prayer; after which the following resolutions were passed :

Moved by Rev. J. K. Smith, A. M., seconded by D. Wylie, esq., and

Resolved, That we, the inhabitants of Brockville, in public meeting regularly assembled, hereby express unfeigned sorrow at the death, by assassination, of ABRAHAM LINCOLN, late President of the United States, and our deep abhorrence of the crime committed, a crime at which humanity shudders. We also offer our sympathy with the citizens of that nation in the great loss which they have thereby sustained; and we further express our sincere condolence with the sorrowing widow and family, in the heart-rending bereavement with which, in the inscrutable providence of God, they have been afflicted.

Moved by J. McMullen, esq., seconded by the Rev. Mr. Poole—

That it being highly desirable that the citizens of Brockville should express by some public act, or acts, their profound sympathy with the people of the United States, in the great affliction which the all-wise providence of God has permitted them to be subjected to, be it, therefore,

Resolved by this meeting, That all places of business in the town of Brockville shall be closed on to-morrow (Wednesday) from 12 to 2 o'clock, that being the period for the late lamented President LINCOLN's public funeral services; that the bells of the town be tolled, all flags raised at half-mast, and every other mark of sympathy and respect be shown that may be practicable.

Moved by Lieutenant Colonel Edmondson, seconded by J. McMullen, esq., and

Resolved, That this meeting cannot permit itself to separate without expressing a hope that the melancholy death of the late President will not complicate the public affairs of the United States, that peace will soon happily be restored, and that the good understanding which now subsists between the governments of the United States and of Great Britain will remain undisturbed for all time to come.

Moved by R. W. Kelly, esq., seconded by Wellington Landon, esq., and

Resolved, That the chairman of this meeting forward a copy of the above resolutions to the Secretary of State, at Washington ; and also give direction that they be published in each of the local journals of Brockville.

Moved by Rev. Mr. Poole, seconded by W. H. Willson, esq., and

Resolved, That the chairman do now leave the chair, and that Dr. Edmondson do take the same.

A vote of thanks was then passed to the chairman and secretary, when the meeting broke up.

A. B. DANA, *Mayor, Chairman.*

D. WYLIE, *Secretary.*

Dated at Brockville, Canada West, this 19th day of April, 1865.

At an adjourned meeting of the inhabitants of Belfast, held in tne Music Hall, on Monday, the 8th day of May, 1865, the mayor in the chair, the following resolutions were unanimously agreed to :

Moved by Thomas Sinclair, esq., chairman of the harbor commissioners, seconded by John Shelly, esq., collector of her Majesty's customs, and

Resolved, That this meeting have heard with feelings of profound sorrow of the assassination of his Excellency ABRAHAM LINCOLN, President of the United States, and desire to express their utmost detestation of that atrocious crime.

Moved by James Bristow, esq., director of the Northern Bank, seconded by Rev. Henry Cooke, D. D., LL.D., and

Resolved, That this meeting desires to express its sincere and deep sympathy with the government and people of the United States, under the severe loss which they have sustained in the sudden and cruel death of the President.

Moved by Rev. James McCosh, LL.D., Professor Queen's College, seconded by John Hind, esq., and

Resolved, That this meeting express its deep sympathy with the Hon. W. H. Seward, Secretary of State of the United States, and with his family, and their utter abhorrence of the brutal and murderous attack made on him and his sons, in his own house, while confined to a sick bed.

Moved by the Rev. John Macnaughten, seconded by Theobald Bushell, esq., J. P., and

Resolved, That this meeting humbly offers its sincere and heartfelt condolence to Mrs. Lincoln, under the sore trial that has bereaved her of an honored and affectionate husband, and while not wishing to intrude on the sorrow of a stricken heart, fervently commends her to the support and care of a gracious God.

Moved by William Mullan, esq., seconded by Thomas McClure, esq., D. L. J. P., and

Resolved, That copies of the foregoing resolutions be placed in the hands of the Hon. C. F. Adams, the American minister, for transmission to his Excellency the President of the United States, Mrs. Lincoln, and the Hon. W. H. Seward.

JOHN LYTLE, *Mayor of Belfast.*

[SEAL.] JAMES GUTHRIE, *Town Clerk.*

Copy of resolutions passed at an open-air meeting of the inhabitants of Bradford, on Saturday, the 29th April, 1865.

Resolved, That this meeting expresses its deep horror and detestation at the deed of assassination perpetrated on the person of ABRAHAM LINCOLN, President of the United States of America ; with like feelings it also regards the attempt on the life of the foreign minister, Mr. Seward, and shudders with disgust at such brutal acts of low, mean, dark, cowardly atrocity, unequalled in the annals of history.

Resolved, That the workingmen and women of Bradford, in public meeting assembled, express their deep sympathy with the government and people, their brethren and sisters in America, in the loss they have sustained by the lamented death of Mr. President LINCOLN.

Resolved, That the worshipful the mayor, as chairman of this meeting, be requested to sign and forward a copy of the above resolutions to the representatives of the American government, its sorrowing people, and the bereaved wife and family of Mr. President LINCOLN.

CHARLES SEMON, *Mayor.*

Copy of resolutions passed at a meeting of inhabitants of Bradford, on the 28*th day of April,* 1865.

Resolved, That the inhabitants of Bradford, in public meeting assembled, do hereby express their strongest feelings of abhorrence and grief at the atrocious assassination of the President of the United States of America, and also at the dastardly attempt upon the life of Mr. Seward, the Secretary of State.

Resolved, That this meeting do express their deep sympathy with the American people in the loss they have sustained by the cruel death of Mr. President LINCOLN.

CHARLES SEMON, *Mayor.*

BRADFORD CHAMBER OF COMMERCE, *April* 26, 1865.

SIR: The council of the Bradford Chamber of Commerce beg most respectfully to express to you, and through you to the people of the United States, the horror and grief which they, in common with the whole civilized world, must feel at the news which has reached the town this day of the assassination of President LINCOLN. Just at the very moment when the arduous struggle which he had so gloriously conducted for the last four years was concluded in the field, and when the world was admiring the wise and conciliatory spirit which he had shown in his endeavors to allay conflicting passions and to heal the wounds of his country, he was struck down by a cowardly assassin. The horrible event is too recent to admit of anything more than the mere expression of the most heartfelt sympathy and grief, and the council are sure that in thus addressing you they only give expression to feelings which are common to their constituents and to the whole community of Bradford.

I have the honor to remain, sir, your faithful servant,

HENRY W. RIPLEY, *President.*

JOHN DARLINGTON, *Secretary.*

GEORGE J. ABBOT, Esq.

BOROUGH OF BIRMINGHAM.

At a quarterly meeting of the council of this borough, held in the council chamber at the public office, Moor street, on the 4th day of May, 1865, Henry Wiggin, esq., mayor, in the chair, it was moved by the mayor, seconded by Mr. Alderman Holliday, and

Resolved unanimously, That this council desires to express to the government of the United States its abhorrence and detestation of the atrocious crime which has deprived the American nation of its chief; that while manifesting its horror at the foul deed which sacrified the life of the President, at the moment when victory had crowned his efforts with success, this council desires to record its deep and earnest sympathy with the government and people of the United States on this great calamity.

[SEAL.]   HENRY WIGGIN, *Mayor.*

At a public meeting of the inhabitants of Birmingham, convened by the mayor and held in the Town Hall, on Friday, the 28th day of April, 1865, the right worshipful the mayor (Henry Wiggin, esq.) in the chair, it was moved by the mayor, seconded by John Jaffray, esq., and

Resolved unanimously, That this meeting desires to express the deepest regret at the irreparable loss which the people of the United States of America have sustained by the untimely death of President LINCOLN; that this meeting regards with horror and detestation the crime by which the President's life was sacrificed, and that on behalf and in the name of the inhabitants of Birmingham this meeting respectfully offers to the government and people of the United States the most sincere and earnest sympathy under the calamity which has befallen them.

It was moved by Rev. R. W. Dale, seconded by Mr. Alderman Hawkes, and

Resolved unanimously, That this meeting further desires to record its deep regret at the attempt to assassinate Mr. Seward, the Secretary of State, and expresses an earnest hope that, by the blessing of Divine Providence, his life may be spared to the service of his country.

HENRY WIGGIN,
Mayor, Chairman of the said Meeting.

Address of " The Ladies Negroes' Friend Society" to Mrs. Lincoln.

EDGEBASTON, BIRMINGHAM, *June* 16, 1865.

Mrs. Edmund Sturge, with deep feelings of respectful sympathy for Mrs. Lincoln, thinks it may be of some interest to her to know that the address has been signed by the wife and daughter of John Bright, esq., M. P., as well as the daughter of J. Angell James.

BIRMINGHAM, *May* 30, 1865.

MADAM : We, the undersigned, members and friends of "The Ladies Negroes' Friend Society," assembled at our fortieth annual meeting at the residence of the late Joseph Sturge, cannot refrain from offering you the expression of our deep and respectful sympathy at this time of your bitter sorrow. We trust in the conviction of our hearts that, though personally unknown to you, we may ask permission to share your grief, because we are associated to promote the same great cause of human freedom which your honored and beloved and lamented husband, the late President LINCOLN, espoused in early life, and so religiously and beautifully enforced in his last message to Congress ; that we earnestly desire the sentiments therein contained may be engraven on the hearts of all who read them the world over.

We have placed on record his saying, so full of truth, "If slavery be not wrong, nothing is wrong." Thus may it be bound more closely on our consciences and memory, and stimulate us to do all that is in our power towards realizing the final triumph of the great anti-slavery cause to which President LINCOLN was honored to render such vast services. In commemorating these services, we would tenderly remember how afflicting is the dispensation that through them has been allotted to you, even the surrender of a life dearer than your own.

We have been comforted by the knowledge that in the representative of your departed husband, you had one near you, in the first hours of your "agonizing sorrow," who gave expression to the reflection that even from its depths God could bring good to others. May our Heavenly Father, " who doeth all things well," supply you with his richest consolations. May you be permitted to see, with admiring and reverential wonder, such beneficial results as may fill your smitten heart with resignation and peace. Even now we implore you to take comfort from the fact that already blessed thoughts of peace and good will between the British and American people have been nourished by the community of feeling awakened by our common loss Cherishing this belief, we also cling to the hope that henceforth both nations will unite in carrying forward the sacred cause now afresh consecrated by the sacrifice of such a life.

With heartfelt sympathy and respect, we are, madam, yours, sincerely,

LOUISA J. MORLLIET, } *Treasurers.*
MARIA CADBURY,

LYDIA EDMUND STURGE, } *Secretaries.*
ANNA MARIA HARRIS,

ELIZABETH BRADY, Jr.
MARY L. M. GODDARD.
ELLEN STURGE.
MARTHA DALE.
MARIANNE GIBBS.
M. A. PHIPSON.
ELIZABETH T. PHIPSON.
REBECCA PIERCY.
ANNIE MANTIN.
MARY HILL THORNTON.
MARIA TUCKER.
MERCY STEADMAN.
JANE PLANT.
HENRIETTA W. MORGAN.
MARY MIDDLEMIRE.
HANNAH PERRY.
ELIZABETH GORVE.
S. R. BUCKTON.
DOUDECIMA CROWLEY.
JULIA A. SNEPP.
GULIELMA A. W. BAKER.
MARY GEORGE B. LLOYD.
SOPHIA SARAH TAYLOR.
EMMA WHATRUNE.
ANN CADBURY.
ANNA H. RICHARDSON.
MARY W. POLLARD.
RACHEL A. ALBRIGHT.
HESTER S. SPRIGGS.
MARY E. MARSHALL.
S. H. BUCKMAN.
HANNAH FOWLER.
M. A. HALL.
HARRIET ANN HEATON.
SARAH LIGHTWOOD.
ANN YATES.
M. A. YEOMANS.
ELIZABETH HOWELL.
SARAH SCOTTIN.
FRANCIS FORD.
MARY ANNA AVERY.
MARY CLARK.
E. F. TAUNTON.
J. B. BULLINANT.
M. G. WARREN.
MARY BOOTH.
MAY BOOTH.
HANNAH J. SURGE.
TAMERSIN CHRISTIE.
SARAH SOUTHALL.
ANNA J. BAKER.

EMMA J. GIBBONS.
ANN MARY GOODRICK.
MARY ANN KING.
SOPHIA SEEKINGS.
SUSAN KING.
ANNA LLOYD.
ANN SNOWDEN.
MARY H. PEASE.
H. B. BOTTOMLEY.
H. B. BOTTOMLEY, Jr.
SUSANNAH REYNOLDS.
KEZIAH YATES.
CAROLINE SARGEANT.
JULIA GODDARD.
CAROLINE DAYKEN.
CATHARINE W. THORNTON.
ESTER M. PARTRIDGE.
MARY KENT.
EMMA HULEY.
EMMA WAINWRIGHT.
HANNAH BOLTON.
HANNAH B. SMITH.
MARGARET A. WATSON.
ELEANOR STURGE.
MARY WATSON.
ELIZABETH HUNT.
ANNIE CHIPMEN.
SARAH J. BARNARD.
CATHARINE JANE MENE.
MARY BIDDLE.
MARIA JONES.
HANNAH M. JOSEPH.
SARAH ANN JAMES, daughter
  of the late J. A. James.
H. P. KENWAY.
E. PUMPHREY.
ELIZABETH K. NEELE.
CAROLINE LLOYD.
FANNY JOHNSON.
SUSAN H. BURROWS.
MARY GREVIN.
ELLEN JENNERS.
SARAH E. PAUSLU.
CATHARINE MARSH.
ANNIE E. WALLER.
ALICE BURTT.
MARIA BAKER.
HANNAH GORE.
REBECCA FEARSON.
EMMA CROFT.
ELIZABETH JENKINS.

EMMA HUDSON.
MARY BIRCH.
MARCIA H. CADBURY.
HANNAH CADBURY.
SARAH E. LORD.
SARAH ALLEN.
FRANCIS JENKINS.
ELIZA M. STURGE.
BELSEY MORRIS.
M. A. S NORTHOUSE.
PRISCILLA IMPREY.
SOPHIA STURGE.
ESTER S. WRIGHT.
EMMA WRIGHT.
ELLEN G. DYMOND.
E. WHITE.
MARGARET HAUTIN.
MARY ANN SMESIN.
ELIZABETH BRADY.
ELIZABETH GRECE.
MARIAN DAVIES.
JANE CATTELL.
S. N. MAPPLEBECK.
CATHARINE KEA.
MARTHA GAUSLEY.
MARY GARLAND.
EMMA GREAVES.
HANNAH PARKER.
EMMA EAGLE.
SARAH HEATON.
JANE PYE.
M. FAIRFIELD.
ELIZABETH MIDDLEMIRE.
JANE GOODMAN.
SARAH COLEMAN.
FRANCIS DAY BLADES.
ELIZABETH R. CABURY.
LUCRETIA CUDBURY.
MARY HUXLEY.
HELLEN HOLBECHE.
MARY ANN ROSE.
ANN MARY SCOTT.
JANE BAKER.
ELIZA M. SOUTHALL.
M. FELTON.
M. STOCKWIN.
A. STOCKWIN.
E. T. MILES.
HELLEN P. BRIGHT.
MARGARET E. BRIGHT.

Address of the representatives of the Baptist churches of England, on the death of President Lincoln.

To his Excellency the honorable Charles Francis Adams, envoy extraordinary and minister plenipotentiary of the United States of America at the court of her Most Gracious Majesty, Queen Victoria:

SIR: We, the representatives of the general Baptist churches of England, at our annual association held this year at Birmingham, most respectfully beg leave to express, through you, our intense sympathy with your people on the occasion of the tragic death of your late honored President, by the abhorred act of an assassin, and to pay our tribute of earnest and affectionate admiration to the memory of that great and good man, whose purity of motive, firmness of purpose, and kindness of heart have endeared him to all well-wishers of the human race. We would particularly tender our sincere condolence with his widow and family under their irreparable loss; and at the same time offer our heartfelt congratulations to President Johnson, and the people of the United States, on the termination of that dreadful conflict which has, for four years, been productive of so much bloodshed and misery, and very especially because in this instance the restoration of peace is associated with one of the most welcome and gladdening events in the history of the human race—the abolition of slavery throughout your country.

For this we give most hearty thanks to the Almighty Disposer of all events; and to Him we present our fervent prayers that your great nation may, through all time, enjoy the manifold blessings of unity and liberty, intelligence and piety, peace and prosperity.

Signed on behalf of the association.

THOMAS W. MATHEWS, *Chairman*,
Pastor at Boston, in Lincolnshire.
THOMAS BARRASS, *Secretary*,
Pastor at Peterborough.

Blaydon local board.

The following resolutions were passed at a meeting held May 4, 1865:

That this board desires to give utterance to the feelings of grief and horror with which it has heard of the assassination of President LINCOLN, and the murderous attack upon Mr. Seward, and to convey to Mrs. Lincoln, to President Johnson and his colleagues, and to the people of the United States, its profound sympathy and heartfelt condolence.

That a copy of the foregoing resolution be placed in the hands of the honorable C. F. Adams, the American minister, for transmission to his Excellency the President of the United States, Mrs. Lincoln, and the honorable William H. Seward.

[L. S.]

BOROUGH OF BRIDGEWATER, IN THE COUNTY OF SOMERSET.

At a meeting of the council of the said borough, held at the Council House or Burgess Hall of the said borough, this 5th day of May, 1865, it was

Resolved, That the council desires to record the expression of its indignation and sorrow at the assassination of ABRAHAM LINCOLN, the late President of the United States of America, and its sympathy and condolence with the people of that country, and also with the bereaved widow, at the severe and irreparable loss which they have sustained.

Resolved, That the corporate seal be affixed to the foregoing resolution, and that the same be forwarded by the mayor to Mr. Adams for transmission to the United States.

[L. S.]

JOHN BROWNE,
Mayor of Bridgewater.

From the Bridgewater Methodist Free Church.

This meeting desires to express its unfeigned regret that the triumphant course of the late President LINCOLN should have been cut short by the hand of an assassin.

This meeting also desires to express its deep sympathy for the American people in this hour of trial and conflict. Nevertheless, they venture earnestly to desire that, as truth is stronger than ever, the Almighty will be graciously pleased to overrule all things for good, and to redound to his glory.

At a general meeting of the commissioners acting under and by virtue of the Bury improvement act 1846, held on the 3d day of May, 1865, Mr. John S. Walker in the chair, it was moved by Mr. Thomas Grundy, seconded by Mr. Thomas Roberts, and carried unanimously—

That the commissioners, as the governing municipal body of the town of Bury, in the county palatine of Lancaster, desire to express their horror and sincere regret at the assassination of Mr. LINCOLN, the late President of the United States of America, and to convey to the government and people of the United States their profound sympathy in the great loss they have sustained, and to Mrs. Lincoln their heartfelt condolence in her cruel bereavement.

Extracted from the minutes.

WM. HARPER, *Clerk.*

Resolutions passed at a meeting held by the inhabitants of Bury.

ASSASSINATION OF PRESIDENT LINCOLN.

Public meeting at Bury—Fred. Anderton, esq., in the chair.

Moved by the Rev. F. Howorth, seconded by Mr. J. Stockdale—

That this meeting regards with horror, indignation, and abhorrence the appalling crime which has put an end to the life of the great and good President LINCOLN, and the attempted assassination of the chief secretary, Mr. Seward.

Moved by the Rev. W. Roseman, seconded by Mr. William Hoyle—

That this meeting desires to record its profound sympathy with the people of the United States, in this hour of national bereavement, and especially with the widow of their twice elected chief, the intensity of whose grief is increased by the atrocious nature of the deed which has snatched her husband from her side.

Moved by the Rev. W. R. Brown, seconded by Mr. Welsby—

That this meeting earnestly hopes that the mantle of the murdered President may fall upon his successor in office; that he may be equally distinguished for his firmness of principle, the wisdom of his decisions, the clemency of his actions, and the general kindness of his heart.

Moved by Mr. D. Thomas, seconded by Mr. William Pickstone—

That this meeting sincerely hopes that a fraternal feeling may pervade the lately divided sections of the great republic, and that its future prosperity may be guaranteed by the removal of slavery, the return of peace, and the development of the unlimited resources of the country.

Moved by the Rev. G. Fletcher, seconded by Mr. Wormald—

That a copy of the foregoing resolutions be sent to Mr. C. F. Adams, the American minister in London, with a request that he will kindly forward them to his government at Washington.

MAY 6, 1865.

Resolution passed at a meeting of the Northern Presbytery of Antrim.

At a stated quarterly meeting of the Northern Presbytery of Antrim, held at Ballyclare on the 6th day of July, 1865, the Rev. William Bruce, A. B., moderator, in the chair, it was

Resolved unanimously, That at this our first meeting since the lamented death of the honorable ABRAHAM LINCOLN, President of the United States of America, we feel called upon to record our detestation of the atrocious crime by which he was suddenly cut off in the midst of his days and his usefulness;

our participation in the sorrow of the members of his family under the loss which they have thus sustained; and our sympathy with the people of the United States, deprived of a high-minded Chief Magistrate, at the very moment when his invincible firmness and undaunted fortitude had been rewarded with success more complete than usually attends on the wisest of human counsels ; and when, from his high character, there was every reason to expect that moderation in victory, and that merciful consideration towards a vanquished enemy, which, accompanying the glorious emancipation of the slave, would have forever associated the name of LINCOLN with that of Washington as marking the introduction of a new and happy era in the history of his country.

That we desire to express our earnest hope that the government and people of the United States will employ their utmost efforts to consummate their great victory in the manner most consistent with Christian principle, most accordant with the soundest policy, and best corresponding with the dignity of a great and magnanimous nation.

Signed in the name and by order of the presbytery.

WILLIAM BRUCE, A. B., *Moderator.*

J. SCOTT PORTER, *Clerk.*

At a meeting of the local board of health for the district of the township of Barnsley, in the west riding of the county of York, held at the court-house in Barnsley aforesaid, on Tuesday, the 9th day of May, in the year of our Lord 1865—present, Alfred Badger, James Buckley, Thomas Cope, William Day, William Hopwood, Frederick Gervis Jackson, John Ostcliffe, Charles Newman, Joseph S. Parkinson, Charles Lacey Rogers, James Taylor—it was *(inter alia)*

Resolved unanimously, That this board, although representing but a small community of Englishmen, yet desires to participate in the public expression of horror and indignation at the crime of assassination, and especially when directed against the chief rulers of a nation.

The recent atrocious murder of President LINCOLN, and the attempted assassination of Mr. Secretary Seward, call forth our most profound sympathy and heartfelt condolence with the government and citizens of the United States of America, deprived as they are, at a most momentous crisis in their history, of the benevolent, energetic, and patriotic guidance of their lamented late President.

[Signed by the above eleven members of the same local board.]

[SEAL.]

Resolutions, numbered respectively 1, 2, 3, and 4, adopted unanimously at a joint meeting of the inhabitants of the towns of Berlin and Waterloo, Canada West, held at the court-house at Berlin, on Wednesday, the 19th day of April, A. D. 1865, in compliance with the proclamations of the reeves of aforesaid corporations, for the purpose of affording the citizens an opportunity of giving expression to their sympathy with the American people, and the bereaved family of the late President, as well as to manifest the deep sorrow and horror felt at the atrocious and appalling crime that resulted in the death of ABRAHAM LINCOLN, the late lamented President of the United States of America—Ward Hamilton Bowlby, esq., reeve of the town of Berlin, presiding as chairman, and Israel D. Bowman, esq., county clerk, acting as secretary.

RESOLUTION No. 1.

Moved by William Jaffray, esq., postmaster, and seconded by Dougall Mc-Dougall, esq., county registrar, and

Resolved, That this meeting of the inhabitants of the towns of Berlin and Waterloo, in the province of Canada, assembled on the funeral day of ABRAHAM LINCOLN, late President of the United States, desires, with the deepest sincerity, to express its heartfelt indignation at the cowardly and wanton act by which the President and patriot, the ruler and friend of the republic, has been lost to his country, at the moment of his greatest usefulness, and when he could have almost said of the great work he had undertaken, " It is finished." In the death of ABRAHAM LINCOLN this meeting feels that, while the United States as a nation have lost a firm yet merciful and amiable ruler, and the people individually a counsellor and friend, the world at large has been bereft at the same time of one whose large-hearted humanity and innate love of freedom and liberal institutions placed him at once in the fore rank of nature's noblemen.

RESOLUTION No. 2.

Moved by the Rev. Dr. Schulte, and seconded by Henry F. J. Jackson, esq., superintendent of schools, and

Resolved, That this meeting tender the American people, bowed down this day in overwhelming sorrow over the mortal remains of their late illustrious Chief Magistrate, the expression of their heartfelt sympathy at the national calamity with which it has pleased an all-wise Providence to afflict them. That they regard the dastardly and barbarous murder of President LINCOLN not only as an irreparable loss to the American nation in the present momentous crisis of their history, but as a common loss to humanity, liberty, and the brotherhood of mankind all the world over.

RESOLUTION No. 3

Moved by John J. Bowman. esq., editor, and seconded by the Rev. F. A. Kaessman, and

Resolved, That this meeting would desire, most respectfully and tenderly, to express their sympathy for Mrs. Lincoln and family, in the sore and affecting bereavement which, in the inscrutable dispensation of an overruling Providence, they have sustained, having at one fell blow, "in a moment, in the twinkling of an eye," been robbed of husband, parent, and friend. May He who ruleth all things well comfort and sustain them in this hour of their deepest grief.

RESOLUTION No. 4.

Moved by John A. Mackie, esq., justice of the peace, and seconded by Henry S. Huber, esq., crown land agent, and

Resolved, That a copy of the foregoing resolutions be forwarded to his excellency the governor general of British North America, respectfully requesting that he transmit the same to the Secretary of State of the United States of America.

Certified to be true copies.

W. H. BOWLBY, *Chairman.*

ISRAEL D. BOWMAN. *Secretary.*

Dated at Berlin, county of Waterloo, and province of Canada, this 19th day of April, A. D. 1865.

Resolution of the Birkenhead Working Men's Association.

GLASNEVEN, BALL'S ROADS, BIRKENHEAD,
May 3, 1865.

SIR: I beg to communicate to you the following resolution, proposed by the Rev. Mr. Downe, and seconded by Mr. Graham, and which was unanimously carried at a large meeting of the Birkenhead Working Men's Association, held in the Craven Rooms here last night, and which I, as chairman, was requested to forward to you:

"*Resolved*, That this meeting views with deep concern and indignation the late atrocious murder of Mr. LINCOLN, the able and popular President of the United States of America, and expresses its sympathy with the great American people in the present crisis of their affairs."

In addition to this unanimous expression of the feelings of those present at the meeting, I may be permitted to add that I myself cordially respond to the sentiments expressed, and view with deep grief the melancholy end and sad loss of one whom I regarded as a just and good man, and a wise and merciful ruler, and that I hope it may please God to dispel the dark cloud that this event has cast over the American nation, and out of the present evil to bring forth future and lasting good, for the welfare and happiness of our afflicted kinsmen.

I have the honor to be, sir, your most obedient servant,

ROBERT GEORGE KELLY.

T. H. DUDLEY, Esq.,
American Consul, Liverpool.

GOVERNMENT HOUSE, NASSAU,
May 1, 1865.

SIR : I cannot doubt that the government and people of the United States will be gratified at learning that in the Bahamas, as, I believe, throughout her Majesty's dominions, the atrocious act which has struck down their late President, at so critical a period of the national affairs, and at a moment of such intense interest to himself and the nation, is viewed with the utmost abhorrence and detestation, and that it has aroused the liveliest sympathy for the widow and family of the late Mr. LINCOLN, and for the nation thus cruelly robbed of its Chief Magistrate, whom it had so lately delighted to honor by a triumphant re-election to his exalted post.

It is, therefore, a great satisfaction to me that I am able to add to the personal expression of my own sentiments of regret and sympathy on this mournful occasion, two resolutions, in original, passed unanimously in the legislative council and house of assembly of this colony, now in session, which I request you will have the goodness to lay before the new President in such a manner as you may think most fitting, together with the enclosed copy of my message to the two houses, which led to this hearty, and, I believe, thoroughly sincere response.

I have, &c., &c.,

RAWSON W. RAWSON, *Governor.*

Extract from the speech of Governor Rawson on the closing of the Bahamas legislature. May 3, 1865.

MR. PRESIDENT, AND GENTLEMEN OF THE LEGISLATIVE COUNCIL AND OF THE HOUSE OF ASSEMBLY : The startling and painful intelligence which has lately reached us of the atrocious crime that has deprived a neighboring state of its Chief Magistrate, has awakened here, as elsewhere in her Majesty's dominions, the liveliest feeling of detestation of the act, and of sympathy with Mr. LINCOLN's family and nation. You have judged it to be a fitting occasion, as the chosen representatives of the people of these islands, to give expression to their sentiments. I shall have much pleasure in forwarding the resolutions which you have presented to me to her Majesty's minister at Washington, for the purpose of being laid before the new President, and I cannot doubt that they will be very acceptable to the officer and people to whom they are addressed.

Whereas, while the house considers itself bound, in general, to abstain from the expression of any opinion on subjects relating to foreign nations, yet, viewing the lamentable occurrence by which the Chief Magistrate of a friendly power has been struck down by the hand of an assassin, as constituting an exceptionable state of circumstances, calling as well for an expression of sympathy towards the bereaved family and nation of the victim as of abhorrence of the crime—

Resolved, nemine contradicente. That this house has with deep regret heard of the act of atrocity by which the late President of the United States was suddenly deprived of life, and the house hereby tenders to the family of the deceased President and to the people of the United States this expression of sincere sympathy at the calamitous event.

That a copy of this resolution be transmitted to his excellency the governor, with a request that he will forward the same to the British minister at Washington, to be communicated, as he may think proper, to the authorities of the United States.

Extracted from the minutes of the house of the 27th of April, 1865.

G. C. ANDERSON, *Speaker.*

Resolved unanimously, That the legislative council deeply laments the death of Mr. LINCOLN, late President of the United States, and sympathizes profoundly with his family and with a kindred and friendly nation, deprived of its Chief Magistrate in so melancholy a manner by a detestable and monstrous crime, of which the board of council cannot adequately express its condemnation and horror.

By order of the board:

W. H. DOYLE, *President.*

COUNCIL CHAMBER, *May* 1, 1865.

Lieutenant Governor Hamley to C. M. Allen, Esq., U. S. Consul.

MOUNT LANGTON, *April* 26, 1865.

SIR: I have the honor to acknowledge your communication of yesterday, conveying to me the shocking intelligence of the death, by assassination, of the

President of the United States of America.   Believe that I am deeply sensible of the magnitude of the loss which the people of the United States have sustained, and that I have read with interest the tribute to the late President's high qualities which this melancholy occasion has drawn from you.

I have the honor to be, sir, your most obedient servant,

W. G. HAMLEY, *Lieutenant Governor.*

GOVERNMENT SECRETARY'S OFFICE,
British Guiana, May 22, 1865.

SIR: The governor directs me to acknowledge the receipt of your official communication of this day's date, announcing the death of his Excellency ABRAHAM LINCOLN, late President of the United States of America, and I am to convey to you the expression of his very deep regret on the occasion.

I have the honor to be, sir, your obedient, humble servant,

WALTER HOWARD WARE,
Acting Government Secretary.

P. W. FIGGELMESY, Esq.,
United States Consul, Demerara.

Lord Monck to Sir F. Bruce.

QUEBEC, *April* 17, 1865.

SIR: The intelligence of the perpetration of the atrocious outrage by which the United States has been deprived of their Chief Magistrate has filled all classes of the community in this province with awe and horror.

Immediately that I received a confirmation of the sad news, I gave directions, in conjunction with the lieutenant general commanding her Majesty's troops in this province, that at all civil and military stations the flags should be hoisted half-mast high.

I shall feel much obliged if you will take a fitting opportunity of communicating to the Secretary of State of the United States, on the part of the government and people of this province, their deep feeling of abhorrence of the crime which has been committed, and their profound sympathy with the government and citizens of the United States at the loss which they have sustained.

I have, &c.,

MONCK.

Honorable SIR F. BRUCE, *G. C. B., &c.*

BENGAL CHAMBER OF COMMERCE,
Calcutta, June 3, 1865.

SIR: As chairman of a general meeting of the Bengal Chamber of Commerce held this day, I have the honor to place in your hands a copy of a resolution unanimously adopted by the meeting, and to request you will have the goodness to transmit the same to the Secretary of State of the government of the United States.

The resolution records the horror with which the commercial community of this city view the assassination of the late President of the United States, their sympathy in the calamity which the American nation has suffered by the lamented death of their eminent Chief Magistrate, and their earnest hope that the long-continued war may be happily terminated by an early restoration of peace, lasting and prosperous.

I have the honor to be, sir, your most obedient servant,

JOHN BULLEN.

NATHANIEL P. JACOBS, Esq.,
 Consul General for the United States of America.

Resolution passed at a meeting held by the Bengal Chamber of Commerce.

Resolved, That this meeting desires to place on record the horror with which they, in common with all ranks and classes of her Majesty's subjects, view the assassination of the late Mr. LINCOLN, President of the United States of America; the deep sympathy which they feel for the people of that country under the great national calamity which this event has brought upon them; and their earnest hope that the war from which they have suffered so severely may soon be brought to a close, and be followed by peace, lasting and prosperous.

A true copy :

JOHN BULLEN.

Meeting of the American community.

The American merchants and ship-masters of Calcutta assembled to the number of thirty or forty, at the counting-house of Messrs. Atkinson, Tilton & Co., on Wednesday afternoon, June 7, to do honor to the memory of their deceased President, LINCOLN. The meeting was opened by the appointment of the American consul general for India, Nathaniel P. Jacobs, esq., to preside, and of the reverend Mr. Dall as secretary.

A committee was then appointed to draught resolutions embodying the sense of the meeting. It consisted of Messrs. Eldridge, Whitney, Dall, Hamlin, and Knowles.   The following were, after a brief conference in the committee-room, presented, and received unanimous approval :

Resolved, That we, Americans of Calcutta, India,, desire to add our testimony of respect and of sorrow to that which has been, and is now being, expressed in various parts of the world for ABRAHAM LINCOLN, the justly honored and beloved President of the United States of America, murdered while on duty—martyred in the hour of triumph of his arduous and successful labors for us and for humanity.   We mourn, in his death, the unreturning departure of a true patriot, ruler, and friend.

Resolved, That with our grief is mingled a grateful and deep satisfaction at the general outburst of sympathy in this our national bereavement, and at the expression of fellow-feeling which seems to come to our native land from every region in which Christianity has found a home or a mission.

Resolved, That we recognize the hand of the Ruler of all nations in the loss which we have sustained ; and while, to us, the blow comes with double force at this particular time, when his wisdom and abilities were peculiarly needed, we bow to the divine will, and doubt not that God's protecting hand will be extended to our suffering country, and that good will come out of what now seems to us an irreparable loss

Resolved, That, in these expressions of sorrow, we specially desire to remember the widow and family of our late President, and to convey to them, as to our fellow-countrymen, our earnest sympathy at the calamity which has befallen them.

Resolved, That as a token of our present relation to the deceased, and out of respect to his memory, we will wear crape on the left arm for the next thirty days ; and that the masters of American ships in port be requested to set their colors at half-mast for one week from this date.

Resolved, That a copy of these resolutions be handed to the consul general of the United States of America for British India, with the request that he will have them transmitted to the proper authorities at home.

F. F. Wills, esq., moved that the resolutions, as now read, be accepted and adopted as an expression of American feeling in Calcutta ; and, on the seconding of Mr. H. B. Goodwin, they were carried unanimously, and the meeting was dissolved.

Special general meeting of the justices of the peace for the town of Calcutta, held on Tuesday, the 13th June, 1865.

Present, the chairman and vice-chairman, Hon. W. S. Seton-Karr, Colonel Nicolls, R. E., and fifty-five others.

The honorable W. S. Seton-Karr proposed the following resolution :

That the justices for the town of Calcutta, in meeting, view with the utmost abhorrence the diabolical act which has deprived the United States of America of their President.

The resolution being seconded by Baboo Ramanath Tagore, was carried unanimously.

Mr. J. H. Ferguson then moved the following resolution :

That the justices desire to express their deep sympathy for the widow and the children of the late President, and for the American people, under the loss they have sustained.

The resolution was seconded by Dr. Brougham, and carried unanimously

Mr. Remfry then moved—

That these resolutions be communicated to the consul general for the United States in this city, with a request that he will transmit the same to the widow of the late President and to the American government.

The resolution being seconded by Mr. J. B. Roberts, was carried unanimously.

True copy :

V. H. SCHALCH,
Chairman to the Justices of the Peace.

Vestry of the Parish of Chelsea.

Resolved, That we, the vestry of the parish of Chelsea, representing about seventy thousand inhabitants, having heard with the deepest horror and indignation of the death of the President of the United States of America by the hand of a dastardly assassin, desire to express to the American minister, and through him to the American people, our heartfelt sympathy with them in this their time of national sorrow.

We further desire to record our deep sympathy with Mrs. Lincoln under the sudden and overwhelming bereavement which she has sustained, and we earnestly hope that this sad and appalling event may be overruled by Providence to the welfare of America, and that the future of that great country may be one of peace and prosperity.

Resolutions at a meeting of the inhabitants of Camden town.

1. That this meeting desires to give utterance to the feelings of grief and horror with which it has heard of the assassination of the late President LINCOLN and the murderous attack upon Mr. Seward, and to convey to Mrs. Lincoln, the United States government and people, an expression of its profound sympathy and heartfelt condolence.

2. That this meeting hails with delight the prospect of returning peace in America and the total abolition of slavery.

3. That copies of the foregoing resolutions be placed in the hands of the honorable C. F. Adams, the American minister, for transmission to his Excellency the President of the United States, to Mrs. Lincoln, and the honorable W. H. Seward.

On behalf of a public meeting of the inhabitants of Camden town, held in Camden Hall, Friday evening, May 5, 1865:

DUGALD CAMERON,
Chairman.

RAYMOND JAVENY, *Secretary.*

Resolutions at a meeting held by the inhabitants of Chatham.

At a large and influential meeting of the inhabitants of Chatham, held in the lecture hall, on Tuesday, the 16th of May, at the close of an earnest and eloquent address by Henry Vincent, esq., of London, " On the rise and fall of the slaveholders' rebellion against moral obligations and human freedom, to the culminating crime, the murder of honest President LINCOLN," Henry Everest, esq., justice of the peace, in the chair, the following resolution was moved by the reverend G. L. Herman, and seconded by S. Steele, esq., justice of the peace, and carried unanimously:

That this meeting expresses its affectionate sympathy with Mrs. Lincoln, the American people and their government, under the sad loss they have sustained by the atrocious murder of the late illustrious President LINCOLN, but at the same time offers its warm congratulations that the crime of a vile assassin has not arrested the progress of the republic towards a complete and full victory over all its opponents, and it most earnestly rejoices in prospect of the speedy restoration of the Union and the complete destruction of negro slavery.

Signed on behalf of the meeting:

HENRY EVEREST,
Chairman.

Resolutions passed at a meeting held at West Cramlington, Northumberland, Saturday, May 20, 1865.

That this meeting desires to convey to Mrs. Licnoln, President Johnson, Mr. Seward, and the people of the United States, the expression of its utter abhorrence of the assassination of President LINCOLN, its condolence for the loss sustained, and its heartfelt hope that peace and freedom may bless forever the land of promise in the west.

That the Hon. Charles Francis Adams, United States ambassador in London, be respectfully requested to transmit to Mrs. Lincoln, President Johnson, and the Hon. William H. Seward, copies of the foregoing resolutions.

Excerpt from minutes of meeting of the town council of the royal burgh of Crail, in the county of Fife, Scotland, dated eighth day of May, eighteen hundred and sixty-five.

Inter alia, the council expressed their detestation and abhorrence of the atrocious assassination of the President of the United States and the attempts to assassinate the Secretary, and also their sympathy with the American government and people under the calamity which has befallen them; and the provost was requested to communicate this expression of the feelings of the council in the proper quarter.

Extracted from the minutes by—

MAT. F. CONOLLY, Clerk.

At a quarterly meeting of the council of the city of Chester, held the third day of May, 1865, it was moved by the right worshipful the mayor, Robert Frost, esquire, seconded by Mr. Councillor Henry Ford, and

Resolved unanimously, That this council desires, before proceeding to the business of the day, to express its horror and indignation at the assassination of President LINCOLN, and at the atrocious attempt made on the life of the Hon. William H. Seward, and to convey to Mrs. Lincoln and the people of the United States its deep sympathy and condolence with them in their bereavement.

It was moved by the right worshipful the mayor, Robert Frost, esquire, seconded by Mr. Alderman John Trevor, and

Resolved unanimously, That copies of the foregoing resolution, under the common seal of the city, be forwarded to the United States minister, in London, for transmission to his Excellency the President of the United States, Mrs. Lincoln, and the Hon. William H Seward.

Given under the common seal of the city of Chester, this fifth day of May, one thousand eight hundred and sixty-five.

[SEAL.] R. FROST, Mayor.

To his Excellency the Minister of the United States of America:

Sir: We, the mayor, aldermen, and councillors of the borough of Chippenham, in the county of Wilts, in council assembled, beg to join our fellow-countrymen in expressing our profound indignation and sorrow at the assassination of the President of the United States.

At any moment and under any circumstances the English nation would have been filled with horror on hearing that a powerful ruler, trusted and beloved by millions, had been struck down by the hand of violence; but that this act of odious wickedness has been committed now, when Mr. Lincoln's life was so precious to himself, to his country, and to the world, is an event far more than commonly distressing.

We feel anxious, sir, to assure you, not only of our earnest and heartfelt sympathy, but that every sentiment of wisdom and gentleness, conciliation and peace, uttered by your late lamented President, will be deeply treasured in England, and will not fail to secure our affectionate gratitude. And while we mourn with all and for all who suffer from the event, especially for her to whom he was bound by the tenderest ties, we yet trust that even this awful bereavement will be overruled for good—that your statesmen and warriors may be filled with stronger desire and with greater power to overcome the difficulties in the way of peace; and, not least, that between America and England there will always be the harmony and the confidence so natural in their near relationship, and so essential to their mutual prosperity.

Signed on behalf of the town council of the borough of Chippenham:

[SEAL.]   JOHN WILSON, M. A, *Mayor.*

Chippenham, Wilts, *May* 9, 1865.

At a quarterly meeting of the mayor, aldermen, and common councillors of the borough of Cardigan, held the 9th day of May, 1865, it was—

Resolved unanimously, That we, the mayor, aldermen, and councillors of the borough of Cardigan, in council assembled, desire to give expression to the feelings of horror and indignation with which we have heard of the atrocious assassination of President Lincoln and the murderous attack upon Mr. Secretary Seward and his sons, and beg to convey to Mrs. Lincoln and the American people an expression of our profound sympathy and heartfelt condolence at the irreparable loss which they have sustained.

Signed in behalf of the members of the corporation of Cardigan by—

RICH. W. JENKINS, *Mayor.*

That the corporation of Carnarvon desires to record its detestation of the atrocious crime perpetrated by the cruel murder of the President of America, and to express its ·deep sympathy with the people who have been suddenly deprived of their Chief Magistrate by the hand of a cowardly assassin.

That copies of this resolution, signed by the mayor, be forwarded to his excellency the American minister.

[SEAL.]   **LLEWELYN TURNER,** *Mayor.*

CITY AND BOROUGH OF CANTERBURY AND COUNTY OF THE SAME,
April 27, 1865.

At a special meeting of the council held at the Guildhall, on Thursday, the 27th day of April, 1865, present the mayor in the chair, the following resolution was unanimously adopted by acclamation:

We, the mayor, aldermen, and councillors of the metropolitical city of Canterbury, have learned with startling surprise and deep regret of the death of the President of the United States by the hand of a cowardly assassin; and we desire to express our sympathy with the American minister in London, and through him with his country at large, at this mournful event which deprives them of their Chief Magistrate, and the world of one of the greatest friends to humanity.

By order:

[SEAL.]   **WILLIAM FLINT,** *Town Clerk.*

Resolution passed at a meeting of the town council of the borough of Cork.

At an assembly of the town council of the borough of Cork, held on Monday, the 1st of May, 1865, the right worshipful Charles J. Cantillon, mayor, in the chair, on motion of Councillor Lyons, seconded by Alderman Casey, it was—

Unanimously resolved, That this council desire to express the deepest regret at the great loss which the people of the United States have sustained by the untimely death of President ABRAHAM LINCOLN; that this council view with feelings of horror the atrocious crime by which the President's life was sacrificed, and desire respectfully to offer to the government and people of the United States the sincerest expression of profound sympathy.

That copies of this resolution, signed by the mayor and countersigned by the town clerk, be sent to the American minister in London, with a request that he will transmit one to the Secretary of State at Washington, and the other to Mrs. Lincoln.

CHARLES J. CANTILLON,
Mayor of Cork.
ANDREW CASEY, Jr., *Town Clerk.*

At a meeting of the town council of the borough of Congleton, in the county of Chester, held on Wednesday, the 3d day of May, 1865, the following resolution was unanimously passed, on motion of the mayor, seconded by Mr. Alderman Hadfield:

That this council hereby expresses its feelings of extreme sorrow and indignation at the dastardly and cruel assassination of President Lincoln, and desires hereby to show its sympathy with our kindred people, who have been so suddenly deprived of the head of their government, at a time so critical and in a manner so atrocious.

BENJ. RADLEY, *Mayor.*
CHRIS. MOORHOUSE, *Town Clerk.*

At a public meeting of the inhabitants of the borough of Congleton, in the county of Chester, held on Wednesday, the 3d day of May, 1865, Benjamin Radley, esq., the mayor of the borough, in the chair, the following resolutions were unanimously passed:

1. That this meeting desires to express its heartfelt sympathy with the government and people of the United States in their present calamity, and its abhorrence of the atrocious crimes by which the late President has been deprived of life and the republic has been bereft of a ruler of patriotic integrity and large-hearted beneficence, and by which his principal minister has almost fallen under a dastardly assassin while lying on the bed of sickness; and that it is the earnest desire of the meeting that these cruel and disastrous events may be overruled by Providence for good in drawing together, in stricter accord than ever before, the sympathies and affections of the great Anglo-Saxon race.

2. That this meeting wishes most respectfully to convey to Mrs. Lincoln and her family the deepest sympathy of the inhabitants of this borough in their affliction, which they trust may be in some degree alleviated by the knowledge that it is shared by the princes and peoples of the whole civilized world, and especially by the Queen and people of this kindred nation.

BENJ. RADLEY, *Chairman*

Resolution passed at a meeting held at Cardiff.

The following resolution was passed unanimously at a public meeting in Cardiff, on the 12th of June, 1865, after a lecture delivered by the Rev. J. B. Balmer, of Bridgewater, on the late President LINCOLN and his assassination :

" That this meeting desires to express its horror and indignation at the assassination of ABRAHAM LINCOLN, the late distinguished President of America, and to assure the bereaved widow and the American people of its deepest sympathy with them in this hour of great trial. It would further express the ardent prayer that America may yet come out of this struggle trusting in God, who has hitherto been its helper, and that, guided by Him, it may be led to permanent peace, great prosperity, and entire national freedom "

APRIL 29, 1865.

We, the undersigned, the merchants, brokers, and others at this port, beg to convey to you our sympathy, indignation, and horror at the assassination of Mr. LINCOLN, the President of the United States. We feel that his loss will be deplored not only by the British nation, but throughout the civilized world, and we sincerely trust and believe that the great nation you represent will be able to bear with dignity, and that its future progress will in no way be impeded by, the great and irreparable loss it has sustained.

JOHN PRIDE, *Mayor.*

WILLIAM ALEXANDER,
Alderman and Justice of the Peace.

D. HOWELL,
Treasurer of St. John's, Cardiff.

SAMUEL NASH.

SYDNEY D. JENKINS.

THOS. HODGE.

JOHN WILLIAMS.

JOSEPH ELLIOTT.

J. H. WILSON.

AND SOME FIFTY OTHERS.

CHARLES EDWARD BURCH,
Consul for the United States of America at Cardiff.

Resolution passed at a meeting held by the council of the city of Coventry.

At a meeting of the council of the city of Coventry held at the justice room, St. Mary's Hall, in the said city, on Tuesday, the 9th day of May, 1865, Robert Harvey Minster, esq., mayor, presiding, it was—

Resolved unanimously, That this council, on this first occasion of its meeting since the receipt of the intelligence from America of the deplorable assassination of President LINCOLN, desires to express its cordial sympathy with the government and people of the United States of America under that great calamity, and its horror at the detestable crime.

That this council also desires to express its feelings of deep and respectful sympathy with Mrs. LINCOLN in her loss of a husband whose rare virtues under the most trying circumstances the civilized world had learned to recognize and admire.

That a copy of the foregoing resolutions, under the common seal, be presented to the American minister in London.

In testimony whereof, the common seal of the said city of Coventry is hereunto affixed this 9th day of May, 1865.

[SEAL.]   R. HARVEY MINSTER,
Mayor of Coventry.

At a public meeting of the citizens of Coventry held at St. Mary's Hall, in the said city, on Thursday, the 4th day of May, 1865, Robert Harvey Minster, esquire, mayor, presiding, it was—

Unanimously resolved, That the citizens of Coventry, in public meeting assembled, do hereby wish to convey to the American people their grief and horror at the atrocious and cowardly assassination of ABRAHAM LINCOLN, their single-minded, kind-hearted, and noble President, and their deep sympathy with the government under the loss of one whose firm, mild, and conciliatory character had worn the respect and admiration of both friends and enemies.

That the mayor be requested to transmit to the American minister the resolution just passed.

R. HARVEY MINSTER,
Mayor of Coventry.

BOROUGH OF CAMBRIDGE.

At a council holden at the Guildhall there on Tuesday, the 2d day of May, 1865, Swann Hurrell, esq., mayor, it was—

Unanimously resolved, That this council takes the earliest opportunity of declaring that it participates in the general feeling of horror and indignation at the murder of the President of the United States of America, and desires to convey to the government and people of that country its sympathy on this sad occasion, and to tender to the afflicted widow an assurance of most respectful and heartfelt condolence.

Ordered, That a copy of the foregoing resolution be transmitted to the honorable Charles Francis Adams, minister of the United States in London.

C. H. COOPER, *Town Clerk.*

The Chancellor of Cambridge to Mr. Adams.

DEVONSHIRE HOUSE, *May* 12, 1865

SIR: It is my agreeable duty, as Chancellor of the University of Cambridge, to transmit to your excellency the enclosed letter, expressing the indignation of the university at the assassination of President LINCOLN, and its sympathy with your countrymen on the loss they have sustained.

I have the honor to be, sir, your excellency's most obedient servant,

DEVONSHIRE.

Address to his excellency the Hon. Charles Francis Adams, minister of the United States of America at the court of her Majesty the Queen of Great Britain and Ireland.

SIR: We, the chancellor, masters, and scholars of the University of Cambridge, desire to assure you, as the representative in this country of the United States of America, that we cordially share those sentiments of indignation and abhorrence which have been called forth throughout England by the intelligence of the assassination of President LINCOLN. Removed, as we are, from the arena of political discussion, we still cannot forbear to say that crimes of this nature are essentially opposed to the interests of peace and civilization. The circumstances of peculiar atrocity which characterized the murder of President LINCOLN must ever stigmatize it as a most foul blot on the history of our times.

We beg leave to request your excellency to make known in some suitable manner to your countrymen this respectful tribute of our sympathy and condolence with them on the great loss which they have sustained.

Given under our common seal, in our senate house at Cambridge, this 11th day of May, in the year of our Lord 1865.

[SEAL.]

BOROUGH OF COLCHESTER.

At a meeting of the council of the said borough, held on the 3d day of May, 1865, the following resolution was unanimously passed:

"That the council of this ancient borough desire to unite with all classes of British subjects in expressing their utter detestation of the atrocious crime by which the United States have been deprived of the life and services of their true-hearted and able President and citizen, ABRAHAM LINCOLN; and the council, on behalf of themselves and of the inhabitants of the borough of Colchester at large, would respectfully offer their most sincere and heartfelt sympathy and condolence to Mrs. Lincoln in her deep personal desolation and sorrow, and also to the whole of the American people and their government under their overwhelming national bereavement."

[SEAL.]

To his Excellency ANDREW JOHNSON, *President of the United States:*

SIR: At a public meeting held in the public hall, Colchester, Essex, England, on Thursday evening, May 4th, 1865, it was—

Resolved, That this meeting has heard with the profoundest regret the sad and mournful news of the assassination of President LINCOLN, a man whose life was of such great value, not only to the American people, but to all free peoples everywhere, and desires to express its sincerest sympathy and condolence with the government and people of the United States in the distressing bereavement they have sustained, and their deep abhorrence of the diabolical deed by which so precious a life has been sacrificed.

It nevertheless desires to express its firm conviction that the work begun and so nobly carried on by ABRAHAM LINCOLN, in connection with slavery, can never be undone, and it trusts that you, his successor, will effect the work, both of the extinction of slavery and the reconstruction of the Union.

That this meeting desires to express its gratitude to Divine Providence that the attempted assassination of Mr. Seward has not been successful, and hopes that he will be spared to render valuable service in the utter extinction of slavery and the complete reconstruction of the Union.

That this meeting desires to express its heartfelt sympathy and condolence with Mrs. Lincoln in the distressing bereavement she has sustained, and also its deep abhorrence of the deed which has so suddenly removed her lamented husband.

Signed, on behalf of the meeting, by the chairman:

THOMAS CATCHPOOL,
Justice of the Peace.

Resolution passed at a meeting held by the council of the city of Carlisle.

At a meeting of the council of the city of Carlisle, held at the Town Hall, on Tuesday the 9th of May, 1865, Thomas Nansom, esq., mayor, in the chair—

Resolved, That this council views with feelings of the utmost horror the atrocious crime by the commission of which the people of the United States of

America have been deprived of their Chief Magistrate, and it desires to tender to the government and people of the said States, and also to the afflicted widow and family of the late President, its sincere sympathy and condolence, under the great calamity which has befallen them and the grievous loss they have sustained.

By order :   JOHN RANCON, *Town Clerk.*

At a meeting called by the mayor of the city of Carlisle, to express sympathy with Mrs. Lincoln and the American people, held in the Athenæum, on Monday, the 15th day of May, 1865, Caleb Hodgson, esq., deputy mayor, in the chair—

Resolved, That this meeting regards with feelings of detestation and horror the assassination of ABRAHAM LINCOLN, President of the United States ; the attempted murder of Mr. Seward, Secretary of State, and of his two sons ; and desires to express its profound sympathy for Mrs. Lincoln, who has been cruelly bereft of a devoted husband, for her children, who have lost an honored father, and for the people of the United States, who have been deprived, at a critical moment of their career, of a wise, humane and noble ruler.

Moved by Robert Ferguson, esq.; seconded by the Dean of Carlisle ; supported by Rev. J. E. Hargraves.

Resolved, That this meeting tenders its best wishes to Andrew Johnson, the new President, and earnestly hopes that, with the blessing of God, he may be enabled to carry out the enlightened policy of his predecessor, and lead the great country over whose destinies he has been unexpectedly called upon to preside, on the way of peace, prosperity and freedom.

Moved by Rev. W. A. Wrigley; seconded by Mr. Cowin; supported by Mr. John Hargraves.

CALEB HODGSON,
Deputy Mayor, Chairman.

Extract from the minutes of the Grand Division of the order of the Sons of Temperance of the province of Canada, (incorporated by act of provincial Parliament,) at its semi-annual session, held at Cobourg, Canada West, on the 29th day of June, 1865.

Resolved, That this Grand Division has watched with much interest the struggle just brought to a close and successful issue in the United States, and that although party strife ran high, and the blood of thousands of her noble sons have stained the soil, yet we conceive that one of the mightiest achievements in the world's history has occurred, namely, the liberty of her slaves.

And while we rejoice at the general results to this end, we feel that we would fail in our duty did we not express the deepest sorrow and commiseration in the calamitous event and death of President LINCOLN, a gentleman in whom we discovered virtues of the highest order, under whose government the most disastrous civil war the world ever witnessed was brought almost to a successful issue, when his valuable life was taken by the hand of an assassin.

Therefore, we, this Grand Division, do deeply sympathize with the executive government and people of the United States in their great loss; but more particularly would we sympathize and condole with Mrs. Lincoln and family in their irreparable loss and bereavement. The nation may lament over and deplore the loss of their much loved President, but the sorrow of Mrs. Lincoln and family under the unhappy occurrence must be such as to demand the condolence of the civilized world.

We furthermore record our unanimous detestation of the merciless villain and associates who either directly or indirectly plotted and carried into execution this abominable act of assassination.

Resolved furthermore, That a copy of this resolution be forwarded to the executive government of the United States at Washington, and to Mrs. Lincoln and the family of the lamented President.

Attest:

[SEAL.]   EDWARD STACY.
                                        Grand Scribe.

The following resolutions were unanimously passed at the semi-annual meeting of the Grand Division Sons of Temperance of Canada East, on the 6th day of July, 1865:

Resolved, That, while rejoicing over the happy termination of the late destructive war, we desire to record our horror and detestation for the assassination of the late President of the United States, and do hereby tender to his bereaved widow and family our profound sympathy in their sorrow.

Resolved, That while we deeply regret the loss of life and treasure occasioned by the late war, we yet rejoice in the conviction that the blood shed and the treasure expended have not been in vain, but, under Providence, have resulted in the overthrow of that sum of all villany, slavery, and the establishment of freedom to a hitherto oppressed race.

Resolved, That we express our earnest hope that the bands of union may be drawn closer than ever, and that, as the result of peace, the blessings of temperance, prosperity, and religion may be universally diffused throughout the United States

[SEAL.]   JOHN S. HALL,
                                        Grand Scribe.

Resolutions passed at a meeting held by the municipal commissioners of Cape Town, Wednesday, June 7, 1865.

Unanimously resolved, That this board desire to convey to Walter Graham, esq., United States consul residing in this city, an expression of the deep sorrow which the painful intelligence from Washington has inspired, of profound sympathy with the great people who have lost their Chief Magistrate, and abhorrence of the dastardly acts which deprived President LINCOLN of life, and imperilled the lives of other high officers of state.

Further resolved, That a deputation, consisting of the chairman and vice-chairman of the board, be appointed to wait upon Mr. Graham and present him with a copy of the foregoing resolution.

Resolution passed at a meeting held by the Chamber of Commerce of Cape Town.

CHAMBER OF COMMERCE, EXCHANGE BUILDINGS,
June 13, 1865.

SIR: I have the honor to forward the following resolution, passed at a special meeting of the Chamber of Commerce of this city, held this day, and to request that you will be good enough to convey the terms thereof to your government by the out-going mail:

"The Chamber of Commerce of Cape Town desire to convey to Walter Graham, esq., consul for the United States in this colony, the profound regret with which they have heard of the assassination of ABRAHAM LINCOLN, esq., President of the United States, and beg to offer their sincere condolence on the sad calamity, and to express their deep detestation of the atrocious nature of the crime which has so suddenly deprived the American nation of its ruler."

I have the honor to be, sir, your most obedient servant,

THOMAS WATSON,
Vice-President.

WALTER GRAHAM, Esq.,
United States Consul, Cape of Good Hope.

To his Excellency C. F. Adams, American minister in London:

The memorial and address of the provost, magistrates, and town council of Cupar, Fife, in Scotland, showeth that your memorialists, forming the corporation of Cupar, the head burgh of the county town of Fife, in common with the entire body of their fellow-citizens, and of the people generally throughout the British nation, desire to express, as they hereby do, their utter abhorrence of the atrocious crime by which the United States of America have been so suddenly and cruelly deprived of so able and upright and (especially to the British nation) so friendly a Chief Magistrate and President as the late President LINCOLN, and their sincere sympathy with the government and people of that great country on so sad and trying an occasion.

Signed, in name and by appointment of the memorialists, by

WILLIAM CAGAN,

Provost of Cupar, Fife.

CUPAR, FIFE, *May* 4.

Address of the commissioners of supply of the county of Fife, Scotland.

CUPAR, FIFE, *May* 1, 1865.

SIR: We, the commissioners of supply of the county of Fife, Scotland, in annual general meeting assembled, desire very respectfully to convey, through your excellency, to the government and people of the United States of America, the horror, indignation, and sorrow with which we have heard of the atrocious acts of assassination of which the city of Washington has recently been the scene, and particularly our grief at the lamented death of President LINCOLN, by the hands of an assassin.

In the extremely painful and trying circumstances into which the government and people of the United States have, by such a sudden and unexpected calamity, been brought, we beg, in common with the people of this country, most warmly to tender them our profound sympathy and regard.

We beg also respectfully to request your excellency to accept, on behalf of Mrs Lincoln and the family of the late lamented President, our heartfelt sympathy for her and them in the midst of their deep sufferings, and to express our earnest prayer that Divine help and consolation may be abundantly granted to them.

We have the honor to be your excellency's most obedient servants.

Signed in name and by appointment of the meeting:

WHYTE MELVILLE,

Convener of the County of Fife.

His Excellency CHARLES FRANCIS ADAMS, Esq.,

    Minister of the United States of America, London.

CAPE COAST CASTLE,
Salt Pond Road, No. 3, *July* 12, 1865.

SIR: I am convinced that you will not refuse to accept the expression of African feeling to which the enclosed letter bears witness, and which I am charged to convey to you in behalf of my countrymen.

I have the honor to be, sir, your obedient servant,

S. M. GOOD.

Hon. WILLIAM H. SEWARD,
Secretary of State.

To Mr. Seward.—Letter from Africa.

CAPE COAST, GOLD COAST OF AFRICA,
July 10, 1865.

SIR: We, the undersigned, representing the natives of this part of Africa, as well as persons of African race resident here, desire to show, by the expression of our sorrow for the death of President LINCOLN and our hearty abhorrence of the manner in which that death was brought about, that we are able to appreciate the benefits that our race has derived from the results of events that have occurred during the administration of that great and good man.

During this administration it has pleased God to bring about the emancipation of millions of unfortunate persons of our race and color held in bondage. We rejoice in this; we are thankful to Providence; we bless those who achieved such a result, and we hope for better days for Africa.

We beg to assure the American people that all true sons of Africa will mourn for the cruel and untimely fate of President LINCOLN, whose destiny it was to be ruler over your mighty nation at a time when events took place having such immense importance for the children of our country.

We most respectfully and sincerely sympathize with the bereaved widow of the late President, and we cannot sufficiently express our detestation of those cowardly and atrocious attempts which had nearly deprived America of the service of the eminent statesman whom we now have the honor to address, and in whose return to health and strength all Africans are deeply interested, as being essentially necessary to the final accomplishment of that great work which has, under God's providence, been hitherto so successfully carried on.

We are, sir, your obedient servants and well wishers,

JOHN AGGERY,
King of Cape Coast.

QUOW ATTAH,
Chief of Donasie.

CHIEF MAYAN.

SAMUEL WOOD, Sr.,
Interpreter to the Governor.

CHAS. BANNESMAN,
*On behalf of the People of the Eastern Districts of the
Gold Coast of Africa.*

GEORGE SLANKSON.

GEO. SLANKSON, Jr.,
On behalf of the People of Anamaboe District.

KOFFEE AFFADIE,
King of Anamaboe.

HENRY ARQUAH,
King of Winnebah.

CHAS. H. GARDNER,
Colonial Schoolmaster of Massachusetts, U. S. of America.

JOSIAH M. ABADOO,
On behalf of the People.

DEAL, KENT, *May* 6, 1865.

SIR: At a meeting of the town council for this borough held on Wednesday, the 3d instant, the resolution hereunder written was unanimously carried, and that the same be presented through your good self to the government of the United States.

I have the honor to be, sir, your obedient servant,

EDWARD DREW, *Town Clerk.*

Hon. C. F. ADAMS, *&c., &c., &c.*

" That this council hereby express their sincere regret at the severe loss which the people of the United States have sustained by the untimely death of President LINCOLN; that they regard with the utmost horror the crime by which the President's life was taken and sacrificed, and that on behalf and in the name of the inhabitants of this borough (Deal) they most respectfully offer the government of the United States their sincere and earnest sympathy under the dreadful calamity that has befallen them."

Hon. CHARLES FRANCIS ADAMS,
United States Minister at the Court of St. James:

SIR : We, the mayor, aldermen, and burgesses of the borough of Dorchester, in the county of Dorset, in council assembled, beg to approach your excellency with an expression of our deepest indignation and horror at the recent murder of the President of the United States of America, and the attempted assassination of Mr. Secretary Seward under circumstances of unheard of atrocity, and we desire through you to offer to Mrs. Lincoln our respectful and heartfelt condolence under her sad and awful bereavement; to Mr. Seward our sincere congratulations at his providential escape; and to him and the American people our genuine sympathy with them at the loss of a ruler of whom Americans were so justly proud.

Given under the common seal of the borough of Dorchester the 2d day of May, 1865.

[SEAL.]   JOHN PETTY ALDRIDGE, *Mayor.*

We, the mayor, aldermen, and burgesses of the borough of Dover, in the county of Kent, in council assembled, desire to record our deep regret at the melancholy and untimely end of the late President of the United States of America, ABRAHAM LINCOLN. We regard with horror and detestation the diabolical crime by which his life was sacrificed to the remorseless weapon of a dastardly assassin, at a time, too, when the position of the great republic over which the President ruled seemed especially to require the guiding hand of one who had become thoroughly acquainted with the circumstances of the nation.

We have marked with much pleasure the profound wisdom, unwearying assiduity, and temperate zeal which have characterized the career of the late President during his term of office, and through all the trying circumstances in which he has been placed; and we have greatly admired the manner in which he has used the successes of his victorious armies for the advancement of the cause of peace.

We beg, therefore, respectfully to offer our most sincere and earnest sympathy to his bereaved and sorrowing widow, to his family, and to the President, government, and people of the United States, under the great calamity which has befallen them.

Given under our corporate seal in our council chamber this 3d day of May, 1865.

[SEAL.]   W. R. MURRAY, *Mayor.*

To his excellency the ambassador of the United States of America at the court of London:

The humble address of the provost, magistrates, and town council of the royal burgh of Dumbarton, in council assembled:

That this council, in common with all classes of their fellow-citizens, have heard with horror and indignation of the foul and execrable murder of the President of the United States of America.

That this council deeply sympathize with the great American republic under the heavy loss which it has sustained by the unexpected and untimely decease, under such revolting circumstances, of a ruler whose personal excellence and high endowments have rendered him an object of honest pride to his own countrymen, and of just admiration to the rest of the world, and whose earnest endeavor to cultivate and maintain friendly relations with Great Britain must ever endear his name and memory to the people of this country.

That this council also deeply sympathize with Mrs. Lincoln and family under their heavy bereavement, and earnestly pray that they may be sustained and supported by Him who is "the husband of the widow and the father of the fatherless."

And this council requests that your excellency will kindly forward these their sentiments to your government.

Signed in name and by authority of the provost, magistrates, and town council of the royal burgh of Dumbarton this 10th day of May, 1865.

JOHN McAUSLAND,
Provost and Chief Magistrate.

Excerpt from the monthly meeting of the town council of the royal burgh of Dumfries, held May 5, 1865.

Before proceeding to business, Provost Turner moved that this council record an expression of the deep regret and sorrow with which they and the whole inhabitants of the burgh have learned of the death, by assassination, of the President of the United States of America; that, in common with the entire community, the council regard with feelings of horror and indignation the cruel and atrocious deed, and desire to express their participation in the feelings of profound sympathy entertained by the people of this country towards the people of the United States under the painful and trying circumstances in which they are placed.

That the council also express their deepest sympathy with Mrs. Lincoln and the family of the late President on account of the severe affliction with which they have been visited.

This motion was seconded by Bailie Newbigging, and unanimously agreed to, and the clerk was directed to send a copy of these resolutions to the American minister in London.

Extracted by—

WM. MARTIN, *Town Clerk.*

COUNCIL CHAMBER, GUILDHALL,
Doncaster, May 9, 1865.

At a public meeting of the mayor, aldermen, and burgesses of the borough of Doncaster, in the West Riding of the county of York, it was proposed by Alderman Shirley, seconded by Councillor Wright, and

Resolved unanimously, That this council desires, in its corporate capacity, to unite in the universal expression of indignation and sorrow at the assassination of the late President of the United States of America, and solemnly to record its horror and detestation of the treasonable and wicked act which has deprived that country of its chief at a time when his services were so important. This council desires, also, in its corporate capacity, to convey to Mrs. Lincoln and her family the expression of its deepest sympathy, and sincerely to condole with them in their heavy bereavement.

[SEAL.] Given under our corporate common seal in council assembled.

Extract from the minutes of a special meeting of the town council of the city of Dunfermline, held on May 4, 1865.

Before proceeding to the transaction of the special business for which the present meeting had been called, the provost took this the earliest opportunity of moving the adoption of the following resolutions, expressing condolence and sympathy with the people of the United States of America on the assassination of President LINCOLN, viz:

Resolved, That this council do record a unanimous expression of the feelings of profound sorrow and indignation with which they and the whole community of the city of Dunfermline have heard of the foul assassination of Presdient LINCOLN of the United States of America, and of the attempted assassination of Mr. Secretary Seward and his son—acts the atrocity of which is scarcely paralleled in the annals of political crime.

That they sincerely sympathize with the government and people of the

United States under this great national calamity, and the peculiar and trying circumstances in which they have been placed by the untimely and unexpected removal of such an able administration; but they earnestly hope that matters may be so ordered by Divine Providence that peace and tranquillity shall soon be restored to the United States, and that the feelings of brotherhood, amity, and good will which it is the earnest desire of this council should ever subsist between that great country and England may be strengthened.

That the council also sympathize most deeply with the widow and family of the late President in their afflicting bereavement.

That a copy of these resolutions be transmitted to his excellency the minister of the United States in London, with a request that he will take the earliest opportunity of communicating the same to his government, and also to Mrs. Lincoln.

Which, being seconded by Bailie Alston, were unanimously adopted.

Extracted from council minutes by—

JOHN LANDALE, *Town Clerk.*

Resolution passed by the mayor, aldermen, and burgesses of the borough of Dewsbury, in council assembled, on the 2d day of May, 1865.

That this-council desires to give expressions to the feelings of horror and indignation with which it has heard of the assassination of President LINCOLN, and the attempt upon the life of Mr. Seward; and it also desires to convey to Mrs. Lincoln and the people of the United States an expression of its heartfelt sympathy and condolence; and that a copy of this resolution be forwarded to the honorable Charles Francis Adams, the American minister, for presentation.

Extracted from the minutes:

CHARLES WALKER, *Town Clerk.*

Resolution passed by the Chamber of Commerce, Dewsbury.

Resolved, That this council expresses its utter abhorrence and detestation of the foul crime which has deprived a kindred nation of its President at such a momentous crisis in its history; and that such expression of the indignation of the council, together with its sympathy, be conveyed to the American consul at Leeds.

The AMERICAN CONSUL, *Leeds.*

DARWEN.

At a public meeting of the inhabitants of Darwen, Lancashire, held on Saturday, April 29, 1865, the following resolutions were passed:

1. That this meeting desire to express the feelings which they, as Englishmen, entertain in regard to the assassination of the late ABRAHAM LINCOLN, President of the United States of America. They profoundly sympathize with the people of those States in the heavy calamity which has befallen them by his sudden and lamented death, while they view with the utmost horror and detestation the atrocious crime which has so cruelly deprived his family, his country, and the world of his valuable life.

2. That copies of the foregoing resolution be sent to the United States minister in London, with a request that he will convey one to his government at Washington, and one to Mrs. Lincoln.

RALPH SHORROCK ASHTON,
Justice of the Peace, Chairman.

BOROUGH OF DERBY.

Resolutions passed at a meeting held by the inhabitants of Derby.

At a public meeting convened by the mayor, in the Guildhall, Derby, on Monday, the eighth day of May, 1865, upon the requisition of a large number of the inhabitants, for the purpose of expressing indignation at the assassination of ABRAHAM LINCOLN, late President of the United States, and of condolence with his bereaved widow and family, as well as of sympathy with the American people in their present trying position, the following resolutions were passed unanimously—Thomas Roe, esq., mayor, in the chair:

Moved by the Rev. W. F. Wilkinson, M. A., seconded by Herbert Holmes, esq., and supported by Josiah Lewis, esq.:

Resolution 1. That the inhabitants of Derby have heard with horror and indignation of the assassination of ABRAHAM LINCOLN, President of the United States of America, whose genuineness of character, whose desire for peace, and whose faithful discharge of the duties of his high position must endear his memory to all Americans; and whose friendly feelings towards this country will ever be recalled in England with melancholy interest and satisfaction.

Moved by the Rev. E. W. Foley, M. A., seconded by the Rev. J. Merwood, and supported by the Rev. William Griffith:

Resolution 2. That we, the inhabitants of Derby, desire especially to express our deep sympathy with Mrs. Lincoln in the bereavement which this atrocious crime has inflicted upon her, and humbly hope that the veneration of her countrymen, the pitying love of her countrywomen, the respectful commiseration of the whole civilized world, and the remembrance of her husband's great career, in which he was never unmerciful, even to an enemy, may help to sustain her in her sore distress.

Moved by the Rev. John Hyde, seconded by the Rev. William Jones, and supported by Frederick Longdon, esq. :

Resolution 3. That this meeting earnestly hopes that the eminently conciliatory policy of the late President may not be without its due effect upon his countrymen, but may be carried forward by his successor to the speedy re-establishment of peace, and the securing of prosperity to the great American nation.

Moved by the Rev. H. Crassweller, and seconded by the Rev. J. Baxendale :

Resolution 4. That two copies of the resolutions passed at this meeting be made, and that his worship the mayor do forward them to his excellency the American minister in London, with the request that one copy shall be sent to Mrs. Lincoln, and the other to the government of the United States.

THOMAS ROE, *Mayor.*

Moved by John Flewker, esq., and seconded by Benjamin Wilson, esq. .

Resolution 5. That the thanks of this meeting be given to his worship the mayor, for his kind compliance with the request of his fellow-townsmen in granting the use of the Guildhall; also for consenting to preside over the meeting, and for the able and impartial manner in which he has discharged the duties of chairman on this occasion.

JOSEPH JONES,
Honorary Secretary.

Resolutions passed at a meeting held at the Town Hall, Devizes.

At a public meeting held at the Town Hall, Devizes, on Tuesday, the 9th May, 1865, the mayor in the chair—

It was moved by the Rev. S. S. Pugh, seconded by W. Brown, esq., and

Resolved, That this meeting takes the earliest convenient opportunity of following the example of the two houses of Parliament, and of the representative councils of certain larger towns, in expressing a deep-felt sorrow at the assassination of the President of the United States; regarding it as a crime of astounding magnitude, fraught with manifest evil, not only to the great commonwealth with which we have long held friendly relations, but in all its attendant features, especially in the dastardly mode of its consummation, as quite unparalleled in modern times; and that as Englishmen, possessing an instinctive abhorrence of assassination, our sympathies are in the present case peculiarly called forth by the circumstances that the victim of this pitiless murder was one whose honest boast it was that his origin, language, and blood were British, and whose avowed sentiments as towards this country were cordially pacific.

It was moved by R. W. Biggs, esq., LL.D., seconded by S. Wittey, esq., and

Resolved, That we warmly sympathize with the citizens of the United States, who are thus at a critical juncture deprived of their Chief Magistrate, and in an especial manner with Mrs. Lincoln and the other members of the late President's family, on the blow that has so suddenly and appallingly fallen upon them.

It was moved by the Rev. R. Dawson, and

Resolved, That our abhorrence at the attempted assassination of the American Secretary of State and his attendants, in all its atrocious and frightful incidents, is scarcely less than at its fellow outrage; the higher rank of the latter in the scale of crime being derived from its combining treason with foul murder, and that we hereby tender our kindliest sympathies to the honorable Mr. Seward, and the afflicted members of his household.

Moved by Edward Waylen, esq., seconded by the Rev. S. S. Pugh, and

Resolved, That we tender to the citizens of the United States our best wishes for their prosperity and happiness as a nation, sprung from the same stock as ourselves and following the mother country in removing from their midst the dark stain of slavery; while in the enlightened sentiments so promptly and frankly expressed by their present President, Mr. Andrew Johnson, to her Majesty's minister plenipotentiary at Washington, viz., "that the friendship of the United States towards Great Britain is enjoined by every consideration of interest and sentiment," we are pleased to recognize a guarantee of that pacific and mutually advantageous relationship which has for so long a period marked the intercourse of the two countries.

It was proposed by Mr. Hart, seconded by Mr. H. Knight, and

Resolved, That the worshipful the mayor be requested to send a copy of the foregoing resolutions to Mr. Adams, to be forwarded to his government and to Mrs Lincoln.

Resolutions of the inhabitants of Darlington.

At a meeting held in the Central Hall, Darlington, on the 2d of May, 1865, and at which a large number of the inhabitants of the town were present, the Rev Henry Kendall in the chair—

It was moved by John Forster Clapham, esq., seconded by John Henry Backhouse, esq., and

Unanimously resolved, That this meeting express to the President and people of the United States of America its horror and detestation of the crime by which the late illustrious President LINCOLN has been deprived of life; and earnestly prays that this awful event may strengthen their determination to uproot and utterly destroy the slave institution, and to reconstruct and consolidate their union upon the basis of free labor and political liberty.

It was moved by Henry Fell Pease, esq., seconded by William Fothergill, esq., and

Unanimously resolved, That this meeting respectfully and affectionately offers to the honorable Mrs. Lincoln its profound sympathy under her terrible affliction, and prays God to cover her with the mantle of His love, and to console her by His all-prevailing grace.

HENRY KENDALL, Chairman.

DARLINGTON, May 12, 1865.

The following resolutions were passed at a meeting of the 15th Durham rifle volunteers on the above date:

At a special parade of the 15th Durham rifle volunteers (Darlington) it was unanimously resolved—

1st. That the officers and members have heard with horror and regret of the foul murder which has been perpetrated on Mr. LINCOLN, the President of the United States, and they beg leave to tender their sympathies to Mrs. Lincoln and the people of the United States.

2d. That Lieutenant Colonel Scurfield be requested to forward this expression of the feelings of the 15th Durham rifle volunteers to Mr. Adams, the representative of the United States of America in London.

GEORGE JOHN SCURFIELD,

Lieut. Colonel commanding 4th Art. Batt. D. R. V.,

and Captain commanding 15th Durham R. V.

CITY HALL, TOWN CLERK'S OFFICE,

Dublin, May 13, 1865.

SIR: I have the honor to transmit to you the accompanying resolutions unanimously adopted by the municipal council of this city, and to request that you will submit the same to the President and Congress of the United States at your earliest convenience.

I have the honor to remain, sir, your obedient servant,

W. J. HENRY, Town Clerk.

SECRETARY OF STATE, *Washington.*

At a meeting of the municipal council of the city of Dublin, held in the council chamber, City Hall, Cork Hill, on Monday, the 1st day of May, 1865—the right honorable the lord mayor in the chair—

It was moved by Alderman Atkinson, justice of the peace, seconded by Alderman Carroll, and

Unanimously resolved, That we regard with abhorrence the dreadful deed which has deprived the people of the United States of their Chief Magistrate.

Moved by Councillor Devitt, seconded by Councillor Byrne, and

Unanimously resolved, That we tender to the government of the United States our profound sympathy with them under so great and terrible a calamity as the loss of their President.

Moved by Councillor Sullivan, seconded by Alderman Durdin, and

Unanimously resolved, That while we abstain from the expression of any opinion whatever upon the fratricidal strife in which the States of America are unfortunately engaged, we desire to offer the tribute of our sincere respect for and appreciation of the character of the lamented deceased, President LINCOLN.

[SEAL.]   JOHN BARRINGTON, *Lord Mayor.*
                            W. J. HENRY, *Town Clerk.*

CITY HALL, TOWN CLERK'S OFFICE,
Dublin, May 13, 1865.

MADAM : I have the honor to transmit to you herewith a resolution unanimously adopted by the municipal council of the city of Dublin, expressive of their condolence and sympathy in the sad bereavement you have sustained in the loss of your lamented and esteemed husband, the late President LINCOLN.

I have the honor to remain, madam, your obedient servant,

                            W. J. HENRY, *Town Clerk.*
Mrs. LINCOLN, *Washington.*

At a meeting of the municipal council of the city of Dublin, held in the council chamber, City Hall, Cork Hill, on Monday, the 1st day of May, 1865, the right honorable the lord mayor in the chair—

It was moved by Councillor Warren, seconded by Councillor Draper, and

Unanimously resolved, That we offer the expression of our condolence and sympathy to the widow and family of the lamented President LINCOLN, in their sad bereavement.

[SEAL.]   JOHN BARRINGTON, *Lord Mayor.*
                            W. J. HENRY, *Town Clerk.*

35 MOLESWORTH STREET, *April* 28, 1865.

To the Right Honorable the Lord Mayor:

We, the undersigned, citizens of Dublin, request your lordship to convene a public meeting, at your very earliest convenience, to express our indignation and sorrow at the assassination of President LINCOLN, and our sympathy with the people of the United States.

The above was signed by Joseph Wilson, D. L., and 426 other names and firms.

MANSION HOUSE, *April* 28, 1865.

In compliance with the above influentially-signed request I hereby convene a meeting of the citizens of Dublin, to be held in Oak Room, Mansion House, on to-morrow, Saturday, April 29, at 2 o'clock.

JOHN BARRINGTON, *Lord Mayor.*

DUBLIN, *April* 29, 1865.

At a meeting of the citizens of Dublin, convened and presided over by the right honorable the lord mayor, in pursuance of a requisition signed by a large number of the citizens of Dublin, and held at the Mansion House on Saturday, the 29th of April, 1865, for the purpose of expressing their indignation and sorrow at the assassination of President LINCOLN, and their sympathy with the people of the United States, the following resolutions were unanimously agreed to:

It was proposed by the right honorable the attorney general for Ireland, seconded by the right honorable Joseph Napier, ex-lord chancellor of Ireland, and

Resolved, That we, the citizens of Dublin, view the atrocious assassination of his Excellency ABRAHAM LINCOLN, President of the United States, and the attack on the life of the Hon. William Henry Seward, Secretary of State, with feelings of indignation and sincere sorrow. We feel assured that throughout the civilized world there can be but the one sentiment of horror at so revolting a crime, and, in common with the rest of our fellow-countrymen, we desire to express our deep sympathy with the people of the United States under this great national calamity.

It was proposed by Alexander Parker, esq., J. P., seconded by Professor John Elliot Cairns, and

Resolved, That while we scarcely venture to hope that any words of ours can avail to alleviate grief so profound, yet we cannot forbear expressing our heartfelt condolence with the widow and family of the late President, and our trust that they may be sustained by a merciful Providence under their sad and awful bereavement.

It was proposed by Sir Robert Kane, seconded by Alderman J. B. Dillon, and

Resolved, That the foregoing resolutions be signed by the right honorable the lord mayor and the secretaries of this meeting, on behalf of the citizens of Dublin, and that they be this day forwarded to Washington for presentation, and that copies of the same be sent to the United States minister in London, informing him that we have sent them direct in order to go forward by the present mail.

The right honorable the lord mayor having left the chair, and the Earl of Howth being called thereto,

It was moved by the archdeacon of Dublin, seconded by A. M. Sullivan, J. C., and supported by the Rev. Dr. Urwick—

That the marked thanks of this meeting are due and hereby given to the right honorable the lord mayor for his dignified conduct in the chair

[SEAL.]   JOHN BARRINGTON,
Lord Mayor of City of Dublin.
THOMAS PIM, JR.,
ALFRED WEBB,
Secretaries.

Resolutions passed at a meeting of the democratic classes of Dublin.

At a meeting of the democratic classes of Dublin, held in the Mechanics' Institute, on Friday evening, the 28th day of April, 1865, it was, by a large and enthusiastic meeting, unanimously resolved—

1. That the scheme of assassination concocted by a gang of dastardly conspirators in the name of the southern cause, and partially carried into execution on the evening of the 14th instant by the treacherous murder of ABRAHAM LINCOLN, America's best and greatest President since the days of Washington, excites our horror and indignation, and calls aloud for the execration of mankind.

2. That, while expressing our abhorrence of the foul deed by which the cause of human liberty has lost one of its purest and best defenders, we confidently cherish the belief that the perpetration of a crime so horrible can have no other effect than to hasten the completion of LINCOLN's glorious work, the restoration of the Union, the extinction of slavery, and the establishment of a solid and durable peace.

[SEAL.]   ISAAC S VARIAN, *Chairman.*
WILLIAM M. STACK, *Secretary.*

MAY 4, 1865.

At the regular monthly meeting of the Grand Lodge of Ireland, held at Freemasons' Hall, Dublin, on Thursday, 4th of May, 1865, the following address was unanimously adopted:

The Grand Lodge of Freemasons of Ireland desire to convey to the government of the United States of America the unanimous feeling of execration and horror with which they have learnt the assassination of the late President LINCOLN, and they beg to convey to the citizens of that great republic the sentiment of their sincere condolence on this most deplorable occurrence, as well as to the bereaved widow and family of the departed statesman the expression of their heartfelt sympathy for the grievous loss they have sustained.

[SEAL] LEINSTER, *Grand Master.*

CHARLES WALMISLEY, *Deputy Grand Secretary.*

---

8 LOWER ABBEY STREET, DUBLIN, *May* 13, 1865.

May it please your excellency, I have the honor to enclose to your excellency a copy of the resolution of sympathy adopted at our late district meeting, and acquiesced in by the Wesleyan church in this country.

Humbly praying that "He by whom kings reign and princes decree justice" may be your excellency's refuge and strength and bless your great country with peace and prosperity,

I have the honor to be your excellency's most obedient servant,

ROBERT G. JONES.

His Excellency the PRESIDENT OF THE UNITED STATES,
Washington.

P. S.—Enclosed is also the chairman's letter to your excellency

---

94 STEPHEN'S GREEN, DUBLIN, *May* 10, 1865.

SIR: I have the honor to transmit to you the accompanying resolutions, passed at a meeting of the Wesleyan ministers and stewards of the Dublin district, and concurred in by the other districts in Ireland, which met at the same time.

I have the honor to be your excellency's very obedient servant,

ROBERT WALLACE,
Wesleyan Minister.

His Excellency the PRESIDENT OF THE UNITED STATES.

Resolutions passed at the annual meeting of the Wesleyan ministers and stewards of the Dublin district.

It was moved by the Rev. Robinson Scott, D. D., and seconded by John Jamison, esq., steward of the Dublin Centenary Chapel circuit, supported by the Rev. John F. Mathews, ex-secretary of the Irish conference, and passed unanimously:

1st. *Resolved,* That we avail ourselves of this opportunity to express our utmost abhorrence of the atrocious and diabolical assassination of his Excellency ABRAHAM LINCOLN, late President of the United States, and of the cowardly and wicked attempt upon the life of the honorable William H. Seward, Secretary of State. That we deeply sympathize with the President, Congress, and the people of America in the dire calamity by which, in a manner that scandalizes all civilized nations, they have been deprived of the great ability of him who, under God, succeeded in guiding the republic through a period of unprecedented difficulty in such a manner as to secure the admiration of the world.

That we fervently pray not only that peace may be speedily and completely restored, but that the noble aims of the late and present President, and the illustrious statesmen by whom they have been surrounded, may be fully realized in the utter extinction of the last vestige of slavery, without impairing the ability of the country to fulfil her high mission among the nations of the earth.

And that along with this prayer, we shall offer our fervent supplication on behalf of Mrs. Lincoln and family, who have sustained such sudden and irreparable loss.

Moved by the Rev. Thomas T. N. Hull, seconded by Samuel McComas, esq., steward of the Dublin Abbey Street circuit, and supported by the Rev. Gibson McMillen, secretary of the Hibernian Wesleyan Missionary Society, and passed unanimously:

2d. *Resolved,* That a copy of the foregoing resolutions be engrossed and transmitted, as speedily as possible, to his Excellency the President of the United States.

Signed on behalf and by order of the meeting:

ROBERT WALLACE, *Chairman.*

ROBERT G. JONES, *Secretary.*

CENTENARY CHAPEL, *Dublin, May* 2, 1865.

We, the ministers and stewards of the Waterford district, concur in the above resolution.

Signed by order:

HENRY J. GILES, *Chairman.*

ROBT. HUSTON, *Secretary.*

Signed on behalf and by order of the Londonderry district:

HUGH MOORE, *Chairman.*

JOHN OLIVER, *Secretary.*

Signed on behalf and by order of the Belfast district:

HENRY PRICE, *Chairman.*

WILLIAM CATHER, *Secretary.*

Signed on behalf and by order of the Portadown district:

WILLIAM P. APPLBE, LL.D., *Chairman.*

JOHN GILCHRIST, *Secretary.*

Signed on behalf and by order of the Enniskillen district:

THOMAS MEREDITH, *Chairman.*

EDW'D M. BANKS, *Secretary.*

His Excellency the PRESIDENT OF THE UNITED STATES,

Washington.

Excerpt from minutes of meeting of the magistrates and town council of Dundee, held on the 28th day of April, 1865.

ASSASSINATION OF THE PRESIDENT OF THE UNITED STATES OF NORTH AMERICA.

To his excellency the ambassador to the court of Great Britain for the United States of America:

The provost called the attention of the council to the intelligence recently received of the assassination of the President of the United States of North America, and of the attempt to murder Mr. Seward.

On the motion of the provost, seconded by Bailie Ower, the council unanimously resolved—

1. That the provost, magistrates, and town council have heard of the horrible acts of assassination in the city of Washington with sorrow and indignation, and unite in desiring humbly and respectfully, but in the kindest spirit, to represent to the government of the United States of America, and the whole people, their sincere sympathy, and the sympathy of every class of the people of this town, young and old, rich and poor, in feelings of abhorrence towards the miserable actors and their adherents, wherever and whomsoever they be.

2. When such events happen the good part of human nature asserts its sway. The people of the United States are part of ourselves, sharers with us in a common ancestry; cross interests, and chance events, and the evil part of our nature may create temporary estrangement and distrust, but when trouble comes we are all one—brethren in origin and in progress; and it is in this spirit we seek to approach the people of North America, in sincere affection and good will and sympathy.

3. That the provost do transmit, in the name of the magistrate and council and whole people of Dundee, and under the seal of the burgh, to the representative of the United States in Britain, through the United States consul in this town, an official declaration of these feelings of sympathy and love entertained by this large community towards our brethren in North America, in this the hour of their affliction.

4. That the provost do cause a special communication to be made to his excellency the ambassador of the desire of the council to tender, in the way which the ambassador shall consider to be best suited to the circumstances, to Mrs. Lincoln, the widow of the President, the respectful sympathy of this corporation and community, and their earnest prayer that the Almighty will be pleased to lighten her affliction in the way accordant with His infinite goodness and mercy.

5. That there be a like communication to Mr. Seward.

Extracted from the records of the magistrates and town council of Dundee.

[SEAL.] CHAS. OWEN, *Town Clerk.*

DUNDEE, COUNCIL CHAMBER, *May* 12, 1865.

To his excellency the ambassador to the court of Great Britain for the United States of America:

At a public meeting of the magistrates, merchants, bankers, manufacturers, and other inhabitants of the royal burgh of Dundee, in Scotland, held in the Town Hall, on Tuesday, the 2d day of May, in the year 1865, called by due public notice, the provost of the burgh in the chair, it was moved and resolved, without a dissenting voice, as follows:

That the meeting unite in declaring the profound sorrow and indignation with which they have heard of the atrocious assassination of President LINCOLN, and of the attempted assassination of Mr. Seward and his son; further, they desire to express their sincere respect for Mr. LINCOLN'S personal character, and in particular their admiration of the forbearance and moderation which he evinced in the hour of success; and they would respectfully express their deep sympathy with the American people and with the afflicted families of the sufferers.

It was then moved and

Unanimously resolved, That a copy of the foregoing resolution be transmitted to the United States embassy in London, through their consul in Dundee.

Signed in the name and by appointment of the meeting:

CHARLES PARKER,
Provost and Chief Magistrate of the Royal Burgh of Dundee.

Meeting of American citizens in Dundee.

At a meeting of American citizens held at the United States consulate, Dundee, on the 3d of May, 1865, Dr. Smith, consul at Dundee, having been called to the chair, spoke as follows :

The object of our present meeting, as you are aware, is to express our sorrow at the appalling calamity which has befallen our people and nation in the sudden removal, by cowardly assassination, of our excellent and beloved Chief Magistrate, and at a time when that great and good man had, under God, by his fortitude, consistency, prudence, and sagacity, brought the nation safely and triumphantly through one of the most dreadful conflicts ever witnessed upon the earth; also to express our detestation and abhorrence of the conduct of those who devised, and the tools who carried into effect, but too successfully in the case of our beloved President, the diabolical purpose, while we trust the attempt upon the worthy Secretary of State, and his son Frederick, has proved abortive.   Another object we have in view is to convey to the bereaved widow and orphans our sentiments of deep sympathy and condolence under the heavy affliction which God, in His inscrutable wisdom, has permitted to befall them ; also, to convey to Secretary Seward and his family our sentiments of sorrow and sympathy with them under the great calamity which has befallen them, and to express our earnest desire that they may be restored to health, and their lives be long spared as a blessing to our beloved nation.   In the circumstances, it will be also becoming to express our high confidence in the ability and integrity of our present Chief Magistrate, Andrew Johnson, whose antecedents are our guarantee for the future, and our assurance that, by his energetic, judicious, and Christian course, he will live down the vile slanders heaped upon him by the enemies of our great republic.

Mr. Mackenzie having been chosen secretary, the following resolutions were unanimously adopted :

"1. Whereas we have heard with ˙deep and heartfelt sorrow, and at the same time with a just indignation, of the cowardly and brutal assassination of our excellent and illustrious President, ABRAHAM LINCOLN, and of the dastardly attempt on the lives of Secretary and Assistant Secretary Seward, &c., we hereby tender to our sorrowing countrymen and fellow-citizens our heartfelt sympathy, and would desire to mingle our tears with theirs over the grave of the best and greatest citizen of our country, whose death at this critical period of our nation's history we feel to be a most fearful calamity.   We mourn with them the loss of the sagacious statesman, the true patriot, and the pious Christian, whose name and fame will be a sweet savor in the memory of his countrymen in the ages to come.

" 2. That we deeply sympathize with Mrs. Lincoln and her afflicted family in the heavy blow which has so unexpectedly deprived them of the kind husband

and the fond and affectionate father. and trust that He who has heretofore by His heavenly grace sustained her in previous trials will continue to support her in this her greatest sorrow; and that the affectionate remembrances of a great nation for him who died a martyr's death for the cause of liberty and justice may prove a solace to her in her widowhood.

"3. That while we deeply sympathize with Mr. Seward and his family in their heavy affliction, we congratulate the nation that the life of him whose wise councils and prudent action have done so much for his country at home and abroad is likely to be yet spared; and we would fervently pray that his invaluable services may long be continued to guide his country in her path of progress and civilization.

"4. That we trust speedy and condign punishment may soon overtake the villanous and cowardly wretches that devised, planned, and carried out these nefarious and diabolical deeds, from which universal humanity has recoiled with horror.

"5. That we have perfect confidence in the integrity and ability of our present Chief Magistrate, Andrew Johnson, believing that his antecedents are sufficient guarantee of his energy, wisdom, and prudence in the future, and that under his leadership the nation may soon arrive at a righteous and lasting peace.

"6. That a copy of these resolutions be forwarded through our minister, Mr. Adams, signed by the chairman and secretary of this meeting."

The meeting then terminated.

JAS. SMITH, *Chairman.*

JAMES M. MACKENZIE, *Secretary.*

At the annual meeting of the Welsh Baptist Association, in the county of Glamorgan, South Wales, assembled in Dowlais, in the borough of Merthyr Tydfil, on Tuesday and Wednesday, June 20 and 21, 1865, representing 131 separate congregations, 92 ordained ministers, 96 assistant preachers, 15,163 members in full communion, 17,000 hearers not being communicants, 1,990 Sabbath-school teachers, with 14,745 Sunday-school scholars—

Resolved unanimously, That the ministers and the messengers in this conference express their deep and heartfelt sympathy with the bereaved widow and fatherless children of the late lamented ABRAHAM LINCOLN, together with the whole loyal people of the American continent, on the occasion of the tragical death of the able, honest, and upright man who had been twice chosen by his fellow-men to preside over the affairs of the nation. We further view with intense abhorrence the foul manner by which the death of so good a man and so just a ruler was encompassed ; but while we deeply lament the death of

ABRAHAM LINCOLN at so important a moment in the history of America, we beg to express our sincere regard for and unflinching faith in Andrew Johnson, his successor in the presidential chair, believing that his long practical experience, his honesty of purpose, and his firm determination to do what is right and just, will enable him to do more than carry out the great purposes of the late able ruler, and that through the instrumentality of Andrew Johnson, as Chief Magistrate, assisted by the wise and good around him, under the blessing and guidance of the Most High God, we shall again, and soon, see the States of America united, peaceful, happy, and prosperous, the fetters of slavery being forever broken, and all men declared free in name and in fact.

Resolved secondly, That the foregoing resolution be signed by the three officers of the association, in the name and on behalf of this conference, and that the moderator be respectfully requested to forward the same to the Hon. Charles Francis Adams, the American minister in Great Britain, for transmission to Washington, United States of America.

> NATHANIEL THOMAS, *Moderator.*
> PHILIP JOHN, *Treasurer.*
> BENJAMIN EVANS, *Secretary.*

To the President of the United States of America:

SIR: We, the mayor, aldermen, and burgesses of the city of Exeter, in the Kingdom of England, feeling the deepest abhorrence at the atrocious crime which has deprived America of her late President, ABRAHAM LINCOLN, by a cruel murder, desire to express that feeling to the President and people of America, and our sorrow that such a crime should have been perpetrated.

The sentiments which animate the mayor, aldermen, and burgesses of Exeter, influence also the government and people of England generally, and call forth our sympathy with a nation which has suffered such a calamity.

We regret that the murderer should have met his fate otherwise than by the hand of justice.

Given under our common seal at the city of Exeter, the 10th [SEAL.] day of May, in the year of our Lord one thousand eight hundred and sixty-five.

BOROUGH OF EVESHAM, IN THE COUNTY OF WORCESTER.

At a quarterly meeting of the town council of the borough of Evesham, held at the Guildhall, the 3d day of May, 1865, present: Thomas White, esq., mayor; Aldermen Edge, Burlingham, and New; Councillors Martin, Perry, Rodd, Collins, Allard, Bicknell, Field, Hunt, New, and Smith.

Proposed by Mr. Mayor, seconded by Mr. Alderman Burlingham, and carried unanimously : That the mayor, aldermen, and councillors of this borough share the public sorrow and indignation of this country at the assassination of the President of the United States, and desire that an expression of their feelings should be conveyed to the government and people of the United States, and an assurance of sympathy to the family of the late President; and that our town clerk do cause a copy of this resolution to be engrossed and forwarded to the minister of the United States in London.

THOMAS WHITE, *Mayor.*

Resolutions passed at a meeting held by the provost, magistrates, and council of Edinburgh.

At Edinburgh, the second day of May, in the year eighteen hundred and sixty-five, which day the right honorable the lord provost, magistrates, and council of the city of Edinburgh being in special meeting assembled, on motion of the lord provost, it was unanimously

Resolved, That this council do record an expression of the sorrow with which they and the entire community of the city of Edinburgh have learned of the assassination of President LINCOLN—an act the foul atrocity of which has excited the horror and indignation of the whole civilized world. That, warmly participating in the feeling of profound sympathy entertained by the people of this country towards the people of the United States of America, under the circumstances of unprecedented trial and difficulty in which they are placed, the council desire very respectfully to offer them the expression of that sympathy, the spontaneity and universality of which the council trust will be accepted by the great people to whom it is addressed as the best evidence of the existence in this country of that feeling of brotherhood which should ever hallow the relations between the two great branches of the same race. That the council also sympathize most deeply with Mrs. Lincoln and the family of the late President, and earnestly pray that the terrible event which has caused them so much suffering may, in the hands of Him who in His inscrutable providence often " causes the wrath of man to praise Him," be so ordered as to facilitate the re-establishment of peace and order in the United States, and to strengthen feelings of amity and good will towards them all over the world.

Resolved, That a copy of these resolutions be transmitted to his excellency the minister of the United States, with a request that he will take the earliest opportunity of communicating them to his government, and to the widow of the late President.

Extracted from the council record upon this and the two preceding pages by—

[SEAL.]   J. D. WARWICK, *City Clerk.*

EDINBURGH, *May* 3, 1865.

MADAM : When the sad intelligence of the death of your great and beloved husband reached this city, a large and influential meeting of the inhabitants was held, at which I had the honor of presiding, to express the great and universal sympathy with yourself and the people of America which pervaded the whole community here.

One of the resolutions adopted by the meeting was thus expressed : " That an address prepared in accordance with these resolutions be transmitted by the lord provost of Edinburgh to the American minister in London, and that his lordship be also requested specially to transmit, along with the expression of the warmest sympathy of the inhabitants of Edinburgh, a copy of the foregoing resolutions to Mrs. Lincoln."

On the part of the inhabitants of this city, therefore, I have now the honor to transmit to you a copy of the resolutions referred to, and to convey to you an expression of the deep and universal sympathy which is felt for you in the sudden and heartrending trial which Providence has lately permitted to overwhelm you, your family, and the people of the United States of America.

Your late husband, the President of the United States, was as much respected and admired here as he was beloved in his home and his country, and if, in such a severe affliction as yours has been, it is any consolation to possess heartfelt and widely spread sympathy, this consolation must be yours in great abundance, and from none more sincerely or warmly than from the people of the city of Edinburgh.

I have the honor to be, madam, your most obedient, humble servant,

CHARLES LAWSON,
Lord Provost and Chief Magistrate of Edinburgh.

Copy of resolutions unanimously adopted by public meeting of the inhabitants of the city of Edinburgh, held Wednesday, 3d May, 1865, the Right Honorable Charles Lawson, lord provost of the city of Edinburgh, in the chair.

1. Moved by John Thomson Gordon, esq., sheriff of the county of Edinburgh, seconded by Duncan McLaren, esq., chairman of the Chamber of Commerce—

That the inhabitants of Edinburgh have learned with the deepest sorrow and indignation of the assassination of the President of the United States of America.

2. Moved by the Very Reverend Doctor Candlish, principal of the Free Church College at Edinburgh, seconded by Sir John McNeills, G. C. B.—

That the inhabitants of Edinburgh desire to express their most sincere sympathy with the government and people of the United States under their terrible national calamity.

3. Moved by the Right Reverend Doctor Merrill, bishop coadjutor, seconded by the Reverend William Arnot, one of the ministers of Free Church, Edinburgh—

That the inhabitants of Edinburgh having heard with similar feelings of the infamous attempt on the life of Mr. Seward, Secretary of State, warmly congratulate the people of the United States on the failure of that attempt, and pray that his life may long be spared for the benefit of his country.

4. Moved by James Y. Simpson, esq., M. D, one of the professors of the University of Edinburgh, seconded by the Reverend W. H. Gray, one of the ministers of Edinburgh—

That an address prepared in accordance with these resolutions be transmitted by the lord provost of Edinburgh to the American minister in London, and that his lordship be also requested specially to transmit along with the expression of the warmest sympathies of the inhabitants of Edinburgh a copy of the foregoing resolutions to Mrs. Lincoln.

5. Moved by James Richardson, esq., seconded by Admiral Sir William Hope Johnston, K. C. B.—

That a vote of thanks be given to the lord provost for calling the meeting and for his conduct in the chair.

EDINBURGH, *May* 3, 1865.,

At a special meeting of the Edinburgh Chamber of Commerce and Manufactures held this day, it was moved by James Richardson, esq., merchant, seconded by George Harrison, esq., merchant, both of Edinburgh, and unanimously adopted—

That this chamber have learned with the deepest grief and indignation of the assassination of President LINCOLN and of the attempt on the life of Secretary Seward, and desire to record their admiration of the ability, honesty, and patriotism of the late President, and their warmest sympathy with the government and people of the United States on account of the sad affliction under which they are now suffering.

It was moved by William Law, esq., merchant, and seconded by Josiah Livingston, esq., merchant, both of Edinburgh, and unanimously adopted—

That an address in accordance with the above resolution be forwarded to the government of the United States through their ambassador.

JAMES GREIG, *Secretary.*

At the monthly meeting of the Edinburgh Ladies' Emancipation Society, held on Thursday, May 4, 1865, the following minute was adopted and recorded:

It is with sentiments of profound grief and indignation that we have received the tidings of the death, by the hand of an assassin, of ABRAHAM LINCOLN, the noble President of the United States.

We desire to record an expression of our sympathy with Mrs. Lincoln and the American people in the terrible calamity they have sustained. We feel as if a great personal loss had befallen ourselves, for we have long believed that the interests of the slave were safe in the hands of President LINCOLN, and had fondly hoped that the cause we have so long had at heart was about to be brought to a triumphant issue by him who has thus suddenly been laid low.

We the more deeply deplore this mysterious event from its occurring at a crisis of the nation's history when the wise, magnanimous, and merciful policy of President LINCOLN was so peculiarly needed to readjust the sorely troubled elements of the republic, and to effect a reconciliation between the North and the South, with freedom for its basis.

We can only bow before this awful dispensation, knowing that the Most High still ruleth in the kingdoms of men, and that He who raised up ABRAHAM LINCOLN can raise up other instruments for his work.

We earnestly desire that the just and generous policy initiated by the late President may be pursued by his successor, and that the great republic may be again united in the bonds of peace, the plague-spot of slavery (the true secret of its past weakness) forever wiped from its escutcheon.

Then, in connection with this glorious consummation, the name of ABRAHAM LINCOLN will be held in grateful and loving remembrance by generations yet unborn.

AGNES LILLIE,   ELIZABETH P. NICHOL, *President.*
ELIZA WIGHAM,
  Secretaries.

His Excellency CHARLES FRANCIS ADAMS,
 Envoy Extraordinary and Minister Plenipotentiary for the
  United States of America at the Court of Great Britain and Ireland:

SIR: We, John Whyte Melville, esq, of Bennochy and Strathkinness, most worshipful Grand Master Mason, the right worshipful the office-bearer, and the worshipful the members of the Grand Lodge of Free and Accepted Masons of Scotland, beg leave to assure your excellency that the very sudden and atrocious crime which has plunged the American nation into grief and mourning has produced a feeling of the utmost horror and indignation, not only in the masonic craft of Scotland, and the great mystic family of the world, but also, we doubt not, throughout the enlightened portion of the civilized globe.

We seize the earliest opportûnity afforded to us of expressing these our sentiments and the sorrow we so deeply feel at the loss sustained by the American people in the cowardly assassination of their late President LINCOLN.

While we offer our fraternal sympathies with the distress occasioned to our brethren of the United States and the people in general by this melancholy event, we would request your excellency to convey to Mrs. Lincoln and her family our sincere and heartfelt condolences on their afflicting bereavement, assuring that lady how deeply she has become, in her sudden misfortune, the object of our earnest and warmest sympathy.

Trusting it may graciously please the Great Architect of the Universe to take her and her family into His sure keeping, and bestow upon them every consolation, and strengthen them to bear up against their present affliction, is the united prayer of the Freemasons of Scotland.

Given at Freemasons' Hall, in the city of Edinburgh, in full Grand Lodge assembled, the eighth day of May, in the year of our Lord 1865, and of light 5865.

[SEAL.]

J. WHYTE MELVILLE,
Grand Master Mason of Scotland.
WM. H. LAURIE,
Grand Secretary Grand Lodge of Scotland.

Excerpt from the minutes of the annual general meeting of the commissioners of supply for the county of Elgin, North Britain, on the 1st day of May, 1865.

Sir Alexander Gordon Cumming, of Altyre and Gordonstown, baronet, acting convener of the county, in the chair.

On motion of Sir Alexander Gordon Cumming, seconded by Sir George MacPherson Grant, it was

Unanimously resolved, That the commissioners of supply of the county of Elgin, North Britain, assembled at their annual general meeting, desire to take the opportunity of expressing their sympathy with the American nation, and their horror and detestation of the atrocious acts to which the President of the United States of America has fallen a victim, which is rendered the more lamentable by the high integrity and ability of his career, by the important and eventful crisis at which it occurred, and by the consideration and clemency which he had evinced towards the vanquished in the hour of triumph.

Resolved further, That this resolution, signed by the chairman, be transmitted to his excellency the American ambassador in London, with the view of its being forwarded to the American government.

ALEX. P. GORDON CUMMING, Baronet,
Convener of County of Elgin. North Britain, Chairman.

BORÒUGH COUNCIL CHAMBER,
Emerald Hill, August 4, 1865.

SIR: I have the honor, by desire of the council of the borough of Emerald Hill, to forward herewith a copy of a resolution unanimously passed by the council at the last meeting, being an expression of the council's sympathy with the widow of the late and lamented President of the United States of America in her sore bereavement; and also the council's deep abhorrence of the dastardly act which has removed from the sphere of his usefulness one of the greatest men of modern times, and one who no doubt, had he lived, would have restored America to her original tranquillity and prosperity. I am further desired to request the favor of your kindly forwarding the enclosed to Mrs. Lincoln by the first opportunity.

I have the honor to be, sir, your most obedient servant,

JOHN WHITEMAN, J. P., *Mayor.*

WILLIAM BLANCHARD, Esq.,
Consul of the United States of America.

Resolution unanimously passed by the council of the borough of Emerald Hill, in the colony of Victoria, on the 3d day of August, 1865.

Resolved, That this council place upon record an expression of its abhorrence of the cruel and dastardly assassination of the late President of the United States of America, and its deep sympathy with Mrs. Lincoln in her bereavement ; and that a copy of this resolution be conveyed to that lady through the American consul.

[SEAL.]   JOHN WHITEMAN, J. P., *Mayor.*
                JAMES EVILLE, *Town Clerk.*

Excerpt from the minutes of a meeting of the provost, magistrates, and council of the burgh of Falkirk, held on the 3d day of May, 1865.

Provost Kier in the chair.   It was moved by Provost Kier—

That this meeting agrees to enter on its records an expression of deep sympathy with the government and people of the United States of America under the calamity which has befallen them through the assassination of President LINCOLN, and its entire concurrence in the universal detestation with which that crime is looked on in Great Britain.

The motion was seconded by Bailie Wyse, and unanimously carried.

Excerpted from the minutes of council by—

ROBERT HENDERSON, *Town Clerk.*

Unto the government and people of the United States of America—the address of the provost, magistrates, and town council of the royal burgh of Forfar, in Scotland.

We beg to approach you with heartfelt regret upon the atrocious deed recently perpetrated, through which you have been so suddenly and cruelly bereaved of the wise and patriotic counsels of your honored chief. We have watched his career since he was first elected President of your great country, and he has more and more proved that his subdued firmness and energy, steadfastness to truth and morality, calm and farseeing practical wisdom, and kindly and forgiving nature, fitted him for his high office, and specially qualified him for rightly steering the vessel of the state in its present perilous trials. It is therefor that we, in common with our countrymen, mourn his loss. We hope and trust that, chastened by the sad event, and guided by and following his noble example, you will, in this time of affliction, treat tenderly all who have departed from the path of loyalty, and through your clemency command the admiration of the civilized world, heal shattered and embittered feelings, and engender kindly intercourse, so long rudely dislocated.

Signed in name and behalf of the council, in council assembled, by me, provost and chief magistrate of Forfar, and the seal of the burgh attached, this first day of May, eighteen hundred and sixty-five.

[SEAL.]   JAMES CRAIK, JR.,
Provost and Chief Magistrate.

At Forfar, and within the County Hall there, the 1st day of May, 1865, in the statutory general meeting of the commissioners of supply and justices of the peace of the county of Forfar, of which meeting the right honorable the Earl of Dalhousie, K. T., G. C. B., &c., &c., lord lieutenant of Forfarshire, was chairman—

Before proceeding to the ordinary business of the meeting, the lord lieutenant submitted the following resolution, which was unanimously agreed to :

The justices of the peace and commissioners of supply of the county of Forfar, having read with horror of the tragical event which has recently occurred in the United States of America, by the cold-blooded and cowardly assassination of President LINCOLN, desire to express their cordial sympathy with the people and government of the United States in this most grievous calamity.

Whatever opinion may be held by individuals of their body, there is not one of them who does not bear a willing tribute to the honesty of purpose and the patriotism of the late President, and his deep sense of the responsibility which lay upon him of maintaining the Constitution of his country unimpaired.

The meeting desire that a copy of this resolution, signed by the lord lieutenant of the county, may be transmitted to his excellency Charles Francis Adams, the United States minister in London.

By desire of the meeting :

DALHOUSIE, *Lord Lieut.*

Resolutions passed at a meeting held by the inhabitants of Friockheim, Scotland.

At a largely attended meeting held on the 4th day of May, 1865, of the inhabitants of Friockheim, county of Forfar, Scotland, called for the purpose of consideration of the recent tragedy in the United States of America, resulting in the death of President LINCOLN, and the serious disablement of Secretary William H. Seward, the following resolutions were unanimously passed :

Doctor John Todd was called to the chair.

1. Moved by Mr. Francis Patterson, quarry-master, and seconded by Mr. A. R. Laing, manure merchant, " That this meeting desire sincerely to sympathize with their brethren in the United States of America in the great loss which they have sustained by the death of President LINCOLN, and to express their deep abhorrence at his atrocious murder."

2. Moved by Mr. W. G. Oliver, saddler, and seconded by Mr. James Christie, laborer, " That this meeting wish to express their heartfelt condolence with Mrs. Lincoln in the irreparable loss which she and her family have sustained in the death of her illustrious and worthy husband."

3. Moved by Mr. John Glass, shoemaker, and seconded by Mr. John Scott, gas-manager, " That this meeting likewise desire to express their feelings of detestation at the murderous attack upon Secretary Seward, their sympathy with the American government and people on this most deplorable event, and their heartfelt hope that he will be so far recovered at an early date as to resume the reins of office."

It was agreed that a copy of these resolutions be transmitted through Mr. Adams, the United States representative in London, for being forwarded to the proper quarter.

JOHN TODD, *Chairman.*

At a special meeting of the town council of the burgh of Greenock, called by order of the provost, and held within the Council Hall there, on Friday, the 5th day of May, 1865, the honorable the provost in the chair—

The provost having stated the object of the meeting, it was unanimously resolved—

That this council, in common with all classes of their fellow-citizens, have heard with horror, indignation, and profound regret, of the foul and execrable murder of the President of the United States of America.

That this council deeply sympathize with the great American republic under the heavy loss which it has sustained by the unexpected and untimely decease, under such revolting circumstances, and in the midst of his illustrious career, of a ruler whose personal excellence and kingly endowments have rendered him an object of honest pride to his own countrymen, and of just admiration to the rest of the world, and whose earnest endeavors to cultivate and maintain friendly relations with Great Britain must ever endear his name and memory to the people of this country.

That this council also deeply sympathize with Mrs. Lincoln and family under their heavy bereavement, and earnestly pray that they may be sustained and supported by Him "who is the husband of the widow and the father of the fatherless"

That the provost be authorized to sign the resolutions now unanimously approved of by this council, and that the provost, Treasurer Fleming, and Councillor Morton, be requested to present the same to the American minister in London, with a request that he will kindly forward the same to his government.

[SEAL.]   JAMES I. GRIERS, *Provost of Greenock.*

BOROUGH OF GRANTHAM.

Resolutions passed at a meeting held by the council of the borough of Grantham.

Extract from the minutes of a quarterly meeting of the council of the said borough held at the Guildhall there, on Thursday, the 11th day of May, 1865—present, Richard John Boyall, esq., mayor, and others:

Resolved unanimously, That we, the mayor, aldermen, and burgesses of the borough of Grantham, in council assembled, desire to give expression to the feelings of horror and indignation with which we have heard of the assassination of President LINCOLN, and the murderous attack upon Mr. Seward, and beg to convey to Mrs. Lincoln, and the government and the people of the United States, our sincere and profound sympathy and heartfelt condolence at the sad events.

[SEAL.]   RICH'D JOHN BOYALL, *Mayor.*

To his Excellency ANDREW JOHNSON,
     President of the United States of America:

SIR: We, the mayor, aldermen, and citizens of the city of Gloucester, in England, desire to convey to the people of your great country the feelings of sorrow and abhorrence with which we, in common with all classes of this kingdom, received the lamentable intelligence of the death, by the hands of an assassin, of your late distinguished President, ABRAHAM LINCOLN, and of the dastardly attack upon the life of another officer of your government, Mr. Secretary Seward.

While deploring with all civilized nations the commission of these heinous and detestable crimes, we would offer to the people of the United States an expression of our sympathy and good will; and we would also add our sincerest condolence with the widow and family of the late eminent statesman.

Given under our common seal, the 1st day of May, 1865.

[SEAL.]   W. C. TUNSTALL, *Mayor.*

TOWN HALL, GEELONG, *August* 22, 1865.

MADAM : I have the honor, on behalf of the town council of Geelong, in the colony of Victoria, Australia, to forward (through William Blanchard, esq., the American consul) the accompanying address from that body, of sympathy and condolence with you in your deep affliction on the lamented death of your husband, the late President of the United States of America.

I have the honor to be, madam, with the most profound respect, your most obedient, humble servant,

[SEAL.]   CHARLES KEENOT, *Mayor.*
          WILLIAM WEIRE, *Town Clerk.*

Mrs. LINCOLN, *Washington, America.*

Address of sympathy to Mrs. Lincoln, on the death of her husband, the late President of the United States of America, from the mayor, aldermen, council, and burgesses of the town of Geelong, in the colony of Victoria, Australia.

We, the town council of Geelong, in council assembled, hereby desire to place on record our abhorrence and detestation of the atrocious murder of ABRAHAM LINCOLN, late President of the United States of America.

We desire also to offer our unfeigned and sincere sympathy and condolence to Mrs. Lincoln, in her deep affliction and great bereavement.

Given under my hand, and the seal of the corporation of Geelong, this 22d day of August, in the year of our Lord 1865.

[SEAL.]   CHARLES KEENOT, *Mayor.*
          WILLIAM WEIRE, *Town Clerk.*

TOWN HALL, *Geelong.*

[Handbill.]

SYMPATHY WITH AMERICA.

Base assassination of the President, Abraham Lincoln, and attempted murder of Mr. Seward.

A public meeting will be held at the Town Hall, Great Bardfield, on Wednesday evening, May 3, 1865, to express its utter abhorrence of the above foul crimes, and to pass a resolution of condolence with Mrs. Lincoln and the people of the United States in their present painful position.

Chair to be taken at eight o'clock by Francis J. Freelove.

All classes are earnestly invited to attend. Admission free.

Resolutions unanimously adopted at the above meeting :

1st. That this meeting deeply sympathizes with the people of the United States in the great loss they have sustained in the sad death of their worthy President, ABRAHAM LINCOLN, and expresses its horror and indignation both at the foul crime which was the cause of his decease and of that which meditated the murder of Mr. Seward.

2d. That this meeting records its heartfelt condolence with Mrs. Lincoln in her irreparable loss, and fervently hopes that she may be supported in her overwhelming trouble.

Signed on behalf of the above meeting :

FRANCIS J. FREELOVE, *Chairman.*

GREAT BARDFIELD, *May* 3, 1865.

Honorable WILLIAM H. SEWARD,

Secretary of the United States of America, Washington :

We, the inhabitants of the town of Galt, Canada West, being British subjects, on hearing of the base assassination of the late honored President of the United States, and also of the foul attempt made upon your own life and that of your sons, have, through our properly constituted authorities, called a public meeting of the inhabitants of this place, to give expression to our sense of horror at these acts, and to express deep sympathy with the bereaved widow and family, yourself and family, and your nation at large, at which this address and the following resolutions were unanimously adopted, and we have instructed our chairman and secretary to sign the same, and to affix to them the seal of our corporation, respectfully soliciting you to present the same to Mrs. Lincoln and family, and also to your nation, as expressive of our deep sympathy with them in this their great affliction; and most earnestly would we pray that the day may never come when such scenes shall be repeated; that peace to your nation may soon be restored, and that the bonds of national and Christian brotherhood which now unite us so closely into one may never be dissolved; that your health may soon be restored, and that you may long live to fill the high station you occupy, to assist in maintaining the unity of the nations in the bonds of peace.

The foregoing address was moved by the Rev. J. A. Miller, and seconded by William McLaughlin, esq.

1st. Moved by the Rev. Mr. Acheson, seconded by James Young, esq., and

Resolved, That we hereby express our heartfelt indignation and horror towards the spirit that planned, and the monster in human form that perpetrated, the foul act of assassinating the late honored President of the United States. We cannot but regard it as a base violation of every principle of right, both human and divine, and as such at variance with the spirit and law of all civilized nations.

2d. Moved by the Rev. Mr. M'Ghee, seconded by the Rev. Mr. M'Rae, and

Resolved, That in accordance with the common sympathies of our nature, and in the spirit of our holy Christianity, we hereby beg to present our deep sympathy for, and condolence with, the bereaved widow and her afflicted family in the loss they have sustained by the removal, especially in such a manner, of an affectionate husband and a kind father.

3d. Moved by the Rev. Mr. Campbell, seconded by James Cowan, esq., M P. P., and

Resolved, That we also hereby beg to express our earnest sympathy with with the people of the United States in being thus deprived, at a critical period of their history, of the services of one whom they called to fill the office of Chief Magistrate at a time when that position was beset with most unparalleled difficulties, and yet who so conducted himself as to secure not only the confidence and love of his own people, but also the admiration and esteem of foreign nations, who, from his consistent character, were led to regard him as a sagacious, conciliatory, honest, yet firm chief ruler.

4th. Moved by the Rev. Mr. Murdoch, seconded by William Osborne, esq., and

Resolved, That we mourn the untimely death of ABRAHAM LINCOLN as one honestly desirous of maintaining peace with the British nation, a firm friend of what is dear to us as Britons and as Christians, the cause of emancipation, and it is our confident hope, while it will ever be our prayer, that Divine Providence may grant to his successor the same wise and Christian policy.

Dated at Galt, in the county of Waterloo, this 17th day of April, A. D. 1865.

MORRIS C. LUTZ, *Mayor, Chairman.*

THOMAS SPARROW, *Town Clerk, Secretary,*

Resolutions passed at a meeting held by the inhabitants of Galway.

Public meeting in Galway, May, 1865.

At a public meeting held in the town court-house on Thursday, 4th instant, the following resolutions were unanimously adopted—

Thomas M. Persse, esq., chairman of town commissioners, in the chair:

Proposed by Rev. Peter Baly, P. P., seconded by A. O'Flaherty, esq., D. L.:

Resolved, That we, the citizens of Galway, have heard with feelings of horror and indignation of the atrocious murder of the President of the United States, ABRAHAM LINCOLN, and the attempted assassination of Mr. Secretary Seward, and we hereby join our fellow-countrymen in offering our sincere sympathy to the American people on the national bereavement they have sustained.

Proposed by Professor Moffett, LL.D., seconded by R. N. Somerville, esq.:

Resolved, That although we cannot believe our good words will have much effect in soothing the sorrow of Mrs. Lincoln, yet we cannot separate without expressing our condolence with her on the great calamity that has befallen herself and family in the untimely end of her illustrious husband, and our hope that the universal sympathy of the world may in some measure assuage their great grief.

Proposed by James Campbell, esq., seconded by Rev. J. D'Arcy, rector of Galway:

Resolved, That copies of the foregoing resolutions, signed by the chairman and secretaries of this meeting, on behalf of the people of Galway, be sent to the American minister in London for transmission to Mrs. Lincoln and the United States government.

THOMAS M. PERSSE, J. P., *Chairman.*
JAMES CAMPBELL,
THOMAS W. MOFFETT, LL.D.,
Honorary Secretaries.

At Glasgow, on Tuesday, the 2d day of May, 1865, and within the Trades' Hall, there was held a meeting of the inhabitants called by the chief magistrate.

The hall was filled.

Andrew Galbraith, esq., merchant in Glasgow, moved that the acting chief magistrate be requested to take the chair, and that the city chamberlain be requested to act as secretary.

The motion was carried by acclamation.

Thereafter the secretary read the following requisition addressed to the honorable the lord provost of the city, and signed by a large number of the leading citizens:

"We, the undersigned, hereby request your lordship to call a meeting, upon an early day, of the inhabitants of Glasgow, for the purpose of expressing their abhorrence of the crime by which America has been deprived of her President and their sympathy with the American people." Together with the following reply by the acting chief magistrate, in the necessary absence of the lord provost, who is in London:

"In compliance with the foregoing requisition, I hereby call a public meeting to be held in the Trades' Hall, Glasgow, upon Tuesday, the 2d of May, at one o'clock.

"ROBERT GILKISON,

"Acting Chief Magistrate."

The secretary then read the following telegram, addressed to him by the lord provost:

"GLASGOW, *May* 1, 1865.

"Be good enough to deliver the following message to the chairman of the American meeting in the Trades' Hall. Please to inform the meeting that I much regret not being able to be present, and as lord provost of the city to join with the citizens in the expression of their feelings of abhorrence at the barbarous crime which has been committed in the assassination of President LINCOLN and the attack on Mr. Seward, grief at the national loss sustained by the United States of America from the death of so great and honest a President, and sympathy with his bereaved widow."

The Very Reverend Thomas Barclay, D. D., principal of the University of Glasgow, moved the first resolution, which was seconded by Charles Gairdner, esq., manager of the Union Bank of Scotland, as follows:

"We, the citizens of Glasgow, in public meeting assembled, have heard with grief, and do hereby express our unmitigated horror of the crime which has suddenly deprived the United States of America of an upright and honored ruler."

The resolution was carried by acclamation.

Henry Glassford Bell, esq., one of the sheriff substitutes of the county of Lanark, moved the second resolution, which was seconded by Sir Andrew Orr, of Harvieston and Castle Campbell, as follows:

"We embrace this opportunity of assuring the citizens of the United States of our deep and earnest sympathy with them under this grievous dispensation."

The resolution was carried by acclamation.

James Lumsden, esq., merchant, Glasgow, moved the third resolution, which was seconded by Walter Paterson, esq., merchant, as follows:

"That the chairman be authorized to subscribe these resolutions in the name of this numerous and influential meeting; and that the secretary be requested to transmit them to the lord provost for presentation at the American embassy in London."

The resolution was carried by acclamation.

Signed by me, in name and by appointment of the meeting, and I have caused the common seal of the city of Glasgow to be hereunto affixed, this 2d day of May, 1865

[SEAL.]   ROBERT GILKISON,
Acting Chief Magistrate.

The right honorable the Lord Belhaven and Stenton, lord lieutenant of the county of Lanark, then moved that the thanks of this meeting be offered to Bailie Gilkison for the promptitude and courtesy with which he called this meeting and occupied the chair.

This resolution also was carried by acclamation.

WM. W. WATSON, *Chamberlain,*
Secretary of the Meeting.

At a special meeting of the Chamber of Commerce, held at Glasgow, the 28th April, 1865—present, Messrs. John M'Ewen, Henry Dunlop, James Sterling, James Watson, John Ramsay, James Lumsden, Walter Paterson, James A. Campbell, James White, John Mathieson, jr., Patrick Playfair, J. C. Bolton, and William M'Kinnon—Mr. M'Ewen in the chair—

It was moved by the chairman, and seconded by Mr. Dunlop—

That this chamber desire to record their utter abhorrence and detestation of the crime by which the United States have been so suddenly deprived of the services of their President, ABRAHAM LINCOLN ; that the chamber beg to express their sincere sympathy with the people of the United States of America on so trying an occasion, and trust that the sad event may be so overruled as not to be prejudicial to the continued prosperity of the United States of America and the best interests of the nation.

[SEAL.]   JNO. M'EWEN, *President.*

At Glasgow, and within the Merchants' Hall, this 3d day of May, 1865, at a meeting of the members of the Merchants' House, called by public advertisement for the purpose of "expressing abhorrence at the detestable crime which has deprived the United States of President LINCOLN, and to vote an address of condolence to them on this melancholy occasion," Archibald Orr Ewing, esq., lord dean of guild, in the chair—

The clerk read the advertisement calling the meeting, after which the lord dean of guild proposed the following resolution :

That this house have received the intelligence of the assassination of President LINCOLN of the United States of America with sentiments of horror and pain.

That they desire to express their heartfelt sympathy and condolence with the people of the United States, who, in a manner so shocking to every feeling of humanity and so subversive of social order, have been suddenly deprived of their Chief Magistrate at a momentous crisis in the history of their country.

That this house would record their high respect for the character of the late President LINCOLN, and their grateful remembrance of his endeavors, at all times, to preserve and cultivate friendly relations with Great Britain; and they would express their earnest hope and prayer that the prospects of internal peace which had opened to the United States during the last days of Mr. LINCOLN's life may not be materially affected by the execrable deed which has brought that life prematurely to an end.

Which resolution, having been seconded by Sir James Campbell, of Stracathro, was unanimously agreed to.

It was then moved by Alexander Harvey, esq., that the lord dean of guild be authorized to sign the resolutions now read and approved by this house, and that he thereafter forward them to the United States government through the American minister in London.

Which motion, having been seconded by William M'Ewen, esq., was also unanimously carried.

The lord dean of guild having declared the business of the meeting terminated, it was thereupon moved by Peter White, esq., that a vote of thanks be accorded to the lord dean of guild for the promptitude with which he had called the meeting, and for the able manner in which he had presided.

Which motion having been carried by acclamation, the meeting separated.

Signed and sealed with the corporation seal of Merchants' House, in name and by appointment of said house, at Glasgow, this 3d day of May, 1865.

[SEAL.]   ARCHIBALD ORR EWING,
Dean of Guild.

His Excellency ANDREW JOHNSON,
    President of the United States of America:

SIR : We, the members of the Union and Emancipation Society of Glasgow, desire to express through you to the great nation of which you now are chief, our profound sorrow for the loss it has sustained through the cruel and atrocious assassination of ABRAHAM LINCOLN, and our utter detestation and abhorrence of the foul deed which has brought this calamity upon your people.

We mourn with your nation; for we have long reverenced ABRAHAM LINCOLN as a great and good man, discharging the solemn duties intrusted to him, not only with high ability, but with purity of purpose and simplicity of heart, and ever seeking righteous ends through honorable means.

Called to power in the direst crisis of your national history, he has proved to the world that high-principled integrity is practical wisdom, and that the greatest difficulties in the affairs of nations are best mastered by the spirit of simplest nobleness.

We would also ask your excellency to convey our sorrowing sympathy to Mrs. Lincoln, and assure her of our prayer that the Everlasting Arm may be outstretched to uplift and give her strength in her terrible bereavement, and the tender mercy of our Father in Heaven minister the peace which passeth understanding.

We would further beg your excellency to express to Mr. Seward our indignant horror at the vile blows inflicted on him by an assassin's hand, and our earnest and hearty hope that he may soon be restored to his accustomed place in the councils of your government.

We believe, sir, that the universal indignation excited by these crimes, which have disgraced humanity, will bind even more closely our nation to yours, and that we only utter the feeling of the aroused heart of the mass of our people when we pray that those beneficent purposes of ABRAHAM LINCOLN (which, expressed upon the day of his death, are his last legacy to his countrymen) may have their happy and abundant fulfilment in a peace which shall conclude war with mercy, and, while securing freedom for those heretofore held in bondage, shall unite all sections and parties in one nation, whose prosperous future will be the best monument to the memory of the great ruler over whose sad grave we mourn with a common sorrow.

Signed, in behalf of the society, by—

JAMES SINCLAIR,
Secretary.

GLASGOW, *April* 28, 1865.

His excellency Hon. CHARLES FRANCIS ADAMS,
United States Minister, &c., &c., at London:

SIR: We, the undersigned, Americans, resident in Glasgow, have heard with the deepest grief, horror, and detestation that the President of the United States has been deprived of life by violence.

We beg to convey to you, as the representative of the American government in London, our heartfelt sympathy, on learning this sorrowful event. We also ask permission to record our loving admiration of the stainless and heroic presidency of ABRAHAM LINCOLN, and to express our hope and confidence, that through the veneration inspired by his lofty virtue, his influence may now become more powerful than ever to guide the Union, of which he was the fruit and ornament, to victory and peace.

J. M. BAILEY.

A. F. STODDARD.

WM. COOK.

W. B. HUGGINS.

M. M. MOORE.

LEWIS T. MERROR.

At a meeting of native-born Americans, convened at the United States consulate in Glasgow on the 28th instant, for the purpose of expressing their feelings with respect to the late distressing news from the United States, J. M. Bailey, esq., consul of the United States of America, in the chair, and A. F. Stoddard, secretary, it was unanimously resolved—

1. Whereas we have heard with profound sorrow and indignation of the assassination of our honored Chief Magistrate, ABRAHAM LINCOLN, and of the dastardly attempt upon the life of Mr. Seward, Secretary of State, we tender our deep and heartfelt sympathy and grief to our weeping countrymen at home, and would mingle our tears with theirs over the grave of one of nature's noblest sons, whose loss at this critical and eventful period of our nation's history is wholly irreparable. We mourn for the fall of one whose every impulse was characterized by pure patriotism and unflinching devotion to the cause of liberty, and who combined in a pre-eminent degree those heavenly attributes, mercy, justice, and truth.

2. That while mourning over the great loss which has befallen our country, we deeply sympathize with Mrs. Lincoln and her afflicted family in the heavy blow which they have so suddenly and so unexpectedly sustained, and trust that the love of a great nation may in some degree compensate for him who has thus been ruthlessly snatched from their side.

3. That while conveying to Mr. Seward and his stricken family our sincere grief and sympathy for the sad calamity which has befallen them, we earnestly pray that their lives may all be spared to their country.

4. That we, in common with humanity the world over, unite in expressing our unmitigated abhorrence and detestation of the vile hearts that conceived this diabolical plot, and the villanous hands that executed the cowardly deeds.

5. That we have confidence in the integrity and ability of Andrew Johnson, the present Chief Magistrate of the United States, and fondly trust that by following in the footsteps of his illustrious predecessor, he may, under God.

speedily see consummated the desire of a nation's heart; when the United States shall emphatically become the "land of the free," as she has proven herself on many a sanguinary field "the home of the brave."

6. That the foregoing resolutions be signed by the chairman and secretary, and forwarded to our minister in London, for transmission to the President of the United States.

J. M. BAILEY, *Chairman.*
A. F. STODDARD, *Secretary.*

GLASGOW, *April* 28, 1865.

Resolutions of the synod of the Reformed Presbyterian church in Scotland.

To the Honorable ANDREW JOHNSON,
      President of the United States of America :

HONORED SIR : The following resolutions were unanimously passed at the meeting of the synod of the Reformed Presbyterian church in Scotland, held in Glasgow, 10th of May, 1865. As clerk to that synod, I have been instructed to forward them to you, as expressive of our sympathy with your great nation in the crisis through which it has been passing.

JOHN KAY,
      Clerk to Reformed Presbyterian Synod.

1. That this court, recognizing the duty of Christian churches to consider those momentous evolutions of Providence which may seriously affect the moral and spiritual welfare of mankind, record an expression of deep sympathy with the people of the United States, under the attempts made on the life of their Secretary of State, and more especially under the loss of their chief ruler, President LINCOLN, by a foul assassination, and deplore it as an event which would have been painful and startling under any circumstances, but which is much more distressing from the gravity of the crisis in which it occurred, and from the evidence which the deceased President had given of a firm purpose, in combination with great benignity of temper—the very qualities that seem chiefly requisite to meet the remaining difficulties of the American government in its efforts to restore peace and order and unity throughout its extensive dominions.

2. Although this court never could regard with any feelings but the deepest abhorrence the attempt to rear a government with slavery as its corner-stone, and while due regard must be had to the interests of law and justice, the hope is confidently cherished that the American government will be enabled to signalize the reality of its success in restoring the "Union," and to give the

world some assurance of its own conscious strength, by adherence to the same magnanimous and merciful policy to the vanquished, which ABRAHAM LINCOLN would appear to have recommended and inaugurated.

In name and by authority of the synod of the Reformed Presbyterian church in Scotland.

WILLIAM McLACHLAN, *Moderator.*
JOHN KAY, *Clerk of Synod.*

Resolutions of the Chamber of Commerce.

CHAMBER OF COMMERCE, GUERNSEY, *May*, 1865.

At a general meeting held on the 2d of May, 1865—

Resolved, That this chamber, deeply impressed with horror at the intelligence recently received from America of the assassination of President LINCOLN and others, thinks it a duty to publicly express its abhorrence of such dastardly crimes, the authors of which deserve the execration of mankind.

The inhabitants of these Norman islands of the channel, the apex of the great Norman Anglo-Saxon social edifice, venture to hope that the fratricidal struggle that has endured in America during a period of four years, and affording on both sides so many proofs of heroism and endurance, may be closed, and, uniting again, peace and prosperity may be restored throughout America; and that the great Norman Anglo-Saxon family in all its branches throughout both hemispheres, all sprung from the same race, may hereafter live in brotherly union and love, contributing to the happiness and welfare of each and all, and giving to the world a bright example of concord, progress, and civilization.

THOS. HELARY AGNEW, *Secretary.*

Resolutions of sympathy with America, passed at a meeting of working men and women held in the Temperance Hall, Gateshead-on-Tyne, on Sunday evening, May 7, 1865.

Mr. George Lucas in the chair.

Moved by Mr. Blagburn, seconded by Mr. Gammell, and carried unanimously—

1. That the workingmen who constitute this meeting have looked with much interest upon the struggle which has been so long pending in America, and they devoutly trust it will issue in the entire overthrow of slavery throughout the American continent.

Moved by Mr. Wheater, seconded by Mr. D. Rule, and carried unanimously—

2. That the workingmen now assembled desire to express their regret that persons in this country have spoken and written in justification of the rebellion of the South, especially during the earlier periods of the conflict; but they have observed with much satisfaction, that as the spirit and objects of the contending parties have become more fully understood throughout this country, a different tone has prevailed; and it is hoped the event now so much deplored may tend to cement the two nations in bonds of lasting brotherhood.

Moved by Mr. Tweddle, seconded by Mr. Wordsworth, and carried unanimously—

3. That the workingmen now assembled wish to express their deep admiration of the manner in which the late President has conducted the affairs of the government of America during the period of his office, but they most of all admire that spirit of wise moderation which he manifested towards the enemies of the Union in periods of especial difficulty and provocation.

Moved by Mr. Thomas Rule, seconded by Mr. Smith, and carried unanimously—

4. That the workingmen now congregated wish to express their utter detestation of the diabolical crime which has deprived a wife of her husband, children of their father, the American commonwealth of its President, and the world of one of its distinguished benefactors.

Moved by Mr. J. B. Anderson, seconded by Mrs. Tweddle, and carried unanimously—

5. That the working men and women who compose this meeting desire to express to Mrs. Lincoln their unfeigned condolence in her present affliction, and to direct her mind to that source of true consolation which her late husband knew so well how to value.

Moved by Mr. Townsend, seconded by Mr. Rutherford, and carried unanimously—

6. That this meeting earnestly hopes that should events arise between England and America which appear of a complicated character, a wise forbearance may be manifested on the part of both nations, and differences be settled on the principles of equal justice.

Moved by Mr. Mackin, seconded by Mr. Swanson, and carried unanimously—

7. That the resolutions now passed be forwarded by the chairman to the American minister in London, for presentation to the American commonwealth.

GEORGE LUCAS,
Chairman of the Meeting.

GATESHEAD-ON-TYNE, *May* 8, 1865.

Resolutions of the mayor, aldermen, and burgesses of the borough of Huntingdon

At a meeting of the mayor, aldermen, and burgesses of the borough of Huntingdon, held in the council chamber of the said borough, this 10th day of May, 1865, it was proposed by Mr. Foster, seconded by Mr. Charles Veasey—

That this council unanimously desire to convey to the government of the United States of America the sorrow and indignation felt by this council at the assassination of the late President of the United States, and their deep sympathy with the people of America at the loss sustained thereby.

Proposed by Mr. Cooch, seconded by Mr. Foreman, and

Resolved, That a copy of the foregoing resolution be signed by the mayor, and the corporate seal affixed thereto, and that the same be then transmitted to the American minister.

[SEAL.]   ROBERT MARGETTS, *Mayor.*

Resolution of the mayor, aldermen, and burgesses of the borough of Hastings.

TOWN CLERK'S OFFICE,
Hastings, May 6, 1865.

SIR: At a meeting of the mayor, aldermen, and burgesses, the council of the borough of Hastings, held on the 5th instant, it was

Resolved, That this council has heard with extreme horror and indignation the news of the assassination of the late President of the United States, and desires that the people of those States do understand that the people of this municipality are full of sympathy with them, under the disgraceful act by which President LINCOLN lost his life.

At the above-named meeting of the council of this borough I was instructed to forward a copy of the resolution to the American ambassador.

I have the honor to be your most obedient servant,

ROBERT GROWSE, *Town Clerk.*

C. F. ADAMS, Esq., *American Ambassador.*

At a quarterly meeting of the council of the borough of Hertford, held May 10, 1865—present: Jasper Gripper, esq., mayor; Aldermen Squire, Austin, and Young; Councillors Armstrong, Cocks, Haggar, Hancock, Neale, Pollard, Manser, Twaddle, Willson, and Woodhouse, M. D.—it was

Unanimously resolved, That this corporation wishes, emphatically, to express the feelings of indignation and grief with which they have heard of the atrocious acts by which the United States of America have been suddenly deprived of their President, and the life of his chief Secretary endangered; and that they recall with sorrowful interest the friendly feelings invariably displayed by the late President LINCOLN towards this country.

PHILIP LONGMORE, *Town Clerk*

Hon. CHARLES F. ADAMS,
    Minister of the United States in England:

HONORED SIR: We, the mayor, aldermen, and citizens of the city of Hereford, in council assembled, view with the utmost detestation and horror the flagitious crime by which the life of Mr. President LINCOLN has been so cruelly sacrificed, and desire to express the deep sympathy we entertain with the government and people of the United States of America under the severe calamity which this atrocious act has inflicted upon them.

We also beg most respectfully to offer to Mrs. Lincoln our sincere condolence under the awful bereavement which she has sustained.

And we are most anxious to convey to the American nation our sentiments of deep grief and indignation at the cowardly attack which has been made upon the life of Mr. Secretary Seward, together with our earnest hope that he may very soon recover from the severe wounds which have been inflicted upon him.

As the representatives of the inhabitants of this ancient city, we request that you will do us the favor to forward to the President of the United States, to Mrs. Lincoln, and to Mr. Secretary Seward these expressions of our sentiments, with the assurance that it is our anxious desire that no other feelings than such as are consonant with those above expressed will ever prevail between the people of this realm and those of the United States.

Sealed with our corporate common seal, at our council chamber, in the Guildhall of the city of Hereford, this 2d day of May, 1865.

[SEAL.]   THOMAS CAM, *Mayor.*

Resolution passed at a meeting of the mayor, aldermen, and town council of the borough of Hanley.

TOWN CLERK'S OFFICE,
Hanley, Staffordshire, May 11, 1865.

We, the mayor, aldermen, and town council of the borough of Hanley, have heard with feelings of grief and abhorrence of the foul assassination of President LINCOLN, and the murderous attack on Mr. Seward, and desire to convey to Mrs. Lincoln and the United States government our heartfelt sympathy and earnest wishes for the prosperity of their country.

The corporate seal of the borough of Hanley was hereunto affixed this 11th day of May, 1865, in the presence of—

[SEAL.]   EDWARD CHALLINOR, *Town Clerk.*

His Excellency the PRESIDENT
    of the United States of America :

 May it please your Excellency, we, the provost, magistrates, and council of
the burgh of Hawick, in that part of her Britannic Majesty's dominions called
Scotland, in public council assembled, having heard with the deepest sorrow
and indignation of the assassination of President LINCOLN, hasten to express to
you the feelings of horror and execration with which such an atrocious crime is
regarded by this whole community, and to tender our sincere sympathy and
condolence with the government and people over whom you preside, under the
terrible national calamity they have thereby sustained.

 May it please your Excellency also to convey the deep sympathy and condolence we feel towards the widow and family of the lamented late President,
under the sudden and overwhelming bereavement over which they have, in an
especial manner, been called to mourn.

 That the terrible catastrophe which has befallen your country may be
mercifully overruled by Him who is Governor among the nations, for the
speedy pacification and prosperity of the American people, is the earnest prayer
of your Excellency's most obedient servants.

 Signed in name and by authority of the provost, magistrates, and council of
the burgh of Hawick.

 [SEAL.]   GEO. WILSON, *Provost.*

---

*Address to President Johnson, unanimously adopted at a public meeting of the
friends of union and emancipation, held at Hawick., Scotland, May 5, 1865.*

His Excellency ANDREW JOHNSON,
    President of the United States of America :

 Having heard with profound sorrow of the assassination of his Excellency
President LINCOLN and the attempted assassination of the Hon. Mr. Seward,
we tender to you this expression of our deep sense of the wickedness of the
atrocious crime that has been perpetrated, and of our heartfelt sympathy with
the American people under the heavy loss they have sustained in the untimely
close of Mr. LINCOLN's great career.

 While feeling deep sorrow for the death of that great and good man, to
whose inflexibility of purpose and unswerving fidelity to great principles the
American people have been so much indebted throughout the gigantic struggle
in which they have been engaged, we cannot help expressing, at the same time,
our high satisfaction at the recent great victories of your armies, under General
Grant, over the confederates at Richmond and Petersburg, the capture of those

cities, the surrender of General Lee with the shattered remnant of his once formidable rebel army, and the subsequent successes of the army under General Sherman, resulting, as that brilliant series of events does, in the entire overthrow of one of the most gigantic conspiracies against the rights of mankind of which history contains any record, and giving confident hope of the complete restoration of the Union and of the emancipation of the negro race.

We cannot doubt that the same policy which was so steadfastly and ably carried out by Mr. LINCOLN will be continued by yourself, on whom the highest responsibilities of the state have now devolved; and we trust that ere long the great issues of the Union and emancipation may be fully and happily consummated; and that the United States, emancipated from the evil and disorganizing institution of slavery, and from the dominating power of a slave aristocracy, may come out of this great crisis a yet purer, stronger, and freer nation, and that between her government and ours, and her people and ours, feelings of amity and brotherhood may ever be maintained, and that the two nations advancing together in righteousness, in commerce, and in moral power, may lead forward the nations of the world to higher conditions of prosperity, happiness, and justice than any that have yet been attained.

Signed in name and by authority of the meeting:

ANDREW WAUGH, *J. P.*,
Chairman of the Meeting

Hon. M. H. Richey. mayor of Halifax, to the United States consul.

MAYOR'S OFFICE,
Halifax, Nova Scotia, April 18, 1865.

SIR: I have the honor to enclose, by request of the city council, a resolution passed by that body, at its session yesterday, upon receiving intelligence of the tragic and terrible event which has thrilled with horror and lamentation the great nation of which you are the chief representative at this post.

Permit me, in conveying to you this expression of sympathy on behalf of the city council, to add emphatically my own, as deeply sensible of the overwhelming grief which must pervade the United States of America upon so truly calamitous an occurrence as the violent death of their honored President.

I have the honor to be, sir, your most humble and most obedient servant,

M. H. RICHEY, *Mayor.*

M. M. JACKSON, Esq.,
United States Consul, &c., &c., &c.

Extract from minutes of city council, Halifax, Nova Scotia, April 17, 1865.

Resolved, That this council have heard with deep regret that the President of the United States has fallen a victim to the foul assassin, and they desire to express their sincere sympathy with the bereaved family of the illustrious deceased and the great nation of which he was the head.

To publicly mark their sense of regret, this body respectfully requests his worship the mayor will order the city flag to be drooped over this building on the day of the obsequies ; and further, that his worship the mayor be requested to direct a copy of this resolution to be forwarded to the representative of the United States residing in this city.

For and on behalf of the city council :

J. NONCRAGG, *City Clerk.*

CITY COURT-HOUSE, *April* 18, 1865.

BOROUGH OF HALIFAX, IN THE COUNTY OF YORK.

At a meeting of the council of the borough of Halifax, holden in the Town Hall, Halifax, on the 3d day of May, 1865, William Irving Holdsworth, esq., the worshipful the mayor, in the chair, it was—

On the motion of the mayor, seconded by Mr. Alderman Ramsden

Resolved, That we, the mayor, aldermen, and burgesses of the borough of Halifax, in council assembled, desire to give expression to the feelings of horror and regret with which we have heard of the assassination of President LINCOLN, and beg to convey to Mrs. Lincoln and the United States government and people an expression of our sincere and profound sympathy and heartfelt condolence at the sad event.

On the motion of Mr. Alderman Collenson, seconded by Mr. Alderman Dennis—

Also resolved, That the mayor be requested to sign and affix the corporate common seal of the borough to a copy of the above resolution, and to transmit the same to the American minister now in London.

[SEAL.] W. I. HOLDSWORTH, *Mayor.*

Resolutions unanimously passed at a public meeting of the inhabitants of Halifax, in the West Riding of the county of York, held on Thursday, the 4th day of May, 1865.

William Irving Holdsworth, esq., the worshipful the mayor, in the chair.

Moved by John Crossley, esq., J. P., seconded by Mr. John Snowden, and supported by Mr. Thomas Scarborough—

That we, the inhabitants of Halifax, in public meeting assembled, express our deep sympathy with the people of the great American republic in the loss they have sustained in the death, by cruel assassination, of their honorable and honored Chief Magistrate, President ABRAHAM LINCOLN; and we cannot shut out of view the atrocious political significance of the crime as evidenced by the fact that it was accompanied by a murderous attack upon Chief Secretary Seward.

Moved by G. Buckston Browne, esq., J. P., seconded by Mr. William Brook, and supported by the Rev. William Roberts—

That we feel profound horror at the barbarous murder of President LINCOLN, but at the same time we feel such unabated confidence in the sound principles on which the American Constitution is based, that we cannot doubt that even this afflictive dispensation of Providence will in nowise retard the final accomplishment of that glorious object of the late President, the utter extinction of slavery.

Moved by Mr. George Garfitt, seconded by Mr. Henry Ambler—

That a copy of the foregoing resolutions, signed by the mayor, be sent to James Stansfeld, jr., esq., member of Parliament, with a request that he will hand the same to the Hon. C. F. Adams for transmission to the American government.

W. I. HOLDSWORTH, Mayor.

HASLINGDEN, LANCASHIRE, May, 1865.

The following resolutions were unanimously adopted at a public meeting of the inhabitants of Haslingden, held in the Town Hall, Haslingden, on the evening of May the 3d, 1865:

First. That this meeting desires to give utterance to the deep feelings of grief and horror with which it has heard of the assassination of President LINCOLN and the murderous and diabolical attack upon Mr. Seward, the Secretary of State.

Secondly. That this meeting also desires to tender to Mrs. Lincoln, the United States government and people, an expression of its profound sympathy and heartfelt condolence in this the hour of their affliction, and deeply lament that, by the hand of an assassin, the one should be bereaved of a husband and the other deprived of a wise and benevolent ruler.

Signed on behalf of the meeting.

LAURENCE WHITAKER, JR., Chairman.

His Excellency the PRESIDENT OF THE UNITED STATES.

39

HALSTEAD, *April* 29, 1865.

His Excellency C. F. ADAMS, *London :*

We, the undersigned, inhabitants of Halstead, Essex, England, desire to express our deep horror and regret that the President of the United States has been deprived of life by an act of violence, and our sympathy with the citizens of the United States in the great loss they have sustained.

[Signed by 67 names.]

Forwarded by R. L. Hughes, proprietor of the " Halstead Times."

Resolutions passed at a meeting held by the inhabitants of Heckmondwike.

At a meeting of the inhabitants of Heckmondwike, held on the 8th of May, 1865, at the Freemasons' Hall, convened in pursuance of public requisition to the chairman of the local board of health, to express sympathy with the American people in the great loss they have sustained at so critical a period of their national history, and to express a hope that the same wise and generous policy which distinguished Mr. LINCOLN and his government will also characterize the new President and his advisers; and also to express sympathy with Mrs. Lincoln in her sad and deplorable loss—William Rhodes, esq., in the chair—

It was moved by L. H. Firth, esq., seconded by Rev. E. Vickridge, and

Unanimously resolved, That this meeting has heard with indignation and horror of the foul murder of ABRAHAM LINCOLN, President of the United States of America, at perhaps the most critical period of his career, and at a time when his wise, prudent, and conciliatory conduct was commanding the admiration of the world. That we tender our deep sympathy to a brave people suddenly deprived of their Chief Magistrate, and hope the murderers may speedily be discovered and brought to condign punishment.

It was moved by Rev. Mark Howard, seconded by George Burnley, esq., and

Unanimously resolved, That we deeply mourn the great and overwhelming affliction which has so suddenly fallen upon the bereaved widow and family of the martyred President LINCOLN, and humbly offer to them such condolence as can be derived from sympathizing hearts in the great loss which they and the cause of humanity throughout the world have sustained.

It was moved by Benjamin Rhodes, esq., seconded by Mr Jacob Green, and

Unanimously resolved, That we rejoice to hear that the cowardly and murderous attack on the life of the Hon. W. H. Seward (while lying in a helpless condition on a bed of sickness) has not proved fatal. We trust he will soon be enabled to resume the duties of his important office; that President Johnson may retain him to assist in guiding and directing the affairs of his country, helping to meet and overcome every trial; that they may succeed in purging their nation from everything that would blot its future fame, and preserve it in honor and peace with all the world.

It was moved by Mr. W. B. Micklethwaite, seconded by Rev. R. Bowman, and

Unanimously resolved, That this meeting avails itself of the opportunity of expressing sympathy with President Johnson and his advisers in their present perilous circumstances, and hopes the wise and humane policy which distinguished the noble-minded LINCOLN may inspire and influence them; that they may prosecute the work of reconstruction so consistently begun by their illustrious predecessor, until the glorious republic be rendered still more glorious by the total and complete extinction of slavery in every part of its dominions.

It was moved by Mr. J. Leadbeater, seconded by Mr. J. Crabtree, and

Unanimously resolved, That the chairman be authorized to sign the above resolutions on behalf of this meeting, and forward them to the Hon. C. F. Adams, the American minister in London, for transmission to his Excellency President Johnson, Mrs. Lincoln, and the Hon. William H. Seward.

WILLIAM RHODES, *Chairman.*

HAMILTON, BERMUDA, *May* 11, 1865.

Resolved, That, in the opinion of this meeting, the recent barbarous assassination of the late President of the United States of America was an atrocious outrage upon all the principles of humanity and good government, and deserves to be met with the just indignation and fixed abhorrence of every peaceable and well-ordered community.

Proposed by his honor the chief justice; seconded by the attorney general.

Resolved, That this meeting desires to express its sympathy with a neighboring nation, deprived by this outrage of the Chief Magistrate of its choice, and also to convey to the bereaved family and personal friends of the late President LINCOLN a heartfelt expression of condolence with them in their deep affliction.

Proposed by honorable the speaker; seconded by Hon. M. G. Keon, colonial secretary.

HENRY JAMES TUCKER.
Mayor and Chairman.

Hon. Miles Gerald Keon to C. M. Allen, Esq., United States Consul.

HAMILTON, BERMUDA, *April* 28, 1865.

DEAR SIR: Although you will need no assurance of this kind for your own information, I can keep silence no longer, and am constrained both by my principles and by my feelings, (and certainly not prohibited by the commission which I hold from her Majesty, as one of her principal servants in this community,) to express to you, however feebly and inadequately, the grief and indignation with which the horrible crime of the 14th instant has filled me. I trust we shall have a public meeting, at which we can attest solemnly before the world the sentiments which this community entertains respecting so foul and detestable a deed.

I speak only the feelings everywhere paramount, nay, the natural language of human society itself, and beyond a question in that fragment of it in which I am living, when I beg you to believe that the deepest reprobation of every man who dares to look his fellow-creatures in the face awaits the wretch who has deprived a great nation of its Chief Magistrate, just when he had shown that he was as merciful in victory as he had been stern in conflict, and at a moment of cruel public difficulty, by one of the most doltish and objectless, as well as wicked and truculent murders, that history has ever had to record.

I have been urging all my friends to hold a meeting, and say jointly before the world what they are saying severally in their homes. Men of all parties, of all countries, can unite in this. During a struggle which could not be settled save by Americans, and on American principles, some of us felt commiseration and sympathy for the gallant few fighting so splendidly on the defensive; others for the cause of obvious political order and central authority; but all remained officially neutral. When, however, Providence has decided the conflict, and assassination is introduced among the factors of political science, I trust no British gentleman and no honest man will ever show neutrality.

I have the honor to be, dear sir, your most obedient servant,

MILES GERALD KEON.

CHARLES M. ALLEN, Esq.,
 Consul of the U. S. of America in Bermuda.

Resolutions passed at a meeting held by the Alexandria Lodge of the G. U. O. of Odd Fellows, Bermuda.

Whereas, by recent arrivals from New York, we do learn of the death of ABRAHAM LINCOLN, President of the United States of America, by assassination: therefore, be it—

1st. *Resolved,* That in this dispensation of the Divine will, our race has lost an invaluable friend, one who in public and private life failed not to do honor to his country, who in the support of freedom, equality, and the rights of man, fell by the hand of a ruthless assassin.

2d. *Resolved,* That this meeting do hear of his untimely decease with feelings of deep and deserved regret, and in view of the said mournful intelligence do make such public demonstration of the same as is consistent with us, members of the fraternity of Odd Fellows.

3d. *Resolved,* That the members of this lodge do on Thursday, the 4th proximo, at its annual celebration, appear in mourning costume, in token of respect for the deceased President, and that badges of mourning be continued to be worn by the brethren for thirty days.

4th. *Resolved,* That we do heartily sympathize with the worthy consul here, C. M. Allen, esq., and the friends of the Union, as also with Mrs. Lincoln, and their bereaved family abroad, in this hour of trying moment.

5th. *Resolved,* That the secretary be directed to notify " Somers Pride of India Lodge, No. 899," and "Victoria and Albert Lodge, No. 1,027," of their intention in accordance with the 3d resolution, and to request a compliance of the same.

6th. *Resolved,* That a copy of these resolutions be forwarded to the United States consulate at St. George's, and to the Anglo-African papers, New York, for publication.

The foregoing resolutions were submitted to the meeting at Hamilton, on Tuesday, the 25th of April, ultimo, by P. G. M. Brother J. T. Richardson, supported by Senior G. M. Brother Joseph H. Thomas, and ably seconded by Brother Joseph H. Rainey, and unanimously carried by the brethren, some one hundred and fifty or more being present.

DAVID TUCKER,
General Secretary.

MAYOR'S OFFICE, HAMILTON, CANADA WEST.,
April 26, A. D. 1865.

SIR: I have the honor, by direction of the municipal corporation of the city of Hamilton, Canada West, to enclose a copy of resolutions passed by that body on hearing the sad news of the assassination of the late President, ABRAHAM LINCOLN, and to respectfully request that you will be pleased to lay the same before the President.

I have the honor to be, sir, your most obedient servant,

CHARLES MAGILL,
Mayor of Hamilton, Canada West.

Hon. WILLIAM H. SEWARD,
Secretary of State.

Resolutions passed by the municipal corporation of the city of Hamilton, Canada West, on the 18th day of April, A. D. 1865.

Whereas this council having heard the melancholy news of the assassination of the late President of the United States, ABRAHAM LINCOLN: therefore, be it

Resolved, That we, the mayor, aldermen, and commonalty of the city of Hamilton, in council assembled, deeply lament the sad occurrence, and also sincerely sympathize with the widow and bereaved family of the late President, and with the nation thus afflicted and wrongfully deprived of its Chief Magistrate; and we also feel that in thus expressing our views on this mournful subject, and in deprecating the diabolical act which deprived a neighboring nation of its chief head, we are only giving expression to the feelings entertained by the inhabitants of this city.

Resolved, That, as a mark of respect to the deceased President, the mayor be instructed to request the citizens to close their respective places of business during the time the funeral obsequies are being performed, which will take place on Wednesday, the 19th instant, between the hours of 12 o'clock noon and 2 p. m., and that the city bells toll during those hours.

[SEAL.]   CHARLES MAGILL,
                          Mayor of Hamilton, C. W.

Resolutions of the Huddersfield Chamber of Commerce.

CHAMBER OF COMMERCE,
Huddersfield, May 1, 1865.

Extract from proceedings of special meeting of council, May 1, 1865:

Moved by W. R. Haigh, esq., vice-president, seconded by T. Creswell, esq., and

Resolved unanimously, That this chamber desires to record the expression of its profound sympathy and condolence with the government and citizens of the United States of America on the occasion of the recent assassination of President LINCOLN, and the attempted assassination of Mr. Secretary Seward. These most atrocious crimes must excite the horror and indignation of all civilized nations, and cannot at this momentous crisis of American affairs be too deeply deplored by all who recognize, as this chamber does to its fullest extent, the single-minded patriotism and great ability with which President LINCOLN has guided the destinies of his country through almost unparalleled difficulties.

The chamber would also express its respectful sympathy with the widow and family of the deceased President.

Moved by W. P. England, esq., seconded by H. Brooke, esq., and

Resolved unanimously, That the foregoing resolution be communicated to the American consul in Huddersfield, with a request that he will forward the same through the proper channel to the American government.

W. R. HAIGH. *Vice-President.*

JOSEPH BATLEY, *Secretary.*

Resolution passed by the Huddersfield improvement commissioners.

At a monthly meeting of the Huddersfield improvement commissioners held on Wednesday, the 5th day of May, 1865, it was

Unanimously resolved, That the Huddersfield improvement commissioners, in monthly meeting assembled, feel that they cannot but give expression to their feelings of horror and indignation at the atrocious acts by which the United States of America have been suddenly deprived of their late President, and by which the lives of Mr. Secretary Seward and his two sons have been endangered.

The commissioners would also record their deep sympathy with the people of the United States, and with the widow of the late Mr. President LINCOLN, in the irreparable loss which they have sustained through his death.

JOSEPH TURNER,

Chairman of Commissioners.

J. W. CLOUGH,

Clerk to the said Commissioners.

From the council of the Huddersfield Union and Emancipation Society.

HUDDERSFIELD, *April* 27, 1865.

THOMAS STEPHENSON, Esq.,

Consular Agent of the United States at Huddersfield :

SIR: We have learned with the deepest horror and regret that the President of the United States of America has been basely assassinated, and we desire to express our profound sympathy in the sad event, with his family and friends, a sentiment which must be shared by the friends of liberty everywhere.

Signed, on behalf of the council of the Huddersfield Union and Emancipation Society :

MATHEW HALE.

THOMAS DENHAM.

JOHN GLAISZER.

HENRY REVILL.

WILLIAM R. CROFT.

J. K. GLAISZER, *Honorary Secretary.*

HULL, *May* 1, 1865.

At a meeting of the directors of the Hull Chamber of Commerce and Shipping held this day, the president, Henry J. Atkinson, in the chair—

It was moved by Stephen West, vice-president, seconded by Edmund Philip Maxsted, vice-president, and carried unanimously—

That the American minister be assured of the sympathy of this chamber with the government and the people of the United States, under the mournful circumstances in which they are placed by the assassination of President LINCOLN.

HENRY J. ATKINSON, *President.*

Resolution of the Holmfirth Chamber of Commerce.

At a meeting of the council held on the 8th of May, 1865, the following resolution was unanimously adopted:

" That this chamber desires to express its abhorrence of the assassination of the late President of the United States of America, and to offer its sympathy to Mrs. Lincoln and family, and the American people, in their painful bereavement."

BENJAMIN CRAVEN, *President.*

SAMUEL S BOOTH, *Secretary.*

Resolutions passed at a meeting held by the working men of Hinton Martel, Dorset county.

At a public meeting of the working men, held (by permission) in the school-room, Hinton Martel, near Wimborne, in the county of Dorset, on Wednesday, May 17, 1865, the following resolutions were unanimously adopted:

That this meeting having heard with great regret of the assassination of Mr. President LINCOLN, beg most humbly, but very respectfully, to tender through his excellency the American ambassador residing in this country, to the government and people of the United States of America, their most earnest sympathy and condolence, and to express their detestation and horror of the crime.

That his excellency be requested to convey to Mrs. Lincoln the assurance, that by no class in this country will there be felt for her a more earnest and true sympathy under this great trial than that experienced by us, a few of the agricultural laborers of Dorset.

Signed on behalf of the meeting:

HARRY STOKES, *Chairman.*

HINTON MARTEL, *Wimborne, May* 19, 1865.

SIR: As chairman of the above meeting, I have the honor to hand you the resolution passed by the workingmen of this district.

I would take this opportunity to express my earnest hope that the prospect now presented of a termination of the conflict that has been raging so long in your country may be speedily realized, and that you, sir, may be long spared to watch over the interests of your country at the court of our beloved Queen.

With great respect, I beg to remain, sir, your very obedient, humble servant,

HARRY STOKES.

His Excellency C. F. ADAMS, Esq.

To the President of the United States of America:

We, the town commissioners of West Hartlepool, in the county of Durham, beg to convey to you and, through you, to the people of the United States, our deep abhorrence and detestation of the foul crime which has so suddenly deprived you of your late President, ABRAHAM LINCOLN.

We share with all classes and creeds in this country in feelings of mingled grief and indignation at so atrocious an outrage.

Called to the high office of supreme director of the destinies of a great nation, and engaged in the active and conscientious performance of his vast and arduous duties, such a life might well have been regarded as peculiarly sacred.

We would desire to express our deep sympathy and condolence with your government and people at this untoward and melancholy event, and our hope that, under the blessing of Almighty God, even this sad event may be overruled to the welfare of your country and the restoration of national peace and prosperity.

Given under our common seal this 3d day of May, 1865.

The common seal of the West Hartlepool commissioners was hereunto affixed in the presence of—

[SEAL.]   WM. W. BRUNTER, *Clerk to the Board.*

To Mrs. Lincoln:

We, the town commissioners of West Hartlepool, in the county of Durham, desire to express to you our earnest sympathy in your recent great and irreparable bereavement. So foul an outrage against the life of the illustrious President is received by us with but one united feeling of abhorrence and detestation. All classes and creeds unite in one common expression of mingled grief and indignation at the foul and dastardly assassination.

We desire to convey to you our deepest condolence in this your great trial and affliction, and our earnest hope that if anything will tend to assuage your great grief, it will be the united sympathy of all classes and all countries, and your consciousness that the life so dear to you was sacrificed while engaged in the honest and noble discharge of his duty in that high sphere to which, under God's providence, he had been elected by his fellow-countrymen.

Given under our common seal this third day of May, 1865.

The common seal of the West Hartlepool commissioners was hereunto affixed in the presence of—

[SEAL.]   **WILLIAM W. BRUNTER,**
                                     Clerk to the Board.

BOROUGH OF HARTLEPOOL, COUNTY OF DURHAM.

At a public meeting of the inhabitants of the borough of Hartlepool, convened by the mayor in response to a numerously signed requisition from the rate-payers, and held in the Town Hall on Tuesday, May 2, 1865, James Groves, esq., mayor, in the chair, it was unanimously resolved—

On the motion of Mr. William Hall, seconded by Mr. B. T. Ord—

First. That this meeting deeply sympathizes with the people of the United States of America, in the bereavement which they have sustained in the death of their President by the hand of an assassin.

On the motion of George Blumer, esq., seconded by Thomas Belk, esq.—

Second. That this meeting desires, while giving expresions to the feelings of grief and horror with which it regards the assassination of President LINCOLN, to convey to Mrs. Lincoln an intimation of its profound sympathy and heartfelt condolence.

On the motion of the Rev. B. J. Hall, seconded by Mr. S Armstrong—

Third. That this meeting of the inhabitants of the ancient borough of Hartlepool rejoice to learn that it is the intention of President Johnson to carry out the policy of which the lamented late President's career was the embodiment, believing, as they do, that that policy had for its object the preservation of the Constitution of the United States and the emancipation of the slave.

On the motion of Mr. J. H. Bell, seconded by Mr. Councillor Graham—

Fourth. That copies of the foregoing resolutions be placed in the hands of the Hon. C. F. Adams, the American minister, for transmission to his Excellency the President of the United States, to Mrs. Lincoln, and to the honorable William H. Seward.

Signed on behalf of the meeting:

[SEAL.]   **JAMES GROVES,** *Mayor.*

And the chair having been vacated—

On the motion of Mr. Councillor Taylor, seconded by Mr. Councillor Harrison—

Fifth. That the best thanks of the meeting be accorded to his worship the mayor, for having so promptly convened and so ably presided at this meeting

MAY 4, 1865.

MY DEAR SIR: The United Methodist Free Church, West Hartlepool, in a special congregation, desires that you will convey to the government of the United States, and to Mrs. Lincoln and to Mr. Seward in particular, its deep detestation of the crime and of the men who have struck down the noble life of the late President. We have ever felt towards him while alive a personal friendship, and now, that he is no more of this world, we love his memory. "The memory of the just is blessed." But this is not a time for many words. We have faith in the future of the United States, and we say, God prosper and bless the American people. God bless the policy of emancipation.

On behalf of the church:

J. MARTIN, *Pastor.*

Hon. C. F. ADAMS, *American Legation, London.*

Resolutions passed at a public meeting held at Ipswich, in the county of Suffolk, on Thursday, the 11th day of May, 1865, Samuel Harrison Cowell, esq., mayor of the borough of Ipswich, in the chair.

On the motion of the Rev. Charles Hicks Gaye, seconded by Henry Footman, esq.—

That this meeting regards the assassination of President LINCOLN with unmitigated abhorrence, and desires to express the deepest sorrow and indignation at the occurrence.

On the motion of the Rev. James Robert Turnock, seconded by Edward Grimwade, esq.—

That this meeting sincerely condoles with Mrs. Lincoln and all others whom this event has bereaved, and entertains the greatest respect for the memory of the late Mr. LINCOLN, whose talents, integrity, and peaceful disposition so eminently qualified him for the high position he held at the present crisis of American affairs.

On the motion of the Rev. James Webb, seconded by George Green Sampson, esq.—

That we deeply sympathize with our American kinsmen in the great national affliction that has befallen them, and trust that they may ere long be delivered from their present distress, to enjoy the blessings of peace and prosperity, and, above all, the utter extinction of slavery.

On the motion of Joseph Fison, esq., seconded by the Rev. John Gay—

That copies of the foregoing resolutions be sent to the honorable Mr Adams, the United States ambassador in London.

SYMPATHY WITH AMERICA.

Resolutions passed at a public meeting of the working classes held in the borough of Ipswich, in the county of Suffolk, May 22, 1865.

First resolution : That this meeting desires to express the detestation and profound sorrow with which it regards the assassination of President LINCOLN, and the barbarous attack on Mr. Seward, and to offer its sympathy and heartfelt condolence with Mrs. Lincoln, President Johnson, the government, and the people of the United States.

Second resolution : That this meeting, while it deeply laments the loss of President LINCOLN, at a time when his influence and abilities were most needed to complete the ·work of slave emancipation in America, confidently trusts that President Johnson and his colleagues, upon whom the conduct of national affairs in America devolves, will succeed in accomplishing that desirable result.

Signed on behalf of the meeting :

W. D. SIMS,

(of Burlington Road, Ipswich,) *Chairman.*

Hon. W. H. SEWARD,

    Secretary to the Government of the United States of America.

Address of the Niagara annual conference of the Methodist Episcopal church in Canada to Mr. Johnson.

We, the ministers composing the Niagara annual conference of the Methodist Episcopal church in Canada, desire to express our heartfelt sympathy with Mrs. Lincoln and family, yourself, and the people of the United States of America, because of the melancholy death of the lamented late President LINCOLN, who was assassinated in the prime of life, and at a period in the history of the republic when he appeared to be the mainspring of the nation.

We feel that in the demise of Mr. LINCOLN his country lost a patriot, and the whole civilized world a friend.

The cause and spirit of the execrable southern rebellion, which evidently dictated the barbarous crime, as well as the assassins who attempted the destruction of the Hon. W. H. Seward and sons, and succeeded in killing President LINCOLN, deserve the reprobation of the universal brotherhood of mankind.

Our sincere prayer to Almighty God is, that He may console Mrs. Lincoln and family under their bereavement; preserve the life of the present Chief Magistrate of the republic, and direct him and his administration to such wise conclusions as shall fully restore the Union, extinguish slavery, and give permanent peace to the nation.

Done by order of conference at Strashrog, on the 24th of April, A. D. 1865.

M. BENSON, *Secretary of Conference.*

His Excellency ANDREW JOHNSON,
President of the United States of America.

At a meeting of the provost, bailies and councillors of the royal burgh of Jedburgh, in Scotland, held on the 8th day of May, 1865, it was

Resolved, That this council, on their own part and as the exponent of the feelings of the entire community of the royal burgh of Jedburgh, do record an expression of the deep sorrow universally experienced on receiving the intelligence of the assassination of President LINCOLN—an act the foul atrocity of which has excited the horror and indignation of all classes of her Majesty's subjects.

That this council, in expressing their most sincere sympathy with the government and people of the United States under their terrible national calamity, fervently hope and pray that the death of their Chief Magistrate, in a manner so shocking to every feeling of humanity and so subversive of social order, may be regulated by an all-wise and overruling Providence so as not materially to affect their country's prospects of internal peace, amity, and good will.

That this council further express their sympathy with Mrs. Lincoln, and the family of the late President in their sorrowful bereavement, and earnestly pray that He who has revealed himself heretofore as the "father of the fatherless, and judge of the widow," may be to them an all-abiding consolation in this their hour of trial.

It was further

Resolved, That the provost transmit a copy of these resolutions to the American minister in London, with a request that he will take the earliest opportunity of communicating them to the government, and to the widow of the late President.

WILLIAM DEANS, *Provost.*

At and within the Town Hall of the burgh of Kilmarnock, in the county of Ayr, on the 3d of May, 1865, convened the provost, magistrates and council of said burgh; whereupon it was

Resolved, That this council have learned with the greatest indignation and profound regret of the atrocious murder of Mr. ABRAHAM LINCOLN, President of the United States of America.

That this council deeply sympathize with the American republic, under the great loss which it has sustained by the untimely decease under such revolting circumstances, and in the midst of the illustrious career of a ruler whose personal excellence has made him an object of honest pride to his own countrymen, and of just admiration to the rest of the world, and whose earnest endeavor to maintain friendly relations with Great Britain must ever endear his name and memory to the people of this country.

That this council also deeply sympathize with Mrs. Lincoln and family under their heavy bereavement, and sincerely pray that they may be supported by Him " who is the husband of the widow, and the father of the fatherless."

That these resolutions be subscribed by Provost Dickie, in name and on behalf of the council, and presented by him to the minister in London of the United States of America.

JOHN DICKIE, Provost.

At a meeting of the town council of the borough of Kidderminster, in the county of Worcester, held Wednesday, the 3d day of May, 1865—

Moved by Mr. Councillor P. Talbot ; seconded by Mr. Councillor Boycott—

That this council, representing the inhabitants of the borough of Kidderminster, desires to give utterance to the feelings of grief and horror at the assassination of President LINCOLN, and the attempted murder of Mr. Seward, and to convey to the United States government and people, and to Mrs. Lincoln, an expression of its profound sympathy and sincere condolence.

Carried unanimously.

KING'S LYNN—GUILDHALL.

At a congregation there holden on Friday, the 19th day of May, A. D. 1865—present, William Monement, esquire, mayor; Aldermen Francis J. Cresswell, Walter Moyse, John G. Saunders, and William Seppings; Councillors Henry W. Allen, Robert Cook, Joseph Cooper, Richard Coller, W. D. Harding, Geo. Holditch, S. Marsters, William Plews, H. B. Plowright, James Seals, T. M. Wilkin—it was moved by Mr. Alderman Moyse, seconded by Mr. Councillor Cook, and resolved unanimously—

That the mayor, aldermen, and burgesses of this borough, in common council assembled, desire to record their feelings of horror and indignation at the atrocious assassination of the late President of the United States, ABRAHAM LINCOLN, and the murderous attack on Mr. Secretary Seward, and to express their deep sympathy with the people of the United States under the great national calamity which has befallen them; and with Mrs. Lincoln and her bereaved family in the irreparable loss they have sustained.

That copies of the above resolution be forwarded through one of the members for the borough to Mr. Adams, the American minister in London, for transmission to the American government and to Mrs. Lincoln.

[SEAL.]   **WILLIAM MONEMENT,** *Mayor.*

Address of the provost, magistrates and town council of the royal burgh of Kirkcaldy, Scotland.

MAY 9, 1865.

SIR: The provost, magistrates and town council of the royal burgh of Kirkcaldy, Scotland, desire to express their unfeigned sorrow at the tragic termination of the career of the late loved and lamented President of the United States of America, ABRAHAM LINCOLN.

They join in the universal cry of horror and detestation at the dreadful crime which has inflicted so deep a wound in the heart of the nation, and has awakened so keen a sympathy with you throughout the civilized world.

They recognize in the late President a man who, by his honesty, vigor, and ability, secured the intense affection and respect of the people; one fitted to rule in the midst of the greatest civil conflict the world has seen, and to temper with forbearance and clemency the triumph over the vanquished. They join in earnest hope that your severe and protracted struggles may terminate with his intentions and desires fully accomplished, in the downfall of slavery, and in the entire removal from your great nation of an evil which has hitherto trammelled and distressed it. They anticipate a bright future for America in the reign of freedom, intelligence, and Christian worth; they desire an intimate and friendly understanding between her and the government and people of Great Britain; and trust that, together, they may long continue the pioneers and promoters of civilization and freedom.

They will feel obliged by your communicating these sentiments to the government of America.

Signed in name and by authority of the provost, magistrates and town council of the royal burgh of Kirkcaldy, and the seal of the burgh hereunto appended.

[SEAL.]   **PATRICK D. SWAN,**
                    Provost Magistrate of Kirkcaldy, N. B.

CHARLES FRANCIS ADAMS, Esq.,
      Envoy Extraordinary and Minister Plenipotentiary
            for the United States of America, London.

*Address of the provost, magistrates and town council of the royal burgh of
Kirkcaldy, Scotland, to Mrs. Lincoln.*

MAY 9, 1865.

MADAM: Permit us, the provost, magistrates and town council of the royal
burgh of Kirkcaldy, Scotland, to approach you in order to express our deep
sympathy with you under your sore bereavement, and the dreadful shock which
the removal from your side, by such foul means, of a husband who had earned
the respect, love, and admiration of so great a people, must have given you.

We commend you to the care and protection of the Almighty Father, who
alone can heal the wound which this great calamity has inflicted.

We pray that He may be your God and guide through life, your constant
protector and stay, and that, to soothe your sorrow, you may enjoy the attachment of the great people over whom your lamented husband ruled with so much
ability and success, and whose virtues we doubt not will be embalmed in the
hearts of their grateful posterity.

Signed in name and by authority of the provost, magistrates and town
council of the burgh of Kirkcaldy, and the seal of the burgh hereto appended:

[SEAL.]   PATRICK D. SWAN,
Provost of Kirkcaldy, N. B.

Address of the corporation of Kendal to Mrs. Lincoln.

The corporation of Kendal approach Mrs. Lincoln with their respectful
expression of sincere condolence on the incalculable loss she has so suddenly
and so painfully sustained.

It having pleased the Almighty Ruler of events to permit the newly
re-elected head of the American people to be removed on the threshold of his
continued possession of the chair of state, thus overturning a nation's plans for
its own government, the corporation feel that, in the solemn presence of such
a lesson of the instability of the schemes of man, the death of the President
must have come upon his afflicted family as a national as well as a domestic
bereavement. But it is with regard to the latter deep sorrow that the corporation venture to offer their sincere sympathy to Mrs. Lincoln and her children.
The amiability and kindliness of the departed President were not limited to his
connections, but extended to his opponents; his prayers for peace, and the
dignity of his benevolence in the hour of successful triumph, have left behind
a light pure and bright for those who succeed him.

[SEAL.]   JOHN WHITWELL,
Vice-Mayor of Kendal.

Address of the corporation of the borough of Kendal to the government of the United States.

The corporation of the borough of Kendal, moved by indignation at the foul and treasonable assassination of the late President of the United States, hereby transmit to his excellency Charles Francis Adams, for communication to the American government, the sincere expression of sorrow that the life of the chief ruler of the American people has been sacrilegiously taken at the moment he was designing, by conciliatory and kindly measures, to heal the discord and anarchy that has so grievously afflicted the United States. It will rejoice the corporation of Kendal to learn, in the process of time, that the sanguinary struggle, during which so many precious lives on both sides have been sacrificed, has eventually resulted in freedom to the whole family of man on the North American continent—a consummation necessary to the sacred character of a free constitutional state.

[SEAL.]   JOHN WHITWELL,
                                        Vice-Mayor.

At a public meeting of the inhabitants of Kendal, convened on behalf of the mayor by John Whitwell, esq., the ex-mayor, and held the 6th day of May, 1865, the following proceedings took place :

The following resolution, proposed by Mr. Henry Wilson, seconded by Mr. John Robinson, and supported by James Cropper, esq., (by request,) was carried unanimously :

The inhabitants of the borough of Kendal in public meeting assembled—

Resolved, That it is their bounden duty to express their horror and detestation of the treacherous assassination of the Chief Magistrate of the United States, the late President LINCOLN, and of the murderous attack on the life of Mr. Secretary Seward ; and they request his excellency Mr. Adams to convey from them to the authorities of the United States and to the American people the expression of condolence on the death of the head of their government by the hand of treason and crime.

The following resolution, proposed by the Rev. William Taylor, and seconded by Charles Lloyd Braithwaite, esq., was carried unanimously :

Resolved, That the honorable widow and children of the late President of the United States be respectfully informed that this meeting enters deeply into their great sorrow, sympathizing with them in their sudden and most afflictive bereavement, and trusts that it may please the great Ruler of the Universe, in

41

this His inscrutable dispensation, to comfort those who mourn, and to visit with His healing presence the widow and fatherless in their affliction.

Signed on behalf of the meeting:

JOHN WHITWELL,

Ex-Mayor, Chairman.

Address of condolence with the American people.

We, the inhabitants of Keighley, in public meeting assembled, having learned with deepest sorrow and regret the horrible act of foul assassination of his Excellency ABRAHAM LINCOLN, President of the United States of America, and the attempt upon the life of Mr. Seward, Secretary of State, do hereby express our sympathy with the American people, and especially with Mrs. Lincoln, her family, and the members of the late President's cabinet, for the great loss they are thus called upon to sustain in that pure, kind-hearted, forgiving, and persevering friend to the human race, so violently removed from his high and responsible position in life. We deplore the loss of such a good and great man, and deprecate the foul deed as a blot upon the human character. We recognize among the American people many of our beloved relatives and friends, and to all we offer the right-hand of human brotherhood, expressing our earnest wish for the future peace, prosperity, and amicable relations of the nation with this and every other country; and we pray the God of all peace to guide them in all domestic affairs, to preserve them from discord at home and abroad, and especially from further deeds of dark and fiendish assassination and lawless violence, which they with us equally abhor.

JOSEPH CRAVEN, *Chairman.*

We, the undersigned inhabitants of the town of Kettering, in the county of Northampton, desire to express, through his excellency the American minister, our horror at and detestation of the atrocious crime by which the President of the United States has been deprived of his life, and our deep sympathy with the people and government, as well as with the family of the late President.

H. LINSAY, *Rector.*

JAMES MURSELL, *Wesleyan Minister.*

MILES B. PICKERING, *Baptist Minister.*

(The above memorial of the inhabitants of Kettering was signed by eight hundred persons.)

Resolutions passed at a public meeting of the inhabitants of the city of Kingston, in the island of Jamaica, held at the Baptist chapel, East Queen street, on Thursday, June 1, 1865, the honorable L Q. Bowerbank, custos, in the chair.

RESOLUTION 1.

That this meeting rejoices in the prospective termination of the fratricidal war which has for four years desolated the United States of America, and trusts, by the blessing of God, that soon peace may be permanently established in that country; that all its institutions, social, political, and commercial, may be speedily restored to their former order and prosperity; and that all classes of its citizens may be once more united together in peace, amity, and love.

Moved by Rev. W. Gardner; seconded by Rev. E. Nuttall.

RESOLUTION 2.

That this meeting would reverently and thankfully acknowledge the overruling providence of Almighty God, in having evolved from the late terrible war the blessings of emancipation to four millions of human brings, and congratulate the United States that their country has thus become delivered from the curse and dishonor of slavery, and is now throughout its entire and vast extent a land of liberty, in which every man, woman, and child, without any distinction of class, country, or color, may enjoy the benefits of its charter—life, liberty, and the pursuit of happiness.

Moved by Rev. Seth Wolcott; seconded by the Rev. Mr. Dilavante.

RESOLUTION 3.

That this meeting would express its deep sympathy with all those families whose homes the late awful struggle has made desolate, and prayerfully commend the widows who have been deprived of their husbands, and orphans whose fathers have been slain, to the loving care and protection of Him who is the widow's friend and the father of the fatherless; and most especially would it mingle its sympathies with the nation, on account of the awful calamity which has fallen upon it in the moment of its greatest triumph, by the assassination of its late President, as also with his bereaved widow and family whom this terrible event has deprived of one whom they so tenderly and reverently loved, and who was so highly and deservedly honored by a great and mighty nation.

Moved by Rev. W. Holdsworth; seconded by Rev. W. Hamilton

RESOLUTION 4.

That this meeting cannot refrain from its expression of horror and detestation of the foul crime which has so suddenly deprived President LINCOLN of life by the hand of an assassin; that it would pray the Father of Mercies to watch over the interests and welfare of the United States in this eventful and perilous crisis of their history, and by the communication of His grace to him who has succeeded the late lamented President in the government of the republic, by the impartation of wisdom and discretion to those officers of state in whose hands is placed the solemn trust of directing public affairs, and to the people at large a spirit of mutual forbearance, conciliation, and good order, so that no further evils may result from the awful tragedy that has filled the land with mourning.

Moved by Rev. James Watson; seconded by Rev. W. Raw.

RESOLUTION 5.

That this meeting would record its profound veneration and highest respect and admiration for the character of him whose untimely death it deplores, and its conviction that history will not only enshrine his name among the noblest patriots and most enlightened statesmen that have ever presided over the destiny of nations, but that the memory of ABRAHAM LINCOLN will be embalmed in the hearts of millions as one whose private virtues, simple honesty of purpose, and enlarged philanthropy rank him as one of the greatest and most honorable of men.

Moved by Rev. S. Oughton; seconded by Rev. E. Palmer.

RESOLUTION 6.

That John Camp, esq., vice-consul of the United States of America, be requested to forward a copy of these resolutions to his government, with an assurance of the deep sympathy of the inhabitants of Jamaica in their present bereavement, and earnest interest in their future prosperity and happiness.

Moved by Thomas Oughton, esq.; seconded by Richard C. Hitchins, esq.

LEWIS Q. BOWERBANK,

Custos Rotulorum, Chairman.

KINGSTON, JAMAICA, *June* 5, 1865.

His Excellency ANDREW JOHNSON,

President of the United States of America:

May it please your Excellency: By desire of a numerous meeting of the inhabitants of this city, held at the Tabernacle on the 1st instant, in condolence on the assassination of your beloved late President, I have the honor to hand herewith a copy of resolutions and address which were unanimously adopted, and also to state that the sympathies of the people of Jamaica have ever been with your government. I have further to ask the condescension of your Excellency towards the meeting, by placing the enclosed letters in possession of Mrs. Lincoln and the honorable William H. Seward, giving expression to our sincere and respectful wishes.

I have the honor to be, with the highest respect, your Excellency's most obedient servant,

GEORGE W. GORDON, *Chairman.*

Address of the inhabitants of Kingston, Jamaica, to President Johnson.

KINGSTON, JAMAICA, *June* 1, 1865.

SIR: We, the inhabitants of Kingston, Jamaica, on this melancholy occasion, seek the opportunity of conveying to you and the people of America the inexpressible grief we feel, and the sympathy which touches our hearts, on the sad event which has not only overtaken the nation of America, but, we may say, the whole world, in the tragical end of the great and renowned Mr. LINCOLN, your late President.

Our feelings revolt at the atrocious, cowardly, and heartless manner in which his valuable life was taken, and by which the cause of truth, liberty, and righteousness has been deprived of one its greatest supporters the world ever produced.

When we reflect on his fixed principles of humanity and truth, from which he could not be moved by threats nor tempted by selfish interests to swerve, we find that he was of a singularly great mind. He accomplished, under God, great purposes, and his memory claims a reputation which can never be tarnished. We could wish that his most valuable life had been spared to see the unnatural and terrible war, which he had so nearly subdued, brought to a conclusion; "but though dead, he yet speaketh." We hope that that freedom which has cost the penalty of life may be ever a memento of him, dear in the heart of the people of America, in present and succeeding generations. We beg you, as the representative of the American people, and, through you, his surviving widow, to accept this our special condolence in the sudden bereavement which has caused such general sorrow, and we hope that it will please God to grant sustaining grace in the hour of need, and that the dispensation may be sanctified in its influences.

We have also to convey to the honorable William H. Seward, Secretary of State, our heartfelt congratulations on the narrow escape of his life from the hands of the base ruffian, who so barbarously assaulted him on a bed of sickness. We hope that Almighty God may be pleased yet to spare his valuable life, and that his remaining days on earth may be peace.

destruction on a bed of sickness, and thanks God for this token of mercy to Mr. Seward, whose life it is hoped may be yet long spared for future usefulness

We heartily convey to yourself our best wishes for the success of your administration, and the happiness and prosperity of the nation, whose greatness is so truly enhanced by the blessings of freedom to all its subjects.

By desire and on behalf of the meeting:

GEO. W. GORDON, *Chairman.*
JNO. H. CROLE, *Secretary.*

His Excellency ANDREW JOHNSON,
President of the United States of America.

Resolutions passed at a meeting held by the citizens of Kingston, Jamaica.

At a numerous meeting of the inhabitants of Kingston, Jamaica, held at the Tabernacle Parade, on Thursday, 1st of June, 1865, to give expression of deep sympathy with the United States of America, which have suffered sad bereavement by the assassination of their late distinguished President, ABRAHAM LINCOLN, George W. Gordon, esq., was unanimously called to the chair, and the following resolutions were passed:

Moved by Mr. W. K. Smith; seconded by Rev. Mr. Dingwall:

Resolved, 1st. That this meeting records with profound grief the overwhelming calamity which has afflicted the cause of humanity and freedom, and also the civilized world, by the tragical and sad manner in which the most useful and valuable life of the great and justly beloved President of the United States of America, ABRAHAM LINCOLN, was suddenly terminated by the barbarous act of an unscrupulous assassin.

Moved by Rev. Mr. Crole; seconded by Mr. J. Williamson:

Resolved, 2d. That this meeting desires to express its sense of gratitude to the memory of the lamented late President of the United States, and also to his surviving Secretary, the Hon. W. H. Seward, for their discreet, untiring, and successful labors in the most critical crisis of American history, and during which protracted period, by their persevering and courageous efforts, they were able to subdue a most stubborn and unnatural rebellion, and, by the mercy of God, defended the cause of truth and righteousness to an extent which shall hand down their memories to posterity with lustre on the pages of history.

Moved by Mr. M. A. Hearse, of the United States of America; seconded by Mr. W. H. Bercley:

Resolved, 3d. That this meeting congratulates the Hon. W. H. Seward on the narrow escape of his life from the hand of the base ruffian who sought his to his fellow-creatures; and when it may please God to remove him from this present sphere of labors may he receive the welcome approbation of his heavenly Benefactor.

Moved by Rev. J. F. Roach; seconded by Mr. J. Gordon:

Resolved, 4th. That this meeting glories in the fact, and humbly acknowledges with devout gratitude the hand of Almightly God, in the near approach of the entire abolition of slavery in America, and trusts that a similar blessing awaits at an early period all other slaveholding countries.

Moved by Mr. J. Goldson; seconded by Mr. W. Harris:

Resolved, 5th. That a copy of the foregoing resolutions and the address herewith be signed by the chairman and secretary and forwarded to the President, and also a copy of the resolutions to Mrs. Lincoln and the Hon. W. H. Seward, in the most acceptable manner, and the chairman, the Rev. J. F. Roach, Rev. J. H. Crole, and Messrs M. A. Hearse and W. K. Smith, be a committee for such purpose.

Moved by Mr. J. G. Surgeon; seconded by Mr. M. A. Hearse:

Resolved, 6th. That a copy of these resolutions be sent to each of the newspapers of this island, and to the New York Herald, and also to the London Times.

Moved by Mr. M. A. Hearse; seconded by Mr. W. K. Smith:

Resolved, 7th. That the thanks of the meeting be tendered to the chairman for the able manner in which he presided over the meeting.

GEO. W. GORDON, *Chairman.*
JNO. H. CROLE, *Secretary.*

Resolution passed at a meeting held by the inhabitants of Kingston-upon-Hull.

TOWN HALL, KINGSTON-UPON-HULL, *April* 29. 1865.

At a meeting of the inhabitants of Kingston-upon-Hull, duly convened by the mayor, it was

Unanimously resolved, That the inhabitants of Kingston-upon-Hull, in public meeting assembled, desire to express the feelings of horror and indignation with which they heard of the assassination of the President of the United States, and the barbarous attempt on the life of the Secretary of State, and also their deep sympathy with the government and people of the United States, as well as with the widow and the family of the late President, at the great loss which they have sustained.

[SEAL.]   HENRY J. ATTKINSON,
Mayor of Kingston-upon-Hull, and Chairman of the Meeting.

At the quarterly meeting of the mayor, aldermen, and council of the borough of Ludlow, held in council chamber, the 4th day of May, 1865, the following resolution was unanimously agreed to, and it was ordered that the corporate common seal be affixed thereto:

Resolved, That this council express their sorrow and indignation at the atrocious murder of ABRAHAM LINCOLN, the late President of the United States, and record their deep sympathy with the people of the great American nation in the heavy affliction that has befallen them.

[SEAL.]　　　　　　　　　　　　　JOHN HARDING, *Mayor.*

At a quarterly meeting of the council of the borough of Llanidloes, in the principality of Wales, Great Britain, held pursuant to summons, on the 5th day of May, A. D. 1865, it was moved, seconded, and carried *nem. con.*—

That the council of the borough of Llanidloes hereby unanimously express their extreme abhorrence of the assassination of the lamented late President LINCOLN, and their deep sympathy and condolence with Mrs. Lincoln upon her great bereavement, and also with the American people for the great loss they have sustained, and at a very critical period of their history, in that most honest, sagacious, and conciliatory statesman and patriot, their late President.

Signed on behalf of the council:

[SEAL.]　　　　　　　　　　　　　THOS. F. ROBERTS, *Mayor.*

Resolution passed by the town council of the borough of Lymington, May 2, 1865.

Resolved, That this meeting, having heard of the great loss the American commonwealth has sustained in the horrible assassination of its President, and the murderous attack upon Mr. Seward, desire to convey to the United States government and people, and to Mrs. Lincoln, its sympathy and condolence; and that the town clerk do forward a copy of this resolution to the American minister in London.

E. H. MOORE, *Town Clerk.*

At a quarterly meeting of the town council of the borough of Leominster, in the county of Hereford, held on the 11th day of May, 1865, it was moved by Mr. Alderman James, and seconded by Mr. Rudge, and carried unanimously—

That this council, feeling deep indignation at the cowardly and brutal assassination of the American President, ABRAHAM LINCOLN, and the attempt on the life of Mr. Seward, are desirous of expressing their sympathy with Mrs.

Lincoln and the American citizens at the great loss they have sustained, and the heavy affliction with which they have been visited.

That a copy of this resolution be duly signed and sealed by the mayor, and transmitted by the town clerk to the American minister of the United States in this country.

[SEAL.]   JOHN JACKSON, *Mayor.*

BOROUGH OF LANCASTER, IN THE COUNTY PALATINE OF LANCASTER

At a quarterly meeting of the council of the said borough, held in the council chamber in the Town Hall, within the said borough, on Wednesday, the 3d day of May, 1865—present, James Williamson, esq., mayor, in the chair—it was

Unanimously resolved, That this council shares in the spontaneous and deeply felt indignation and horror of the people of this country at the atrocious assassination of the late President of the United States, and the barbarous attack on Mr. Secretary Seward—deeds most cowardly and détestable, which no political considerations can palliate, and which must shock the whole civilized world.

That this council desires to express, through the American minister now in London, its deep sympathy and condolence with the United States government and people, and with the widow and family of the late President, at the loss they have sustained.

That copies of these resolutions be presented to Mr. Adams, the resident American minister.

JAMES WILLIAMSON, *Mayor.*

Extracted from the minutes:

THOMAS SWAINSON, *Town Clerk.*

CITY OF LINCOLN.

At a meeting of the council of the mayor, aldermen, and citizens of the city of Lincoln, held at the Guildhall in the said city, on Tuesday, the 9th day of May, 1865, it was proposed by the worshipful the mayor of Lincoln, Richard Sutton Harvey, esq., and seconded by Mr. Thomas John Nathaniel Brogden, and carried unanimously—

That the mayor, aldermen, and citizens of the city of Lincoln, England, in council assembled, are desirous of expressing their most profound sympathy with Mrs. Lincoln and the people of the United States, now plunged into the deepest sorrow by a deed which has in a moment not only deprived her of a beloved husband, but them also of their elected chief, and filled the mind of every member of their great and intelligent republic, as well as the mind of every thoughtful individual throughout the world, with feelings of the utmost horror, indignation, abhorrence, and grief.

That the mayor, aldermen, and citizens, in council assembled, are desirous, most respectfully, to present to Mrs. Lincoln their sincere and heartfelt sympathy and condolence on the melancholy loss she has sustained in the death of her illustrious husband.

That the mayor, aldermen, and citizens rejoice that the dastardly attempt upon the life of Mr. Seward was frustrated, and sincerely hope that he may long be spared, to continue that assistance to his bereaved country which he has hitherto afforded, and with the help of his great colleagues may succeed in speedily restoring it to a position of freedom, happiness, and peace.

[SEAL.]   RICHARD SUTTON HARVEY, *Mayor.*
                 JOHN THOMAS TWEED, *Town Clerk.*

At a meeting of the citizens of Lincoln, convened by public notice, and held in the Guildhall in the said city, on Saturday, the 20th day of May, 1865, at which meeting the mayor, Richard Sutton Harvey, esq., presided, the following resolutions were proposed and unanimously carried:

Proposed by Mr. Coroner Hitchins, and seconded by the Rev. A. F. Macdonald—

Resolved, That the citizens of Lincoln deeply regret the melancholy termination, by assassination, of the life of President LINCOLN, and more especially at a time when the continuance of his career of usefulness was in the greatest need.

Resolved, That they deplore the irretrievable loss which Mrs. Lincoln has sustained, and fervently sympathize with her in her sorrow and bereavement.

Resolved, That the citizens of Lincoln sincerely hope the pleasing recollection of the many virtues of her departed husband may in a measure tend to alleviate the sorrows of Mrs. Lincoln.

Resolved, That they rejoice that the deadly intentions of the cowardly assassin upon the valuable life of Mr. Seward and his sons were thwarted, and they cheerfully congratulate him upon his providential deliverance.

[SEAL.]   RICHARD SUTTON HARVEY, *Mayor.*

At a public meeting of the inhabitants of the borough of Leicester, England, held in the Temperance Hall, on Friday, the 28th day of April, 1865, Alfred Burgess, esquire, mayor, in the chair, it was unanimously resolved—

First. That this meeting records its unqualified abhorrence of the assassination of his Excellency ABRAHAM LINCOLN, the late President of the United States of America.

Second. That the inhabitants of Leicester greatly deplore the loss which the citizens of the United States have sustained in the violent death of their patriotic and honest President, and deeply sympathize with them at this important crisis.

Third. That this meeting desires to express its deep sympathy with the widow and family of the late President of the United States, trusting that, in the midst of their unparalleled affliction, they may find comfort from the memory of the high character of the deceased, and from the gratitude of a great nation.

Fourth. That this meeting, whilst receiving with feelings of thankfulness an improved account of the state of the honorable W. H. Seward, desires to express its strong sympathy with himself and his family.

Fifth. That the foregoing resolutions be signed by the mayor for transmission to the honorable C. F. Adams, the American ambassador.

ALFRED BURGESS, *Mayor.*

TOWN HALL, *Limerick, May* 9, 1865.

SIR: At a public meeting held in this city on Saturday, the 6th instant, to express the opinion of the citizens of Limerick on the assassination of President LINCOLN and the attempt on the life of Mr. Seward, a series of resolutions were passed unanimously, and which I now enclose, with a request that you will have copies sent to Mrs. Lincoln, also to Mr. Seward.

Assuring you of my own feeling of sympathy with the American people, and abhorrence of the cowardly act which has been committed,

I have the honor to remain your obedient servant,

JOHN R. TINSLY,
Mayor of Limerick.

His Excellency C. F. ADAMS,
United States Minister, London.

LIMERICK, *May* 6, 1865.

Proposed by Richard Russell, esq, J. P., seconded by Councillor Synan, J. P., and unanimously passed:

That this meeting view with the deepest abhorrence the assassination of the President of the United States, and desire to record their most heartfelt sympathy with the American people in the great national loss sustained by the removal from the head of the government of a man who displayed in the discharge of his duties the greatest ability and zeal for the interest of the people over whom he presided.

Proposed by Caleb Powell, esq., J. P., seconded by Eugene O'Callaghan, esq., J. P., and carried unanimously:

That as Irishmen we feel it our duty to express our deep sorrow and indignation at the attempt to assassinate Mr. Seward, Foreign Secretary of the States of America.

Proposed by Alderman Quintiran, J. P., and seconded by Thomas Boyse, esq., J. P.:

That copies of the resolutions now passed be forwarded to the American minister in London, and to Mrs. Lincoln and Mrs. Seward.

JOHN R. TINSLY,
Mayor of Limerick, Chairman of Meeting.

Resolution passed at a meeting held by the town council of the royal burgh of Lanark.

LANARK, May 8, 1865.

At an ordinary monthly meeting of the town council of the royal burgh of Lanark, before proceeding to the ordinary business of the meeting, the following resolution was unanimously agreed to:

That this council desire, in common with every public body in the British nation, to express their feelings of horror on learning of the dastardly murder of ABRAHAM LINCOLN, President of the United States of America. This crime, which would have been atrocious under any circumstances, is rendered doubly so in this instance, from its having been committed upon a man whose honesty of purpose, gentleness of disposition, and greatness of character were becoming fully appreciated by the whole civilized world, and were of peculiar value in the crisis which the American nation had just reached. This council cannot, under such circumstances, refrain from expressing their deep sympathy with the people of that country in the great loss they have just sustained, and more especially with Mrs. Lincoln, to whom the loss must be altogether irreparable, and for this purpose order a copy of this minute, signed by the provost on behalf of the council, to be forwarded to the ambassador of the United States of America in London.

[SEAL.]   ALEXANDER MAXWELL ADAMS,
Provost.

COUNTY OF LANARK, SCOTLAND.

At a general meeting of the lord lieutenant, sheriff, and commissioners of supply of the county of Lanark, and of the provosts and chief magistrates of the city of Glasgow, royal burghs of Lanark, Rutherglen, and burghs of Hamilton and Airdrie, holden at Lanark, on the 1st day of May, 1865, it was, on motion of the Right Honorable Lord Belhaven and Hamilton, K. T., &c., &c., lord lieutenant of the county, seconded by Sir Archibald Alison, baronet, sheriff of the county—

Unanimously resolved, That the meeting do give expression to the feelings of profound sorrow and of deep horror and detestation with which they, in common with all the inhabitants of the British islands, regard the late atrocious murder of President LINCOLN, and the murderous assault upon the honorable Secretary Seward.

It was also

Unanimously resolved, That a copy of this resolution be forwarded to his excellency the minister of the United States for presentation to his government.

BELHAVEN AND HAMILTON,
Lieutenant and Convener of the County.

At a meeting of the mayor, aldermen and burgesses of the borough of Liverpool, in common council assembled, held in the Town Hall within the said borough, on Wednesday, the 3d day of May, 1865—present, Edward Laurence, esq., mayor, &c.—it was

Unanimously resolved, That this council desires to record its horror and indignation at the atrocious murder of ABRAHAM LINCOLN, President of the United States, and to express its sympathy with the American nation under their severe loss, as well as to Mrs. Lincoln in the sad bereavement she has sustained.

And it was also

Resolved, That a minute of the foregoing resolution, under the common seal, should be sent to Mrs. Lincoln through the British minister at Washington.

[SEAL.] EDWARD LAURENCE, *Mayor.*
WILLIAM SHUTTLEWORTH, *Town Clerk.*

LIVERPOOL, *April* 27, 1865.

At a meeting of the inhabitants of Liverpool, held in St. George's Hall, on the evening of Thursday, the 27th of April, 1865, called for the purpose of expressing sorrow and indignation at the assassination of ABRAHAM LINCOLN, President of the United States of America, the following resolutions were passed unanimously :

1. That this meeting of the inhabitants of Liverpool records its horror and detestation of the atrocious assassination perpetrated at Washington on the fourteenth of this month.

2. That this meeting desires to express its deepest sympathy with the families of President LINCOLN and Mr. Seward in the great affliction which has befallen them.

3. That this meeting desires, also, to express its profound sympathy with the people of the United States in the loss they have sustained by the death of President LINCOLN, and its earnest hope that the events we now deplore may not imperil or delay the triumph of freedom and of right, or the restoration of peace in America.

4. That the resolutions now passed be signed by the chairman on behalf of the meeting, and be transmitted through the proper authorities to Washington.

CHARLES WILSON, Chairman.

Resolution passed at a meeting held by the inhabitants of the borough of Liverpool.

At a public meeting of the inhabitants of the borough of Liverpool, held in St. George's Hall, on Thursday, the 27th day of April, 1865, Edward Laurence, esq , mayor, in the chair, it was

Resolved unanimously, That the inhabitants of Liverpool, in public meeting assembled, do hereby express their deepest sorrow and indignation at the atrocious assassination of ABRAHAM LINCOLN, President of the United States, and of Mr. Frederick Seward, Assistant Secretary of State ; and at the dastardly attempt, about the same hour, on the life of Mr. Seward, Secretary of State. They desire that the government and the people of the United States should understand that no difference of opinion on the merits of the conflict of the last four years avails to prevent the unanimous condemnation of so great a crime against our common humanity.

EDWARD LAURENCE, Mayor.

At a meeting of the American Chamber of Commerce of Liverpool, held on the 28th day of April, 1865—present, Wellwood Maxwell, (W. A. & G Maxwell & Co.,) president; J. Spence, (Richardson, Spence & Co.,) vice-president; F. A. Hamilton, (Brown, Shipley & Co.;) Stewart H. Brown; M. Hyslop, (W. A. & G. Maxwell & Co.;) Henry W. Gair, T. K. Twist, (Rathbone Brothers & Co.;) C. W. Pickering, (T. H. Schroeder & Co.;) Charles MacIver, (C. & D. MacIver;) Charles Forget, Charles P. Melly, George Melly, (Melly, Forget & Co.; William Rome, (Eyre, Evans & Co.;) H Stolterfoht, H. Stolterfoht, jr., (Stolterfoht, Sons & Co.;) Thomas Boyde, Thomas Stolterfoht, (Boyde, Edwards & Co.;) Ferdinand Karck, (Drake, Kleinwort & Cohen;) Edgar Garston, (George Green & Co.;) George Martin, Meadows Frost—it was

Unanimously resolved, That this chamber begs to express to the American minister, and through him to the government of the United States, its deep abhorrence of the foul deed that has been perpetrated by assassins in the ruthless murder of the President of the United States and the dastardly attempt upon the life of Mr. Secretary Seward.

The chamber offers to the whole American people its heartfelt condolence on the terrible loss they have sustained in the person of their Chief Magistrate.

To Mrs. Lincoln and Mrs. Seward the chamber would respectfully tender the expression of its most sincere sympathy in their great affliction.

WELLWOOD MAXWELL, *President.*

At a special general meeting of the Liverpool Chamber of Commerce, held on Friday, the 5th of May, 1865, H. W. Meade King, esq, vice-president, in the chair, the following resolutions were unanimously adopted:

Resolved, That this chamber, in special meeting assembled, hereby record the profound sorrow and indignation with which they have heard of the assassination of the honorable ABRAHAM LINCOLN, and the attempt on the life of the honorable W. H. Seward. While expressing their deep sympathy with the Chambers of Commerce of the United States of America, and through them with the nation at large, in this national calamity, they fervently hope that it may not delay the return of peace and confidence to an afflicted country.

Resolved, That the president be requested to forward a copy of this resolution to his excellency Charles Francis Adams, the American minister, for transmission to his government at Washington, and that copies be also sent to Mrs. Lincoln and the honorable W. H. Seward, and also to the New York Chamber of Commerce, with a request that that chamber will kindly send copies to every other Chamber of Commerce or Board of Trade in the United States.

Mercantile Marine Service Association, Liverpool.

At a meeting of the council of the Mercantile Marine Service Association, held at the office of the association, 66 Tower buildings, Water street, Liverpool, on Monday, the 1st of May, 1865, Captain Benjamin Sproule in the chair, it was

Unanimously resolved, (on the motion of Captain James W. Jeffrey, seconded by Captain James R. Rea,) That this association desires to express, in the strongest possible terms, its deep feelings of sorrow and indignation at the recent foul assassination of Mr. ABRAHAM LINCOLN, President of the United States of America, and also at the diabolical attempt, made about the same hour, upon the lives of Mr. Secretary Seward and his son, Mr. Seward, the under-secretary.

It was further

Unanimously resolved, That this association also ventures to place on record its heartfelt sympathy with Mrs. Lincoln and her family in the irreparable loss they have sustained in the awfully sudden and truly sad and unlooked for departure from among them of the late President of the United States, and the association earnestly hope that consolation be ministered to them in this bitter hour of trial and distress.

It was also

Unanimously resolved, That the secretary do transmit copies of the foregoing resolutions, through the proper channel, to Mr. President Johnson, as representing the American people, and to Mrs. Lincoln.

BENJ. SPROULE, *President.*

Vice-President of the Liverpool Cotton Brokers' Association to Mr. Dudley.

LIVERPOOL, *April* 28, 1865.

SIR : At the usual weekly meeting of the Cotton Brokers' Association of this town, held this morning, the appalling assassination of the late President of the United States and the atrocious attempt on the lives of Mr. Secretary Seward and his son, were the theme of unanimous execration and abhorrence.

I have been requested to convey to you, as the representative of the United States at this port, the expression of the deep sympathy and condolence of this association, in common with the country at large, in a calamity so awful, and which has impressed our body with the strongest feelings of profound regret and indignation, as well as of commiseration for a people with whom we are so closely allied in the bonds of good will, as well as in the daily business of our lives. I trust you will favorably receive this imperfect assurance that in this terrible blow which it has pleased God to inflict on your great nation they and you have the utmost possible sympathy of the members of our association, both individually and collectively. In the absence (from ill health) of our president, Edgar Musgrove, esq., I beg to subscribe myself, on behalf of this association, with all respect, sir, your obedieut, humble servant,

D. C. BUCHANAN, Vice-President.

THOMAS H. DUDLEY, Esq.,
American Consul, Liverpool.

At a meeting of the committee of the Liverpool Emancipation Society, held May 3, 1865, the following resolutions were passed unanimously, and ordered to be forwarded to his excellency the Hon. C. F. Adams, for transmission to the government of the United States :

That the Liverpool Emancipation Society, in recording its deepest sorrow for the death of President LINCOLN, cut off as he has been in the midst of a life of usefulness rarely equalled, expresses its sympathy with his bereaved family in their affliction, and with the people of the United States in their loss.

That the society expresses at once its sympathy with Mr. Seward and his family in their sufferings, and its heartfelt satisfaction that the purposes of the assassin were in this case frustrated.

That, in conveying to the people of the United States this testimony of sorrow for their bereavement, this society also records its profoundest thankfulness that in the good providence of God, the great cause of emancipation, so nobly carried out during the last four years by President LINCOLN and the legislature, is in the safe keeping of a people fully awakened to a sense of its responsibility ; a people resolved to make peace on the basis of freedom only, and thus hand down to succeeding generations a heritage enlarged, ennobled and consecrated by the precious blood of martyrs.

Signed on behalf of the society :

CHARLES WILSON, Chairman of Committee.

ROBERT TRIMBLE, Secretary.

FINANCIAL REFORM ASSOCIATION, LIVERPOOL—MONTHLY MEETING, FRIDAY, APRIL

28, 1865—(E. K. Muspratt, esq., in the chair.)

Extract from proceedings.

Moved by Owen Williams. esq.; seconded by Joseph Coventry, esq., and resolved unanimously—

Believing that it is the duty of all associated bodies of Englishmen to give expression to the feelings of horror and indignation excited in every English mind by the execrable murder of the wise, patriotic, and magnanimous ruler of a great people, and this at a moment when triumphant in the terrible struggle which has so long devastated his native land, he had no thoughts but those of clemency toward the vanquished; no desire but to assuage all animosities, and to confer on all classes of his fellow-countrymen, without distinction of color, the blessing of equal rights and privileges; and regarding with equal horror and detestation the murderous assaults on the chief Secretary of State and members of his family, the council of the Liverpool Financial Reform Association desire to convey to the President and people of the United States, to the bereaved widow and family of ABRAHAM LINCOLN, and to the Hon. Mr. Seward, if his life be happily spared, or to his family, if deceased, an assurance of their sincere sorrow and sympathy, in contemplation of the atrocious deeds which have converted the hour of triumph for them and their country into one of universal mourning; and, also, an expression of their earnest hope that, whatever differences of opinion or causes of complaint there may have been on one side or the other, the knowledge that there is not one person in America not closely related to the victims that detests and deplores these savage deeds and their consequences more than every honest man in the United Kingdom, will have the effect of burying in oblivion the remembrances of all such grievances, real or imaginary, and of permanently restoring those feelings of cordial amity which ought ever to prevail between two great nations, one in race, language, laws, and religion, and, henceforth, in really free institutions.   And the council further desire that the Hon. Mr. Adams, resident American minister at London, will have the goodness to transmit this resolution to the proper parties in the United States.

CHARLES EDWARD MACQUEEN,

Secretary.

Resolution passed at the ordinary meeting of the Albert Literary Society.

THE LATE PRESIDENT LINCOLN.

At the ordinary meeting of the Albert Literary Society, on the 4th instant, held at the Royal Institution, Colquitt street, Mr. G. H. Ball in the chair, the following resolution was proposed by Mr. A. B. Hayware, the vice-president, seconded by Mr. E. J. Parr, the treasurer, and carried unanimously—

   " That this society record its deep horror of the enormous crime which has deprived the American people of their Chief Magistrate, and tender to the late President LINCOLN's family, and the nation at large, its sincere sympathy, and also its appreciation of his singular ability, rare integrity, and progressive spirit."

WILLIAM EVANS, *Hon. Secretary.*

LIVERPOOL, *May* 5, 1865.

ABRAHAM LINCOLN.

" *Sic semper tyrannis !*" the assassin cried,
  As LINCOLN fell. O villain! who than he
More lived to set both slave and tyrant free?
Or so enrapt with plans of freedom died,
  . That even thy treacherous deed shall glance aside
  And do the dead man's will by land and sea;
  Win bloodless battles, and make that to be
Which to his living mandate was denied!
Peace to that gentle heart! The peace he sought
  For all mankind, nor for it dies in vain.
Rest to the uncrowned king, who, toiling, brought
  His bleeding country through that dreadful reign;
Who, living, earn'd a world's revering thought,
  And, dying, leaves his name without a stain.

ROBERT LEIGHTON, *of Liverpool.*

At a public meeting of the inhabitants of the borough of Leeds, in the county of York, held in the Town Hall, on the 1st of May, 1865, convened by the mayor, in accordance with a requisition presented to him by the inhabitants—present, the mayor, in the chair—

Resolved, That the inhabitants of Leeds, in public meeting assembled, would emphatically express the feeling of horror and intense regret with which they have heard of the atrocious acts by which the United States of America have been suddenly deprived of their President, and the life of his chief Secretary has been endangered; and that they recall with melancholy interest the friendly feeling invariably displayed by the late President LINCOLN towards this country.

Resolved, That while deeply lamenting the removal of President LINCOLN from his exalted position, at a time when his combined wisdom and benevolence seemed peculiarly needful to secure the peaceful and harmonious reconstruction of the American nation, this meeting earnestly hopes the surviving statesmen of that great republic may succeed in speedily and happily surmounting every obstacle to such a reconstruction, in accordance with the immutable principles of justice and freedom.

Resolved, That a copy of the preceding resolutions, signed by the mayor, on behalf of the meeting, be forwarded to the United States government, and that the American consul at Leeds be requested to transmit such copy to the embassy in London.

Resolved, That copies of the foregoing resolutions be also forwarded to Mrs. Lincoln, with an expression of the deep sympathy entertained by the inhabitants of Leeds for herself and her family in their heavy bereavement and affliction.

J. D. ZUNOCK, *Mayor.*

At a large meeting of work-people, in the Leeds Working Men's Hall, on Thursday evening, April 27, held to hear a dramatic reading, opportunity was taken to show the deep feeling of sympathy felt among the working classes for their brethren in America on the sad loss of President LINCOLN.

The following resolution was unanimously carried, with a request that the American consul in Leeds would kindly forward it to the proper quarter:

Resolved, That this meeting desires to express its deep and heartfelt sympathy with the people of the United States on the terrible bereavement they have just experienced in the assassination of President LINCOLN, and its feeling of horror at the cowardly murder by which they have been deprived of a sound leader, a wise counsellor, a beloved friend, and an honest man. In ABRAHAM LINCOLN the working classes of this country have long had the fullest confidence, as the uncompromising enemy of the detestable institution of slavery; and although recent victories had placed his enemies at his feet, his noble-heartedness and kindly disposition led him to extend forgiveness to them, in the hope of restoring peace and unity among the American people.

This meeting prays that God, in his infinite mercy, will so direct the rulers of America that peace may be soon-restored, the Union cemented, and slavery forever abolished.

FRED. R. SPARK, *Vice-President, Chairman.*

Mr Adams to Mr. Seward.

No. 936.   LEGATION OF THE UNITED STATES,
London, April 28, 1865.

SIR: I had the grief to receive the day before yesterday the telegraphic despatches from Mr. Stanton, the Secretary of War, and from Mr. Hunter, the chief clerk of your department, announcing the afflicting event of the 14th instant, which has thrown our whole people into such deep distress. They also give a narrative of the simultaneous savage onslaught upon yourself in your sick-room, and upon your son, the Assistant Secretary, which had not at the latest date, and which I yet permit myself to hope will not prove fatal to either of you.

I immediately took the requisite measures to communicate the intelligence to the different legations on the continent.

It is but consistency that a rebellion which began in perjury, treachery, and fraud, should close with private assassination.

The whole of the day was one of the greatest excitement. Few events of the present century have created such general consternation and indignation. Many people called personally at the legation to express their deep sympathy, and many more sent me notes of the same tenor.

The notices taken by the press are almost all of them of a most honorable character.   I transmit copies of the leading newspapers.   There seems, at last, to be a general testimony borne to the noble qualities of the President, and the friendly disposition of the Secretary of State.

If all this eulogy be found mingled with the alloy of unworthy aspersions of the Vice-President who succeeds, he has abundant consolation in the reflection that when his predecessor began he was not a whit better treated.   It is a weakness of the press and the people of the country not to value some men properly until they are lost; the case of the late Prince Consort is a remarkable instance.

The proceedings in the two houses of Parliament last evening mark out the line proposed to be adopted by the government on this occasion.

I have the honor to be, sir, your obedient servant,

CHARLES FRANCIS ADAMS.

Hon. WILLIAM H. SEWARD,
Secretary of State, Washington, D. C.

Mr. Adams to Mr. Hunter.

No. 943.]

LEGATION OF THE UNITED STATES,
London, May 4, 1865.

SIR : The death of the President and the fearful circumstances under which it was brought about have occupied the public mind, all over this kingdom, almost exclusively during the past week.

At the desire of the Americans residing in this city, I called a public meeting of all such as might happen to be here, for Monday last.   It was very well attended.   I have the honor to transmit a copy of the proceedings.

I have the honor to transmit a number of addresses, resolutions, or other form of public action taken by various corporate bodies in England, Scotland, and Ireland on this subject, and forwarded to me down to this time, according to the list which is attached to this despatch.

As a further evidence of the extent of the public feeling, I transmit a considerable number of newspapers from different parts of the kingdom which have been sent to me as containing comments upon the late calamity.

A very large number of persons have called at this legation, including most of the members of the corps diplomatique, in token of their sentiments on this occasion.   The labor devolved upon the members of it, in acknowledging all these demonstrations, is not small.   It will also become a serious question to decide upon the most suitable mode of responding to them.   On mature reflection, I should rather recommend one brief, comprehensive communication, which

I might be authorized to print, in some form or other, and send to the respective parties concerned.

I have the honor to be, sir, your obedient servant,

CHARLES FRANCIS ADAMS.

Hon. WILLIAM HUNTER,
    Acting Secretary of State, Washington, D. C.

[Extract.]

A REQUIEM FOR ABRAHAM LINCOLN : AN ADDRESS TO THE LIBERALS OF EUROPE.

" Awake! thou shalt and must !"

BROTHERS : One of our best friends, and one of the best men the world has ever seen, has been called suddenly from us.   We will not say that he is dead, for there is no death for such as he: nothing but life—a glorified and immortal life—both on earth and in heaven.   It will be as wise as consoling for us to reflect that this good man, instead of dying, as his wretched enemies have supposed, has attained to a higher existence—has gone to a companionship more worthy of his exalted merits—has been welcomed home like a good servant to repose from his labors—and is henceforth to be known as one of that sublime brotherhood of sages and heroes who have died that men may be wiser and better.

   *   *   *   *   *   *   *   *

I. THE GLORY OF MR. LINCOLN.

Grandest among the sages and heroes of this generation ! the most perfect embodiment of the genius of a free and mighty people ! the noblest benefactor of his species that has ever toiled and suffered among men ! the glorious father of a whole world's regeneration ! the great prophet of the speedy emancipation of every man on the earth who is burdened and wronged ! there is no mortal name beneath the stars that can be placed beside that of ABRAHAM LINCOLN. He has lived and died, not for America alone, but for the people of England, the people of France, the people of Germany, the people of Italy, the people of every land under heaven.   He has lived and died, not only for American unity and brotherhood, but for the unity and brotherhood of all the groaning and oppressed peoples of Europe.   As simple as a child in the sublime faith that moved him, as sound in every attribute as the sturdy oaks of his native hills, as kindly towards all mankind as a loving mother to her children, as unselfish and as spotless in all his attributes as an angel from heaven, it is not for naught that he has been elevated in the providence of God to the highest pinnacle of glory, where the eyes of all the sons of men can behold him, as a bright and deathless example.   When the foremost of the liberals who had called him to his high office were calling sternly for judgment upon the rebels, he knew how to temper judgment with mercy; when all around him were discouraged by unexpected reverses, his faith remained calm and unshaken. When sympathizers with rebellion obtruded themselves upon him, and told him that certain proposed measures would be the certain destruction of his country, he smilingly bowed them out of his presence, and went on with his labors as steadily as though these croakers of evil had never existed. When a hundred different cliques and parties endeavored to sway him in as many different directions, he wisely selected the right course, and placed his foot firmly upon the precise road that his far-seeing wisdom and humanity pointed out to him. A mental and moral giant, he did not waste his strength upon the little expedients of politicians, but he charged directly upon the great towers of human wretchedness, assaulted incessantly the strongholds of the misguided men who had taken up arms against human liberty; and nobly and gloriously did he carry his warfare to the hour of victory. Patient and long-suffering, animated by a trust in God that gave him sufficient endurance for the onerous duties devolving upon him, looking hopefully towards heaven for the regeneration of mankind, and loving even those who had pointed their weapons at his throat, it was in keeping with all his thoughts and actions that *he spoke kindly of Lee and others in the confederacy*, in the last hours preceding his assassination, and thus grandly sealed the yearnings and tender affection he had so long displayed towards the brave but mistaken men who had attempted the life of the republic.

Brothers! the world is too small to furnish a grave for ABRAHAM LINCOLN, and the spirit of the glorious martyr must continue to dwell among us!

II. THE POWER AND GRANDEUR OF THE AMERICAN REPUBLIC.

In the land beyond the sea, where the spirit of ABRAHAM LINCOLN still animates his people, there is honor and glory. There is weeping, too; there is sorrow too great for utterance, but there is also a hope as radiant as the morning of that blessed eternity to which we are all hastening. The great prophet has indeed left us, but the true seer of God lives forever in the fulfilment of his aspirations, and greater than all surviving voices is that voice which has been so rudely silenced. Over the sea, towering supremely above all the mighty things of the world, there is a redeemed and ennobled nation, quickened into universal life by the spirit of its great leader, and ordained by Almighty God to be the bulwark and the impregnable fortress of universal freedom.

The initial battles of a universal regeneration have been won!

If Mr. LINCOLN did not live to perform all that he intended, and all that we had reason to expect of him, he did certainly live to set in motion the forces that will soon sweep from the face of the earth the enemies of mankind who hated and abused him.

A great change for the better has already been accomplished, and it only remains to carry Mr. LINCOLN's work to its completion.

If the dungeons built by tyranny have not been destroyed, they have at least been shattered by the lightnings of progress, and the light of liberty is to-day shining into them, never more to be darkened.

Glorious light! all hail!

If we are not all of us fully awake to the duties devolving upon us, and if we have not yet entered fully into possession of our promised land, and if we are still loaded unjustly with burdens grievous to be borne, and if many of us are still driven to and fro like cattle, the glad truth is nevertheless manifest that the spirit of God is working lovingly among us, and that the long-desired morning of the world's regeneration will soon dawn upon us.

If there is yet sin and suffering around us, and if weary men are still toiling hard and long for the bare necessities of existence, and if the most vital titles and claims of manhood are yet denied by our governments, and if cruelty and injustice are still potent in many of the affairs touching our personal honor and happiness, it is nevertheless easy to see that the idea of *a government of the people for the people* will soon be realized among all the civilized nations of the earth.

Once more, O glorious era of freedom and freemen, all hail!

*   *   *   *   *   *   *   *   *

Fraternally your brother,

LEON LEWIS,
A Citizen of the United States.

[Translation.]

LONDON, NO. 3 PERCY STREET, BEDFORD SQUARE,
May 5, 1865.

MR. PRESIDENT: In presence of the sombre tomb which encloses the body of citizen ABRAHAM LINCOLN, President of the United States of America, and member of the Grand Lodge of New York, the undersigned, delegates from the lodge of Gymnosophists in London, have the honor of transmitting to you the expression of their fraternal regret for the loss of one of the greatest citizens of the republic of America.

ABRAHAM LINCOLN is no more! He has given his blood for the social restoration of the most pitiable portion of humanity. Death to him is not annihilation, but the beginning of a new life that will endure as long as the memory of man.

The lodge to which we belong has decided to wear mourning for a month in commemoration of that heroic and unfortunate death, and takes this occasion of requesting you, Mr. President, to accept the expression of the regrets which we send in the name of our brethren, and our best wishes for the prosperity of your country and your own personal happiness.

J. P. BERJEAN, (33,)
Grand Venerable Master of the Lodge.
J. LORGUE, *First Warden.*
CHAPERON, *Second Warden.*
L. WOLFF, *Deputy of the Lodge.*
P. LEFEVRE, *Orator.*
CRESPELLE DESIRÉ, *Treasurer.*
L. ARNAUD, *Levite.*
GROT, *Expert.*
DAUTEAUBEL, *Brother Collector.*
T. CHARLES BERJEAN, *Secretary.*

[MASONIC SEAL.]
His Excellency ANDREW JOHNSON,
President of the United States

A common council holden in the chamber of the Guildhall, of the city of London, on Thursday, the 27th day of April, 1865, Hale mayor—

Resolved unanimously, That this court desires, before proceeding to the business of the day, to express its profound sympathy with the people of American at the loss sustained in the death, by assassination, of Mr. LINCOLN the President of the United States, and to record its detestation of the atrocious crime which has been perpetrated.

WOODTHORP.

BEEHIVE OFFICE, 10 *Bolt Court, Fleet street, London.*

At a meeting of the workingmen of London, held at St. Martin's Hall, on Thursday evening, May 4, 1865, Mr. Thomas Bayley Potter, M. P., in the chair, it was

Unanimously resolved, That in addition to expressing their deep sympathy with the people of America for the great loss they have sustained, this meeting also desires to convey to the President, government, and people of the United States, their congratulation on the decisive successes which have lately attended the federal arms, affording a just hope of a speedy suppression of the rebellion, and the entire extinction of the accursed slave institutions, and therefore adopt the following address :

To the President, government, and people of the United States :

We, the workingmen of London, send you greeting ! For more than four years have we watched, with the deepest anxiety, the momentous and stupendous struggle in which you have been engaged; we have sympathized with your reverses, rejoiced over your successes, and hailed with delight your late decisive triumph over the men who raised the standard of rebellion, not for the advancement of liberty, but that they might establish in your midst an empire with the avowed object of maintaining, extending, and perpetuating the accursed slave institution, for so long a period the dark spot in your national history. We were about to congratulate you on your late glorious victory, and on the extirpation from your great republic of that foul stain of slavery, when we were shocked at receiving the intelligence that the man who had done so much to bring about this desired end, gradually and constitutionally, who had pursued steadfastly his anti-slavery policy, braving alike the opposition of the open foe, the fears of the timid, the prejudice of the ignorant, and the abuse of the aristocrat, had fallen a victim to the fiendish attack of an assassin, on the eve of witnessing the consummation of his great and glorious labor, and while the words of conciliation and mercy to the vanquished enemy were yet hovering on his lip.

People of America, we deeply feel with you the great loss you have sustained by the untimely death of your late illustrious President, ABRAHAM LINCOLN, who had endeared himself to his country and mankind, especially to the toiling millions of the civilized world, not less by his pure and stainless character than by his great services to his country in its time of agonizing trial. We feel that the loss of such a man is ours as well as yours. We feel that the loss of such a man is not only a loss to the nation over which he presided, but a loss to the world at large. Raised by the force of his own character and genius from a humble position in the ranks of industry to be the first citizen of a great and glorious republic, his memory will be endeared to and enshrined in the hearts of the toiling millions of all countries, as one of the few uncrowned monarchs of the world. ABRAHAM LINCOLN has been sacrificed in the cause of negro emancipation, and the freedom of the slave has been consecrated by the blood of his deliverer.

People of America, in your grief and affliction we, the workingmen of London, offer you our heartfelt sympathy. We also have to lament the recent loss of a man among us whose life was devoted to our interests and whose political career, like that of your ABRAHAM LINCOLN, though less troubled, was equally pure and stainless, Richard Cobden. May we, acting in the spirit of these two great men, draw closer the bonds of unity between us, and may peace and good will always exist between our respective nations. That man is a traitor to humanity and freedom who would lift his voice or his pen to provoke hostile proceedings between England and America; that man, be he peer or plebeian, be he in the senate or on the platform, or in the press, who would say or write anything in favor of a war between the two countries is little less a miscreant than that assassin who has lately struck down the foremost man among you. Be assured, whatever you may have heard to the contrary, either in a parliament with which we have nothing in common, and in which we are not yet represented, or in the leading articles of the corrupt and venal portion of the press, the workingmen of Great Britain have always been sound upon the great struggle in which you have been engaged, and, while you have been fighting, they have been anxiously watching and awaiting that time, now, it would appear, so happily approaching, when the rights and dignity of labor shall be acknowledged to exist equally in the black man as in the white. It was for this ABRAHAM LINCOLN lived and labored. It was for this ABRAHAM LINCOLN died the martyr of freedom. May his glorious example be as a beacon-light to his successor. May he and those associated with him in the government carry out the principles and policy of ABRAHAM LINCOLN, tempering justice with mercy, and triumph with conciliation, and the blood and treasure poured out during the last four years will not have been sacrificed and expended in vain.

Accept, people of America, the pledge of sympathy and the hand of fellowship and fraternity, from the workingmen of England's great metropolis.

Signed on behalf of the meeting:

THOMAS BAYLEY POTTER,
Chairman.

THOMAS BAYLEY POTTER, *M. P.*,
P. A. TAYLOR, *M. P.*,
EDMOND BEALES, *M. P.*,
JOHN ROBERT TAYLOR,
PROFESSOR BEESLY.
MASON JONES,
F. W. EDGE,
S. ENGLANDER,
J. A. NICHOLAY,
D. D. ROGERS,
Committee.

GEO. POTTER,
W. S. NORTHHOUSE,
Honorary Secretaries.

AND FORTY-TWO OTHER NAMES.

Address of the workingmen of South London to Mrs. Lincoln, Mr. Johnson, and the people of America.

SOUTH LONDON, *April* 28, 1865.

BEREAVED FRIENDS : We, a public meeting of many hundreds of working-men of South London, assembled in front of Surry Chapel, Blackfriars' Road, Surrey, desire to convey to you our sincere and sorrowing sympathy in reference to the sad loss you have sustained by the cruel and blood-thirsty assassination of the truly magnanimous and patriotic President, ABRAHAM LINCOLN, and to record our unmitigated disgust and horror at the brutal treachery and unparalleled baseness of the savage deed of blood which has placed your own and every civilized land in mourning.

The name of ABRAHAM LINCOLN had already become famous to the working people of England ; he appeared as one of themselves, fighting the battle of freedom for all lands ; he is now, and for all coming time, the hero martyr of liberty and right. The American people have acted right nobly under his wise, conscientious, and upright rule. We believe they will not depart from the splendid course he has marked out for the nation. The assassin's hateful blow has sealed with sacred blood the bond which secures freedom in perpetuity to every man on the American continent, irrespective of color or race.

Peace be to the slain ! We mourn the mighty dead ! Never, in the whole range of the world's history, were hopes so gloriously bright so rudely, suddenly, and atrociously dashed ; but we earnestly pray that from out the thick darkness and the fearful evil good may ultimately flow. The twice elected President—the man of the people—is no more ; but Sampson-like, in a moral sense, there will be more slain by his death than in his life ; for we see, even now, in clearer character, the diabolical vindictiveness which obtains among the baffled abettors of slavery, and to see a subtle and gigantic evil in its native hideousness is the certain forerunner of its complete and final overthrow. The blow which aimed, alas ! too surely, at ABRAHAM LINCOLN's life, will send its echoes wherever slavery is felt or known, and will, we trust, prove the key-note of freedom for the oppressed in every land.

We mourn with bitterness and lamentation for the dead ; we sorrow for the living ; but not as for those who have no hope. The comforter will surely come for them, and their wounds, though many and severe, shall be healed. We pray for the future of America, that it may be indeed a glorious future of liberty, prosperity, and peace, and notwithstanding the last fearful climax to the treachery and rebellion so recently and gallantly quelled by the victorious bravery and courageous persistence of the northern arms, we trust that moderation and clemency may still rule ; justice, as in the past, being ever tempered with mercy, and that the national counsels may be always under the guidance of Him who has said, "Vengeance is mine, I will repay."

Signed on behalf of the meeting, and at its unanimous request :

GEORGE M. MURPHY,
Chairman, 55 Finchley Road, London.

To Mrs. ABRAHAM LINCOLN,
His Excellency the PRESIDENT OF THE UNITED STATES, and
The PEOPLE OF AMERICA.

Meeting held by the members of the "Workingmen's Christian Institute," Drury Lane, W. C.

DEAR SIR : We, the members of the "Workingmen's Christian Institute," Parker street, Drury Lane, W. C., in meeting assembled, beg leave to convey to Mrs. Lincoln, to the United States government, and to the American people, our deep sympathy with them in the great loss they have sustained by the *martyrdom* of President LINCOLN, and we fervently hope that the principles of Union and emancipation which were so dear to the lamented late President, and in the defence of which his blood was shed, may become still dearer to the American people, and that from the present struggle the United States may come forth a glorious, a united, and a free nation.

In behalf of the meeting :

R. NICHOLLS, *Chairman.*

His Excellency C. F. ADAMS,
Minister of the United States of America, London.

LONDON, W., 18 *Greek Street, May* 13, 1865.

SIR: The demon of the peculiar institution, for the supremacy of which the South rose in arms, would not allow his worshippers to honorably succumb in the open field. What he had begun in treason he must needs end in infamy. As Philip the Second's war for the inquisition bred a Gerards, thus Jefferson Davis's pro-slavery war, a Booth.

It is not our part to cull words of sorrow and horror, while the heart of two worlds heaves with emotion. Even the sycophants who year after year, and day by day, stuck to their Sisyphus work of morally assassinating ABRAHAM LINCOLN and the great republic he headed, stand now aghast at this universal outburst of popular feeling, and rival with each other to strew rhetorical flowers on his open grave. They have now at last found out that he was a man, neither to be browbeaten by adversity nor intoxicated by success—inflexibly pressing on to the great goal, never compromising it by blind haste; slowly maturing his steps, never retracing them; carried away by no surge of popular favor, disheartened by no slackening of the popular pulse; tempering stern acts by the gleams of a kind heart; illuminating scenes dark with passion by the smile of humor; doing his Titanic work as humbly and homely as heaven-born rulers do little things with the grandiloquence of pomp and state; in one word, one of the rare men who succeed in becoming great without ceasing to be good. Such, indeed, was the modesty of this great and good man that the world only discovered him a hero after he had fallen a martyr.

To be singled out by the side of such a chief, the second victim to the infernal gods of slavery, was an honor due to Mr. Seward. Had he not, at a time of general hesitation, the sagacity to foresee and the manliness to foretell "the irrepressible conflict?" Did he not, in the darkest hours of that conflict, prove true to the Roman duty to never despair of the republic and its stars? We earnestly hope that he and his son will be restored to health, public activity, and well-deserved honors within much less than "ninety days."

After a tremendous civil war, but which, if we consider its vast dimensions and its broad scope, and compare it to the Old World's one hundred years' wars, and thirty years' wars, and twenty-three years' wars, can hardly be said to have lasted ninety days, yours, sir, has become the task to uproot by the law what has been felled by the sword, to preside over the arduous work of political reconstruction and social regeneration. A profound sense of your great mission will save you from any compromise with stern duties. You will never forget that, to initiate the new era of the emancipation of labor, the American people devolved the responsibilities of leadership upon two men of labor, the one ABRAHAM LINCOLN, the other Andrew Johnson.

Signed on behalf of the International Workingmen's Association, the central council:

CHARLES KAUB.	H. CLUWOSKY.
EDWIN COULSON.	JOHN WESTON.
FERD. LESSNER.	HENRY BOLLETER.
CARL PFAENDER.	BENJAMIN LUCRAPT.
N. P. HANSEN.	JAMES BUCKLEY.
KARL SCHAPPER.	PETER FOX.
WILLIAM DELL.	N. SALVATELLA.
GEORGE LOCKNER.	GEORGE HOWELL.
GEORGE ECCARIUS.	BORDAGE.
JOHN ASBEUN.	A. VALTIER.
EMILL HATTORP, *Secretary for Poland.*	ROBERT SHAW.
KARL MARX, *Secretary for Germany.*	JOHN H. LONGMAID.
GEORGE WILLIAM WHEELER.	M. MORGAN.
J. WHITLOCK, *Financial Secretary.*	JOHN D. NICASS.
P. PETERSEN.	WILLIAM C. WORLEY.
ALO TÄNKO.	DIXON STAWTZ.
EUGENE DUPONT, *Secretary for France.*	G. T. DE LASSARIE.
H. JUNG, *Secretary for Switzerland.*	J. CARTER.
W. R. CREMER, *Honorary General Secretary.*	G. ADGER, *President.*

ANDREW JOHNSON, *President of the United States.*

LONDON, *May* 1, 1865.

SIR : We, the undersigned, merchants, bankers, and traders of the city of London, are anxious to express to you, as the. representative of the United States of America, the horror and indignation with which we have heard of the assassination of the late President, Mr. LINCOLN. This event, which, under any circumstances, would have called forth these feelings, seems to do so more strongly at this time, when so much appeared to depend upon Mr. LINCOLN's well known character for integrity, and his kindly desire of conciliation in the great task to which he was about to address himself—of restoring peace and concord in that great country over the councils of which he presided.

We also desire to express our deep and heartfelt sympathy in the irreparable loss which his family have sustained; and we beg you will convey to them the assurance of this feeling, which we believe to exist universally throughout this country.

H. L. HOLLANDS,
Governor of the Bank of England.

THOMAS N. HUNT,
Deputy Governor of the Bank of England,
AND THREE HUNDRED OTHER NAMES OR FIRMS.

His Excellency Hon. C. F. ADAMS,
Minister of the United States of America, London.

THE LATE PRESIDENT LINCOLN

At a great meeting held under the auspices of the Emancipation Society, at St. James's Hall, London, on Saturday evening, the 29th of April, 1865, (Mr. William Evans, president of the society, in the chair,) the following resolution was proposed by Mr. W. E. Forster, M. P., seconded by Mr. P. A. Taylor, M. P., supported by Mr. E. A. Leatham, M. P., and carried unanimously :

That this meeting desires to give utterance to the feelings of grief and horror with which it has heard of the assassination of President LINCOLN and the murderous attack upon Mr. Seward; and to convey to Mrs. Lincoln and to the United States government and people an expression of its profound sympathy and heartfelt condolence.

Mr. Stanfield, M. P., moved, Mr. T. B. Potter, M. P., seconded, and Mr. W. E. Baxter, M. P, the honorable Lyulph Stanley, Mr. Henry Fawcett, professor of political economy in the University of Cambridge, and Mr. G. Shaw Lefevre, M. P., supported the following resolution :

That this meeting desires also to express the entire confidence which it feels in the determination and the power of the government and people of the United States to carry out to the full the policy of which ABRAHAM LINCOLN's presidential career was the embodiment, and to establish free institutions throughout the whole of the American republic.

It was further resolved, on the motion of Mr. Caird, M. P., seconded by Mr. Grenfell, M. P., and supported by Mr. Crum Ewing, M. P., the Rev. Newman Hall, and Mr. Mason Jones :

That copies of the foregoing resolutions be placed in the hands of the honorable C. F. Adams, the American minister, for transmission to his Excellency the President of the United States, Mrs. Lincoln, and the Hon. W. H. Seward.

Mr. F. W. Chesson, the honorable secretary, announced the receipt of letters expressing deep sympathy with the objects of the meeting from Lord Houghton, Sir Charles Lyell, bart., Mr. Göschen, M. P., Colonel Sykes, M. P., Mr. Thomas Bazley, M. P., Mr. Charles Buxton, M. P., Mr. Thomas Hughes, and Dr. Frederick Tomkins.

A vote of thanks to the chairman was moved by Mr. Edmond Beales, and seconded by Mr. Cyrus W. Field, of New York.

WILLIAM EVANS, *Chairman.*

P. A. TAYLOR,

WILLIAM V. MALLESON,

Treasurers.

F. W. CHESSON, *Honorary Secretary.*

Address of the Freedmen's Aid Society of London.

Sir : The committee of this society deems it its melancholy duty to give expression to its deep sorrow on account of the sudden removal of President Lincoln, and its intense abhorrence of the crime by which his valuable life has been terminated. This committee has long cherished the highest admiration for the character, and felt full confidence in the constitutional and genuine anti-slavery policy, of the lamented late President. It has never traced the sufferings of the freed people to that policy, but to the cruel and unrighteous war which the slaveholders originated, which having begun, Mr. Lincoln turned to the advantage of the enslaved, by making it the constitutional ground of their emancipation.

This committee tenders its deep sympathy with the widow and other members of the bereaved family, and also to the entire nation which at such a crisis has been so suddenly deprived of its great leader. But this committee, while sorrowing for the loss of this great and good man, and deeply sympathizing with all the American people, has strong faith in the glorious cause of emancipation, to accomplish which the President has fallen a sacrifice.

He by whom kings reign and princes decree justice can easily supply the lack of service which has now arisen, and will, it is confidently believed, raise up and duly qualify all needed agency for effecting the absolute extinction of slavery, the reconciliation of contending parties, and the establishment of universal peace.

Signed on behalf of the above society by—

T. FOWELL BUXTON, *Bart., Chairman.*
SAMUEL GURNEY, *M. P., Treasurer.*
WILLIAM ALLEN, *Sub-Treasurer.*
FRED. TOMKINS, *M. A., D. C. L.*
F. W. CHESSON.
SAMUEL GARRATT, *M. A.,*
JOHN CURRVEN,
Honorary Secretaries.

Hon. CHARLES FRANCIS ADAMS,
Minister of the U. S. of America at the Court of St. James.

At a general meeting of the committee of the British and Foreign Anti-Slavery Society, held at No. 27 New Broad street, E. C., London, on Friday, the 5th day of May, 1865, the following resolution was unanimously adopted, and the secretary was instructed to forward to the Hon. C. F. Adams, United States minister in London, copies of the same for transmission to Andrew Johnson, President of the United States of America:

RESOLUTION.

The committee desire to record the feelings of dismay and sorrow with which they have heard of the assassination of ABRAHAM LINCOLN, President of the United States of America, and of the murderous attempt upon the life of his colleague, the Hon. W. H. Seward. While they regard these crimes as unparalleled in atrocity, deserving, as indeed they have justly excited, universal reprobation, they consider that the peculiar circumstances under which they were perpetrated remove them out of the category of ordinary crimes, and give them a deplorable prominence as the natural manifestations of the execrable system of slavery directed against the exponents of a policy of freedom.

The committee deem it especially their duty to bear their testimony in appreciation of the high qualities which distinguished ABRAHAM LINCOLN as the ruler of a great people, who during a season of unprecedented difficulty consistently adhered to principles which have happily been accepted by the nation, and in their application will secure the liberty of four millions of our fellow-creatures, held oppressed and degraded in the very worst form of bondage. As the emancipator of the slaves in the United States, ABRAHAM LINCOLN is entitled to the gratitude of all mankind.

The committee, in condoling with the people of the United States on the occasion of the signal loss they have sustained in the sudden removal of their late President, would express the confident hope that they will remain steadfast to the policy of emancipation, to the steady development of which his life was consecrated, and to which he fell a martyr, and will strengthen the hands of his successor to pursue the same noble course. They also fervently trust that in the high and responsible position which Andrew Johnson, now President, has been called to fill, he may be guided by the wisdom which cometh from above; that he may be endowed with the forbearance which tempereth justice with mercy, and be spared to bring to a happy and peaceful consummation the work ABRAHAM LINCOLN began.

The committee would further express their profound sympathy with the family of ABRAHAM LINCOLN, under their bereavement, which bows them down with grief. At such a solemn time they will derive consolation from the world-wide manifestation of sorrow and regret which the violent death of him who was their head has elicited, and will be strengthened to bear up against this grievous calamity, and be cheered by the reflection that he and his descendants will bear an honored name, which the ever-increasing multitudes of a once down-trodden race will hold enshrined in their hearts, to be transmitted to remotest posterity, as that of one of the greatest benefactors of mankind.

SAMUEL GURNEY, *President.*
EDMUND STURGE, *Chairman of Committee.*
L. A. CHAMEROVZOW, *Secretary.*

London Committee of Deputies of the British Jews.

4 GREAT STANHOPE STREET, MAY FAIR, *May* 2, 1865.

SIR: I am deputed, as president of this board, to express to your excellency, and to request that your excellency will convey to Mrs. Lincoln and the United States government, the assurance of its deepest sympathy in the sad event which has aroused the indignation of all classes of persons in this country, and excited their most heartfelt sorrow.

This board is mindful of the full measure of equal liberty so long enjoyed by its co-religionists in the United States, and trusts that in thus conveying its condolence, it may be permitted to express its grateful appreciation of this blessing.

I have the honor to remain your excellency's faithful and obedient servant,

J. M. MONTEFIORE.

CHARLES FRANCIS ADAMS,
*Envoy Extraordinary and Minister Plenipotentiary
for the United States of America, London.*

ARGYLE SQUARE JUNIOR MEMBERS' SOCIETY,
24 *Grafton Place, Euston Square, London, May* 6, 1865.

SIR: I beg to hand you a copy of a resolution passed at a general meeting of this society, held last evening, expressing condolence with the American nation on the late disastrous assassination of Mr. LINCOLN.

I have the honor to be your excellency's most obedient servant,

H. FRANCIS MOORE, *Honorary Secretary.*

Hon. C. F. ADAMS.

Resolved, That this meeting desires to give utterance to the feelings of grief with which it has heard of the assassination of President LINCOLN, and to convey to Mrs. Lincoln, and to the United States government and people, an expression of their deepest sympathy and condolence.

THE BANK OF BRITISH COLUMBIA,
80 *Lombard Street, E. C., London, April* 28, 1865.

SIR: We are deputed by the court of directors of this bank to convey to you, and through you to the government of the United States of America, the expression of their sincere sympathy at the heavy calamity which has befallen, not only your country, but our own, and, in fact, the whole world, by the cruel assassination of your high-minded and patriotic President.

We have the honor to be, sir, your excellency's most obedient servants,

THOS. W. L. MACKEAN, *Chairman.*
ROBERT ESTERSFIE, *Deputy Chairman.*
HENRY McCHELSEY, *Director.*

His Excellency Hon. CHARLES F. ADAMS,
Envoy Extraordinary and Minister Plenipotentiary
from the United States.

BRITISH HONDURAS COMPANY, LIMITED,
London, E. C., 2 *Great St. Helen's, April* 28, 1865.

SIR: I am intrusted by my colleagues, the directors of the British Honduras Company, Limited, with the expression of our deep sympathy with you and your nation on the sad event of the assassination of your late excellent President.

Somewhat of the tenderness of private personal feeling mingles with our sense of a great public calamity in which the whole civilized world shares. As Mr. LINCOLN showed great kindness to our manager when seeking labor in the United States, and took an interest in the company's affairs, we thus deem ourselves called on, peculiarly, to express that sincere sympathy which is universal, for the sad loss which the people of the United States have sustained by the death of so honest, so humane, so sagacious, so good, and so great a chief.

Permit me to add to yourself the expression of our personal respect and regard.

I am, sir, your excellency's most obedient servant,

J. R. ROBERTSON, *Chairman.*

His Excellency Hon. CHARLES F. ADAMS,
*Envoy Extraordinary and Minister Plenipotentiary
from the United States.*

---

*An address of condolence from the members of the " Temple Discussion Forum,"
Fleet street, London, to the illustrious widow of the late President Lincoln.*

ILLUSTRIOUS LADY—illustrious by position, and still more by sorrow: We, the supporters and frequenters of the "Temple Discussion Forum," Fleet street, London, approach you with liveliest sentiments of profound respect, deep sympathy, and unfeigned regret. Our society, which numbers in its ranks the representatives of all nations and forms of government throughout the civilized world, and in the free exercise of its opinions once evoked the censure of the most potent sovereign in Europe—established in dark and troubled days in the history of our country, for the fearless and open expression of opinion—has ever held in utter detestation the crimes of conspiracy and assassination, which in all ages have been the most deadly instruments which despotism could supply, and have ever been inimical to the cause of civil and religious liberty throughout the world.

In a society constituted as ours, it is useless to say, a variety of opinions necessarily exist as to the merits of that mighty struggle which has marked with the furrows of age a glorious and youthful republic. But, we rejoice to think, not a single dissentient opinion exists in the condemnation of a deed which has taken away so cruelly and abruptly from this life the husband, father, and uncrowned monarch of millions of men whose language is the language of Shakespeare and Milton.

Upon sorrow so sacred and so recent we will not presume further to intrude ourselves; but, illustrious lady, be pleased to place upon that narrow bed of eternal rest where your own heart now lies entombed, this well-meant tribute of an ancient body, a tribute already sanctioned by the sorrows of our august Sovereign, a tribute which the great ornament of our hereditary legislature declared in his senatorial place, "every man, woman, and child agreed in."

Praying that He who "tempers the wind to the shorn lamb," and filled in the old days the stricken heart of the royal Psalmist with celestial rays of promised joy, may guard you from every ill and sustain you in your terrible bereavement,

We remain, illustrious lady, your devoted and faithful servants,

WILLIAM CORNTIER, *Proprietor.*

JOSEPH BENJAMIN FRANKLIN, *Chairman.*

M. N. DEYBURGH,

Scotchman, Editor of the Illustrated Times.

EDWARD BAKER, *London.*

JOEL H. TALUM, *of Alabama.*

WILLIAM CHAPMAN,

Citizen of Antwerp, Belgium.

The directors of the Atlantic Telegraph Company, while occupied on the eve of accomplishing their enterprise for drawing closer the ties of friendship and cordial intercourse between the two kindred nations of America and the British empire, have heard with horror of the atrocious and recent acts by which the people of the United States have been deprived of their Chief Magistrate, in the person of their estimable and patriotic President, and have lost for a time the active services of Mr. Seward, who is one of their foremost ministers and statesmen.

The directors desire to record their deep sympathy with the people of the United States on this calamitous occasion, and hoping that these wicked and disastrous crimes will be traced to individual malignity, wholly foreign and abhorrent to the feelings of any section of the American people, they share with them in the sorrow and indignation which they have excited in this kingdom, and throughout the civilized world.

The directors further desire respectfully to tender to Mrs. Lincoln, and the bereaved families and friends of the eminent men who have thus fallen and suffered under the hands of assassins, their joint and individual condolence on their cruel bereavement and sorrows.

Given under the common seal of the Atlantic Telegraph Company, at the offices of the company, within the city of London, this 8th day of May, 1865.

[SEAL.] GEO. SAWARD, *Secretary.*

COVENT GARDEN THEATRICAL FUND,

May 4, 1865.

Resolved, That this honorable corporation, the Covent Garden Theatrical Fund, desires to give utterance to the feelings of grief and horror with which it has received the fearful intelligence of the assassination of ABRAHAM LINCOLN, President of the United States, and to convey to his sorrowing widow and the

American people its profound condolence and sympathy, together with the expression of its sad and solemn regret that the unnatural parricide who deprived the father of his country of existence, and the wife of his bosom of her loved protector, should in any, the slightest, way have been connected with the profession this corporation represents, whose honor and loyalty have ever been its most cherished pride.

Signed for the committee of the Covent Garden Theatical Fund:

DRINKWATER MEADOWS, *Secretary*,

6 *The Grange, Michael's Grove, Brompton, S. W.*

CHARLES FRANCIS ADAMS,

Minister of the United States in England.

[Translation.]

CONCORD LODGE, LONDON, *May* 22, 1865.

To the Citizen ANDREW JOHNSON,

President of the Republic of the United States, thrice greeting:

Stricken by the ball of a serf of tyranny, ABRAHAM LINCOLN is dead—victim to his love for the cause of our brethren, the black laborers of the southern States.

Descendants of slaves, it is with feverish anxiety that we have followed the great movements of the drama of emancipation, for which the blood of the upholders of right have been shed.

Independent operatives, our bosoms have swelled with joy at the news of the downfall of oppression beneath the heroic efforts of the soldiers of emancipation.

Our brethren are free! Slavery is abolished! Such is the cry which, throughout the Old World, the down-trodden of our day repeated with joy, when the death of the great martyr came to add new brilliancy to the glorious halo which surrounds the sacred cause of right and of justice.

Mourning is in our hearts! our grief is great! We weep with you for the loss of the great citizen who represented the nation of freemen. Faithful to his memory, we shall tell our sons of the actions of this just man, who has passed from this life to the life immortal.

L. LUBAY, *President of Concord Lodge.*

P. BORDAGE, *Secretary.*

LARDON, *Orator.*

L. PAIRIER, 1*st Supervisor.*

L. RIDET, 2*d Supervisor.*

DE ROUX, *Treasurer.*

EMILE HATTORFF, *Expert.*

AZERNA, *Architect.*

Resolution of the German National Verein in London.

SEYD'S HOTEL, FINSBURY SQUARE, LONDON,
May 6, 1865.

SIR: At to-day's meeting of the German National Verein in London, to which meeting the Germans resident in London were invited, it was resolved to express at the same time our joy at the victory of the free States of the Union, and our horror of the crime perpetrated upon the life of your noble President, whose fidelity to the cause of humanity we admired, long before his kindness to the conquered and his glorious martyrdom reconciled to him even those who had so long been his antagonists.

We consider it an important sign of our time that, as this great and good man, who held the helm of your state during this tempest, had, by his own energy and virtue, risen from the working class, so your actual worthy President, likewise, shows us a workman of former days, raised to the head of a grand and mighty community, by his own merit and the free election of his people.

Germany has assisted the giant struggle of freedom in your hemisphere, not by idle sympathy, but with blood and treasure; because, throughout the country the feeling is universal that, as a reverse of the North must have given the severest blow to the growth of democratic institutions in Europe, so your glorious conquest will powerfully influence and accelerate the triumph of our own freedom. America, during these four years, has fought the battle of liberty for all mankind; for the cause of liberty is the same cause everywhere. The abolition of slavery and the reconstruction of your state into a powerful republic will conduce to the elevation of the laborer, and to the establishment of such forms of government as will secure to the will of the true majority the sway over the destinies of every nation in Europe.

May we be allowed to convey to your excellency these sentiments of our countrymen, and to sign, with the expression of our highest consideration,

The committee of the German National Verein in London.

GOTTFRIED KINKEL, *Chairman.*
L. LOEFFLER, *Secretary.*

His Excellency the AMBASSADOR
of the United States of America at the Court of St. James.

LONDON, *April* 27, 1865.

DEAR SIR: In view of the distressing intelligence which has just reached us from America, we have to ask your excellency to convoke a meeting of

Americans resident here, in order to obtain an expression of their feelings on this sad occasion. If convenient to your excellency, we propose Monday, May 1, at 3. p. m., for such meeting, at some place to be hereafter designated.

Respectfully, yours, obediently,

GEORGE PEABODY.	W. R. BALLARD.
RUSSELL STURGES.	W. N. NEWMAN.
J. S. MORGAN.	FREEMAN H. MORSE.
C. M. LAMPSON.	OSGOOD FIELD.
JAMES McHENRY.	E. G. TINKER.
J R. BLACK.	SEWELL WARNER.
ELIHU BURRITT.	DENNIS R. ALWARD.
H. E. SOMERBY.	JOHN NORRIS, Jr.
BENJAMIN MORAN.	WINSLOW LEWIS.
CRAUMOND KENNEDY.	WM. D. COOLIDGE.
HENRY T. PARKER.	E. C. FISHER.
DANIEL BLISS.	C. M. FISHER, &c., &c.
R. HUNTING.	

His Excellency CHARLES FRANCIS ADAMS,
Minister of the United States.

LONDON, *April* 27, 1865.

GENTLEMEN: In accordance with the desire expressed in your note of this day, and with what I presume to be the general wish of Americans in London, I consent to your proposal, and hereby invite my countrymen, so disposed, to meet for the purpose designated on Monday next, May 1, at 3 p. m., at St. James's Hall.

I am your obedient servant,

C. F. ADAMS.

Messrs. GEORGE PEABODY,
    RUSSELL STURGES,
    J. S. MORGAN,
    C. M. LAMPSON,
    JAMES McHENRY,
        &c., &c., &c.

At a meeting of Americans resident in London, holden at St. James's Hall on the first day of May, 1865, his excellency Charles Francis Adams in the chair, it was resolved unanimously

That we have heard with the greatest indignation and the most profound sorrow of the assassination which has deprived our country of its beloved Chief

Magistrate, as well as of the audacious assault which has greatly perilled the lives of the Secretary and Assistant Secretary of State, and that we regard the taking of the life of our chief executive officer, while our country is passing through unparalleled trials, after all loyal Americans had learned to love him, and, with good men the world over, to confide in him, and when so much of national and individual welfare and happiness depended on his existence, as the great crime of the nineteenth century, memorable in its atrocity and entailing on its perpetrator the execration of mankind.

That we tender to Mrs. Lincoln our heartfelt sympathy and expressions of condolence in the great affliction that she and her family and the nation have sustained.

That in the long public career of Andrew Johnson, now President of the United States, the early and pre-eminent sacrifices he made from his devotion to the cause of the Union, and his pledges to maintain the great principles of human liberty, we have every assurance that he will faithfully prosecute to its final success the wise, humane, and statesmanlike, domestic and foreign policy of President LINCOLN.

That, as loyal Americans, we have witnessed with peculiar pleasure the expressions of indignation and sorrow throughout Great Britain at the assassination of President LINCOLN, and the cordial and hearty sympathy which has been extended by the people of this realm to the government and people of the United States in this great bereavement and public calamity.

That copies of these resolutions be transmitted to the President of the United States and to Mrs. Lincoln.

R. HUNTING, Secretary.

[From the London Evening Star, May 2, 1865.]

THE ASSASSINATION OF PRESIDENT LINCOLN.

Important meeting of Americans.

In accordance with an influentially signed requisition to Mr. Adams, the American ambassador, a public meeting of Americans, resident in London, was held yesterday at St. James's Hall, in order to give expression to their feelings respecting the late distressing intelligence from America. The hall presented the same singularly effective and sombre appearance as on the occasion of the great demonstration last Saturday evening, under the auspices of the Emancipation Society, the entire front of the balconies being draped with black cloth, bordered with white lace, and festooned with cord of the same hue, and the front of the upper gallery being tastefully decorated with three American flags grouped together, and whose drooping folds were looped with crape, while the staves of the wand-bearers were tipped with the same material. Although the hour appointed (three ó'clock) might be considered rather inconvenient, the attendance was very numerous. An hour before the time appointed the principal corridors leading to the hall were quite thronged with ladies and gentlemen waiting for admission, and soon after the doors were thrown open the spacious hall became comfortably filled. By the time appointed for commencing the proceedings the platform, which it is well known is of very large dimensions, presented quite a crowded appearance. Some few minutes after three o'clock Mr. Adams, accompanied by a large number of gentlemen, ascended the platform. His appearance was the signal for loud applause, and after taking the chair his excellency had several times to bow his acknowledgments. Among those present were Mr. Benjamin Moran, secretary of legation; Mr. Dennis R. Alward, assistant secretary of legation; Hon. F. H. Morse, United States consul, London; Mr. Joshua Nunn, deputy United States consul, London; Mr. G. H. Abbott, United States consul, Sheffield; Mr. H. Bergh, late United States secretary of legation. St. Petersburg; Lord Houghton, Alderman Salomons, Hon. A. Kinnaird, Hon. Lyulph Stanley, Mr. H. T. Parker, Mr. C. M. Fisher, Mr. James McHenry, Mr. Gerald Ralston, consul general of Liberia; Mr. T. B. Potter, M. P.; Mr. John Goddard, Dr. W. R. Ballard, Dr. J. R. Black, Mr. C. M. Lampson, Mr. J. S. Morgan, Mr. Russell Sturgis, Judge Winter, Dr. Howard, Mr. Mason Jones, Colonel J. S. Chester, Captain E. G. Tinker, Mr. Gilead A. Smith, Mr. B. F. Brown, Mr. Nathan Thompson, Dr. E. G. Ludlow, Mr. C. Coutoit, Mr. H. G. Somerby, Mr. Horatio Ward, Dr. W. Darling, Mr. John Brougham, Mr. Charles Button, Rev. Dr. Storr, Mr. W. R. Dempster, Mr. James Beal, Mr. Marshall Woody, Captain Tomkin, General Tom Thumb, Commodore Nutt. Rev. Cramond Kennedy, Mr. Henry Stevens, Dr. Fred. Robinson, Dr. C. R. Nicholl, Mr. George Ross, Captain Richardson, (San Francisco,) Rev. Daniel Bliss, Rev. E. L. Cleveland, Mr. C. F. Dennet, Mr. E. G. Coates, Mr. T. B. Hubbell, Mr. George Atkinson, Mr. Edmond Beales, Mr. R. Hunting, Mr. Bartlett, Mr. Osgood Field, Mr. Edward Thornton, Mr. John B. Stephenson, Mr. Levi Coffin, (Cincinnati, Ohio,) Mr. Stafford Allen, Mr. Peach, Mr. Massey, Mr. Phillips, (Wisconsin,) Mr. Westerton, Mr. John H. Goodnow, United States consul at Constantinople, Mr. M. D. Conway, &c.

The chairman, on entering the hall, was received with most enthusiastic applause, which was repeated on his rising to address the meeting. Silence having been restored, he said:

LADIES AND GENTLEMEN : I have been desired to call you together for the sake of giving some common form of expression to our emotions, stirred up as they have been by the late fearful calamity. In presence of such an awful event we are forcibly impressed, not merely with the commonplace idea of mortal vicissitude, but with the more solemn idea of keeping ourselves wholly free from the indulgence of any unworthy passion. The ordinary jars of human life are hushed before such a catastrophe. A great Virginian statesman once said that "he trembled for his country when he reflected that God is just." The dreaded visitation appears to have come upon us in the third and fourth generation. Let us endeavor to bear ourselves with patience and humility. But while acknowledging our shortcomings, let us draw closer and closer together while we unite in one earnest wail of sorrow for our loss, for I may be permitted to observe that in this loss the bereavement is wholly our own. We are entirely to bear the responsibility of it. The man who has fallen was immolated for no act of his own. It may well be doubted whether, during his whole career, he ever made a single personal enemy. In this peculiarity he shone prominent among statesmen. No; he who perpetrated the crime had no narrow purpose. It was because ABRAHAM LINCOLN was a faithful exponent of the sentiments of a whole people that he was stricken down. The blow that was aimed at him was meant to fall home upon them. The ball that penetrated his brain was addressed to the heart of each and every one of us. It was a fancied short way of paralyzing the government which we have striven so hard to maintain. It was, then, for our cause that ABRAHAM LINCOLN died, and not his own. If he was called a tyrant who was elevated to his high post by the spontaneous voices of a greater number of men than had ever been given in any republic before, it is only because he was obeying the wishes of those who elected him. It is we who must stand responsible for his deeds. It is he who has paid the penalty for executing our will. Surely, then, this is the strongest of reasons why all of us should join, as with one voice, in a chorus of lamentation for his fall. It is one of the peculiar merits of Mr. LINCOLN that he knew how to give shape in action to the popular feelings as they developed themselves under his observation. He never sought to lead, but rather to follow, and thus he succeeded in the difficult task of successfully combining conservatism with progress. This surely was not like tyranny. His labor was always to improve. Hence it was that he conducted a war of unexampled magnitude, always bearing in mind the primary purpose for which it had been commenced, at the same time that he associated with it broader ones as the opportunity came. He had pledged himself at the outset to accomplish certain objects, and he never forgot that pledge. The time had at last arrived when he might honestly claim that it would be fulfilled. It was in that very moment he was taken away. On the very same day of the year when the national flag, which just four years before had been lowered to triumphant enemies at Fort Sumter, was once more lifted to its original position by the hand of the same officer who had suffered the indignity that commenced the war, ABRAHAM LINCOLN fell. His euthanasia is complete. For him we ought not to mourn. His work was done: he had fought the good fight; he had finished his course. The grief is all for ourselves alone. And now we who stand around his body may well cry, "Go up, go up, with your gory temples twined with the evergreen symbols of a patriot's wreath, and bearing the double glory of a martyr's crown. Go up, while for us here remaining on earth your memory shall be garnered in the hearts of us and our latest posterity, in common with the priceless treasures heaped up by the great fathers of the republic, and close by that of the matchless Washington." But although we profoundly lament this loss, it must not be presumed that we do so having no hope. We have parted with a most faithful servant. But the nation has not lost with him one atom of the will which animated others of its servants as fully as it did him. It is one of the notable features of this great struggle that it is not particular men who have attempted to lead on the people, but rather that the people have first given the tone, to the level of which their servants must come up, or else sink out of sight and be forgotten. They have uniformly designated to them their wishes. To one man they have said "Come up," and to another, "Give way," and in either case they have been as implicitly obeyed. Whoever it be that is employed, the spirit that must animate him comes from a higher source. The cause of the country, then, does not depend on any man or any set of men. It has now called to the front the individual whom it had already elevated to the second post in the government. He had been pointed out for that place by a sense of his approved fidelity to the Union at the moment when all around him were faltering or falling away. In the national Senate he stood Abdiel-like, firm and determined in encountering with truth and force the fatal sophistry of Jefferson Davis and his associates, and in denouncing the course of action which was leading them to their ruin. Four years of intense and continued trials within the borders of his own State have been passed in the effort to reconstruct the edifice of civil government, which they had overthrown. No one has braved greater dangers to his person and to all that was held most precious to a man in this world than he. Those four years have not been passed without at once proving the firmness of his faith and the progressive nature of his ideas. He, too, has been susceptible to the influence of the national opinion. He, too, has gradually been brought to the conviction that slavery, which he once defended, has been our bane, and the cause of all our woe. And he, too, will follow his predecessor in making the recognition of the principle of human liberty the chief pathway to restoration. May be that he will color his policy with a little more of the sternness gathered from the severity of his own trials. He may give a greater prominence to the image of justice than to that of mercy in dealing with notorious offenders. But if he do, to whom is this change to be imputed? LINCOLN leaned to mercy, and he wa staken off. Johnson has not promoted himself. The magician who worked this change is the enemy himself. It would seem almost as if it were the will of Heaven which has interposed the possibility of this marvellous retribution. Yet, even if we make proper allowances for this difference, the great fact yet remains clear that Andrew Johnson, like his predecessor, will exert himself to the utmost of his power fully to re-establish in peace and harmony the beneficent system of government which he has clearly hazarded so much to sustain. And should it happen that he, too—which Heaven avert—should by some evil design be removed from the post now assigned to him, the effect would only be that the next man in the succession prescribed by the public law, and inspired from the same common source, will be summoned to take his place. And so it would go on, if need be, in a line like that in Macbeth's vision, "stretching out to the crack of doom." The republic has but to command the services of any of her children, and whether to meet open danger in the field or the perils of the more crafty and desperate assassin, experience shows them equally ready to obey her call. So long as the heroic spirit animates her frame the requisite agents will not fail to execute her will. Any attempt to paralyze her by striking down more or less of them will only end, as every preceding design to injure her has ended, in disappointment and bitter despair. Let us, then, casting aside all needless apprehensions for the policy of our land, now concentrate our thoughts for the moment upon the magnitude of the offence which has deprived us of our beloved chief in the very moment of most interest to our cause, and let us draw together as one man in the tribute of our admiration of one of the purest, the most single-minded, and noble-hearted patriots that ever ruled over the people of any land.

The Hon. Mr. Morse, in moving the first resolution, said : If he were to consult his own feelings, he should allow the resolution to pass in silence. To attempt to add anything to the atrocious crime which had brought them together was useless. All human language failed to make it clearer, or to convey any stronger impressions than the fact itself. Having expressed his profound sorrow at the fact, and his admiration of the noble character of the late President, he said there was this consolation—the lamentable event was calculated to hasten the coming of the day which the North and all who sympathized with their cause longed to see, namely, the restoration of the Union and the promulgation of liberty throughout the land. [Cheers.] This was not a fit time to go into the question of slavery, but they well remember the various stages through which Mr. Lincoln had carried his country with the view to wipe out that black stain upon its banner. [Applause.] Now that the head of the state was dead, it was necessary to take a calm survey. What remained, now that Lincoln was no more ? Lincoln was dead, but America was not—it still lived. [Applause.] This brought him to consider who were left behind to fill up the gap. First, as regarded President Johnson ; of him he could speak from personal experience. Twenty-one years ago he entered the Congress of the United States with Andrew Johnson, who was then the representative of the State of Tennessee. He was on a committee with him, and sat three or four times a week with him perhaps for the space of two years, and he said here, that throughout the whole of that period, and for three or four years subsequently, during which time his acquaintance with Andrew Johnson continued, he never heard one word whispered against his fair fame. [Loud cheers] He never heard the reproach of intemperance cast upon him. [Hear, hear.] He had seen him daily, and knew him well, and he knew that to charge him with habitual intemperance was one of the vilest slanders that could be brought against him. [Cheers.] Johnson came from the ranks of the people. He had now been in public life some thirty years; commencing as an alderman, then mayor, afterwards a member of the lower House, from which he was in time advanced to the Senate, eventually made Vice-President, and now, by the providence of God, President of the United States. [Applause.] He was a little particular in making these facts known, because after what had been represented against him, it was not to be wondered at if a want of confidence should manifest itself in regard to the stability, and particularly the foreign policy, of a government with such a man presiding over it. [Cries of "No, no." "No, no."] He was glad to hear that, for he believed in his heart there need not be the slightest mistrust of that noble man—a man, in whose honor let it be added, who had made his way from the ranks of the people upward to his present eminence by his own untiring perseverance and manly conduct. [Applause.] As had been remarked by the chairman, when, in 1861, the United States seemed to be fast crumbling away; when senator after senator and member after member boldly gave in his resignation, or left his seat without making any sign that they intended joining in the rebellion—while Slidell and Mason were plotting underground—where was Andrew Johnson? He was contending loudly against the adversaries of the Union; he was protesting loudly against secession; he was upholding the flag of his country like a brave and patriotic man, as he was, and as he remained, doubtless, to this day. [Cheers.] There was no faltering in his case; he went straight on; it mattered not who lagged behind, he was ever stoutly defending the front. He had suffered, as they had heard. He came from a State in which, more than anywhere else, it was dangerous to be a known Unionist—where hundreds and hundreds of men were shot down in cold blood, hanged upon trees, and hunted to the mountains for no other reason than that they had a leaning towards the North. He lost all his property. His wife was imprisoned, and became an invalid through the sufferings she endured while in prison. Was that the man to fail them in these times? [Cheers.]

Mr. C. M. Lampson briefly seconded the resolution, which, as was the case also with all the subsequent ones, was unanimously adopted.

Henry Bough, Esq., of New York, moved the next resolution. With manifest emotion he expressed his detestation of the crime that inflicted such a blow on America. From Italy, Germany, Spain, France, Russia, and England—the cradle of the American race—[applause]—had already gone forth addresses and letters of condolence with the American nation generally, and the widow in particular. Within these very walls, only on Saturday night, a thrill of unfeigned sympathy and grief was excited by the noble utterances of those who took part in the proceedings of the occasion. He concluded an impassioned harangue by powerfully appealing in the language of Shakspeare to the sympathy of the Christian worlds—

" Canst thou minister to a mind diseased ?" &c.—

and declared his belief that, by the aid of that Divine Providence which tempers the wind to the shorn lamb, they could, " with some sweet oblivious antidote, wipe out the written troubles of the mind" of the widow and family, bereaved by this shocking event.

Mr. J. S. MORGAN seconded the resolution.

Dr. BLACK, in moving the third resolution, remarked upon the faults found with the late President by those whose sympathies favored the South. LINCOLN was wrong in everything when he was living. What was said now he was dead ? He had no villifiers now, and before long it would be difficult to find a man to dare acknowledge ever having said a wrong word against such a noble character. Andrew Johnson was now the man at whom attacks would be directed ; it would not be many years, he (Dr. Black) apprehended, before his villifiers would also hang down their heads. Johnson had a very difficult task before him, and not the least difficult part of it was the question of slavery—where to place the slaves, how to provide for them, and what privileges to accord them. But it was not by far so difficult to deal with as the enemies of the North tried to make out. People in this country pointed to Jamaica, and said, " Look what difficulties we had there." But Jamaica and America were two different places, and presented very different aspects in reference to the slave trade. In Jamaica, where fresh supplies were continually arriving from Africa, the negroes kept up the superstitions and bad habits of their race ; their masters lived in England and knew nothing about them, had no sympathy with them ; in fact, they never associated with anybody but their drivers, until at last slavery and labor became synonymous. Afterwards, when the slaves were made free, freedom and laziness became synonymous. In the United States the slaves had some degree of intelligence ; since 1808 there had been no admixture with fresh importations from Africa ; and let him say here, it was America who first abolished the African slave trade, Great Britain following the example. Leaving this question, he glanced at the financial condition of the United States, and replying to the alarm felt in certain quarters in this country that America would repudiate its liabilities, said that when this country came out of the Napoleonic war its debt was nearly twice as much as that which America has now entailed upon itself; the commerce of England was very little more than that of America even now while she was at war ; the people of England were half the number of the American population ; the leading men of America were English in origin, religion, language, morality, and habits of business ; surely, then, if England was in a position to pay its way, America would be. If anybody supposed, indeed, that the Americans had any other than honest and honorable intention, they did them an injustice. Moreover, it was their interest, as well as their duty, to pay their just debts, and it was pure nonsense to talk any other way. [Hear.] In conclusion, he expressed his hope that the event which had called them together, and which had excited such universal sorrow, would be the starting point from which to establish amicable relations between this country and America—amicable relations in their truest and widest sense—from which both should march, treading down all past prejudices, to an honorable and lasting peace and unity, and from which to inaugurate the natural alliance, the most powerful combination the world ever knew—not for tyranny, but for the prosperity and happiness of mankind throughout the world. [Cheers.]

Mr. H. T. PARKER seconded the resolution. He made a very able speech, hopefully picturing the future of America.

Mr. R. STURGIS, in moving the next resolution, remarked that an address of sympathy had that day emanated from the Bank of England and passed through city circles preparatory to being placed in the hands of Mr. Adams. He also stated that had that gentleman been well enough in health, Mr. Peabody, whose noble heart and liberal hand has spread blessings over both lands, [cheers,] would have occupied his place. He then proceeded to show that it was the interest as much of England as of America to cling closely to each other. The two countries had not only a common lineage and common language, but a common heart: and whatever differences of sentiment existed as to the issue of the present conflict, the heart was found in the right place when such a crime as this occurred. There was not one single throb on the American side but what had a corresponding movement on the English side. [Applause.]

Mr. E. M. FISHER seconded the resolution.

Mr. CYRUS FIELD proposed a vote of thanks to his excellency the chairman. In doing so, he remarked that just before he left America for this country he had an interview with Mr. LINCOLN, and he was convinced, from what then transpired, as well as by what he knew of his character and policy, that he heartily desired peace in America, and America to be at peace with all the world [Applause.]

The CHAIRMAN said it was a great comfort and pleasure to him to meet so many of his fellow-countrymen, and to perceive, as he did, such unanimity of sentiment on the melancholy subject which had brought them together.

The meeting then dispersed.

LONDON, *Saturday, April* 29, 1865.

SIR: We, the undersigned, Mauritian colored gentlemen, resident in London, assembled in committee, have resolved to send this address to the representative of the United States in England, as the tribute of our warm admiration for the patriotic deeds of the Chief American Magistrate, whose assassination has horrified the civilized world.

We, colored men, natives of Mauritius, have placed an implicit faith in all those liberal views of the late Mr. ABRAHAM LINCOLN'S government, acting as barriers against the lawless attempts of a slave-holding community to destroy the glorious, free, and united republic of George Washington.

Be assured, sir, that by expressing our abhorrence of the murder of Mr. ABRAHAM LINCOLN, we echo the opinion of our colored brethren in Mauritius.

The fiend-like assassin who cruelly butchered your late illustrious President at the time when the Union armies were successful everywhere and the slave empire was crumbling to the dust, has not only deprived the United States of one of its noblest citizens, of one of its most virtuous patriots, but also the suffering and enslaved colored race living in abjectness in your country of their kind and stanch protector.

We beg, sir, that you will convey to the authorities of your great and free republic the expression of our sentiments of admiration for the chivalrous conduct of your late lamented and deeply regretted President in the hour of triumph, and of our feelings of horror and disgust on hearing of his assassination.

We subscribe ourselves, yours, obediently,

POLYXENES VAUDAGNE, *President.*

TH. LIONEL JENKINS, *Vice-President.*

J. D. MURRAY.

DÜBOIS.

E. VAUDAGNE.

ARTHUR BÉNERS

His Excellency Mr. ADAMS,

American Ambassador of the United States.

LONDON, *April* 27, 1865.

SIR: We, the undersigned, speaking the feelings of a large number of Germans resident in England, express our sincere grief at the destruction of the life of the President of the United States, whose very forbearance and leniency in the hour of national triumph has not been able to stay the hands of assassins.

Whilst deeply deploring that the joy we have felt at the recent victories of the American republic should thus be marred by the untimely and violent death of its Chief Magistrate, we firmly trust that the people of the United States, who have carried on during four years a gigantic war in the cause of freedom and civilization, will only feel nerved to further exertions in rooting out the hateful institutions from which the slaveholders' rebellion, with all its attendant crimes, has sprung.

We beg you, sir, to convey these sympathetic sentiments of ours to the authorities of your free and great republic, and we subscribe ourselves yours obediently,

> KARL BLIND.
> A. HEINTZMANN.
> P. H. BERNDES.
> FERDINAND FREILIGRATH.
> ERNST ZUCH.
> E. G. RAVENSTEIN.
> NICOLAUS TRUBNER.
> GOTTFRIED KINKEL.

His Excellency Mr. ADAMS,
United States Ambassador in London.

SIR: We, the undersigned, merchants and others of the Greek race resident in London, have heard with the profoundest regret of the cruel assassination of ABRAHAM LINCOLN, the President of your great republic.

When we ourselves were struggling for our freedom against our oppressors, no nation was more generous in its sympathy for our cause than the great free republic of the west: gratitude, therefore, as well as every feeling of humanity, calls upon us to express to your excellency, and through you to the people which you so worthily represent, the intense feelings of horror and abhorrence with which we have heard of the unprovoked and unprecedented crime and of our sincere and heartfelt wishes and prayers for the future well-being and prosperity of your great and glorious people.

> A. A. RALLI,
> 9 *Grace Church street.*
> M. E. MAVROCORDATO.
> DEM. F. RANA.
> ALEXANDER BALLI.
> AND ONE HUNDRED AND ELEVEN OTHER NAMES.

His Excellency Mr. ADAMS,
Ambassador of the United States.

Resolutions passed at a meeting held by the Welsh residents in London.
SYMPATHY WITH AMERICA.

At a meeting of Welsh residents in London, held at the Young Men's Christian Association institution, Aldersgate street, on Monday, the 8th of May, the Rev. Owen Thomas, Jewin Crescent, in the chair, the following resolutions were unanimously adopted:

I. Moved by Rev. Henry Richard, seconded by J. Owen, esq., Holloway and supported by Rev. W. Rees, Liverpool:

Resolved, That this meeting desires to express its utter abhorrence of the execrable crime by which Mr. ABRAHAM LINCOLN, President of the United States, was stricken down by the hand of an assassin, at a time so inexpressibly critical and momentous in the history of that country, while it cordially joins in the tribute of admiration so universally paid to the many admirable qualities of the deceased statesman, the honesty, simplicity, and firmness of his character, the rare self-control which he showed amid the excitement of conflict, and the moderation and mercy with which he was prepared to use the advantages of victory.

II. Moved by Mr. John Griffith, seconded by Mr. J. Williams, London city mission, supported by Dr. Nicholas, Dr. Rees, Swansea, Rev. W. Lloyd, Aldersgate street, and Thomas Williams, esq., Pendarran:

Resolved, That the meeting would convey to the people of the United States the assurance of its profound sympathy under the appalling calamity that has overtaken them, and earnestly hopes they will not suffer themselves to be driven, even by the supreme atrocity of this act, from the disposition, so honorable to their national character, which they had previously displayed, to act towards their vanquished brethren in the spirit of true Christian kindness and conciliation.

III. Moved by Rev. J. Kilsby Jones, seconded by Rev. H. C. Parry, supported by Rev'ds W. Edwards Aberdare, D. Davies, London, and D. Rowlands, B. A., Llanbrynnmair:

Resolved, That the meeting would further record the expression of its respectful sympathy with Mrs. Lincoln in the midst of the awful affliction that has befallen her, and trusts that she may be enabled to find solace in the thought that the father of the fatherless and the judge of the widow is God in his holy habitation.

Signed on behalf of the meeting:

OWEN THOMAS, *Chairman.*

His Excellency Hon. CHARLES F. ADAMS:

SIR: We, on behalf of our countrymen resident here, hasten to tender, through you, to the American people, our profound sympathy with them under the heavy affliction they have sustained in being deprived of their deeply lamented and much beloved President.

We fondly hoped that he would have enjoyed for the full term that position and those honors which a grateful country had conferred on him, and that, in the increased happiness and prosperity of the United States, he would have seen the desires of his great and generous soul realized and continued on a scale commensurate with the high destiny and splendid fortunes of the American republic.

It must be consoling, under this bereavement, to recall that it was reserved for him to see his country emerge, great and glorious, from the perils which menaced her existence as a nation, and thus disappoint the anticipations of those who desired her dismemberment.

We feel proud that our countrymen have contributed to this great result, and proved, by their fidelity and heroism, that valor and gratitude are among the many virtues which Irishmen cultivate and extend to their friends and benefactors in whatever position they may be placed, whether in social or military life.

As good citizens, they have been true to the national cause, and we refer, with especial satisfaction, to those among them whose names will enter into the history of your great republic, associated with its principles, hallowed by its sacrifices, and identified with its glory.

We beg you, sir, to be the interpreter of our feelings to the American people, and to assure them that our attachment has been unalterable, neither springing from expediency nor inspired by self-interest, but that it is the warm impulse of a people whose generous sensibilities are among the most prominent of their national characteristics.

Signed on behalf of a meeting of the Irishmen of London, held at the Arundel Hall, Arundel street, Strand, on Monday, the 1st of May, 1865.

O'DONOGHUE, *M. P.*,	WALTER M. O'DWYER.
JOHN FRANCIS O'DONNELL.	FRANCIS SCANNELL.
RICHARD ARCHER.	JAMES W. GILLIGAN.
WILLIAM DOYLE.	FRANCIS J. MORAN.
ROBERT E. MURRAY.	C. SAVAN DUFFY.
P. B. HALL.	

At a meeting of the corporation of the city of London, in the province of Canada, held on the seventeenth day of April, in the year of our Lord 1865, the following resolution was unanimously adopted :

Resolved, That, in view of the lamentable occurrence which has taken place in the neighboring nation of the United States, by which their Chief Magistrate has been deprived of life by the hand of an assassin, we, the corporation of the city of London, deem it incumbent upon us to offer to our sorrowing neighbors this expression of our sympathy for the great loss they have sustained, and our abhorrence of the act by which they have been made to suffer.

In testimony whereof, I, David Glass, esq., mayor of the said city of London, have hereunto set my hand, and caused to be affixed the corporate seal of the said city, on this eighteenth day of April, 1865.

[SEAL.]   DAVID GLASS, *Mayor.*

Resolutions adopted at a large public meeting, held in the city of London, Canada West, on Wednesday, the 19th of April, in the year of our Lord 1865.

First. That we, the citizens of London, Canada West, in public meeting assembled, at the hour when the solemn obsequies of ABRAHAM LINCOLN are being performed at Washington, are moved by our common feelings of humanity and our regard for the American people to express our profound sorrow at the sudden and mournful death of the late excellent and humane President of the neighboring and friendly republic; and we hereby record our heartfelt sympathy with the nation that has been visited by such an appalling calamity, with the widow and other relatives of the deceased President, who are plunged into grief by his assassination, and with the Hon. W. H. Seward and his family in the barbarous cruelty inflicted on his person.

Second. That we regard the assassination of President LINCOLN and the attempted assassination of the Hon. W. H. Seward, whoever were the agents and whatever were their motives, as most cowardly, bloody, and diabolical crimes, a daring and lawless outrage on humanity, and a lasting disgrace to the civilization of the nineteenth century.

Third. That a copy of these resolutions, signed, in name of this meeting, by the chairman and secretary, be forwarded through the proper channel to Andrew Johnson, President of the United States, to Mrs. Lincoln, widow of the lamented late President, and the Hon. W. H. Seward, Secretary of State.

DAVID GLASS, *Mayor.*

WARREN ROCK, *Secretary.*

Address of the Board of Trade of the city of London, Canada West, to Mr. Johnson.

OFFICE OF THE BOARD OF TRADE,
London, C. W., April 19, 1865.

The Board of Trade of the city of London, Canada West, desire to express their deep sympathy with the government and people of the United States, in the great loss the nation has sustained by the untimely death of ABRAHAM LINCOLN, their late President, who has fallen in the prime and vigor of life by the hand of an assassin. They feel that the act is one deserving the deepest execration of all civilized communities, and that at this critical period of the history of the United States, it is a great calamity to the government and people of that country and to the whole civilized world The Board of Trade also desire respectfully to offer their condolence with Mrs. Lincoln and her family, and hope that with the blessing of God they will be sustained under this trying bereavement.

CHARLES JAMES POPE, *President.*

THOMAS CHURCHER, *Secretary.*

ANDREW JOHNSON,
    President of the United States of America.

At the half-yearly general meeting of the Grand Trunk Railway Company of Canada, held at the London Tavern, London, on Thursday, the 27th of April, 1865, Edward W. Watkin, esq., M. P., in the chair, it was moved by Mr. Fildes, seconded by Mr. Champness, and carried unanimously, in solemn silence—

That this meeting of holders of property, much of which is protected by the laws and institutions of the United States, desires to express its horror and detestation of the crime of assassination by which the invaluable life of President LINCOLN has been sacrificed, and that of Mr. Secretary Seward placed in extreme jeopardy, and to record its conviction that a grievous loss has thereby been occasioned not only to the United States, but to the civilized world at large.

Certified copy:

EDWARD W. WATKIN, *President.*

JOHN W. GRANT, *Secretary.*

We, the local board of health for the town and district of Luton; in the county of Bedford, do hereby desire to record the expression of sorrow which we and this town and district have deeply felt since informed of the diabolical assassination of President LINCOLN, a deed the nature of which has excited and must continue to excite the indignation of all right-minded people.

We strongly unite with the rest of our countrymen in the expression of our sympathy and good feeling, which we always have, and shall ever entertain towards the people of the United States of America, and more so at the present juncture, when we contemplate the fearful trials and difficulties which have been placed in their way, but which can only retard for a very brief period that great work of civilization and progress which has eminently characterized them. Sprung from the same nation, there always will be a strong manifestation of interest with the people of this country in American affairs, and upon every matter which will advance the welfare and happiness of the American people.

We, the said local board of the town and district of Luton, do hereby likewise most sincerely condole with, and beg to express our sincere and heartfelt sympathy with, Mrs. Lincoln and her family in their great and irreparable loss, and humbly hope that an inscrutable Providence may support them under the very heavy trial which they are now undergoing, and which we hope and pray may be overruled for their and their country's good.

Given under our hand and official seal this 5th day of May, in the year of our Lord 1865.

[SEAL.]

> WILLIAM T. PLEDGE, *Chairman.*
> SAMUEL TOYN.
> A. V. WEBSTER.
> FREDERICK PRAIMAN
> JAMES HIGGINS.
> JNO. AMBERLAND.

Countersigned:

> GEORGE BAILEY,
> *Clerk of the said Local Board.*

[SEAL.]

At·Leith, tne second day of May, one thousand eight hundred and sixty-five, which day the honorable the provost magistrates and council of the borough of Leith being assembled, unanimously resolved to record their abhorrence of the atrocious assassination of President LINCOLN of the United States of America, and their deepest sympathy with the people of the United States under the calamity which has befallen them.

Extracted from the council records by—

> H. H. COUPER, *Town Clerk.*

At a meeting of the Leith Chamber of Commerce, incorporated by royal charter, held the 2d day of May, 1865, the following resolution was moved by John Warrack, esq., chairman of the chamber, seconded by Adolph Robinow, esq., and unanimously adopted:

The Leith Chamber of Commerce desire to join with all classes of their countrymen in expressing their indignation, horror, and sorrow at the assassination of President LINCOLN, and resolve to communicate to the American people and government the sympathy of the chamber for the loss which is felt, not by the United States alone, but by the whole civilized world.

The secretary was instructed to transmit a copy of the above resolution to his Excellency Mr. Adams, the United States minister in London.

Signed in name and by authority of the chamber:

[SEAL.]

> JOHN WARRACK, *Chairman.*

METHODIST NEW CONNECTION CONFERENCE,
Assembled at Lynden, C. W., June 13, 1865.

Resolution 109: That we, as a branch of the Church of Christ, beg to express our feelings of detestation and abhorrence at the spirit that planned, and the monster in human form who perpetrated, the foul act of assassinating the honored late President of the United States; and while we thus give utterance to our deep feelings of sympathy with his bereaved family and nation, most earnestly would we pray that the day may never come when such scenes of horror shall be repeated in any nation; that human slavery may soon be brought permanently to an end; and that the commercial interests and bonds of Christian brotherhood which now so closely unite the American and British nations may never be lessened.

110. That the secretary of this conference transmit a copy of the above resolution to the American Secretary of State.

[SEAL.]   WILLIAM TINDALL,
                                      Secretary of Conference.

Resolution of the mayor, aldermen, and burgesses of the borough of Margate.

We, the mayor, aldermen, and burgesses of the borough of Margate, in the county of Kent, learn with deep regret the death of his Excellency ABRAHAM LINCOLN, President of the United States of America, by the hand of a cowardly assassin, and desire to express our warmest sympathy with the American nation at so lamentable and horrible an event, which has deprived the people of the greatest ornament of their country, and the world of one of the best friends of humanity.

Given under our common seal the second day of May, A. D. 1865.

[SEAL.]   THOMAS H. KEBLE, *Mayor*.
                                      WM. BROOKE, *Town Clerk.*

Resolution of the council of the borough of Morpeth.

Resolution passed at a quarterly meeting of the council of this borough, on the fourth day of May, one thousand eight hundred and sixty-five:

"That the mayor, aldermen, and councillors of Morpeth desire to express their feelings of sorrow and indignation at the assassination of the President of the United States of America, and at the attempt to obtain the life of his chief Secretary, Mr. Seward."

Resolution of the council of the borough of Macclesfield.

At an assembly of the council of the said borough, held at the Town Hall there on Thursday, the fourth day of May, one thousand eight hundred and sixty-five—

Resolved, That this council embraces the earliest opportunity (before proceeding with the business of this day) of expressing its deep and profound sympathy with Mrs. Lincoln, and the government and people of the United States of America, in the melancholy bereavement they have sustained in the brutal and cowardly assassination of Mr. President LINCOLN, and begs to record its horror and abhorrence of so malignant and atrocious a crime.

That the mayor be respectfully requested to communicate this resolution to his excellency Mr. Adams, the minister of the United States, and to desire that he will be pleased to transmit the same to the President of the United States and to Mrs. Lincoln.

[SEAL.]   JAMES JACKSON, *Mayor.*

Extracts from the minutes of the meeting of the town council of the borough of Maidstone, in the county of Kent, held at the Town Hall on Wednesday, the 10th day of May, 1865.

Ordered, That the mayor, aldermen, and burgesses of the borough of Maidstone view with horror and indignation the atrocious assassination of the late President of the United States, and desire to express their unmitigated regret at the commission of so foul and unprovoked a crime.

Ordered, That a copy of the foregoing resolution be forthwith transmitted by the town clerk to Mr. Adams, the American ambassador in London.

Given under the corporate seal of the said borough, this 10th day of May, 1865.

[SEAL.]   CHARLES ELLIS, JR., *Mayor.*

His Excellency Hon. CHARLES FRANCIS ADAMS,
        Envoy Extraordinary and Minister Plenipotentiary
                of the United States, London :

We, the mayor and corporation of the borough of Maldon, in council assembled, desire to express through you to the people of the United States of America the feelings of sorrow and indignation with which we have received intelligence of the assassination of President LINCOLN.

Our regret at his untimely end, at a moment when his life appeared to be of the utmost importance to the welfare of the state, is greatly increased by the recollection of his well-known character, but especially by the just and friendly sentiments he entertained towards England, and we venture to hope that the general expression of horror which his violent death has excited throughout our land will show to the American people that England reciprocates these feelings of kindness and good will to their fullest extent.

We also beg to offer to Mrs. Lincoln our respectful sympathy in her afflicting bereavement, and we trust she will find great consolation in the thought that the memory of the late President will long be affectionately cherished by the people who twice chose him to fill the highest office in the land.

Given under our common seal this 9th day of May, 1865.

[SEAL.]   JAMES BARRITT, *Mayor.*

Hon. CHARLES FRANCIS ADAMS,
  Envoy Extraordinary and Minister Plenipotentiary
    of the United States of America

May it please your excellency : We, the provost, magistrates, and members of council of the burgh of Musselburgh, in Scotland, participating as we do in the feeling of distress universally existing in this nation on account of the atrocious crime which has been committed in the country which you represent, by the assassination of its Chief Magistrate, grievously aggravated by its being perpetrated on one of such commanding talents and estimable qualities as President LINCOLN unquestionably possessed, deeply sympathize with the great people of whom he was the head, and especially with the lady who has by this foul deed been so unexpectedly and sadly rendered a widow, as well as with the family who have been deprived of their honored parent.

We embrace also this opportunity to express our regards towards your excellency, and remain yours, very faithfully,

GEORGE LAURIE,
Provost and Chief Magistrate.

Signed in name and on behalf of the town council of the burgh of Musselburgh, and the seal of the burgh affixed, upon this 11th day of May, 1865:

[SEAL.]   GEORGE LAURIE,
              Provost and Chief Magistrate of Musselburgh.

THOMAS LEES, *Town Clerk.*

At Montrose, the 3d day of May, 1865, the which day the magistrates and town council met and convened in council, William Mitchell, esq., provost, in the chair, the following resolution was proposed by the provost and unanimously agreed to:

The magistrates and town councillors of the royal burgh of Montrose, in the county of Forfar, having heard with profound regret and horror of the cowardly assassination of his Excellency ABRAHAM LINCOLN, President of the United States of America, have resolved to express their abhorrence and detestation of the cold-blooded and murderous deed, and their sincere and earnest sympathy and condolence with the people of the United States, in being thus bereft of the services of a man whose honest devotion to what he considered the principles of right and justice had won for him an eminent name and position in the world's history. The council further desire that a copy of this minute, signed by the provost and chief magistrate, and having the corporation seal affixed, be forwarded to his excellency Mr. Adams, the United States minister in London, to be communicated to the proper quarter.

[SEAL.]
WM. MITCHELL,
Provost and Chief Magistrate.

CITY OF MANCHESTER.

At a meeting of the council of this city, held the 3d day of May, 1865, it was

Unanimously resolved, That this council seizes the first opportunity which has arisen since the painful intelligence was received, to record the feelings of horror and of indignation, as well as of deep sorrow, with which they have heard of the cruel and cold-blooded assassination of President LINCOLN, and to express their sincere sympathy with the citizens of the United States in the grievous loss which they have thereby sustained.

That the mayor be respectfully requested to communicate this resolution to his excellency Mr. Adams, the minister of the United States, with the assurance that, in the opinion of this council, the sentiments therein expressed are entirely in accordance with the feelings universally entertained by the inhabitants of this city, and to desire that his excellency will be pleased to transmit the same to the President of the United States.

J. M. BENNETT, Mayor.

JOSEPH HERVEY, *Town Clerk.*

Resolutions passed at a meeting held by the citizens of Manchester.

ASSASSINATION OF PRESIDENT LINCOLN.

At a public meeting of the citizens of this city, convened by the mayor, and held in the Town Hall, King street, on Thursday, the 4th day of May, 1865—J. M. Bennett, esq., mayor, in the chair—it was

Unanimously resolved, That the citizens of Manchester, now assembled, desire to express their horror and detestation of the deplorable crime which has resulted in the violent death of the Chief Magistrate of the American republic, ABRAHAM LINCOLN, and of the attempt to murder Mr. Seward and some members of his family, and they desire most earnestly and respectfully to convey to the authorities of the United States their deep sympathy with the American people in the heavy loss they have sustained.

Resolved unanimously, That this meeting desires most respectfully to present to Mrs. Lincoln its sincere sympathy and condolence on the melancholy loss she has sustained in the death of her husband.

Resolved, That the mayor be requested to transmit the resolutions this day adopted to his excellency the Hon. Mr. Adams, the American minister at the court of St. James, London.

J. M. BENNETT, Mayor.

Resolutions of sympathy with the Hon. William H. Seward, Secretary of State, Washington.

At a public meeting of citizens of Manchester, held in the Free Trade Hall, April 28, 1865, to express sympathy and condolence with Mrs. Lincoln and the American nation on the assassination of the late President of the United States, the following resolution was unanimously adopted:

Moved by Dr. John Watts, seconded by Mr. Edward Hooson—

Resolved, That this meeting also desires to record an expression of profound sympathy with the Hon. William H. Seward and the members of his family, in regard to the atrocious attempt to assassinate that distinguished and able statesman while lying in a helpless condition on a bed of sickness; and this meeting earnestly hopes that the foul attempt may not have proved successful, but that Mr. Seward may soon be restored to health and vigor, to render efficient service in the government of his great nation under a restored Union based on the eternal principles of freedom, justice, and equal rights to men of all races.

Signed on behalf of the meeting:

FRANCIS TAYLOR, Chairman.

His Excellency ANDREW JOHNSON,
 President of the United States of America:

The board of directors of the Manchester Chamber of Commerce desire to convey to the government and people of the United States of America, in the most emphatic terms, the expression of their horror and indignation at the dastardly assassination of the late Chief Magistrate of the republic, as also at the murderous assault made upon Mr. Secretary Seward and his son; and they desire to assure the American people that those diabolical outrages have evoked sentiments of the deepest execration from all classes in the United Kingdom.

The directors of the chamber further desire most respectfully to express towards Mrs. Lincoln, and other members of her sorrowing family, their profound sympathy and condolence under the heavy affliction which has befallen them.

Signed for and on behalf of the directors:

MALCOM ROSS, *President.*

HUGH FLEMING, *Secretary.*

Address of the Union and Emancipation Society of Manchester to Mr. Johnson.

SIR: We have heard with profound regret that your late distinguished President, ABRAHAM LINCOLN, has fallen a victim to a vile conspiracy, and that he has been suddenly removed from your midst by the hands of a cowardly assassin.

We have watched his career from the period of his election in 1860 down to his lamented death, as well through all the darkest hours of the struggle in which your country has been engaged as at the time when success seemed to be within his grasp, and we have ever recognized in him a self-denying patriotism, a devotion to the principles of right and justice, and a determination to surmount, by constitutional means, every obstacle which stood in the way of the final triumph of those principles. His unswerving faith never forsook him in the hour of depression and gloom, and he has left behind him a noble example of magnanimity and moderation in the hour of victory, which cannot fail to secure the admiration of the whole civilized world.

Elected on the basis of a limitation of the area of slavery in the United States, he gradually and cautiously developed an anti-slavery policy, which resulted in the issue of an emancipation proclamation, by which every slave in the rebel States is now free; and he lived to see adopted by Congress an amendment to the Constitution abolishing forever slavery in the United States.

He has not been permitted to witness the final achievement of this great work, but his name will ever be associated in history with the removal of this dark stain from your national escutcheon.

It is not alone or chiefly on grounds of philanthropy that we have sympathized in his objects and aims. From the period when we beheld a section of your community, when defeated at the ballot-box, appealing to the arbitrament of the sword, without even the pretence of a grievance, excepting the alleged danger to the institution of slavery, we regarded free constitutional government as on its trial, and we have viewed with unvarying satisfaction the uniform consistency with which he always upheld the maintenance of the Union as paramount to every other consideration.

In the recollection of these things we desire now, through you, to express our deep sympathy with your loyal fellow-citizens in the grievous loss you have sustained—a loss which, at this important crisis in your country's history, cannot fail to produce serious and anxious concern.

In the midst of gloom, however, we are consoled by the reflection that the world is ruled by principles, not by men; and that while the most distinguished statesmen are constantly passing away, the principles which they have propounded are immortal.

Mr. LINCOLN, it is true, has departed, but he has bequeathed to posterity an example which cannot fail to exercise a powerful influence on the future of your country.

The Constitution places you in the office of Chief Magistrate of the Union at a solemn crisis in your national affairs, which has no parallel in the past history of the nation; but we cheerfully recognize the fact that the same ballot which secured the triumphant re-election of Mr. LINCOLN also placed you in the distinguished position to become his successor; and our faith in the instincts of a great people forbids us to doubt that the noble principles which animated him will ever find a response in your heart.

For and on behalf of the Union and Emancipation Society of Manchester:

THOMAS BAYLEY POTTERS,
President.

FRANCIS TAYLOR,
For self and other Vice-Presidents.

SAMUEL WATT, *Treasurer.*

JOHN H. ESTCOURT,
Chairman of Executive.

JOHN C. EDWARD,

EDWARD OWEN GREENING,
Honorary Secretaries.

His Excellency ANDREW JOHNSON,
President of the United States.

At a public meeting held in the Free Trade Hall, Manchester, April 28, 1865, it was moved by Alderman Heywood, ex-mayor, seconded by the Rev. S. A. Steinthall, and passed unanimously—

That the address to President Johnson, expressive of sympathy with the American people in the loss they have sustained by the lamented death of President LINCOLN, be adopted, and that the chairman be authorized to sign it on behalf of this meeting.

FRANCIS TAYLOR, *Chairman.*

Address of the Union and Emancipation Society of Manchester to Mrs. Lincoln.

51 PICCADILLY, MANCHESTER, *April* 27, 1865.

MADAM: It is not for us to invade ·the privacy of domestic sorrow, nor fitting that we should add to the sharpness of your grief by characterizing as it deserves the deed which has deprived you of a husband and your country of its Chief Magistrate. We desire, however, to express our deep sympathy with you in this mournful affliction, and our earnest hope that you may be supported through the trial by the consciousness that your husband though called to the helm in the midst of tempest and storm, never failed to respond to the call of duty, and that throughout a period of unparalleled difficulty he has guided the affairs of the nation in a manner which will ever connect his name with all that is noble, magnanimous, and great in your country's history. His name will be associated with the cause of human freedom throughout all time, and generations yet unborn will learn to lisp his name as synonymous with liberty itself, and to connect the atrocious deed by which his career was closed with the expiring throes of that foul system of slavery against which his life was a standing protest, and the fate of which he had sealed.

For and on behalf of the Union and Emancipation Society of Manchester :

THOMAS BAYLEY POTTERS,
President.

FRANCIS TAYLOR,
For self and other Vice-Presidents.

SAMUEL WATT, *Treasurer.*

JOHN H. ESTCOURT,
Chairman of Executive.

JOHN C. EDWARD,
EDWARD OWEN GREENING,
Honorary Secretaries.

Mrs. LINCOLN.

At a public meeting held at the Free Trade Hall, Manchester, April 28 1865, it was moved by the Rev. G. W. Conder, seconded by Jacob Bright esq., and passed unanimously—

That the address of sympathy and condolence with. Mrs. Lincoln, now read, be adopted, and that the chairman be authorized to sign it on behalf of this meeting.

FRANCIS TAYLOR, *Chairman.*

At a conference of the British Temperance League, held in the city of Manchester on the 17th day of May, 1865, Joseph Thorp, esq., in the chair, on the motion of the Reverend J. C. Street, of Newcastle, seconded by the Reverend William Cain, of Manchester, it was

Unanimously resolved, That this conference expresses its feeling of grief and indignation at the assassination of the late President of the United States of America, who was for upwards of fifty years a consistent temperance man, and desires to convey to Mrs. Lincoln and to the people of that country its profound sympathy with them in this great affliction; its horror and detestation of the atrocious crime against humanity which has been committed, and its fervent hope that the event may be overruled by the Almighty for the preservation of the great republic and the complete overthrow of human slavery— these being the objects for which Mr. LINCOLN lived and worked, and for fidelity to which he died.

JOSEPH THORP, *President.*

WM. J. CLEGG,
     Secretary to the Conference.

Resolution passed at a meeting of the Sons of Temperance of Manchester.

27 DEVONSHIRE STREET, MANCHESTER.

At a meeting of the officers and representatives of the twenty-nine divisions under the Manchester Grand Division of the Order of the Sons of Temperance, England, in session assembled, April 29, 1865, it was—

Unanimously resolved, That this Grand Division expresses its utter abhorrence at the revolting and cowardly assassination of the late President of the United States of America, by which act we feel that America has lost one of its brightest ornaments and our cause one of its noblest champions, and desires to offer its deepest sympathy with Mrs. Lincoln and the people of America in the sad and bereaving dispensation under which they have had to groan, and prays that the arm of Omnipotence may surround and sustain them.

Signed on behalf of the Manchester Grand Division:

[SEAL.]   HENRY HULME, *G. W. P.*

JOHN HARRISON, *G. S.*

Mrs. LINCOLN and the PEOPLE
    of the United States of America.

Resolutions adopted by the Executive of the United Kingdom Alliance for the Total Suppression of the Liquor Traffic, Manchester.

OFFICES, 41 JOHN DALTON STREET,
Manchester, May 5, 1865.

MADAM: I am instructed to convey to you the enclosed copy of resolutions of the Executive of the United Kingdom Alliance.

In performing this official duty, allow me to add that no words can express to you our deep and tender sympathy.

May God bless and comfort you under your great bereavement.

Ever very faithfully yours,

THOS H. BARKER, *Secretary U. K. A.*

Mrs. LINCOLN.

Resolutions of sympathy and condolence on the assassination of President Lincoln, adopted by the Executive of the United Kingdom Alliance.

Resolved, That the Executive of the United Kingdom Alliance for the Legislative Suppression of the Liquor Traffic has heard with feelings of profound horror and inexpressible grief of the assassination of the President of the United States by the hands of a reckless murderer, inspired by political rancor.

That this Executive, while recording an expression of its deep sympathy and sorrowful condolence with the widow and nation of ABRAHAM LINCOLN, cordially recognizes the great personal worth and noble civic virtues of that large-hearted patriot and magnanimous ruler, twice elected by the people as the Chief Magistrate of a great nation, the emancipator of four million slaves, and the savior of his country from armed rebellion, anarchy, and ruin.

That, while this Executive shares most earnestly these sentiments entertained by all parties, ranks, and classes, it feels very keenly the death, by the hand of a murderer moved by drink, of a man whose long adhesion to the principles of total abstinence and prohibition, and whose faithful adherence to them even during the war, have proved that to these, as to all forms of enlightened philanthropy, the late President of the United States of America devoted his high intelligence and his noble heart.

That this Executive earnestly hopes that the fearful civil war in America has now ceased, and that peace will speedily be proclaimed and permanently established on the righteous bases of union and nationality, justice and freedom, with equal civil and political rights to loyal men of all creeds, races, and conditions.

WILLIAM HARVEY, *Chairman.*
SAMUEL POPE, *Hon. Secretary.*
THOS. H. BARKER, *Secretary.*

MANCHESTER, *May* 3, 1865.

His Excellency ANDREW JOHNSON,
     President of the United States of America:

SIR: We, the inhabitants of Mossley, in public meeting assembled, pray your acceptance of our heartfelt condolence at the heavy loss sustained by the government and people of the United States in the death of their truthful, righteous, and self-sacrificing President, ABRAHAM LINCOLN.

We have suffered long and severely in consequence of the cruel war which has cursed your land; for it has crippled our industry, blasted our hopes, and caused many of our sons to seek a home among strangers. But our sufferings sink into insignificance when we think of this horrid crime, which stands without a parallel in the history of the world.

Feeling conscious that the assassin's blow was not only aimed at your worthy predecessor and his worthy colleagues, and, through them, at your glorious Constitution, but also at the cause of liberty throughout the world, we share your heavy grief, and sincerely pray that the spirit of him whose name will be ever dear to freedom's worthy sons may not be buried with him, but that it may influence your counsels as his successor until the last remnant of slavery shall be annihilated and your Union cemented by love.

We are happy to learn that Mr. Seward and his son are likely to recover.

We have every confidence in your nation's heart, and in your firmness, integrity, and heroism as President, and sincerely hope that you will be able so to temper justice with mercy that the future of your country may be unclouded, and its peace unbroken.

GEORGE ANDREW, *Chairman.*

MOSSLEY, *May* 4, 1865.

DEAR WIDOWED LADY: Permit us, as subjects of a widowed Queen, whose mighty heart and spotless life have not only made our native land more dear to us, but bid us long to see the reign of love universal, to express our deep sympathy with you in your great affliction, and our ardent prayer that He who overrules all events may fill up the painful void in your heart which the loss of such a treasure must create, and so control the spirits of men that your beloved country may soon become what your beloved husband toiled to make it—the abode of peace and purity, liberty and love.

We have suffered deeply in consequence of your dreadful war. It has made us familiar with poverty and grief, desolated many of our homes, and blighted many of our prospects; but our sufferings are nothing to yours.

Dear lady, God bless you and yours!

GEORGE ANDREW, *Chairman.*

Mrs. LINCOLN.

The address of the inhabitants of Merthyr Tydvil, in the county of Glamorgan, in public meeting assembled.

To the President and Congress of the United States of America:

In desiring to convey to you our expression of painful sympathy in the heavy loss which the government and people of the United States have suffered by the death of President LINCOLN, we express our unqualified detestation and execration of so hideous a crime.

We are the more deeply shocked that the event has occurred at a moment when the triumph of the United States seemed on the point of completion; and as the murderous and simultaneous attack upon Mr. Seward, the faithful minister of President LINCOLN, who so well supported him through the whole of this eventful crisis, betrays the object of the crime, we are constrained to believe that their death was intended to rob the people of the United States of their devotion to right and law, and to postpone the time when the long-desired peace would be obtained.

But we sincerely hope that the great work of the restoration of the Union will not, by this deplorable event, suffer, or that it will cause it to be long delayed. The death of him who so wisely and efficiently worked for that great end will, we confidently trust, have only the more striking effect of strengthening the Union for which he died.

In the invincible respect which the people of the United States have manifested for law and freedom, during the terrible struggles of this war, we recognize the best guarantee of a future obedience to the authority of the government, and of submission to the will of the people, as expressed by popular representation.

We confidently anticipate they will express most unmistakably that the policy of which their late President was the embodiment is to be carried out in all its extent, and that institutions in which perfect freedom for life, for speech, and for property, will be extended over the whole of the United States, so that integrity and worth, not color and class, shall henceforward be recognized as the proper qualifications of those who govern.

We consider that the long services of Andrew Johnson are sufficient guarantees that, in succeeding the late President, the people of America will find a man eminently qualified to carry to a successful issue the policy inaugurated by his predecessor, and we fervently hope that, in the hands of Divine Providence, he will prove to be the humble instrument of bringing peace and tranquillity to a land torn by warfare and bloodshed, and that in the future relation of America with foreign nations, truthfulness, honesty, and forbearance will be its foremost consideration.

Finally we pray that the ruthless passions which have been engendered may totally cease, and that under a united people the remembrance of the fearful struggles of civil warfare will forever be buried in oblivion.

JOHN JONES, *High Constable, Chairman.*

Resolution passed at a meeting held by the inhabitants of Merthyr Tydvil, Wales.

To Mrs. Lincoln, widow of the late ABRAHAM LINCOLN, President of the United States of America:

The following resolution was unanimously adopted at a public meeting of the inhabitants of Merthyr Tydvil, in the county of Glamorgan, Wales:

That this meeting expresses its sincere condolence with Mrs. Lincoln on her sudden and mournful bereavement, and wishes to convey to her its deep sympathy under her heart-rending trial.

Dated this 10th day of May, 1865.

JOHN JONES, *High Constable, Chairman.*

MELBOURNE, *July* 4, 1865—58 Elizabeth street.

SIR: We, the undersigned, on behalf of the few remaining Polish and Hungarian refugees resident in the colony of Victoria, beg most humbly to request you, as the only representative of the American United States government, to accept the expression of our most deep and sincere sorrow at the untimely death, by a most cowardly assassination, of his Excellency ABRAHAM LINCOLN late President of the United States of America.

May the great Providence, which has chosen to visit one of the greatest nations upon the earth with such an indescribable calamity, inspire the present and many generations yet unborn, not only how to support this great loss, but to venerate the sacred memory of its greatest citizen forever.

We again beg that you may accept this from, sir, your most humble servants,

GEORGE G. WOINARSKI,
Late Officer in the Polish and Hungarian Army.
MARTIN FARKAS,
Late Captain in the Hungarian Army.
WILLIAM BLANCHARD, Esq.,
United States American Consul, Melbourne.

At a meeting of the council of the city of Melbourne, held in the council chamber in the Town Hall, Swanston street, in the said city, on Monday, the 24th day of July, 1865, it was

Resolved, That this council, for and on behalf of the corporation of the mayor, aldermen, councillors, and citizens of the city of Melbourne, desires to record its unmitigated horror and detestation of the atrocious murder of ABRAHAM LINCOLN, the late President of the United States of America; to express its profound sympathy with the American people in the incalculable loss of so great and good a citizen, councillor and ruler; and to offer its deep and respectful condolence to Mrs. Lincoln under her most grievous and terrible bereavement.

[SEAL.]   GEO. WRAGGE, *Mayor.*
        E. G. FITZ GIBBON, *Town Clerk.*

Extract from the minutes of a meeting of the council of the city of Montreal, held on Wednesday, the 19th day of April, 1865.

Present: his worship the mayor, J. L. Beaudry, esq.; Aldermen Grenier, Rodden, Contant, Gorrie, David Rolland, Stevenson, McCready; Councillors McGibbon, Devlin, Lamoureux, Goyette, McNevin, Higginson, McGauvran, Leduc, Donovan, Alexander, Ogilvie, Brown, Isaacson, Cassidy, Bastien.

Before proceeding to business, his worship the mayor stated that since the meeting was called a great calamity had befallen the American people in the assassination of their Chief Magistrate, and his worship submitted to the meeting whether it would not behoove this council to adjourn, as a mark of respect to the memory of the late President. It was, therefore,

Unanimously resolved, That in respect to the memory of the late President of the United States, and as a mark of sympathy with the great public calamity which has befallen our neighbors, and also as an expression of the profound regret and horror felt by this council at the foul crime perpetrated on the revered person of the late Chief Magistrate of the United States, this council do now adjourn.

[SEAL.]   J. L. BEAUDRY, *Mayor.*
                               CHS. SLACKMEYER, *City Clerk.*

Resolutions passed at a meeting held by the citizens of Montreal.

MONTREAL, *April* 20, 1865.

In compliance with a very numerously signed requisition, a public meeting of the inhabitants was called by his worship the mayor, and held on the 19th instant, at which the following action was taken :

1. Moved by honorable Thomas Ryan, seconded by honorable A. A. Dorion, and

Unanimously resolved, That the citizens of Montreal, in public meeting assembled, desire to express most emphatically the sentiment of horror and detestation with which they regard the great crime recently perpetrated at Washington, by the base and cowardly assassination of ABRAHAM LINCOLN, late President of the United States.

2. Moved by honorable T. D. McGee, seconded by honorable James Ferrier, and

Unanimously resolved, That we regard this unprovoked and most atrocious assassination, the greatest crime of our age, as committed not merely against the people of the United States, but against our common humanity and common Christian civilization.

3. Moved by honorable P. J. O. Chauveau, seconded by honorable L. H. Holton, and

Unanimously resolved, That on behalf of the city of Montreal, we desire to tender to the people of the United States the assurance of our sincere sympathy and condolence with them, in this awfully sudden and afflicting loss of their Chief Magistrate.

4. Moved by Benjamin Holmes, esq., seconded by Tancrede Bonthillier, esq., and

Unanimously resolved, That his worship the mayor, and the secretaries, be requested to transmit copies of the foregoing resolutions to the honorable John F. Potter, United States consul general for British North America.

J. L. BEAUDRY, *Mayor.*
F. P. POMINVILLE,
WM. J. PATTERSON,
                               Secretaries.

Resolutions passed at a meeting held by the New England Society of Montreal.

At a meeting of the members of this society, and other Americans, held in the American Presbyterian church on Wednesday, April 19, 1865, in commemoration of the memory of ABRAHAM LINCOLN, late President of the United States, the following resolutions were unanimously adopted:

Whereas ABRAHAM LINCOLN, President of the United States, has perished by the hand of an assassin, at the time when the military power of the rebellion was conquered, and when his wisdom seemed most necessary to the well-being of the country; and whereas the Americans resident in Montreal are deeply interested in anything which concerns the honor or welfare of the United States: Therefore resolved—

1. That the members of the Montreal New England Society, and other Americans resident in Montreal, tenderly sympathize with the government and people of the United States, and bereaved family, in deploring this calamitous event, and in their grief at this sore affliction, and that as an evidence of our grief we wear mourning thirty days.

2. That in the acts and character of ABRAHAM LINCOLN as President of the United States, in a time of unparalleled difficulty, we recognize the true patriot and sagacious statesman, as well as that fidelity to sacred trust, that regard to individual rights, that kindly consideration for all classes, as manifested in his reluctance to wage war until forced upon him, his tender care for the soldiers, and words of sympathy to their relatives, his emancipation proclamation, and his clemency to conquered cities and captured armies, which will forever link his name with that of the illustrious Washington, as one of the greatest, wisest, noblest, and kindliest men of the race.

3. That in the career and character of ABRAHAM LINCOLN as farm laborer, boatman, school teacher, lawyer, legislator, and President, we recognize the influence and power of American institutions to develop manhood, and to confer honor and rewards upon the capable and deserving.

4. That although ABRAHAM LINCOLN has perished by the hand of an assassin, we thank God that he was permitted to live to see the arm of this most gigantic and guilty rebellion broken; that although we ardently desired he might have been spared to carry out his schemes for the reconstruction of government in the conquered and returning States, yet we bow in submission to God's will, entertaining undoubting faith in the righteousness of the Divine government, and the speedy and thorough pacification of the country, so that the United States, purged of its heirloom of slavery, and strengthened by the discipline of war, shall be in the future, as in the past, the home of the free and hope of the oppressed, the refuge for the poor and down trodden of every race and creed.

5. That seeing in this dreadful crime, at which "humanity shudders and civilization grows pale," a fresh proof of the lawless and degrading tendencies of slavery, we pledge ourselves anew to aid in every legitimate way in the overthrow of the last vestige of human slavery on this continent.

6. That the foregoing resolutions be published in the newspapers of this city, and that a copy of them be sent through the United States consul general to the United States government, and to the family of the lamented deceased.

A true copy of the original minute:

P. D. BROWNE, President.

E. F. AMES, Secretary.

[Translation.]

MOTTOES ON THE SEAL:

> Altius Tendimus.
> Travail et Concorde.
> Canadian Institute, founded
> in 1844, incorporated in
> 1853.

To his Excellency ANDREW JOHNSON,
President of the United States:

May it please your Excellency: With profound sentiments of affliction and indignation the Canadian Institute heard of the horrible murder that has spread consternation among the people of the United States, and of the execrable attempt of assassination upon the person of the honorable Secretary of State.

The premature and tragic death of the eminent man, so universally respected and admired, who was the political chief of the great nation that your Excellency is now called upon to govern, is, in the opinion of the Canadian Institute, not only a terrible national calamity, but an event that brings sorrow and mourning upon all true friends of liberty and progress, and upon the enemies of slavery and tyranny throughout the world, and sincere grief to the believers in democratic institutions; who were proud to see one of the most upright and blameless men that ever governed a nation at the head of the freest people on the face of the earth.

The members of the Canadian Institute, in their humble sphere, admired ABRAHAM LINCOLN as much for his rare modesty and the self-denial of which he gave so many glorious examples, as they esteemed him for his elevated conception of political and private probity, which even his enemies could not refuse to acknowledge in him.

Slavery had already sacrificed enough victims; and it was truly lamentable that the great chief of the nation, who had destroyed the monster, should become its last and most illustrious martyr. It is, indeed, deplorable that this great and renowned patriot, the impersonation of national unity, of fidelity to the Constitution and devotion to duty, should be added to the hecatomb of sacrifices of defenders of the Constitution and the laws, caused by the accursed institution of slavery.

The Canadian Institute, watching with interest the various events in the social or political progress of a people towards civilization, ventures to express to your Excellency the great pleasure it feels at the abolition of slavery in the glorious American republic. The consequence of this act will be the blotting out of the only stain upon democratic institutions, which have been so often corrupted, perverted, and turned from their true path by an accursed institution which was an emphatic denial of all human rights, and a violation of every divine law; and the restoration of peace in the United States, a peace that must endure, since the sole cause of the terrible war that has desolated the great country has disappeared with slavery.

The Canadian Institute rejoices that your Excellency escaped the assassin's dagger, and expresses its most sincere wish for the success of your administration; it hopes you may overcome the existing obstacles in the way of a perfect peace and reunion, with the same success that attended your illustrious predecessor, and wishes you may fill the honorable and glorious position in the history of the United States which was promised by your memorable assurances of devotion to the integrity of your country and to its glorious and admirable Constitution.

L. A. DESSAULEES, *Clerk of the Crown,*
GONZALVE DOUTRE, *B. V. L.,*

Committee.

J. J. DURAND, *President of the C. I.*
LEO SASSRON, *Secretary Arc. C. I.*
JOS. BOUCHARD, *Secretary Cor. C. I.*

MONTREAL, *April* 22, 1865.

To his Excellency ANDREW JOHNSON,

President of the United States:

SIR: We, the mayor, aldermen, and burgesses of the borough of Newark, in the county of Nottingham, England, in council assembled, desire through you to express to our brethren in America, on our own behalf, as well as of the inhabitants of the town of which we are the municipal representatives, our deep commiseration on the melancholy event which has so suddenly and unexpectedly placed you in your present high and difficult position, and our profound abhorrence of the dastardly crime which, at so important a period of his valuable life, has deprived his country of the services of your distinguished predecessor.

Although the perpetrator of an act of unparalleled atrocity appears hitherto to have escaped detection, we trust that he may soon receive the just reward of his villany, and that through Divine assistance you may be enabled, by a wise and beneficent policy, to effect the object which at the time of his premature removal appeared nearest the heart of ABRAHAM LINCOLN, namely, the restoration to peace and prosperity of your magnificent but now afflicted country.

Given under our common seal at the council chamber, in the Town Hall of the said borough, the 2d day of May, 1865.

[SEAL.]   JOHN GILBIET, *Mayor.*

BOROUGH OF NEWCASTLE-UNDER-LYME, IN THE COUNTY OF STAFFORD.

At an assembly of the council in the Town Hall, on Wednesday, the 3d day of May, 1865, it was

Resolved unanimously, That this council desires to express its feelings of horror and detestation at the death, by the hand of an assassin, of President LINCOLN, the chosen and trusted chief of the United States of America; and to record its heartfelt sympathy and condolence with Mrs. Lincoln, and the government and people of those States, upon the grievous loss they have sustained.

[SEAL.]   THOMAS HARDING, *Town Clerk.*

TOWN CLERK'S OFFICE, GUILDHALL,
Neath, May 8, 1865.

At a quarterly meeting of the town council of the borough of Neath, in the county of Glamorgan, holden at the council chamber of the Guildhall of the said borough, on Monday, the 8th day of May, 1865,

On the motion of Mr. Alderman Gwyn, seconded by P. Charles, esq., mayor, it was resolved—

1. That this council desires to record the sentiments of horror and detestation with which it regards the assassination of President LINCOLN and the attack on Mr. Seward, the American Secretary of State; and wishes to offer its sincere condolence to the widow and family of the late President, and to express its deep sympathy with the American people in the severe loss which they have sustained.

2. That the foregoing resolution be transmitted by the mayor to the American minister for presentation in due course.

[SEAL.]   P. CHARLES, *Mayor.*

Resolutions passed at a meeting of the magistrates and town council of the royal burgh of Newburgh, Fifeshire, held on the 5th of May, 1865.

The magistrates and council unanimously agree to place on their records an expression of their own and fellow-townsmen's condemnation and abhorrence of the barbarous murder of the President of the United States of America, and also an expression of their sincere sympathy with the people of the United States on the afflicting calamity which has befallen them.

That the chief magistrate be requested to transmit to his excellency the American minister in London an address in accordance with these resolutions, and also that a copy of them be sent to Mrs. Lincoln, with an expression of the magistrates' and council's sympathy with her under her severe and distressing bereavement.

ANDREW MILNE, Chief Magistrate.

NEWBURGH, *May* 10, 1865.

Address of the magistrates and town council of the burgh of Newburgh.

To his Excellency CHARLES FRANCIS ADAMS,
  Envoy Extraordinary and Minister Plenipotentiary
    for the United States of America, London.

May it please your excellency: We, the magistrates and town council of the burgh of Newburgh, in the county of Fife, North Britain, in common council assembled, do hereby express deepest sorrow and indignation at the atrocious assassination of ABRAHAM LINCOLN, President of the United States of America, and at the dastardly attempt about the same hour on Mr. Seward, Secretary of State.

We desire that the government and people of the United States should understand that no difference of opinion on the merits of the conflict of the last four years avails to prevent the unanimous condemnation of so great a crime against our common humanity. No fouler crime stands chronicled in all history.

We hereby offer our sincere sympathy with the people of the United States on the afflicting and heavy loss which they have thus sustained, and trust that the event may be overruled for their good.

May it please your excellency to forward this humble address to the proper quarter, in order that the American people may know they have the sympathy of the council and inhabitants of this burgh.

Signed by the chief magistrate at Newburgh, May 10, 1865.

[SEAL.]   ANDREW MILNE, *Chief Magistrate.*

Resolution passed at a meeting held by the Newmilns Anti-Slavery Society.

NEWMILNS, *May* 5, 1865.

In public meeting assembled it was unanimously resolved to present the following unto the honorable Andrew Johnson, President of the United States of America:

HONORED SIR: We, the members of the Newmilns Anti-Slavery Society, having early espoused the side of humanity in the great struggle going on in your beloved country for the emancipation of mankind from bondage—a bondage which made the humane of every land shudder to contemplate—proud as we were over him who undertook the task to grapple with this gigantic evil, what are we to think, or how can we express our feelings, when we know that he who was the appointed instrument to erase from the land of America the accursed blot which had so long stained your honored and will-be respected flag, and he who with calmness, fortitude, and dignified mercy, held in the one hand the palm of victory, in the other the olive-branch, crying peace! peace! being struck down and deprived of life by the assassin's hand, when on the very verge of seeing his long-wished-for desire successfully consummated; and, honored sir, in our lamentations over the sad event, may we be permitted to congratulate you, upon the knowledge we have, through the honorable Mr. Adams, the American ambassador, London, and Mr. Stodart, Glasgow, of the high attainments you possess for the important office you have been so unexpectedly called upon to fill. We therefore tender unto you, and along with you, our sincere sympathy for the bereaved widow of the late honored and respected President, ABRAHAM LINCOLN, acknowledging our gratitude to God for the miraculous preservation of the honorable Mr. Seward and family; and while we mourn, along with every true friend of humanity, the unparalleled event that has befallen your country, and although the horizon seemed dark for a time after such a calamity, we are again hopeful when we see the sun emerging from behind the cloud in your own likeness, supported by General Grant and the gallant army, Farragut and the navy, the patriotic people of America, and all who stood forward so nobly in time of need in defence of those institutions for the good of mankind contained in the glorious republic of America, all deserving and receiving our best thanks.

Signed in behalf of the meeting:

MATTHEW POLLOCK, *President.*
ALEXANDER DYKES, *Secretary.*

Resolved, That the foregoing be forwarded to the honorable Charles Francis Adams, American ambassador, London, for transmission to the honorable Andrew Johnson President of the United States of America.

M. P.
A. D.

SALT CHAMBER OF COMMERCE,
Northwich, Cheshire, May 6, 1865.

YOUR EXCELLENCY : The salt trade of England, represented by this chamber, have, perhaps more than any other mercantile community of this country, cause to identify their interests with those of the great American people.

The council of this chamber have therefore instructed me, by unanimous resolution, to convey to your excellency their profound grief and heartfelt sympathy with the American nation at the great calamity which has befallen them through the dastardly assassination of their late President.

In thus representing their condolence, this chamber pray you to accept their earnest assurance of profound respect for your excellency.

JOHN MOORE,
Secretary of the Salt Chamber of Commerce.

His Excellency the PRESIDENT OF THE UNITED STATES.

At a meeting of the watch committee of the corporation of Newport, in the county of Monmouth, held at the council-house on Tuesday, the 2d day of May, 1865, E. J. Phillips, esq., mayor, in the chair, the following resolution was unanimously agreed to :

That we view with the greatest horror and detestation the atrocious crime by which the President of the United States has been deprived of his life, and that our deep sympathy with the people of the United States for their loss be conveyed with this resolution to the United States consul of this town.

THOS. WOOLLETT, *Town Clerk.*

BOROUGH OF NEWPORT, ISLE OF WIGHT.

The following is a copy of a resolution passed at the quarterly meeting of the council of this borough, held on the 2d day of May, 1865, at the Guildhall.

Proposed by Mr. Councillor Pinnock, seconded by Mr. Alderman Way, and carried unanimously—

That this council desire to record their abhorrence and detestation of the crime which has deprived the American nation of the services of their President, and respectfully offer to the government and to the people of the United States their heartfelt sympathy.

[SEAL.] HY. MEW, *Mayor.*

At a meeting of the mayor, aldermen, and burgesses of Nottingham, in council assembled, held the 1st day of May, 1865, it was unanimously resolved—

That this council desires, in its corporate capacity, to express its extreme sorrow and indignation at the assassination of the late President of the United States of America, and to convey the expression of its condolence and sympathy at the loss which his widow and that nation at large have thereby sustained.

That the members of this council also express their regret at the attempt made upon the life of Mr. Seward and his sons, and the pleasure with which they this morning receive the news of their improved condition.

Given under the common seal of the said mayor, aldermen, and burgesses.

[SEAL.]   WILLIAM PAGE, *Mayor.*

At a public meeting of the inhabitants of Nottingham, held at the Exchange Hall on the 1st day of May, 1865, it was unanimously resolved—

That this meeting regards with horror, indignation, and abhorrence the appalling crime which has put an end to the life of President LINCOLN, while it rejoices that the dastardly attempt on the life of Mr. Seward has not resulted in his death, and trusts that he may long be spared for the benefit of his country.

That this meeting desires to record its profound sympathy with the people of the United States in this hour of national bereavement, and more especially with the widow whose grief is intensified by the atrocious nature of the deed which has snatched her husband from her side.

That this meeting devoutly trusts that the wise, statesmanlike, and eminently conciliatory and Christian policy of the late President, so peculiarly suited to bind up the wounds of his bleeding country, may not die with its author, but be carried forward by his successor to the speedy establishment of an enduring peace.

Signed by order and on behalf of the meeting:

WILLIAM PAGE, *Mayor, Chairman.*

Resolutions passed by the annual assembly of the United Methodist free churches, held in Nottingham, August, 1865.

THE AMERICAN WAR AND SLAVERY.

1. *Resolved,* The members of this assembly, having during the past four years watched with intense interest and painful anxiety the progress of the civil conflict upon the American continent, would now express their gratitude to Him by "whom kings reign and princes decree justice" that the said sanguin-

ary struggle has closed, and upon this auspicious circumstance this assembly most cordially congratulates both the government and people of the United States.

2. *Resolved,* This assembly is exceedingly grateful to have observed that God in his providence has so overruled the discussions of Congress and the conflict of armies as to have removed from among the American people that which has been their dishonor and scourge—chattel slavery; and upon this issue this assembly congratulate not only the American nation, but also all others, believing that the abolition of slavery in the United States will be the prelude to its abolition all over the world.

3. *Resolved,* This assembly rejoices at the seasonable and well-sustained efforts which have been made by the American people, in order to lessen the distress which has arisen from the immediate emancipation of the slaves of the south, by the feeding and clothing of the aged and infirm and the opening of schools for the education of the young; and this assembly recommends the members of our churches to do what they can by the contribution of both apparel and money, in order to further the object of the "freedmen's aid societies."

4. *Resolved,* This assembly records its unmitigated abhorrence of, and indignation at, the crime of assassination by which the American people have, in the hour of returning order and peace, been deprived of one of the most praiseworthy of modern rulers—the patient, sagacious, and philanthropic ABRAHAM LINCOLN.

This assembly also expresses its deep and sincere sympathy with the Executive and people of the United States upon their loss; and also, in harmony with the promptly-presented utterances of the British press, platform, senate, and throne, tenders its condolence to the honored widow of the deceased President.

This assembly, moreover, trusts, now that the war has ceased in the triumph of the northern arms, that henceforth England and America, as they are one in origin, language, and religion, will cultivate towards each other the most amicable relations, and, being banded together not only as profitable traders but true friends, will by their powerful example and moral influence elevate and bless the world.

5. *Resolved,* That a copy of the aforesaid resolutions be communicated to the honorable Charles Francis Adams for presentation to Mrs. Lincoln and to his Excellency the President of the United States.

Signed on behalf of the assembly:

WILLIAM ROBERTS BROWN, *President.*
MARMADUKE MILLER, *Secretary.*

At a meeting of the citizens of Norwich, in Common Hall assembled, on Tuesday, the 2d day of May, 1865, pursuant to a requisition to the mayor, numerously and influentially signed, for the purpose of expressing the sympathy of the city of Norwich to the American government and people for the great loss they have sustained by the atrocious murder of their President, the following resolution was unanimously passed, and the mayor was requested to sign and affix the corporate seal thereto, and forward it to the American minister in London :

Resolved, That this meeting desires to express the greatest regret at the calamity brought upon the people of the United States of America by the assassination of President LINCOLN.

That this meeting regards with horror and detestation the crime by which the President's life was sacrificed, and that, in the name of the citizens of Norwich, this meeting begs to offer to the government and people of the United States the most sincere and earnest sympathy under the loss which has so suddenly befallen them.

[SEAL.]   S. E. TUCK, *Mayor.*

Resolution passed at a meeting of the council of the borough of Newcastle-upon-Tyne.

At a quarterly meeting of the council of the borough of Newcastle-upon-Tyne, held in the council chamber, Town Hall, Newcastle-upon-Tyne, on Wednesday, the third day of May, 1865, Anthony Nichol, esq., deputy mayor, chairman, it was unanimously resolved, on the motion of Mr. Joseph Cowen the younger, seconded by Mr. Alderman Laycock—

That this council desires to give utterance to the feelings of grief and horror with which it has heard of the assassination of President LINCOLN, and the murderous attack upon Mr. Seward, and to convey to Mrs. Lincoln, President Johnson, and his colleagues, and to the people of the United States, its profound sympathy and heartfelt condolence.

[SEAL.]   ANTHONY NICHOL, *Chairman.*

Resolution passed at a meeting held by the inhabitants of the borough of Newcastle-upon-Tyne.

At a meeting of the inhabitants of the borough of Newcastle-upon-Tyne, convened by the mayor on requisition and held in the Town Hall, on Thursday evening, the 4th of May, 1865, the sheriff of Newcastle in the chair,

On the motion of the Rev. W. Walters, seconded by Councillor Mawson, and supported by the Rev. J. C. Street, it was unanimously resolved—

1st. That this meeting desires to give utterance to the feelings of grief and horror with which it has heard of the assassination of President LINCOLN, and the murderous attack upon Mr. Seward, and to convey to Mrs. Lincoln, to President Johnson, and his colleagues, and to the people of the United States, its profound sympathy and heartfelt condolence.

On the motion of Councillor Benson, seconded by Mr. Ralph Curry, and supported by Councillor Harford, it was unanimously agreed—

2d. That copies of the foregoing resolution be placed in the hands of the honorable C. F. Adams, the American minister, for transmission to his Excellency the President of the United States, Mrs. Lincoln, and the honorable W. H. Seward.

Signed on behalf of the meeting:

WILLIAM LOCHEY HARLE, *Sheriff.*

To his Excellency ANDREW JOHNSON,
President of the United States of America:

The following resolution was adopted by the sixty-ninth annual conference of the Methodist New Connection, assembled in Salem chapel, Hood street, Newcastle-upon-Tyne, on the thirteenth day of June in the year of our Lord eighteen hundred and sixty-five:

Resolved, That the conference of the Methodist New Connection, assembled in Newcastle-upon-Tyne, would record the expression of its devout thanksgiving and joy on the termination of the war which for four long years has been waged at so fearful a cost of human life and human treasure between the northern and southern divisions of the United States of America. While in the war itself the conference would recognize the supreme justice of Eternal Providence in making a nation, however mysteriously and by whatever means, yet ultimately and surely, responsible for the legislative or social wrongs it either authorizes or countenances, it would nevertheless and equally recognize the mercy of that Providence in the conclusion to which the war has been finally conducted, in that a great nation, so intimately allied to our own in all the interests of human civilization and Christian enterprise, has been redeemed from disorder and anarchy by the triumph of the national wisdom and courage, and especially that this has been so done as effectually to annihilate the evil out of which the war really though not ostensibly sprang, restoring to the position and privileges of manhood four millions of human beings who had previously been held as mere property by those who claimed to be their owners.

The conference also desires to unite with the whole English nation, and, indeed, with the entire civilized world, in giving emphatic utterance to its horror and abhorrence of the fearful crime by which the close of the war has been signalized, in the assassination of the much lamented late President of the United States, to whose practical wisdom and singular goodness of character may be largely attributed the continuance of the peaceful relations existing between this country and America, amid the jealousies and perplexities which the war occasioned, as well as by whose prudence and perseverance, together with the prudence and perseverance of those united with him in the conduct of public affairs, the result now enjoyed has been happily reached.

And yet the conference would express an earnest hope that no irritation thence resulting, however natural and reasonable, will be allowed to influence the regular course of justice in dealing with those who have taken a leading part in the attempt to divide the Union, by establishing a separate confederacy, and that in fact no means will be adopted but such as will, under the superintendence of the Great Ruler, tend to conciliate the affections and interests of the parties hitherto so much divided, and so restore them to a condition of permanent harmony and peace.

Signed on behalf of the conference :

WILLIAM BAGGALY, *President.*
JOSHUA POLLARD, *Secretary.*

Resolution adopted at a meeting of the Executive Council of Newfoundland, on Saturday, May 6, 1865.

That the council avail themselves of the earliest opportunity of expressing their deepest regret and horror at the foul assassination of President LINCOLN ; and on behalf of the people of this colony they beg to tender their respectful sympathy in the sorrow that has so justly been awakened throughout the American Union at the loss of their illustrious head.

Resolved, That his excellency the governor be requested to transmit a copy of the foregoing resolution to her Majesty's minister at Washington.

THE CITIZENS OF THE SWISS REPUBLIC IN NEW SOUTH WALES,

To the honorable the President, the Senate, and the House of Representatives of the United States of America :

We, the citizens of the Swiss republic, resident at New South Wales, have been requested by Signor John Baptist Modini, one of our countrymen, to assemble in order, as sons of another free republic, to condole with you, the Congress of America, on the very sad calamity that has befallen your nation, and to express our heartfelt sorrow and sympathetic grief for the immense loss you have sustained by the atrocious murder of your great devoted champion of liberty, President ABRAHAM LINCOLN.

We, by birth sons of another free republic, cannot refrain from giving expression of sympathy for your great loss, being ourselves brought up under free principles, and we owe it to ourselves and to the republic of which we are citizens to declare our abhorrence of the crime which has deprived humanity of one of its greatest ornaments.

To Mrs. Lincoln and family we offer the respectful condolence of our sympathy with the sufferings which it is some consolation to know are in a degree shared by the world at large, but which are assuaged by the consideration that Mr. LINCOLN's work and best efforts had already gained the approval and admiration of every free and enlightened people.

J. B. MODINI.
AUGUSTO ANDREOLI.
ORIOLA MIRO.
LORENZO BERTA.
GIOVANNI GAGLIARDI.
FRANCESCO GALLI.
AND FORTY OTHER NAMES.

At a meeting of the mayor, aldermen, and councillors, being the municipal council of the borough of Northampton, held at the Town Hall in the same borough, on the 1st day of May, 1865—present, the worshipful the mayor, Thomas Osborn, esquire, in the chair—it was

Unanimously resolved, That the members of this council, including persons of all parties in the state, desire to record the deep feeling of horror with which they have heard of the late atrocious murder of the President of the United States of America, and the attempted assassination of his Secretary of State, crimes deserving the execration of mankind, and which the members of this council doubt not will prove to have been the acts of the guilty perpetrators exclusively.

The council desires further to record their sympathy with the widow of the murdered Chief Magistrate under her bereavement, their condolence with the citizens of the republic, and their sincere trust that under the providential guidance of the Great Disposer of events the path of mercy and conciliation on which Mr. LINCOLN had entered may be steadily trodden by his successor, and that the great and kindred nation over which he is summoned to preside may speedily recover from the deep wounds of civil war, and enjoy a bright future of liberty, peace, and prosperity in ever closer and more cordial alliance with our own branch of the English race.

That two copies of the above resolutions be fairly made on vellum, authenticated by the signature of the worshipful the mayor and the common seal of the borough, and sent to his excellency the United States minister in this country, with a request that he will forward one copy to the proper authority of his own government and the other to Mrs. Lincoln.

[SEAL.]   THOMAS OSBORN, *Mayor.*

ABINGTON TERRACE,
Northampton, May 19, 1865.

RESPECTED SIR : Your well known courtesy encourages me to forward the enclosed lines to you, at the request of an invalid sister, whose composition they are, as a tribute to the memory of that great and good man, your late President.

If it will not be out of place, and should meet with your approbation, my sister desires you would enclose them in your future despatches for Mrs. Lincoln, with a sincere hope that they may afford her some comfort in her heavy affliction.   Trusting you will pardon the liberty I have taken,

I remain, your most obedient servant,

WILLIAM GRAY.

C. F. ADAMS, Esq., *United States Ambassador.*

ACROSTIC ON ABRAHAM LINCOLN.

A nation—nor one only—mourns thy loss,
Brave LINCOLN, and with voice unanimous
Raise to thy deathless memory
A dirge-like song of all thy noble deeds.
High let it rise ; and I, too, fain would add
A loving tribute to thy priceless worth,
More widely known since banished from the earth.

Laurel shall now thy brow entwine
In memory's ever faithful shrine ;
Nor shall it fade when earth dissolves.
Caught up to meet thee in the air,
Old age and youth shall bless thee there ;
Love shall her grateful tribute pay,
Nor cease through heaven's eternal day.

NORTHAMPTON, ENGLAND.   GRACE W. GRAY.

GOVERNMENT HOUSE,
Halifax, Novia Scotia, April 17, 1865.

SIR: I have the honor to ackowledge the receipt of your communication of Saturday, the 15th instant, announcing the atrocious assassination of President LINCOLN. I feel I need not assure you of my own personal sympathy for your countrymen under an affliction so sudden, and accompanied by special circumstances so appalling.

The adjournment of both branches of the legislature, on receipt of the melancholy intelligence, the flags hoisted half-mast on all forts and public buildings, together with the unanimous and outspoken feeling of the press, sufficiently attest the profound and painful impression which the intelligence has produced on this community.

You thus have at least the sad gratification of knowing that the misfortunes of your countrymen can evoke from their kindred here only feelings of kindly sympathy and good will.

I have the honor to be, sir, your most obedient humble servant,
RICHARD GRAVES MACDONNELL,
Lieutenant Governor.
Judge JACKSON, *United States Consul,*
Halifax, Nova Scotia.

LEGISLATIVE COUNCIL CHAMBER,
Halifax, Nova Scotia, April 15, 1865.

SIR: By the direction of the legislative council of Nova Scotia, I have the honor to transmit to you two resolutions passed by that house on receiving the sad intelligence of the assassination of the President of the United States of America, and to request that you will forward the same to the Secretary of the Department of State of the United States.

I have the honor to be, sir, your most obedient humble servant,
JOHN C. HILLBURTON.
MORTIMER M. JACKSON, Esq.,
United States Consul, Halifax, N. S.

Resolutions passed by the legislative council of Halifax.

LEGISLATIVE COUNCIL CHAMBER,
Halifax, Nova Scotia, April 15, 1865.

Resolved unanimously, That this house has heard with most profound regret that the President of the United States of America has fallen by the hand of an assassin, and that as a mark of sympathy with the people who have thus been deprived of their chief ruler, and of abhorrence of the atrocious crime that has been committed, this house do now adjourn.

Resolved, That the clerk of this house be directed to forward a copy of the foregoing resolution to the consular officer of the United States resident in this city, with a request that the same be respectfully transmitted to the Secretary of the Department of State of the United States.

JOHN C. HILLBURTON,

Clerk of the Legislative Council of Nova Scotia.

THE NEWS IN THE HOUSE OF ASSEMBLY.

[From the Reporter.]

The house of assembly met this morning at 11 o'clock, and the provincial secretary immediately moved a resolution to adjourn until Monday next. He said : I need not say that this house has been deeply shocked by the intelligence which has just been received of the death of President LINCOLN. Both branches of the legislature having been on Thursday last informed that his excellency would come down at three o'clock for the purpose of assenting to several bills which have passed, I felt it my duty, proposing as we do to adjourn this house, to put myself in communication with his excellency, who entirely concurs in the appropriateness of this house marking its sympathy with the people of the United States, who have thus lost their Chief Magistrate, and its deep abhorrence of the crime by which he has been removed. This house is aware that when, exactly four years ago this day, the first intelligence reached this country of the commencement of hostilities in the American republic, this house placed on record its sentiments by the following resolution :

" *Resolved unanimously,* That the house of assembly of Nova Scotia have heard with deep regret of the outbreak of the civil war in the United States ; that this house, without expressing any opinion upon the points in controversy between the contending parties, sincerely lament that those who speak their language and share their civilization should be shedding each other's blood, and offer up their prayers to the Father of the Universe for the speedy restoration of peace."

This resolution sufficiently marked the feelings with which this house viewed the beginning of hostilities which have so long and so terribly distracted the neighboring republic. It is not to be denied that as that struggle advanced, when the people of British North America witnessed the heroic resistance that a comparatively small number of men in the southern States made against overwhelming odds, a large amount of sympathy was excited in the minds of many— that sympathy which is always excited when a small body is seen contending with great bravery against superior numbers—in favor of the South. But although that feeling has existed to some extent—although there have been persons in this country who believe that the material interests of British America would be promoted by a separation between the northern and southern States, and that great republic being thus divided into two governments; yet I am confident that there is not a British subject in British America who will learn the untimely death of President LINCOLN, and the circumstances under which it has occurred, without the feeling of the most unfeigned sorrow and the most profound regret.   It is well known that President LINCOLN was elected the President of the United States of America by the intelligent and freely expressed voice of the people of that great country; and no man who has observed the course he has pursued can entertain a doubt that he has regarded it as a conscientious duty—a duty from which under no circumstances he was able in the slightest degree to shrink —to maintain the sovereignty of his government over the entire country.   That he has persistently pursued that policy with an inflexibility of determination and strength of purpose which must forever mark him as a man of commanding talents no one can deny, and I am satisfied that the sentiment of the people, and of those who are placed over the people throughout British North America, will agree in the opinion that he has been actuated by a conscientious discharge of what he believed to be a patriotic duty in that crisis of his country's history.   Under these circumstances, I feel that it is right that the neighboring governments in British North America should, as far as their means would permit, exhibit on the present occasion their deep sympathy with the people of the neighboring States, who have lost their chief ruler, and at the same time mark their deep abhorrence of the atrocious crime by which he has been removed.   I have, therefore, to offer to the house the following resolution:

Resolved unanimously, That this house have heard with the most profound regret that the President of the United States of America has fallen by the hand of an assassin, and that as a mark of sympathy with the people who have thus been deprived of their chief ruler, and of their abhorrence of the atrocious crime that has been committed, this house do adjourn until Monday next.

Mr. Stewart Campbell, who seconded the resolution, said: On any ordinary occasion I should regret the absence of the learned member for Colchester, who occupies a position in this house which would peculiarly call upon him to second any resolution demanding the united action of all parties in this house.   But this resolution is of no party, and requires not that any particular individual should second it.   It is, indeed, one that need not be formally seconded by the lips, for it is sustained by the feelings of every gentleman around these benches. The honorable provincial secretary has referred to the awful tragedy of which we have just received the painful intelligence, in terms so feeling and so appropriate and just, that although, according to parliamentary usage, I have undertaken my present duty, but little observation is required on my part to confirm or indorse those sentiments.   We all feel, sir, that an occurrence has taken place which, at the present age of the world, is not only an outrage upon an individual and a nationality, but is an outrage upon .mankind and the civilization of the world at large; and although we belong to another empire than that in which this dreadful scene has been enacted, we are deeply moved by the awful fact that there has been a gross outrage committed against those feelings which are, and ever will be, respected in every country that prides itself in the possession of the privileges of civilization and the blessings of Christianity. I think the course taken by the government in adjourning this house, as a mark and testimony of its feelings on the present melancholy occasion, is extremely appropriate, and will be sure to meet with the cordial approval of every member in this house, and of every man in this country.

The resolution passed unanimously, and the house adjourned.

At a meeting of the council of the borough of Oldham, in the county of Lancaster, held at the Town Hall in Oldham, on Wednesday, the 3d day of May, 1865, it was

Resolved, That this council hereby expresses its horror at the crime recently perpetrated, in the assassination of the President of the United States of America, and the attempted assassination of Mr. Seward, and desires to lay before the United States their wish that the government may still be carried on efficiently, and in the interests of peace, notwithstanding the loss sustained by them and the world.

[SEAL.]   JOSIAH RADCLIFFE, *Mayor.*

Resolution passed at a meeting of the council of the borough of Oldham.

At a meeting of the council of the borough of Oldham, in the county of Lancaster, held at the Town Hall in Oldham, on Wednesday, the 3d day of May, 1865, it was

Resolved, That this council expresses to Mrs. Lincoln its sincere and strong sympathy with her in the sorrow which she must feel, and the loss she has sustained, by the foul crime that has been committed in the assassination of the President of the United States, and trusts she may have strength to bear the great sorrow that has been thrown upon her, and power to look beyond the present.

[SEAL.]   JOSIAH RADCLIFFE, *Mayor.*

At a public meeting of the inhabitants of the borough of Oldham, in the county of Lancaster, convened upon a requisition to the worshipful the mayor, held at the Town Hall in Oldham, on Monday, the 1st day of May, 1865, Josiah Radcliffe, esq., mayor, in the chair, it was

Resolved, That this meeting desires to express its deep and unqualified abhorrence of the foul and atrocious crime which has been perpetrated on the person of the President of the United States, as well as the diabolical attempt to assassinate Mr. Seward, while helpless and prostrated on a bed of sickness. The tragic event has suddenly deprived the people of the United States of a Chief Magistrate whom they had learned to love and revere, and thus plunged them into the deepest sorrow and distress. It has also caused all right-minded people in every land to feel the strongest horror and disgust at its cowardly and dastardly character. We denounce not only the instrument of Mr. LINCOLN's death, but all who may have aided and abetted him, and any who may be so lost to honor and justice as to approve of such a diabolical deed. We desire to acknowledge our sympathy with the people of the United States, who have been thus ruthlessly deprived of a wise and good ruler at a time when his moderation and sagacity were so needful to the cause of peace. While we are conscious that the cruel act which we all deplore is so eminently calculated to rouse the deepest indignation, still we trust that in the order of Providence the same wise forbearance which President LINCOLN has manifested may be shown by his successor, President Johnson, and that peace and harmony may be speedily restored to the whole country.

It was also

Resolved, That in accordance with the deep sorrow which animates our own breasts, we feel constrained to express our heartfelt sympathy and condolence with Mrs. Lincoln in her sudden and overwhelming bereavement, and we trust she may be enabled to derive some consolation from the fact that she has the sympathy of the whole civilized world, and from the consciousness that her husband was actuated by the noblest motives and the most generous designs; that he harbored no resentment in his lofty soul, but sought to heal the wounds which have lacerated his country by kindness and conciliation, and by a Christian forbearance, which ought to have disarmed the malice of all, and which have won for him the approbation of mankind.

It was further

Resolved, That the mayor be requested to forward the foregoing resolutions to his excellency Mr. Adams, the American minister at London, as the expression of the feelings of the people of Oldham, in public meeting assembled, on the tragic event which has recently been enacted in the United States.

JOSIAH RADCLIFFE, *Mayor.*

Resolutions passed at a meeting held by the Ancient Order of Foresters.

Court Duchess of Sutherland, No. 3,212, held at the Roman Arms, Roman Road, Old Ford, in the county of Middlesex, at the meeting on Tuesday, 2d May, 1865, it was proposed by P. C. R. Bro. Walsham, seconded by P. C. R. Bro. Davis, and carried unanimously—

That the members of this court, who are in connection with the London United District, numbering upwards of 47,000 members, and a branch of the order, comprising nearly 150,000 members, in all parts of the globe, enforcing no creed in religion or code in politics, do hereby tender to the people of the United States of America, many of whom must be tied to them by the bonds of brotherhood, their expression of deep sympathy upon the loss they have sustained by the death of their President by assassination—a crime of such deep guilt and magnitude that it is justly held in abhorrence by all nations and people ; and further, to offer Mrs. Lincoln their sincere condolence and regret that she should be deprived of her husband by such a cowardly and inhuman act.

It was further proposed by P. C. R. Bro. Walsham, seconded by P. C. R. Bro. Davis, and carried unanimously—

That a copy of the foregoing resolution be forwarded the Hon. Charles Francis Adams, American minister in London, desiring him to offer it for the acceptance of the Secretary of State at Washington, and Mrs. Lincoln.

Extracted from the minutes, this 3d day of May, 1865.

WM. H. WALSHAM, *Secretary.*

His Excellency the Hon. ANDREW JOHNSON,

President of the United States of America :

We, the mayor, aldermen, and citizens of Oxford, in council assembled, express through you, sir, to our brethren the great American nation, the abhorrence and detestation with which, in common with the whole British nation, and indeed the whole civilized world, we regard the foul crime by which the late President has been deprived of his life, his wife and family of a faithful and loving husband and father, and his country of a true citizen.

We pray, sir, that under your auspices, the United States may shortly be restored to peace, and thus be reinstated in happiness and prosperity.

Given under our common seal the 18th day of May, 1865.

[SEAL.]

The Chancellor of Oxford to Mr. Adams.

ST. JAMES SQUARE, *May* 6, 1865.

SIR : As chancellor of the University of Oxford, I have the honor of transmitting to you an address under the seal of the university, unanimously adopted
by convocation, expressive of their condolence with the government and the
people of the United States on the calamity which has recently befallen them
in the assassination of the President; their abhorrence of the act of the assassination ; their friendly feeling towards a kindred nation, and their earnest prayers
for the restoration of peace and national prosperity to your now suffering country.   It is, I hope, unnecessary for me to assure your excellency of my entire
personal concurrence in the sentiments of which I am made the official organ ;
but the departure on this occasion by the university from its almost invariable
practice will afford an additional proof, if any were required, of the strength
and genuineness of the feelings which this atrocious crime and lamentable
catastrophe have evoked from all classes and all shades of political opinions,
from the sovereign downward, throughout the whole of the United Kingdom.

I have the honor to be, with the highest respect, your excellency's most
obedient servant,

DERBY.

His Excellency Hon. CHARLES FRANCIS ADAMS,
Minister of the United States.

---

*Address to his excellency the envoy extraordinary and minister plenipotentiary of
the United States of America.*

May it please your excellency : We, the chancellor, masters, and scholars
of the University of Oxford, request your excellency to convey to the government and people of the United States of America the assurance of our sincere
condolence, on the occasion of the appalling calamity which has recently befallen
your country.

It is not the practice of this University to notice, in its corporate capacity,
events which do not directly affect the well-being of our own country.   But at
this singular and lamentable crisis we are conscious of the full force of those
recollections of the past which must at all times lead the British nation to regard
with a community of interest the fortunes and destinies of a friendly and a
kindred people.   In accordance with these sentiments, it is the anxious desire
of the university to express to your excellency the abhorrence with which we,
together with the whole civilized world, regard the assassination of the President of the United States.   We would also at the same time express, in common
with all ranks of our countrymen, our earnest hope that by the orderings of a

merciful Providence the American people may speedily enjoy the restoration of internal peace and national prosperity.

Given at our house of convocation, under the common seal, this fifth day of May, in the year of our Lord God 1865.

[SEAL.]

MAYOR'S OFFICE, CITY HALL,
Ottawa, April 19, 1865.

SIR : I have the honor to enclose herein a copy of a resolution adopted unanimously by the municipal council of this city, the same being but an imperfect expression of the most sincere sympathy of this community towards the American people, on the melancholy occasion of the recent tragical death of the late President of the United States of America at the hands of an assassin.

I would also beg leave to express my regret at the atrocious attempt made upon your own life and others of your family and household, and have great pleasure to learn this day by public report of the certain and gradual improvement in the condition of yourself and those who unfortunately suffered with you.

I have the honor to remain your obedient servant,

M. K. DICKENSON,
Mayor of Ottawa.

Hon. WILLIAM H. SEWARD,
Secretary of State, Washington, D. C.

Resolutions of the city of Ottawa.

Resolved, That this corporation deems it its duty to express its sincere regret for the untimely and tragical fate of ABRAHAM LINCOLN, President of the United States of America, which calamitous event has bereft a friendly nation of its Chief Magistrate and mankind of a character noble for his integrity and firmness. And that as an expression of the deep sympathy felt by this community for the afflicted people who have thus suddenly been deprived of their chief ruler, the mayor be requested to order the national ensign to be raised on the public buildings of this city, and the citizens of Ottawa are hereby respectfully requested to follow such example.

[L. S.]   M. K. DICKENSON, *Mayor.*
Certified :   WM. P. LETT, *City Clerk.*
CITY HALL, OTTAWA, *April* 19, 1865.

Excerpt from minutes of the meeting of the magistrates and commissioners of the burgh of Patrick, near Glasgow, Scotland, held on the 8th day of May; in the year 1865.

. *Inter alia*, it was unanimously resolved, on the motion of Allan Arthur, senior magistrate of the burgh—

That this meeting desires to express their grief and abhorrence at the crime by which, in an eventful crisis, the United States of America have been deprived of a wise and good President, and the life of one of their Secretaries of State has been endangered; their sympathy with the people of the United States in the trying circumstances; respectful condolence with the widow and family of the lamented late President, ABRAHAM LINCOLN; and the hope that the life of Mr. Seward may be spared to his country and to his family.

And, further, this meeting desire to express the fond trust that under the favor of Almighty God the blessing of peace may soon be restored to those States, so long suffering the horrors of war.

That a copy of the foregoing resolution be excerpted from the minutes by the clerk to the commissioners, signed by the senior magistrate in the name of the meeting, and sent to his excellency the minister of the United States in London.

ALLAN ARTHUR,
Senior Magistrate of the Burgh of Patrick.

MAT. WALKER, *Clerk.*

At Pollokshaws, and within the council chamber there, on Friday, the 5th day of May, 1865:

At a meeting of the magistrates and town council of the burgh of Pollokshaws—present, Provost Austin, Bailie King, Treasurer Nicol, Counsellors Watson, Baird, McIntire, Mackay, Brownlie, and Steel—the provost in the chair—Provost Austin moved that the magistrates and town council express their sympathy with the community of the United States of America, and especially with Mrs. Lincoln and her family, on the melancholy bereavement they have sustained through the assassination of the late President of those States.

This motion was seconded by Bailie King, and unanimously agreed to, and the clerk was instructed to forward to the American minister in London a copy of this minute.

In respect whereof:

WILLIAM AUSTIN, *Provost.*

I certify that the foregoing is a true copy.

JOHN KENART, *Town Clerk.*

At a meeting of the council of the borough of Portsmouth, holden at the council chamber, the 1st day of May, 1865,

The mayor having addressed the council in reference to the recent death by assassination of the President of the United States, he moved therein, seconded by Louis Arnoldus Vandenberg, esquire, and it was thereupon

Unanimously resolved, That this council, representing the feelings of all classes in the borough, has heard with the greatest sorrow and indignation of the recent death of the President of the United States of America by the hands of an assassin, and of the attempt made at the same time on the life of Mr. Seward, the American Secretary of State.   And while declaring its abhorrence at these hateful crimes, it desires earnestly to express its deep sympathy with the American people in the grief and distress into which they have been plunged by those sad and cowardly events.

It was then moved by Mr. Alderman Scale, seconded by W. G. Chambers, esq., and

Unanimously resolved, That the mayor be requested to forward a copy of the foregoing resolution to Mr. Adams, the representative of the United States to this country, with a request that it may be communicated to the American government, and that the mayor do at the same time offer the sincere condolence of the council to Mrs. Lincoln, in her sudden and cruel bereavement.

Extracted from the minutes of the proceedings of the council of the borough of Portsmouth, the 9th day of May, 1865.

JOHN HOWARD, *Town Clerk.*

Address of the provost, magistrates, and town council of the burgh of Paisley, in Scotland.

SIR: That the provost, magistrates, and town council of the burgh of Paisley have received the intelligence of the death of his Excellency ABRAHAM LINCOLN, late President of the United States, by the hand of an assassin, and of the attempt to assassinate the honorable William H. Seward, an illustrious member of his government, with sentiments of detestation and abhorrence.

That they desire, for themselves and the inhabitants of the burgh they represent, to express their detestation of these atrocious crimes whereby the American nation, by the untimely death of Mr. LINCOLN, has been deprived of an upright ruler, and the life of Mr. Seward endangered, and their deep sympathy and condolence with Mrs. Lincoln in her severe affliction.

They have also to express their sympathy with the government and people of the United States in being deprived of their Chief Magistrate at a momentous period of their country's history.

They would express a hope that the prospects of a returned peace may not be impeded by the lamented death of Mr. LINCOLN, and that the measures to be adopted by your government may tend to the restoration of the blessings of peace.

Signed in our name and behalf, and by our authority, and the common seal of the burgh affixed thereto, the sixth day of May, eighteen hundred and sixty-five.

[SEAL.]   DAVID CAMPBELL,
                          Provost and Chief Magistrate of Paisley.

His Excellency the PRESIDENT
    of the United States of America.

Resolutions passed at a meeting held by the town council of the city of Perth.

At Perth, and within the Town Hall thereof, Monday, the first day of May, eighteen hundred and sixty-five, at ten o'clock, forenoon, sederunt in council— John Kemp, esq., present, lord provost of the city of Perth, &c.—

On the motion of the lord provost, it was

Unanimously resolved, That the town council of the city of Perth record the heartfelt concurrence with which they and the people of this locality, in common with the whole British nation, reprobate with abhorrence the foul crime which has recently been committed in and against the United States of America by the assassination of Mr. LINCOLN, the twice elected President of that great nation; and that the council express their participation in the grief which the sad event has universally created.   The crime is atrocious from every point of view, eminently dangerous to society, and deeply distressing to the relatives of the exalted victim, as well as to the great community over which he presided with so much justice, intelligence, and ability.

And resolved, That the council offer their condolence and sincere expressions of sympathy with the American people and relatives of the deceased President, by forwarding an extract of the present resolutions to his excellency the American ambassador in London.

Extracted by—

                         WILLIAM GREIG,
                            Joint Town Clerk.

The improvement commissioners of the city of Peterboro', in the county of Northampton, Old England, being the local authority of the city, at their meeting held on the 2d day of May, 1865, unanimously passed the following resolution:

Resolved, That this meeting desires to express its grief and horror at the cruel assassination of President LINCOLN, and the murderous attack upon Mr. Seward, and to convey to Mrs. Lincoln and the United States government an expression of profound sympathy.

Signed on behalf of the meeting:

W. STRONG, *Chairman.*

MILLFIELD, PETERBORO', *May* 13, 1865.

SIR: At a public meeting held here on the 12th instant, in the "Assembly Rooms," which meeting was called by some workingmen, (although others assisted at the meeting,) "to express sympathy with the people of America in the sad loss they have sustained in the assassination of President LINCOLN," the following resolutions were unanimously passed. As secretary of the committee calling the meeting, I am requested to forward them to you, praying you to transmit them to the authorities at Washington:

Resolved, That this meeting, having heard of the assassination of President LINCOLN, desires to express its profound sorrow at, and detestation of, the deed by which he was striken down.

Resolved, That this meeting desires to condole with Mrs. Lincoln in this the hour of her sad bereavement, and would earnestly pray that God, the "husband of the widow," may be graciously pleased to grant her the rich consolations of his grace.

Resolved, That this meeting desires to express to the people of America its deep sympathy with them in the irreparable loss they have sustained in one so wise, so honest, and so generous as ABRAHAM LINCOLN, and sincerely hopes that the good work so gloriously inaugurated by him may be carried on to its final issue.

Allow me to add that the meeting, although not so numerous as it would have been but for the severity of the weather, (it had been raining incessantly during the whole of the day, and during the time of the meeting,) from 250 to 300 present, was very enthusiastic in its approval of the principles and polity of the lamented late President, and rejoiced with joy unfeigned at the overthrow of the slaveocracy of the South.

With deep sympathy for yourself in this trying moment of your country's history, I have the honor to be, your obedient servant,

H. BEECH.

Hon. Mr. ADAMS, &c., &c.

PUDSEY, NEAR LEEDS, *May* 4, 1865.

The local board of surveyors for the township of Pudsey, near Leeds, in the West Riding of the county of York, at their public meeting yesterday, passed the following resolution with a deep feeling of sorrow:

Resolved, That this board desires to take this its earliest opportunity to record its utter detestation of the atrocious crime of assassination committed at Washington, in the United States of America, on the honorable the President of the United States, in consequence of which ABRAHAM LINCOLN, their noble and beloved Chief Magistrate, has lost his life.

And this meeting wishes to express its profound sympathy with the people over which he was called to preside, in the grievous and irreparable loss the nation has sustained by his death at this critical period of their country's history.

Signed on behalf of the meeting:

BENJAMIN TROUGHTON, *Chairman.*

Hon. C. F. ADAMS,
 American Minister, London.

Resolutions passed in the borough of Preston, in the county of Lancaster.

At a meeting of the council of the said borough, held on the 27th day of April, 1865, present the right worshipful Joseph Isherwood, mayor, in the chair, it was

Unanimously resolved, That this council desire to express their utter abhorrence of the assassination of the President of the United States of America, and to condole and sympathize with the American nation upon the loss they have sustained through the sudden and lamented death of their President.

Given under the common seal of the said borough, the day and year above mentioned.

[SEAL.]   JOSEPH ISHERWOOD, *Mayor.*

ROBERT ASHCROFT, *Town Clerk.*

Resolution passed at a public meeting held in Preston on the 4th of May, 1865.

Resolved, That the inhabitants of Preston, in public meeting assembled, do hereby express their deep sorrow and indignation at the atrocious assassination of ABRAHAM LINCOLN, President of the United States, and the dastardly attempt about the same hour on the life of Mr. Seward, Secretary of State. They desire to express their profound sympathy with Mrs. Lincoln in this mournful affliction, and with the American government and people in the loss, at such a crisis, of one so recently elected a second time to the office of President. In the state of affairs consequent upon the recent successes of the federal arms, the kindly feeling and the evident anxiety to smooth the way to the removal of animosities displayed by President LINCOLN in the hour of triumph, render his removal, in the opinion of this meeting, a calamity not only to America, but to Europe.

JOSEPH ISHERWOOD,

Mayor, Chairman.

His Excellency ANDREW JOHNSON,
President of the United States.

Address of the Preston Anti-Slavery Society.

To his Excellency ANDREW JOHNSON,
President of the United States:

SIR: Permit us, in thought and feeling, to join with the great multitude of mourners, and with them utter our deep sorrow over the loss of one so noble-hearted, so gentle and wise, as the late President of the American republic.

We are shocked at the atrocious and dastardly mode by which so valuable a life was destroyed, and can only attribute it to the corrupting influence of the foul system of slavery, which engenders the most cruel and inhuman passions We desire to express and offer, through you, our deep sympathy with the American government and people in their grief over this cruel deed, which is truly the crowning enormity of that catalogue of crimes committed in the name of slavery. With them we execrate the brutal assault on Mr. Seward and his sons, and join in gratitude for their spared lives.

Permit us to hope that the anti-slavery policy so wisely inaugurated and so firmly executed by your predecessor, may under your governance be practically completed, until in America shall be found only the freed man and the citizen, and unjust prejudice, disappearing from all classes of society, shall follow as a shadow the departed form of slavery.

Our sense of the inestimable worth of the departed checks the disposition to congratulate you upon your ascension to the presidential chair; but remembering your manner of life from your youth up, your steadfastness and sufferings on behalf of your convictions, and the gifts with which you have been so liberally endowed, and have so diligently cultivated, we beg to express our earnest hope and confidence that your future career will testify your worthiness of the honor and your ability to sustain the responsibility so unexpectedly conferred upon you.

Accept, sir, for yourself and the great republic of America, our best wishes. Signed for and on behalf of the Preston Anti-Slavery Society:

> JNO. McKEAN, *President.*
> ROBT. BENSON, *Treasurer.*
> SARAH J. CLEMESHA,
> EDWIN COX,
> *Honorary Secretaries.*

Address of the Preston Anti-Slavery Society.

To Mrs. LINCOLN:

MADAM: We desire not to invade the privacy of domestic sorrow—a sorrow into the agony and solitude of which only one, the Divine Comforter, can and does fully enter—but we wish to assure you of our sincere and deep sympathy by which, in some degree, we share your grief, and of our earnest hope that you may be sustained in this time of bitter trial by the memory of the Christian character and noble life of the late Mr. LINCOLN, as also by the universal sympathy which his untimely loss has excited, by the general tribute already offered to his wisdom and nobility as the Chief Magistrate of the American republic, and above all, by that religious faith which he so truly manifested, and which sheds upon his grave the light of a better hope exclaiming: "Blessed are the dead which die in the Lord; yea, saith the spirit, for they rest from their labors and their works do follow them."

Signed for and in behalf of the Preston Anti-Slavery Society:

> JNO. McKEAN, *President.*
> ROBT. BENSON, *Treasurer.*
> SARAH J. CLEMESHA,
> EDWIN COX,
> *Honorary Secretaries.*

SIR: Having followed the fortunes of the federal government and people during the terrible war of the last four years with intense and undisguised sympathy, we cannot now refrain from expressing our profound and grateful joy in the magnificent triumph which has crowned the northern arms—a triumph which, in sealing forever the fate of the most infamous of rebellions, also pronounces the final doom of the foulest slavery the world has ever known; a triumph, not of arms merely, but of principles—the principles of "liberty, equality, and fraternity."   Alas, sir, that a nation's joy should be so suddenly eclipsed—that a short-sighted malignity, born only of slavery, should rob the world of a man so true and noble-hearted, so just yet gentle, so sagacious and humane, as ABRAHAM LINCOLN. While, sir, we are shocked at this accursed deed, and execrate the foul conspiracy of which it formed but a part, we cease to be astonished when we remember that the history of the slave power is a history of crime and corruption, of satanic cruelty and baseness. Having first sought to murder liberty, we do not wonder that its guilt should culminate in the assassination of the great liberator. But, sir, though he dies, liberty survives! It lives in the aspirations of a race uprising from beneath the burden of centuries of wrong and misery. It is seen emerging from the dismal night of a dead past, rejoicing in its native air and the early morn of its redemption. The redeeming sacrifice has indeed been precious, but around its altar stand a chastened but disenthralled, a purified and ennobled people, who bow the head and exclaim with their martyred chief: "The judgments of the Lord are true and righteous altogether;" "for the Lord knoweth the way of the righteous, but the way of the ungodly shall perish."

We rejoice, sir, that the control and governance of the great republic in this crisis of its history have been committed to one who, by a long and honorable career of public service, by fidelity to constitutional law and moral conviction, has merited the entire confidence of the American people. In the presence of the manifold and great difficulties involved in a state of social and national transition, our congratulations upon your ascension to the presidential chair may fittingly assume the form of sincere desire and earnest hope that, endowed with wisdom and knowledge, strengthened by conscious rectitude and the love of truth, you may tread the future as firmly and as nobly as the past, maintaining justice, yet delighting in mercy, healing the nation's wounds, and rebuilding her waste places, until "peace be in her walls, and joy in all her palaces, her cottages and halls."

Accept, sir, for yourself and the American people, this assurance of our sympathy in your joy and in your grief, and of our best wishes for your prosperity and welfare, and for the maintenance and increase of our mutual amity and friendship.

Signed on behalf of the Preston Union and Emancipation Society:

JNO. HASLAN, *President.*

His Excellency ANDREW JOHNSON,
    President of the United States.

We, the mayor, aldermen, and burgesses of the borough of Pembroke, in council assembled, are anxious to express to you, as the representative of the United States of America, the feelings of disgust and abhorrence with which we heard of the assassination of Mr. LINCOLN, the late President of the United

States, and more especially at a time when the councils of that great nation required the benefit of his valuable services and judgment.

We also request that you will convey to Mrs. Lincoln and the other members of the family of the late President the expression of our deep and heartfelt sympathy with them under their present bereavement and in the irreparable loss which they have so suddenly sustained ; and which feeling of deep sympathy is, we believe, universally entertained throughout the United Kingdom.

We further venture to express our earnest hope that the most friendly feelings may ever exist between the people of the United States and of this country.

Signed on behalf of the mayor and council, and under the corporate seal of the said borough, this 9th day of May, 1865.

[SEAL.]   JONAS DAWKINS, *Mayor.*

His Excellency the Hon. C. F. ADAMS,
> *Minister of the United States of America, resident in London.*

Resolutions of the independent ministers of the counties of Carmarthen, Cardigan, and Pembroke on the death of President Lincoln.

A resolution passed unanimously at the annual association of the independent ministers of the counties of Carmarthen, Cardigan, and Pembroke, held at Maenclochog, Pembrokeshire, June 6, 1865, Rev. Evan Lewis Brynberian presiding ; and also at the annual association of the independent ministers of the counties of Glamorgan, Monmouth, Dadnor, and Brecon, held at Neath, Glamorganshire, July 5, 1865, Rev. Dr. Rees, of Swansea, presiding.

(These two associations represent 289 ministers and 438 churches.)

That this conference desires to inform our fellow-Christians, and especially our fellow-countrymen in America, of our deep interest in the past history and our full confidence in the future progress of the United States. That we acknowledge in the late war the righteous judgment of God on the northern and southern States, and also on Great Britain, in the distress occasioned by the war, and see in it an instance of retributive providence, as a temporal judgment for the commencement, continuance, and defence of the polluted system of slavery, reducing the man created in God's image to the status of the animal.

That we have personally and socially prayed for the speedy termination of the war in the complete overthrow and everlasting destruction of the slave system, and for the progress of liberty and virtue in America.

That we congratulate the American people on the quashing of the rebellion ; and desire that they may have wisdom from above in the reconstruction of the Union on principles and by laws acknowledging that men of all colors and languages are equal.

That in common with the whole civilized world we have felt deeply indignant on reading the account of the treacherous murder of the benevolent President, ABRAHAM LINCOLN; and while deeply sympathizing with the sorrowing widow so mysteriously bereaved of her husband, and the nation so suddenly deprived of her leader, we earnestly pray that that "righteous man has not been taken away from the evil to come."

That we see in the whole history of the "irrepressible conflict" between slavery and freedom in the States a fresh proof that "righteousness exalteth a nation, but sin is a reproach to any people."

And, lastly, we trust that with the restoration of peace there will be a vigorous renewal of those philanthropic and religious efforts that have made America so conspicuous in the past for moral reformations and religious revivals; so that she may become in the future still more eminent for powerful and more enduring revivals, having been freed from the curse of slavery, that defiled with its touch everything with which it came in contact; and that she may be a free country, living in peace at home and in peace with all other nations, according to the wish so beautifully expressed by the ever to be remembered ABRAHAM LINCOLN on his reinauguration as President, on the 4th of March, 1865.

> EVAN LEWIS, *Chairman.*
> THOMAS REES, *Chairman.*
> SIMON EVANS, *Secretary.*
> ELLIS HUGHES, *Secretary.*

BOROUGH OF PLYMOUTH.

Record of the mayor, aldermen, and councillors of the borough of Plymouth.

We, the mayor, aldermen, and councillors of the borough of Plymouth, in council assembled, desire to record our feelings of indignation and sorrow at the atrocious crimes by which the United States of America have been deprived of their Chief Magistrate, and the life of a principal officer of state has been endangered, and to join our voices in the universal condemnation of the authors of these deplorable events.

We desire to tender to the government and people of the United States the assurance of our profound sympathy under this great calamity, and to offer to the widow of the lamented President our respectful condolence at her bereavement. We earnestly hope that in this universal sentiment, and the cordial recognition which has found so world-wide an utterance of the eminent qualities and kindly nature of the deceased, they may derive all the consolation which human sympathy can impart.

We confidently trust that the same spirit which was seen to animate Mr.

LINCOLN when arrested in his career will continue to guide the successors to his government; that by a generous and conciliatory policy, peace and harmony, involving the recognition of justice to all members of the community, may be restored to a distracted nation, and that the intimate relations which connect this country with the United States of America may be maintained with increasing friendship and cordiality.

[SEAL.]   CHARLES NORRINGTON, *Mayor.*

Resolutions passed at a public meeting held at Plymouth, May 3, 1865.

At a public meeting held at the Plymouth Mechanics' Institute, in aid of the freedmen in the United States, Mr. Charles Norrington, mayor of Plymouth, presiding, the following resolutions were unanimously adopted:

Moved by the Rev. H. A. Greaves, and seconded by Mr. Rowe—

That while this meeting deeply deplores the severe and long-continued war in the United States, it records its gratitude to Almighty God that the consequent manumission of more than two millions slaves has prepared the way for absolute and universal emancipation.

Moved by Mr. Alfred Rooker, and seconded by the Rev. J. E. Risk—

That this meeting, avowing its deep indignation at the recent assassination of the President of the United States, desires to express its deep sorrow at the mysterious event which has suddenly deprived the slaves of a prudent benefactor, and the state of a ruler who had inaugurated a policy of conciliation.

Moved by the Rev. T. C. Page, and seconded by Mr. S. Elliot—

That this meeting, considering the sufferings of the freedmen in their transition from slavery to freedom, pledge itself to render them such assistance as may tend to mitigate present want and prepare for future prosperity, and that gentlemen and ladies' committees be constituted to give effect to this resolution.

On motion of Mr. T. C. Brian, seconded by Mr. T. Nicholson, a vote of thanks was accorded to the mayor for his kindness in taking the chair. Mr. Norrington having briefly acknowledged the compliment, the meeting closed.

From the inhabitants of Plaistow, Essex, England, in public meeting assembled, to the people of the United States of America:

Permit us, as a small portion of the English nation, to add our sentiments of sympathy and sorrow to those felt by you on the recent lamentable events which have plunged your whole community into intense grief.

The base assassination of President LINCOLN, with the attempted murder of a chief member of your government, is one of those events which merge in common unity those minor political differences which are essential to the freedom of great nations, but without necessarily inferring antagonism. Permit us, therefore, as one with you, to offer our profound sympathy and sorrow, to unite in detestation of a crime disgraceful to humanity, and to assure you that the blow struck at yourselves recoils on us.

But, further, we heartily sympathize with that national action which, as expounded by your lamented President, had for its result the emancipation of slaves, and in the destruction of rebellion the destruction also of that system which we believe to have been its moving cause, even if not the prompting cause, also, of President LINCOLN's assassination and the murderous attack on Mr. Seward. That as a united and universally free nation your present position may be unendangered by recent events and your future course attended by increasing stability and glory is our earnest desire, thus expressed through the medium of your official representative at St. James.

Signed on behalf of the meeting :

REV. JOHN FOSTER, *Chairman.*

From the inhabitants of Plaistow, Essex, England, in public meeting assembled.

To Mrs. LINCOLN :

DEAR MADAM : Many words in your present grief would be an intrusion. We have expressed in another form our sympathy with the loss sustained by the United States as a nation. Here, and to you, we would only say that, as men and women of kindred race to your own, and, therefore, of the same Christian family, we fully share in the grief felt by those more immediately near to you. Distance does not create division in a common sorrow ; may that sorrow felt most keenly by yourself be assuaged by the Great Healer, and to his tender mercy we affectionately commit you and yours.

Signed on behalf of the meeting :

REV. JOHN FOSTER, *Chairman.*

Resolutions passed at a meeting of the citizens of Port Rowan, province of Canada.

PORT ROWAN, *April* 24, 1865.

SIR : In conformity with a numerously signed requisition addressed to John B. Hutchinson, esquire, reeve of the township of Walsingham, county of Norfolk, and province of Canada, a large and influential meeting was held in the Town Hall, in the village of Port Rowan, on the evening of Thursday, the 20th instant, for the purpose of affording the inhabitants of said township of Walsingham an opportunity of expressing their sympathy with the American people, and of offering their condolence to the late President's afflicted widow in the loss of so good a husband and father, and of expressing their abhorrence of the treacherous and bloody deed. At which meeting Hugh Mabee, esquire, was appointed chairman, and T. A. Hall, esquire, was chosen secretary, when the following resolutions were unanimously adopted:

Moved by Henry J. Killmaster, esquire, and seconded by P. Bennett, esquire.—

Resolved, That in view of the lamentable occurrence which has taken place in the neighboring nation of the United States, by which their Chief Magistrate has been deprived of life at the hands of a blood-thirsty assassin, we, the inhabitants of the said township of Walsingham, deem it incumbent upon us to offer to our mourning neighbors this expression of our sympathy for the great loss they have sustained in thus being deprived of a patriot and statesman.

Moved by John A. Backus, esquire, and seconded by Benjamin Killmaster, esquire—

Resolved, That this meeting desire respectfully to offer their condolence to Mrs. Lincoln and her family, and hope, with the blessing of God, they will be sustained under this trying bereavement.

We have the honor to be, sir, your obedient servants,

H. A. MABEE, *Chairman.*
T. A. HALL, *Secretary.*

Resolution passed at a meeting held by the city council of Quebec.

CITY HALL, *Quebec, April* 22, 1865.

At a special meeting of the city council, held on the 21st April instant, it was

Resolved, That this council has learned with the most profound regret the death of the honorable ABRAHAM LINCOLN, President of the United States of America, caused by one of the most dastardly outrages recorded in history, and that as a token of respect for his memory and of sympathy for the great nation with whom we are on friendly terms, and which is now plunged into the deepest grief for the loss of its Chief Magistrate by the perpetration of the most atrocious murder, this council do immediately adjourn, and that a copy of this resolution be transmitted to the American consul.

Certified:

[SEAL.]

L. A. CANNON, *City Clerk.*

Resolution of the town council of Rochester.

CITY OF ROCHESTER.

At a quarterly meeting of the town council of the said city, holden at the Guildhall, of and within the said city, on Friday, the twelfth day of May, 1865—

Resolved, That we, the mayor, aldermen, and citizens of the city of Rochester, in council assembled, take this opportunity of giving expression to our extreme feelings of horror and regret at the atrocious crime which has been recently perpetrated in America, whereby the United States of America have been deprived of their President, ABRAHAM LINCOLN, who was thus suddenly cut off while honestly devoting his best energies to the service of his country, and whereby the lives of Mr. Seward and some of his family have been endangered, and we desire most respectfully to convey to the authorities of America our deep and earnest sympathies with them in the great loss they have sustained, and to express the satisfaction which we feel in the intelligence that, under the mercy of God, the ultimate recovery of Mr. Seward may reasonably be anticipated.

At Rothesay, the 8th day of May, 1865, the magistrates and council of the royal burgh of Rothesay, in council assembled, unanimously resolved—

That this council desires to express the feelings of abhorrence and profound grief with which they have received the painful intelligence of the assassination of the President of the United States of America.

That this council heartily sympathizes with the people of the United States, who, by a detestable and shocking crime, have been suddenly deprived of their chief ruler at a momentous crisis in the history of their great country.

That this council record their high respect for the admirable character of the lamented late President LINCOLN and their grateful remembrance of his endeavors, in times of peculiar trial and difficulty, to preserve and cultivate friendly relations with Great Britain.

That this council also deeply sympathize with the late President's widow and family under their sore bereavement, earnestly praying that they may be sustained and comforted by the Almighty and Merciful Disposer of all events.

Signed in name and by appointment of the magistrate and council of Rothesay by the provost and chief magistrates of the said royal burgh.

[SEAL.]   CHARLES DUNCAN.

At a meeting of the council of the town and borough of Rochdale, in the county of Lancaster, in England, held in the council rooms, Rochdale, on the 3d day of May, 1865, John Tatham, esq., mayor, in the chair, it was

Resolved unanimously, That this council has heard with profound regret and horror of the dastardly assassination of President LINCOLN, and hereby expresses its deepest abhorrence of such a deed, and its sincere sympathy with the citizens of the United States, and the widow and family of the late President, in the great and irreparable loss which they have sustained.

[SEAL.]   JOHN TATHAM, *Mayor.*

At a public meeting of the inhabitant householders of the borough of Rochdale, in the county of Lancaster, in England, convened by the mayor of the said borough, on a requisition to him for that purpose signed by such inhabitants, held in the Public Hall in the said borough, on Thursday, the 4th day of May, 1865, the mayor in the chair, it was

Resolved, That this meeting desires to give utterance to the feelings of grief and abhorrence with which it has heard of the assassination of President LINCOLN and the murderous attack upon Mr. Secretary Seward, and to convey to Mrs. Lincoln, Mr. Seward, and to the United States government and people an expression of its profound sympathy and condolence.

JOHN TATHAM, *Mayor.*

At a public meeting held at the Town Hall of Ramsgate, Kent, on Saturday, May 6, 1865, the deputy, Thomas Whitehead, esq., J. P., in the chair, the following resolutions were unanimously passed:

Resolved, That we, the assembled inhabitants of Ramsgate, desire to give utterance to the deep indignation and profound sorrow with which we have heard of the assassination of President LINCOLN, and the murderous attack upon Mr. Seward, and to convey to Mrs. Lincoln and to the United States government and people an expression of the warmest sympathy and heartfelt condolence.

Resolved, That we desire to add to this expression of deep condolence our earnest hope that the wise and merciful counsels of which President LINCOLN was the exponent may speedily crown the dark years now closed by this deplorable event with a lasting peace and firm prosperity.

THOMAS WHITEHEAD.

At a public meeting of the inhabitants of Reading, in the county of Berks, holden at the Town Hall there on Monday, the 1st day of May, 1865, Charles James Butler, esq., mayor, in the chair, the following resolutions were carried unanimously:

Resolved, That this meeting, having heard with great sorrow and indignation of the assassination of Mr. President LINCOLN, by which the United States have been so suddenly deprived of his services, desires to express its utter abhorrence and detestation of the crime, and its sincere sympathy with the people of the United States on so trying an occasion, and trusts that the sad event may be so overruled as not to be prejudicial to the continued prosperity of the best interests of the nation.

Resolved, That a copy of the foregoing resolution be signed by the mayor on behalf of this meeting, and placed in the hands of the Hon. C. F. Adams for transmission to his Excellency the President of the United States.

Signed on behalf of the meeting:

CHARLES JAMES BUTLER, *Mayor.*

THE ASSASSINATION OF PRESIDENT LINCOLN.

Resolutions of the Rhyl improvement commissioners.

At the monthly meeting of the Rhyl improvement commissioners, held this day, the following resolution was unanimously agreed to:

Resolved, That this meeting desires, before proceeding to the business of the day, to express its detestation of the assassination of President LINCOLN and of the wicked attempt made on the life of the Hon. W. H. Seward, and to convey to Mrs. Lincoln and the people of the United States its deep sympathy with them in their loss, and the expression of our hope that our friendly relations with the United States may be continued.

Resolved, That copies of the above resolution be forwarded to the United States minister in London for transmission.

The common seal of the commissioners affixed by order, this 12th day of May, 1865.

[SEAL.]   JOHN PRYDDERCH WILLIAMS,

Clerk to the Commissioners.

TOWN HALL, RHYL, *North Wales.*

Excerpt from the minutes of a meeting of commissioners of supply of the county of Roxburg, held at Jedburg, the 1st day of May, 1865.

The commissioners of supply of the county of Roxburg, at their meeting held this day, unanimously resolved to record their heartfelt indignation at the atrocious murder of Mr. ABRAHAM LINCOLN, the President of the United States, and the attempt to assassinate Mr. Seward, the Secretary of State. They feel assured that throughout the whole of the States, as in every civilized country, the sad event will be equally deplored, and they desire by this resolution to intimate their deep sympathy and condolence to the people of the States, and to Mrs. Lincoln, under the heavy bereavement which this disgraceful crime has occasioned.

That this resolution be signed by the chairman, on their behalf, and thereafter transmitted to the American minister in London, with a request that the same may be communicated to the people in the States, and to Mrs. Lincoln, in such a way as he may think proper.

WILL. OLIVER RUTHERFORD,
Chairman.

TOWN HALL, RYDE.

SIR: We, the Ryde commissioners, incorporated by act of Parliament, beg beg to express our great sorrow and indignation at the lamentable assassination of your late respected President, whereby the American nation has lost the services of an enlightened ruler and noble-minded patriot.

We respectfully tender through you to his bereaved widow, and to the government and people of the United States, our heartfelt sympathy on this melancholy occasion; and we sincerely hope that the era of peace, mercy, and liberty, which your late illustrious chief so happily inaugurated, may be carried by his successor to a just and satisfactory termination.

Given under our common seal, this 9th day of May, 1865.

[SEAL.]   THOMAS DASHWOOD,
Chairman of the Ryde Commissioners.

His Excellency Hon C. F. ADAMS,
Minister of the United States to the Court of St. James.

At a public meeting held in the Congregational church, George street, Ryde, on Monday, May 1, 1865, the pastor, Rev. George Allan Coltart, in the chair, the following resolutions were carried unanimously:

That this meeting desires to record its horror and indignation at the atrocious assassination of President LINCOLN; to express its sympathy with the

American people in this terrible calamity with which they have been visited, and the desire that it may be overruled for the welfare of the whole nation; and its earnest hope that He who has declared Himself to be the husband of the widow may grant His comforting mercies to Mrs. Lincoln.

That this meeting has heard with the deepest solicitude that millions of those who, by the event of the war, have been freed from slavery, are in circumstances of great physical and spiritual destitution; rejoices in the formation of organizations called the Freedmen's Aid Society, intended to supply their wants and raise them in the social scale; and desires to make such contributions as may be within the power of its members to assist this good work.

GEORGE ALLAN COLTART,

Chairman.

BOROUGH OF SUDBURY, COUNTIES OF SUFFOLK AND ESSEX.

Resolutions of the mayor, aldermen, and burgesses of the borough of Sudbury.

At a meeting, or court, being a quarterly meeting of the mayor, aldermen, and burgesses of the said borough, held at the Town Hall there on Friday, the 5th day of May, 1865—moved by Samuel Higgs, esq., mayor, seconded by Mr. Alderman Andrews, and

Unanimously resolved, That the following resolution, on the subject of the lamented late assassination of the President of the United States of North America, be now adopted by this meeting; and that a copy thereof, under the seal of this corporation, be sent to the Hon. Charles F. Adams, the American minister, to be forwarded by him to his Excellency the President of the United States:

Resolved, That the members of this council desire to express the horror and indignation they have felt at the atrocious crime by which the late excellent and much-esteemed President of the United States of North America, Mr. ABRAHAM LINCOLN, has been deprived of life, and the hope they also entertain that the great work of pacification, on which his heart was evidently set, may not be retarded by his lamented and untimely death.

Given under the seal of the mayor, aldermen, and burgesses:

[SEAL.]   SAMUEL HIGGS, *Mayor.*

We, the mayor, aldermen, and burgesses of the borough of Stratford-upon-Avon, in council assembled, having heard with feelings of indignation and profound sorrow of the cruel assassination of the President of the United States of America, express our heartfelt sympathy with the American government and people on this overpowering calamity.   We feel deeply grieved at the distressing affliction and bereavement which has thereby fallen upon Mrs. Lincoln, and earnestly pray that she may be sustained in her sad trial, and that comfort and support may be afforded her and her family in this their hour of need.

The murderous attack upon Mr. Seward, the Secretary of State, and the frightful crimes of which his house was the scene, have also impressed us with the same feelings.   May God in his mercy overrule all for the good and welfare of the American people, and may their future be one of peace and prosperity.

We respectfully request his excellency Mr. Adams, the American minister, to convey this expression of our sentiments to those whom it may concern.

Given under our common seal, the 3d day of May, in the year of our Lord, 1865.

[SEAL.]

Resolution passed at a meeting of the council of the borough of Scarborough, in the county of York, held in the Town Hall, on Monday, May 8, 1865.

Resolved unanimously, That this council desires to express its feelings of horror and indignation at the assassination of the President of the United States, and the barbarous attempt on the lives of Secretary Seward and his son; and also its deep sympathy with the people of the United States, as well as with the widow and family of the President, at the great loss they have sustained.

Signed on behalf of the council:

AMBROSE GIBSON, *Mayor.*

BOROUGH OF SHREWSBURY.

Resolutions passed at a meeting of the mayor, aldermen, and burgesses, in council assembled, on the 8th day of May, 1865.

That this council desires to record their unanimous concurrence in the feelings of horror, detestation, and regret entertained throughout the length and breadth of this kingdom, at the late atrocious murder of the Chief Magistrate of the United States of America, and in those sentiments of sorrow and sympathy which have already been expressed on this most melancholy event by our most gracious Sovereign, and by all classes of her subjects, towards the family, the friends, and the fellow-countrymen of Mr. President LINCOLN.

That this resolution be duly sealed and signed by the mayor, and transmitted to the minister of the United States in this country.

[SEAL]   J. GREGORY BRUYNE, *Mayor.*

Excerpt from minutes of meeting of the town council of the royal burgh of San-quhar, Dumfriesshire, Scotland, dated May 10, 1865.

" The council record that, in common with the whole community, they have heard of the death, by assassination, of the President of the United States, with feelings of abhorrence of the crime, and profound sympathy for the people of the United States in the calamity which they have sustained; and they express their deepest sympathy with Mrs. Lincoln and the family of the deceased President, in the bereavement which they now mourn."

Certified to be a true excerpt, by—

W. O. MACQUEEN, *Town Clerk.*

Extract from the minutes of a meeting of the council of the borough of St. Alban's, in the county of Hertford, held the 12th day of May, 1865.

Resolved unanimously, That this council desires to express, in the name of the inhabitants of this borough, their feelings of sorrow and indignation at the assassination of the President of the United States of America, and to convey to the government and people of that country the assurances of their deep and earnest sympathy under this most grievous calamity.

[SEAL.]   B. CAGG, *Town Clerk.*

ASSASSINATION OF PRESIDENT LINCOLN.

BOROUGH OF SOUTHAMPTON, *Wednesday, May 3, 1865.*

A meeting of the council of the borough of Southampton was this day held at the Audit House, in the said borough, the worshipful the mayor, Thomas Bowman, esq., in the chair.

At this council it was moved by Mr. Alderman Palk, J. P., seconded by Mr. Councillor Stebbing, J. P., and

Unanimously resolved, That this council have heard, with just indignation and abhorrence, of the atrocious crime committed against the government and people of the United States of America, by the assassination of President LINCOLN, and hereby express their deep sympathy and condolence with that people at this lamentable termination of a life which, during his presidency, had been devoted, with great self-sacrifice, to the good of those over whom he was called upon to preside as Chief Magistrate.

The council desire likewise to express their admiration of President LINCOLN's declared feelings of kindness and mercy upon the occasion of the remarkable successes so conspicuous during the latter period of his government, exhibiting up to the last sad closing hour of his existence a brilliant example of those humane principles which always actuate men of distinguished attainments.

This council likewise most respectfully tender to Mrs. Lincoln and family their heartfelt sympathy and condolence at the sad and afflictive bereavement which they have been called upon to sustain by this detestable and tragic event.

That the foregoing resolution be forwarded to his excellency the American minister in London, with a request that he would be pleased to transmit the same to the government of his country, and that a copy be forwarded to the American consul at this port.

CHARLES E. DEACON, *Town Clerk.*

BOROUGH OF SALFORD, COUNTY OF LANCASTER.

At a meeting of the council of the said borough, held on the 3d day of May, 1865, Wright Turner, esq., mayor, in the chair, it was, upon the motion of the mayor, seconded by Mr. Alderman Davis,

Resolved, That this council desires to give utterance to the feelings of grief and horror with which it has heard of the assassination of President LINCOLN and the murderous attack upon Mr. Seward, and to convey to Mrs. Lincoln, and the United States government and people, an expression of its profound sympathy and heartfelt condolence.

WRIGHT TURNER, *Mayor.*

GEORGE BRENT, *Town Clerk.*

AT STIRLING, *the 4th day of May,* 1865.

Which day the magistrates and town council of the burgh of Stirling being convened, *inter alia,* the provost moved that the magistrates and town council resolve to record the profound sorrow and indignation with which they and the whole community of Stirling have heard of the atrocious assassination of President LINCOLN, of the United States of America, their respect for his private and public character, their admiration of his moderation and conciliation in the hour of success and triumph, and their deepest sympathy with the people of the United States under the terrible calamity which has befallen them. Which motion was *unanimously agreed to,* and the clerk was instructed to send a copy of this resolution to the American ambassador in London.

Extracted from the records of said burgh, by—

THOMAS L. GALBRAITH, *Town Clerk.*

STIRLING, *May* 1, 1865.

SIR: We, the commissioners of supply and landed proprietors of the county of Stirling, in annual meeting assembled, wish to express to you, and through you to the people and government of America, our horror and detestation of the great crime committed in the base and cruel murder of the President of the United States.

We feel the deepest sympathy for the loss which a people so nearly connected with our own nation has sustained in the unnatural death of a ruler so good and so honest, at a time when his value had come to be so thoroughly known and so highly appreciated, not only at home, but throughout the rest of the civilized world.

We pray that God may so direct events that this dreadful crime may not prevent peace, freedom, and good government from being soon established in your mighty country.

Signed in name and by appointment of the meeting, by Alexander Graham Speirs, of Culcrench, convener of the county.

A. G. SPEIRS.

His Excellency Hon. CHARLES FRANCIS ADAMS,
Envoy Extraordinary and Minister Plenipotentiary
of the United States of America, at London.

At a public meeting of the inhabitants of the borough of Stalybridge, in the counties of Lancaster and Chester, duly convened by his worshipful the mayor, and held in the Town Hall, in the borough of Stalybridge, on Friday, the 5th day of May, 1865, James Sidebottom, esq., mayor, in the chair, it was

Unanimously resolved, That this meeting would convey the expression of its heartfelt feelings of sympathy with Mrs. Lincoln, together with the government and people of America, under their great affliction, and would hail with delight the carrying out of the conciliatory policy indicated by the late President, and the restoration of peace upon a just and enlightened basis.

JAMES SIDEBOTTOM, *Mayor.*

SUNDERLAND, *May* 2, 1865.

At a meeting of the inhabitants of the borough of Sunderland, in the county of Durham, the right worshipful the mayor in the chair, it was

Unanimously resolved, That this meeting express its profound horror and detestation of the assassination of President LINCOLN, and the murderous attack upon Mr. Seward. That it believes the death of the President at this great crisis of American history is an unspeakable loss to the people of America, and at the same time to the people of England and to humanity at large.   That this meeting desires to convey to Mrs. Lincoln, and to the United States government and people, its deepest sympathy and heartfelt condolence.

EDWARD T. GOURLEY,

Mayor of Sunderland and Chairman of the Meeting.

STAPLEHURST, *May* 2, 1865.

HONORED SIR: Amid the numerous expressions of sorrow, indignation, and sympathy which you are now receiving from the metropolis and chief towns of Great Britain, in reference to the assassination of President LINCOLN, be pleased also to receive one from the village of Staplehurst, in Kent.

At a public meeting held last evening it was—

Resolved, That this meeting regards with intense horror and indignation the assassination of President LINCOLN, and desires to express its sympathy with Mrs. Lincoln, the government, and the people of America in their severe trial.

Resolved, That this meeting expresses its sympathy with Mr. Andrew Johnson in the responsible office to which he is thus suddenly called, and sincerely hopes he may be able so to conduct the affairs of the country as to complete the emancipation of the slave, and secure the establishment of permanent peace.

I am, sir, with much respect, yours most obediently,

JOHN JULB, *Chairman.*

His Excellency Mr. ADAMS,

United States Ambassador.

STEWARTON, AYRSHIRE, N. B., *May* 6, 1865.

1. *Resolved*, That the inhabitants of Stewarton, in public meeting assembled, have heard with grief of the assassination of President LINCOLN, and do hereby express their unmitigated horror of the crime which has so suddenly deprived the United States of America of an upright and honored ruler.

2. We embrace this opportunity of assuring the citizens of the United States of our deep and earnest sympathy with them under this grievous dispensation.

3. We also sympathize most deeply with Mrs. Lincoln and the family of the late President, and earnestly pray that they may be sustained under the terrible affliction which has befallen them, and that their personal loss may, in the providence of God, become a national gain.

A. POLLOCK, *Chairman.*

Resolutions passed unanimously at a meeting of the inhabitants of St. Helen's, Lancashire, convened in compliance with a numerously signed requisition, and held at the Volunteer Hall, St. Helen's, on the 3d of May, 1865.

1. *Resolved*, That the inhabitants of St. Helen's, in public meeting assembled, do hereby express their strongest feelings of abhorrence and indignation at the atrocious assassination of the President of the United States, and also at the dastardly attempt upon the life of Mr. Seward, the Secretary of State.

2. That this meeting hereby records its deepest sympathy with Mrs. Lincoln and her family under their present heart-rending bereavement, and trusts that the universal condolence of all the rightminded and virtuous throughout the world may be some solace to them in their grievous affliction.

3. That this meeting desires to convey to the people of the United States an expression of heartfelt sympathy in the loss they have sustained by the cruel death of their most excellent President.

ROBERT McNICOLL, Chairman.

Resolutions passed at a public meeting of the inhabitants of the town and borough of Stroud, held at the Subscription Rooms, Stroud, on Friday evening, the 5th of May, 1865.

First resolution : That this meeting desires to record the sentiments of grief and horror with which it regards the assassination of President LINCOLN and the attack upon Mr. Seward; to offer its sincere condolence with Mrs. Lincoln and her family, and to express its deep sympathy with the American people in their great calamity.

Second resolution : That this meeting hopes the government of the United States will ever be animated by the spirit of moderation and conciliation which characterized the late President, and that the deplorable struggle in which the people have been so long engaged may be brought to an early conclusion, and result in the freedom and happiness of all the American people.

Third resolution : That the chairman be requested to forward the foregoing resolutions to the Hon. Mr. Adams, the American minister in England, as the expression of the feelings of the inhabitants of this town and borough in public meeting assembled.

S. S. DICKINSON, Chairman.

Resolutions passed at a meeting held by the inhabitants of the borough of South Shields.

At a public meeting of the. inhabitants of the borough of South Shields, in the county of Durham, duly convened by his worship the mayor at the request of the town council, and held on the 10th of May, 1865, William James, esq., mayor, in the chair, the following resolutions were unanimously passed, viz:

On the motion of James C. Stevenson, esq., seconded by the Rev. Robert E. Hoopell—

1. That the dastardly and wicked crimes so recently perpetrated in the United States of America by the assassination of the President and the cowardly attack upon Mr. Seward, the Secretary, have been received with horror and indignation by the people of this country from one end of the kingdom to the other, a feeling in which the inhabitants of this the borough of South Shields most sympathetically concur, in common with the Crown, the Parliament, and the people at large.

On the motion of James Mather, esq., seconded by Mr. Alderman Glover—

2. That great as the loss of their President would have been to the United States at any period of the civil strife in which that country has been so unhappily engaged, it is specially now to be deplored, in the present eventful crisis of the contest, when, by his experience, moderation, character, and prudence, the pain and animosity engendered by the war might have been alleviated, and its attendant exasperation tempered and removed, to the probable advantage and satisfaction not only of the northern but the southern States.

On motion of the Rev. Samuel B. Brasher, seconded by Mr. Alderman Moffett—

3. That therefore these the sentiments and resolutions of the meeting, and the sympathy of the inhabitants of South Shields with the government and people of the United States on their sad deprivation, be conveyed by the mayor to Mr. Adams, the American minister in London, for transmission through him to the proper authority in America; accompanied at the same time with an offer of our heartfelt condolence to the unhappily bereaved widow of the murdered President on the irreparable loss which she has sustained, under circumstances of such sudden and peculiar atrocity.

WM. JAMES, *Mayor.*

Resolutions passed at a meeting held by the inhabitants of Southport.

At a public meeting of the inhabitants of Southport, held in the Town Hall, on Saturday, the 6th day of May, 1865, Samuel Boothroyd, esq., chairman of the Southport improvement commissioners, in the chair, the requisition and notice calling the meeting having been read by the clerk to the commissioners, it was moved by the Rev. B. S. Clarke, seconded by W. G. Talbot, esq., supported by the Rev. J. C. Millson and W. Halliwell, esq., and carried unanimously—

That the inhabitants of Southport, in public meeting assembled, would record their deep abhorrence and indignation at the cruel and cowardly assassination of President LINCOLN and the murderous attack upon Mr. Secretary Seward and his son.

That this meeting hereby expresses its sincere sympathy with the people of the United States in the great loss they have so unexpectedly sustained in the death of their Chief Magistrate, and its earnest hope that the fearful war which has been carried on for four years in that country may speedily be brought to an end.

That this meeting respectfully tenders to Mrs. Lincoln its heartfelt condolence in the deep sorrow into which she and her family are plunged by this awful occurrence.

Moved by the Rev. John Chater, seconded by R. Craven, esq., and carried unanimously—

That the preceding resolution be engrossed, signed by the chairman of the meeting, and forwarded to the Hon. Mr. Adams for presentation to the American government, and to Mrs. Lincoln, the bereaved widow of the late President.

SAMUEL BOOTHROYD.

The undersigned, inhabitants of the town of Selby, desire to give expression to the feelings of horror, regret, and indignation with which they have heard of the assassination of President LINCOLN, and of the attempt on the life of Mr. Secretary Seward.

The undersigned wish to convey the assurance of their deep sympathy with the people and government of the United States under the death of one whose character had won the respect and admiration of both friends and enemies, and of their heartfelt condolence with Mrs. Lincoln on the irreparable loss which she has sustained.

They also desire to express their satisfaction at the prospect of a speedy return of peace, to be accompanied by the extinction of negro slavery in America.

JAMES ANDUS, *Justice of Peace.*
HENRY GREENE, *Curate in Charge.*
CHARLES WILDHON, *Curate.*
JOHN RHODES, *Wesleyan Minister.*
GEORGE ABBOTT, *Wesleyan Minister.*
JOHN D. JULIAN, *Wesleyan Minister.*
PARKINSON MILLSON, *Primitive Methodist Minister.*
DAVID CLEGG, *Independent Minister.*
ROBERT MORRELL, *Bank Manager.*
WM. SWENSEDGE, JR., *Merchant.*

AND TWO HUNDRED AND SIXTY OTHER NAMES.

At a public meeting held in St. Catharine's, presided over by William Eccles, esq., mayor, the following resolutions were unanimously passed :

Moved by Dr. T. Mack, seconded by Rev. Dr. Cooney—

That we feel it to be our duty to express our heartfelt sympathy with our neighbors of the American Union in the great loss they have sustained by the untimely death of their beloved President, the late ABRAHAM LINCOLN.

Moved by Rev. Mr. Burns, seconded by Rev. Mr. Morton—

That we recognize with religious awe and humble submission the will of the Almighty in permitting such a man, at such a time, to fall by the hand of an assassin.

Moved by Delas Beadle, esq., seconded by Rev. Mr. Cary—

That his virtues as a private citizen, his ability, benevolence, and sterling integrity as the head of a great people, make his loss a calamity not to the United States alone, but to the whole brotherhood of civilized nations.

Moved by Hon. J. G. Currie, seconded by Rev. Mr. Howard—

That united as we are with the American people by the ties of kindred and by social and commercial intercourse, it is our earnest desire and our fervent prayer that "He by whom kings reign and rulers decree justice" may direct the counsels of the government of the United States and of our own empire so that the pacific policy propounded by the late President may be pursued, and that peace and amity between these two great Christian nations may be perpetuated.

Moved by Rev. Mr. Holland, seconded by James R. Benson, esq.—

That we deeply sympathize with the family and relatives of the deceased President in their sad and unexpected bereavement; and that the following gentlemen be a committee to forward an address of condolence to Mrs. Lincoln, accompanied by a copy of the resolutions adopted at this meeting, viz : Hon. J. G. Currie, James R. Benson, and the mayor.

Address of the inhabitants of St. Catharine's.

ST. CATHARINE'S, CANADA, *April* 22, 1865.

MADAM : On behalf of a large and influential public meeting of the inhabitants of this town, we beg to enclose you the accompanying resolutions, and desire to address you in this hour of trial and sorrow, and to tender you the heartfelt sympathy of our people for the great and irreparable loss you have recently sustained by the sad and sudden death of your late husband, the President of the United States.

In common with the people of this province, we have ever admired the ability, benevolence, sterling integrity, and private worth of your deceased husband, and we feel that while it has pleased Almighty God in His wisdom, by the hand of death, to deprive you of a kind husband, and your family of an affectionate parent, the United States have lost a prudent counsellor; and we have also to mourn the loss of one whose earnest desire it always was to promote the cause of humanity, and so strengthen the ties of friendship between the United States and the British empire.

We earnestly pray that the God of all grace, the Father of the fatherless, and the Comforter of all that are cast down, may restore you at an early day to bodily health, and vouchsafe to you and family that consolation which he has promised in seasons of trial, and that strength which will enable you to bear this heavy affliction which it has pleased Him to send.

We have the honor to be yours, respectfully,

WM. ECCLES, *Mayor.*

J. G. CURRIE, *M. S. C.*

J. R. BENSON.

Mrs. ABRAHAM LINCOLN, *Washington.*

Resolutions passed at a public meeting of the citizens of the town of Sherbrooke, province of Canada, on Wednesday, the 19th day of April, 1865.

SHERBROOKE, CANADA EAST, *April* 19, 1865.

Resolved, That this meeting is shocked at the fearful tragedy which took place at Washington, the capital of the United States, on Friday night last, in the fiendish and dastardly murder of the honorable ABRAHAM LINCOLN, President of the United States, and filled with the most painful emotions that a man holding so high a position, upon whose life so many hopes were resting, and whose character was such as to give promise of so much good, should fall by the hands of a brutal assassin, in the presence of a peaceful audience.

Reesolved, That we sincerely sympathize with the widow and family of the late President in the sudden and unexpected death of one so near and dear to them; who amidst the unceasing cares and responsibilities devolving on him as the ruler of a great nation, at the same time retained those social and domestic qualities which so endeared him to his family, and to all those privileged with meeting him in the social circle.

Resolved, That we deeply feel for and deplore the loss our friends and neighbors in the adjoining republic have sustained in the removal of their Chief Magistrate—a man eminently qualified for his high position, and combining in his person those characteristics which, at the present critical juncture of their national affairs, rendered him, under Almighty God, the instrument of great good to their country.

Resolved, That we trust the mysterious dispensation of Almighty God, in permitting at this juncture of affairs in the United States the removal of ABRAHAM LINCOLN by the hand of death, will be so ordered and overruled as not to prove detrimental to the best interests of the republic, and that although the leading instrument in the conduct of affairs during their present unhappy struggle to an issue giving promise of peace has been removed from his high position, the progress of true freedom will be onward, and the principles of liberty perpetuated throughout the length and breadth of the land.

Resolved, That as Canadian citizens connected with the British empire, we but express, we believe, the opinions of all our fellow-subjects in deploring the removal of ABRAHAM LINCOLN at this present important epoch in the world's history, believing him to be desirous of maintaining friendly relations with other nations; and that, in connection with the honorable Mr. Seward, he was prepared to promote and advance the best interests of the world, by endeavoring to perpetuate the good feeling and friendly intercourse which have so long existed between the United States and European powers.

Resolved, That we feel grateful for the kind interposition of Almighty God in preventing the cowardly assassination of the honorable Mr. Seward and his son, on the evening of Friday last, and trust that their lives will be spared to prove a blessing to their country in carrying forward to completion those plans inaugurated by their late President for the restoration of peace, and the re-establishment of liberty on a firm basis.

Resolved, That the mayor of this town, as chairman of this meeting, be requested to forward a copy of these resolutions to Washington on behalf of the citizens of Sherbrooke.

J. G. ROBERTSON, Mayor.

St. Thomas, Canada West, April 19, 1865.

At a public meeting of the inhabitants of St. Thomas, Canada West, on Wednesday, the 19th of April, 1865, the mayor, Thomas Arkell, esq., presided, and the following resolutions were passed unanimously.

The meeting was opened by religious services, in which the ministers of different denominations took part.

Moved by Doctor Southwick, ex-M. P. P., seconded by the Reverend Doctor Caulfield—

1. That we, the mayor and inhabitants of St. Thomas, in public meeting assembled, hereby declare our unutterable horror at the crime by which the valuable life and labors of the excellent late President of the United States were so dreadfully closed.

Moved by Daniel Hauvey, esq., seconded by his honor Judge Hughes—

2. That we regard the assassination of President LINCOLN and the diabolical assault on Secretary Seward as indelible stains upon the civilization of the age, and a special disgrace to our race and language.

Moved by Sheriff Munro, seconded by the Reverend Mr. Cuthbertson—

3. That we desire to express our sincere sympathy with the people of the United States in the great and awful loss which they have sustained by the murder of their President—an act which has this day draped that nation in mourning, and will cause a shudder of horror to run through every civilized nation in the world.

Moved by the Reverend Mr. Ames, seconded by W. E. Murray, esq., of Aylmer—

4. That we express our deepest sympathy with the widow and family of President LINCOLN, in their bereavement.

Moved by Colin McDougal, esq., seconded by Mr. Hodge—

5. That the proceedings of this meeting be engrossed and forwarded to the British ambassador at Washington, and published in the local newspapers, the London Free Press, and the Globe and Leader, of Toronto.

Moved by C. D. Paul, esq., seconded by Nelson Moore, esq.—

6. That the mayor leave the chair and Doctor Southwick take the same.

The thanks of the meeting were then given to the mayor, and the meeting was closed by the Reverend Doctor Caulfield pronouncing the benediction.

[SEAL.]   THOMAS ARKELL,
                                                      Mayor, Chairman.

THOMAS HODGE, *Secretary.*

At a meeting of the town council of the borough of Sheffield, held on the 3d day of May, 1865, it was

Unanimously resolved, That this council unites in the universal expression of indignation and profound sorrow at the assassination of Mr. LINCOLN, the late President of the United States of America, and desires to record its horror and detestation at the treasonable and wicked act which has deprived that country of so able and good a man, at a time when his services were so important; and to express its entire sympathy with the government and people of the United States of America.

This council also desires to convey the expression of its deepest sympathy to Mrs. Lincoln and family, and begs sincerely to condole with them in their heavy bereavement.

[SEAL.]   THOMAS JESSOP, *Mayor.*

*Resolution passed at a meeting held by the inhabitants of the borough of Shef-
field, England.*

At a meeting of the inhabitants of the borough of Sheffield, in the county
of York, England, held on Monday, May 1, 1865, Thomas Jessop, esq., in the
chair, it was

Unanimously resolved, That this meeting condemns in the strongest possible sense the dastardly and cruel murder of President LINCOLN, in the hour of
his clemency, and records its utmost abhorrence of the atrocious miscreants
who planned and the wretches who perpetrated the hideous, detestable, and
unparalleled crime; and that the Right Honorable Earl Russel be requested to
transmit this resolution, in the manner most befitting the occasion, to the
government and citizens of the United States, assuring them of the profound
and sincere regret of the inhabitants of Sheffield at the bereavement, and their
firm hope that, as in the past, so with this sad occurrence, the United States
will show by their calmness, wisdom, and energy, that though of appalling
magnitude, their loss is not irretrievable.

THOMAS JESSOP,
Mayor and Chairman.

Address of the inhabitants of Sheffield, England.

SHEFFIELD, ENGLAND, *May* 1, 1865.

MADAM: The inhabitants of Sheffield, in public meeting assembled, beg
permission to approach you in the hour of your grief, to assure you how deeply
and tenderly they sympathize with you in your great sorrow.

They are mournfully reminded of the bereavement of their own beloved
sovereign, and are well aware that time alone can heal the deep and terrible
wound which has been inflicted upon you.

Without trespassing further upon the sanctity of your sorrow, they desire
to express the fervent hope that you may find consolation in the contemplation
of the noble and righteous life of him who has been so suddenly taken away,
in the thought that his influence over the minds of his countrymen, and his
power to promote the great cause for which he would willingly have died, has
been increased by his tragical martyrdom; and, above all, in the love of that
God whom he served, and who has promised "to comfort all them that mourn,"
"to be the Father of the fatherless and the husband of the widow."

Signed on behalf of the meeting:

THOMAS JESSOP,
Mayor and Chairman.

Mrs. LINCOLN,
*Widow of his Excellency Abraham Lincoln,
late President of the United States of America.*

THE LATE PRESIDENT LINCOLN.

Public sympathy—Sheffield Chamber of Commerce.

At a meeting of the council of the Sheffield Chamber of Commerce and Manufactures, held at the office of the chamber the 27th of April, 1865, the president (Robert Jackson, esq.) in the chair, it was moved by Joshua Moss, esq., seconded by W. C. Corsan, esq., and resolved—

That the council take this the earliest opportunity of expressing, in the strongest terms, the horror and disgust which they feel at the outrage recently perpetrated in Washington, in consequence of which his Excellency President LINCOLN has lost his life, and the lives of Mr. Secretary Seward and other persons of distinction have been greatly endangered, if not actually destroyed.

That the council beg also to express their deep sympathy with the American people in the loss, at such a crisis, of one so recently selected for a second time to fill the office of President. In the state of affairs consequent upon the recent successes of the federal arms, the kindly feeling and the evident anxiety to smooth the way to the removal of animosities displayed by President LINCOLN in the hour of triumph render his removal, in the opinion of this council, a calamity to all sections of the community.

That in thus giving expression to their feelings of disgust and abhorrence at the crime which has been committed, and their sympathy with the American people, the council are convinced that they are giving utterance to the feelings which these terrible occurrences have excited in the breast of the whole British nation.

ROBERT JACKSON,
President of the Sheffield Chamber of Commerce.

CUTLERS' HALL, *Sheffield, April* 29, 1865.

DEAR SIR: I am directed by the Cutlers' Company to send you the accompanying resolution passed yesterday by the company on the assassination of Mr. President LINCOLN, and have to request that you will forward it to the proper quarter.

I am, dear sir, yours faithfully,

CHARLES ATKINSON,
Master Cutler.

G. J. ABBOT, Esq., *American Consul, Sheffield.*

Resolved, That this company desires to express its deep sorrow and indignation at the assassination of Mr. LINCOLN, President of the United States, and to record, in common with the whole British nation, its profound sympathy with the government and people of America at the very serious loss they have sustained by the atrocious crime which has just been perpetrated.

Address of the Sheffield Secular Society.

HONORED MADAM: From this country there will reach you addresses of condolence and respect from all classes. The English nation has spoken with one voice of deep and sincere sympathy for the fate of your illustrious husband, of detestation of the vile and cowardly murderer who struck him down, and of grief for the bitter bereavement you have sustained. From the Queen upon our throne, from the leaders of our parliamentary parties, from our municipal and public bodies, down to the humblest associations, there has gone forth the most earnest and unanimous expression of sorrow for the deplorable loss the great American republic has suffered, in the violent death of its eminent and honored President; and the Sheffield Secular Society desires to put upon record, and to convey to you and to your family, its sincere concern for this the most grievous event of our times. Our principles teach us to regard reason and liberty as the two great forces of political progress. We are attached to that great doctrine of democracy which regards the whole people as entitled to equal conditions of personal improvement, of social prosperity and civil equality ; and when the head of the great American federation, which represents these principles, is struck down, we regard it as a crime against humanity and the liberties of the human race.

Another reason why we regret the fate of Mr. LINCOLN, and why we honor his memory, is, that Mr. LINCOLN not only rose from the people, but he exalted the people among whom he arose. His career is a historic proof that industry applied to study, animated by honesty, sustained by patience and perennial good will, may result in a commanding capacity, placing the possessor on a level with the most distinguished statesmen of Europe, and higher than any king. The courage, persistence and moderation with which he advanced, and the impassable heroism with which he became the deliverer of the slave, crowned his life with a kinglier glory than any which attaches to any name in the history of men

We trust that these considerations, which the heart of the English nation ratifies, will be to you and to your family some consolation in this hour of your sorrow.

We are, honored madam, your sincere friends,

JAMES DODWORTH, *President.*
GEORGE JACOB HOLYOAKE.
H. WM. BELLS.

(Signed on behalf of the Sheffield Secular Society)
Mrs. LINCOLN.

446   ASSASSINATION OF ABRAHAM LINCOLN.

Resolution of the provost, magistrates, and town council of the royal burgh of Selkirk.

To the President of the United States of America:

We, the provost, magistrates, and town council of the royal burgh of Selkirk, for ourselves, and as representing the community of the said burgh beg to express our feelings of abhorrence in regard to the assassination of President LINCOLN, and our sympathy with the American people under the loss they have sustained by the sudden and violent death of the head of their government.

Signed by the magistrates, by authority of the town council, and the seal of the burgh affixed, this 11th day of May, 1865.

[SEAL.]   JOHN JOHNSTON, *Provost.*
THOMAS DALYLEITH, *Bailie.*
GEORGE LEWIS, *Bailie.*
JAMES MILLAR, *Dean of Guild.*
BASIL HENDERSIN, *Treasurer.*

Resolution of the noblemen, gentlemen, and commissioners of supply of the county of Selkirk, in public meeting assembled.

Resolved, That this meeting do record an expression of heartfelt sorrow and indignation with which they have heard of the assassination of Mr. ABRAHAM LINCOLN, the President of the United States of America, feeling assured that an event so terrible in its nature, and so calamitous to the people whose chief man has been thus suddenly cut off, has excited sentiments of the deepest horror and commiseration, not in this kingdom only, but in every civilized country throughout the world. They desire to convey this expression of their individual sympathy to the people of the United States, as well as to the widow and family of the late President; and for that purpose they authorize their chairman to sign the present resolution, in their name and on their behalf, and to transmit the same to his excellency the American minister in London, with a request that he will communicate it to the government of the United States and to Mrs. Lincoln in such way and manner as he may think proper.

Signed in name and by appointment of the meeting, by

R. WAITT, *Chairman.*

MAY 1, 1865.

Resolutions adopted at a meeting of the corporation of Sligo, held on Thursday, the 4th day of May, 1865.

Resolved, That we, the members of the corporation of Sligo, in council assembled, hereby tender our most profound sympathy to the President and people of the United States of America on the great loss sustained by them in the death of their late President, ABRAHAM LINCOLN, and that we regard the means by which his life was sacrificed with horror and indignation.

Moved by Alderman Lyons; seconded by Alderman McGill.

Resolved, That the resolution this day adopted be suitably engrossed and signed by the mayor, with the corporation seal attached thereto, and forwarded to the American minister at London for presentation to the American government.

Moved by Councillor Gillmor; seconded by Councillor Doherty.

[SEAL.]   W. A. WOODS, *J. P., Mayor of Sligo.*
S. WHITTAKER, *Town Clerk.*

Extract from minutes of proceedings of the Board of Guardians at their meeting 9th of May, 1865, the right honorable John Wynne, P. C., in the chair.

Notice having been given on last board day by H. Griffith, esq., D. L., that an address of sympathy and condolence to the American government and people on the late atrocious murder of President LINCOLN, and attempted murder of Mr. Secretary Seward, be prepared and forwarded for presentation, it is this day

Unanimously resolved, That having heard with feelings of the deepest regret the great loss which the American nation have sustained in the death of their late President, ABRAHAM LINCOLN, whose honesty, courage, and perseverance in the fulfilment of the duties of the high position he occupied have gained the highest respect and esteem for him, even among those who may have differed from him on questions of state policy, and by whom terms of conciliation tending to an honorable peace with the southern portion of the States so anxiously awaited in these countries were about to be perfected, we desire to express our heartfelt sympathy with the American government and people, and our deep abhorrence of the atrocious murder committed, as well as of the attempted murder of Mr. Seward; and we also tender our sincere condolence to the bereaved widow, Mrs. Lincoln, and to the family of Mr. Seward, and add our earnest prayer that the death of the brave, good man, who has died for his country, may be the last sacrifice of a war apparently about to expire, and that peace, on a substantial basis, may speedily follow.

JOHN WYNNE, *Chairman.*
DAVID CLARK, *Clerk of Union.*
BOARD ROOM, SLIGO, *May* 10, 1865.

Stourbridge resolutions.

Moved by Mr. Henry Hughes, seconded by Mr. William Rollinson, and carried unanimously—

That this meeting, on behalf of itself and the inhabitants of the town of Stourbridge, takes this opportunity of giving expression to its feelings of condolence and sympathy with the family of the late President of the United States of America and the nation at large on the occurrence of that great calamity to themselves and to the whole civilized world, the assassination of their able, beloved, respected, and revered Chief Magistrate.

STOURBRIDGE, *May* 1, 1865.

STOURBRIDGE UNION.

Moved by Mr. Chance, seconded by Mr. Wood, and carried unanimously—

That this board has heard with the deepest regret of the assassination of ABRAHAM LINCOLN, President of the United States; and, while it expresses its utter detestation of so diabolical an act, begs to offer to the American people its sincere condolence on the heavy calamity which has befallen their nation.

BOARD-ROOM, WORKHOUSE, *April* 20, 1865.

UNION AND EMANCIPATION SOCIETY.

STAFFORD AUXILIARY, *April* 29, 1865.

SIR: We, the undersigned, on behalf of the committee and members of the above society, beg respectfully to tender to your excellency our most sincere condolence upon the loss the United States of America and the civilized world have sustained by the atrocious murder of President ABRAHAM LINCOLN.

Trusting that Providence will direct his successor, President Johnson, as an instrument for perfecting the work so honestly begun to a speedy termination, when the South may see that to be prosperous a nation must be both free and united,

> We are, sir, yours most obediently,
> WM. SILVESTER, *President.*
> W. J. LAPWORTH, *Secretary.*

His Excellency the AMERICAN MINISTER *in London.*

BOROUGH OF STOCKPORT IN THE SEVERAL COUNTIES OF CHESTER AND LANCASTER.

At a meeting of the council of the borough of Stockport, held in the council chamber, on Wednesday, the 3d of May, 1865, William Linton Eskrigge, esq., mayor, in the chair, it was

Unanimously resolved, That the council of Stockport, at its first meeting since the terrible news reached this country that President LINCOLN had fallen the victim of a dastardly assassin, and that a like attempt had been made on the life of Mr Secretary Seward, unanimously passes a vote of sincere condolence with the United States of America, with Mrs. Lincoln, and with Mr. Secretary Seward, expressive of the horror felt by the council, and its deep sympathy with those afflicted by these most diabolical acts.

That this resolution be transmitted to the envoy extraordinary and minister plenipotentiary of the United States in London, with a request that he will duly communicate it to his government, to Mrs. Lincoln, and to Mr. Secretary Seward.

The common seal of the borough of Stockport was hereunto duly affixed in the presence of—

⌈SEAL.⌉   HENRY COPPOCK, *Town Clerk.*

Resolutions passed at a meeting held by the Sunday School Union of Stockport.

At a meeting of the teachers, superintendents, and representatives of the schools composing the Sunday School Union of Stockport, held on the eighth day of May, 1865, Mr. Councillor George Barber in the chair, it was

Unanimously resolved, That the Sunday schools of Stockport, embracing all the evangelical denominations of the Christian church, have heard with feelings of the deepest horror and the most inexpressible grief of the brutal assassination of ABRAHAM LINCOLN, President of the United States of America, by the hand of a vile and reckless murderer.

That this Union, while recording this expression of the most heartfelt sympathy and sorrowful condolence with the bereaved widow and the great American republic, most cordially recognizes the eminent personal worth, the high-toned religious principle, and the noble civic virtues of that large-hearted father of the American people, twice elected as Chief Magistrate by the popular voice, beloved by the children of two hemispheres, admired by the vast army of Sunday school teachers in the free countries of Europe and America, and revered by the great and good of every clime, as the heroic emancipator of four millions of abject bondsmen, and the saviour of his country from armed rebellion, anarchy, and ruin.

That while this Union cherishes these sentiments with the deepest emotion, it feels most keenly the death, by the hand of a wretched drunkard, of so good a man, whose persistent advocacy of the importance of an education based upon religious principles, and his bright example as a steady and consistent abstainer from intoxicating drinks, afforded strength and encouragement to our bands of hope, and proved that, even under circumstances of the most severe trials ever imposed upon the ruler of a great nation, the late President of the United States of America devoted the full strength of his lofty intelligence and the warmest sympathies of his noble heart.

While our Sunday schools are bowed with sorrow, feeling that each has lost a friend, the prayer is raised continually that this fearful rebellion may be speedily brought to a close, and that a permanent peace may soon be proclaimed, established on the only righteous basis, viz: that of union, nationality, justice, and freedom, with equal civil and political rights to all loyal men, of whatever creed, race, or condition, and the inestimable blessings of a healthy religious education secured to all rising and future generations of the republic.

Signed on behalf of the Union:

GEORGE BARBER, *Chairman.*

JAMES H. MIDDLETON,
Honorary Secretary.

STOCKPORT, *May* 8, 1865.

At a meeting of the vicar, church wardens, and vestrymen of the parish of St. Martin in the Fields, in the county of Middlesex, specially convened and held at the vestry hall of the said parish, on Friday, the 5th day of May, 1865— present, the Reverend William Gelson Humphrey, B. D., vicar, in the chair—it was moved, seconded, and

Unanimously resolved, That the following address be forwarded to his excellency the American minister at the Court of St. James, viz:

SIR: We, the vicar, church wardens, and vestrymen of the parish of St. Martin in the Fields, desire to express to you the strong feelings of grief and indignation with which we have heard of the assassination of President LINCOLN, and the attempted murder of Mr. Seward.

We are not without hope that it may be some consolation to the American people, and to the widow of the late President, in this their bereavement, to receive the sympathy of the people of this country; and we trust that the dreadful events which have called forth our sympathy will, by the Divine Providence, be so overruled as not in any way to retard the restoration of peace, concord, and prosperity in the United States.

W. G. HUMPHREY, *Chairman.*

Hon. CHARLES FRANCIS ADAMS,
Envoy Extraordinary and Minister Plenipotentiary
of the United States of America.

At a public meeting of the inhabitants of the town and borough of Swanson, held at the Guildhall, in said town, on Thursday, the 4th day of May, 1865, it was

Unanimously resolved, That this meeting desires to manifest its profound abhorrence and indignation at the great crime by which the United States of America have been deprived of their late Chief Magistrate, ABRAHAM LINCOLN; and further to express its unfeigned sympathy with the government and people of the United States, and the widow and family of the late President, in the depth of their calamity and bereavement.

J. CLARKE RICHARDSON, *Mayor.*

SWANSEA WORKINGMEN'S INSTITUTE.

At a special general meeting held at the institute on Tuesday, May 9, 1865, Mr. Benjamin Davies in the chair, it was

Unanimouly resolved, That the members of the Swansea Workingmen's Institute, being desirous of manifesting their sincere regret at the revolting act which has deprived the American republic of an able President, and society at large of one of its brightest ornaments, beg to tender to Mrs. Lincoln and the government and people of the United States their heartfelt sympathy in their present hour of sorrow.

And it was further

Unanimously resolved, That the resolution just passed be forwarded, through the medium of the American minister at London, to Mrs. Lincoln, and government and people of the United States.

ST. MARYLEBONE, *April* 27, 1865.

At the vestry—present, Mr. Churchwarden Baddely in the chair—

Resolved unanimously, That the vestry of Saint Marylebone, having heard with the profoundest regret of the assassination of the President of the United States, beg respectfully and earnestly to convey, at the earliest possible opportunity, to his excellency the American minister the expression of their horror at the detestable and cowardly crime that has been committed, and their deepest sympathies with the American people and his excellency in the lamentable national catastrophe which has befallen them.

Extracted from the minutes:

W. E. GREENOCK, *Vestry Clerk.*

PARISH OF ST. PANCRAS, IN THE COUNTY OF MIDDLESEX.

At a general meeting of the vestrymen of the said parish, held at the vestry hall, King's road, Pancras road, on Wednesday, the 10th day of May, 1865— Mr. Churchwarden Robson in the chair, and sixty-eight other vestrymen present—it was moved by John R. Collins, esq., pursuant to notice, seconded by Henry Farrer, esq., F. S. A., and

Resolved unanimously, That this vestry desires to express its feelings of grief and horror at the untimely death of President LINCOLN, by the hands of an assassin, and to avow its high appreciation of the great ability, moderation, and patriotism displayed by him as Chief Magistrate of the United States of America, at a period of extraordinary civil commotion. This vestry desires further to express its deep sympathy with the widow and family of the late President, and also with the people of the United States, in being thus ruthlessly deprived of the guiding influence of so high-principled a statesman at a time of national difficulty and distress, and would fervently hope that the wise and moderate policy of ABRAHAM LINCOLN may be adopted by both President and people in the pacification of their distracted country.

The common seal of the vestry of the parish of St. Pancras, Middlesex, affixed hereto by order of the said vestry.

[SEAL.] FRANCIS PLAW, *Vestry Clerk.*

At a meeting of the corporation of the borough of Stockton, in the county of Durham, held at the Town Hall in the said borough, on the 5th day of May, 1865—present, the mayor; Aldermen Wren, Craggs, Ord, Jackson, and Richardson; Councillors Grey, Trowsdale, Brashay, Thompson, Knowles, T. Wren, jr., Henderson, Bigland, Clough, T. Nelson, Barnes, J. Smith, W. Nelson, T. Harrison, Brown, and Appleton—it was

Resolved, That the mayor, aldermen, and council of the borough of Stockton have learned with feelings of horror and detestation of the awful crime committed on the President of the United States and of the murderous attack on Mr. Seward, and they desire to record their sense of these cruel and cold-blooded villanies, and to express their sincere and heartfelt feelings of sorrow and regret for the calamity that has befallen that country, and for the grievous loss which its citizens have sustained.

And it was

Resolved, That the American ambassador be requested to convey to Mrs. Lincoln and the American nation the expression of their profound sympathy and condolence for this lamentable and grievous occurrence.

[SEAL.]

At a public meeting of the inhabitants of the borough of Stockton-on-Tees, in the county of Durham, held at the Borough Hall in Stockton-on-Tees aforesaid, on the 5th day of May, 1865—Joshua Byers, esq., mayor, in the chair—the following resolutions were passed :

That the inhabitants of Stockton-on-Tees, in a public meeting called by the mayor, would express, in the strongest manner possible, their abhorrence of the dastardly crimes which have suddenly deprived the United States of America of their President and seriously endangered the life of his chief secretary, and their deep sympathy with the government and people of that country in the affliction into which the loss they have sustained has plunged them.

That this meeting deeply regrets that President LINCOLN should have been cut off at the time when his firm but conciliatory policy was about to reap the noblest fruit, and when his earnestness, simplicity, and clear insight into realities would have enabled him successfully to carry on the work of reconstruction, and devoutly hopes that those upon whom his labors must now devolve may succeed in speedily and happily overcoming every obstacle and effecting that reconstruction on the immovable basis of freedom and justice.

That this meeting would express its earnest desire that the sympathy for the government and people of the United States of America, called forth by the astounding intelligence of the assassination of their Chief Magistrate, and the remembrance of his conciliatory bearing towards this country, may tend to cement the friendship between England and America.

That this meeting learns with sincere gratification that the Queen of the realm has with such promptness and characteristic kindness written with her own hand to the widow of his late Excellency President LINCOLN, a letter of condolence and sympathy with her in her great affliction and bereavement.

That this meeting respectfully requests the mayor to sign and afterwards forward the foregoing resolutions expressing our sympathy with the American government and people to the American ambassador in London.

JOSHUA BYERS, *Chairman.*

In memoriam.

OFFICE OF THE GRAND SCRIBE OF THE GRAND DIVISION
SONS OF TEMPERANCE OF NEW BRUNSWICK, B. N. A.

At the regular session of the Grand Division Sons of Temperance of the province of New Brunswick, British North America, held at the city of St. John, on Wednesday evening, 26th day of April, A. D. 1865, on motion of Representative William Wedderburn, P. G. W. P., seconded by Representative William H. A. Keans, grand scribe, the following resolutions were unanimously adopted :

Whereas his Excellency ABRAHAM LINCOLN, late President of the United States, has suddenly been cut off in the zenith of his great career by the hand of an assassin; and whereas we deeply feel for the affliction in which our brethren and the people generally of the United States have therefore been involved—

Resolved, That we, the members of the Grand Division of New Brunswick Sons of Temperance, while we acknowledge allegiance only and loyalty to the crown of Great Britain, take the first opportunity afforded us to express our deep and sincere sympathy with our brethren in the Order, and the people generally of the United States, upon the death of ABRAHAM LINCOLN, their honored and beloved Chief Magistrate.

Resolved, That irrespective of our individual political sympathies and associations, we have recognized in ABRAHAM LINCOLN a true friend of virtue, and one who has publicly expressed his hearty approval of the cardinal principles of our Order and of all similar institutions; as a pure-minded and upright magistrate, an able statesman, a devoted Christian, an honest man.

Resolved, That we abhor and denounce the assassination of ABRAHAM LINCOLN as a deed which can only become memorable for its ineffable infamy, as a treason against the commonwealth of nations, a crime against Christianity and civilization, and a wickedness unparalleled in the pages of history for the horror and villany of its conception, and the inhuman character and circumstances of its commission.

Resolved, That the foregoing resolutions, suitably engrossed and under the seal of this Grand Division, be transmitted to the British minister at Washington, to be laid before the American government in such manner as he shall deem best, to the widow of the late President, to the most worthy scribe of the Order, and the press of this city for publication.

Extracts from the minutes.

[SEAL.]   W. H. A. KEANS, *Grand Scribe.*

Address of the colored people of Bermuda.

SAINT GEORGE'S, BERMUDA, *April* 28, 1865.

SIR: We, the undersigned, beg leave to submit to you, the lawful representative of the United States of America for Bermuda, our expressions of sympathy on our part, and in behalf of the colored people of this community, on the melancholy intelligence which has reached us of the death of the good ABRAHAM LINCOLN, at Washington, on the 15th instant, by assassination. Knowing his many virtues as a man, while in office as Chief Magistrate of America, we consider his untimely removal a loss of no common degree, not only to the people of his country, but to many foreign to his domains.

We do not make these expressions as a mere formal observance, but are prompted by purer motives. We feel that a great and good man has passed from us.

We therefore most respectfully tender to you, and through you to his bereaved family across the "ocean's foam," our heartfelt sympathy and condolence in this hour of trial and affliction, when, by the hand of a ruthless assassin, a wise and patriotic ruler has been stricken down, at a time when his work was near its consummation.

We remain, dear sir, with profound respect, your very obedient servants,

J. T. RICHARDSON,
E. B. M. FRITH,
J. H. RAINEY,
JOSEPH H. THOMAS,
BENJAMIN BURCHALL,
Committee.

C. M. ALLEN, Esq.,
United States Consul.

SAINT GEORGE'S, BERMUDA, *May* 11, 1865.

SIR: It has fallen to my lot to have the honor of presenting you with the enclosed address from the three divisions of the order of the Sons of Temperance located in these islands; and while I regret the delay the said divisions have shown in the discharge of so important a duty, do conceive it would have been a greater blunder, a greater omission, to have neglected it altogether. Therefore trusting you will pardon their error in this respect,

I am, sir, yours respectfully,

GEORGE OXBORROW,
General Deputy Grand Worthy Patriarch, Sons of Temperance.
C. M. ALLEN, Esq.,
United States Consul.

SAINT GEORGE'S, BERMUDA, *May* 11, 1865.

SIR: We, the undersigned, representing the divisions of the Sons of Temperance in Bermuda, convey to you the following resolutions, expressive of the sympathy felt by that body in reference to the lamentable occurrence which has so lately afflicted the American nation, by the cruel assassination of its President.

Resolved, That recognizing the hand of Almighty God in this afflictive stroke, the divisions of the Sons of Temperance in the Bermuda islands have received the intelligence of the brutal murder of ABRAHAM LINCOLN, late President of the United States, with feelings of horror and detestation.

Resolved, That to the bereaved wife and family of the late chief ruler of the American nation we tender our sincere sorrow and sympathy for his untimely death. Allow us, in conclusion, to convey to you our deep regret at this unfortunate event.

We are, sir, yours, very respectfully,

[L. S.]   GEORGE OXBORROW, G. D. Grand W. Patriarch,
              JOSEPH M. HAYWARD, Treasurer,
                        Star of Hope, No. 190, *St. George's.*

[L. S.]   CHARLES W. B. FOYARD, D. G. W. Patriarch,
              BENJAMIN P. ELDRIDGE, R. S.,
              NEIL McK. McLEOD, W. P.,
                        Reid Division, No. 192, *Hamilton.*

              JOSIAH W. FRITH, W. P.,
              JOSEPH H. FRITH, R. S.,
                        Argus, No. 210, *Warwick.*

C. M. ALLEN, Esq.,
        United States Consul.

Address of the municipal council of the city of Sydney, N. S. W.

MADAM: We, the municipal council of the city of Sydney, in the British colony of New South Wales, desire, on behalf of the citizens of this city, to express to you our deeply felt sympathy on the lamentable occurrence which has led to the untimely death of your husband, the late President of the United States of America.

If any consolation can be experienced on such an occasion, when the almost universal feeling is that of the deepest sorrow, it must arise from the knowledge that in the history of your country there does not exist a name which, from its association with the momentous events of his time, will be more honored and reverenced than that of ABRAHAM LINCOLN.

The unostentatious simplicity and uprightness of his character in private life; the wise and useful influence which he exercised over the public institutions of his country; his worthy ambitious desire to support and maintain the Constitution of the State, and the undeviating firmness and admirable sagacity which he evinced during the extraordinary struggle of the past few years, have exhibited to the world one of those great and attractive characters which commands the profoundest respect from every rank of life. The unhappy event which has removed such a man from the social circle, and has deprived the nation of such valuable aid and guidance, must excite the most heartfelt sympathy for the relatives and friends who mourn his disastrous fate, and the deepest regret that his country should have lost so noble and devoted a patriot.

We earnestly hope that the condolence which has been offered you from all parts of your own land and from foreign nations may tend in some degree to assuage your great affliction, while we are confident that the people whom your husband so wisely governed will bear his name in honored remembrance, and that it will stand side by side with the greatest in the history of the New World.

[SEAL.] JOHN WOODS,
Mayor of the City of Sydney.

Adopted by the municipal council of the city of Sydney, this seventeenth day of July, A. D. 1865.

CHARLES W. WOOLCOTT, *Town Clerk.*

Mrs. LINCOLN.

New South Wales branch of the Irish National League.

COMMITTEE ROOMS, 106 KING STREET,
Sydney, July 22, 1865.

To the honorable the President, the Senate,
and House of Representatives of the United States of America:

The members of the New South Wales branch of the Irish National League have instructed us, their central committee, to condole with you (the Congress of America) on the calamity that has befallen your nation, and to convey to you their heartfelt sorrow and sympathy for the loss which, in common with the cause of freedom throughout the world, you have sustained by the foul murder by the hand of an assassin of that great, energetic, untiring, and devoted champion of freedom, ABRAHAM LINCOLN.

We, as inhabitants of New South Wales, are actuated to this expression of sorrow for America's great loss by the feeling, among others, that as possessors of free institutions we were greatly benefited by the talent, energy, and Christian virtues displayed by one in the proud position of President of the greatest republic of modern times.

In the high and responsible position in which he was placed, his powers were great for the accomplishment of good or evil, and how those powers were used is manifest to the world. By the efforts of the great mind with which he was endowed, he overcame obstacles which to the most experienced statesmen in Europe seemed insurmountable ; he suppressed a rebellion, more formidable than the annals of any other country can record ; united and brought into amicable intercourse many who were previously actuated in their opposition by the influence of party spirit or sectarian prejudices, and by his powerful abilities he brought his country safe and triumphant from that terrible ordeal through which she has been passing for the last four years.

The members of the Irish National League are also actuated in this far-off land of Australia by gratitude, which is a national characteristic, to express their feelings on the present occasion ; they cannot and do not forget that when a code of the most ill-conceived laws deprived them of freedom and prosperity at home, and even seemed to threaten the total extirpation of their race ; when unable to meet their landlords' call, they were expelled from the homes in which they were born ; when they appeared deserted by the world, and nothing seemed to remain but death from cold and starvation by the wayside, it was then that America, noble America, with outstretched arms welcomed them to her shores and bestowed upon them her fertile plains and teeming valleys, where now, beside the grand and majestic rivers that beautify and fertilize your country, they reside in freedom and happiness, with honor and credit to themselves, a lasting memorial of the benefits to be derived from that Constitution and that country whose laws they acknowledge and respect.

For these among other reasons we desire to express our warmest sympathy with America, and to pay a tribute of respect and admiration to the memory of the great departed. In conclusion, we beg to express a hope that the united exertions of America's patriotic sons will secure her peace and happiness, and that the mighty republic of the west, the great home of freedom, the United States of America, may continue to retain her exalted position as one of the great and free nations of the world.

JOHN ROBETSON, *President.*
OWEN HARUHER,
PATRICK O'DOND, *Vice-Presidents.*
THOMAS McCAFFERY, *Treasurer.*
P. J. GROGAN, *Secretary.*
JAMES P. GARVAN,
WILLIAM DOLMAN,
RICHARD MOONELY,
J. J. CURRAN,
MICHAEL RILEY,
JAMES COLEMAN,
LAWRENCE MORAN,
JAMES BUTLER,
J. I. McDERMOT, *Committee.*

Resolution passed by the council of the corporation of the city of Toronto, Canada.

TUESDAY, *April* 18, 1865.

Resolved, That this council, on behalf of the citizens of Toronto, deplore the impious act that has convulsed society, in the death, by violence, of ABRAHAM LINCOLN, late President of the United States of America. Esteeming the same a national calamity, they mournfully sympathize with his countrymen, and recognizing in them a great co-operating Christian power, feel deeply sensible of the melancholy gloom it must create. And, further, that in honor of the dead the business of the city be suspended for two hours from noon on Wednesday, to-morrow.

Truly extracted from the journals of the council:

F. H. MEDCALF, *Mayor.*

[SEAL.]   JOHN CARR, *City Clerk.*

A. T. McCORD, *Chamberlain.*

His Excellency ANDREW JOHNSON,
President of the United States of America:

We, the mayor, aldermen, and burgesses of the borough of Tewksbury, in England, desire to give utterance to our feelings of grief and horror at the assassination of your late distinguished predecessor, President LINCOLN, and the attempted murder of Mr. Secretary Seward, and to convey to the people of the United States an expression of our sympathy and good will, and at the same time to add our sincere condolence with the widow and family of the late eminent statesman.

Given under our common seal, at the Tolsey, in the said borough. this 15th day of May, 1865.

[SEAL.]   W. ALLARD, *Mayor.*

We, the mayor, aldermen, and burgesses of the ancient borough of Thetford, in council assembled, having received with great sorrow the intelligence of the assassination of President LINCOLN, desire to express our utter abhorrence at the detestable crime, and beg to offer to the American nation our sincere condolence and sympathy upon the loss it has sustained.

Given under our common corporate seal, this 22d day of May, 1865.

[SEAL.]   W. P. SALTER, *Mayor.*

His Excellency the MINISTER *from the United States.*

At a public meeting of the inhabitants of the borough of Tynemouth, in the county of Northumberland, held in the Town Hall, on the 2d day of May, 1865, the mayor in the chair, it was

Unanimously resolved, That the inhabitants of the borough of Tynemouth, in public meeting assembled, desire to express their feelings of sorrow and indignation at the assassination of the President of the United States of America, and at the attempt made upon the life of his chief secretary.

That while deeply lamenting the removal of President LINCOLN, at a time when his influence was most urgently needed to secure a happy and peaceful termination of the war in America, this meeting sincerely hopes that the statesman upon whom the conduct of national affairs of America has now devolved may succeed in attaining that most desirable result.

That a copy of the preceding resolutions, signed by the mayor on behalf of this meeting, be forwarded to the American government through their ambassador in London.

That a copy of the foregoing resolutions, signed by the mayor, be also forwarded to Mrs. Lincoln, with an expression of the deep and sincere sympathy of the inhabitants of this borough with herself and her family in their great sorrow and bereavement; and another copy to Mrs. Seward, coupled with the expression of an earnest hope that Mr. Secretary Seward may eventually recover from the attack made upon his life.

GEORGE JOBLING,
Mayor of Tynemouth, Chairman.

VANCOUVER'S ISLAND, VICTORIA, *April* 22, 1865.

SIR: I have the honor to transmit the copy of a resolution adopted by the legislative assembly of Vancouver's Island, on the 20th instant, expressing their sympathy in the calamity which has befallen the United States of America, in the death of their President, ABRAHAM LINCOLN, in which expression of sympathy I fully join.

I have the honor to be, sir, your most obedient servant,

A. E. KENNEDY, *Governor.*

ALLEN FRANCIS, Esq.,
    United States Consul, &c., &c., &c., Victoria.

Resolution passed by the legislative assembly of Vancouver's Island, on the 20th day of April, 1865.

Resolved, That this house, taking into consideration the great calamity which has befallen the United States of America, and the rest of the civilized world, in the assassination of President ABRAHAM LINCOLN, does adjourn till to-morrow as a mark of respect to the memory of the great departed, the chief of a nation connected by the nearest ties with our own, and glorying in the same origin, the same traditions, and the same freedom.

R. W. TORRENS,
Clerk of the House.

To her most gracious Majesty the Queen :

We, your Majesty's faithful subjects, the members of the legislative assembly of Victoria, in Parliament assembled, crave leave to approach your Majesty with fresh assurances of our loyalty and affection.

We desire to express our abhorrence of the foul crime by which the United States have been deprived of their late President, ABRAHAM LINCOLN, and our profound sympathy with the American government and people in their national calamity.

We desire also to record our unfeigned condolence with Mrs. Lincoln in her deep affliction ; and we humbly beg that your Majesty will be graciously pleased to communicate these our heartfelt sentiments to the government at Washington.

FRANK MURPHY, *Speaker.*

To her most gracious Majesty the Queen :

We, your Majesty's faithful subjects, the members of the legislative council of Victoria, in Parliament assembled, crave leave to approach your Majesty with fresh assurances of our loyalty and affection.

We desire to express our abhorrence of the foul crime by which the United States have been deprived of their late President, ABRAHAM LINCOLN, and our profound sympathy with the American government and people in their national calamity.

We desire also to record our unfeigned condolence with Mrs. Lincoln in her deep affliction; and we humbly beg that your Majesty will be graciously pleased to communicate these our heartfelt sentiments to the government at Washington.

PALMER, *President.*

Resolutions adopted at the annual conference of the Welch Baptist Association, held in Victoria, county of Monmouth, May 30, 1865.

Resolved, That this association takes the earliest opportunity of expressing its intense sorrow and deep abhorrence at the assassination of the late President of the United States, the honest and upright ABRAHAM LINCOLN, and its heartfelt sympathy with the American people in the peculiarly trying circumstances in which, by this sad event, they have been placed; its ardent desire for their peace and prosperity, and the maintenance of their amicable relations with Britain and all other European states; and its fervent gratitude to God for the prospect of a speedy termination of the war, and the total abolition of slavery throughout their land.

Signed on behalf of the conference:

WILLIAM ROBERTS, *Moderator.*
TIMOTHY THOMAS, *Secretary.*

MEETING OF AMERICAN RESIDENTS.

At a meeting of the American residents of Victoria, V. I., held at the consulate of the United States of America, on Tuesday, April 18, 1865, it was

Unanimously resolved, That a committee of five be appointed by the chairman to draught resolutions expressive of our feelings in regard to the assassination of the President of the United States, and to make the necessary arrangements for a suitable observance of the sad event, and to pay proper respect to his memory.

In compliance with the foregoing, Messrs. A. H. Guild, J. A. McCrea, G. Sutro, Julius Lowey, and S. A. Moody were appointed such committee, and on motion the president and secretary were added to the same. The meeting then adjourned.

ALLEN FRANCIS, *Chairman.*
JNO. P. COUCH, *Secretary.*

NOTICE.

The committee to whom was referred the matter of making arrangements on behalf of the American residents of Victoria to take some suitable notice of the death of the late President of the United States and to pay proper respect to his memory, beg leave to report that the Hon. S. Garfield has kindly consented to address the people of Victoria on the subject of the recent national calamity at the Victoria theatre, at 3 o'clock this (Wednesday) afternoon, April 19.

The committee respectfully recommend those so disposed to close their places of business throughout the day, and pay every respect to the occasion. The committee also desire to extend a cordial invitation to every resident of Victoria to attend the meeting at the theatre. Ladies are expected to attend.

THE COMMITTEE.

Mr. Garfield concluded his oration amid prolonged applause, and moved the adoption of the following preamble and resolutions, which were carried by acclamation:

Whereas it has pleased the Almighty Ruler of the universe, in the all-wise dispensation of His providence, to afflict the people of the United States by permitting ABRAHAM LINCOLN, their Chief Magistrate, to be stricken down in the prime of life and in the midst of usefulness by the hand of the assassin; and whereas the intelligence of this great calamity, not only to our country, but to the cause of truth and humanity throughout the world, has been received by us with feelings of the most profound sorrow, we deem this hour of our country's bereavement a fit and proper occasion to express the deep sympathy we feel for her affliction, as well as the grief which afflicts our hearts at this sudden and lamentable event. But how shall we give expression to our sorrow? In what words shall we speak of the mighty dead who has fallen, or bewail his loss? To us, on these distant shores, he was not only the Chief Magistrate of our beloved country, but the embodiment and representative of the principles we cherish, and which we had hoped, through him, to see carried out and established. Called to preside over the destinies of our country at the most critical period of its history, and all inexperienced as he was in the administration of government, many doubted his ability to cope with the mighty difficulties and dangers which encompassed the nation. Questions the most momentous and altogether new in the country's history were presented, and upon their solution depended not only its welfare, but its existence as a nation. To meet these successfully required the greatest wisdom, firmness, and moderation. But He who holds in the hollow of his hand the destinies of nations mistakes not His agents in the accomplishment of His vast designs; and, therefore, ABRAHAM LINCOLN was found to possess the necessary qualifications to conduct his country through the trying ordeal to which she has been subjected; to preserve the stability of the government, and at the same time vindicate the correctness of the principles upon which it was founded. He brought to the discharge of his great and arduous duties a heart so honest and sincere, a wisdom so practical and sound, and a moral courage so steady and unwavering, as to eminently fit him for his exalted position. But his most distinguished trait was his humanity—humanity in its largest sense. His was the heart to feel that every man was his brother. Surely, in the great day of reckoning his name will be found "foremost in the Book of Life, as one who loved his fellow-man." But time will not permit us further to allude to his deeds and virtues. His work was accomplished, and he has passed from his labors, and however much we deplore his loss, we can but bow in all humility to the fiat of Him who—

> Deep in unfathomable mines
> Of never-failing skill,
> Treasures up His vast designs,
> And works His sovereign will.

We, therefore, the citizens of the United States residing in Victoria, Vancouver's Island, for the purpose of expressing our sense of our country's loss, have

Resolved, first, That while humbly bowing to the decrees of an all-wise Providence which has permitted our beloved country to be afflicted by the death of its Chief Magistrate at a period so momentous in its history, our hearts are filled with the deepest grief, and with our country we mourn in its affliction.

Resolved, second, That in the death of ABRAHAM LINCOLN—the wise, the noble, the good—the nation has suffered a great and irreparable loss, and the kindly nature of the departed President has enshrined his name deeply in the affections of his afflicted countrymen, who feel that liberty wept when LINCOLN fell.

Resolved, third, That we feel the keenest sorrow for the bereaved widow and family of the deceased President, and tender to them our warmest sympathy in their great distress.

Resolved, fourth, That we bow in humble submission to the inscrutable decrees of Almighty God, and invoke His blessing upon William H. Seward, Secretary of State of the United States of America, and we fervently hope that he may be speedily restored to his wonted health and faculties, and that our country may long continue to enjoy the benefits of his known wisdom and ability.

Resolutions passed at a meeting held by the working classes of Wigan.

At a meeting of the working classes, held in the Public Hall, Wigan, on the 17th day of May, 1865, the following resolutions were enthusiastically adopted:

1. That this meeting tenders its heartfelt sympathy to Mrs. Lincoln upon the loss of her noble and devoted husband, and to the people of the United States in their sudden deprivation of a wise, just, and merciful head; that, expressing its utmost abhorrence and detestation of the foul and treacherous assassination of President LINCOLN, and the attempt upon the life of Mr. Secretary Seward, it at the same time expresses its conviction that it was but the culminating point of a crime, if possible, of still darker hue—the attempt to perpetuate the bondage of millions of men, and to achieve the destruction of a great nation; that it expresses its gratitude to Almighty God for the termination of the rebellion, and the destruction of the institution of slavery in the United States; rejoices at the complete falsification of the statements that American institutions were a failure, and expresses its warmest wishes for the welfare of the great American republic, and its desire that the bond of brotherhood between the two people (England and America) may grow ever stronger, and the possibility of war between them ever more remote.

2. That the chairman be requested to send the foregoing resolution to Mr. Adams, the American minister in London, desiring him to forward it to the American government and to Mrs. Lincoln.

Signed on behalf of the meeting:

TIMOTHY COOP, *Chairman.*

White Chapel district, comprising the parishes of White Chapel, Spitalfields, Oldgate, Minories, Saint Catharine, Mile End, New Town, Norton Folgate, Old Artillery Ground, and Tower.

OFFICE OF THE BOARD OF WORKS, WHITE CHAPEL DISTRICT,
51 *Great Alie street, White Chapel, East London, May* 1, 1865.

SIR: The board of works for the White Chapel district, at their meeting held this day, have directed me to communicate to your excellency, as the representative of the government of the United States of America in this country, their feelings of abhorrence and disgust at the assassination of the late President of the United States of America, and of the attempt upon the life of the Secretary of State, and also to express their feelings of warm sympathy with the people of America for the loss of a Chief Magistrate who, under circumstances of the most trying description, by his ability, kindness of heart, and honesty of purpose, did so much to endear himself to all over whom he was called upon to preside.

I have the honor to be your excellency's most obedient servant,

ALFRED FURNET, *Clerk.*

Hon. CHARLES FRANCIS ADAMS,
        Minister of the United States of America,
                Upper Portland Place, West.

We, the mayor, aldermen, and citizens of the city of Winchester, in town council assembled, desire to express our extreme sorrow and indignation at the foul assassination of the late President of the United States of America, and to convey our sympathy and condolence at the loss which that nation and his widow have thereby sustained. We also express our regret at the attempt made upon the life of Mr. Seward and his son, and the pleasure with which we have received the intelligence of their improved condition.

Given under our corporate seal this 4th day of May, 1865.

[SEAL.]   WM. BUDDEN, *Mayor.*

His Excellency the Hon. C. F. ADAMS, *American Minister.*

At a meeting of the council of the city of Worcester, holden this 2d day of May, 1865, it was

Resolved, That this council has heard with great sorrow and indignation of the assassination of the President of the United States, and of the atrocious attempt on the lives of other persons connected with the government of that country, and feels the deepest sense of horror at such detestable crimes. The council also wishes to assure the family of the late President, and the American people, of its heartfelt sympathy with them under their irreparable loss.

RICH. WOOF, *Town Clerk.*

Address of the mayor, aldermen, and burgesses of the borough of Walsall, in the county of Stafford, to the government and people of the United States of America, and to Mrs. Lincoln.

The mayor, aldermen, and burgesses of the borough of Walsall, in council assembled, unanimously desire to express to the government and people of the United States of America their abhorrence of the foul and cowardly crime which has lately deprived the States of the life of their President, and embittered the happiness which all must feel at the prospect of approaching peace. The council desire also to express their deep sympathy with Mrs. Lincoln and her family under the terrible bereavement, and their earnest wishes for tranquillity and prosperity to their brethren of the States.

Given under the common seal of the borough the 3d day of May, 1865.

[SEAL.]   THOS. HAZLEDINE, *Mayor.*

SAM'L WILKINSON, JR, *Town Clerk.*

TOWN HALL, WELLS, *May* 1, 1865.

Third quarterly meeting of the council. Moved by Dr. Purnell, seconded by Mr. Welsh, and

Resolved, That the council has heard with horror and indignation of the atrocious outrages which have unhappily deprived the United States of America of their President, and threaten a similar calamity in the death of his Secretary of State, and they take the earliest opportunity, in the name of the municipality which they represent, of recording their detestation of these outrages, and of expressing their regret at the loss which the American people have sustained, and of sympathy in the calamities which have thus befallen them.

Extracted from the minute book of the proceedings of the council of Wells:

W. J. S. FOSTER, *Town Clerk.*

Resolution of the council of the borough of Warwick.

We, the mayor, aldermen, and burgesses of the borough of Warwick, in council assembled, desire to give expression to the feelings of horror, indignation, and regret with which we have heard of the assassination of President LINCOLN, and beg to convey to Mrs. Lincoln and the United States government and people an expression of our sincere and deep sympathy and heartfelt condolence at the melancholy event.

Given under our common seal the ninth day of May, one thousand eight hundred and sixty-five.

[SEAL.]   THOMAS B. DALE, *Mayor.*

CITY OF WATERFORD, IRELAND,
Council Chamber, May 2, 1865.

Resolved unanimously, That this council take the present opportunity of expressing its unfeigned sorrow and intense indignation at the foul and atrocious assassination of his Excellency Mr. ABRAHAM LINCOLN, President of the United States, and the attempted murder of the Hon. William H. Seward, the Secretary of State; and that we most respectfully desire to convey to the American people and government, as well as to the bereaved widow and family of President LINCOLN, our warmest sympathy and heartfelt condolence on the sad and melancholy event, and for the irreparable loss they have sustained by such a vile, treacherous, and cowardly assassination.

That copies of the foregoing resolution be transmitted to the Hon. Mr. Adams, the American minister at London, the Secretary of the United States government, and the widow and family of the late Mr. LINCOLN.

[L. S.]   JOHN LAWLER, *Mayor.*
                                     JOHN O'BRIEN, *Town Clerk.*

TOWN CLERK'S OFFICE, WATERFORD, IRELAND,
Monday, May 8, 1865.

SIR: By direction of the right worshipful the mayor of Waterford, I have the honor to transmit to your Excellency a copy of a resolution unanimously adopted at a meeting of the citizens, in reference to the late melancholy event which unhappily deprived your government of its head.

Permit me, sir, to offer you the assurance of my sincere sympathy and condolence, which I feel in common with all classes of my fellow-citizens.

I have the honor to be your excellency's most obedient, humble servant,

GEORGE J. BRISCOE, *Secretary.*

The PRESIDENT OF THE UNITED STATES,
Washington, D. C.

City of Waterford, Ireland.

At a meeting of the citizens of Waterford, held at the Town Hall, on Thursday, the 4th instant, to express the sympathy and condolence with the people of America, shared in by all classes of the city of Waterford, the right worshipful John Lawler, mayor, in the chair—

Resolved, una voce, That we, the citizens of Waterford, feel called upon to unite in the very general expression of indignation and horror at the cowardly and most atrocious assassination of Mr. ABRAHAM LINCOLN, President of the United States, and also the similar brutal attack on the life of Mr. Secretary Seward; and we request that our chief magistrate, John Lawler, esq., will forthwith transmit to Mr. President Johnson the expression of these our sentiments, as well as of our deep and sincere sympathy with the people of America for their sufferings under so dreadful a national calamity as this heinous act has given rise to.

Resolved, una voce, That although at the risk of intrusion on her intense grief, we cannot allow ourselves to separate without offering to Mrs Lincoln our deep sympathy and sorrow for the very sad and sudden bereavement which she has endured in the loss of her husband, whom we have recognized to have been so good a man while holding the reins of the American government.

To attempt on our part to afford consolation would, we feel, be an impossibility; but we most humbly and prayerfully commend her to the care and protection of Him who alone can dispense full and adequate comfort and consolation under the severest circumstances of affliction, whether of a national or a domestic character.

By order of the mayor:

GEORGE J. BRISCOE, *Secretary.*

Town Clerk's Office, Town Hall,
Waterford, Ireland, Monday, the 8th of May, 1865.

ASSASSINATION OF PRESIDENT LINCOLN.

Resolutions passed at a public meeting convened by the mayor of Warrington, in pursuance of a numerously signed requisition, and held at the public hall, in Warrington, Lancashire, on the 2d May, 1865.

That we, the inhabitants of Warrington, view the atrocious assassination of his Excellency ABRAHAM LINCOLN, President of the United States, and the attack on the life of the honorable William Henry Seward, Secretary of State, with feelings of indignation and sincere sorrow. We feel assured that throughout the civilized world there can be but the one sentiment of horror at so revolting a crime; and, in common with the rest of our fellow-countrymen, we desire to express our deep sympathy with the people of the United States under this great national calamity.

That this meeting wishes to express its heartfelt condolence with the widow and family of the late President, and trusts that they may be sustained by a merciful Providence under their sad and mournful bereavement.

That our best thanks be given to the mayor for convening this meeting, and that he be requested to send copies of both resolutions to Mr. Adams, the American minister in London.

[L. S.]   PETER SMITH, *Mayor.*

At a public meeting of the inhabitants of the borough of Wakefield, in the county of York, held at the Court-house in Wakefield, on the first day of May, 1865, the worshipful the mayor in the chair, it was unanimously resolved—

1. That the inhabitants of Wakefield, in public meeting assembled, express their strongest hatred and grief at the horrible murder of the President of the United States of America, and also at the foul attempt to kill Mr. Seward and his sons ; and they hereby express their earnest sympathy with the American people and government in the loss they have thus sustained.

On the motion of Mr. Robert Bownas Mackie, seconded by Mr. Ralph Linfield, supported by the Rev. James Bewglass, LL.D.

2. That this meeting records its deep sorrow and heartfelt sympathy with Mrs. Lincoln and her family in their fearful affliction, caused by the cruel murder of Mr. LINCOLN.

On motion of the Rev. Goodwyn Barmby, seconded by Mr. William Kitching.

3. That copies of these resolutions be forwarded by the mayor to the honorable C. F. Adams, the ambassador of the United States to Great Britain, with a request to forward the same to the President of the United States, Mrs. Lincoln, and the honorable Mr. Seward.

On the motion of Mr. William Ralph Milner, seconded by Samuel Holdsworth, M. D., supported by Mr. William Thomas Lamb.

Resolutions passed at a meeting held by the inhabitants of the borough of Wolverhampton.

TOWN HALL, WOLVERHAMPTON,
May 5, 1865.

At a public meeting of the inhabitants of the borough of Wolverhampton, in the county of Stafford, held at the Town Hall on Friday, the 5th day of

May, 1865, John Ford, esq., mayor, in the chair, the following resolutions were unanimously passed :

That this meeting desires to express its detestation and abhorrence of the horrid crime of assassination by which the valuable life of the President of the United States has been sacrificed, and, on behalf of the inhabitants of Wolverhampton, to offer to the government and people of that country, and to the family of the late Chief Magistrate, its heartfelt sympathy in the great calamity that has befallen them.

That this meeting also desires to record the deep regret of the inhabitants of this borough at the attempted assassination of Mr. Secretary Seward, and their earnest wishes for his complete recovery.

That the mayor be respectfully requested to forward copies of the foregoing resolutions to the honorable E. M. Stanton, the Secretary of War at Washington, and also to the honorable C. F. Adams, the United States minister in London.

JOHN FORD, Mayor.

Woodstock, April 20, 1865.

May it please your Excellency : In accordance with a resolution adopted at a public meeting held yesterday in this town for the purpose of expressing horror at the committal of a deed which makes every civilized mind shudder, and sympathy for the bereaved family and the people in the neighboring republic in the lamentable and untimely death of ABRAHAM LINCOLN, President of the United States, by the hand of a cruel and relentless assassin, I beg, respectfully, to transmit a copy of the proceedings of said meeting, with the respectful request that your excellency may be pleased to transmit the resolutions to the proper authorities of the United States of America.

Yours, &c.,

T. McWHENNIE, Mayor.

His Excellency the Rt. Hon. CHARLES STANLEY MONCK,
Governor General of the Province of Canada.

Moved by the Rev. Wm. J. McMullen, seconded by the Rev. U. S. Griffin, and

Resolved, That we, the citizens of Woodstock, having heard of the assassination of ABRAHAM LINCOLN, President of the United States, do hereby record our sincere grief and inexpressible horror at the unnatural tragedy by which our neighbors of the American republic have been deprived of a President who has proved himself so well qualified to fill in such a national crisis the distinguished position to which his fellow-countrymen had a second time called him We deplore his untimely end by a hand so worthless, not only as a great public calamity, falling at a time so critical on a friendly neighboring nation, but also as a heavy blow inflicted on the cause of humanity itself, with which the name of ABRAHAM LINCOLN must ever be associated.

Moved by the Rev. D. McDermid, and seconded by the Rev. J. Lacy, and

Resolved, That the occurrences of Friday last, in the capital of the neighboring republic, by which the Chief Magistrate of the American people met his death at the hands of an assassin, prostrating in the gloom of bitterest despair an exalted family and bowing a nation in tears of deepest grief, evoke our heartfelt commiseration as well for the sorrowing family as the afflicted people. It is, therefore,

Resolved, That the ministers of the various churches in Woodstock be requested to utilize the occasion on Sabbath next by a service special and pertinent to the terrible calamity, and indicative of the abhorrence felt by this community at the commission of an act so revolting to all Christian men, and so subversive of that obedience to constituted authority which is the keystone of individual liberty.

WEDNESBURY LOCAL BOARD OF HEALTH,
May 5, 1865.

SIR : I am instructed by the above Board of Health, as representing the inhabitants of the town of Wednesbury, containing upwards of 23,000 population, to forward to you a copy of a resolution passed at the last meeting of the board held on the first of this present month of May, as follows :

Resolved, That this board expresses its detestation of the assassination of President LINCOLN, and of the brutal attack upon Secretary Seward, and also its sympathy with the people of the United States of America upon the great and irreparable loss they have sustained thereby.

I am, sir, your most obedient servant,
WILLIAM TANLY BAYLEY,
Clerk of the Board.

CHARLES F. ADAMS, Esq.,
Ambassador of the United States, London.

At a meeting of the council of the mayor, aldermen and burgesses of the borough of Yeovil, in the county of Somerset, held at the Town Hall on the 1st day of May, 1865—present, the worshipful the mayor in the chair—it was

Unanimously resolved, That the council desire to unite in the general expression of deep sorrow and indignation excited throughout the kingdom by the foul assassination of the President of the United States of America, and most respectfully tender to the government and people of that nation, as well as to the widow and family of the late President, an assurance of the sincere sympathy of the council in the unprecedented calamity which has befallen them.

And further, that the town clerk do transmit a copy of the foregoing resolution to his excellency the United States minister in London.

Resolutions passed at a meeting held by the inhabitants of the city of York.

At a public meeting of the inhabitants of the city of York, held at the Guildhall of the said city, on Thursday, the 4th day of May, 1865, the right honorable Edwin Wade, lord mayor of the said city, in the chair, the following resolutions were unanimously adopted, viz:

Moved by Mr. Alderman Richardson, seconded by the sheriff of York—

That this meeting desires to express its horror and detestation at the atrocious crime by which the life of Mr. LINCOLN has been sacrificed, and its warm sympathy with the American people in the loss they have sustained by the death of their distinguished President.

Moved by W. D. Husband, esq., seconded by A. E. Hargrove, esq.—

That this meeting desires to convey to Mrs. Lincoln its warm expression of sympathy and condolence at the bereavement she has sustained by the sudden and untimely death of her distinguished husband.

Moved by John Smith, esq., barrister at law, seconded by Henry Watson, esq.—

That copies of these resolutions be forwarded to Mr. Adams for transmission to the government of the United States and to Mrs. Lincoln.

EDWIN WADE, Mayor.

EXTRACTS FROM THE PRESS OF GREAT BRITAIN.

[From the Ardrossan and Saltcoats Herald and West Coast Advertiser, Saturday, April 29, 1865.]

IN MEMORIAM—ABRAHAM LINCOLN.

ABRAHAM LINCOLN is dead. The news has sent a thrill of horror through the country, for his death was the result of none of the ordinary causes which remove men from the scene of their labors, but he was foully and cowardly assassinated. In the hour of their triumph the northern States have been deprived of their trusted ruler—the genial, warm-hearted, kindly, honest man—the man, above all public men in the North, who did his duty from a sense of what he owed to his country; who prosecuted the war without vindictiveness, without vaunting, without threats of extermination, and without the smallest grain of self-glorification; who conducted his intercourse with other countries with rare sagacity and moderation; and who, but a few days before his death, now that the hard fighting he hoped was over, indicated in his own homely, kindly way, the best use which could be made of their recent great victories, and that was by showing mercy to their erring brethren. It is no matter for wonder that when intelligence was received of the great crime, New York was draped in black. In this country the act everywhere is viewed with deep abhorrence, and whatever the difference of views regarding the war, there is but one universal feeling of regret for the victim, and strong commiseration for a country deprived of its Chief Magistrate at the most critical crisis of its history. What, then, must be the public feeling in the industrious towns of New England, in the cities on the seaboard, all over the western States, and in the armies? Craftsmen and clerks, fishermen along the shores, toilers in the rich fields of the west, wanderers in the prairies—the working world of the States—were allowed but bare time to cast aside their holiday attire, put on to hold high festival for the downfall of Richmond. The news would reach them when still surrounded with much of the confusion and trappings of a merry-making time. It would come with the shock of a death immediately on a marriage; the enactment of a fearful tragedy after a farce. Would it be inhuman if the enraged feelings of the nation should find utterance in a call for vengeance? God grant they may not! That in this sad hour of trial the innocent may not be called upon to suffer for the guilty. But none, under the circumstances, need be surprised if they should. We remember Lucknow, and deemed the atrocities committed by Nina Sahib and his myrmidons as only too mercifully punished when the captured were blown from the cannon's mouth.

ABRAHAM LINCOLN has died with his work incompleted; but he has done enough to place his name next to that of Washington on the broad roll of his country's great men. Without any special training for government, he will stand second to none for having conducted the affairs of his country, both at home and abroad, with great firmness and sagacity. He was reputed a humorist, but his jokes were neither rude nor ill-natured; and although for the most part of his life he has followed manual employments, he so conducted himself in his personal intercourse with all classes and with all men whom curiosity or business brought to the seat of government, that he gained for himself general respect, if not admiration. He acted with extreme caution, and it would be difficult to point to a single act in his presidential career which was either mistimed or a mistake. He never vituperated the South; and after four years of protracted struggle to force their return to the Union, if he has not gained their confidence, he has commanded their respect. His name will ever be associated with the freedom of the slave, and the abolition of the cursed slave system in the States of America.   Like our own Sir Robert Peel and protective duties, he was slow in perceiving and acting upon the policy of emancipation as necessary to the triumph of the northern arms and the future well-being of his country. But when he did take hold of the principle, with the firmness inherent in his character, unhesitatingly he made it the chief ground on which he sought his late re-election to office, and the one point he was determined to insist upon in any reconstruction of the Union in which he was to play a part.   Although he was aware that an opposite policy might rally round him the democratic party of the North, and possibly change somewhat the sentiment of the South, and make them less difficult to manage when once the war is over, he solemnly accepted the nobler alternative.   It was he who exalted the issue of the war. He changed it from a war waged to enforce the return of the seceded States into the Union to one which, while accomplishing the end first contemplated, secured the emancipation of the negro race.   The blacks call him the "liberator," and as this, as well as the nation's martyr, his name will descend in the annals of his country's history.

It is needless to speculate on the effect which his death will have upon the war.   His assassination is more than a crime—it is a great mistake.   Apart altogether from the influence which the deed will have upon the public opinion of Europe, it will have an evil influence, we fear, upon the future of the South. It will not delay for a day the further prosecution of the war—Grant, and Sherman, and Sheridan are still alive to press the advantages already gained.   But the most humane and sagacious man in the cabinet has been taken away, and taken away when planning how best and most mercifully he could assuage the animosities of a four years' conflict, and reconstruct the Union on a broad and firm basis.   The reins of government are in other and quite different hands— men, we fear, less mercifully disposed to the instigators and fomenters of the rebellion.

[From the Ulster Observer, Belfast, Thursday, April 27, 1865.]

The startling and melancholy intelligence which reached our shores on yesterday is of a nature to overawe with terror and bow down with sorrow every humane and generous heart.   President LINCOLN has been coldly and deliberately assassinated.   At the same time and the same hour his sick and suffering Secretary of State was stabbed in the bed to which illness confined him ; and a double crime, unequalled in infamy and unsurpassed in atrocity, has been perpetrated at a time when consequences of fearful moment and importance are likely to throw into temporary oblivion the enormity of the guilty deeds that have produced them.

When war was fiercely raging, and the angry passions of desperate men, carried away by the whirlwind of unrestrained fury, made every hour pregnant with incalculable danger, even the terrible catastrophe which has now unexpectedly befallen the government of the United States would not then have taken the world greatly by surprise. When impiety raises its head crime rears aloft its blackened brow, and the iron does not clasp more suddenly nor cling more tenaciously to the magnet than do the patrons of a bad cause to the evil agencies by which all wickedness strives after its forlorn ends. But that such a catastrophe as has at once afflicted and disgraced the republic of America should have happened at a moment when all hearts were glad and full of joyous anticipations—at a moment when all danger was seemingly past and all enmity apparently on the decline—is a calamity as unexpected in its occurrence as it is likely to be terrible in its results. The fiery flash which shoots across the summer sky, heralding the thunder and the storm, is but a faint illustration of the sudden and terrible event which shrouds in gloom the joy and hope of a jubilant nation, and turns their hour of triumph into one of mourning and desolation. A few days ago and Europe heard with delight the intelligence that the bloody strife which for four years had been wasting the strength and energies of a noble people was drawing to a close. The civilized world regarded with admiration the magnanimity which rose, spontaneously and with the haughtiness of virtue, in the breasts of the northern people, and turned the occasion of victory into an opportunity for the display, not merely of mercy, but of brotherly sympathy and love. The feeling which welled up from the heart of the nation found a fitting recipient and fitting exponent in the breast and tongue of him who lies wrapped in a bloody shroud to-day; and there is no friend of liberty and humanity who will not sorrow over the fate, so sudden and so undeserved, of one who was a champion of both, and who is the latest and noblest martyr in their cause.

ABRAHAM LINCOLN has fallen at his post. The assassin's hand may take away life; it cannot wound that which is more precious and enduring than life—the reputation which is based on tried goodness and proven greatness. In this respect the admirers of the President of the United States have nothing to regret. His life has been long enough for its purpose—his end is conducive to his fame. With more reason and more truth than their author could claim he might, on the 4th of March (the day at first marked out by his murderers for his doom) have used the memorable words uttered by Cæsar in the senate, and declared that he had lived long enough for his own glory and his country's welfare. He was raised up in a season of danger to be a guide to the state in its difficulties and perils. With steady hand and unfaltering purpose he fulfilled his allotted task. Through good report and evil report; in the midst of the raging storm of battle, when all the land was convulsed and no ark of refuge appeared on the troubled waters; and at the no less dangerous crisis when the tide of victory set in, and vengeance, with glaring eye and bared arm, sought to lead the van of conquest, he was true to his duty, and true to that high mission from which his sense of duty derived its inspiration. Fearless in danger, unshaken in adversity, hopeful when the bravest all but despaired; calm amidst the wild, contagious excitement of success; as imperturbable in the general ecstacies produced by triumph as he was resolute in the general despondency produced by misfortune, he displayed, from first to last, the rare qualities of a good man and a wise ruler. His simplicity of character was mistaken for ignorance; his firmness of purpose was characterized as obstinacy; his perseverance was regarded as infatuation. Caricatured, reviled, and calumniated; sometimes hardly pressed by fortune, and sometimes hardly pressed by designing hostility, he rose, by the sheer force of his integrity and ability, above all opposition and enmity, and in the day of final triumph had his full share in the halo of glory which crowned the conquering arms of the republic. It was not, it is true, permitted him to see the end he would have most delighted to behold. His golden dreams of restored peace and union; of equality without reserve and justice without curtailment; of the full plenitude of righteous freedom poured out upon the land, have been extinguished in his blood; but, having watched through the night, and seen the lustre of the dawn, it may be said that he witnessed the consummation for which his soul longed. And who will say, looking to his zeal and labors, that, had he foreseen his doom, and that his life would be required for his country's triumph, he would not have willingly bowed to destiny, and, accepting his fate, have cheerfully, and with a *nunc dimittis* on his lips, paid the penalty, which is no less a sacrifice because the red hand of the cowardly assassin has exacted it?

It is such thoughts as these that afford to the sympathizing mind its highest consolation under such trying circumstances. LINCOLN has not fallen before the cause to which he devoted his life has been rendered secure. The victorious arms which crushed out the rebellion and drove slavery from the continent cannot be affected by the loss of one man, although he be the most important man in the state. It is the privilege of republics to be free from the perils which beset countries in which power is centred in an individual or a dynasty. The loss of the President of the United States is great, but the Constitution can repair it. A thousand daggers, successfully wielded by a thousand assassins, could not cut off the race of rulers. So long as the people exist, their ranks will supply the men necessary to conduct the administration; and in the present crisis, terrible and pressing as it is—so fraught with danger and calamity —those who have steadily watched the history of the past cannot doubt that the future will prove the stability of the institutions that have survived so many rude and awful shocks. Long after the present panic shall have passed away, and the peace and liberty which have been so dearly purchased shall have been consolidated on a basis too permanent for disturbance, men will look back on the last fearful act of the terrible tragedy that has drawn to a close, and see in it not a peril to the state, but the most valuable pledge of its safety. Great blessings are purchased by great sacrifices, and human suffering is the road to real glory. When President LINCOLN penned the sentence which liberated forever millions of his fellow-creatures from bondage, and gave a death-blow to slavery throughout the world, he did an act which entitled him to everlasting fame. That act is now sealed with his blood; and the consummation, so devoutly wished and prayed for, has received its crowning sacrifice.

But what will be said of the perpetrators and instigators of this horrible deed? If the life of the President appears, as it is, a precious offering on the altar of liberty, the crime by which it was destroyed stands as a hideous blot on the hideous cause in whose behalf it was accomplished. Slavery, born of murder, has ended its days in murder. The hands that gloried in wielding the lash have found congenial delight in the pistol and the dagger. The chivalry which was brave in the scourging of defenceless men and unprotected women, has given one more proof of its valor and spirit; and the assassin who levelled his pistol at the back of an unsuspecting man, filled with kindness and pity for him and his, and the assassin who, with lying tongue and stealthy step, plied his dagger on a defenceless invalid, are worthy companions of the heroes who swept the seas in quest of unarmed vessels, pillaged a defenceless village, and shot, in cold blood, its inhabitants, and made a daring attempt to bury in the smoke and flames of their burning homes the population, young and old, of a crowded and unoffending city. It may be that the assassination of President LINCOLN, and the attempted assassination of Mr. Seward, are solely attributable to the criminals directly engaged in them; but in the account which has reached us of these infamous and cowardly deeds, there is evidence of a conspiracy in which the character of the South is seriously implicated. The murderer of the President had fixed on the 4th of March for the perpetration of his crime. His accomplice refused to act with him until he received further instructions from Richmond. This points to a deliberate plot, formed in the confederate capital, for the perpetration of the foulest crime that human wickedness could commit; and, when it is borne in mind that the St. Albans raiders and the incendiaries who sought to fire New York boasted of having obtained their commission of guilt not merely in the confederate capital, but from men high in authority in it, there is justification for the suspicion that the latest act of southern vengeance has had more than the savage ferocity of individual desperation to prompt it. If this be so, and if, on investigation, it be found that the South, beaten in the field, has had recourse to the bandit's weapon and the assassin's snare, an infamy greater than even slavery has brought upon her will rest upon her name forever. It is melancholy to think that even one man could be found among a people claiming the character of a brave and gallant race to perpetrate, in the name of liberty and independence, a crime which strikes at the root of all justice and humanity. But tyranny is a bad teacher of morality, and traffic in human liberty leads, by a short road, to disregard of human life. It did not need this last awful crime to reveal to the world the ferocious spirit by which but too many of the defenders of slavery are actuated. There have been, heretofore, fitful gleams of the fierce truculence which the system could not fail to foster, and an indignant world will shudder at the excesses in which it has eventuated. But it is time to draw a veil over the terrible tragedy, and from the haggard South—wasted, worn, and infuriated—crying out like the Medea of the poet's creation, in mingled dread and resentment,

"Est-ce assez, ma vengeance, est-ce assez de deux mortes!"—

we invite the attention of our readers to the spectacle presented by the North, where fortitude and magnanimity, constancy and hope, are still in the ascendant. Nor can we for a moment doubt that, in spite of temptation, and in defiance of example, the people who have proved so noble in suffering will not yield to provocation, and that even the dead body of their murdered chief will not rouse within them the baser passions which he would have been the first to control. · It is a great trial for the people and armies of the North; but the greater trial, the greater will be the glory of the victory, which all friends of civilization must pray may be theirs.

[From the Bradford Review, Saturday, April 29, 1865.]

ASSASSINATION OF PRESIDENT LINCOLN.

Many a time during the past four years has mournful news been brought us from the North; but never during the whole of the war has any intelligence of such evil import for America arrived as that which sent a shudder of horror through the length and breadth of England on Wednesday afternoon. President LINCOLN was assassinated on the 14th of April. No remarks of ours can add anything to the intensity of feeling which those few words will excite throughout this nation and the civilized world. For ourselves, we record the event with the bitterest sorrow for the dead, the most burning indignation against his murderer.

From the scanty details which arrived on Wednesday it appears that the President was at Ford's theatre, Washington, on the evening of Friday, April 14th, with Mrs. Lincoln and some friends. A man suddenly appeared in the back of the box, fired at Mr. LINCOLN, and lodged a bullet in the back of his head. The assassin then leaped from the box on to the stage, brandishing a large knife, and escaped at the back of the theatre. The whole affair was the work of a moment, and the audience did not realize the fact that the President was shot till the villain had escaped from the building. Mr. LINCOLN was carried home insensible, and remained in that state all night. No hope was entertained from the first. About half past seven o'clock next morning he died.

About the same hour that the President's murder took place, a man came to Secretary Seward's house and demanded to see him, pleading pressing business. He was met by Frederick Seward, Mr. Seward's second son, and an Assistant Secretary of State. After some colloquy had taken place between them, the fellow suddenly struck young Seward with a "billy" on the head, injuring the skull, and striking him down insensible. He then rushed into the Secretary's sick-room, wounded Major Seward, his eldest son, stabbed two male nurses, who were also present, and next attacked Mr. Seward himself. He stabbed him repeatedly in the throat and face. He then effected his escape from the house. It is not certain that Secretary Seward's wounds are mortal, but it is feared that they will prove such.

This is the story of a deed scarcely paralleled in the world's history for brutal atrocity or wickedness. We look with fear and trembling for its results on the immediate future of America. The policy of President LINCOLN, resolutely persevered in during four long terrible years, had almost completed the suppression of a gigantic rebellion. So far, the President was successful; the first part of his great work was almost complete. But the second part was yet to be effected, and it presented difficulties absolutely stupendous. The settlement of the South—the organization of its society on an entirely new basis, the creation of a new system for it, the healing of the wounds caused by the war—this was the task which Mr. LINCOLN had to perform in his second term of office. Yet gigantic as this undertaking was, the people of the North, and the millions of well-wishers to America in this country and elsewhere, looked with trusting confidence to its adequate performance by the great, pure, single-hearted man who, with unequalled moral courage and resolute perseverance, had steered the vessel of the state through such a time of trial as the world had never before witnessed. And now he has gone—gone with his work but half finished—gone in the midst of another great crisis in his country's history, when the eyes and hopes of all were turned on him, as the man above all best calculated to conduct the nation through the critical time—gone, having lived long enough to see his country's enemies vanquished and broken, but falling before the Angel of Peace had spread her glorious wings over the land. ABRAHAM LINCOLN has died a noble martyr in the cause of America and of liberty.

Nor should we forget to recognize the heavy loss which the United States have, we fear, sustained in Mr. Seward. He was a statesman of the true American type, with some of the faults and very many of the virtues of his nation. For the people to be deprived of his services just when his great chief is struck down, and to lose him, too, in the same horrible manner, is a fearful intensifica-

tion of the calamity.   As we have said above, it is not certain that his wounds
are mortal.   We sincerely hope and pray that this may prove so.

The crime is one which stands in horrid pre-eminence above all ordinary
murders, and perhaps in its double brutality cannot be paralleled in history.
Who were the assassins?   What impelled them to the commission of the crime?
It is stated that the murderer of the President is a "rabid secessionist" named
Wilkes Booth ; and that his accomplice, who struck down Mr. Seward and his
son, is a man of similar character.   Whoever these cowardly wretches may be,
they have assuredly earned for themselves the eternal execrations of civilized
humanity.   We do not believe that there is a single man in all the South, even,
but will join in denouncing the deed, and in pursuing its perpetrators to the
expiation of their monstrous guilt   What will be the ultimate result of the
event it is impossible to say.   The people of the North are just now engaged in
working out a great problem, the settlement of which will have a mighty influence on the cause of liberty throughout the world.   How the death of President
LINCOLN will affect this settlement, how it will modify the future policy of
America, both toward the South and to other nations, what will be its effects
on commerce, it is hard to indicate; but certainly it will have a marked influence
in shaping these great questions.   Theh our of greatest trial for the North has
arrived.   Let us hope that the remarkable love of order which was displayed at
the election a few months since, and on other recent occasions, will restrain the
people, and enable them to pass through the crisis unharmed.   They deserve—
we have no doubt they will receive—the sympathy of all free peoples.

We confess that to us the blow is so sudden and so terrible that we find
ourselves, as yet, scarcely able to realize its truth, utterly incapable of tracing
its results.   We had a deep respect and love for this man, who, quietly and
unpretendingly, was doing a great work.   We attempt no estimate of Mr.
LINCOLN's character.   If he was not a man of brilliant qualities or showy
accomplishments, yet he possessed great grasp and force of intellect, honesty
and singleness of purpose, unsullied integrity, unshaken perseverance, firmness
in authority, an ambition utterly unselfish, the qualities, in short, which go to
make the truest and noblest patriot.   In him, the preserver and restorer of
the republic, the United States have lost a man worthy to rank with George
Washington, the founder of it.   There was a grandeur about his simple purity
and truth which never attaches to more selfish men, however great the height
to which they may attain.   The weapon of a vile and cowardly assassin has
deprived us of one of the greatest men of modern times.   England will mourn
for him, mourn with her kinsfolks across the ocean.

We of course presume that Mr. Vice-President Johnson will at once
become President.   In the first section of article II of the Constitution, it is
declared : "In case of the removal of the President from office, or of his death,
resignation, or inability to discharge the powers and duties of the said office.

the same shall devolve on the Vice-President." In accordance with this provision, Vice-President Tyler, in 1841, became President on the death of General Harrison, who died exactly a month after his inauguration. Again, Vice-President Fillmore, in 1850, succeeded President Taylor on his death. * * * We have the fullest confidence that the American people will be ready to assist their new head in contending with the difficulties of the position in which he is so suddenly placed.

Some facts respecting Mr. Johnson's previous career have been published, which tend to prove that although he may be rough and lacking cultivation, he is still a man of mental powers and of energy. He educated himself while working hard for a livelihood as a journeyman tailor; and from this humble position he rose, by dint of perseverance and political talent, to the high position he now holds. In 1835, when in his 27th year, he was elected to the Tennessee legislature. Eight years afterward, in 1843, he entered Congress, in which he served till 1853. He was then chosen governor of Tennessee, and was re-elected in 1855. In 1857, at the expiration of his second term of office, he was elected senator of the United states for Tennessee. Mr. Johnson was at that time a democrat and a slaveholder; but when the rebellion began, he liberated his slaves, declared for abolition and the Union, and has since adhered firmly to the cause he then took up. He is said to be a man of decision and daring; and in his military government of Tennessee, to which he was appointed by Mr. LINCOLN, he gave many proofs of his administrative power, and of some truly noble qualities.

Mr. LINCOLN was born in February, 1809, and was consequently in the fifty-sixth year of his age. Mr. Seward was born in Florida, in New York State, in July, 1801; he will therefore be in his sixty-fourth year.

[From the Carlisle Examiner, Saturday, April 29, 1865.]

THE CLIMAX OF INFAMY.

A fortnight this Saturday, when the startling news was flashed through Europe of the fall of Richmond, the telegraph was carrying to the remotest cities of the North the story of an appalling tragedy. The capital of the confederacy and the great army of the confederacy were things of the past. The former had been evacuated a fortnight—the latter had surrendered a week ago. The people were rejoicing in the overthrow of the rebellion which they had made such mighty efforts to crush, and on the advent of that reign of peace which was quickly coming with its attendant train of blessings. In the midst of their jubilations they were stricken with an awful blow. Their beloved President—he whose steady hand and wise brain had guided the reeling ship through the hurricane, and was but yesterday full of humane thoughts for its future career—lay dead, the victim of an infuriated assassin. Strange, is it not, that the last of the ten thousand bullets of the war should be reserved for him ? But so it was. The greatest war of any time was consummated by an act to which history reveals no parallel, and which the world will regard with feelings of unutterable horror. The death of Cæsar did not come with such a shock to the assembled senators as the death of the President to his own people and to ours. The Roman had grasped power, and made the liberties of his countrymen and of alien nations subservient to his own imperial will. He lived in an age when *Sic semper tyrannis* was a motto which commended itself to the highest minds. Even the assassinations of William of Orange, of the Russian Paul, of Kotzebue, of Marat, of Percival, were justified by rigid philosophers, whose teachings the world has happily discarded; and the still more recent attempt on the life of Napoleon was mitigated by many who regarded him as the author of Italy's thraldom. But Mr. LINCOLN had nothing in common with any of these high objects of the assassin's knife. He was a plain, homely man, whom the people had placed in power once, and whom they reinstated in power as the best evidence of their devotion. He had nothing of the tyrant either in his office or person. He did nothing of an extrajudicial tendency that was not sanctioned by the Constitution and by Congress. He neither rose to power on the burning ashes of a republic which he had destroyed, nor used a victorious army to enable him to override the laws of his country. As he was at the beginning, so he was at the end. He was sworn to execute laws which bound him equally with the prairie farmer or the city storekeeper. He would have been a traitor to his oath if he had not put those laws in force against those who sought to dismember the Union he was charged to defend. He did so with a magnanimity unparalleled in the history of civil wars, for no man suffered on the scaffold for domestic treason. He brought the war to an end, and was glad of the opportunity it afforded of issuing a liberal amnesty. His generous plans have been frustrated by an event which deprives the North of a noble ruler, and the South of its best friend.

It is almost needless to go over the terrible details of Mr. LINCOLN's untimely death. He went to the theatre, accompanied by Mrs. Lincoln and a couple of friends, on the evening of the day appointed for a national thanksgiving. That, probably, explains the reason why Good Friday should have been chosen for a visit to such a place of entertainment. He was there, in his private box, shot in the head by a ruffian who had slipped in behind. He was never afterwards sensible, and died next morning. On the same night, and about the same time, an accomplice of the murderer made his way into the house of the Secretary of State. Mr. Seward was in bed, slowly recovering from his late accident. The villain rushed to the bedside, and instantly gashed his victim's head and neck. Two of Mr. Seward's sons were summoned by the domestics. One was knocked down with a bludgeon, and the other so terribly wounded that he was reported dead.   One or two of the attendants were also so much injured as to leave little hopes of their recovery.   It is doubtful, also, whether Mr. Seward will get better.   It is said that Mr. Stanton, the Secretary of War, was marked by the assassins, and that General Grant, who was advertised to be at the theatre, but who did not go, was another expected victim.   One of the monsters escaped, but the other was said to have been captured.   They had come to Washington on horseback, and had left their horses at a livery stable.

The first question that arises on reading the particulars of this atrocious series of crimes is, were they the result of accident or premeditation—the freak of madmen, or the deliberate purpose of their employers ?

The madman and fanatic theory falls to the ground at once as worthless. No lunatics would have come to the city on saddle horses, separated each on his diabolical mission, and then run away.   A fanatical patriot would have bid defiance when his revenge had been accomplished.   Brutus justified his deed, and less men than Brutus, inspired with the desire to kill a tyrant, would have quietly stood their ground.   Not so the villains whose object was unquestionably to murder the entire cabinet.   Mr. Stanton charges the crimes against " the enemies of the country," and says that " evidence has been obtained that these horrible crimes were committed in execution of a conspiracy deliberately planned and set on foot by rebels under pretence of avenging the South and aiding the rebel cause."   It is further stated that the murders were to have been committed in March, but were postponed " until Richmond could be heard from."   Who were the conspirators at the rebel capital we shall probably learn before long, though they would have cunning enough to hide the written proofs of complicity· We have not the shadow of a doubt that the actual assassins were the wretched instruments of that slave power which offered rewards for the heads of the Washington government and plotted the murder of Mr. LINCOLN at Baltimore in 1860.   The chivalry which could starve Union prisoners to death, which could butcher negro captives, which could send out pirates to burn defenceless merchantmen, which could burn its own cities, which could break their solemn oaths and rob the public treasury, which could live in barbaric luxury on the spoils of human slavery, which could flog, imprison, and torture human beings as mere brutes, whose chief city was described by Mr. Russell, the Times correspondent, as " a hell upon earth," whose logical weapons for settling every dispute before the war were the revolver, the bowie-knife, and the pine fagot, who planned the burning of New York and murdered the citizens of St. Albans—we have no hesitation in ascribing to some of them the authorship of the black list of assassinations.   It is the worst job they have taken in hand since their famous treason.   It will rouse the soldiers and people of the North to exact a measure of vengeance which Mr. LINCOLN was the only man able to prevent.   They have sent to an untimely, but not an inglorious grave, a man whose simple, honest, grand life will place him next to Washington on the scroll of Presidents, and whose merciful nature would have stood between them and the block.

[From the Freeman's Journal, Dublin, Friday, April 28, 1865.]

The assassination of the President created intense excitement over England. He was respected by all, and among the working classes was as popular as he was in his own country. Simple in his habits—with no pride or pretension—accessible to all, and with a kind word for all—the warm friend of England, though from that country went forth some of the bitterest attacks on his person and character—his loss is the more deeply felt when the future is so uncertain and dark. *All lament the good man and great statesman. We doubt whether modern history contains a grander character than the humble lawyer of Illinois.* Others had more genius, and, perhaps, a deeper insight into the political future, though in that prescience which is one of the highest and rarest gifts of rulers ABRAHAM LINCOLN was far from deficient. *In high moral qualities he was unsurpassed by any public character of the age.* His hands were as free from corruption as his generous soul was indisposed to harshness. None of his enemies ever charged him with appropriating a dollar of the public money beyond his modest salary of four thousand pounds. *His public virtue shone out as brightly as his private worth, and both made him the best beloved man in the United States.* His loss is acutely felt in England and France, for his calm wisdom interposed a barrier against popular passions and mitigated national animosities. *He sent as ambassador to England one of the first and most conciliatory of American statesmen, and his choice has been proved by the esteem in which Mr. Adams is universally held, and the skill with which he has conducted the relations between the two countries in many a perilous crisis.* Whatever differences of opinion about the war may have existed in England, the horror which the murder excited has been universal. The House of Commons, as the representative of the people, testified, in a manner which will be appreciated in the United States, its sense of the calamity. At the sitting of the house on Monday members of all shades—English, Irish, and Scotch—liberal and conservative—signed an address of sympathy to Mr. Adams. Last night Sir George Grey stated that on Monday next he would move an address to the Crown, expressing the horror and condemnation the house felt at the assassination of the President, and praying her Majesty to convey that expression of feeling to the government and people of the United States. In the House of Lords Earl Russell, in graceful language, made a similar statement. Earl Derby wished to know whether in point of form such an address was regular. As to the substance, the noble earl concurred in the indignation and horror which the atrocious act excited among all ranks in England. The Queen will do her part. She entertains great regard for the American people, in which the Prince Consort shared. One of his last acts was to soften the tone of the despatches on the affair of the Trent, a fact stated by Earl Russell in the House of Lords. Her Majesty feels grateful for the universal hospitality the Prince of Wales received in the States, and we may be sure "the noble Queen," as Mr. Seward called her in his last speech, will convey to the American government and people more than a formal expression of the duty imposed on her by the lords and commons. Such displays are calculated to do much good. They soften resentments, soothe the sorrows, and draw closer the bonds of friendship between nations. The American residents in London, in whom the late President had almost frantic admirers—we write, of course, of the northern section— met yesterday to express their sentiments on the mournful occasion, and the Americans (who are still more numerous) in Paris will follow the example. One of the most honored bodies in England—the Emancipation Society— founded in the middle of the last century, and which saw the consummation of its labors in the abolition of slavery, assembled for a similar purpose. In Liverpool, Manchester, Birmingham, Leeds, Newcastle, and other great cities and towns, meetings are about to take place to address the American people. The common council of London—the first municipal body in the world—will also give expression to their feelings. We rejoice to find Dublin active on the mournful occasion. The working classes will meet this evening at the Mechanics' Institute. A preliminary meeting of gentlemen will take place to-day in Molesworth street, to prepare a requisition to the lord mayor to convene a meeting of the citizens on an early day.

[From the Dublin Evening Post, Saturday, April 29, 1865.]

THE MEETING AT THE MANSION HOUSE.

A requisition, signed by men whose names represent every shade of political opinion, has drawn together at the Mansion House to-day a meeting of the citizens of Dublin, presided over by the lord mayor, to give language to their detestation of the crime which has just widowed the United States, and to offer to the American people the expression of their heartfelt sympathy. Dublin, as might be expected, has borne itself worthily on this occasion. We do not think it has ever before happened that a common feeling did so completely unite governments and populations, official and unofficial bodies, hostile parties, and warring opinions, in one spontaneous and irresistible expression of sympathy with a nation, and of homage to a man. There were doubtless many at that meeting entitled, by conscientious conviction, to withhold their sympathies from the cause, noble as we think it, which the victim President has further ennobled and consecrated by his death. Whatever differences of opinion may have existed respecting the great struggle now all but terminated, there is but one universal sentiment of abhorrence for the damning infamy of the crime which has given so tragic a horror to its close. It is impossible, however, not to feel that every homage paid to the memory of the late President, and every message of condolence with the American people in the hour of their solemn grief sent forward to their government, more especially from Ireland, will go to swell the universal tribute of civilization, not less to the cause than to the man. There could not have been any divergence of opinion at the meeting, because no man, in express-ing his abhorrence of assassination and parricide, makes sacrifices of political sentiments or partialities; but we still feel that the expression of sorrow, indignation, and sympathy, perfectly unexampled in the history of the world for breadth and intensity, which will be conveyed to the people of the United States from the ends of the earth, will and must be interpreted as testifying to the greatness of the cause which, under the presidency of ABRAHAM LINCOLN, the American people had conducted to a glorious issue, and which, it is to be hoped, under the surviving inspiration of his firm but merciful policy, they will fix in abiding security.

[From the Dublin Daily Express, Saturday, April 29, 1865.]

The meeting convened for to-day is one in the objects of which all Irishmen, whatever their politics and whatever their predilections, will combine. The assassination of President LINCOLN is, without doubt, the most horrible catas-trophe which has occurred within the memory of man. Nay, it is even doubt-ful whether, in order to find its perfect parallel, we must not go back eighteen hundred years or more, and revert to the assassination of the first Cæsar. The feeling with which the intelligence was received when the first vague sense of incredulity had passed away was one of overpowering sorrow. It was as though there were some great danger impending, some great personal bereavement to be endured, some vague and indefinable horror to be undergone. The feeling was enhanced by the consciousness that we had not done justice to the character or fairly estimated the career of the murdered statesman. We were all of us familiar with the descriptions of the homely and ungainly man—the man that, born and bred a peasant, had carried, in some respects, the manners of a peasant into the lofty station which by his energy of character he had achieved. But we were only beginning to appreciate the homely common-sense which had guided him where mere astuteness would have failed—the homely honesty which, in a community where political honesty is rare, had secured him the name of " Honest Abe," the gentle, affectionate disposition which in the moment of triumph was ready to forget the past, and, in a broad spirit of philanthropy, to receive back his most deadly enemies as countrymen and friends.

The loss of President LINCOLN is great, but we must beware of exaggerating its greatness. The murdered statesman was not what is sometimes called "a necessary man." If the Emperor of the French were to be assassinated, his dynasty would in all probability be ended, France would be in a revolution, and all Europe would be shaken to its centre. The assassination of the President of the United States will, as far as we can forecast the future, be attended with no such terrible results; and the reason is easily to be discovered. In the one case the nation is the creature of the man, in the other the man was the creature of the nation. The Emperor is himself the empire. The French government is the realization of his ideal. He has impressed his individuality on France. The French people are not only ruled, they are governed, and animated, and impelled by him. The case was different with the murdered President. He was not a man of preconceived ideas and predetermined plans. Though he marched with unfaltering step at the head of American opinion, he can scarcely be said to have even lead it. The nation urged him onward. The national thought inspired, the national energy impelled him. The nation found in him its representative, its embodiment, its chief. And here is to be found at once his true merit as a statesman and the explanation of the fact that he was not indispensably necessary to the States. If he was not in advance, he was never in arrear, of public opinion. He yielded freely to the pressure from behind. Urged onward by the nation, he pushed towards the end he did not see with honest purpose and unshaken courage. But his range of vision widened as he advanced. Dangers disappeared and difficulties cleared before him. At the outset of his eventful presidency he was scared at the prospect of secession. Secession, he said, was never contemplated by the Constitution, and the Constitution gave him no power of coercing a seceding State. For the moment the strong man seemed paralyzed. But Sumter was taken, and the national spirit was aroused. The nation rushed to arms, and the President caught the spirit of the nation and took his natural position at its head. Then came dark days of humiliation and disaster. Army after army was defeated. General after general was deposed. But the heart of the President never failed him, and the nation's spirit rose higher the lower its fortunes sank. There was aroused throughout the North a firmer determination to sacrifice everything and to suffer anything rather then abandon its destiny and renounce its place among the nations. Then, for the first time, came the thought that the negro might be emancipated, not, it is true, in obedience to the dictates of religion, not in the interests of humanity, but as a military expedient to meet the stern exigencies of the war. The sentiment of the nation once more found expression in the homely words of its elect. If by maintaining slavery, he said, he could maintain the Union, he would maintain it; if by abolishing slavery he could maintain the Union, he would abolish it. His great, his only object was the Union. But it soon became apparent that the maintenance of slavery would not maintain the Union, and then arose a fierce, loud cry for abolition; a cry in which were mingled the discordant voices of humanity, and worldly wisdom, and political rancor, and unrelenting war. The time was at length come ; the President at length pronounced his emancipation proclamation, and slavery as an institution perished in the war which it had evoked. Then came the hour of triumph. Fortune had changed, the tide had turned, the hour of darkness had passed away. Then followed in quick succession the march of Sherman, the capitulation of Savannah, the storming of the lines before Petersburg, the capture of Richmond, the surrender of Lee, the virtual suppression of the great pro-slavery rebellion. But new tasks awaited the savior of the republic. The Union was to be reconstructed; a torn confederation of States was to be consolidated into a single nation. The element of division and disorder had disappeared with slavery, and the Constitution was to be remodelled to meet the exigencies of the new development of national existence. The pacification of the South, the determination of the future *status* of the blacks, the disbandment of the army, the consolidation of the debt, and the restoration of the finances—these and a thousand other labors awaited the calm sagacity and moderate counsels of the homely statesman. But his hour was come. He was to be cut off in the midst of his triumph. His country was to lose him. In one sense it is an irreparable loss; but the nation survives, though the individual is dead, and the high qualities which have carried the American people through the terrible ordeal of war will, we doubt not, carry it through the ordeal—less terrible, perhaps, but equally trying— of approaching peace. The spirit of the nation now, as heretofore, will animate the spirit of its statesmen and its generals, and mould them to its will. Grant is still at the head of the army of the Potomac, and the death of the President can exert no influence on the conduct of the war. Slavery perished in the lifetime of the murdered man, and cannot be resuscitated by his murder. The consolidation of the confederacy of independent States into a nation will be the work of time, but the process has commenced and cannot be arrested even by an assassination. The only peril with which America is really menaced by the catastrophe which has occurred is a reaction of popular sentiment against the South. The hand of the assassin has destroyed the man of moderate counsels and kindly heart, and those who have succeeded to his place have not, we fear, inherited his virtues. There is, in truth, peril. As for ourselves, the deplorable event which has occurred has been attended with at least one poor consolation and advantage. The universal horror which the intelligence of this foul assassination has evoked, the universal sympathy with the American people in its great bereavement which it has elicited, will go far in the mind of a generous nation to obliterate all those angry feelings which necessary policy and unfortunate accidents have engendered. And the report of the proceedings of the multitude of public meetings throughout the length and breadth of the land, such as that which will be assembled to-day in Dublin, will prove to the American people that, whatever may have been our want of appreciation of the living, we honor and revere the dead, and cherish the memory of the second Washington.

[From the Dublin Reformer, Saturday, April 29, 1865.]

ASSASSINATION OF ABRAHAM LINCOLN.

"ABRAHAM LINCOLN, the President of the United States, was shot by an assassin on the 14th instant, and died the following morning." This was the intelligence which reached Europe on Wednesday, the 26th instant, and never was greater consternation, horror, and grief exhibited than that which appeared in the faces of the millions who crowded the streets of European cities. * * Were it not that official information has been received confirming the diabolical butchery of a man equal in every respect to the immortal Washington, we should scout the statement contained in Reuter's telegram as a most wicked and clumsy imposture. Information subsequently received, however, has gone too far to leave room for any reasonable doubt as to the lamentable fate of this great patriot, statesman, and philanthropist. In an age teeming with intellectual genius and refinement, ABRAHAM LINCOLN, the humble woodman, was called to play an arduous, noble, and conspicuous part in the great drama of civilization and progress. The earliest days of his presidency were employed in raising gigantic armies, money, and all the munitions of war, on a scale never before contemplated or necessary; and which he had to draw from a people who adored peace, and who trampled on all the instincts of selfishness and individual aggrandizement, in order to raise their country to the highest pinnacle of social prosperity, political purity, and moral advancement.

No people in the world have yielded to greater lengths in the cause of peace than the Americans. "Peace with all, and to all," was their motto, until Jefferson Davis plotted for that brutal effusion of blood which has ended so characteristically in the cowardly and brutal assassination of ABRAHAM LINCOLN, the good and the great. This last savage act was only one of the many that were planned and enacted by Davis and his secession aiders and abettors. Davis disappeared with a carpet-bag the moment a signal reverse attended his man-stealing government. And after the massacre by General Lee of the remnant of the army he opposed to Grant's forces, we have the most substantial reasons for believing that southern leaders would not stop at anything, and it would be hard to entertain an idea that they are wholly free from complicity in the savage deed of blood which hurried ABRAHAM LINCOLN to an untimely but glorious grave   As lately as the month of February last General Lee is reported to have said that " he would startle the whole world," which he has not done since that date by his military successes; and let us hope that the death of President LINCOLN, and the attempted assassination of a no less trustworthy and indefatigable public servant, Mr. Seward, are not the tragedies " which were to startle the world." Happily for America, before LINCOLN fell, Grant had proved himself a man of honor, and a military commander of the highest genius, and Sherman, Sheridan, and Thomas had signalized themselves as men of the same stamp, whose names, if not respected for their valor by the South, will long be dreaded by the disturbers of the peace of a people who loathe and despise war, and seek greatness in the harmony and advancement of all nations. Before these men appeared on the stage ABRAHAM LINCOLN was left with armies shattered by intriguing and incompetent leaders, whose place could not be readily supplied. These armies were reorganized by LINCOLN in his cabinet, who never allowed the war and public spirit to flag, until men of honor and consummate skill as commanders led the desponding and almost panic-stricken troops of the North to victory as complete as the contest was great.

While engaged in directing great warlike operations, without leaders, except those who had not been fairly tried, but who have since shown themselves equal to the work, ABRAHAM LINCOLN held together the civil government intact, and left none of the duties of his high office undone. With the greatest power ever placed in the hands of a single man, ABRAHAM LINCOLN never took upon himself any unconstitutional power, but openly conveyed his views and opinions to the criticism of public opinion, and acted in strict accordance with the popular voice. He was an American, and he breathed only for America; and, horrible to think, the soil of America has drunk his blood. But great and deplorable as this calamity is, much as the sympathizers of the South may rejoice over this terrible deed, and secessionists may think that it will open the door to fresh tumult and bloodshed, the great republic, with all its giant powers, genius, and interests, will be safe, and handed down to posterity by Grant, Sherman, Sheridan, and Thomas. Four such men were never seen at any one time in a single battle-field, and if the armies of the North do not wreak their vengeance on Mobile and the other confederate positions still holding out against the North, it will be simply because they respect and honor the names of those commanders who have led them to victory, and delivered their country from further carnage. But before we conclude, we hope that the citizens of Dublin, and of the other large towns in Ireland, will follow the example of Liverpool, Manchester, and other cities in England, and hold meetings to express the horror and disgust with which the assassination of President LINCOLN has filled the public mind of Europe, and to offer the American people all the condolence they can bestow on a nation who has suffered so great and so bitter a loss.

[From the Caledonian Mercury, Edinburgh, Thursday, April 27, 1865.]

"GOD MOVES IN A MYSTERIOUS WAY."

It is with a profoundly solemn sense of the inscrutable wonder-workings of Providence that we announce to-day the assassination of President LINCOLN The news is harrowing in the extreme. It has struck Edinburgh, and will strike Great Britain and the world, with terrible impressiveness. It has come so unexpectedly, so unsuspectingly also, at the very time when the friends of the United States were rejoicing over the extinction of the great rebellion, and when even the opponents of the President and his government were reconciling themselves to fate and contemplating the immediate and peaceful winding up of the four years' war. It is no mere figure of speech, nor is it the slightest exaggeration, to say that when the telegraph first wafted the brief announcement through this city

> " The boldest held his breath for a time."

Nay, more, not a few strong men wept as children, or as if a common father had gone. Among all classes—chiefly, of course, among the friends of the North— there was evidenced a feeling of astonishment, grief, and pain, which could not have been greater had the Sovereign of our realm been taken to her last home. For ourselves, knowing as our readers do the intense admiration we have ever had of the calm, Christian, enlightened statesmanship of " honest old Abe," his firm and inflexible determination to abide by the Constitution of his country, and at the same time to blot out, through that Constitution, the infamous system and institutions of slavery, we feel bound to say that we have not language equal to the expression of our sorrow. President LINCOLN was, in our judgment, " the right man in the right place"—the appropriately chosen ruler of a great people. He was admirably adapted for the arduous work Providence gave him to perform ; and that he thoroughly performed that work during his first term of office no one can deny. Those who take the most comprehensive view of the magnitude of the struggle in which the federal government was involved, and of the conflicting interests to be consulted in that struggle, are most impressed when they reflect how he raised army after army and fleet after fleet ; how he equipped and supported them ; how he met, through sanitary commissions and Christian commissions, every requirement, temporal and spiritual, of which they stood in need; and how, *pari passu* with all this, he smoothed down the rough angles of old prejudices, curbed the impetuous demands of wild and revengeful passions, and led the people on from victory to victory to the goal of universal and unconditional emancipation. Like Moses, he saw the people in bondage ; like Moses, he sympathized with them in their afflictions ; like Moses, he led them through the Red sea out of the reach of their oppressors ; and, like Moses, also, just as he was beginning to realize a Pisgah view of the promised inheritance he is taken away. There are and there will be many who in no irreverential spirit and with no idea of improperly associating the human with the divine will feel and say, in something like the same language as did the disciples on their way to Emmaus, " We had thought that it would have been he who would have redeemed Israel." It has no doubt been the earnest wish of tens of thousands of British hearts, as well as tens of thousands and millions of others in the States and throughout the world, that he would be spared to complete the work he so nobly and so chivalrously begun ; that he would see the consolidation and regeneration of his country after its four years' terrible baptism of blood ; that he would long rule over a united, a happy, and a prosperous people, all the happier and all the more prosperous that both divisions of them had tested each other's courage and skill, and that in the ordeal the original ground of quarrel had completely disappeared. The Great Disposer of events has ordered it otherwise. He has allowed, no doubt for His own wise and excellent purposes, as He allowed the rebellion itself to break out, President Lincoln to fall—to fall, too, by an assassin's hand. Is it not mysterious ? Is it not confounding ? Is it not another illustration of the solemn truth that " His thoughts are not as man's thoughts, nor His ways as man's ways ?" We cannot do otherwise than bow to that Sovereignty whose wisdom is infinite, whose judgments are as the floods, whose hand no earthly power is able to restrain, and to whom no creature he has formed can or ought repiningly to say, " What doest thou ?"

In view of the terrible calamity involved in the death of President Lincoln, and the circumstances connected with it, the first question likely to arise is, " what effect will it have on the future of the war, or on the probability of an early and satisfactory peace ?" To this we believe we can give an answer which the future will demonstrate to be correct. The war will be proceeded with, and the work of reconstruction will go on as certainly, as surely, and as successfully as if the calamity itself had not occurred. The American people readily accommodate themselves to circumstances—adverse as well as favorable—and while they will mourn with sincerest sorrow the loss of one so eminently sagacious and good, they will also prosecute to its early and satisfactory completion the work he so faithfully and firmly showed them how to perform. Vice-President Johnson has already assumed the reins of office. He is a tried man, a more thorough abolitionist even than President Lincoln himself, and one also who will abate neither jot nor tittle of the national demands. Notwithstanding his unfortunate appearance at the occasion of his inauguration, he is believed in and trusted by the American people. He has done much good service to the state in his day ; he has displayed a firmness and fearlessness against the slaveholding faction which has endeared him to the thoroughgoing emancipationists of both north and south ; and while he will want the suave manner and genial temperament and long-sighted perspicacity of " honest old

Abe," he has other qualities which not less fit him to be the wise and powerful ruler of the destinies of a great nation passing like refined gold out of a furnace of fire. We have no doubt he will rise to the dignity of his position and the responsibilities of his office, and that, carrying out the typical idea to which we have given expression, he will perfect, like Joshua with the judges, what Moses was not permitted to perform. Rulers die ; nations live ; God reigns. This is our comfort and consolation in the midst of sudden calamities, overwhelming the spirit and drowning the soul in grief, and this is especially our consolation in the contemplation of the awful end of the father of a regenerated people.

We do not and we will not discuss at present—because we have no certain information on the subject—the circumstances originating the assassination of President LINCOLN. It may have been the result of a southern conspiracy—assassination being a crime almost unknown in the north, and unfortunately too well known in the south—or it may have been the work of a madman. The former seems to us much more likely, especially when the attempt on Mr. Seward the same night, and in his suffering chamber, is taken into account. We prefer, however, to await details and proofs. It is to be regretted that the genial, confiding, honest old man should have exposed himself unprotected at a time when " southern chivalry" must have been writhing under its terrible defeat. If it turn out that his death has been the result of a plot on the part of the southern leaders, then, need we say, it will be atoned for by a sweeping revenge.

[From the Gateshead Observer, Saturday, April 29, 1865.]

One of the foulest deeds in the annals of crime has been committed at Washington. President LINCOLN, sitting in the theatre, accompanied by his wife, was shot to death on the 14th instant by an assassin, who unfortunately escaped, and had not been apprehended when the Nova Scotia, which reached Liverpool on Thursday, left New York.

No wonder that so dreadful a murder, so far as Mr. LINCOLN was concerned, and so great a calamity for the country which he governed with an ability which even his adversaries have not been the last to admit, has aroused the indignation of every people to which its perpetration has been made known, and warmed even the coldest heart into sympathy with her who has been deprived not only of a husband, but of one whose management of state affairs has illuminated a brighter page in the history of his country than any which has been emblazoned since the death of Washington.

The crime, indeed, the more it is looked at, intensifies in atrocity, for Mr. LINCOLN, at the moment of his assassination and in the hour of victory, it is well known, and as we always believed would be the case, was desirous of securing peace with the least possible humiliation to the defeated party, and with a view to an impartial promotion of the interests of every State of the Union, the restoration of which was the great object of his incessant labor, and as he (we believe most honestly) believed the one thing needful to secure the power and happiness of the republic.

The utter hopelessness of further resistance in the South had been proved by the surrender of General Lee, with all that remained of his army, to the federal commander. The terms given by the victorious general, Grant, to his gallant, although unsuccessful opponent, were of themselves an indication of that clement policy on which the President is said to have been resolved. . There was no humiliation—no captivity for either officers or men—all the honors of war were allowed by the victor, and the *parole d'honneur* of the vanquished was considered sufficient security that no resumption of arms would be resorted to by soldiers whose conduct in the field had secured them respect both in the cabinet and the camp of the conquerors.

The ruffian, in striking down the President, struck at the same time at the heart of a nation desirous of forgetting past differences and of changing a bloody war into an everlasting peace. He was the murderer not merely of the President, but of that disposition towards forgiveness which was beginning to manifest itself in almost every department and every class in the federal States. Indeed, it is difficult to say whether the deed ought to be most bitterly execrated in the northern or in the southern States The death-wound of the President, it is true, laid a great man low, but it produced a paroxysm of anguish at the same time in every city, nook, and corner of the vast territories which he ruled, and, we have not the least doubt, in those also which were endeavoring to secure their independence. Murder, in its ordinary acceptation, is a thing unknown to honorable warfare; and as such, we verily believe, this sad and sanguinary act will be regarded in the Confederate States.

It is to be deplored that so great a criminal as Wilkes Booth (as the wretch is called) even temporarily escaped. That he will succeed in evading justice for any considerable length of time we cannot believe. No community, even of literal savages, would harbor such a monster. The mark of Cain will be upon him, and we fain trust will facilitate his apprehension. We only hope that he may have gone to some Confederate State, because we cannot but believe that, despite all the asperities of which civil strife has been productive, he would in that case be immediately given up to the federal authorities; and the doing so would tend to dispel suspicions, which in some quarters seem to prevail, that the murder was planned, not by one or two individuals only, but by the government of the southern confederacy—an atrocity of which we believe the latter to be utterly incapable.

That there were two persons bent on murder on the 14th is evident, because, while Booth was shooting Mr. LINCOLN, another ruffian, whose name is unknown, and who has also escaped, was endeavoring to stab to death Mr. Seward, although lying in a state of great suffering, consequent upon a recent serious accident; and not only was the life of Mr. Seward jeopardized, but his son was grievously wounded by the assassin's dagger while endeavoring to protect his father against the man of blood. Indeed, it was at first reported that young Seward had died of his wounds, but this has been, since, contradicted. We sincerely hope that both father and son may yet live to serve their country and earn its gratitude.

It is an eminently creditable as well as consolatory fact that, in every portion of the United Kingdom, the news of the bloody scene in the Washington theatre produced a thrill of horror and indignation, and that all classes, from the Queen on her throne to the very humblest of her subjects, are desirous of testifying to the people of America their detestation of the crime and their sympathy with those whom the assassin's dagger has deprived at once of a father, a ruler, a statesman, and a friend.

In both Houses of Parliament, on Monday, an address to the Crown will be moved, expressive of sorrow and indignation at the murder of the President, and praying her Majesty to convey that expression of feeling to the American government.

The corporation of London and the great commercial cities and towns of the kingdom have already taken steps for uniting with the lords and commons in giving expression to their feelings on this sad occasion; and there is every reason to believe that few communities of any magnitude or importance will fail to follow the example, for it is one of those special occasions when the hearts of nations throb in unison, and when, in addition, as in our case, the impellent forces of a common origin raise from the lowest depths the well-springs of sympathy, commiseration, and affection.

[From the Glasgow Herald, Monday morning, May 1, 1865.]

The profound and universal impression which the assassination of Mr LINCOLN has made upon the public mind leads us to believe that the people of Glasgow would be glad of the opportunity, which is likely to be afforded them, of giving utterance to the horror and indignation with which this diabolical act has inspired them, and of expressing the profound and painful sympathy which is felt in this dark moment for the people of the United States, on whom this terrible event has fallen as a national calamity. It is a dark and portentous event for the South as well as for the North. It is almost impossible, indeed, to conceive anything that could have occurred more disastrous to southern interests. Southern and pro-southern people will probably shudder at the deed and execrate the doer as much as we do ourselves, and as we see they have already done to some extent in Liverpool. But, unfortunately, the act connects itself by an inevitable link with the political situation; the simultaneousness of the murderous assaults on Mr. LINCOLN and Mr. Seward indicates a conspiracy; and it is difficult for such deeds done on behalf of a cause to be entirely dissociated from that cause itself. We can only pray God that in the present case it may be done, and that the people of the North, who have, even in the exultant hour of triumph, displayed such a spirit of noble and unexampled magnanimity, may be able to withstand the exasperating influence of this accursed deed, and not allow it to change the voice of kindness and conciliation into a cry for indiscriminate revenge. . Much will depend on the way in which the deed is regarded by the people of the South. Were it for a moment conceivable that the southern people would accept it as their own—nay, that they would regard it otherwise than with utter detestation and abhorrence; then, indeed, their cause would deserve execration, and their conflict—beginning with slavery and ending with assassination—would go down to future ages branded with an infamy that all the genius of its champions and all the devotion of its advocates would do nothing to remove. This, however, is inconceivable. We are perfectly satisfied that the South will repudiate this foul deed with indignation, and that southern sympathizers here would be prompt to participate in any public act which would express the abhorrence with which it is regarded in this country by people of every class and of every shade of political opinion.

Under these circumstances, we are not disposed to take such gloomy views as many are taking of the probable consequences of this sad event. The conduct of the North during the whole course of this long and desperate struggle inspired us with a strong and unwavering faith in her good sense, in her self-control, and in the moral grandeur and beneficence of her aims. Mr. LINCOLN was not the leader so much as the fit representative of the great nation that elected him. When he did his best, as he ever did, to preserve the most frank and amicable relations with this country, even under provocation and abuse, of which we believe the authors to be now heartily ashamed; and when, in the very hour of federal triumph, his language was full of mercy and conciliation, he was acting, not upon his own sentiments alone, but upon the magnanimous sentiments of the whole northern people. That people, inspired by the same generous and friendly feelings, still remain, though LINCOLN, who represented them so nobly and so well, is gone. His fall is a loss to the world; it is a loss inflicted under most exasperating circumstances to them; but it will not—we are satisfied that it will not—change their policy. They have already shown themselves most ready to forgive in the very moment when they were most able to avenge; and, therefore, we are not without a strong and earnest hope that, even should the South regard the assassination of Mr. LINCOLN with more callousness than we anticipate, the people of the North will crown their recent acts of magnanimity and forbearance with a moral victory grander and more triumphant than the capture of Richmond itself.

In the mean time let us unite in expressing our deep and genuine sympathy with the people of the United States in their bereavement, and the indignation and horror with which we look upon the act that has deprived them of their constitutional head.   Since the death of Prince Albert, we know of nothing that has filled this nation with such deep and universal sorrow.   Poor ABRAHAM LINCOLN—"honest Abe"—the simple, the noble, the true-hearted ; as blunt and unaffected, as simple-hearted, kindly and playful in his high position as President of the United States as ever he had been when, in earlier days, he drove his team through the forests of Illinois !   The people of this country had all come to love him.   Even those who could or would see nothing in him at first but the quondam rail-splitter and mule-driver, came in the end to recognize the native grandeur and simplicity of his character, and the fitness there was in this blunt, unassuming man to head a great people in passing through a national crisis, and doing battle for a higher civilization.   There was not, we believe, one true British heart in these dominions that did not feel a pang of deep and unaffected sorrow mingling with the horror that was excited by the intelligence of Mr. LINCOLN's violent death.

If there ever was a moment when we as a people could unite with deepest sincerity in expressing our sympathy with the people of the United States, it is now.   Let us have an address of condolence prepared, in which the deeply agitated feelings of the community could find expression.   Were such an address prepared, and a proper opportunity afforded, we believe it would be signed by the whole population of this city.   Let something of this sort be done before the time for it is gone.   Let us join hands with our brethren in America, and mingle our tears with theirs over the grave of this simple, heroic man, who has brought the two nations nearer to each other than they were, and who has now fallen, honored and lamented by them both.

[From the London Morning Post, April 27, 1865.]

The startling intelligence which has reached us from America will excite but one sentiment in the minds of all, no matter what their political predilections.   Northerner and southerner, European and American, slaveholder and abolitionist, must equally concur in reprobating the dastardly crime which has just been consummated.   The President of the United States of America has, in the moment of what he at least considered to be victory, and at the very instant when he had reason to believe that the gigantic enterprise to which he devoted himself was on the point of being crowned with success, fallen by the hand of an assassin.   The event is so astounding that it is with difficulty we can bring ourselves to realize its occurrence, much less to estimate its consequences. It is but a few short days since the great and crowning events of the civil war took place, since Richmond was evacuated and the army of Virginia laid down its arms, and since Mr. LINCOLN, boasting once more to be not only *de jure* but *de facto* President of the entire American republic, proclaimed it to the civilized world, and appointed a day of general thanksgiving to inaugurate the commencement of a new and happier era. On Sunday, the 9th of the present month, General Lee capitulated; on the following day Mr. LINCOLN congratulated his fellow-citizens on the happy issue of the arduous struggle in which they had been so long engaged, and besought their co-operation in that no less arduous work of reconstruction to which he proposed devoting the second period of his official career, and on the Friday following he was brutally murdered. In the annals of history there are to be found but too many instances in which the chief magistrate of a state has fallen by the assassin's hand, but we doubt if there is one which, by its surrounding circumstances, will retain a deeper hold on the memory of posterity than the murder of the American President. What Mr. LINCOLN might have been, and what he might have accomplished, must always remain matters of speculation; but that he should have been arrested midway in his career, and that the wishes of a great nation should be frustrated by the will of a rabid fanatic, points a moral of the futility of all human projects, which, however trite, is not uninstructive. At the very time when most persons would have concurred in approving the policy of the northern States in again electing Mr. LINCOLN to the presidential office, and would have gladly seen him endeavor to reconstruct the edifice which has been so cruelly shaken, he is suddenly carried from the scene. " The king is dead. God save the king." As it is in monarchies, so it is in republics. The same mail that tells us of the assassination of Mr. LINCOLN informs us of the accession of his successor.   *   *   *   *   *   *   *   *   *

The circumstances under which the murder of Mr. LINCOLN took place may be gathered from an official report published by Mr. Stanton on the morning after the commission of the crime; and it is not the least remarkable circumstance attendant on the extraordinary event that at the same time that Mr. LINCOLN was shot down in a theatre, Mr. Seward, the Secretary for Foreign Affairs, should be stabbed in the sick-bed to which he had for some days been confined by a recent accident. On the evening of Good Friday Mr. LINCOLN, accompanied by his wife, another lady, and a Major Rathburn, visited the theatre, and at about half-past nine o'clock a man suddenly entered the box in which the President was seated, and before any one was made aware of his intention discharged a pistol at the President's head. The shot took fatal effect, the ball penetrating the back of the head, and probably lodging in the brain. After effecting his object the assassin is said to have leaped from the box on to the stage, and then to have escaped. While this scene was being enacted at the theatre another assassin succeeded in obtaining an entrance to Mr. Seward's house under the pretence of pressing business, and inflicted on the Secretary wounds which it was believed would prove fatal. Mr. Seward's son, who was in an adjoining room, having hastened to his father's assistance, was struck down by the murderer, and is reported to have since died. In this instance, as in that of the assassination of the President, the ruffian succeeded in effecting his escape. Mr. LINCOLN remained insensible until his death, which took place the following morning at half-past seven o'clock. At eleven o'clock Andrew Johnson took the oath of office, and was duly installed as President of the United States.

The first sentiment, after that horror which will be excited in the minds of most persons, will be one of surprise that such crimes as those we have recorded should have been committed. The late President had for an enemy every man who took up arms or was ready to take up arms for the southern cause. But they were open enemies, and, as the whole history of the civil war has shown, they were chivalrous enemies. We should not have believed it possible, nor can we believe it now, that in the entire mass of the southern population a single man would be found who would have committed the crime which has aroused the indignation of the entire world. We do not mean to say that a southerner may not be a murderer just as an Englishman may be, but merely that we fail to discover the motive which would actuate a southerner to this particular crime. Mr. LINCOLN could not be held individually accountable for the cruel war which has made so many regions of the confederacy desolate, and none who took the trouble of considering the matter would fail to perceive that that war would, in all probability, have equally run its course if another individual of the same political opinions had been elected President four years ago, or if Mr. LINCOLN had died at any period subsequent to his accession to office. The assassination of Butler in New Orleans would have been perfectly intelligible; but that of Mr. LINCOLN in Washington, at the very moment when the war had to all appearances come to an end, is apparently motiveless. The circumstance, however, that an attempt, and probably a successful one, was made to murder Mr. Seward at the same time, shows that the double crime was the result of a carefully organized scheme. We must await the arrival of the next mail to be made apprised, as we hope we shall be, of the capture of the assassins, and then perhaps we may learn the circumstances under which they were led to commit so terrible a crime.

[From the London Evening Standard, April 27, 1865.]

The startling news which was yesterday received from America is such as to throw into the shade even the tremendous catastrophe of the fall of Richmond and the surrender of Lee's army. Mr. President LINCOLN has been assassinated,

and is dead.   Mr. Seward has been stabbed, and is reported in a hopeless state.
Mr. Andrew Johnson is President of the United States.   The blow is sudden,
horrible, irretrievable.   Never, since the death of Henry IV by the hand of
Ravaillac—never, perhaps, since the assassination of Cæsar—has a murder
been committed more momentous in its bearing upon the times.   In the very
height and plenitude of his triumph—at the moment when all his hopes
seemed fulfilled, all his labors rewarded, when the capitulation of his most
powerful enemy had placed within his grasp that prize of empire for which
he had so long and so earnestly striven—ABRAHAM LINCOLN was smitten to
the earth by a dastardly assassin, who shot him through the head from behind.
The commander of armies that the Macedonian or the Roman might have
envied; the leader in the most gigantic struggle of the nineteenth century;
the ruler, or likely soon to be the ruler, of the most populous, and, in the opinion of many, the mightiest nation in the modern civilized world; the man who
had risen from low estate to a power as vast as was ever wielded by a mortal,
whose recent success has astonished and bewildered the universe, is now
reduced to some poor six feet of common clay.   All the texts and sermons of
the mutability of human affairs, and the instability of life, pale into insignificance before this tremendous commentary.   Much as we have condemned the
attitude of the American people during the civil war, and though we have, from
the first, opposed the policy and censured the acts of the late President of the
United States, we must sympathize with the nation which is widowed by this
sudden bereavement.   Now that he is dead, the good qualities of the unfortunate
LINCOLN seem to come into the foreground.   We remember his honesty and
his manliness; we do justice to his consistency; we give him all praise for the
spirit of conciliation which he has shown ; for his refusal to be borne along by
the sanguinary counsels of his friends ; we make some allowance for his frequent
and untimely levity ; we almost excuse his obstinacy in the prosecution of the
war.   Such, we are persuaded, will be the sentiments of every right-minded
Englishman ; and they will be shared in by the vast majority of the confederate
people.   The men who shot LINCOLN and Seward were probably lunatics, or
men who had been crazed by their misfortunes in this terrible war.   There is
no reason to suppose that there was any southern conspiracy to take away the
life of the only man in the northern government who was disposed to deal
leniently with the South.   The confederates, as a nation, are too magnanimous
to plan or approve of such a cowardly method of revenge.   Booth, who killed
LINCOLN, when he jumped upon the stage and shouted " *Sic semper tyrannis*,"
made an unworthy use of the proud motto of the State of Virginia.   The
wretched murderer has been caught, it is said, and will doubtless soon meet
with the fate which he so richly deserves.   But the most ignoble means may
work a stupendous result.   The dagger or the bullet, in the hand of the feeblest
worm in human shape that crawls the earth, may alter the fate of nations or

turn the tide of time. The unfortunate President, shot as he was through the brain, went unwarned and unprepared to his account. No portents accompanied the deed—no omens foretold it. No soothsayer bade him beware of the fatal 14th of April. He is gone; the pilot is gone. His country is left to toss in the sea of a dismal anarchy, a revolution of which no man can presume to foretell the issue. * * * * * * *

[From the London Times, April 27, 1865.]

The American news which we publish this morning will be received, throughout Europe, with sorrow as sincere and profound as it awoke even in the United States themselves. Mr. LINCOLN has fallen at the hands of an assassin, and Mr. Seward has too probably shared his fate. While the President was sitting quietly with his wife and some friends in a private box at a Washington theatre on Friday week, he was shot by a man who entered the box under a treacherous pretence of public business; and, almost at the same hour, an accomplice of the assassin, with similar treachery, forced himself into Mr. Seward's sick-room and stabbed the Secretary of State four or five times in the face and throat. The President died the next morning. Mr. Seward, when the mail left, lay almost beyond hope of recovery; and his son, who acted as his secretary, in attempting to withstand the murderer of his father, was wounded to his death. Deeds of such atrocity cover their perpetrators with everlasting infamy, and discredit the cause they are presumably meant to serve. We trust it will appear that the crimes of Wilkes Booth and his accomplice were conceived and executed in concert with no one but themselves. The South, broken and defeated, could receive no possible benefit from the removal of Mr. LINCOLN and Mr. Seward; the too probable effect of the crime is an accession of madness and anger, rendering all schemes of reconstruction impossible. On the other hand, the waving of a knife before the affrighted audience at the theatre, and the " *Sic semper tyrannis*" pronounced by the assassin, indicate the vanity of men willing to immortalize themselves, like Eratostratus, though the world should perish. Unjust as we believe it to be, the confederate cause will not escape the dishonor cast upon it by the wanton murders of Mr. LINCOLN and the Secretary. The admiration won by the long and gallant defence of Richmond will be lessened; the memory of Lee's lofty bearing and Jackson's deep religious feeling will be obscured by the atrocities committed in the name and on behalf of the South. Arson in New York; theft, under the pretence of war, in Vermont, and assassination in the capital, dim the lustre of a four years' resistance to superior forces, and of many a well-fought field in Virginia.

The critical condition of affairs in America; the position of the southern States at the feet of their victorious antagonists; the gigantic task of reconstruction which must be undertaken by the political leaders of the North—all tend to exalt our estimate of the loss which the States have suffered in the murder of their President. But it would be unjust not to acknowledge that Mr. LINCOLN was a man who could not, under any circumstances, have been easily replaced. Starting from a humble position to one of the greatest eminence, and adopted by the republican party as a makeshift, simply because Mr. Seward and their other prominent leaders were obnoxious to different sections of the party, it was natural that his career should be watched with jealous suspicion. The office cast upon him was great, its duties most onerous, and the obscurity of his past career afforded no guarantee of his ability to discharge them. His shortcomings, moreover, were on the surface. The education of a man whose early years had been spent in earning bread by manual labor had necessarily been defective, and faults of manner and errors of taste repelled the observer at the outset. In spite of these drawbacks Mr. LINCOLN slowly won for himself the respect and confidence of all. His perfect honesty speedily became apparent, and, what is perhaps more to his credit, amid the many unstudied speeches which he was called upon from time to time to deliver, imbued though they were with the rough humor of his early associates, he was in none of them betrayed into any intemperance of language towards his opponents or towards neutrals. His utterances were apparently careless, but his tongue was always under command. The quality of Mr. LINCOLN's administration which served, however, more than any other to enlist the sympathy of bystanders, was its conservative progress. He felt his way gradually to his conclusions; and those who will compare the different stages of his career one with another will find that his mind was growing throughout the course of it. The *naïveté* with which he once suggested to the negroes that they should take themselves off to Central America because their presence in the States was inconvenient to the white population, soon disappeared. The gradual change of his language and of his policy was most remarkable. Englishmen learnt to respect a man who showed the best characteristics of their race in his respect for what was good in the past, acting in unison with a recognition of what was made necessary by the events of passing history. But the growth of Mr. LINCOLN's mind was subject to a singular modification. It would seem that he felt himself of late a mere instrument engaged in working out a great cause, which he could partly recognize, but which he was powerless to control. In the mixed strength and weakness of his character he presented a remarkable contrast to Mr. Seward, who was his coadjutor for more than four years, and who must, we fear, be reckoned his fellow victim. The Secretary of State, long before his elevation to office, was a prominent citizen of New York. More than a quarter of a century ago he was the governor of that State, and for twelve years he represented it in the Senate. In the Empire City and at Washington he had attained a culture which the Illinois lawyer never acquired. But the experience of the politician had, perhaps, weakened the independence of Mr. Seward's character, and he never inspired the same confidence as his chief, because it was not known by what influences his course might not be modified.

What may be the actual destiny of the United States deprived of the guiding hand of Mr. LINCOLN and of the experience of Mr. Seward no one would venture to foretell.   *   *   *   *   *   * The fate of a nation hangs in the balance, and we wait with anxiety to see which way it will turn.

[From the London Daily News, April 27, 1865.]

ABRAHAM LINCOLN.

*   *   *   *   *   *   *   *   *   *   *   *

To trace the events of Mr. LINCOLN's administration would be to write the history of the great revolution through which the United States have passed during the last four years, a task which does not come within the scope of this article. It would be foolish to pretend that Mr. LINCOLN foresaw what no one could foresee, the extent and character of the work before him when he assumed the presidency. It is sufficient if it can be truly affirmed that he brought to his duties qualities and a character which fitted him to grapple with the tremendous difficulties of his position as they arose. Mr. LINCOLN was thoroughly in sympathy with the interests of the American people, and completely imbued with reverence for those ideas of justice, freedom, and humanity which are expressed in American institutions. His first words on taking office were suited to develop that trust of the nation in itself, without which it was impossible to hope to sustain it in a war begun and carried on by an aristocracy based upon the denial of human rights. On his way to Washington in February, 1861, he said, at Indianapolis : "Of the people, when they rise in mass in behalf of the Union and of the liberties of their country, truly it may be said, 'The gates of hell cannot prevail against them;'" and he concluded his address with the words . "I appeal to you again to constantly bear in mind that with you, and not with politicians, not with Presidents, not with office-seekers, but with you, rests the question, shall the Union and shall the liberties of this country be preserved to the latest generation?" Again and again, in the short speeches made by him during his journey to Washington, he dwelt on this idea. "It is with you, the people, to advance the great cause of the Union and the Constitution." "I am sure I bring a heart true to the work. For the ability to perform it, I must trust in that Supreme Being who has never forsaken this favored land, through the instrumentality of this great and intelligent people." And in an address to a returning Ohio regiment delivered last August, he said : "I wish it might be more generally understood what the country is now engaged in. We have, as all will agree, a free government, where every man has a right to be equal with every other man. In this great struggle this form of government and every form of human right is endangered if our enemies succeed. There is more involved in the contest than is realized by every one ; there is involved in this struggle the question whether your children and my children shall enjoy the privileges we have enjoyed." These were in Mr. LINCOLN's eyes the principles by which alone the republic could live.; it was by them that slavery was to be stifled and overthrown.

Mr. LINCOLN's political course in reference to the rebellion was based on the doctrine laid down in his first inaugural address: "I hold that in contemplation of universal law and by the Constitution the union of these States is perpetual." It has often been said that his successive measures against slavery were only adopted for political purposes, and to save the Union. This may be admitted with the explanation that in Mr. LINCOLN's view only the necessity of saving the Union gave him a warrant to attack slavery by some of those measures. At the beginning of the struggle he, in common with the mass of the people of the North, was ready to guarantee to the people of the South protection for slavery within its existing limits. His oath as President to support the Constitution was interpreted by him as depriving him of all lawful right to interfere, directly or indirectly, with the institution of slavery in the States where it then existed. But the progress of events taught him, as it taught the people, that slavery, like every other partial interest or relation, was subordinate to the general interest; that it was subject to the Constitution ; that if, to preserve the Union, slavery must be destroyed, the Constitution, which formed the bond of the Union, could not be pleaded in its defence. His course in this matter was in accordance with the fundamental principles of his political creed. He never pretended to be a crusader like John Brown, or the leader of an agitation, like Mr. Garrison. His duties were those of a statesman and a magistrate, and the very fact that he had never uttered a single revolutionary sentiment qualified him to accompany and guide the remarkable but gradual development of national opinion on this vital subject. He had to unite the people of the loyal States, and to keep them together. Had he not succeeded in this he could have done nothing for liberty, nothing against slavery; and he did succeed.

In this country great alarm has often been expressed for the loss of liberties which it was supposed would ensue in America as a consequence of the exceptional measures to which he more than once resorted in times of emergency. It belongs to American lawyers to decide how far those measures were warranted by the Constitution; and differences of opinion may well exist as to their necessity and policy. The American people, however, showed their appreciation of the trustworthiness of Mr. LINCOLN by re-electing him after he had suspended the habeas corpus and suppressed newspapers. No alarm for the fate of their most precious rights and the establishment of the worst despotism over them prevented them from recording their votes for him last November. Their sentiments on the subject were, as they then showed, more in harmony with those of Mr. LINCOLN's letter to the Hon. Erastus Corning, written on the 13th of June, 1863.

"Nor am I able," said he, "to appreciate the danger apprehended that the American people will, by means of military arrests during the rebellion, lose the right of public discussion, the liberty of speech and the press, the law of evidence, trial by jury, and habeas corpus, throughout the indefinite peaceful future which, I trust, lies before them, any more than I am able to believe that a man could contract so strong an appetite for emetics during temporary illness as to persist in feeding upon them during the rest of his healthful life."

It is given to few men to triumph over the most formidable obstacles, as Mr. LINCOLN triumphed, by the mere force of honesty and sagacity. His simple integrity of purpose, firmness of will, patience, humanity, and the deep sense of accountability which marked every important act, united to form a character which has steadily and visibly gained upon the minds and hearts, not of his own countrymen alone, but also of the world. Even the enemies of his country and foreign powers acknowledged in him a man whom they could trust. In this country Mr. LINCOLN's name is mentioned with regret by many who four years ago half believed that he was the wretched imbecile he was described to be by the Richmond press. And even at Richmond we will undertake to affirm there are those, lately foremost in resisting his authority, who will deeply regret that the political changes which military events have rendered necessary are not to be conducted under his guidance. We will conclude this hasty and imperfect sketch with the words of one of the most distinguished of Mr. LINCOLN's countrymen in the North American Review:

"The results of the policy pursued by Mr. LINCOLN during his administration thus far are its own best justification. The verdict of the future is not to be foreshown. But there can be little doubt that history will record the name of ABRAHAM LINCOLN as that of a pure and disinterested patriot. She may find in his course many errors; she may point out in his character many defects; she will speak of him as a man who had to contend against the disadvantages of imperfect culture, of self-education, and of little intercourse with men of high breeding. But she will speak also of the virtues which the hard experience of early life had strengthened in him; of his homely sincerity and simplicity; of his manly frankness and self-respect; of his large, humane, and tender sympathies; of his self-control and good temper; of his truthfulness and sturdy honesty. She will represent him as actuated by an abiding sense of duty, as striving to be faithful in his service of God and of man, as possessed with deep moral earnestness, and as endowed with vigorous common sense and facuity for dealing with affairs. She will tell of his confidence in the people, and she will recount with approval their confidence in him. And when she has told all this, may she conclude her record by saying that to ABRAHAM LINCOLN more than to any other man is due the success which crowned the efforts of the American people to maintain the Union and the institutions of their country, to widen and confirm the foundations of justice and liberty, on which those institutions rest, and to establish inviolable and eternal peace within the borders of their land."

Such is the man whom Providence, by a mysterious dispensation, decrees to be no longer necessary to his country.

In the hour of his great work done, President LINCOLN has fallen. Not, indeed, in the flush of triumph, for no thought of triumph was in that honest and humble heart, nor in the intoxication of applause, for the fruits of victory were not yet gathered in his hand, was the chief of the American people, the foremost man in the great Christian revolution of our age, struck down. But his task was, nevertheless, accomplished, and the battle of his life won. So he passes away from the heat and toil that still have to be endured, full of the honor that belongs to one who has nobly done his part, and carrying in his last thoughts the sense of deep, steadfast thankfulness that he now could see the assured coming of that end for which he had so long striven in faith and hope. Who shall pity or lament such a death, while the tears of a nation fall upon his corpse, and the world softly speaks how true and good he was? Who will not bow the head submissive to the inscrutable decree which mocks our plans and fancies, but even in our sorrow makes us feel that it is wiser, juster, kinder, than our vain wishes might have been?

For in all time to come, not among Americans only, but among all who think of manhood as more than rank, and set worth above display, the name of ABRAHAM LINCOLN will be held in reverence. Rising from among the poorest of the people, winning his slow way upward by sheer hard work, preserving in every successive stage a character unspotted and a name untainted, securing a wider respect as he became better known, never pretending to more than he was, nor being less than he professed himself, he was at length for very singleness of heart and uprightness of conduct, because all felt that they could trust him utterly, and would desire to be guided by his firmness, courage, and sense, placed in the chair of President at the turning point of his nation's history. A life so true, rewarded by a dignity so majestic, was defence enough against the petty shafts of malice which party spirit, violent enough to light a civil war, aimed against him. The lowly callings he had first pursued became his titles to greater respect among those whose respect was worth having; the little external rusticities only showed more brightly, as the rough matrix the golden ore, the true dignity of his nature. Never was any one, set in such high place and surrounded with so many motives of furious detraction, so little impeached of aught blameworthy. The bitterest enemy could find no more to lay to his charge than that his language was sometimes too homely for a supersensitive taste, or that he conveyed in a jesting phrase what they deemed more suited for statelier style. But against these specks, what thorough nobility have we not set? A purity of thought, word, and deed never challenged, a disinterestedness never suspected, an honesty of purpose never impugned, a gentleness and tenderness that never made a private enemy or alienated a friend—these are indeed qualities which may well make a nation mourn. But he had intellect as well as goodness. Cautiously conservative, fearing to pass the limits of established systems, seeking the needful amendments rather from growth than alteration, he proved himself in the crisis the very man best suited for his post. He held back the ardent while he gave confidence to the timid, his reluctance to innovate did not prevent him from recognizing and accepting the changes in the situation which the progress of events brought to pass, and the firmness with which he refused to proceed faster than they warranted was equalled by the tenacity with which he refused to retire from the position he had at last thought it right to take up. So four years of trial convinced his countrymen that there was none among them who could better fill his place. And there can be no doubt that in his known respect for established rights, as well as in his known justice, impartiality, and benevolence, South as well as North had begun to look upon him as their surest friend, and as the safe arbiter in whom they could both trust to exact no more and to claim no less than might suffice to make their reconciliation perpetual.

But he has fallen, and by a southern hand. We cannot as yet tell the motive that urged the treacherous blow, but the fact that two had conspired to murder, the one the President, the other the Secretary of State, shows that at least there is not insanity to be reckoned as a possible explanation. But we will not, without overwhelming proof, let the horrible conspiracy, or the phrases of its actors, lead us to lay it to the charge of abettors in the South. We will not doubt that from what lately was the southern government and people there will come at once earnest disavowals of any knowledge of the meditated crime, and that if the murderer of Mr. Seward has reached the territory their power yet holds, he will be seized and surrendered as one guilty of a crime against humanity itself. On no other terms, at least, will their English sympathizers believe in southern "chivalry." For though some among us have by growth of prejudice come to think slavery not sin, there is no Englishman yet whom secret assassination does not horrify. And the kindly nature, the earnest desire to do right, which even his opponents confessed in ABRAHAM LINCOLN, will, now that he has gone, turn to him all sympathies, and make all among us call with one voice for vengeance on his detestable murderer.

But a harder task than vengeance lies yet on the North, which they must enter on before the first hours of mourning have passed. They have a government to carry on, a war to finish, a commonwealth to reconstruct. It were vain to conceal how the difficulty of each part of their task is enhanced by the loss of their chosen and tried head. Nor, unhappily, have they made provision for an event so wholly unforeseen. The Vice-President, who, in virtue of the Constitution, has already taken the oaths as President for nearly the term of four years still remaining to be run, is not the man whom they would have selected had they thought of such an event as his sitting in the President's chair. Already, too, there has been removed from his side the Secretary of State, who has during Mr. LINCOLN's tenure of office shared most fully his confidence and his designs. It is a great and terrible crisis. But we have confidence that the people will meet it worthily, and, if they do, that they will surmount all their troubles. Chief among our reasons for this belief is the reflection that Mr. LINCOLN was himself rather a representative than a leader. His personal influence had not formed his party; he was only selected in its exigencies to do its behests. Admirably as he has done them, we must not think that he was the only one who could have substantially done the same. And though Andrew Johnson was not selected to represent the party, but only as a secondary compromise between sections, this is an occasion which it may be hoped will extinguish sections, and unite all in a common effort. Round him will stand the old leaders—Stanton, Chase, and Grant. The responsibilities thus thrust upon him will, it may be expected, force him to guide his acts by their counsels, and by the public opinion of the people which has made him what he is, and which they guide. But in the firm heart of the people, tried and purified as it has been for four years in the furnace of affliction, lies, under God, our hope for the future. Eminently a law-abiding people, they will follow, first of all, and as far as possible, the path their Constitution points out. But if a chance more powerful than their will, if the perversity of this man or of that, renders the effort dangerous, they will know how to save the Constitution by sacrifice. Meantime, their great common sorrow, their great common danger, will obliterate division, and nerve them to energy. As when a beloved captain falls in fight, his men press forward with more impetuous and irresistible force to secure the post to which he led them, the fall of the captain of the people will fill them with the sterner resolve to be victors in the combat in which he was their leader, and to gain the object for which his life was given.

[From the London Morning Star, April 27, 1865.]

The appalling tragedy which has just been perpetrated at Washington is absolutely without historical precedent. Not in the records of the fiercest European convulsion, in the darkest hour of partisan hatreds, have we an example of an assassin plot at once so foul and so senseless, so horrible and so successful, as that to which ABRAHAM LINCOLN has already fallen a victim, and from which William H. Seward can hardly escape. Only in such instances as the murder of William of Orange, of Henri Quatre, or of Capodistria, have we any deed approaching in hideous ferocity to that which has just robbed the United States of one of the greatest of their Presidents. But from the fanatic's hateful point of view there was at least something to be said for men like Balthazar, Gerard, and Ravaillac. They at least might have believed that they saw embodied in their victims the whole living principle and motive power of that religious freedom which they detested. They might have supposed that with the man would die the great hopes and the great cause he inspired and guided. So, too, of Orsini. That unfortunate and guilty being believed, at least, that in Napoleon the Third there stood an embodied and concentrated system. But ABRAHAM LINCOLN was no dictator and no autocrat. He represented simply the resolution and the resources of a great people. The miserable excuse which fanaticism might attempt to plead for other political assassins has no application to the wretch whose felon hand dealt death to the pure and noble magistrate of a free nation. One would gladly, for the poor sake of common humanity, have caught at the idea that the crime was but the work of some maniacal partisan. But the mere nature of the deeds, without any additional evidence whatever, bids defiance to such an idea. While the one murderer was slaying the President of the republic, the other was making his even more dastardly attempt upon the life of the sick and prostrate Secretary. It does not need even the disclosures which have now, too late for any good purpose reached official quarters to prove that two madmen cannot become simultaneously inspired with the same monstrous project and impelled at the one moment to do their several parts of the one bloody business. The chivalry of the South has had much European compliment of late. It has been discovered to be the fount and origin of all the most noble and knightly qualities which the world heretofore had principally known through the medium of mediæval romance. Let it not be forgotten that southern brains lately planned the conflagration of a peaceful city. It never can be forgotten while history is read that the hands of southern partisans have been reddened by the foulest assassin plot the world has ever known; that they have been treacherously dipped in the blood of one of the best citizens and purest patriots to whom the land of Washington gave birth.

For ABRAHAM LINCOLN one cry of universal regret will be raised all over the civilized earth. We do not believe that even the fiercest partisans of the confederacy in this country will entertain any sentiment at such a time but one of grief and horror. To us ABRAHAM LINCOLN has always seemed the finest character produced by the American war, on either side of the struggle. He was great not merely by the force of genius—and only the word genius will describe the power of intellect by which he guided himself and his country through such a crisis—but by the simple, natural strength and grandeur of his character. Talleyrand once said of a great American statesman that without experience he "divined" his way through any crisis. Mr. LINCOLN thus divined his way through the perilous, exhausting, and unprecedented difficulties which might well have broken the strength and blinded the prescience of the best trained professional statesman. He seemed to arrive by instinct—by the instinct of a noble, unselfish, and manly nature—at the very ends which the highest of political genius, the longest of political experience, could have done no more than reach. He bore himself fearlessly in danger, calmly in difficulty, modestly in success. The world was at last beginning to know how good, and, in the best sense, how great a man he was. It had long indeed learned that he was as devoid of vanity as of fear, but it had only just come to know what magnanimity and mercy the hour of triumph would prove that he possessed. Reluctant enemies were just beginning to break into eulogy over his wise and noble clemency, when the dastard hand of a vile murderer destroyed his noble and valuable life. We in England have something to feel ashamed of when we meditate upon the true greatness of the man so ruthlessly slain. Too many Englishmen lent themselves to the vulgar and ignoble cry which was raised against him. English writers degraded themselves to the level of the coarsest caricaturists when they had to tell of ABRAHAM LINCOLN. They stooped to criticise a foreign patriot as a menial might comment on the bearing of a hero. They sneered at his manners, as if Cromwell was a Chesterfield; they accused him of ugliness, as if Mirabeau was a beauty; they made coarse pleasantry of his figure, as if Peel was a posture-master; they were facetious about his dress, as if Cavour was a D'Orsay; they were indignant about his jokes, as if Palmerston never jested. We do not remember any instance since the wildest days of British fury against the "Corsican ogre," in which a foreign statesman was ever so dealt with in English writings as Mr. LINCOLN. And, when we make the comparison, we cannot but remember that while Napoleon was our unscrupulous enemy, LINCOLN was our steady friend. Assailed by the coarsest attacks on this side the ocean, tried by the sorest temptations on that, ABRAHAM LINCOLN calmly and steadfastly maintained a policy of peace with England, and never did a deed, never wrote or spoke a word, which was unjust or unfriendly to the British nation. Had such a man died by the hand of disease in the hour of his triumph the world must have mourned for his loss. That he has fallen by the coward hand of a vile assassin exasperates and imbitters the grief beyond any power of language to express.

Had LINCOLN been a vain man, he might almost have ambitioned such a death. The weapon of the murderer has made sure for him an immortal place in history. Disappointment, failure, political change, popular caprice, the efforts of rivals, the malice of enemies, can touch him no more. He lived long enough to accomplish his great patriotic work, and then he became its martyr. It would be idle to speculate as yet upon the effect which his cruel death will produce upon the political fortunes of his country; but the destinies of that country will be cared for. Its hopes are too well sustained to faint and fall even over the grave of so great a patriot and so wise a leader as ABRAHAM LINCOLN. There are still clear and vigorous intellects left to conduct what remains of LINCOLN'S work to a triumphant conclusion; nor must we allow one day's unhappy misconduct to make us forget the undoubted abilities and patriotic purpose of the man so suddenly and strangely called to fill LINCOLN'S place. Dramatic justice has, indeed, been marvellously wreaked thus far upon the criminal pride of the South. A negro regiment was the first to enter Richmond, and now one of the poor whites, the "white trash" of a southern State, is called to receive from the South its final submission. We trust and feel assured that even in this hour of just indignation and natural excitement the North may still bear itself with that magnanimous clemency which thus far has illumined its triumph. But it may be that the conquered South has yet to learn that it too must mourn over the bloody grave to which ABRAHAM LINCOLN has been consigned by a southern assassin's hand.

ABRAHAM LINCOLN.

In the moment of victory ABRAHAM LINCOLN has been stricken to death Not on the battle-field, where so many noble patriots have laid down their lives for freedom, not by the unseen shaft of disease before which the greatest and noblest must sooner or later fall, but brutally murdered by an assassin of the slave power while he sat beside his wife enjoying a much-needed relaxation from the heavy cares of state. Noble, generous, forgiving, his only thoughts since the capture of Richmond have been of mercy. At a meeting of the Cabinet on the morning of his death he spoke very kindly of Lee and others of the confederates, and while his thoughts were thus all of forgiveness, the miscreant stole behind him and shot him through the brain. Unconscious from the moment he received the fatal wound, the great and noble-hearted patriot breathed his last on the following morning. Nothing else was needed to sanctify the name and memory of ABRAHAM LINCOLN to the people of the United States, and to all lovers of freedom throughout the world, than this his martyr death. Raised from the ranks of the common people to take upon himself the responsibility of the most gigantic struggle the world has ever witnessed between the forces of freedom and slavery, he guided the destinies of his country with unwavering hand through all the terrors and dangers of the conflict, and placed her so high and safe among the nations of the world that the dastards of despotism dare no longer question the strength and majesty of freedom. With a firm faith in his God, his country, and his principles of freedom for all men, whatever their color and condition, he has stood unmoved amid the shock of armies and the clamors of faction; he quailed not when defeat in the field seemed to herald the triumph of the foe; he boasted not of victory, nor sought to arrogate to himself the honors of the great deeds which have resounded through the world; but, gentle and modest as he was great and good, he took the chaplet from his own brow to place it on the lowly graves of the soldiers whose blood has been so liberally poured forth to consecrate the soil of America for freedom. He dies and makes no sign, but the impress of his noble character and aims will be borne by his country while time endures. He dies, but his country lives; freedom has triumphed; the broken chains at the feet of the slaves are the mute witnesses of his victory. It was on the evening of the 14th of April, the day which saw the federal flag raised once more on Fort Sumter amid the hoarse reverberation of cannon and the cheers of liberated slaves, that the President received his death-blow. The wretched conspirators who sought to destroy their country that slavery might triumph over its ruins, panted for LINCOLN's life since the day he was first elected to guide the destinies of the republic. When in the act of passing from his home in Illinois to assume the reins of office, he was apprised by General Scott that the barbarians of slavery had resolved to assassinate him. The plan was to raise a riot in Baltimore as he passed through that city on his way to Washington, and in the midst of the tumult Mr. LINCOLN was to be slain. The messenger who brought the news of the conspiracy to Mr. LINCOLN at Harrisburg was Frederick Seward, son of the statesman who now lies low beside his chief, stricken down by another desperate miscreant on the same day as the President. Mr. LINCOLN, with his usual prudence, at once stopped in his triumphal progress towards the capital, and, disguised as a countryman, passed safely through Baltimore by the night train, and arrived at the White House in Washington. The speech which he made to his neighbors of Springfield when he set out on his perilous mission has a mournful interest in view of his sudden and awful death. At the railway depot on Monday, the 11th of February, 1861, a large concourse of his fellow-citizens had assembled to bid him farewell. "My friends," he said, "no one not in my position can appreciate the sadness I feel at this parting. To this people I owe all that I am. Here I have lived more than a quarter of a century; here my children were born, and here one of them lies buried. I know not how soon I shall see you again. A duty devolves upon me, which is, perhaps, greater than that which has devolved upon any man since the days of Washington. He never could have succeeded without the aid of Divine Providence, upon which he at all times relied. I feel that I cannot succeed without the same Divine aid which sustained him. In the same Almighty Being I place my reliance for support, and I hope you, my friends, will all pray that I may receive that Divine assistance, without which I cannot succeed, but with which success is certain. Again I bid you all an affectionate farewell." The touching address was given with deep emotion, and many of the auditors replied to his request for their prayers by exclaiming, "We will pray for you." Thus this devout, simple-hearted, and courageous man went forth to his high task, not leaning on his own strength, but humbly trusting in the power of an Almighty arm. Those gentle utterances are but the key to all the speeches and proclamations which he has made during his troubled career. No one ever heard him utter a bitter word against the rebels, but many have confessed that they felt rebuked in his presence, his manner was so calm, his thoughts and words were so magnanimous, his great heart was so full of gentleness and compassion And yet it is this man who has been held up to the southern people by the lying politicians and most mischievous journalists of the South as a kind of human demon who delighted in blood, as a man regardless of law and justice, who, when he spoke of God or humanity, spake but in mockery of the sacred name and the sacred rights of the people. The southern heart has been fired, as the phrase went, by the most furious appeals to the passions of an ignorant people against a ruler who never would have touched a single southern right or harmed a real southern man had these truculent politicians not crowned their frenzy by rebellion. Even in the midst of the late most sanguinary outburst of ferocity he has mitigated the woes of war and so tempered justice by mercy that not a single traitor has perished on the scaffold. We would that we could add that the passions of the southern demagogues were sought to be assuaged by the universal efforts of the press and the politicians of those countries where the American struggle excited an overwhelming interest. But history will proclaim, to the eternal humiliation of our country, how an influential section of the English press outbade the journalists of the South in their slander and invective against the great man who has been so cruelly slain; how his every action was twisted and tortured into a wrong, his every noble aspiration spoken of as a desire for blood, his personal appearance caricatured, his lowly origin made the theme for scorn by men as base-born as he, but without the nobleness of soul which made LINCOLN a prince among princes; how even that proclamation which conferred liberty upon four millions of down-trodden slaves was reviled as a base effort to incite the negroes to servile war. The men who penned those revolting slanders were probably alike ignorant and reckless of their effects, but it cannot but be a painful reflection to Englishmen that the deluded southern rebels were encouraged in their efforts to destroy a free nation for the purpose of building a slave empire on the ruins by the writings and speeches of men who could boast of free England as their country. Their virulent abuse, in all probability, never reached him whom it was designed to wound, and even if the miserable writers had been factious Americans instead of degenerate Englishmen, LINCOLN would have had nothing but a smile for their malignant efforts. Nor had these unworthy effusions any effect upon the great body of the people of England. They saw at once the sterling integrity and

appreciated the high purpose of the American ruler; they took the universal
testimony of the people of the country over which he ruled in preference to
the partisan abuse of the pro-slavery organs, so that long before the emancipation proclamation was issued the efforts and intentions of ABRAHAM LINCOLN
were thoroughly understood by the commons of Great Britain. When, however, the moment had arrived for LINCOLN calling a race to freedom, and the
news was received in this country that, so far as the fiat of the President of
the United States in the execution of his constitutional authority during a state
of war could strike the fetters from the slave and purge the commonwealth
from its foul stain, the order had gone forth, and the slaves had a legal title to
their freedom, nothing could thereafter shake the faith of the people in the
liberator. Many touching proofs of the sincerity of these convictions were
afforded during the struggle. In every public meeting of our countrymen,
when the name of President LINCOLN was mentioned it was received with a
burst of ringing cheers. Perhaps the most notable occasion was when Henry
Ward Beecher addressed the inhabitants of London in Exeter Hall. It was
at a time when the pro-slavery press was most rampant, when for days they had
been heaping upon the head of Mr. Ward Beecher, one of the pioneer abolitionists of the north, and upon Mr. LINCOLN, as the leader of the abolitionist
party, all the vials of their abuse, and when, if ever, it might have been
supposed that the cause of right must be overborne by the power of slander
and misrepresentation. No sooner, however, was the name of LINCOLN mentioned by Mr. Beecher in the course of his speech than enthusiastic cheers,
which seemed as if they would never stop, burst forth from the vast assemblage.
It was the same everywhere throughout the country; and the American people
now amongst us, stunned and overwhelmed as they are by the news, may
believe that their feeling of an irreparable loss is shared in by the vast masses
of the English people. For, in truth, a man like ABRAHAM LINCOLN is claimed
by humanity as her own. He was in name and in heart an American citizen,
and his great work had been appointed for him in that new continent where
two great battles have already been won for human freedom; but he soon
showed by his actions and the magnanimity of his character that he belonged
to that illustrious band whose work is for the human race, and whose name
and fame shall never die out amongst men. In his hands was placed a most
sacred trust. In the United States the right of the majority to govern, and
perfect freedom to all to take part in the business of government, was the
basis of the Constitution. It had never been questioned until the southern
leaders, defeated at the ballot-box, sought to achieve by the sword what they
failed to achieve at the polling-booth. The question was the extension or the
non-extension of slavery, and the ultimate issue was the triumph or failure of free
institutions. We need not recall how triumphantly the enemies of freedom
pointed their finger in scorn at what they called the failure of the experiment

of free institutions. The very uprising of the southern slave power was held to be the end of the republic. They never dreamed that the obscure man of the people, who had been raised to the highest post of honor which it was possible for a citizen to fill, would grasp the helm with so vigorous a grasp, and so pilot the ship of state among the fearful breakers as to bring her safe to port with colors flying and not a spar lost. Alas! that the firm hand should now be nerveless, the bold heart cold and lifeless, and that the cup of joy should be so rudely dashed from the lips of the great people whom he had so faithfully served in the crisis of their destiny!

The assassination seems unquestionably to have been the result of a conspiracy to which various southern sympathizers were parties. The villain whose hand struck down President LINCOLN is stated to be a person named Wilkes Booth, a brother of Edwin Booth, the actor, and in his trunk was found a letter which showed that the horrid deed was to have been perpetrated on the 4th of March, when Mr. LINCOLN's second term of office began. It has, therefore, been no sudden inspiration of frenzy caused by the fall of Richmond, but the deliberate calculation of cold-blooded miscreants. The intention was not consummated sooner because some expected instructions, or aid, or encouragement, had not been received from Richmond. We cannot believe that the designs of the conspirators were known to and approved by the heads of the southern government, but it is not at all impossible that some leading secessionists may have aided in the conspiracy and encouraged its execution. It was known that the earlier attempt, when Mr. LINCOLN was about to take office, was known to and approved by many persons of influence and standing, and more than one influential fanatic in the course of the war has openly offered rewards for the heads of northern abolitionists. The murder was at length effected in the most cruel and barbarous manner. Seated in the theatre at Washington beside his wife and another lady, and attended by only one officer, a stranger suddenly made his appearance at the door of the box, and stated that he had despatches from General Grant. That general had been advertised to be present on the same evening, but he and his wife had gone to Burlington on a visit. The simple state of the republican President permitted the stranger easily to get access to his victim, who, it would seem, never turned his head—his thoughts probably far away on those fields of battle where so many have died that the republic might live. The assassin instantly raised his pistol and shot the President in the back of the head, the bullet lodging in the brain. We have as yet no details of the scene of consternation in the theatre, the anguish of Mrs. Lincoln, and the despair of the people when they saw one so beloved so basely smitten; but there needs no description. It is easy to imagine it all—all except the unutterable anguish of the woman who has been the support and solace of the President during many weary months of anxiety and suffering. To his wife Mr. LINCOLN was tenderly attached. His first action after receiving the notice of his election by the Chicago convention of 1860 as the candidate of the Republican party was to leave his political friends with whom he had been waiting for the news, and proceed home saying, "There's a little woman down at our house would like to hear this. I will go and tell her." The barbarians were not content with this one noble victim. About the same time another, and even more callous, southern fiend proceeded to the residence of Mr. Seward, and, under pretence of carrying medicine to the sick-chamber, managed to get access to the chamber where the Secretary of State lay suffering from his recent accident. Mr. Frederick Seward, the son of the Secretary, attempted to prevent him, but was cruelly wounded and has since died. A male attendant was stabbed through the lungs, and then the miscreant sprang forward to the bed and stabbed with many wounds the statesman who lay helpless. When the cries of the nurse and of a young daughter who was by her father's bedside brought Major Seward, another son, to his father's apartment, the assassin likewise fell upon him and severely wounded him. Most foul deed that ever pen recorded or demon perpetrated! A sick man lying helpless on his couch of pain thus barbarously assailed, a son eager to save a father's life thus foully slain! It illustrates in a yet more awful manner the innate barbarism of that system of society based on slavery which can breed criminals of so deep a dye. It is now some years since the writer met Mr. Frederick Seward in New York—an amiable, accomplished, intelligent gentleman, whose conversation showed him to possess a keen intellect and a cultivated mind. The conversation turned upon the sudden death of friends—of those who had sailed from home and been lost at sea, or who had been suddenly cut off by some great calamity. Did the shadow of his own premature and tragic end even then cast a shadow over his spirit? How many of his companions and friends have during these few years passed away amid the din and fury of the battle-field! and now, when peace seemed ready to come, and with her gentle touch restore all things, he too is snatched away to join the company of the martyrs of the anti-slavery war. The official report of Mr. Stanton, which will be found elsewhere, expressly states that these deeds of horror were the result of a conspiracy among the rebels, and the greatness of the enormities must now prove to the world that the attempt to set fire to New York, and to destroy in one horrible holocaust the women and children, the aged and infirm, of a populous city, was no hallucination of the federal government, but a grim reality of desperadoes— the spawn of the slave power. These are specimens of that chivalry of the South over which some English men and women have been heretofore shedding maudlin tears. It is a chivalry which can murder a gentle and noble man in presence of his wife; which can stab a father with furious blows on his sickbed in presence of a little daughter who ministers to his wants, and which can ruthlessly sacrifice two sons as they strive to save a father's life.

*   *   *   *   *   *·   *   *

(Here follows an account of the life and public services of Mr. LINCOLN, concluding as follows:)

The election of Mr. LINCOLN was hailed with delight by the people of the northern States, little dreaming that their right to elect him would have to be sustained in so fearful a manner; and when the time came for him to proceed to Washington to execute the functions of President, the whole country watched his progress with intense satisfaction.   As he passed eastward he had to make speeches at almost every town of any note, and many of the expressions which then fell from his lips were sufficiently remarkable.   When passing through Indiana he thus spoke of State rights: "By the way, in what consists the special sacredness of a State?   If a State and a county, in a given case, should be equal in extent of territory and equal in number of inhabitants, in what, as a matter of principle, is the State better than the county?   On what principle may a State, being not more than one-fiftieth part of the nation in soil and population, break up the nation, and then coerce a proportionately larger subdivision of itself in the most arbitrary manner?   What mysterious right to play tyrant is conferred on a district of country, with its people, by merely calling it a State?"   In New Jersey, he made use of a characteristic expression, which has been frequently quoted since: "I shall do all that may be in my power to promote a peaceful settlement of all our difficulties.   The man does not live who is more devoted to peace than I am; none who will do more to preserve it; but it may be necessary to put the foot down firmly."   How firmly, the South, the North, we and all men now know.   When raising a flag in Philadelphia, he asked whether the Union could be saved upon the Declaration of Independence, and in answering his own question uttered words which sound prophetical after the occurrence which has so troubled the country: "If this country cannot be saved without giving up that principle, I was about to say I would rather be assassinated on this spot than surrender it;" and his last words on the occasion were, "I have said nothing but what I am willing to live by, and, if it be the pleasure of Almighty God, die by."   He has stood by these principles during his life, and he had completed the most triumphant defence of these principles when called on to die; but dying, he bequeathes a new life to the nation; and, being dead, he yet speaketh.

Mr. LINCOLN's policy was to woo the South to submission to the constitutionally expressed will of the people by every argument which would be supposed to have weight with American citizens.   His inaugural address was a pleading with them to give up their mad design to break up the nation, and it was thus he conjured them to think well upon the fatal step they were about to take: "I am loth to close.   We are not enemies, but friends.   We must not be enemies.   Though passion may have strained, it must not break, our bonds of affection.   The mystic chords of memory, stretching from every battle-field and patriot grave to every living heart and hearthstone all over this broad land, will yet swell the chorus of the Union, when again touched, as they surely will be, by the better angels of our nature." His appeal was vain. The men to whom it was addressed, for a long series of years, had been educating themselves into the monstrous delusion that slavery was a divine institution; that it was the natural basis for society; that a slave empire could be established so powerful that abolitionism would forever be abashed, and southern interests reign supreme. The politicians clamored for war, the editors wrote up war, the clergy preached up a war for slavery, until the poor deluded common people rushed blindly into the conflict. The North had no choice; Mr. LINCOLN, as the President, had no choice but to enforce the laws, and to use whatever powers the Constitution gave him for the suppression of the rebellion. This is not the place to recount the varied fortunes of the field. In the west the national arms were almost uniformly successful; in the east the forces of the Union failed to capture Richmond until weary years of effort had been wasted, and several successive generals' tried and removed. But the elasticity of free institutions permitted of these changes of commanders, and the patriotism of the people supported the President in whatever appointments he deemed best for the furtherance of the cause, until by his happy selection of Grant, who had proved victorious in the west, and Grant's no less admirable appointments of Sherman, Sheridan, Thomas, and others, the power of the South has been completely crushed. President LINCOLN, at first, incurred much odium among many sincere friends of the slave in this country, and was taunted by the supporters of the slave confederacy, because he did not from the outset inaugurate an anti-slavery war. But his true position began to be appreciated. Some of the border slave States remained loyal, and he could not at once attack slavery without encroaching upon the right of these loyal people to regulate their own affairs. The northern democrats, moreover, polled more than one million of votes, while the purely abolitionist element among his own supporters was comparatively small. Had he at once raised an anti-slavery banner, in all likelihood he would have retarded in place of advancing the cause. He repressed all attempts prematurely to proclaim emancipation, until perfectly satisfied in his own mind that he had the constitutional power during a state of war to do so, and that the proclamation would tend to lessen the power of the rebels and more speedily bring peace to his torn and bleeding country. The policy has been the saving of the Union. The slaves crowded the federal lines in order to gain their freedom, and eagerly availed themselves of the privilege to enlist under the federal banners to aid in the freedom of their friends and brethren of the negro race. The emancipation proclamation of ABRAHAM LINCOLN was a grand and sublime act; and when, in announcing his policy to Congress, he declared that they who were at the head of affairs in those times could not escape history, he truly shadowed forth that all who had in any way contributed to that crowning act of justice would occupy in history a most conspicuous and enviable place.   The cause of the Union has prospered from the day the proclamation was issued, until at length the greatest army of the rebels has surrendered to the great soldier whom President LINCOLN's sagacity selected as the fit man to lead the armies of the republic.

The personal appearance of Mr. LINCOLN has often been described.   He was six feet four in height, and of that thin, wiry build which is somewhat characteristic of Americans.   But all observers unite in describing his countenance as singularly pleasing, and the eye mild and gentle.   One English observer, not particularly prepossessed in his favor, describes his countenance as peculiarly soft, with an almost feminine expression of melancholy.   While all observers unite in thus describing the late President, those who knew him more intimately are equally of one opinion as to his disposition being as kind, courteous, and gentle as his mild expression denoted.   He was never heard to say a bitter word against the rebels, but invariably in his public proclamations, and by his acts, he sought to win them back to their fealty without undue shedding of blood.   But with all this gentleness, he was inexorably firm.   Men of all parties have gone to him to attempt to move him from some of his positions; but while listening courteously to their statements, he never failed to indicate that what he had himself resolved, after careful consideration, he should abide by until he saw that it was unsuited to the circumstances of his country. He had an overflowing and ready humor.   This trait in his character has given many shafts to the venomous slanderers of the great man who has been so suddenly removed from his proud position; but it is scarcely necessary to say that all the *bon-mots* attributed to the President are not genuine.   One slander which has been often repeated by his enemies it may be as well to contradict here, once for all.   It has been asserted and reasserted, and is now apparently deemed to be beyond the reach of cavil, that Mr. LINCOLN, when riding over the field of Gettysburg, called for a comic song to drive away serious thoughts. The statement is a gratuitous and baseless calumny, invented by those who would as readily destroy a reputation as the southern assassins would wreak their vengeance upon a helpless victim.   These have, indeed, accomplished the death of a noble-hearted patriot; but while they have killed the body, they cannot touch his deathless fame; they cannot mar his glorious work; they cannot rob him of his immortal reward.

[From the London Evening Star, May 2, 1865.]

The Parliament of Great Britain, in a spirit worthy of its ancient fame, has unanimously expressed its deep and earnest feeling of sympathy with the government and people of the United States in the hour of their dire affliction.   The addresses to the Crown which were voted by both houses last night were no merely formal acts. They represented the solemn and deliberate sentiments of both branches of the legislature—they embodied that sense of grief which has weighed upon the heart of the nation ever since the perpetration of the atrocious crime has been known in this country. The appearance of the two chambers indicated the serious nature of the business which was announced for discussion. The attendance of members was unusually large, and the languor of an uneventful session was once more broken by a mournful-episode. The crowd which assembled in Westminster Hall, and filled the corridors and lobbies, showed the deep interest which the subject excited among the classes who are never attracted to this quarter unless the popular mind is stirred by some deep emotion. While such was the temper of the spectators, we may justly affirm that those who more directly assisted on the occasion were moved by no vague curiosity to be present at the deliberations of Parliament, and that the chief actors performed their appointed task with befitting dignity and earnestness. It would be too much to say that the evil spirit of a faction which cruelly maligned the martyred patriot when he was living was quenched; but in the presence of the awful calamity which has befallen our American kinsmen, it at all events exhibited the grace of silence and held its peace. Even that faction, while it could not recant its recorded opinions or atone for the past, with the memories of which it must be forever dishonored, without doubt concurred heartily in those execrations of the assassin's cruel deed which were uttered by the chiefs of the two great parties in the state. Both houses were absolutely unanimous in their expressions of horror at the crime; and no voice, no sound was heard which did not imply profound sympathy with the character of the illustrious man who, by the common consent of every civilized nation, has been elevated to a position in history which a long line of the world's greatest heroes have coveted, but in vain.

It would be difficult to say who among the speakers last night gave proof of the most discriminating appreciation of the peculiar excellencies of Mr. LINCOLN's large-hearted nature. But although they differed in form, they agreed in essence. All combined to do justice to his manliness, his sincerity, and his generous feeling. Lord Russell, who appropriately reminded the assembly which he addressed that the late President was twice legally elected the Chief Magistate of the American nation, declared that he was exactly suited by his natural disposition for the conjuncture which taxed his energies during his four years of power. With honesty and frankness he combined conciliation, the quality which would temper the pride of victory. The noble speaker was singularly felicitous in his eulogy of Mr. LINCOLN's moderation on the slavery question, the gradual but sure measures he adopted to effect the abolition of what he saw from the beginning was the one crime of his country, and the only source of her civil troubles; and he was equally just in pointing to the influence of that same moderation in smoothing over the difficulties which had arisen from time to time between the two governments. If Lord Derby spoke in more guarded terms on the political aspects of the American war, he was not less energetic in his reprobation of the dastardly murder which has disgraced the annals of that contest, and not less happy in the tribute he paid to the virtues of Mr. LINCOLN's character, that singular wisdom and prudence combined with conciliation, which he said had distinguished his conduct of public affairs. In the lower house Sir George Grey, in the unavoidable absence, through indisposition, of Lord Palmerston, proposed the motion in an admirable speech. The only expression of dissent was provoked by his perfectly true statement that the majority of this country have sympathized with the North during its arduous struggle. The few gentlemen below the gangway on the tory side of the house who sought to cast distrust upon the assertion, provoked a counter-cheer which served to make their own insignificance the more conspicuous. Sir George Grey dwelt forcibly upon the wise forbearance and generosity of President LINCOLN—qualities which, as the speaker truly said, would, if he had lived, have added greater lustre to the fame he had already acquired. But to Mr. Disraeli once again attached the honor of elevating a mournful theme by the inspiration, not only of a genuine feeling, but of a classic eloquence. His words blended the graces of the orator with an acute perception of the noble traits of Mr. LINCOLN's nature and the true dignity with which death had invested him. It was a genuine power of discrimination and no mere trick of rhetoric which enabled him to point out that the homely and innocent character of the victim and the accessories of his latest moments "take the subject out of the pomp of history and the ceremonial of diplomacy, and make it touch the heart of nations and appeal to the sentiments of mankind." Never did the conservative leader appear to greater advantage, never did his acknowledged genius seem to be more closely allied with all that is great and good in human sympathy, than when he affirmed that President LINCOLN in a time of sore trial had performed his duty with "simplicity and strength," and when he reminded the English people of his kinship with them, and expressed his faith that the United States would emerge from the ordeal of discipline and suffering elevated and chastened by what they had endured. The reassuring words, founded upon the experience of mankind, to which he gave utterance, may well make us believe that the assassin's arm in striking down Mr. LINCOLN had no power to injure the cause of which he was the elected representative; but his profound declaration of sympathy with the American people will do something more than allay groundless alarms. It will essentially assist to consolidate those friendly relations between England and America which Lord Stratford de Redcliffe and every other speaker desired to see established upon a firm and lasting basis.

The two houses have agreed to address the Queen, praying that she would communicate their sentiments as well as her own to the government of the

United States. In advance of the action of Parliament instructions have been sent out to the British minister at Washington to make known the feelings of the imperial government. There was only one other manifestation of grief and indignation at the great tragedy which could have been desired, and that has been given. The Queen has with her own hand written a letter of sympathy to Mrs. Lincoln. The act is as graceful as it is touching. The royal widow seeking to afford consolation to her sister in affliction is an incident of which history will be proud. Every Englishman will feel that this last instance of tenderness on the part of the Sovereign—this truly gentle and womanly deed—binds him by a closer tie of loyalty and affection to the illustrious lady who sits upon the throne of these realms. It is an act which will serve as much as anything to bury all discord in a common grave. Queen Victoria is as much revered in America as she is in her own land; and we believe that if Mr. Adams had delivered his admirable speech to-day instead of yesterday, he would feel himself able to assert that no circumstance could have occurred which would be more certain to afford consolation to his countrymen or to reunite the two nations.

[From the London Daily Telegraph, April 27, 1865.]

ABRAHAM LINCOLN.

One universal feeling of horror and grief will thrill through the breasts of Englishmen this morning, if we do not mistake our countrymen, as they read in our columns the sad news which has come to us across the Atlantic. ABRAHAM LINCOLN has fallen by the assassin's hand; fallen as Julius Cæsar fell on those fatal "Ides of March," but by the hand of a baser Brutus; fallen as, to our human eyes and fallible judgment, he little deserved to fall—shot through the head with a pistol fired by a wretched conspirator, as he sat in a private box at Ford's theatre, Washington, on the evening of the 14th instant. The wound, it was at once seen, was mortal, and the President expired soon after sunrise on the following morning; his colleague, Mr. Seward, having, about the same time and hour, sustained a similar attack from the dagger of the same or a fellow-assassin.

Such is the sum and substance of the melancholy news which is told in another column, with additional victims and details of butchery; and we have elsewhere attempted to give an estimate of the probable effect of this sad event on the war and on the politics of America. It is our duty, however, to offer here an outline of the career and public character of the eminent man who has thus been suddenly cut off when scarcely past his prime, and at the outset of a second period of rule, having fallen, as even the stanchest southerner must admit, like Epaminondas of old, and like Wolfe in modern times, in the very hour of victory.

* * * * * * * *

(Here follows an account of the life and services of Mr. LINCOLN, concluding with the following:)

The rest of the President's life, if we were to write it, would really be little less than the history of the fearful and fatal war which has laid waste America for the last four years. The chief event in it, perhaps, is the re-election of ABRAHAM LINCOLN to the presidential chair last summer. At that time, as will be remembered, the leaders of the abolition party seemed bent on withdrawing from him their support. He was, however, so firmly rooted in the affections of the mass of the electors, who identified him with the Union cause, that it was deemed unwise to bring forward a rival republican candidate. Had that party become divided, as seemed probable at one time, General McClellan would certainly have been returned. Thanks to the forbearance and foresight of the abolitionists, Mr. LINCOLN was elected by a triumphant majority, with full power to control the destinies of those States at least which had elected him for a new term of four years.

"Man proposes, but God disposes." Within a few short months the assassin's pistol has set aside the wishes of the northern people, thrown transatlantic politics into the most sad confusion, and caused all New York to array itself in robes of black.

The face of "Honest Abe" has been made familiar to most English readers by the aid of photography; but the following sketch of his person, from the pen of one who knew him well, is so perfect that we may be excused for repeating it here: "Old Abe is a gaunt giant, more than six feet high, strong and long-limbed. He walks slowly, and, like many thoughtful men—Napoleon and Wordsworth for example—he keeps his head inclined forward and downwards. His hair is black and wiry; his eyes are dark-gray; his smile is frank, sincere, and winning. Like most American gentlemen, he is loose and careless in dress, turns down his flapping white collars, and wears habitually what we should call evening dress. His head is massive, his brow full and wide, his nose large and fleshy, his mouth coarse and full; his eyes are sunken, his face is bronzed and thin, and drawn down into strong corded lines, which disclose the machinery that moves his broad and formidable jaw."

Honest, straightforward, practical, energetic, and indifferent to censure so long as he was conscious of his own integrity, ABRAHAM LINCOLN seems to have been one of those men whose latent talents are called forth by great emergencies, and hence his sudden death is a national loss. Under a rough and even forbidding exterior he concealed a great and good heart, and it deserves to be recorded to his credit that, throughout this long and painful struggle, he never once signed the death-warrant of a political enemy, though often urged to do so.

It is perhaps too early as yet to pronounce sentence definitively on his character; for that we must appeal from the bar of contemporary criticism to the verdict of posterity; and there is little doubt that future generations will accord a very high position to him who, as President of the United States, has just fallen by the same cruel and horrible fate which half a century ago robbed us of our own Premier, Spencer Perceval.

No fouler crime stands chronicled in all history than the murder of ABRAHAM LINCOLN. The sorry pleas of state necessity or political interest that have been advanced time out of mind to palliate assassination cannot even be heard with toleration in such a case as this, for the act is one that outrages humanity and shocks the common conscience of the world. It is accursed and supremely infamous; it is most cowardly, most cruel. Every war has its horrors, and the great fight between the North and the South has been no exception to the rule; but there never was anything more atrocious than this—never anything more base than the slaughter of a man who, during the years of great excitement, had scarcely made a single personal enemy. In the agony and crisis that preceded Robespierre's reign of terror, Danton said, "The Revolution, like Saturn, is beginning to devour its own children!" ABRAHAM LINCOLN was the child—in no invidious sense, we may even say the puppet—of the passions of his time, and now he has become their victim. A fine spirit of popular enthusiasm made him Chief Magistrate of the greatest republic ever known; the ferocity and the madness of a few desperadoes have abruptly ended a career which already loomed so largely. A wonderful life was LINCOLN's—a life quite as startling and surprising as his death; but, at any rate, the worst part of his work seemed over. The resistance of the South had been crushed. A sturdy, sensible western man, with long limbs and a longer head, Mr. LINCOLN had worked his way in the world without any dishonorable subterfuges or mean devices. Clear, direct, simple, and straightforward, he had already, during his brief term of office, outlived many suspicions, jealousies, misconstructions, and dislikes. He bore his honors well, and was settling down into a quiet simple dignity of manner, and a kindly moderation of thought and temper. Terrible had been the trial through which he had victoriously passed. He was emphatically one of the people, but his homespun virtues seemed to justify the people's choice. At any rate, he had diligently, faithfully, and not unskilfully, labored according to such light as was given him; and now, as he seemed to touch the goal, his course is abruptly checked. To-day, all party feeling, all political jealousies, must be hushed and suspended; to-day, no man is a sympathizer with North or South; we are all mourners over the fate of an honest citizen.

The war was practically over. When the news came that Lee had surrendered, when people like Butler were crying for vengeance, President LINCOLN stepped forward and made a speech that was eminently conciliatory. His last public oration was also his best; it was just, manly, sage, and charitable. We have now the authority of Mr. Stanton for saying that in council his tone was precisely the same; and there is something which should touch all honest hearts in that one sentence, "He spoke very kindly of Lee." This was in the morning; in the evening of Friday, April 14, he was at a theatre in Washington. He had been to Richmond; had authoritatively marched into Jefferson Davis's house; had received the salutes of negro regiments in the capital of the confederacy; but, so far from allowing this singular turn in the whirligig of fate to excite him, he grew more moderate; he had obviously made up his mind to act as pacificator. He sat in a private box at Ford's theatre, with his wife, another lady, and Major Rathburn. It was easy enough to approach him; *that*, indeed, had never been very difficult. The Jacques Clement or Ravaillac of the occasion had not to thrust his way through any guards, for LINCOLN had always lived in the open air, fearlessly and frankly. At half past nine o'clock the door of the box was opened, and before the President could turn around to meet the intruder with his broad genial smile, a pistol was clapped to the back of his head. The shot went through his brain. The assassin, drawing a huge knife and brandishing it, leaped out from the box to the stage, yelled "*Sic semper tyrannis!*" and fled from the theatre. ABRAHAM LINCOLN was never again conscious. His last words had been said before he repaired to the theatre, and they were words of friendliness and conciliation. We do not know that he even spoke once after the bullet pierced his brain; but he lingered on through the night, dying hard, as became a man of his tough, indomitable temper. While he was thus agonizing, another murderer had obtained admission to the sick-room of Secretary Seward, and had stabbed the sufferer in his bed; then, confronted by his son, had stabbed *him* too, and made his escape. It was to have been a night of wild, hellish butchery; for Stanton's life also had been threatened, and it is supposed that Ulysses Grant, who was likewise to have attended at Ford's theatre, was down in the list of the doomed. On the morning of Saturday, the 15th, President LINCOLN died; Andrew Johnson succeeded him at the White House; and the assassin was arrested. He proved to be one Wilkes Booth, brother of Edwin Booth, an actor of some repute. The news is so sudden and so startling that its full import can hardly be realized at once. That shot in a private box—the wild stir and alarm of the audience—the horror of the actors, as the assassin jumped upon the stage and mocked their mimic drama by his own awful crime—these things picture themselves as a dim, confused, terrible vision, whose outlines can scarcely be traced even by the steadiest eye and the calmest hand. The deed seems all the more frightful because it was so easily committed; because no soldiery with drawn swords and glittering helmets guarded the approach to LINCOLN's box; because any citizen could approach him, just as any citizen the day before could have walked, scarcely questioned, into his official residence. This splendid reliance upon the people has hitherto been safe; but every land has its felons, and the miscreant

Booth has perchance murdered that mutual confidence between ruler and ruled which was the essence of republicanism.

ABRAHAM LINCOLN's life was not particularly happy. He was a sagacious, toilsome, dogged, patient man; he rose by his energy and his shrewdness from a very humble position to the presidential chair; but the presidential chair itself was not a luxurious resting-place, and even the strong Kentuckian frame of the man was sorely tried. Mr. Tennyson speaks of the fierce light which beats upon a throne; fiercer yet, even more broad, open, dazzling, and glaring, was that which played so terribly around the President. It has lit up many noble points in his character, to which, as the years roll on and as party passions fade away, full justice will assuredly be done; but even viewed in this utter publicity, this sheer nakedness of life, his character stands singularly clear of all that was mean or base. It was easy to caricature his ungainly form, and it was often necessary to dwell upon his mental limitations and defects; his jests were sometimes in bad taste, his language exaggerated and heedless; yet upon everything that he said or did there was the stamp of strong individual manhood. In truth, those who knew him best were convinced that his life was really sad; that his jokes were but the efforts of a jaded, melancholy nature to relieve its sense of weariness; that, knowing he had no time to cry, he laughed as often as he could. Be this said to his honor—whatever cruel things have been done by his subordinates, ABRAHAM LINCOLN himself never sent a man to the scaffold. The journalists of his own country have not spared him; yet, after all, the sum of their accusations was also the basis of his glory. ABRAHAM LINCOLN, who had been a "rail-splitter" and then a "village lawyer," contrived by shrewd mother-wit and robust integrity of character to win the esteem of the stout men of the west—a nobler type of Americanism than the motley tribes of New York; whilst at last he became the foremost man in the greatest republic of the world at the hour of its supremest need. His acts are on record—they fill a large volume; and whoever may study them as a part of history, not as material for party polemics, they will prove, upon the whole, singularly sagacious and astute. It has often been our lot to blame them— often been our lot to question the wisdom of the policy which he pursued; nor do we retract what we have said, even now that we have to review it so solemnly and sadly. But from vulgar corruption, from factious hatred, from meanness, jealousy, uncharitableness, this ruler was nobly free. The strange grim face, that was yet illuminated so often by a gleam of honest humor or a glance of genuine kindliness, has been quietly covered by the sere-cloth; the almost gigantic frame, lifeless and limp, has been coffined and palled. He had given the republic all he had—his time, his peace, his reputation, his children. One son, his eldest, he had sent to the front with General Grant; another he lost while the war was raging; and yet the office-seekers would not give him an hour's rest, but almost tortured him into madness by their importunities.

Throughout the dreariest time of national reverses and calamity, he never despaired. Almost solemn now are those well-remembered familiar phrases, "I have put my foot down," and "We must keep pegging away." They were but rough translations of a sentiment which, expressed in more knightly phrase, we should regard as heroical. And at last came what seemed to be the fruition of his labors, the reward of his patience and his courage. He, the man of Kentucky and Illinois, entered Richmond as a conqueror; but he launched no decree of proscription; for the fight appeared over, and it was not in the man's large heart to bear malice against a beaten foe. "He spoke very kindly of Lee," said Stanton; and on the night of that memorable council, where he pleaded for peace and for mercy, a villain killed him. Not for Lincoln himself can the end be considered as unhappy. To the extent of his power he has done his duty, with singleness of heart, with honesty of purpose; and if ever man needed rest, he needed it. That rest he has obtained, and, with it, the reward that follows honest service. There is a wonderful old song of Shirley the dramatist—a song of which Charles II is said to have been strangely enamored—which tells us that "the glories of our birth and state are shadows, not substantial things," and which preaches the sublime equality, the sacred fraternity, of the tomb. In the last verse of that famed lyric we read: "Upon death's purple altar now, see where the victor-victim bleeds!" The victor-victim of democracy was Abraham Lincoln, twice President of the United States.

[From the London Daily Telegraph, April 28, 1865.]

Last night in both houses of the legislature the representatives of the English government announced that on Monday next our senate would give expression to the feeling of indignation which had been occasioned in this country by the murder of President Lincoln. The course taken is undoubtedly the best. Even on the most important night of the parliamentary year there would have been no lack of generous eloquence upon such a theme; but it was more especially desirable that the sympathy of the whole people should be formally expressed by the Queen and her responsible advisers. Had the matter been left to the feelings of individual members, no delay need have occurred; but then the words of condolence would have represented merely the personal opinions of the speakers. In this case it was essential that not only the leaders of party and the chieftains of debate should rise to denounce the infamous atrocity, but that the voice of the British empire itself should be heard in solemn reprobation of a most hideous crime. Nor are there many grander things in history than such an expression of a whole nation's mind. Doubtless from every court upon the continent messages of sympathy and regret will be forthcoming; but it behooved the one people of the Old World that is absolutely free to rise to the height of so great and terrible an occasion, and to speak in tones which would be remembered centuries hence. So, not disregarding ancient rule and order, but adapting them with a wise liberality to the actual necessities of the day, lords and commons will desire her Majesty to speak for them as well as for herself. Whatever may be the faults of our Parliament, it is in all cases involving national reputation or national sentiment substantially at one with the people. We never look to it in vain when there is an outrage to be resented or a generous action to be performed; we can trust it safely with our honor—confide to it without misgiving the keeping of our conscience. France, Russia, Austria, young Italy, and the states of Europe may vie with each other in their expressions of regret; but, unless the civil war has strangely altered the nature of Americans, the first inquiry across the Atlantic must be, "What will they think of this at home?" Nor will they be left long in suspense. Were the little, throbbing, eloquent, electric wire now working at the bottom of the ocean, there would have been flashed hours ago a message from Windsor Castle to Washington—a message from Queen Victoria to Andrew Johnson, which would have been practically a message from one great people to another. The petty jealousies, the small bickerings, that may have been engendered in a time of war, must end in presence of so stern and horrible a fact. Be it ours, as a nation, to show that whatever we may have thought of the contest while it lasted, we sympathize with the affliction of a kindred race; that we loathe, we men of the old mother-land, the dastardly crime which has been committed; that we honestly wish our cousins good speed through a sad time of trial. Party, as we have said, has nothing to do with this simple question. If anywhere abroad there is a notion that upon the American war we are split into two hostile factions of aristocrats and democrats, we may as well nail that base coin to the counter at once, before it passes any further, and clear the good name, the honest repute of England in the eyes of the whole land. From the leader of the conservatives—the fourteenth Earl of Derby, the Stanley whose ancestors influenced our history before Christopher Columbus set sail for the "unknown world"—there will come as eloquent and as honest an expression of manly sympathy as from any radical member of the House of Commons. Our peers, our squires, the representatives of past glories, and the tribunes of modern wants, can have but one thought just now; and that thought will find its highest and most constitutional expression in the letter of the Queen herself.

The people of England, however, who were not bound over to silence, and who had no considerations of parliamentary etiquette to guide or to restrain them, have already expressed in a hundred ways their abomination of the crime, and their sympathy for its victim. No man who walked in the streets of London at noon on Wednesday will readily forget the scene as the news spread throughout the great city. There was one vast, universal sense of horror and dismay ; for the act, in truth, seemed an outrage upon humanity itself—an outbreak of devilish passion which menaced all society. That sense of abhorrence was not confined to London. We could only assume yesterday what we can assert to-day—that from one end of the land to the other there has been a cry of rage at this most foul assassination. The men of Liverpool have, on the whole, been southern in their sympathies, but when the news reached them they grieved as earnestly as the most fervid abolitionist of Massachusetts. A creature, indeed, there was—and we wish we could pillory the offender by his name—who cried "Hurrah," but a southerner seized him, and helped to kick him from the room. National, indeed, was the sorrow and the anger. Southampton heard the news, and instantly a meeting for condolence was resolved upon ; far away in the north Newcastle heard it, and the dwellers by the Tyne gave vent to their wrath with unmistakable Northumbrian emphasis ; Dublin learnt the horrid tidings, and the warm-hearted Irish people at once grew eloquent in their indignation ; at Manchester, at Birmingham, everywhere throughout the land—from the great centres of industry to the quiet little country towns— there was but the same expression of opinion. The London press, always unanimous on such a point, had already spoken out, and its words of sympathy may have done more to restore an absolutely friendly feeling between the two great sections of the Anglo-Saxon race than a host of diplomatic despatches. The corporation of London—interesting whenever it becomes a spokesman for the whole metropolis—postponed all business until it had placed upon official record its "detestation of the atrocious crime." The demonstrations of feeling were not, of course, confined to Englishmen. The Americans in London assembled, under the chairmanship of a gentleman who was among the late President's political opponents, and although the meeting was adjourned, there can be no doubt that citizens of both sections of the States will join in expressing on Monday night their condemnations and their regrets. Meanwhile, the Germans in London had also gathered together, and helped to swell the general shout of human indignation—a shout which is now echoed from the other side of the channel by the journalists of France.

Little enough that is new has yet reached us from America ; to-day we have only a summary that is but five hours later than the telegrams we published yesterday morning, but in this intelligence there are some items of importance. Chief of these is the statement that hopes were still entertained of Mr. Seward's recovery, and that, at any rate, he was still living. We cannot profess to feel very sanguine on this point ; the Secretary of State is growing old, and his recent accident was almost enough to kill a stronger man, without the foul supplementary violence of the assassin. As he threw himself from his carriage before, so he seems, when the murderer's knife had gashed his face, to have thrown himself from his bed, and thus to have escaped the last deadly thrust; but it is difficult for a man of his age to survive such an accumulation of physical calamities. His son, who was reported to be dead, survives; but his condition is most critical, and the many Englishmen who knew Frederick Seward well must wait with a painful anxiety for the next telegrams. The last item in the news is the saddest; the assassins are still at large, and in such a time of general confusion they may possibly contrive to make their escape. If they go south and reach any part of the country which is still under confederate authority, their summary arrest and subsequent surrender to their pursuers may be reckoned as certain. Wherever they go, the curse of Cain is perhaps more markedly upon these men than on any other political murderers in the world's history.

[From the Spectator. April 29, 1865.]

THE MURDER OF MR. LINCOLN.

It is hard sometimes to abstain from accusing Providence of irony. In the supreme hour of his career, when the enfranchisment of a race and the future of a continent seemed to hang upon his safety, when, after four years of battle, the peace for which he had longed throughout appeared almost in sight, and after four years of depreciation, the whole world at last recognized his value, when men had ceased to speak of the importance of his life because the thought of his death seemed to impugn the kindness of Heaven, America has lost Mr. LINCOLN. It has lost him, too, in the only way, which his death could by possibility have neutralized any of the effects of his life. There never was a moment in the history of his country when firmness and shrewdness and gentleness were so unspeakably important, and the one man in America whose resolve on the crucial question was unchangeable, whose shrewdness statesmen indefinitely keener than himself could never baffle, whose gentleness years of incessant insult had failed to weary out, who, possessed of these qualties, was possessed also of the supreme power, and who had convinced even his enemies that the power would be exerted under the influence of these qualities, has been taken away from his work. The future of the black race still oscillates between serfage and freedom, and the one man sure to have preferred freedom, and, preferring, to have secured it, has been removed; the feeling of the white race fluctuates between forgiveness and vindictiveness, and the one whose influence would have insured mercy has been murdered amidst the race who are striving to forgive by the class towards whom he forbade vindictiveness. As if to show that the South is unworthy of pardon, a southerner assassinates the ruler who on that very day was contending with his cabinet for the policy of pardon to the South, and who must be succeeded by a man who, avowedly worshipping the people, can scarcely, even to conciliate that people, restrain his own desire for a policy of vengeance. Whatever of vindictiveness is latent in the northern heart has been supplied at once with an excuse which even the South will not deny, and with the very agent whom vindictiveness in full swing might have prompted the nation to elect. It is the very irony of fate, a calamity for which the single consolation lies in the old expression of a trust to which political faith is mere suspicion, "Shall not the Judge of all the world do right?" With the ship barely over the bar the pilot falls dead upon the deck—and it must be well, but the sailors may be pardoned if for the moment they feel as if the harbor would never be attained. It is hard to estimate even the immediate effects of a disaster so great and so unexpected; the consequences are so vast, the data so numerous, that the mind is bewildered by the effort preliminary to calculation. The main datum of all is, however, secured; the law-abiding North rejects the idea of revolution, and intends to accept Mr. Andrew Johnson as its Chief Magistrate, and that fact once granted, two or three results will, we think, seem to reflecting men almost inevitable: 1. The North has suffered an immense loss of power. 2. The prospect of peace has been weakened, if not materially, still perceptibly; but (3) the triumph of the great cause itself is as secure as ever.

1. The North has lost in Mr. LINCOLN an advantage of organization great always, but greatest in a democracy—a ruler whose power was based upon the laws, but who was in action nearly absolute. Mr. LINCOLN entertained from the first a high idea of his own responsibility as the elected representative of the nation, and four years of incessant strife, passed almost without a blunder, had secured him a popular confidence which made his will almost irresistible. Not originally a statesman, and always hampered by defective knowledge, as, for example, in finance, he had risen gradually above circumstances till his enemies denounced him as an autocrat, till his ministers became clerks, his generals instruments, his envoys agents to carry out his commands. So thoroughly had the belief in his honesty and capacity penetrated the national mind, that had he, five hours after the fall of Richmond, dismissed General Grant from the service without a reason, the people would, while still sore and wondering, have believed that the reason must be adequate. When once resolved on his course no politician ventured to dictate to him, no general to disobey him, no State to lock the wheels of the machine. "In the end," he said once, "the decision must rest with me," and the people had learned to know that it was best it should so rest. An authority so wide gave coherence to the national action, brought to it all the advantages of Cæsarism without the tendency to dependence which is apt to be its heaviest drawback. The nation still thought and decided for itself, but so perfect was the harmony between it and its head that his command had the irresistible force of an utterance of the national will, against which any individual, whether he represented, like Frémont, a great territorial section, or, like Mr. Seymour, a compact organization, or, like General

McClellan, an entire party in the army and the nation, shattered himself in vain. Mr. LINCOLN had come to be, like Cavour, a man whose spoken word carried with it the crushing authority of a popular vote, who, while in appearance only representative, was in reality as absolute as if the people itself had been embodied in him. Such a man is the necessity of every revolution, and in losing him the Union has lost the strongest link in its momentary organization.

* * * * * * * * *

2. The chances of peace are diminished, to what degree it is impossible to say, but still diminished. The mad ruffian who has just murdered the representative man of his country as he would have murdered an opponent in a southern tavern broil, has killed the one man on whom the South could have relied for justice and moderation. Mr. LINCOLN's mere existence as President was a permanent offer of peace upon unchangeable terms, a guarantee to every State in the confederacy that if it would do certain acts it would at once be replaced in a certain position—acts and position being alike endurable. Where is the guarantee now? Mr. Andrew Johnson is probably far more merciful than his talk, may follow his predecessor's policy, may indeed have only expressed a wish for severity because as Vice-President he had no other means of being individual at all. But there is and can be no proof of all this, and till it is proved, till, for instance, it is certain that the new President is no advocate for confiscation, every State which can hesitate, will, even if its mind had been previously made up. Mr. Johnson has lived the life of a border abolitionist, a man whose one great idea has forced him daily to take his life in his hand, who has learned to regard the slaveholders as deadly personal foes, to view them as a class deserving neither mercy nor justice. That, as far as the system is concerned, is well; but it is the worst mood in which a reformer can approach the individuals whom his reform affects. The South by its own act has exchanged a conqueror whom it could trust for a conqueror it has reason to dread, and it must therefore hesitate, if it can, to place itself finally in that conqueror's hand, Add to this cause of delay the shock to the negroes, who, like all half-civilized men understand a principle chiefly through a name; the new excitement to southern imagination in the prospect of northern confusion; the new hope which will spring in southern statesmen that Mr. Johnson may affront France or menace England, and we shall see ample cause to fear the protraction of the war. Fortunately the catastrophe occurred when success had been in substance achieved, and it is not the fact but only the time of victory which is in question, but still there may be delay.

3. And yet the cause must win, not only because Providence governs as well as reigns—though events like the one we deplore force even politicians to recall the single certainty of politics—not only because a cause never hangs upon a single life, but because of the special circumstances of this individual case. This war, from first to last, has been a people's war, commenced, con-

ducted, and sustained by the instinct of a whole nation, slowly shaping itself into action and finding for itself expression. The singular position of Mr. LINCOLN—a position unparalleled, we believe, in modern history, or paralleled by that of Cavour alone—was that, while intensely individual, he was in the most perfect and complete degree a reflector of the national will His convictions, originally those of an average American of the western States, advanced in perfect independence at the same rate as those of the country, from recognizing the need of an expedition to enduring the sacrifices of continued campaigns, from a distrust of the extension of slavery to an iron resolve that it should cease, until at last his public utterances attained something of that volume of sound and depth and variety of meaning which belong to the expression of genuinely national opinions. When Cavour resigned after Villafranca, men knew without telling that Italy had made up its mind that Villafranca should be a phrase; when Mr. LINCOLN declared that, should the negroes ever be re-enslaved, "another, not I," would be the agent, the world perceived that abolition had become a fixed constituent in the national creed. The people have lost their mouthpiece, but not the determination which he so clearly expressed. His death, whatever else it may do, will certainly not diminish their hatred of slavery, or of that habit of violence, that contempt of all obstacles, human and divine, when they stand in the way of self-will, which slavery engenders. "The black man resists—lash him ; the white man defies us—kill him ;" that is the syllogism of slavery, which Wilkes Booth has worked out in the face of all mankind. He killed Mr. LINCOLN as he would have killed a man who preached abolition, or crossed his speculations, or defeated him at cards, as men used to be killed every day in New Orleans, if they gave offence to men trained from boyhood to regard their own will as almost sacred. The North will not love the slaveholders the more for perceiving so clearly whither their system tends, for realizing that in the murder of Mr. LINCOLN, as in the assault on Mr. Sumner, lawless force is the natural expression of the spirit of the institution. Slavery was doomed before—it will be hated now ; and the motive power of the revolution is the necessity of ending slavery. Nor is the organization framed for that end shattered by Mr. LINCOLN's death. The framework has been terribly tested by that great shock ; but it has stood. * * *

MR. LINCOLN AND HIS FATE.

It is but seldom that men kick against the pricks of a foreign political calamity as they do against those of a sudden private grief; seldom that they feel as if to realize it were almost too painful, and feed their mind on those futile "ifs" and "might-have-beens" which give an intellectual relief by restoring the old natural point of view at the expense of the keener pang which reminds them that all these probabilities of yesterday are the impossibilities of to-day. Yet there were many Englishmen, not a few passionless Englishmen, who, though knowing nothing personally of the late President of the United States, felt thus rebellious against the news received on Wednesday of Mr. LINCOLN's murder. This was no doubt in some degree due to the political *anxiety* excited by the murder of a ruler pledged to a policy of gentleness towards the South and peace towards the rest of the world, and his murder in a manner likely to unloose the worst passions of civil war. But it was due in a far greater degree to the moral and imaginative shock of the event itself, to the striking incompatibility between Mr. LINCOLN's mild and patient temper and slow constitutional methods, and the deed of treachery and blood which has closed his career. No one felt this peculiar bitterness when John Brown, a man in some respects of more fascinating and picturesque, though not of more noble character, was hanged in Virginia for his attempt on Harper's Ferry. Then we could but say that "the blood of the martyrs is the seed of the church," and acquiesce in the noble old man's own expressed faith that he was "worth inconceivably more to hang than for any other earthly purpose." He had made up his mind to the chivalric duty of laying down his life for the slave, to precipitate the conflict between slavery and freedom; and though many condemned this apparent impatience of the slowly ripening purposes of Providence, all felt that it would not be laid down in vain. He had chosen his own fate, and there was something of satisfying moral sublimity in the tragedy of his heroism. It was impossible to blame a slave State for executing a violent destroyer of its institutions and invader of its peace, though our deepest sympathies were with the sufferer and against his judges.

But there is nothing of this consolation in the violent and apparently unmeaning tragedy of this second and far more shocking martyrdom. Although Mr. LINCOLN's official life began with a foiled attempt at assassination, and has closed thus awfully when he had just succeeded in nearing the end of the country's troubles—though his short four years' service in the cause of freedom has been framed as it were in blood—there is nothing which seems less consonant to Mr. LINCOLN's character than the violent death which wicked men planned for him. Unlike John Brown, it was his first and dearest wish to avoid appealing to the sword. There was absolutely nothing of the impatience of revolutionary feeling about him, nothing of the spirit which cries to God for vengeance on the oppressor. If there was any one remarkable characteristic about Mr. LINCOLN, it was his almost undue disposition to wait upon Providence, and not to act till the one duty that was clearly visible to his mind and thoroughly grasped by his conscience required him to act. Instead of precipitating the conflict like John Brown, and appealing hastily to the arbitrament of the sword, Mr. LINCOLN's whole heart was set on the desire to *avert* judgment, to see if God had not some better way in store for the salvation of the country than the fiery trial of battle. When in the autumn of 1858, the year before John Brown's raid, Mr. LINCOLN canvassed the State of Illinois as senator against Mr. Douglas, (the advocate of the spread of slavery into the Territories,) his speeches literally teemed with declarations of his ardent desire to delay and. if possible, prevent the conflict which he anticipated. "I have again and again said," reiterated Mr. LINCOLN, "that I would not enter into any of the States to disturb the institution of slavery." All he demanded—and he demanded it expressly to *avert* this otherwise inevitable conflict—was a "national policy with regard to the institution of slavery that acknowledges and deals with that institution as being *wrong*." This was two years before the possibility of the presidency was even a dream to him. But all he said in this struggle with Mr. Douglas was singularly characteristic of the future President—all was patience, moderation, conspicuous lucidity as to matters of principle, distinct determination not to hurry the course of events as to matters of policy. He was as much the opposite of John Brown as one noble and good man could be of another noble and good man. The one was anxious to cut knots with the sword; the other to loose them gradually, though it should take generations, even centuries, to effect it. The one chafed under the slowness of God's purpose; the other shrank from the rashness of precipitating His judgments through not adequately understanding them. The one was of the fiery, revolutionary temperament which assumes its divine commission and rushes into the battle; the other of the vigilant, naturalistic temperament which watches the issue, and cannot believe that it has any commission to fight till the tide of war interferes with the discharge of some plain and long accustomed duty. Hence while the martyrdom of John Brown seems the natural close to a noble but half-presumptuous career, the murder of Mr. LINCOLN looks like an anomaly in history—an act of bloody personal revenge committed on the most impersonal, the most patient, the most tardy, though the most firm of rulers—a violent death inflicted on a cautious exponent of national convictions who never in his life expressed an uncharitable view of his enemies, who never stirred into activity one hostile feeling which could single *him* out as its individual object, who moderated, even while he gave effect to, the will of the nation which he governed. Such an end to such a man is less tragic than terrible, for it does not tend to "purify by pity and by fear," but rather to distress by the jar of incoherent feelings.

Yet from another point of view there is something grand and pathetic about the sacrifice. It is, we may fairly say, representative of the great conflict. We do not mean for a moment to suppose that this cruel and cowardly act has received any sanction from the confederate government. Even Mr. Davis is probably not evil enough for that, and General Lee would abhor it with his whole soul. But, no doubt, as Mr. LINCOLN may be fairly considered especially representative of the northern movement, this violent and treacherous Baltimore rowdy may fairly be called especially representative of the southern movement—

of the party which proposed and attempted to carry out the treacherous murder of a nation for the sake of revenging the gentle curb which had been imposed on their lust for extended power and extended slavery. The leaders in the South, nay, we believe, the mass of the southern people, have been better, far better, than the principle which impelled them into this strife. But what that principle was there has been no manner of doubt from the moment when the South Carolinian bully, Brooks, half murdered Mr. Sumner in the Senate house for attacking slavery, and became himself almost an object of apotheosis in his native State for his brutal and cowardly act, up to the moment when the evil passions of southern society culminated in this foul murder of Mr. LINCOLN. No doubt Mr. Davis sanctioned these passions only in moments when he himself succumbed to them, as when he called upon the Georgians the other day to " whip the Yankee spaniels," and teach them their true masters; but it is none the less true that he used these passions for his own purposes, and that without them he could never have hounded on the South to battle. Wilkes Booth may have, we trust has, no accomplice but the cowardly wretch who at the same time attempted and probably effected the murder of Mr. Seward and his son; but yet no one who looks at history can deny that his act is symbolic of the passions of the slave society, from which it proceeds, and is, indeed, but one new and more fatal explosion of the same destructive forces which engendered the rebellion. Mr. LINCOLN, no doubt, has shown a spirit as much higher than the average spirit of the North as this dastardly act is below the average spirit of the South. But his murder by this self-styled tyrannicide is not on that account less representative of the struggle; for it is the highest spirit in the North—the true birth of freedom, which has at last secured its conquest; and it is the worst spirit in the South—the true birth of slavery, which has at last secured its defeat. Mr. LINCOLN said at Philadelphia, when his life was first threatened, just before he assumed the presidency, in 1861 : " If this country cannot be saved without giving up the principle of the Declaration of Independence, I was about to say, I would rather be assassinated on this spot than surrender it;" and the sacrifice was accepted. For refusing to give up that principle—the vital principle of northern liberty—he was some years later assassinated, though not till after he had firmly secured, as we may hope, the triumph of that principle.

And if he did not secure it by his life, we may hope that he secured it by his death. To all appearances, indeed, the prospect seems gloomy enough. Succeeded by a man of very different character, and called to lead a people whose first instinct can scarcely be otherwise than bitterly resentful, nothing short of the example which Mr. LINCOLN has set to the nation, no less than to his successor, could arrest revenge. But with Mr. LINCOLN's administration before them—with the evidence they have of the sincere patriotism, the reverence for law, and the religious faith with which he took every great step in his short but eventful official life, it is scarcely possible that they should fall into the temptation of treating the South with southern passion. Only Washington among the Presidents of the United States could compare with Mr. LINCOLN for temper and scrupulous self command under extraordinary trials. Indeed, when Mr. LINCOLN assumed office, he did not disguise from himself that he had a part no less arduous than Washington to play, and that it could be played with equal credit only by the help of the same Power. " My friends," he said, when leaving his home in Illinois, in 1861, "no one not in my position can appreciate the sadness I feel at this parting. To the people I owe all that I am. Here I have lived more than a quarter of a century, here my children were born, and here one of them lies buried. I know not how soon I shall see you again. A duty devolves upon me which is, perhaps, greater than that which has devolved upon any man since the days of Washington. He never could have succeeded without the aid of Divine Providence, upon which he at all times relied. I feel that I cannot succeed without the same divine aid which sustained him. In the same Almighty Being I place my reliance for support, and I hope you, my friends, will all pray that I may receive that divine assistance without which I cannot succeed; but with which, success is certain." The same tone of trust and self-distrust ran through all Mr. LINCOLN's official acts, from the first message in which, before the war broke out, he declared his intention to do the very *least* that was consistent with his duty, by "holding" United States property wherever he had the power, to that last affecting message in March last, when he confessed the complicity of the North in the guilt of the South, and, while praying for peace and for the opportunity "to bind up the nation's wounds," confessed that "if it be God's will that the scourge of war continue until the wealth piled up by bondsmen during two hundred and fifty years of unrequited toil shall be sunk, and that every drop of blood drawn by the lash shall be repaid by another drawn by the sword, as it was said two thousand years ago, still it must be true, that the judgments of the Lord are true and righteous altogether." With such an example of pure and self-forgetful patriotism running in their memories, it will be barely possible for the North to give themselves up to vindictive feeling. The memory of their simple-hearted and noble-minded ruler would be a greater hindrance to such a course than his living authority. And we may well hope that the strong and gentle nature whose last official words were words of sympathy for his foes, will inspire the future policy of the North as completely as if Mr. LINCOLN could still rule them. The greatest revenge the North could take on the society which nourished the spirit of Mr. LINCOLN's assassin would be to make it reverence his memory. The time will no doubt come when the rustic Illinois lawyer who showed so great an equanimity alike in adversity and success will be ranked with Washington by North and South alike, and when perhaps his murder may be spoken of as the turning-point which taught his enemies to know what spirit they were of.

[From the John Bull, London, April 29, 1865.]

THE NEWS FROM AMERICA.

Among all the surprises by which this wonderful war in America has been signalized, none is so amazing in its dramatic outbursts—none so fraught with the elements of pity and horror as the fall of ABRAHAM LINCOLN, in the proudest moment of his triumph, by an assassin's dastard blow.   The story discloses just such an argument as would have impressed itself most forcibly on the imagination of a Greek dramatist; indeed it may almost be said to be but a repetition of that tragic theme which the greatest of Greek dramatists has wrought out with such consummate genius.   Agamemnon returning to his home at the summit of his pride—" the lord of ships and conqueror of Troy "— only to perish at his own threshold by the stab of a murderess, does but stand out of the old epic legend as a type of the late President as he sat in the theatre on that eventful evening of the 14th of April.   For four terrible years Mr. LINCOLN had borne the weight of the most fearful responsibility which was ever cast upon man.   He had felt himself called upon by an imperious sense of duty to plunge his country into a civil war, and he had seen that war deepen and widen beyond all calculations that could have been formed—he had seen the opposition arrayed against him erect itself into a power which bade fair to beat back even the swarming soldiery which his vast resources had enabled him to call forth—and had still held on with a tenacity which all must own to be heroic, and which would have been sublime if it had been shown in a better cause.   And now it seemed as if the reward had come.   The North had at all events made up its mind that the capture of Richmond and the surrender of Lee amounted to a virtual overthrow of the "rebellion;" and when Mr. LINCOLN took his seat in the theatre it was perhaps under haughtier circumstances of success than ever a ruler of men secured for a public appearance.   He has wrestled with the Titans, so he may think, and has overthrown them.   There is a yet more difficult task before him—the task of reconstruction.   But there is a glory about this task that may well compensate for the difficulty.   If he can accomplish it, surely his name will be one of the most memorable in history. As he stands between so grand a past and so glorious a future, the foot of the crawling assassin is behind him, and he drops a dying man on the floor.

Who shall say that we live in a tame and prosaic age in the face of the marvels which recent events in America have yielded us?   It has been a surprise to many to see the utter *bouleversement* of those theories which were built on the assumed regard of Americans for popular rights—to find the solemn formula that all legitimate power is based on the will of the people, treated with as much contumely by the northern majority as ever it could have been by some incarnation of oriental despotism decked with all the pomp of barbaric pearl and gold. Those shrewd observers, who were fully prepared to see the greed and insolence of human nature crop out under the brave words which inaugurated American republicanism, were still confounded by the unexpected tenacity with which the American people, both North and South, clung through blood and ruin to the purpose which they had respectively formed, carried forward to the most terrific reality that which was at first regarded as merely a game of brag, and gave conclusive evidence that even in America there are popular passions astir that can at once override the influence of the "almighty dollar." The most sanguine calculations as to the resources of America must have been dwarfed by the stupendous efforts made on both sides, and the gigantic scale on which the war has been carried on. And it is more startling than all—to an Englishman no less startling than humiliating—to find that, while among ourselves the outbreak of a war passion is assuming a more and more debased type, all the ferocities engendered by civil discord were not sufficient to prevent the Americans from carrying into their great contest much of that chivalry and generosty which was characteristic of medieval warfare. The worst atrocities of Butler leave him a paladin and courteous knight in comparison with many an English "officer and gentleman" who claimed honor and reward at the hands of his country for services rendered during the Indian mutiny. The most rowdy journals of NewYork would never have stooped to degrade themselves to the brutalized level of our Anglo-Indian press at the same period. And if there were at the time of which we speak peculiar circumstances of aggravation that might palliate the popular yell for blood, we must not forget that during the Russian war—a struggle remarkably free from any elements of popular excitement—many of our journals at home turned the same cowardly thirst for human slaughter to excellent pecuniary account, as far as they themselves were concerned, and left us to bear the discredit and the pain of so unpleasant a remembrance. And now, last of all, comes this assassination of the President, rivalling in its appalling interest the blow which Brutus struck at the foot of Pompey's statue, the murder of Henry IV, and the avenging arm of Charlotte Corday uplifted over Marat's bath.

What will be the result of this foul crime, and in what manner is it likely to modify the future history of America? It is difficult to speculate on the answer to this question. Mr. LINCOLN had not certainly during the period of his power shown himself a statesman of high capacity. It may be doubted whether if he had had the opportunity he would have proved himself equal to the herculean and delicate task of reconstructing the American Union—even assuming that its constituent States are willing to be united.

[From the London Punch, May 6, 1865.]

ABRAHAM LINCOLN.

Foully assassinated April 14, 1865.

YOU lay a wreath on murdered LINCOLN's bier;
   You, who with mocking pencil wont to trace,
Broad for the self-complacent British sneer,
   His length of shambling limb, his furrowed face,

His gaunt, gnarled hands, his unkempt, bristling hair,
   His garb uncouth, his bearing ill at ease,
His lack of all we prize as debonair,
   Of power or will to shine, of art to please;

You, whose smart pen backed up the pencil's laugh,
   Judging each step as though the way were plain:
Reckless, so it could point its paragraph,
   Of chief's perplexity or people's pain.

Beside this corpse, that bears for winding-sheet
   The Stars and Stripes he lived to rear anew,
Between the mourners at his head and feet,
   Say, scurril-jester, is there room for *you?*

Yes, he had lived to shame me from my sneer,
   To lame my pencil, and confute my pen;
To make me own this hind of princes peer,
   This rail-splitter a true-born king of men.

My shallow judgment I had learnt to rue,
   Noting how to occasion's height he rose,
How his quaint wit made home-truth seem more true,
   How, iron-like, his temper grew by blows.

How humble yet now hopeful he could be;
   How in good fortune and in ill the same;
Nor bitter in success, nor boastful he;
   Thirsty for gold nor feverish for fame.

He went about his work—such work as few
   Ever had laid on head and heart and hand—
As one who knows, where there's a task to do,
   Man's honest will must Heaven's good grace command;

Who trusts the strength will with the burden grow,
   That God makes instruments to work his will,
If but that will we can arrive to know,
   Nor tamper with the weights of good and ill.

So he went forth to battle on the side
   That he felt clear was liberty's and right's,
As in his peasant boyhood he had plied
   His warfare with rude nature's thwarting mights.

The uncleared forest, the unbroken soil,
    The iron bark, that turns the lumberer's axe,
The rapid, that o'erbears the boatman's toil,
    The prairie, hiding the mazed wanderer's tracks,

The ambushed Indian, and the prowling bear;
    Such were the needs that helped his youth to train.
Rough culture, but such trees large fruit may bear,
    If but their stocks be of right girth and grain.

So he grew up, a destined work to do,
    And lived to do it; four long-suffering years'
Ill-fate, ill-feeling, ill-report, lived through,
    And then he heard the hisses change to cheers,

The taunts to tribute, the abuse to praise,
    And took both with the same unwavering mood;
Till, as he came on light, from darkling days,
    And seemed to touch the goal from where he stood,

A felon hand, between the goal and him,
    Reached from behind his back, a trigger prest,
And those perplexed and patient eyes were dim,
    Those gaunt, long-laboring limbs were laid to rest!

The words of mercy were upon his lips,
    Forgiveness in his heart and on his pen,
When this vile murderer brought swift eclipse
    To thoughts of peace on earth, good-will to men

The Old World and the New, from sea to sea,
    Utter one voice of sympathy and shame!
Sore heart, so stopped when it at last beat high,
    Sad life, cut short just as its triumph came.

A deed accurst! Strokes have been struck before
    By the assassin's hand; whereof men doubt
If more of horror or disgrace they bore;
    But thy foul crime, like Cain's, stands darkly out.

Vile hand, that branded murder on a strife,
    Whate'er its grounds, stoutly and nobly striven;
And with the martyr's crown crownest a life
    With much to praise, little to be forgiven!

[From the Liverpool Daily Post, April 27, 1865.]

ABRAHAM LINCOLN.

In the hour of northern victory the northern President has been martyred. His faithfulness to his sworn duty has cost him his life. A few hours after he had uttered in council sentiments of kindness and conciliation towards the prostrate South, the remorseless aim of an assassin robbed the almost reunited republic of its wise and honest guide. The world will echo with loud and bitter detestation the hellish act by which ABRAHAM LINCOLN was sacrificed; while those who have watched with sympathy the conduct of the departed President will rejoice that he lived just long enough to be consoled by appreciation and success.

It were futile to endeavor to express the feelings which the horrible occurrence at Washington has excited, for as yet they are too poignant for utterance. The vast issues which impend almost daze the understanding and numb the sensibilities. It is only possible at such a moment to retrace the story of the life so sadly ended, and to balance with forced calmness the elements of the character which now lies like a fallen tree, unchangeable, with no trait to be developed and no lineament to be added. If there ever was a man who in trying times avoided offence it was Mr. LINCOLN. If there ever was a leader in a civil contest who shunned acrimony and eschewed passion, it was he. In a time of much cant and affectation he was simple, unaffected, true, transparent. In a season of many mistakes he was never known to be wrong. Where almost all were dubious, he was clear; where many were recreant, he was faithful. Yet there was nothing ill-timed or blunt in his sincerity and straightforwardness. By a happy tact, not often so felicitously blended with pure singleness of soul, ABRAHAM LINCOLN knew when to speak, and never spoke too early or too late. True from the first to his solemn purpose, the restoration of the Union, many who remembered that he had been chosen as a man opposed to slavery deemed him almost a traitor because he did not constantly thrust forward, as imprudently as they hoped he would, the principle of emancipation. But those who approached him never failed to discover what was nearest his heart and what most truly animated his policy. The result has justified his conduct, for it was ABRAHAM LINCOLN who put an end to American slavery, against which men who seemed greater—for Heaven's ways are not as ours—had long contended in vain.

It is especially to be remembered that one of the sublimest state papers of modern times was that simple message in which, at the turning point of the war, LINCOLN expressed, in language worthy of the grandest theocratic eras, his faith in the justice of Heaven, and his devout willingness to accept in common with the leaders of the rebellion the character of instruments in the hand of Providence. The English press deserves little honor for its behavior towards America; but the Americans will not forget that, even before success had tinged Mr. LINCOLN's career with what has sadly proved a setting glory, the simple grandeur of his recreant speeches, delivered, be it observed, at the earliest proper moment, had extorted even from organs which deeply sympathized with the confederacy the acknowledgment that he was a good, a strong, a generous, a stately man. Fine gold such as this could not be dimmed by the breath of calumny, nor will it be shattered by the shot of the assassin. The mortal part of ABRAHAM LINCOLN will be consigned to an honorable and long-remembered tomb; but the memory of his statesmanship, translucent in the highest degree, wise above the average, and openly faithful more than almost any this age has witnessed to fact and right, will live in the hearts and minds of the whole Anglo-Saxon race as one of the noblest examples of that race's highest qualities. Add to all this that ABRAHAM LINCOLN was the kindliest and pleasantest of men, that he had raised himself from nothing, and that to the last no grain of conceit or ostentation was found in him, and there stands before the world a man whose like we shall not soon look upon again.

Happily it is not needful as yet—let us hope it will not be—to sketch the character of Mr. LINCOLN's Secretary of State. Mr. Seward may yet recover; and though nothing can mitigate the horrors of the attack to which he was subjected, every one would be well pleased to evade the duty of dwelling upon an event so horrible.

As to the future, the speculations of yesterday were very anxious. The reputed character of the Vice-President, Mr. LINCOLN's legal and actual successor, filled many who were friendly towards the United States with vague uneasiness, and more than one scheme was suggested by which the dangers of Mr. Johnson's accession might be averted. Some told us that General Grant would at once become provisional dictator, and keep Washington calm and the ark of the Union secure, until some new and safe arrangement could be made for the carrying on of the government. Others suggested that Andrew Johnson would be induced to resign, so that both offices might be left vacant, an understanding being entered into with him that he should be re-elected to his old office of Vice-President. These were the most moderate of the ideas which prevailed; many not hesitating to anticipate anarchy of the wildest kind, and a complete collapse of American institutions. But, before the afternoon had worn over, the telegraph bore to us a rebuke of these imaginings. The Americans have done the best thing possible to reassure the world, and to attest the immobility of their government. Immediately after Mr. LINCOLN's decease, the Vice-President was sworn in before the Chief Justice of the Supreme Court, and Andrew Johnson is now *de jure* and *de facto* President of the United States. It is said that he exhibited the most appropriate emotion, and indeed the circumstances could hardly have failed to solemnize any mind; but the satisfaction to be derived from his demeanor is not so solid as that which is afforded by the regular and simple manner in which the installation of Mr. LINCOLN's successor has been proceeded with. No Amurath ever succeeded Amurath, or Harry Harry, with more certainty or less disturbance. The Americans know, if we do not, that institutions such as theirs depend upon no one man for their stability. Even when assassination rudely severs the line of the presidential succession it is instantaneously and noiselessly repaired. Englishmen have learned much of late about America and the Americans. They have now an opportunity of understanding that to an American the idea of a break in the chain of his government's history is as little likely to occur as is the notion of a hiatus in the English succession among ourselves.

We shall indulge in no guesses as to the effect of Mr. LINCOLN's assassination on the settlement of American affairs. Some prophesy the application of vengeful rigor to the defeated South. We would rather foretell such a ready and unanimous burst of manly indignation throughout the southern States as will effectually disarm the North and unite the whole republic in abhorrence of the atrocious crime which has sullied the conclusion of a gallant war, and in yearnings for a renewal of the Union which was the object of the dead President's dutiful devotion. Who can believe that men who have astounded the world by the noblest virtues of warfare, and the boldest determination of policy, could be driven even by the chagrin of failure to the degrading, cowardly, and criminal expedients of the bravo and the cutthroat? Rather let us suppose that these horrible catastrophes were the result of individual fanaticism, or even, as the name of Booth suggests—though one laments to find a name long linked with genius associated with crime—from theatrical and bombastic excitement. Any hypothesis rather than affix to a brave and noble people, who but lately were deemed a nation, the black bloodguiltiness of these terrible deeds! There will probably be no violence and no general vengeance; but in repentant mournfulness the ashes of good, brave, sterling ABRAHAM LINCOLN will be strewn upon the grave of civil discord.

[From the Leeds Mercury, Thursday, April 27, 1865.]

ASSASSINATION OF PRESIDENT LINCOLN.

The heart fails and the hand trembles as we record the fearful news which reaches us like a knell from the other side of the Atlantic. The North has gained its triumph, but the great man to whose wise counsels and brave spirit that triumph is so largely attributable lies a corpse in the capital of the States which he had once more united. On the 14th of April, on the very day after the federal flag had been triumphantly hoisted on the fort at which the first shot was fired, President LINCOLN fell by the hand of an assassin. His chief Secretary of State, not yet recovered from the effects of the injury he had sustained by his recent accident, was a second victim, and was lying apparently at the point of death when the mail which brings this fatal news quitted America. God only knows to what this terrible crime may lead. For ourselves, we tremble to think of the possible consequences. In that one head and heart seemed to be shut up the better genius of the reconstructed States. There are times when the fate of even the strongest nations seems to hang upon a thread; when a little event, the murder of a single man, may determine its doom for weal or woe, almost for life or death.

While the vessel is in the open sea, it can matter little whether the helm is turned a trifle too much to the right hand or to the left. But when driving through narrow and intricate channels, with dangerous banks and sharp ledges of rock on either side, the smallest mishap in the guidance of the rudder may send the vessel to destruction. God grant it may not be so with that noble vessel, which, after surviving a tempest of unparalleled fury and duration, seemed at last, in calmer seas, but through winding and difficult channels, reaching the longed-for haven! We have still faith in that large-hearted, broad-minded view which the mass of the northern people have continued to hold, even in the midst of the great agony which has convulsed the nation for the last four years. A certain amount of froth and folly there has been, as in all great disturbances, but underneath this spray of angry words and hasty counsels the deep, strong, majestic roll of the thoughts and feelings of a mighty nation, basing its strength on justice, and animated by motives at once pure and elevated, has been visible to every discerning eye. But the greatest and wisest nation needs at the head of its executive one who can give form to its feelings and practical expression to its wishes. LINCOLN has been the very man to embody the national policy at such a moment. As a lawyer, acquainted with technical forms and deeply imbued with the spirit of the written Constitution, he was admirably qualified to carry out the great half-conservative, half-revolutionary work of reconstructing the nation on the old basis, made new by the excision of slavery, without shocking those prejudices or violating those principles to which the American mind always clings with such peculiar tenacity. As a man of great good sense and cool judgment he was able to read the signs of the age with more clearness than most of his contemporaries, and thus acquired the rare faculty of not only doing the right thing, but of doing the right thing at the right time. His great resolution, shown by his unflinching firmness of purpose during four of the most eventful years in the world's history, would have enabled him steadily to pursue his wise and benevolent purpose amid all the conflict of opinions and the confusion of counsels by which he was surrounded. Lastly his large-hearted philanthropy, the truly patriotic and Christian spirit in which he has ever viewed this great national crisis, would have shut out any fear of that bloody retribution which in almost any other country, and in any other age, would have visited the leaders, and perhaps even the people, of the revolted States. Was ever such a man cut off at such a season? Truly it may be said in this case that "man proposes, but God disposes." The prop and hope of the nation suddenly broken. The destroyer of his country's peace marked out by the popular voice for forgiveness; its restorer struck down by the shaft of a vengeance which counted everything noble and good its mortal foe, a vengeance which we earnestly pray may not bring down a fearful retribution on the heads of those in whose supposed interest the blow was struck.

President LINCOLN'S career has been one of the most remarkable ever recorded. Born in Kentucky; educated, so far as he was educated at all, in Indiana; in youth settled in the recently formed State of Illinois, he spent his whole life far away from the refining influences of large cities and polished society. Uncouth in figure, plain in features, endowed with neither the natural advantage of a good address nor the derived advantage of a careful education— an orator only in the greatness of his thoughts, not in the purity of his language, the poetry of his ideas, or the graces of his manner—modest in demeanor, utterly averse to all ostentation or idle display—he seemed the very last man in the United States likely to captivate the multitude, or to win the lofty position to which he was twice elected, and from which he has now at length been deposed by the hand of the great leveller. The speeches which won him so high a reputation as to suggest his name for the Presidency of the Union are not speeches which in this country would be called fine or eloquent; still less are they speeches of the kind usually supposed to constitute the staple of American oratory. The crowds which flocked from all parts of Illinois to hear his great encounters with the celebrated Douglas, the crowds which filled the Cooper Institute when he addressed the republicans of New York after the canvass of his own State, were not drawn by any hope of listening to withering invective, exquisite humor, delicate pathos, grand bursts of oratorical splendor, or loud-sounding praises of the country and flattery of the national prejudices. Never were speeches more devoid of clap-trap. He treats his opponent with a calm respect and courtesy from which neither the sarcasms with which he was attacked nor the growing warmth of the contest ever induced him to swerve. He dealt with slavery as one who strongly disapproved it, but was prepared to leave it wherever it constitutionally existed, and was never for a moment led to confound the system with the men, or to denounce the slaveholders in the language of indignation and invective. For the rest, his speeches are remarkable only for the clear, broad definition of constitutional principles, the unerring logic with which he applies these principles to existing facts, and the startling fairness and candor with which he always states the arguments of his opponents. Many men can speak eloquently who cannot act wisely. But no man ever spoke with the sound sense, clearness of view, and definiteness of purpose which mark his speeches, without having the wisdom which will make him great in action. His speeches are a photograph of his character. Full of transparent honesty and candor; without the smallest infusion of political rancor or personal vanity; singular in their forgetfulness of self; singular in their devotion to the cause of truth; never skimming the surface, but always grappling fairly with the whole question at issue; never shirking difficulties or shrinking from admissions, but meeting the one, and making the other, as calmly as if they were a part of his own case; overflowing with great thoughts, and strong in manly sense, which the very boldness of expression seemed, like the severe simplicity of the Egyptian architecture, to set off in more massive proportions: such were his speeches; such was his mind; such, too, was his policy.

Apart from the future, there is something singularly affecting in his murder at this particular crisis. His great work of crushing the rebellion, a work especially uncongenial to such a spirit, at last accomplished; the bright dawn of peace already breaking, and his heart beginning to expand to the happier duties which seemed now about to engage his attention; the dark frown vanishing from his brow, and the smile of gentle loving welcome beginning to play upon his features; all that was necessarily stern and repulsive in the character of his administration clearing away, and sunshine and brightness bursting out over the scene; at such a moment to be quenched in terrible, total, sudden eclipse! It is indeed a hard fate. And by whom was this ever-detestable crime, which will rank its authors with the worst assassins in history—with the murderers of William of Orange and Henry IV of France—by whom was this act of hideous wickedness committed? By the South we cannot and will not say; with all its crimes, the nation which produced Lee and Jackson cannot be chargeable with such a deed; but by a party, a faction, a knot of dark, cowardly assassins in the south, whose names and numbers it is impossible yet to know. Yes, it was the moment when his mind was revolving schemes of reconstruction and reconciliation, when his heart was yearning to forgive all that it had suffered, when peace was in all his thoughts and mercy in all his words, that this treacherous blow was aimed at his life. His great work was cut short, its sadder features alone brought to light, its brighter hidden and now blotted out forever. But posterity will give him his due. It will tell that though his work was bloody, his heart was kind; it will tell with what joy he was preparing to cast aside the sword, and welcome back those who had forced him to use it; it will tell how he loved peace, how he sought it, and how, when it seemed on the point of coming, when his arms were stretched out to welcome it, he fell dead, struck down by a murderous hand, at the post of duty and of honor. It will tell, too—and distant generations will repeat the story with growing enthusiasm—how, before his day's toil was done, the colossal fabric of negro slavery had been shivered to its base. For this he lived. His work accomplished in the appointed way, he met his tragic end. While the echo of joyful salvoes was yet ringing in his ears, joyful to him more because they heralded peace than because they celebrated victory, he passed away—leaving the world half stupefied with the horror of the crime and the magnitude of the loss.

History, which embalms few reputations so spotless and so sacred as his, will do justice to his memory. The present generation, and especially his own countrymen, can best mark their sense of his worth by following in his footsteps. In the few dignified words which he so lately uttered when asked to consecrate the cemetery of the heroes who fell at Gettysburg, President LINCOLN said : " It is not we that consecrate them, but they that consecrate us." May his own memory consecrate the great nation it was his lot to rule. His successor is unfortunately very unfavorably known, and is certainly not the person we should like to see in the place of the great statesman whose office he now holds. But Andrew Johnson, with all his faults, is not a man without abilities or without virtues. His words on accepting the new office were words indicating a due sense of the solemn nature of the duties he is called upon to perform. With a cabinet trained to official duties under his noble predecessor, with a people resolute in maintaining the wise and moderate policy to which they have so magnanimously adhered, there is no reason to despair of the prospects of the federal States. They have had a fearful loss, but the greatness of LINCOLN was that he embodied the public feeling, not at all that he created it. In a free state this feeling will find its natural expression, and LINCOLN's work may survive, and LINCOLN's spirit may still rule, though his voice is quenched in the silence of death, and a bleeding nation mourns over his tomb. It may well mourn—but it may also rejoice. In that tomb lies the corpse of slavery.

ABRAHAM LINCOLN.

The great man whose assassination has left so remarkable a blank in the history of the world was not one of those who enjoyed the favors of fortune. He was bred in poverty, and whatever greatness he attained was attained by his own abilities and his own exertions.

(Here follows an account of the life, services, and assassination of Mr. LINCOLN, concluding with the following:)

So died this great and good man, after one-half of his work was completed, but while another half, which no one can execute as he would have done, remains to be finished. The mildest and most peace-loving of men, it was reserved for him, during the comparatively short period in which he has played a prominent part in the history of the world, to be but the minister of a terrible and desolating war. The firmness of his character, the comprehensiveness of his acts, the wisdom of his policy, have been fully displayed. The largeness of his heart, the noble forgivingness of his nature, and the temperate wisdom which can at once conciliate and command, have been nipped in the bud. Alas, for the hopes of the country that has lost such a man !

[From the Renfrewshire Independent, Paisley, Saturday, April 29, 1865.]

THE ASSASSINATION OF PRESIDENT LINCOLN—THE CONFEDERATE CUTTHROATS.

The "chivalry" of the the American slave States has found a frightful vindication in the assassination of President LINCOLN, and the attempted assassination of Mr. Secretary Seward.   This crime—the most atrocious political outrage of modern times—is but a fitting close to the revolt of the southern slaveholders—the heroes of the lash, the bowie-knife, and the revolver.   When General Lee had surrendered, and had washed his hands of the filthy business of defending the right to lash black men and outrage black women, it is not an unexpected result that the confederates should have chosen to put in force a matured plan of assassination, and have attempted to win back by the dagger what they had lost by the sword.   In the south, where assassination has been an habitual practice, the murder of "Honest ABE LINCOLN" will be received with applause, and will renew confidence in a lost cause.   When the brute Brooks, of South Carolina, attempted to assassinate Senator Sumner at Washington, instead of being execrated for his ruffianism, he became a hero in his own State, and was especially honored by the "ladies" of the South, who have a real admiration for ruffianism, especially when practiced on such helpless people as negro men and women.   On this side the Atlantic the execrable deed already finds abundance of apologists in the commercial scoundrelism that has been engaged in blockade-running and building privateers.   The public organs devoted to the interest of our commercial speculators, and the whole class of Jews and hucksters who desire the perpetuation of slavery, take care to express no exultation, but they at the same time show the want of that indignation which every honest heart must feel.   There is, Heaven be praised, a class undemoralized by the ledger and the yard-stick, and to them the infamous tragedy is a sincere regret.   Those Englishmen who in reality abhor slavery have had reason to regard President LINCOLN as in some measure the scourge of the curse, raised up to crush it, not by the merciless slaughter of all who dared to defend it, but by a combination of military and political measures that have finally trampled out the accursed system.   Recognizing in the federal President an instrument of Providence appointed to fill one of the most merciful missions ever committed to man, liberal and intelligent men have watched with an anxious dread every step of the avenger.   How wisely, how humanely, and how effectually he has fulfilled his beneficent duty, his bitterest enemies have at last been obliged to declare.   No paper has more ferociously vituperated Honest ABE than the London Times, and but a few days since, and when no warning of the President's death had reached that journal, it passed an eulogium upon him such as no man of our day and generation dare lay claim to.   The London Times has declared that during the trying ordeal of his presidency— an ordeal unsurpassed for danger and difficulty, as his death has proved it to be—ABRAHAM LINCOLN had done nothing he had any means to feel ashamed of. The warmest admirer of President LINCOLN, and the hottest partisan of his administration, could have said nothing further in laudation, and we shall not attempt to add a higher compliment. That the abominable and odious language used towards the President by a large section of our own press was false and calumnious could find no fuller refutation than the Times has written; but it is to be feared the brutal words of low-bred scribblers may have produced effects the recantation of the Times will not suffice to efface. That the republican party of the States should have had the sagacity to pick out of a private station a man so rarely gifted for the work he has had to do is a wonderful tribute to the sagacity of the American people. And the election of Mr. LINCOLN has no less clearly proved the intense dislike of a large section of our mercantile and aristocratic classes to the progress of such liberal institutions as flourish in America. Because ABRAHAM LINCOLN had begun life as a rail-splitter, had educated himself, and, we may add, did not consider it proper to own human cattle, the Tory papers, written to please the upper-class flunkies, and the unprincipled journals that serve the interest of the upstart commercial gentility of Glasgow and other commercial communities, described the President as a vulgar, low-bred fellow, a brute, buffoon, tyrant, and baboon. Such language can only fall back upon those who so undeservedly have made use of it; but the liberal class, and especially the working men belonging to it, should never forget the ebullition of rage which has been directed against a plain man of the people like Honest ABE, because he had it in his power to dictate terms to "a real gentleman" like Jeff. Davis, who had aristocratic notions about keeping negroes under the lash. The language which has been used by a portion of the public press of this country to support the cause of slavery in the confederacy, and vituperate those who have attempted to suppress it, has been a scandal the most abominable that has befallen us for many a year, and we must confess that it is passing strange no voice has been raised against it even in our own town, among a population so sensitive to political questions of import. But, indeed, the ignorance and prejudice shown upon the American question by the same class of working men who have in past times been in some measure regarded as political oracles leads to the suspicion that political zeal is dying out, and that a generation of idlers and fools are supplanting the same race whose intelligent views and energetic action won in times past for the middle classes such large concessions from the upper. While we thus lament over the untimely death of good honest ABRAHAM LINCOLN, and, worse still, grieve over the vile spirit of tyranny and oppression so rampant among ourselves, we do not think the federal cause will now suffer much from the loss of its ablest leader. The struggle between freedom and slavery was closed by the capture of Richmond and Lee. The confederates still in the field might safely be left to one the armies now in pursuit of them. The remnant of troops still led by Joe

Johnston are being pursued by Sherman's army, Grant's troops, and Hancock's division.   If they should escape from the Carolinas, Thomas, who is in Alabama, will fall upon their rear; and if Davis and an escort of runaways reach the Mississippi and escape into Texas, it is more than can be expected.   Some of our Tory papers believe that the confederates will escape to the Rocky mountains—a sad plight, it must be confessed, for the heroes who were to burn Washington and New York; but if they do, it will be but a scattered remnant who will find a fraternal refuge among the savage Indians and outcast thieves of the far west.   While the armed hordes of the confederacy will thus be speedily accounted for, the new federal President, Andy Johnson, will find means to pacify the South in a way which may prove to the assassins of LINCOLN that in him they have lost their best friend.   Educated among "southern gentlemen," and habituated to the paradise of a slave State, Johnson, it is believed, will turn out to be a man after the southern heart.   Belonging to the slave State of Tennessee, the new President, it is rumored, has imbibed the savagery so characteristic of southern chivalry, and has already been advocating the gallows pretty freely.   ABRAHAM LINCOLN was not the man to desire his death to be avenged in any way, but it is feared Andy Johnson will take upon himself what he may consider to be a public duty with some zeal for the work.   Now that Robert Lee has left behind him the patrons of the assassin Booth, not much regret will be expressed among the humane and intelligent of this country if Jeff. Davis and his whole gang expiate on the gallows the crime they have been guilty of in instigating a rebellion without better reason for it than the preservation of southern rights in human cattle.   If it be still denied that slavery was the mainspring of the revolt, we have but to point to the demands of the southern leaders to save the confederacy by making soldiers of the negroes, and to the fact that up to the last hour the slaveholders would not part with their black chattels.   There is not, however, a shred of argument to support the southern revolt, and it is but fitting that those who inspired it for the most foul purpose should now suffer for the guilt of all the desolation that has been caused.   In Andy Johnson vengeance may have a terrible minister, but let us remember that the crimes committed against the negro race for half a century have likewise to be cast into the scale.   As for the pacification of the South, that will be an easy matter.   Some two hundred thousand black troops quartered upon their old masters, and officered by a few Butlers and Blenkers, will solve the difficulty readily enough.   It may perchance happen that under such a régime the white men may occasionally get their throats cut, and the white women may find their old servants rather unpleasant masters; but if murder and outrage occur, it will only be a continuance of southern customs, with the difference that black instead of white men will be in the ascendant.   We write with an indignation of the fiendish crime committed that we expect will appeal to not a few of our readers; and to these we especially recommend the propriety of some immediate public expression of sympathy with the families of President LINCOLN and Secretary Seward. The contemptible silence Paisley has observed during the whole course of the American conflict goes far to blot out the recollection of the public and liberal spirit our town once had a reputation for; but the present emergency offers an opportunity for asserting our sympathy with the triumph of emancipation on the American continent, and the admiration we had for the honest old man whose life has been so ruthlessly sacrificed in the struggle.

In furthering this purpose we will readily aid in any way, give publicity to letters, or make public such suggestions as may be communicated to us, and we only hope the proposal may meet with an immediate and fitting response.

[From the West Surrey Times, Saturday, April 29, 1865.]

ABRAHAM LINCOLN, the kind and good President of the United States, has been assassinated, and among all the news of startling import which reaches us this week—the death of the amiable Czarowitz of Russia, the uncertain state of the health of the king of the Belgians, the assassination of the assistant secretary of the Russian legation at Paris, the capitulation of his army by General Lee, and the confession of the murder of her little brother, five years ago, by Constance Kent—that is the one subject which engrosses public attention and occupies the minds of all thinking men. A full account, so far as it has yet reached us, of the assassination of the President will be found in another column. Let us briefly recapitulate a few of the events which have been hurrying forward with such terrific rapidity in the United States within the last few weeks, and drop a tear to the memory of a man who, in circumstances of unparalleled difficulty, did as much for his country as any of his predecessors in the high office which he held—Washington or Adams, Jefferson or Madison, Monroe or Quincy Adams, Jackson or Van Buren, Harrison or Tyler, Polk or Taylor, Fillmore, Pierce, or Buchanan; and these names constitute the whole of the men who have presided over the United States of North America since their government was fairly established on its present basis in 1789.

* * * * * * * * *

LINCOLN was, withal, so good a man; his country looked to him so earnestly in her hour of need; his patriotism was so great; his honesty so sterling; his clemency so marked; his piety so pure; his firmness so inexhaustible, that none but miscreants such as these could have entertained for a moment the atrocious idea of a crime like this. In the magnificent language of Macbeth, when soliloquizing upon the proposed murder of the gentle Duncan—

> " He hath borne his faculties so meek, hath been
> So clear in his great office, that his virtues
> Will plead like angels, trumpet-tongued, against
> The deep damnation of his taking off;
> And pity, like a naked, new-born babe,
> Striding the blast, on Heaven's cherubim horsed,
> Upon the sightless couriers of the air,
> Shall blow the horrid deed in every eye,
> That tears shall drown the wind."

GREECE.

[Translation.]

MINISTRY OF FOREIGN AFFAIRS,
Athens, May 9, 1865.

The infamous assassination attempted lately against the person of Mr. LINCOLN, the President of the United States of America, as also against the enlightened Secretary of Foreign Affairs, Mr. William H. Seward, has filled with horror and indignation the whole Greek nation and the government of his Royal Highness, so much more as at the moment when this dreadful crime was being perpetrated the end of the sanguinary war was being ushered in which for so many years had shaken a free and intelligent country, to which Greece has never ceased feeling the greatest sympathy.

The death of a man of such high fame as the now immortal LINCOLN is an irreparable and common loss, felt not only by the United States, but by mankind in general, because, as a truly great politician, Mr. LINCOLN proved by results that he knew how to protect the real interests of the nation by turning the laurels of his victorious troops towards the common good of his country and mankind, and by endeavoring to cement a union by clemency.

You are solicited, Mr. Botassii, to express, officially, to the government of the United States the deep sympathy of the Greek nation and the condolence which it would convey to them for the disaster which has occurred, and you will add in your despatch that we will in Greece pray that the United States will pass unshaken through this ordeal, being confident in the capacity of the man who has succeeded in the government of his country.

The Minister,
D. BRAÏLAS.

Mr. D. N. BOTASSII,
Consul of his Royal Highness in New York.

70

HANSEATIC REPUBLICS.

Mr. Rösing to Mr. Hunter.

HANSEATIC LEGATION,
Washington, April 16, 1865.

SIR: It was with deep commotion and profound sorrow that I learned the sad events of which your note of yesterday bears intelligence.

The death of President LINCOLN will be lamented throughout this country not only, but throughout the world.

My heartfelt sympathies are with the much-tried Secretary of State and the Assistant Secretary. A benign Providence may spare their precious lives and let them witness their nation's resurrection from the mortal blow it has suffered.

I trust President Johnson will inherit the people's respect and confidence, of which his predecessor was possessed to such a remarkable degree.

With feelings of high personal regard, sir, I have the honor to be your most obedient servant,

JOHANNES RÖSING.

Hon. WILLIAM HUNTER,
Acting Secretary of State of the United States, Washington.

BREMEN.

[Translation.]

The Senate of the city of Bremen to President Johnson.

The appalling news of the atrocious deed which brought to so sudden an end the life and labors of President LINCOLN has caused horror and indignation wherever it has gone, but perhaps nowhere in a higher degree than in our city, whose citizens have ever since the first foundation of the American Union maintained with its people uninterrupted friendly relations of commerce and personal intercourse, and which at the present time has more numerous connections, comparatively, with the great transatlantic republic than any other state of the European continent.

Indeed the loss which the government and people of the United States have sustained by the hand of a fanatical assassin is felt the same as a public calamity in our midst, and it is this universal sentiment of deep sorrow and indignation which prompts us, the representatives of the Bremen republic, to express to your Excellency, as the successor of President LINCOLN, the feelings of hearty sympathy with which we in common with all our citizens regard this severe visitation upon your country.

May Almighty God, who, in His inscrutable providence, has permitted the commission of this awful crime, avert a similar calamity from the United States in all future time; and may He by His richest blessings heal the wounds from which the Union is suffering, and crown by an early peace the patriotic labors in which ABRAHAM LINCOLN has died as a martyr.

We avail ourselves of this mournful occasion to commend ourselves, and the republic which we have the honor of representing, to the friendly consideration of your Excellency, and to express to you our sentiments of distinguished esteem and regard.

The senate of the free Hanseatic city of Bremen:

The President of the Senate,

J. D. MEIER.

His Excellency the PRESIDENT
of the United States, Washington, D. C.

[Translation.]

Address of sympathy and condolence of the Bremen House of Burgesses to the United States, on the occasion of the death of President Lincoln.

BREMEN, *May* 3, 1865.

In consideration of the assassination of President LINCOLN, the committee of the House of Burgesses of the free state of Bremen wishes to express its warmest and most cordial sympathy with the United States for the loss of a man who devoted his life to the cause of freedom and equality among all men.

At a moment when the deceased President and the people of the United States were hoping to see the end of a terrible war that had been waged for years, with desperate efforts to perpetuate the work of the immortal Washington and his successors, and to restore a lasting peace to the country by conciliation and lenity, the weapon of a ruthless murderer destroyed the man who did not waver in days of the greatest trouble, but humbly bent before the Lord of Hosts, and, always mindful of his high duty, marched before his fellow-countrymen in the path of rectitude, giving them and the world a grand example, to show how a real honest citizen could finally accomplish a difficult and dangerous task by constancy and determination.

While we earnestly lament the death of such a distinguished man, who had already merited the highest consideration for his civic virtues, understood and appreciated by the citizens of Bremen before all other political corporations, we regret the attack made on his true and consistent friend and helper Mr. Seward, the Secretary of State, and cherish the hope that it may please Divine Providence to preserve that distinguished statesman yet many years to do good to his native land and bless his fellow-countrymen.

The close and friendly relations which have long existed between the United States and the free state of Bremen, the deep interest we take in the success of your affairs, and the just indignation which the bloody deed of assassination has caused among our people of every rank, induce us to hope that the expression of our sympathy and condolence with the people of the United States will be kindly received as a feeble testimonial of our good wishes, to be added to the many honors that have already been paid by many nations to the memory of your lamented President.

May his successor, by the help of Providence, be enabled to carry out the great plan of peace, the result of distinguished victories, and show the world that a republican government has been saved through all its trials and troubles, and that the helm of the ship of state is placed in strong and skilful hands.

In conclusion, we beg you to act as the interpreter of these our cordial sentiments to your fellow-citizens, and request you to communicate this address to the proper authorities, while we remain your devoted friends of the free state of Bremen.

In the name of and by order of the Bremen House of Burgesses:

Dr. FRIEDRICH ADOLPH MEYER,

President.

Mr. HENRY BOERNSTEIN,
  United States Consul.

HAMBURG.

[Translation.]

The Senate of the city of Hamburg to President Johnson.

HAMBURG, *May* 8, 1865.

Mr. PRESIDENT: The news of the criminal deed which so unexpectedly terminated the life and usefulness of President LINCOLN has, everywhere else, evoked in all circles of our republic just indignation and sincere grief. The many friendly and important relations which connect our two republics forcibly urge us to express to your Excellency our warmest sympathy for the great loss which the United States have sustained in the death of their esteemed President by the hand of an assassin.

The assembly of citizens of Hamburg, in their session of the 3d instant, resolved unanimously to join us in the expression of our feeling of profound mourning. May it please Providence to avert further calamities from the United States, and allow them soon to enjoy again the blessings of peace, of which they have been so long deprived, and may your Excellency be convinced that we shall always take the warmest interests in the destiny of the United States.

With the assurance of our distinguished regard, we subscribe ourselves, the Senate of the free and Hanseatic city of Hamburg.

N. F. HALLER, Dr.,
The President of the Senate.
W. CROPP, Dr., *Secretary.*

HAMBURG, *May* 2, 1865.

At a meeting of American citizens held this day in Hamburg, it was

Resolved, That whereas our Almighty Father has permitted to be removed from us our beloved President, ABRAHAM LINCOLN, we afflicted citizens, at this time distant from our country, desire to place on record the overwhelming grief which this sad event inspires. God in his mercy permitted him to live long enough to impress upon us a deep and everlasting affection for his virtues, and in our hearts he can never die. His memory will remain to us, and he will share with the "father of our country" the honored place of being first in the hearts of his countrymen.

Resolved, That our chairman, Hon. James R. McDonald, vice-consul of the United States in this city, send a copy of this resolution, with our heartfelt condolence, to Mrs. Lincoln and the Secretary of State.

JAMES R. McDONALD.	JOHN H. KLIPPART, *of Ohio.*
ALEX. SOTTAN.	FREDERIC WIPPERMANN.
FR. MEISSNER, *New York.*	JOHN R. WARBURG.
EMANUEL LYON.	P. J. BENJAMIN,
RUD. BORMANN.	EDWARD NIEBUHR.

AND THITY OTHER NAMES.

LUBEC.

Mr. Schumacher to Mr. Seward.

BALTIMORE, *June* 3, 1865.

SIR: The senate and people of the republic of Lubec, not content with the oral assurance of their sincere sympathy for the loss the American nation has suffered in the untimely end of their beloved President—which the undersigned had the honor of giving in their name—desire also to add a testimony in writing of these sentiments. They are embodied in the accompanying letter, which you are respectfully requested to hand to his Excellency the President; and if, as I hope, he will favor the senate with a reply, it will afford me pleasure to transmit the same to that body.

I remain, with sincere regard, your obedient servant,

A. SCHUMACHER,
Acting Chargé d'Affaires of the Hanseatic Republic.

Hon. WILLIAM H. SEWARD,
Secretary of State, Washington.

[Translation.]

LUBEC, *May* 10, 1865.

EXCELLENCY: The news of the assassination which terminated the life of the universally honored and very worthy President, ABRAHAM LINCOLN, has filled our city with equal horror at the crime, and pain and sorrow for the loss of the distinguished man who fell a victim.

It is this sentiment of sincere participation in the mourning for ABRAHAM LINCOLN pervading our senate, citizens, and the entire community, to which we now desire to give heart-felt expression.

We comprehend the magnitude of the loss which the government and people of the United States have sustained; we most sincerely wish prosperity to the Union, and commend our republic to the good will of your Excellency, feeling ourselves honored in tendering you the assurance of our particular regard and unaltered esteem.

The senate of the free and Hanseatic city of Lubec:

H. BREHMER, Dr.,
Presiding Burgomaster.

C. H. OVERBECK, Dr., *Secretary.*

DUCHY OF HESSE DARMSTADT.

CONSULATE OF THE GRAND DUCHY OF HESSE DARMSTADT,
Philadelphia, June 7, 1865.

SIR: I have been directed by his Royal Highness the Gand Duke of Hesse, through his prime minister the Baron von Dalwigk, to express to your Excellency the sincere sympathy of his Royal Highness, and of all his faithful subjects, at the assassination of the justly beloved and esteemed ABRAHAM LINCOLN, late President of the United States of North America, and the wish and hope that under your Excellency's administration the constitutional authorities may soon be re-established, and that peace and plenty may reign again over the whole of the land.

Enclosed I have the honor to transmit to your Excellency a letter of condolence (with a translation attached) addressed to me by the prime minister of Darmstadt, the Baron von Dalwigk, and I avail myself of this opportunity to renew my expression of abhorrence at the unhallowed crime which deprived this country of its first magistrate, and at a moment when friend and foe began to pay their just tribute of admiration to the deceased martyr for the almost accomplished suppression of a rebellion that finds no parallel in the past, and which, it is to be hoped in God, will never be equalled in the future. Allow me to express the hope that under your Excellency's administration this land may again teem with plenty, that its commerce may flourish more than ever and unmolested in all the waters of the world, under the bright stars and stripes under which such glorious deeds have been achieved.

I have the honor to remain your Excellency's most humble servant,

C. F. HAGEDORN,
Consul General of Hesse Darmstadt.

His Excellency ANDREW JOHNSON,
President of the United States of America.

[Translation.]

DARMSTADT, *May* 12, 1865.

SIR: It has pleased Providence to cut short, by the hand of an assassin, the life of ABRAHAM LINCOLN, late President of the United States of North America, at the moment when the great and just cause to which his life had been devoted was on the point of obtaining a complete triumph through the victories of the armies of the Union.

The news of this tragic event was received here, as in all the civilized states of the Old and the New World, with the most painful surprise, and the grand ducal government feels itself impelled to give utterance to this feeling to the government of the United States.

By order of his Royal Highness the Grand Duke, my most gracious lord, I therefore request you, sir, to express to his Excellency Andrew Johnson, the present President of the United States, in a becoming manner, the sincere sympathy which is felt here at the much to be lamented decease of President LINCOLN. At the same time I request you, sir, to express the wish and the hope that the Union, which has become the second fatherland of so many Germans, and especially of so many who belonged to the Grand Duchy of Hesse, under the guide of the present President, will soon rejoice in the re-establishment of the constitutional authorities over the whole of its territory, and with it the enjoyment of a new period of peace and prosperity.

Allow me to avail myself of this opportunity to express to you the renewed assurance of my perfect esteem.

BARON VON DALWIGK.

C. F. HAGEDORN, Esq.,
  Consul General of the Grand Duchy of Hesse Darmstadt.

HAYTI.

[Translation.]

HAYTIEN LEGATION IN WASHINGTON,
New York, April 17, 1865.

SIR: Your note of the 15th instant brings me sad confirmation of the horrid crime that ended the days of President LINCOLN, and news of the atrocious attempt to assassinate Mr. William H. Seward, Secretary of State, and Mr. Frederick Seward, Assistant Secretary.

These unfortunate events, which have thrown the whole United States into consternation and mourning, will everywhere excite the same wail of sorrow and condemnation.

I trace these lines with a wounded heart, and I can judge by my own feelings how his Excellency the President of Hayti and his people will be affected by the calamity of the 14th of April.

You will oblige me greatly by having the enclosed documents transmitted to their destination, and at the same time I beg you to express to the family of the late President, and of the Secretary of State, my profound sympathy for them in their deep affliction.

You inform me that Mr. Andrew Johnson, the Vice-President, has formally assumed the functions of President, in conformity with the Constitution of the United States, and that you are authorized by him to fulfil the duties of Secretary of State till further orders.

In expressing my wishes that Providence may watch over the American Union and its new chief, and restore Mr. William H. Seward and Mr. Frederick Seward to perfect health, I beg you to accept the assurance of the respectful consideration with which I have the honor to be ever your most obedient and humble servant,

D. BRUNO,
Secretary and Acting Chargé of the Haytien Legation
  near the Government of the United States.

Hon. WILLIAM HUNTER,
  Acting Secretary of State, Washington, D. C.

HAWAIIAN ISLANDS.

NEW YORK, *April* 21, 1865.

SIR : I have the honor to acknowledge the receipt this day of your letter of the 18th instant, enclosing a programme of the obsequies of the late President and inviting my attendance at the religious services at the Executive Mansion.

Indisposition having prevented my presence at Washington on this sad occasion, I take this opportunity to assure you that it was with the deepest regret that I learned the great bereavement which, under such heart-rending circumstances, has befallen the late President's family and the nation. In this regret I am sure his Majesty the King and his government will participate.

Seldom are the living called to mourn the death of a ruler whose noble deeds had gained for him such universal respect and esteem.

I pray you will be pleased to express to the family of the late President the sentiments which I feel on this mournful occasion.

I have the honor to be, with great consideration, your obedient servant,

S. W. F. ODELL.

Hon. WILLIAM HUNTER,
    Acting Secretary of State, &c., &c., &c.

NEW YORK, *April* 29, 1865.

SIR : I beg to express to you the great satisfaction I have in the continued favorable reports of the convalescence of the Secretary of State, as well as of the improving health of his son, the Assistant Secretary. It gives me great pleasure to be able to announce the same to the Hawaiian government by the mail closing this day.

I pray you will kindly make known to the Secretary of State the deep interest I feel in the recovery of himself and son. May the all-merciful God long continue their lives in the service of their country.

I have the honor to be, sir, your obedient servant,

S. W. F. ODELL.

Hon. WILLIAM HUNTER,
    Acting Secretary of State, &c., &c., &c.

[*Address delivered by Rev. E. Corwin, in Fort street church, Honolulu, before a crowded assembly of American and other foreign residents, Tuesday, May 9, on the reception of the news of the murder of President Lincoln.*

AMERICAN FELLOW-CITIZENS : No wonder that so many are congregated here to-day to testify their heartfelt sorrow for our nation's loss. And no wonder that so many of almost every clime and every nationality, deeply sympathizing with our grief, are here with us in the sanctuary to-day. That thrill of anguish which every loyal American felt all across yonder continent, as the sad tidings were borne to them that President LINCOLN had fallen by the hand of an assassin, has been felt not less deeply by every one of us. Why, yesternight, did strong men, little accustomed to weep, shed tears as they met each other on our streets? Why was there mourning in so many households? our children saddened as if by the tidings that one of our dearest kindred had died? Why, but because we all felt that this was to each one of us a personal bereavement—to every true American the saddest intelligence that had ever reached these shores? Our isolation from our fatherland has not bleached out our love of country. Not all the waves that roll between us and yonder far distant shore could wash out our patriotic devotion to that dear land from which for a time we are voluntary exiles—as not all those waves could suffice to wash out that organized crime which to-day causes a whole nation to mourn as they never mourned before. Not that ABRAHAM LINCOLN, great and good as he was, was so much greater or so much better than all others of our illustrious dead. But as none other had ever borne the responsibilities of Chief Magistrate during such troublous times, and thus been permitted to live so useful a life, so neither had any of our great men ever died such a death. The nation, sorely bereaved, had wept for its departed statesmen and heroes before, but never had it mourned the untimely death of so illustrious a martyr. The fathers of the republic, with fitting honors, had been laid to rest. The people, devoted to their chosen rulers with that intelligent devotion which liberty alone can foster, had shed tears of commingled sorrow and gratitude, when the only Washington the centuries could afford died in a good old age in quietness and full of honors. Such statesmen as Clay and Webster, too great to be Presidents, had been almost idolized by the people while living, and sincerely mourned by them when they died. Twice before had they carried to the grave their Chief Magistrate when as yet he had served but a small portion of his official term. But never before had they mourned, as now they mourn, for one stricken down at the very height of his popularity, from the very pinnacle of earthly glory, not by the act of God, but at the instigation of the devil; not by the gradual approach of disease, which might have prepared us for the shock, but suddenly, by the blow of a fiend in human form, a rash and foolhardy, yet calculating and deliberate assassin.

But it is no part of my purpose to rouse your indignation or to intensify your grief, as it is alike needless and impossible to increase your abhorrence of this monstrous crime. Let me the rather, as a minister of the gospel of peace, whose mission it is to comfort the afflicted, indicate some of those elements of consolation which, while they serve not to mitigate the crime or to lessen our loss, may help to assuage our grief.

Think not alone of the nation's loss in the President's death, but also of what the nation has gained by his most useful and laborious life, through more than one official term marvellously preserved.

Nobody doubts that this same malignant, murderous spirit, which has at length culminated in organized assassination, has been cherished in the hearts of multitudes at the south and the north ever since this infernal treason was hatched. It plotted and thought to consummate its hellish purpose at Baltimore, before the man of the people, that man of common honesty and common sense, should be installed in the place of his imbecile predecessor, who was content to see the nation die under his hand without remedy, and who knew of no way in which rebellious States could be coerced; and it has been breathing out threats of assassination and offering bribes and large rewards for assassination ever since. But He, the all-wise preserver of the man and the nation, thwarted the fiendish purpose for more than four long years. The marvel is, not that he is slain at last, but that God has shown His great love to our nation by preserving him so long. Think you that he who for those long anxious years had held with a steady hand the helm of state, while the vessel was outriding the protracted storm, and had, under God, guided it safely through the breakers till it had almost reached the port of peace—think you that when Richmond was taken and Lee surrendered he was not ready to say, with one of old, " Now let me depart in peace !" Ah yes; if it had only been in peace, then we could the better have borne it. But to die a violent death in the midst of his usefulness, when as yet the work was not finished, and the proclamation of peace, signed by that honored name, ABRAHAM LINCOLN, had not as yet been issued to the world—to be murdered when there was seemingly less cause than ever to anticipate it—to fall a victim to that malice which struck at the head of the nation, only because it utterly despaired of destroying the nation itself—to come, like Moses, to the very border of the promised land, and by faith to behold, as from the heights of Nebo, the future glory of the republic, and yet not be permitted to enter the land and see the promise fulfilled—this seems sad indeed. But what if the nation had been left without their great leader while as yet wandering in the wilderness, and no promise of peace had greeted their longing eyes ? Yes, even in the bitterness of our sorrow there is this occasion for gratitude; the dark cloud is fringed with this golden edge, and we can say, thank God, he lived to see this promised land, towards which, with the patience of a patriotic faith, he had so long been journeying. Yes, thank God, he was permitted to behold that promised land ready to become the perpetual and peaceful heritage of a great and strong and united people; but he knew not that the time and manner of his own death should be the miracle by which the Jordan waves of difficulty and doubt should be rolled away, that the united tribes, bearing the sacred ark of liberty, might at once go over to possess it.

O, our bereavement is bitter ; our loss is great ; our hearts are very heavy ;

but we accept all that God has permitted, with an unfaltering faith that He will bring great good out of the monstrous evil, and that He will, by the sympathy of their mutual griefs, bind the hearts of loyal Americans together, as they could have been bound together in no other way. O, my countrymen! was such a sacrifice needed to seal with more than royal blood our bond of love to our country, and our covenant of faith in freedom? Who shall say that he who has died for that faith would not willingly have offered himself a voluntary victim?

It is also comforting to think that ABRAHAM LINCOLN, the poor man's friend, the emancipator of the oppressed, the chosen champion of liberty and law, died at a time and in a manner most favorable for his own already illustrious fame; and so, as a martyr for liberty, is his memory most securely embalmed in the grateful hearts of an affectionate people.

Have you ever thought if Moses, the great leader and lawgiver of Israel, had lived to enter Canaan and to attempt the adjustment of all the difficult questions pertaining to the driving out of the heathen and the peaceful settlement of the tribes, he might have left some slight blot upon the record of his fair fame, and somewhat tarnished the transcendent brilliancy of a most illustrious career? History has no record of shame to make on all those pages devoted to the life of ABRAHAM LINCOLN. As his best legacy to his bereaved country, he leaves a clean record and an unsullied name.

Nor less may we derive comfort from the thought that this awful, this aggravated crime, sweeps away the last vestige of an apology from those misguided sympathizers with treason, at home and abroad, who had done so much to weaken our faith in human nature, and to make us almost ashamed of the race to which we belong. The true spirit of the rebellion is by this act written as in letters of fire across the very heavens, that all may see it, declaring that in theory and in fact it is nothing less than organized assassination. He who in his very heart condemns the crime and detests the perpetrators, the instigators and the sympathizers with it, as the basest of villains, may claim to be your friend and mine. But he who in his heart rejoices, or by word or look justifies it, is our worst enemy. He is himself at heart a murderer, as well as a traitor, and we cannot fellowship with him without ourselves partaking of his guilt.

This event, in itself so evil, will bring forth its legitimate fruits of good, if it shall serve, as it surely will, to show to all men how vile the intent, how malignant the spirit, and how fiendish the hate of those who planned and instigated that wholesale assassination which has slain so many victims, bereaved so many households, and, without a cause, spread desolation and woe over one of the most favored lands that yonder sun in the heavens ever shone upon.

Nor less is it a comfort to think that this event, in its immediate effect, is another illustration of the fact, of late so often impressed upon us, that God maketh the wrath of man to praise Him, and turneth the counsels of the wicked headlong. What those assassins sought to do was to paralyze the nation. But they have only been the unwitting instruments of rousing it to new life, and of calling forth all its latent energies. They thought to help the already doomed, hopelessly doomed rebellion, but they only wrote its death-warrant in the best blood of the nation, and robbed the South of its most kind and con- ciliatory friend. That mock-tragical shout of the fleeing assassin, *Sic semper tyrannis*, was the death-cry of despair, destined to be applied to the real tyrants over the revolted States, the leaders of the rebellion. It was, in behalf of those leaders, a decree against themselves, saying—since in their madness and folly they have rejected the terms of peace so often extended to them, and consummated their guilt by instigating the murder of the most lenient of rulers, the kindest-hearted of men—so let them perish ! Vindicative, but not vindic- tive, our rulers had been disposed to deal too tenderly with traitors—erring, if at all, on the side of mercy. But those plotters of treason have by this act demanded strict justice instead. Henceforth there can be no compromise with traitors ; no sacrifice of principle ; no permission to talk and think treason, much less to act it. To this standard of patriotism and this test of nationality has this last act of infamy brought the great bulk of the nation ; throughout the length and breadth of that land treason can no longer be tolerated in thought, speech, or behavior. Henceforth the only basis of settlement is unconditional surrender and uncompromising loyalty. And what more shall I say, but that this act, if it does not seal the lips, brands with lasting shame the brow of every apologist for that institution, hated of man and accursed of God, which has so far debauched the conscience, and perverted the reason, and maddened the heart of those who, because of their devotion to slavery, have willed that the nation should die, and that liberty should perish. Go read the record of our heroes slain, who have freely poured out their blood, and willingly yielded up their lives to maintain the integrity of the nation ; ask who slew all these, and from the tomb comes back but one response—slavery ! Go look at that casket, all unpolished, which held a diamond of rarest worth—an honest patriot's soul; ask who dealt that death-wound, and listen to the verdict of a mourning nation—it was slavery ! Go stand by the bedside of that great statesman who, with such masterly ability, has conducted the foreign correspondence of the government for more than four years, maintaining the honor of the nation abroad, saving us from ever-threatening complications, and extorting honor and victory from apparent concessions and apologies—go ask who struck that helpless sick man with the knife of a cowardly assassin, and there comes back but one response—slavery !

As Hamilcar, the father of the greatest of the Carthagenian generals, led his son Hannibal to the altar in the temple, at the age of nine years, and there laying the hand of that son upon the bleeding victim, bade him swear eternal hatred to Rome, so let every American father bring his son into the temple of liberty, and there, laying his hand all reverently upon the bleeding victim, exhort him to swear eternal fealty to freedom, eternal hatred to slavery.]

[Translation.]

The residents of the district of Lahaina, Hawaiian Islands, met in the church at Maui on the 13th of May, 1865, at 2 p. m., on account of the death of ABRAHAM LINCOLN, the President of the republic of America.

The meeting was opened with prayer by the Rev. D. Baldwin, after which, on nomination of D. Baldwin, M. Ihilie was chosen chairman, and D. Kahawlilio secretary. On motion of D. Baldwin, Mr. J. W. H. Kawnahie read his resolutions expressive of the sympathy of Lahaina, on account of the assassination of ABRAHAM LINCOLN. The resolutions as approved are as follows, viz:

Kin killeth kin; countryman murdereth countryman; surely this rebellion and calamity verify Sacred Writ—"a man's foes shall be they of his own household." It well becometh us of Lahaina-Maui, Sandwich Islands, to lament and weep together with the republic of America for the murder, the assassination, of the great, the good, the liberator ABRAHAM LINCOLN, the victim of hell-born treason—himself martyred, yet live his mighty deeds, victory, peace, and the emancipation of those despised, like all of us of the colored races: Therefore—

Resolved, That we of Lahaina mourn together with the republic of America, and deeply deplore the death of their Chief Magistrate, ABRAHAM LINCOLN.

Resolved, That we unite our voice of lamentation with that of the widows their cruel war has made, in sympathy with the now widowed mother of all, Mrs. Lincoln.

Resolved, That a committee of eleven be chosen to present our sympathy in this national bereavement to the American consul of this district.

Resolved, That, while weeping with those that weep, we bow in submission to the divine decree of Him "who doeth all things well;" for thus are we taught, and thus shall we be blessed.

Resolved, That copies of these resolutions be forwarded for publication in the newspapers Ke au O-Koa and in the Commercial Advertiser.

Resolved, That a copy be placed in the hands of the American consul for transmission to the afflicted widow.

Resolved, That the committee of eleven present to the American consul the assurances of our highest esteem and regard for the President of the United States.

On motion of D. Kelupuo the resolutions were read a second time by Charles Kalu, and on motion of J. D. Kahookano were fully approved.

On motion of J. W. H. Kawnahie the following committee of eleven were chosen, viz: Hon. J. W. H. Kawnahie, his excellency D. Nahaolelua, M. Ihiki, M. Kenui, C. W. Kenui, J. D. Kahookano, Charles Kalu, Leni Keliipio, D. Alvolo, D. Kahawlilio, and Kaniaw.

On motion of J. W. H. Kawnahie it was decided to incorporate the minutes of the meeting with the resolutions to be forwarded.

On motion of Charles Kalu the meeting adjourned.

D. KAHAWLILIO,
Secretary.

ITALY.

Mr. Marmora to Mr. Marsh.

[Translation.]

TURIN, May 6, 1865.

Mr. MINISTER: I have received the note which you have done me the honor to address me under date of May 5, transmitting to me a copy of a circular of the Department of State at Washington, which conveys the official announcement of the assassination committed on the person of the President of the United States, and of the accession of Mr. Andrew Johnson to the presidency.

On the 28th of April last I hastened to transmit to the minister of Italy at Washington the address which the Italian Parliament has voted to the Congress of the Union, in order to express to that body its sentiments of lively sympathy and the indignation which the execrable crime of which Mr. LINCOLN has been the victim has excited in Italy.

The King, my august sovereign, and his government, fully concur in this manifestation, and I renew to you, Mr. Minister, the warmest expression of the sentiments they have felt in common with the whole Italian nation on this sad occasion.

In forming sincere wishes for the prosperity of the States of the Union, and their worthy President, Mr. Andrew Johnson, I beg you to accept, Mr. Minister, the assurance of my high consideration.

ALPHONSE LA MARMORA.

[Translation.]

TURIN, *April* 28, 1865.

SIR: The news of the assassination of ABRAHAM LINCOLN has caused throughout Italy the deepest and most painful sensation.

The Italian Parliament, by spontaneous act, has resolved to express to the American nation, in this their sad bereavement, all those sentiments of genuine admiration which our nation entertained for the eminent man who, through times so fraught with danger, so wisely and steadily directed the policy of emancipation of the noble republic of North America; and at the same time to represent with what consternation and horror that honorable body apprized the terrible event. The house of representatives, in the morning session of yesterday, on motion by Hon. Mr. CRISPI, seconded by several other members, with the entire approval of the ministry, unanimously concluded "That the flag upon the front of the Carignani palace be clad in mourning during three consecutive days, and that a message of condolence be sent to the Congress of the United States."

Herewith I enclose you said message, received from the president of the house, with my special desire that you will transmit it to its address, and offer in the name of the King's government to the President of the United States renewed expressions of the sympathy and grief which our nation feels, and sincere vows for the welfare of the republic.

Accept, sir, &c., &c.,

The Minister of Foreign Affairs,
ALPHONSE LA MARMORA.

Commander BERTINATTI,
Minister Plenipotentiary of Italy at Washington.

[Translation.]

TURIN, *April* 27, 1865.

HONORABLE SIR: The announcement of the assassination of President ABRAHAM LINCOLN has caused a profound and painful sensation in the Italian house of representatives. From every political party into which this house is divided a common cry was spontaneously raised of condemnation of the deed, and of high commiseration and sympathy for the illustrious victim and the great nation of which he was the worthy chief.

The house, by unanimous vote, has resolved, "That, in sign of grief, the national flag be clad in mourning during three consecutive days;" and requested me to express, in a special message to you, the great sorrow which Italy herself and all the friends of freedom and civilization universally share.

A similar feeling has been awakened by the news of the attempt to take the life of Secretary Seward.

Having thus fulfilled the melancholy duty assigned me, I beg you now, honorable sir, to accept the assurance of my sympathy and high personal consideration.

The President of the House,
G. B. CASSINIS.

Hon. Mr. SPEAKER
    of the House of Representatives of the United States of America.

[Translation.]

ITALIAN EMIGRATION SOCIETY,
Ancona, May 4, 1865.

When the unanimous cry of sorrow arose from every corner of the earth, lamenting the tragic end of your distinguished President, ABRAHAM LINCOLN, and of execration against the authors of the atrocious crime, the Italian emigration resident in the "Marshe," struck by such a misfortune, shared the common sorrow and covered with black crape the flag of the Tiberian wolf and Adriatic lion.

LINCOLN, promulgator of liberty, defender of the rights of man, a faithful follower of the doctrine taught by the gospel, desired to banish slavery from free America, and to put an end to this stigma upon a civilized people. Seeing that any compromise with the oppressor was impossible, he was able, through the energy of his will and eloquent words, to initiate a holy war, which, owing to the valor of his soldiers and the free sacrifices of the northern people, was finished by federal victories and the planting of the holy flag of humanity upon the fortified strongholds of the slaveholders.

Infamous and cowardly men, guided by fanaticism and selfishness, through the arm of an assassin struck the man of the people and benefactor of humanity, with other illustrious victims, at the very moment when the Americans were rejoicing over their triumph, believing the end of the fratricidal contest to be at hand.

LINCOLN was the true friend of humanity.

LINCOLN was a citizen of the whole world.

LINCOLN is a martyr to a holy principle.

The Italian emigration, faithful to their principles of liberty, brotherhood, and sympathy with oppressed nations, have always followed, with great anxiety, the alternations of this war between civilization and barbarism, and rejoiced at the triumph of their brothers, while they wept over their defeats. Now, filled with the most intense sorrow at this tragic and unexpected deed, they scarcely

know how to express their feelings; they can only pray God for the pacification of the United States, and for the abolition forever of the market of beings
made in the image of God, that sublime object which was the aim of the illustrious martyr of whom we now lament the sudden and bloody death.

The commission charged to present this address beg you to receive and
transmit it to the United States government as an expression of their friendship
and sympathy.

M. URGOLINUCCI,
O. CERRNI,
G. BERNARDINI,
S. DORIA,
Committee.

The CONSUL GENERAL
 of the United States, Florence.

[Translation.]

To the people of the United States of America, from the citizens of Acireale, Sicily.

ACIREALE, *May* 10, 1865.

Your President, ABRAHAM LINCOLN, has fallen the victim of an assassin's
arm; may his blood weigh in the balance for the regeneration of your States.
We, a committee, desire to transmit to your proud and brave people a word
that may avail to express the intense grief experienced here on the announcement of the death of so great a man. We assure you that throughout the nation,
as if it were one individual, the human heart could not restrain its grief, and
staggered beneath the weight of so great a calamity.

ABRAHAM LINCOLN was not yours only—he was also ours, because he was
a brother whose great mind and fearless conscience guided a people to union,
and courageously uprooted slavery.

Brothers, the trial is not ended; the country calls for fresh martyrs—the
last contest—and on the news of your victory we will rejoice with you, as we
now grieve with you.

The committee:

PAOLO GRAEJA DIGA.
GIUSEPPE GRAZIE.
AVE MARIANO COSTANZO.
F. ROSSI MUSMEIZ.
DR. FRANCESCO LEOTTO.
DR. GIUSEPPE VIGO LEONARDI.
TYNAVIO BARBAGALTO.
GIUSEPPE COSTARELLI.
SALVATORE CASTARINA.

[Translation.]

Italian Society of United Workmen of Alessandria.

ALESSANDRIA, *May* 5, 1865.

HON. SIR: The Society of United Workmen of Alessandria, impressed with horror at the mighty crime that deprived ABRAHAM LINCOLN of life, that great defender of the oppressed and champion of liberty, has resolved to drape its banner in mourning for thirty days, and cherishes the most ardent hopes for the good of humanity and the liberty of the world, that the grand and holy work begun by this illustrious victim of treason may triumph in the end; and that the brave people of America, in the future development of their glorious republican institutions, may continue to serve as a model to free nations, and be a comfort and hope to those that mourn under the yoke of oppression.

PASTORE CAMILLO, *President.*   [L. S.]

Hon. GEO. P. MARSH, &c., &c., &c.

[Translation.]

BARGA, *May* 12, 1865.

HON. SIR: The Workingmen's Society of Barga, (near Lucca,) at a meeting on the 7th instant, commissioned me, the undersigned, to express to you, the worthy representative of the United States in Italy, its profound sorrow for the death of your most virtuous President, ABRAHAM LINCOLN, who fell by the hand of a treacherous assassin.

The horrid crime caused a shudder in the bosoms of all good men, and a sorrow that will never be blotted from the hearts of those who love liberty and free institutions like the immortal deceased; but it will not delay, for a moment, the triumph of the federal cause, the abolition of slavery and the emancipation of the people.

Accept, illustrious sir, for the generous nation you represent, the best wishes of the Workingmen's Society of Barga for its permanent prosperity and happiness.

ANTONIO MORDINI,
President and member of the Italian Parliament.

Hon. PERKINS MARSH,
United States Minister to Italy, Florence.

[Translation.]

MECHANICS' MUTUAL AID SOCIETY OF BRESIA,
May 10, 1865.

The announcement of the death of President ABRAHAM LINCOLN, slain by the hand of an assassin, has impressed our society with sincere and honest sorrow. The sad news that justly caused consternation and grief in the hearts of all lovers of justice and liberty must deeply move the feelings of all industrial associations, as they have lost a person dear to humanity, a being who was the living incarnation of the principles of equality and fraternity, the embodiment of true patriotism, of honest intentions, of firmness, and integrity.

But if the death of LINCOLN was a sad and serious event, like that of Christ, it may be the cause of the complete triumph of the humane and holy principle of true liberty, contended for by the great citizen, and which, in the generous American nation, does not depend upon one man, is bound to the life of no single individual, but will resurrect with more beauty and effulgence, and reflect its genial rays over Europe with beneficent effects.

With these sentiments, springing spontaneously from the hearts of the members of our association, we beg you, sir, to be their interpreter to Mr. Andrew Johnson, the worthy successor of Mr. LINCOLN; and while we express our best wishes for the restoration of the American Union, and for the prosperity, happiness, and glory of its people, we ask you to accept the expressions of our greatest consideration and esteem.

[SEAL.]

VIRGILIO CHITO,
President.

ANDREA SALSECHI,
GIACOMO DRAGHI,
GIUSEPPE FOCCHINI,
D. BIANCHI,
Members.

FAUSTINO PALAZZI,
Secretary.

A. FRIGERIO.

The UNITED STATES MINISTER.

[Translation.]

WORKINGMEN'S SOCIETY OF BOLOGNA,
(GENERAL GARIBALDI, HONORARY PRESIDENT,)
Bologna, May 11, 1865.

CITIZEN PRESIDENT: Universal grief and mourning was spread abroad at the sad announcement of the violent death of that most virtuous republican ABRAHAM LINCOLN, and the greatest indignation and horror was felt by all good people against the brutal parricide.

He was barbarously assassinated on the eve of the completion of his great task, the abolition of slavery.

May the malediction of God descend upon those who conceived and consummated the most abominable deed!

But the profound sorrow that affected all was greatly alleviated when it was known that the great American nation had called you to be the worthy successor of the illustrious deceased Chief Magistrate; because it is hoped that you will follow in his footsteps and complete the great task that he begun; and not only that, but give aid to a neighboring nation whose people are now subjugated by a foreign sovereign.

In expressing these sentiments of our society, inspired by republican and humanitarian principles, we cherish the firm hope that the day is not far distant when the glorious country discovered by our Italian Columbus will again flourish as formerly among the great nations of the earth.

Accept, Mr. President, the assurances of our highest respect and esteem.

ANNIBALE CALZONI,
Vice-President.

[SEAL.]

DOMENICO SANGIORGIO,
Secretary.

[Translation.]

BOLOGNA, May 12, 1865.

The Ladies' Society of Bologna, of which Teresita Garibaldi is honorary directress, by its committee, beg you, Mr. Minister, to send the enclosed address of condolence for the assassination of the illustrious ABRAHAM LINCOLN, to Mr. Andrew Johnson, the new President of the United States of America.

The society hall shall be hung with mourning, in token of condolence for the memory of the illustrious martyr of liberty, whose holy image shall ever be graven in the hearts of all the members of this society.

Accept, citizen ambassador, the sentiments of our particular esteem, and be kind enough to acknowledge the receipt of this note.

MARIA TECINI, Directress.
NINA BONFIGLIOLI,
CLAUDIA CAMUZZINI,
CARLOTTA TREBBI,
Committee of Members.

Hon. GEORGE P. MARSH, <i>Turin.</i>

[Translation.]

Address of condolence from the Ladies' Society of Bologna to the President.

ABRAHAM LINCOLN was barbarously assassinated at the moment when the abolition of slavery, the only aim of all of his hopes, had just been accomplished. May the grace of God reach the wretch, for man cannot pardon him!

But the cause of nations is not weakened by private misfortunes, and though our hearts are deeply stricken, we are consoled by the thought that the American nation has chosen you, Mr. President, as the worthy successor of the illustrious deceased, knowing that you would follow in his footsteps, put an end to the civil war, and fly to the help of a neighboring nation that a foreign power wishes to oppress.

The maidens, spouses, and mothers of that nation are sending up their prayers for the salvation of their country; and we, maidens, spouses, and mothers of suffering Italy, are waiting hopefully for the time when America, restored to her former strength and glory, and to her rightful station among the great nations of the earth, will come to our aid and relieve us from foreign oppression.

Accept, citizen President, the assurance of our most distinguished consideration.

For the Ladies' Society of Bologna:

MARIA TECINI, *Directress.*
NINA BONFIGLIOLI,
CLAUDIA CAMUZZINI.
CARLOTTA TEBBI,
Committee of the Members.

[Extract.]

No. 106 CONGRESS STREET,
Brooklyn, L. I., July 20, 1865.

I have the honor of informing you that the citizens of Canzo, province of Como, Lombardy, Italy, wishing to express their veneration and sympathy for the great martyr to the cause of emancipation and the Union, our lamented President, ABRAHAM LINCOLN, unanimously passed a resolution to call after his name the new square by the side of the national road in their town. They wished their resolution should reach your Excellency's hands, and intrusted to me the care of fulfilling their desire.

*   *   *   *   *   *   *   *

Please receive my highest feelings of regard, &c.

ACHILLE MAGNI.

His Excellency ANDREW JOHNSON,
President of the United States of America.

[Translation.]

RESOLUTION.

Participating in the sorrow of the rest of the world for the violent death of the President of the United States, the common council of Canzo, in token of sympathy for the champion of human freedom, and sorrow for his death,

Resolve, That the new square fronting on National street shall be called Lincoln square.

The municipal council is charged with the proper inscription.

[Translation.]

MUTUAL AID SOCIETY OF THE WORKINGMEN OF CARRU,
April 30, 1865.

To the United States Minister in Italy:

Even we, honest workingmen of an Italian village, were struck with horror and indignation at the unexpected and sad news from the United States of America, just at the time when all Europe was rejoicing over the splendid victories of the federal army. Even we felt it our duty to express to you, illustrious citizen and worthy representative of the United States in Italy, our profound condolence for the atrocious murder of your President, ABRAHAM LINCOLN, the martyr to a cause that interests all humanity.

As soon as the unlucky news reached us we draped our banner in mourning, as a token of the deep affliction of our hearts. One thought comforts us: the cause for which LINCOLN lived and died is now triumphant; the name of the man whose death we lament, crowned with immortal glory, shall shine in history with that of Washington. If one was the father of the great republic, the other was its saviour.

Unanimously adopted by the Mechanics' Mutual Aid Society of Carru, at a general meeting on the 30th of April, 1865.

GIORGIO ANTONIO FILIPPI, *President.*
GIORGIO BATTISTA GIANINETTO,
Vice-President.

PIETRO MADONNO, *Secretary.*

[Translation.]

CHIETI, *May* 10, 1865.

The Italians of Abrazzo to the people of the United States of America:

From the summits of our mountains, the bulwarks of liberty, from the banks of our rivers and the shores of our seas, a people who wish to be united, free, and independent have long bent their eyes upon events in the great republic whence they expect a new light to radiate upon the world, with a new era of democratic civilization.

Your history is the same as ours. From Camillus and Cincinnatus to Franklin and Washington, from LINCOLN and Seward to Garibaldi and Mazzini, the tradition of the great struggle between good and evil, liberty and slavery, civilization and barbarism, national autonomy and the rule of foreign despots, has ever been the same.

The roar of your battles was borne across the ocean and awaked an echo in our Appenines. Your victories were the triumph of humanity. But very soon the electric spark, drawn from the clouds by Franklin, told us that a parricidal hand had taken the life of ABRAHAM LINCOLN, when the destinies of his country and partly of the world were trusted to his care, and, at the same time, announced the savage attack upon Mr. Seward and his family.

A voice of detestation and of horror arose throughout the world; and symbols of liberty were draped in mourning everywhere; anguish filled our hearts; but we rejoice that the cause of humanity cannot perish. The blood of new martyrs fertilize the earth, and makes it the mother of freedmen.

ABRAHAM LINCOLN gave his life to save the integrity of the Union and the grandeur of his country, to rescue the colored man from slavery, to give to all men liberty and equality.

When peace shall be restored the white and black races will join hands above his grave, and the spirit of liberty, rising from his sepulchre, will renovate the surface of the earth, and make the return of any tyranny impossible.

LUIGI PRELITI.	SCIPIONE VITACOLONNA.
MICHELE D'OTTAVIO.	GIOVANNI PORTA.
IGINO CARLI.	TOMMASO DI CIO.
ENRICO D'FLAMMINEJ.	DOMENICO ORFANELLI.
ZILOTEO MAGNO.	LUIGI DE JANUARIO.
LUIGI GARZARELLI.	VINCENZO DEL MONACO
NICOLA MANA.	VINCENZO BONITATIBUS.
GIUSEPPE DE SIPIO.	GIVACCHINO D'EUGENIO.

AND TWO HUNDRED AND THIRTY OTHERS.

[Translation.]

MUTUAL AID SOCIETY OF CHIETI, *May* 9, 1865.

To the People of the United States:

BROTHERS: The news of the death of ABRAHAM LINCOLN, caused by the hand of a homicide, at a moment when America was about to gather the fruit of four years of immense sacrifice and continued struggle for liberty against the privileges of race, has found a mournful echo wherever the sound of your splendid victories has penetrated, and your glorious triumphs have carried the enthusiasm of magnanimous undertakings.

Fellow-workmen, bound to you in the bonds of brotherhood, we earnestly hope for our own social emancipation. Your efforts in a most holy cause have always had our sympathies, and we now share the indignation you feel at the attack on Mr. Seward.

We are sure the assassin's dagger cannot stop the work of liberty now nearly finished; and we hope the blood of the victim will cleanse the country of barbarism.

For the society:

GAETANO CARUSI, *President.*
GENNARO DE CARLO, *Vice-President.*
DANIELE POLIDORO,
FERDINANDO SANTONI DE SIO,
[SEAL.] FRANCESCO SICARDI,
Commtttee.

[Translation.]

Common council of Chieti to the people of the Republic of the United States of America.

CHIETI, *May* 11, 1865:

At a time when the whole civilized world was hailing the triumph of the abolition of slavery in your free country, the sad news of the violent death of ABRAHAM LINCOLN, the fearless pilot of liberty, changed the universal joy to mourning, and all humanity has raised a single united cry of malediction upon the authors of the horrid deed.

Let our expressions of condolence be joined to the many manifestations of sorrow that come to you from every part of the world; and accept the fraternal greeting of the common council of Chieti, with its wishes for your future prosperity.

Your sacrifice was immense in the four years of gigantic war for the great principles of brotherly love between black and white, and for the murder of John Brown, and on the 14th of April; but you may be proud of it now, for a holy cause was never more bravely sustained, with greater abnegation, in the paths pointed out by Washington, Franklin, and LINCOLN, and you may be sure it will not fail to reach the glorious bourne.

For the common council:

VINCENZO VERO, *President.*
CAMILLO JULIANI,
GUISEPPE DE SIPIO,
GABRIELLE DE SANCTIS,

FRANCESCO SANCUORE, *Secretary.* *Committee.*

[Translation.]

The Workingmen's Union of Catania, Sicily, to the American people.

CATANIA, *May* 11, 1865.

BROTHERS OF AMERICA : The capture of Richmond was the triumph of civilization over barbarism, and we rejoice at the restoration of peace in a great nation that is our friend.

But the news of Mr. LINCOLN's assassination has sent a thrill of horror and indignation through the civilized world, and its echo has penetrated deeply into our hearts.

Americans : The Workingmen's Union of Catania joins this day in the sentiments of sorrow felt for you by all free people.   Accept our congratulations, our best wishes, and our fervent hopes that the national will may complete the work of peace begun by a great citizen, to restore to America her former splendor and great prosperity.

MARCELLINO PIZZARELLI, *President,*
FRANCESCORE RANCORE, *Vice-President,*
SEBASTIANO VILLANI, *Second Vice-President,*
Committee.

A true copy :

MARIO TROFEO, *Secretary*

[Translation.]

The democratic society called the Sons of Labor, in Catania, to the heroic nation the United States, in condolence with their grief.

CATANIA, *May* 4, 1865.

BROTHERS : You fought the war of liberty and independence against slavery and tyranny.   With the anxiety of those who hope and fear, we waited for the news from your battle-fields.   The victories your gallant soldiers gained were victories for us, and their dangers seemed to be ours ; but the good genius of humanity, as unerring as destiny, will lead you triumphantly on in the path of progress.   You were victorious at Richmond, and human rights triumphed with you in your victory there.   It was a great advance in the path of right and justice ; joy was suppressed in the struggle, for it was terrible, and will be long remembered.   But, sad result ! ABRAHAM LINCOLN, the champion of your rights, the great, victorious citizen, remained the victim of a vile assassin. Cursed be the spirit of evil !   Brothers, we feel the blow that struck you : accept the greeting of love and consolation the Sons of Labor send you as a solemn tribute of profoundest sorrow.   But, brothers of America, now that your country is free, swear, upon the tomb of your deliverer, to rescue your brethren from the bonds of slavery.   His memory will be the terrible leader in your battles—the compact of alliance that binds you close together. His love shall be the example to guide you against those who seek to disunite you. The name of the wicked shall perish from off the face of the earth.

Be united, and extend the hand of pardon to your wayward brothers, and thus you will demonstrate to tyrants that the spirit of revenge is blotted from your hearts.

TOMMASO OLMATO, *President.*

[SEAL.]   GIAMBARTOLO ROMEO, *Secretary.*

[Translation.]

The patriotic Catanese and youths of the university to the people of the United, States of America.

CATANIA, *May* 5, 1865.

BROTHERS: The fame of your victories rapidly spread through the world, and humanity applauded your virtues in the strife for emancipation; but her exultation was brief, and was cut short by the terrible news of the assassination of LINCOLN.

Nations have aspirations in common; princes and peoples entertain them in common and abide their destiny. Your victories are the victories of the whole people; such also are your disasters, and in like manner your griefs are in common. The most powerful arm lent by the Almighty in aid of the rights of humanity has been cut off, and all thoughts now dwell on that mournful theme. But the wailings poured forth over the graves of the heroic dead are not in vain; such grief strengthens and graces and renews the virtuous purpose. May you who have enjoyed the vast benefit of the counsels and example of the hero, renew to him your vows consecrated by the blood of millions of martyrs, that the work of emancipation to which he guided you may not remain incomplete. Wherever man moves on earth, let him be regarded as a brother and tread on free soil; remember that liberty is powerful; give aid to the oppressed in distant lands; listen to the divine idea of LINCOLN—free America for Americans!—and humanity, blessing his memory, will also bless the virtues of her brave and generous sons.

The committee in charge:

PAOLO GASTORINO.
COSMO DI ANICY.
PAOLO PETRINA.
CARLO VICCIOLI.
PAOLO GRANDE.
GIOACHINO POTERVO.
COSTILLO BISCARIS.

SOCIETY OF OPERATIVES OF CHIAVENNA.

Resolutions.

CHIAVENNA, *May* 7, 1865.

Filled with profound grief for the death of ABRAHAM LINCOLN, a benefactor of humanity, convinced that the sudden death of such a man is an irreparable loss for the democracy of every country, and a true catastrophe for all the oppressed still in bonds, but persuaded that the brave sons of free America will not lose courage at a moment when they most need it to secure the fruits of victories gained, the Society of Operatives of Chiavenna in this general meeting resolve—

1. To put mourning upon their flag for thirty days.

2. To inscribe the name of LINCOLN beside those of Garibaldi and Mazzini in the list of honorary members.

3. To write to the United States consul at Genoa our word of cheer for the brave operatives of the American Union, to whom the illustrious dead belonged by his birth, by the sympathies of his heart, and by the virtues of his life.

C. PEDRETTI, *President.*

Mechanics' Society of Dogliani to the people of the United States of America.

Humanity is seized with terror; a horrid crime has thrown the minds of everybody into the most afflicting consternation. ABRAHAM LINCOLN, the industrious working-man, the deserving citizen, who, like Cincinnatus, consented to direct the destinies of his country in calamitous times, is no more. The vile assassin's hand has deprived America of its guide, its leader, its father, its second Washington; and now two worlds are lamenting the loss of a man whom only yesterday they were applauding.

Oh, generous man! the weapon of the homicide that took your life has also wounded the future and the hopes of a people that were anxiously awaiting the conclusion of your work of glory and redemption.

Oh, brothers of the New World, accept as a pledge of mutual affection these few but sincere expressions of condolence, sent you by the humble but independent Society of Mechanics of Dogliani, children of that Italy which has always struggled against ignorance. Our banner is draped in mourning as a symbol of our sorrow and affliction.

Let us trust to the unchanging laws of progress. In vain will villains oppose the sword and calumny to arrest the people in their course to happiness and independence.   The goal will be gained, and the day will soon dawn when the barriers of tyranny, prejudice, and ignorance shall be removed, and men shall call each other truly brothers.

May liberty and independence endure forever!   Long life to the republic of North America!

In the name of the society :

[SEAL.]   GIOVANNI CERRINO, *President.*

[Translation.]

MUNICIPALITY OF FERMO.

Resolution of the Municipal Council of Fermo, at the session of May 10, 1865.

PROPOSITION.

The mayor presiding, the Marquis Chevalier Joseph Ignatio Trevisani, read to the council a resolution of the municipality of Palermo, by which public homage is rendered to the glorious name of ABRAHAM LINCOLN, President of the United States of America, barbarously murdered by the propagandists of slavery.   After approving the action of said municipality, he proposed to the council the following order of the day :

This council, struck with horror at the violent death of ABRAHAM LINCOLN, President of the United States of America, considering that the abolition of slavery, in the triumph of which he was sacrificed, is a matter which interests humanity at large, and wishing, by a public demonstration, to do honor to that great name—

Resolved, 1. To give the name of ABRAHAM LINCOLN to the new street opened on the south side of this city.

2. To communicate to the United States consul general at Florence the present deliberation.

All present, standing, applauded the motion of the mayor, which was adopted by acclamation.

J. TREVISANI, *Mayor.*
C. SILVESTRI, *Senior Alderman.*
L. TRANQUILLE, *Secretary.*

[Translation.]

The Workingmen's Mutual Aid Society of Foggia to the people of the American Union.

FOGGIA, *May* 8, 1865.

BROTHERS OF AMERICA : We comprehend the sorrow that afflicts you in the triumphant hour of your humane cause.   When ABRAHAM LINCOLN, your glorious helmsman of liberty, was struck down by the cruel hand of a vile assassin your generous souls were filled with mourning. The sad news reaches us in Italy like the messenger of a day fatal to the destinies of a people, and every true Italian heart was saddened by its coming. Even in the humble families of the working-men of Foggia the deepest grief was felt, and a shrill cry arose for the extermination of the vampires of humanity.

Brothers, be consoled by the thought that ABRAHAM LINCOLN, in the greatest trials, showed himself something more than the President of a transatlantic republic, and that the assassin's pistol was only the instrument of the dealers in human flesh. LINCOLN's tomb with you, and Garibaldi's misfortunes with us, will be known in history as the irrevocable decrees of reason against barbarism and tyranny; but you will let future ages know the good intentions of the two illustrious victims. Be brave, then, brothers of America, in your desolation, and defend the sepulchre where the secret of the emancipation of all the slaves in the world lies buried.

FERDINAND CIPRO, *President.*
MICHELE FIGLIOLINO, *Secretary.*

[Translation.]

DEMOCRATIC REPUBLICAN ASSOCIATION OF FLORENCE.

SIR: As soon as it became known that the southern rebels had been defeated by the federal armies, the Societa Democratica Republicana of Florence commissioned the undersigned to present to you a congratulatory address, and to assist in a public demonstration of satisfaction, which the liberals of Florence had decided to give to you, as the representative of the republic of the United States, when unexpectedly the intelligence of the murder of Mr. LINCOLN changed their hymn into elegy, their joy into sorrow.

The society which sends us to you as interpreters of its sorrow is composed of men who, loving and hoping, followed the various fortunes of the mighty war that your people have sustained, not for their own liberty, but for that of others; not for an idea, or an interest circumscribed by the boundaries of a nation, but for the great principles of morality and justice.

If upon the death of Mr. LINCOLN your people for a moment trembled before the dangers that seemed to threaten your republic, they soon reassured themselves, knowing that he but reflected the character, will, and soul of his countrymen.

Mr. LINCOLN has been assassinated, but the nation is immortal. It will acquire new strength and vigor from this great misfortune, and will know how to crown the work which was brought almost to an end by its chief, because the ancient race and virtues of the Puritan pilgrims, who first landed in New England, have been transmitted, unchanged from generation to generation, to their present descendants.

A people in whom energy is nature, liberty an instinct, equality a belief, law a religion, of which republican institutions are the necessary expression, may suffer great affliction from the tragical and unexpected death of a man like LINCOLN, yet it must be but a passing and surmountable misfortune.

Sir, the democracy of Europe owe to your people an eternal debt of gratitude for preserving, intact and pure, their great republic, from the model of which the nations of the old world may yet be formed anew.

Receive, sir, the assurances of our profound respect,

A. DE GUBERNATI,

G. DOLFI,

A. MARIO,

B. ODICINI,

Delegates of the Democratic Republican Association.

The CONSUL GENERAL OF THE UNITED STATES, *Florence.*

[Translation.]

Democratic Association of Florence to the free people of the United States of America.

MAY 8, 1865.

BROTHERS OF THE AMERICAN UNION: A few days have passed since your people prepared themselves to celebrate, in the decisive victory of Richmond, the proximate, infallible triumph of liberty and of the Union over servitude and disunion, when sad intelligence troubled the sincere joy of all the friends of liberty, and stopped on our lips the festive expressions of triumph and our glad wishes for the future.

LINCOLN, the honest, the magnanimous citizen, the most worthy Chief Magistrate of your glorious federation, a victim of an execrable treason, is no more.

The furies of despotism and of servitude, deceived in their infamous hopes, incapable of sustaining any longer their combat against liberty, before falling into the abyss which threatened them, strengthened the arm of a murderer, and as they opened the fratricidal war with the gibbet of the martyr of the cause of abolition, John Brown, so they ended it, worthy of themselves, in the most ferocious and stupid of all crimes, the murder of a great citizen.

Now liberty, in stigmatizing the cause of her enemies, will have only to show to the world this gibbet and this murderer, and the people looking upon them cannot do otherwise than recollect that despots have had a share in this;

that in some courts of Europe Mason, Slidell, and the ferocious pirates of the Alabama found protection, encouragement, and applause, and finally the wicked instigator of the civil war, Jefferson Davis, obtained consolation, praises, and hopes even in the paternal benediction of the Pope.

Brothers of the American Union, courage! The great cause for which you have supported four years of Titanic combat is the cause of humanity; its triumph can never more be doubted, and has been delayed only for a moment by the worst of actions committed by an abject murderer.

Tyranny, it is true, could sometimes be destroyed by the murder of the tyrant, because it has life only in him; but liberty, which lives in the people, has, like the people, an immortal origin and destiny.

Democratic Association of Florence, May 8, 1865.

For the committee:

P. D. ANNIBALE.
A. CORTI, *Secretary.*

[Translation.]

FLORENCE, *May* 4, 1865.

SIR: The masonic lodge Il Progresso Sociale, of the ancient accepted Scottish rite established in Florence, at their meeting of the 3d instant, after rendering funeral honor to the great martyr of liberty, ABRAHAM LINCOLN, and adopting mourning for three weeks, have resolved to make known their profound sorrow to the noble nation which you represent in Italy, at the same time expressing the confident hope that, notwithstanding the loss of their President, the nation and its institutions will continue as enduring as the great principles for which they are contending.

B. ODICINI, *Master.*
F. PULSZKY, *Senior Warden.*
C. BETTINI, *Junior Warden.*
A. MARTINATI, *Orator.*
M. LE SAIRO, *Secretary.*

Hon. Col. T. B. LAWRENCE,
    United States Consul General for Italy.

[Translation.]

Fraternity of artisans of Italy to the people of the United States.

FLORENCE, *April* 27, 1865.

CITIZENS: When the telegram brought the intelligence that the cause of civilization and justice had obtained a glorious victory, (fit reward for your indomitable constancy and heroic valor,) this brotherhood of artisans was about to testify in a public and solemn manner the fraternal love which unites to you, free citizens, every heart which beats for and desires the complete triumph of the rights of humanity. But, alas! the hand of an infamous assassin (the agent, doubtless, of a mysterious and iniquitous plot prepared against the national liberty) has taken away the precious life of your Chief Magistrate and placed in great danger another one not inferior to it. This barbarous and execrable deed has filled with deep sorrow the souls of our fraternity, and having in consequence cast aside the thoughts of any joyful demonstration, the committee, as interpreter of the sentiments of their association, has resolved to drape with mourning the flag of the society for fifteen days, to express to you their indignation for the terrible murder committed, and to address to you a word of fraternal sympathy.

Free citizens! may the name of ABRAHAM LINCOLN be to you a watchword whereby you may better accomplish the sublime mission which you have begun, and through the sacrament of his blood may all tyrannies be destroyed.

Long life to the American republic! Long life to the federal Union!

GIUSEPPE DOLFI, *President.*
FRANCESCO PECINI, *Secretary.*

[Translation.]

Constitutional Rights Association to the President of the United States.

FLORENCE, *May* 9, 1865.

SIR: At the very moment when all the friends of liberty and civilization on this side the ocean were rejoicing over the approaching close of a contest sustained by you for the great humanitarian principle of the abolition of slavery, sad news arrived to alloy our joy, and we learned with horror of the assassination of the man elected by the American nation as its chief.

Thus the martyrdom of him who promulgated the solemn decree of emancipation (true sign of equality among men) consecrated the second great epoch of your history, not less glorious than that of your independence itself.

America, discovered by our sailors, illustrated by our historians, celebrated by our poets, is for Italy more than a friend—she is a sister, towards whom she looks anxiously during the revolution through which she is passing in her reconstruction.

We Italians, associated to maintain and keep alive the sacred fire of liberty, send a word of affection and condolence, trusting that the federal flag, which was kept aloft by the iron strength of President LINCOLN, and which is now drooping over the tomb, too soon, alas! opened for Honest Old ABE, may not again be attacked by internal enemies or rebellious citizens.

PROF. EMILIO CIPRIANI, *President.*

American meeting in Florence on account of the death of Abraham Lincoln.

FLORENCE, ITALY, *May* 2, 1865.

Pursuant to a call of the consul general, the citizens of the United States resident or temporarily staying at Florence met at the consulate on Tuesday, May 2, to take such measures consequent on the death of President LINCOLN as might seem appropriate. The meeting, numbering nearly one hundred American gentlemen, was called to order by Hiram Powers, esq., and, on his motion, Colonel Lawrence, the consul general, was appointed chairman, and Dr. B. B. Appleton, of Boston, chosen secretary.

Colonel Lawrence, on taking the chair, addressed the meeting as follows:

FELLOW-COUNTRYMEN: We have met here to-day, united as mourners and companions in a common sorrow, to take counsel together in a national calamity, in an unspeakable and overwhelming grief, which bows our heads and fills our hearts. One of the best of Presidents, one of the purest of statesmen, one of the truest of men, is no more, and the lamentation which arises from every part of our land finds a responsive echo in our own bosoms. The appalling tragedy which has removed our Chief Magistrate is absolutely without parallel or precedent in history. Cæsar found a Brutus because he had trampled upon the liberties of his country; Henri Quatre fell by the hand of an insane fanatic; but it has remained for the nineteenth century, for a period when civilization and Christianity are supposed to exert greater influence than ever before, to produce a cold-blooded and cowardly assassin to strike down a President acknowledged, even by his enemies, to be possessor of the highest virtues, and to have been actuated throughout his public career solely by a single-hearted and unselfish patriotism.

It is not my belief that this fearful deed is either indorsed or approved by the people of the south; I believe at home and abroad that they are sincere in ignoring the infamous crime. But the broad fact nevertheless exists, that with the institution of slavery the pistol and bowie-knife have gone hand in hand, and that under its dominion personal revenge has avowedly been permitted to take precedence of established law. As a result of slavery, therefore, we owe this awful deed, and let us thank the Almighty that, as an institution, it has perished forever.

Gentlemen, it is unnecessary for me to pronounce a eulogy upon President LINCOLN—he needs none; there is his record—the world knows it by heart. His memory will gain new lustre as time rolls on, and history will accord him a niche in the temple of fame second only to that occupied by our immortal Washington.

At the conclusion of Colonel Lawrence's remarks the following resolutions were draughted by a committee appointed for the purpose and adopted unanimously:

The American residents and visitors in Florence, desiring to give expression to their profound horror and grief on account of the atrocious crime by which our beloved country has been deprived of its honored and revered Chief Magistrate, hereby resolve—

That while we see in the assassination of President LINCOLN an act of barbarity unparalleled in the annals of crime, yet we are constrained to regard and denounce it as naturally and logically related to the grand conspiracy which has aimed at the overthow of our republican institutions.

That while we recognize the hand of Providence in this great calamity, which has plunged the nation into mourning, we yet feel that the Divine power and goodness will so overrule it as to give stability and prosperity to our people, and to render lastingly triumphant the cause of freedom.

That while we appreciate the great and patriotic work accomplished by our late President, which will secure for him an undying place in history, we believe that his violent death will but lend additional lustre to the noble and manly virtues of this worthy successor of Washington.

That, in common with all loyal Americans at home and abroad, we hereby express our heartfelt sympathy with the bereaved family of the President in this hour of desolating affliction.

That in token of our respect and sorrow we will wear a badge of mourning for thirty days.

It was voted that a copy of these resolutions be transmitted to his Excellency the President of the United States.

The chairman stated that deputations from various public associations existing in Florence had waited upon him to express their sympathy in the dire calamity which had befallen the United States, and that addresses to the same effect had been received by him from other cities of Italy.

After a vote of thanks to the chairman for his opening remarks, and for his acceptable manner of presiding, the meeting was dissolved.

T. BIGELOW LAWRENCE, Chairman.

B. B. APPLETON, *Secretary.*

[Translation.]

The Mechanics' Society and the Society of Progress of Forli to the American people.

FORLI, May 1, 1865.

BROTHERS OF AMERICA: Our soul is grieved because our first utterance to you must consist of words of sorrow and consolation; and our grief is more poignant as the personage whose death we mourn was the idol of a respectful worship, and deserved the homage of the civilized world. The real design of his assassination is a secret still hidden in the mysteries of a deep policy, and we have not the divining power to find it out; but we must trust that the finger of Providence was concerned in it, and permitted it to be done that some great good might arise out of it.

The illustrious deceased has left you his glorious principles as an inheritance, and if you obey them you will not fail to consummate the great aim of freedom, and will extend its influence to Europe, the only country on the globe that is called civilized, while the descendants of your great discoverer are enslaved in spite of your efforts to establish liberty and independence in every corner of the earth.

LINCOLN and Booth! these are two names forming different periods of history: the first promises a future; the second belongs to the horrid past; is a concentration of all villany past and present—the wickedness of a Nero and a Caligula combined, or of other monsters cast up from hell to seek the most illustrious victims.

LINCOLN's is a great name, that will ever be remembered as the name of the champion of all democratic virtues. He has unmasked monarchy by giving true liberty and independence to a weary world. His martyrdom will be a baptism more powerful than that required by the Roman church; it is a sacrament of blood—the other is of water. LINCOLN and progress are synonymous; his course was but the great principles proposed by Washington.

Brothers, your President was one of those wonderful men, like our Mazzini or Garibaldi, who tower above the meanness of common humanity, and show how great a true man can become. All nations ought now to join with one assent, and inscribe this epitaph upon the stone that covers the remains of your distinguished President: "Here lies buried all the wisdom, all the virtue, all the patriotism that ever lived."

Americans, accept, in fine, these words of sincere sorrow, of fraternal love, of congratulation to a people with whom we sympathize and to whom we wish a lasting peace.

Committee of the Mechanics' Society:

AMADIO CAMILLO.
GIUSEPPE MURATORI.
VINCENZO DANIELE.
GIOVANNI TRASFINETTI.
GIUSEPPE PAZZI, *Secretary.*

Committee of the Society of Progress:

PANCIATICHI POMPEO.
GIUSEPPE TAPOCCINI.
FEDERICO BONDI.
FABIO CORTESE.
LIVIO BARBIANI, *Secretary.*

[Translation.]

GENOA, *May* 28, 1865.

SIR: While from all parts of the civilized world your great and noble country receives daily solemn assurances of condolence and of sorrow for the execrable crime which has taken away your Chief Magistrate, permit the undersigned to send from the city which produced the immortal discoverer of America our word of condolence, and at the same time our word of admiration—of grief for that loss which is a loss not only to the United States, but to all humanity; of admiration for the majestic solidity of a social and political edifice in which so great a misfortune does not disturb the movement of public affairs.

ABRAHAM LINCOLN lived long enough to see the triumph of the holy cause of human liberty which he spent his life in defending, and we most warmly desire that the people who, with heroic valor, have fought to obtain this triumph, may soon gather the merited fruits of their toils, under the smiles of peace and prosperity.

On behalf of the citizens of Genoa:

> Y. VALERIO.
> GEROLAMO BOCEARDO.
> E. G. TRABBI.
> E. G. SCHIATHINANO.

The CONSUL GENERAL OF THE UNITED STATES, *Genoa.*

[Translation.]

GENOA, *May* 4, 1865.

HONORED SIR: While the democracy of Europe was exulting with joy at the late victories of the Union, which had secured the triumph of the holiest of causes, the news of an execrable crime suddenly filled them with consternation and mourning. ABRAHAM LINCOLN has been assassinated. The death of this virtuous and great citizen is a universal misfortune. All humanity was struck down in its benefactor, the emancipator of the black race.

In the midst of manifestations of public grief which come from every part of Italy to the representatives of your nation, the Union of the Operatives of Genoa raise their cry against the murderers of LINCOLN, and send, through you, to your brothers in America, the assurance of their profound grief. We hope that the calculations of the assassins will fail, and that this great crime will not arrest the successful progress of your cause.

Your fellow-citizens will have the magnanimity to avenge this crime in a manner befitting a great nation, by consolidating the work of emancipation initiated and carried forward by LINCOLN with such intelligence and courage.

We feel certain that your great republic, which in a few years has displayed so many miracles of valor, constancy and sacrifice, as to fill the world with surprise, purified from the foul stain of slavery, regenerated in blood, and blessed by all humanity, will be more glorious and powerful than before the war, furnish a model for European nations, and lift up the beacon of hope for oppressed people.

Faithful to the Monroe doctrine, you will not, we are sure, tolerate the planting of a foreign monarchy on the borders of your own land, which is the sacred asylum of liberty.

We beg you to convey to your government and fellow-citizens these sentiments of admiration and affection which we cherish for your country and her cause.

[SEAL.]   MICHELE BOERO,
                                   AND OTHERS.

NOTE.—The Union of Operatives has unanimously voted this address, and further resolved to drape its flag in mourning for one year.

[Translation.]

CITIZEN PRESIDENT : The members of the Fraternal Association of Artisans of Leghorn send to the American people a word of sincere condolence and brotherly grief on the occasion of the assassination of ABRAHAM LINCOLN. They are aware that the valorous champion of the American Union was born an artisan, and that liberty made him great and powerful, not to oppress but to strengthen and ennoble an entire nation; for this they have loved him as though they had been his sons or brothers.

The living ABRAHAM LINCOLN we looked upon as a hero; dead, we mourn him as a martyr, and his memory will ever remain in the heart of the artisans as the symbol of a true faith—the faith of liberty.

From the seat of the Fraternal Association of Artisans at Leghorn, May 21, 1865.

                               G. PENCO, *President.*
                               O. CAMPANA, *Secretary.*

Hon. CITIZEN PRESIDENT
         of the United States of America.

[Translation.]

The Lodge Anziani Virtuosi, Orient of Leghorn, Tuscany, to the President of the United States of America.

HEALTH!

ABRAHAM LINCOLN is dead, not from disease in his own bed, surrounded by friends and parents, but in consequence of a wound inflicted by an unknown hand. Nothing positive yet is known as to the reason why the fatal shot was fired; but, unfortunately, men who are useful to their country either die before the accomplishment of the work they had undertaken, or hands bought with the gold of their enemies cut the thread of their lives, hoping that the trunk being severed, the tree will not blossom; but if the roots are sound, it will, though late. So you, citizen President, ought to do. Falter not, because the life of your predecessor was taken, for it is your duty to finish what he traced out, and not only is the most powerful part of America with you, but the whole world represented by the people who, when they love, love from the heart and shed their blood for any just cause. Yours is one of the most just, and let the great try to crush the people and cry out that they are of no account; they are the elect of God, and their cause will triumph, for all the peoples of the earth have their hopes and sufferings in common, and call a man ABRAHAM LINCOLN, or any other name, it matters not, for it is not the body or the soul but the party he represents which calls our attention.

ABRAHAM LINCOLN, the strenuous defender of the rights of the people, is no more; but you, Andrew Johnson, having taken his place, have the task of completing the work.

Receive the best wishes for the prosperity of your republic, from the brothers of the Leghorn Lodge Anziani Virtuosi, Orient of Leghorn.

ALESSANDRO NELLI Y.·.
FRANCESCO ANDREANI.·.
BALDASSARE PAGHINI.·.
LUSTRO V. COEN.·.
ADRIANO CORRANI.·.
GIOVANNI CORRANI.·.
GIUSEPPE GIANNARDI.·.
ISAAC PIPERNO.·.
DANIEL PIPERNO.·.
RAPHAEL DAVIS.·.
M. P. PIPERNO.·.

FRANCESCO PASTORI.·. Secretary.

[Translation.]

Translation of letter from Masonic Lodge Le Lume e la Verita, in Messina, dated June 10, 1865.

To his Excellency ANDREW JOHNSON, *President of the United States :*

We, inhabitants of distant regions, ultimately address a word to you, citizen President, to manifest to you the great grief that afflicted our hearts on the melancholy intelligence of the assassination of the illustrious President, ABRAHAM LINCOLN—mourned for nine days in the temple of our mysterious works.

In vain did that sacrilegious hand raise itself to smite such virtue, for his name will last to eternity. In him America acknowledges the Washington of liberty; to him the slave to-day pours out his benedictions that his chains are loosed, and the civil people from all quarters of the globe spread flowers and tears on the tomb of the just.

It is but too true that the country of virtue is heaven, and its temple the world.

Accept, citizen President, this tribute of regard towards the late Illustrious which all the fraternity of this respectable lodge dedicate to him. In the mean time we beg you to manifest our grief towards the American nation, which is to-day so nobly given to you to represent.

Signed by the venerable

GIOVANNI PIRROTTA,

AND OTHERS.

[Translation.]

An address of condolence, dated the 21st *of June,* 1865, *from the municipality of Messina to the consul of the United States of America.*

To honor the name of a great citizen, one of the most liberal among nations, and to transmit his name to posterity, the municipal council voted in their sitting, the 13th of May last, and decided on giving the name of ABRAHAM LINCOLN to one of the principal streets which is shortly to be opened in the new quarter of Terranova in this city.

This is an attestation of affection to the United States of America, to honor the memory of their indefatigable President, who fell a victim to treachery, but surrounded by the light of a sublime idea, "the freedom of slaves." It is, finally, an homage to the great principles of liberty, without which whatever may be the civil event is false and illusory.

Be pleased, worthy sir, to accept, and have accepted by his Excellency President Johnson, who now represents the government of the United States, this testimony of grief and sympathy which the people of Messina tribute to the great American nation.

G. CHANCIAFARA, *Mayor, President.*

[Translation.]

MILAN, *May* 17, 1865.

Brothers of the United States of America:

Our grief for the death of LINCOLN is as great as our faith in the triumph of the cause for which you fight. The holiness of your cause is equal to the greatness of its martyr.

For the Workingmen's Mutual Help Association in Milan:

MONDOLFO, *President.*

[SEAL.]   FILIPPO BINDA, *Vice-President,*

AND MANY OTHERS.

[Translation.]

PROVINCE OF MOLISE, DISTRICT OF ISERNIA,

Monteroduni, May 1, 1865.

To his Excellency ANDREW JOHNSON,

President of the United States of America:

The entire world, with different feelings, has anxiously awaited the termination of the great contest, the civil war that has lacerated the limbs of the great and happy republic. Tyranny and double-faced diplomacy attempted to rivet the chains of slavery upon the universe; democracy struggled to break the fetters and crush the head of despotism with them, and sound the hymn of victory and liberty. The hour of victory has struck for liberty; tyranny, pale with rage, gnaws its own viscera, and trembles upon its tottering throne.

Long live the government of Washington! Long live the great republic of the United States! They overthrew the slaveholders of the South, who had ruled the country for three-quarters of a century; but the brave republicans broke off the manacles of millions of slaves, raised them to the dignity of manhood, and now embrace them as men and brothers.

But amid the victorious jubilation came the horrid rumor of ABRAHAM LINCOLN's barbarous assassination! He was the honored parent of the newborn liberty; but you, Mr. Johnson, will be the foster-father of the new republic. LINCOLN is dead; but grateful humanity will erect a splendid monument to the memory of the sublime martyr of liberty, and will appease his spirit by scattering the ashes of the cursed assassin Booth to the four winds of heaven, and destroying tyranny and slavery that prompted him to the horrid deed.

GIUSEPPE GIACOMO.	PASQUALE D'ELIA.
ANTONIO GUGLIELMI.	SALVATORE SCIOLI.
SALVATORE GUGLIELMI.	FRANCESCO SCIOLI.
ICILIO D'ELIA.	NICOLA TRIVISON.
DOMINICO FORTE.	SILVIO FORTE.
CLODOMIRO DE GIACOMO.	ANDREA SCIOLI.

MARSALA AT THE TOMB OF ABRAHAM LINCOLN.

Marsala, the heroic and enlightened city, through its mayor, has elevated its voice at the tomb of ABRAHAM LINCOLN.

On the 6th of May, 1866, in the City Hall of Marsala, a meeting was called by the mayor, and presided over by the syndic, who gave official information of the horrible crime perpetrated on the illustrious ABRAHAM LINCOLN, President of the United States of America.

That atrocious deed confirms the political axiom that the glories and misfortunes of a nation are the glories and misfortunes of all mankind; and young Italy, though rejoicing in her new destiny, now joins in tasting the bitter cup of American misfortune.

We Italians see in the misfortunes of America repetitions of our own misfortunes, and all Italy deplores the lamentable event that overwhelms a sister nation; and its sorrow is the greater because its people are united to us by ancient traditionary ties, a people whose country was first discovered by a son of Italy.

Christopher Columbus, Italy's immortal son, discovered the vast continent of America, and carried Christianity and civilization to its benighted shores; and the good and noble LINCOLN, late President of the United States of the New World, delivered the descendants of the children of Africa from the curse of infamy, the yoke of servitude.

It is the duty of every free people to express their sorrow and pay their homage at the tomb of great men, who are to be revered next to God; therefore the president, as the interpreter of this meeting,

Resolves, That the inhabitants of Marsala, on this occasion, express their horror at the crime perpetrated upon the person of ABRAHAM LINCOLN, and signify their sympathy for the American people in this address to the new President and Congress of the United States of America.

The above resolution was unanimously adopted.

G. NOTAR FIGLIOLI,
TOMMASSO PIPILONE,
A. GRIGNANI,
Councilmen.
ANTONIO SPANO,
Secretary.

NAPLES, *May* 20, 1865.

SIR: Great was our affliction on the news of the death of your predecessor, ABRAHAM LINCOLN.

We, men of labor, and of the people, bent on the conquest of liberty and justice for all, we cannot but express our profound grief for so great a loss.

LINCOLN was, like you, the defender of the rights of the people and the emancipator of the slaves. We feel our hearts pulsating violently at the thought that a horrible crime has deprived the American nation of a generous and honest chief.

Happily the principles, if actuated by man, have their origin in the rights of the people, and find in it the force of expansion and of durability.

We, workmen of Naples, have felt the great misfortune which has struck humanity, on the loss of President LINCOLN, and we, therefore, deliberated in solemn council that an address of condolence to the American people should be presented, and that our great standard should be in mourning for thirty days.

We send, moreover, a salute to all the American people, but particularly to our brothers, the workmen, and we remind them that Italy works assiduously for the accomplishment of her liberty and independence; that she confides in herself as well as in the sympathy of free nations, and hopes to see her ardent wishes accomplished.

To you, President, we intrust our fraternal salute, and we are certain that you will communicate it to your people, reminding them that the Italians feel a profound affection for the great American nation.

JOSEPH F. DASSI,
Honorary Perpetual Vice-President.
FRANCISCO ZAVA,
President General.
CESARE FREARI,
General Secretary.
CESARE BATTAGLIA,
Secretary.

Mr. ANDREW JOHNSON,
President of the United States of America.

[Translation.]

GARIBALDIAN MUTUAL AID SOCIETY,
Naples, August 30, 1865.

SIR: In execution of the resolution passed to-day by our assembly, legally convocated, I have the honor to offer you, in the name of our society, the most sincere and heartfelt condolence for the great loss the American nation has sustained in the death of the late President LINCOLN.

Alas! the noble and generous republic, and together with her all the

European nations, have received a cruel wound. We Garibaldians were profoundly afflicted by the sad news, and can only compare our present affliction to that we have felt when our chief and father, Garibaldi, was wounded at Aspromonte.

ABRAHAM LINCOLN was the true and tried friend of liberty. His virtues and undaunted courage were about to achieve a great work, when the hand of an assassin deprived him of life.

But we despair not. We still hope in the sublime mission of the American nation. The effulgent spark of true liberty shall yet come to us through the American republic.

Italy mingles her tears with America, and all deplore the sad event, but place strong reliance upon the happy results which your renowned talents and patriotism are certain to produce, the re-establishment of the glorious Union, so long the admiration of the world.

With sentiments of high esteem, I have the honor to be, most respectfully, yours,

[SEAL.]   GIUSEPPE DASSI, *President.*
EUGENIO MONTINI, *Secretary.*

The PRESIDENT *of the United States of America.*

[Translation.]

WORKINGMEN'S BENEVOLENT SOCIETY OF NAPLES,
Naples, May 4, 1865.

CITIZEN CONSUL: The Workingmen's Benevolent Society of Naples, in the midst of its exultation at the news of the triumph of a holy and benevolent cause, were suddenly struck with horror at the announcement of the cruel death of your excellent President, ABRAHAM LINCOLN.

Our grief is beyond expression; for he who can tell the anguish of his sorrow does not feel it deeply.

Deign to be the interpreter of our sentiments, citizen consul, to the noble and generous people whose welfare is so much desired by us. Tell them the sad tidings of their loss was brought to us upon the wings of the wind, and left us petrified with horror and indignation. Our only comfort was the thought that grand ideas, by the inscrutable commands of Providence, make their way through a thousand obstacles and only gain their goal by passing through a sea of martyrdom and blood.

Liberty has grown and flourished in your land; and we are sure it has taken root so deeply in your soil, it will never be in want of generous souls to inherit the legacy of love for poor suffering human beings, an inheritance left to them by one who was their apostle and a martyr for them. They have been redeemed from the ignominious yoke of slavery—those poor men who were fastened to the sod, deprived of half the spirit that God had given them entire at their birth. The earth has now no race to till its soil with grievous sighs and water it with servile sweat; but the men who mourned in their labors now work with joyous songs that sweeten toil and render the fruits of their labor more abundant.

.Tell them we rejoice in this change—we who believe in progress and the indefinite development of benevolence, thanks to union and mutual assistance— and hope to see the working classes elevated to a more cheerful and respectable condition. We are glad that so much glory falls to the lot of a people who jealously guarded the light-house of liberty, a divinity banished from the Old World to find a refuge in the New, whose once vast solitudes are now filled with inhabitants. Our eyes have long been turned to that beacon, and are bent on it now, hoping to see that torrent of light shed its blessings upon this old and corrupt hemisphere.

We beg you, citizen consul, to convey these sentiments of the Working-men's Benevolent Society of Naples to the American people, and accept our sincere expressions of reverence and esteem.

The society committee:

LUIGI FAZIO.
PASQUALE CARILLO.
VINCENZO GODONO.
STEFANO CAPOREGGIO
ANTONIO DE FELICE.
PASQUALE CIMINI.
TORINELLI NICOLA.

{ LIBERTY, LABOR, AND PROGRESS. }

[Translation.]

AMERICANS OF THE UNION: Despotism, priestly and political, diplomatic hypocrisy, and a tradition of blood have fettered the Italian emancipation with so many snares that we, overwhelmed with grief and disgusted with this depraved Old World, turn with confiding looks to the New one, and our souls rejoice at the grand spectacle you show us. Oh, Americans! you who have conquered your own independence by your virtue only—in the sacredness of the laws constitutes only one a free family, without kings or myrmidons, without priests or deceitful idols.

We followed with our ardent wishes the titanic struggle which you have sustained against the ungodly insurrection of slaveholders. Oh! could slavery exist any longer among men as free as you are; can one be free by the side of or amidst slaves? This stain you have blotted out with your blood, and with the sacrifices you have made of your men and money for the complete liberty of your country.

On the fall of Richmond the soul of the European democracy was exuberant with joy. We Italians of the south were preparing to send you a salute of congratulations, when the news of the assassination of ABRAHAM LINCOLN, your President, filled us with grief.

ABRAHAM LINCOLN, the generous man who neither tarnished nor stained his triumph—the virtuous Cincinnatus of America—the redeemer of those men whose primitive fault was no other than the color of their skin, has been assassinated. However great is our grief, how much greater must be yours! Oh, American brothers! you who have twice confided to ABRAHAM LINCOLN the jealous deposit of power; for you have found in his honesty, his intelligence, and his patriotism the immovable rock of liberty, and certainly your cause of war was a holy one if such a noble creature has been sacrificed, the propitiatory offering of an inexorable demon.

Americans of the Union, every one in Europe does not hold for its divinity the cotton or the sword; permit that our crowns of laurel and of myrtle go to garnish the tomb of LINCOLN. Let our flowers be mixed with yours, with yours our tears, and with yours our oaths; to gratify the spirit of LINCOLN for the complete destruction of slavery, we will encourage and imitate you in the battle for the redemption of humanity.

For the studious youths of Naples:

> SAVERIA FRISSIO, *Deputato.*
> ENRICO MARIANO, *Caprice.*
> GENEVOSO BOZZIUS.
> CINCOTTA ANGELO.
> CARLO DACONO.
> LORETO PAISCHE.
>   AND SOME THIRTY OTHERS.

[Translation.]

The juvenile Society of Progress to the people of America on the occasion of the assassination of Abraham Lincoln.

NAPLES, *April* 30, 1865.

Accept a word of condolence, and also of encouragement, which the Society of Progress of Naples send you. We, also, like you, have felt misfortunes. We also know what it is to suffer, so we can feel for others; but the road of civilization and progress is made in that way, and it is necessary to traverse it, though the footsteps of the nation are bathed in blood. Misfortunes are seeds which carry fruits that are never lost. For your great deeds we paid you a tribute of praise; now for your misfortunes we offer you a word of sympathy, of encouragement, and of condolence.

[SEAL.]

CARLO REBEECHI, *President.*
PASQUALE GALLUCCIO.
FIDELE ALBANEJE.
BALDASSARRE ZIBÔ.
SALVATORE MENICHINO.
VINCENZO PADAVANI.
BARRABA ANTONIO.
LUGI MENICHINO.
GIOVANNI LAVASTANO.
VINCENZO LABANCA.
MORANO ROMAJO.

[Translation.]

ITALIAN ELECTORAL ASSOCIATION—GENERAL GARIBALDI, HONORARY PRESIDENT.

NAPLES, *May* 2, 1865.

With an ardent heart we join in the universal grief occasioned by the death of ABRAHAM LINCOLN. This event has moved the world more than it has ever done before, or will ever do at the death of a pope or reigning emperor, by the will of God, because the man whose loss we deplore was not raised in virtue of chimerical rights, but by the free vote of the people.

And we, in expressing to you these sentiments in the name of the Italian Electoral Association, for whom the national sovereignty is a sacred cause, and whose first duty is to preserve the popular rights, think we interpret correctly rectly the sentiment of the country which fosters Garibaldi for the one that fostered Washington.

[SEAL.]

S. RICCIARDI, *President.*

[Translation.]

THE MUNICIPAL COUNCIL OF NAPLES.

NAPLES, *May* 5, 1865.

ILLUSTRIOUS SIR: The common council, which has met this morning in an extraordinary sitting, has unanimously voted the following address, which you, illustrious sir, will have the kindness to transmit to your government:

"The municipality of Naples, full of horror for the execrable crime which has deprived the great American nation of its magnanimous President, ABRAHAM LINCOLN, express to his successor, who represents that generous people, the profound grief which struck us on the news of that great calamity, and wish that the noble cause to which LINCOLN's life was consecrated, and for which it was lost, will soon obtain the full triumph which will be the greatest conquest of modern civilization."

Accept, illustrious sir, the testimonies of my esteem.

F. DE SUROVA, *Mayor.*

The CONSUL OF THE UNITED STATES, *Naples.*

[Translation.]

THE JUVENILE SCIENTIFIC, LITERARY, AND POLITICAL ASSOCIATION OF NAPLES.

NAPLES, *April* 28, 1865.

The assassination of ABRAHAM LINCOLN has deeply moved all the hearts of those who recognize in him the indefatigable support of the greatest humanitary principles, the assassin striking him at the moment when a series of glorious victories seemed to have put a stop to the sanginary war which for five years agitated the finest and most intelligent part of America.

This association, honorable sir, has manifested itself that you might be the interpreter to the American assembly of its sentiments of grief for the unexpected death of a man whom General Garibaldi called the "Ship of Liberty." The name of LINCOLN must be placed at the head of those brave men who have devoted themselves to the triumph of a great idea, defying courageously all danger, proud in the sacredness of their task.

The idea of LINCOLN will not die with him; that was not struck by the dagger or by poison. That it will triumph in America is the wish of this association, for henceforth will be the struggle of civilization against barbarism. All know on which side will be the victory. America cannot regret having given birth to a man capable of committing such a crime. Assassins, like traitors, have no country.

Accept, illustrious sir, the salutations of our consideration.

FILIPPO DELLI TRANJS, *President.*

[SEAL.] RAFAELE DE ASARY, *Secretary.*

The CONSUL GENERAL OF THE UNITED STATES, *Naples.*

[Translation.]

NAPLES.

This morning took place in the court of the University the reunion of students, of which we gave notice yesterday, assembled to vote an address for the death of LINCOLN.   There were about two hundred of them present, having accepted the address already printed, which was read to them by the deputy Friscia.   If we do not mistake, they named a committee of ten young men, who met at the office of the president, from whence they proceeded together to the residence of the United States consul.

Having obtained the banner of the University, and covered it with black crape, they proceeded in good order and without noise to the Riviera di Chiaja.   They were joined on the way by a large number of the "Societa Giovanile," who, also with their banner, took place in the cortege.   Arriving at the residence of the consul, the committee went up and presented to him the address, accompanied with many words full of sympathy for the American nation, and of condolence for the sad end of the honorable man who so worthily represented it.

The consul, moved by such a demonstration, thanked them in reply for such a proof of sympathy given to his country and to the great man which humanity had lost, and promised to transfer the address to his government, with a faithful narrative of what had taken place.

After having taken leave of the consul, the delegations, with the same order and quietness, went to take back their banners from where they had taken them.

[Translation.]

ANCIENT AND ACCEPTED SCOTCH RITE, M∴ ⊡ C∴ V∴ OF PARMA, E∴ V∴ UNITED ITALY, ORIENT OF PARMA, NO. 126.

A∴ G∴ D∴ G∴ A∴ D∴ U∴

AND

D∴ N∴ P∴ S∴ G∴ D∴ S∴

To you, S∴ F∴ U∴, *Subject:*

On the announcement of the death of ABRAHAM LINCOLN, the ⊡ Italian Una, in the Orient of Parma, at the regular session of the 28th of April, 1865, E∴ V∴, inscribed the following Tar∴

LINCOLN was taken from terrestrial existence; his noble head was elevated to pay the tribute to eternity of a great and finished work, when it was crushed by the assassin's bullet; his strong form was full of the joy of the great triumph of humanity.   Now no more!   But LINCOLN's personality had reached that point where the individual man disappears and the incarnation of a prince beams forth.   Such was LINCOLN, and as such it was not in the power of any violence to destroy him.   He lives in a strong, brave, and determined people; he lives in the midst of struggling humanity, whose faith has been increased, whose heart has been purified, and whose intellect has been enlarged by the example of his virtues."

Hail, in eternity, O spirit of LINCOLN!   Thou hast gone to the embrace of Washington!   Look down from the supernal spheres with the smile of pardon and faith in the human beings that are contending for the triumph of the eternal laws of moral progress.

O, great spirits, welcome the greeting and love of those who remain to struggle, and may your thoughts of great things and of the constant virtue of sacrifice inspire us all, men and nations, to continue in the right.

The Ven'bl∴ A. OLIVA.

A∴ O∴ of Parma, Italian Una.

A. DORNI, Secretary.

[Translation.]

ROYAL UNIVERSITY OF PAVIA,

Pavia, May 12, 1865.

HONORED SIR: A number of the students of this Royal University assembled yesterday to vote an address for the ceremonies about to take place in Florence in honor of the great Italian poet, (Dante;) and remembering the sad event in the United States that put an end to the life of ABRAHAM LINCOLN, they hereby express their profound sympathy for your people, who place justice and liberty above all things, and beg me to be the interpreter of these unanimous sentiments.

With esteem and devotion,

GELASTONI, Rector.

The UNITED STATES MINISTER *in Italy.*

[Translation.]

To the President of the Congress of Representatives of the United States of America.

HONORABLE SIR: A member of the juvenile politico-literary associations of this illustrious Italian city, I have the honor to signify to you, in the name thereof, the sorrow occasioned to our hearts by the unhappy news of the assassination committed on the person of President ABRAHAM LINCOLN, in whom nature and fortune interchangeably blended to render him the man of Providence for bettering the condition of the United States of America. Our grief is not, therefore, the less great and profound than that which affects the hearts of all our free citizens, of all honest and true lovers of the progress of every people and nation in the universe. Nor was the sorrow different that was caused to us by the attempt on the life of Secretary Seward.

We have, however, most confident hope that, in compensation of the bitter grief flowing from such great calamities, the United States of America will gather in the future new acquisitions of greatness, liberty, and power, which will suffice to sustain and render lasting their civil and political existence.

In fulfilling this very sad duty, I pray you, sir, to accept the expression of the sentiments of my highest regard and consideration.

For the Politico-Literary Society of Perugia:

PIETRO DE DONATO GIANNINI.

PERUGIA, *May* 7, 1865.

[Translation.]

The University of Perugia to the representative of the United States near the Italian government.

We, the committe of the students of the University of Perugia, respectfully request you to convey to your government the feelings excited in our breasts by the intelligence of the assassination of Mr. LINCOLN, and the attack on Mr. Seward.

These two great men, who, with General Grant, completed the great work of emancipation begun by Young America, deserve our greatest admiration and our most sincere thanks.

As our opinions are not influenced by fear or political expediency, and as sincerity is common to young minds, we hope it will not be thought improper that we should join our voices to those of all Europe in detestation of the horrid crime that robbed the republic of the United States of its illustrious chief, whose death we mourn with all lovers of liberty.

We hope that the spirit of enterprise will revive with renewed vigor after the term of sorrow, and that the martyr's blood may prove a pledge for future victories.

We have our martyrs too! Let not America forget that she has our sympathy, and let her people remember that we weep with them in their misfortunes.

In the consummation of this mournful duty, we beg you to accept the expression of our greatest respect and most distinguished consideration.

PIETRO DE DONATO GIANNINI,
EMPEDOCLE NACITO,
LEOPOLDO TIBERI,
Committee.

Attested by the rector of the university, this 11th day of May, 1865.

[SEAL.]   FRANCESCO ANTINORI,

Secretary.

[Translation.]

The Montanelli Association for Mutual Education and Assistance, G. Garibaldi, honorary president, to Mr. Andrew J. Stevens, United States consul in Leghorn.

PISA, *May* 12, 1865.

SIR: Have the kindness to send the enclosed letter to your President. It was unanimously approved by the Montanelli Society of Pisa, on the 10th instant, at 9 p. m.

ALFONZO GIARRIZZO BUETTO.

[Translation.]

To the President of the United States of America:

EXCELLENT SIR: The thunderbolt's revenge prepares the poetic rainbow that glimmers in the cloudless sky; so a baptism of blood prepares a regeneration which is a fatal symptom in the poetry of the age, but will beam forth on the morrow in glorious magnificence and sovereign splendor.

ABRAHAM LINCOLN fell a victim to a sacrilegious assassin, but his name is fixed among the stars as the saviour of a nation. We lament his death, but a century of hope and not of mourning is inscribed upon the tablet of his tomb by the unerring hand of fate. LINCOLN left a testament of indignation and not of tears; let it be received as an encouragement to reform. " My grave demonstrates the justice of war," he says; " lay flowers upon it without a thought of revenge, and warm your hearts to a resolution of reform. Then will a pleasant day dawn for all—a day of fraternity and peace."

Your martyr while living was the apostle soldier; and now dead, he is the guardian angel of your liberties; he had no other ambition. You cannot bring him back, but you can imitate his heroic patriotism and sound the fame of one who gave the greatest blessing to the whites as well as the blacks. We sing our feeble elegy to the memory of a man who fulfilled his holy mission. Receive it and make it known to the American people, and tell them we join in their general sorrow.

—

The above address was unanimously adopted by the council, and a resolution was passed to send it to the President of the United States of America, through the consul in Leghorn. It was also resolved to open a subscription to erect a monument in Pisa to the memory of the great man.

A true extract from the original:

ALFONSO GIARRIZZO BUETTO,
President.

F. GAGLIARDI SFORZA, *Secretary.*

Unity, liberty, fraternity !

The Montanelli Democratic Society in Pisa.

———

[Translation.]

REGGIO, *April* 30, 1865.

The Patriotic Mutual Aid Society, at a meeting held on the 30th of April, instant, adopted the following address:

The Patriotic Mutual Aid Society of Reggio, in Emilia, was preparing an address to Mr. ABRAHAM LINCOLN, President of the United States of America, when the sad news of his assassination was announced.

The much afflicted society now addresses the Vice-President, Mr. Andrew Johnson, who by right becomes President, and sends him its best wishes for his efforts to consummate the labor for liberty and equality.

President Johnson, the premeditated assassination of the illustrious ABRAHAM LINCOLN and his unfortunate colleagues calls for revenge, and it is your duty, Mr. Johnson, to see it carried out.

You must rend the sombre veil that hides the iniquitous scheme, and bring the demons to light, so that all good men may curse the traitors to their country and humanity.

The regeneration of the country is intrusted to your care, and you must renew it, and restore it to a higher rank than it ever held; thus demonstrating that, though the standard-bearer has fallen, the great battle is not lost; the true cause triumphs, strengthens, and crushes all disloyal enemies.

You must make the light-house of liberty beam more brilliantly before its holy temple, where even your greatest enemies will finally seek a sanctuary and confess in shame that their tyrannical course was the way of wickedness, full of tribulation and sorrow.

Citizen President, finish the humane work of the complete emancipation of the slaves, to which you have already contributed much, and your name will gain the greatest glory to which it can aspire—the blessing of the redeemed, joined to the benedictions of the entire world, whose eyes are now bent upon you.

And remember, also, that besides the poor blacks, there are many political slaves not less afflicted and oppressed, crying out for their lost liberty, robbed from them by a foreign power; they expect fraternal aid from you in shaking off the yoke imposed upon their necks by brutal force. Help them, and proclaim to the world that America belongs to the Americans.

For the society.

ANGELO MANINI, *President*
C. GRASSETTI, *Secretary.*

[Translation.]

REPUBLIC OF SAN MARINO,
May 5, 1865.

HONORABLE SIR: The news of the horrible assassination committed upon the person of Mr. ABRAHAM LINCOLN has caused a feeling of profound indignation and sorrow in the bosoms of all our people.

In execrating the atrocious deed with the rest of the civilized world, we mourn the loss of the great chief of a sister nation, and remember him as the most illustrious among his fellow-creatures, the greatest among the friends of humanity.

Be pleased, sir, to accept this token of our condolence with your people, and as a sincere tribute of remembrance of the illustrious deceased.

SETTIMIO BELLUZZI,
GIACOMO BERTI,
Chief Regents.

Hon. ANDREW JOHNSON,
President of the United States of America.

[Translation.]

GENOA, *May* 7, 1865.

CITIZEN CONSUL: We all raised a cry of indignation and horror at the news of the assassination of ABRAHAM LINCOLN, whom we had hailed as a new Washington. In him we revered a man, who, guided by the genius of free institutions and the love of his fellow-men, found a way to promote the doctrines of human equality by a great act of emancipation, and in our last meeting we voted an address, expressing our sorrow and sympathy for this great misfortune of the American people.

The good cause has suffered truly a great loss in the death of such a leader, but there remains no doubt that his and the people's firmness of character, spirit of sacrifice, and courage had already triumphed; and we are convinced that this horrid crime will give greater force to your cause, and speedier recognition of human equality.

Happy, O American people, are you who secured your liberties with your own blood, and have had the courage to maintain them at the same great sacrifice. Firm as a rock in the sea, you may defy those of your enemies who still govern in the name of divine right in every corner of the world, and especially in our Europe, where they are stronger than elsewhere, and fear that the blessing of liberty enjoyed in your country may stimulate the people to imitate your examples and overturn those rotten edifices which are called thrones.

To us, who enjoy a shadow of liberty, there remains no other path to the blessings which you possess than to take you for guide, and move after you towards a true democracy.

Virtue and constancy.

For the union of operatives at San Pier d'Arena:

ROTA CARLO, AND OTHERS,
Operatives.

[Translation.]

DEMOCRATIC SOCIETY OF SIENNA.

MAY 22, 1865.

SIR : The undersigned, fraternizing with all those who work for the emancipation of the human race, cannot but highly revere the name of him who has headed the armies of freedom. ·

ABRAHAM LINCOLN shone like a star in the heavens ! The hand of an assassin attempted to extinguish it, and for the moment succeeded; we say for the moment, because he has now arisen again, crowned with the glory of a martyr.

The intelligence of the infamous crime horrified every one who professes to believe in liberty and progress.

We, not the last to curse the ball which crippled the hermit of Caprera, shed our tears to-day over your great misfortune, and have resolved that the name of the republican emancipator of slaves in America should be placed in the hall of our meetings, as a proof of our friendship, and as an evidence to posterity of our eternal condemnation of this infamous assassination.

Desiring you to be the interpreter to your countrymen of the sentiments which animate the members of this society, I have the honor to be, sir, your most obedient servant,

F. CELLESI, *President.*

The CONSUL GENERAL OF THE UNITED STATES, *Florence.*

[Translation.]

ITALIAN UNION COMMITTEE OF SIENNA.

MAY 18, 1865.

SIR: The assassination of the illustrious defender of the sacred rights of humanity, which has cost your country such precious blood, has created a sensation of horror among the nations of the world.

The free fatherland of Washington and of Benjamin Franklin, a hospitable soil to all who emigrate from the despotisms of ancient Europe, mourns, in the murder of its new liberator, an event the equal of which does not exist.

In every civilized nation, upon the arrival of the news of his death, there was a day of mourning; as for ourselves, we cursed the infamous assassin and thought it impossible sufficiently to deplore this atrocious and iniquitous crime.

There are in the world some beings who, when they die, like luminous planets when they set, leave behind them only gloom and obscurity. LINCOLN was one of these.

The committee of the Italian Union in Sienna, sharing the sorrow of the generous sons of America, send you a word of sincere condolence, with a sad salutation.

Noble President! may you be able to dry the tears of your countrymen and of ourselves.

F. BARNARDI, *President.*

F. INNOCENTI GHINI, *Secretary.*

The PRESIDENT OF THE UNITED STATES.

[Translation.]

SISSA, (NEAR PARMA,) *May* 8, 1865.

Mr. PRESIDENT: The sad news that came with lightning speed from the New World, announcing the vile assassination of the illustrious ABRAHAM LINCOLN by the treacherous hand of a hired murderer, has spread over the whole earth, and brought sorrow to the hearts of all lovers of liberty. Yes, the champion of true liberty, the glory of a free people, is no more; but his name and memory will shed a new refulgent light over the benighted world, and may arouse the spirit of progress in the darkness of Europe. Yes, the father of humanity is fallen; but the joyous smile of the emancipated slave, now a man and brother, will resurrect his spirit in a better world. The members of this society mourn the death of this worthy successor of Washington, and heartily execrate the perpetrators of the crime that took him from this world.

To express their sorrow in a proper manner, the members of the Mechanics' Society of Sissa have unanimously resolved to drape their banner in black for six months, as a sign of mourning for the loss of a man so dear to the republicans of the United States of America.

Accept our sympathy and friendship as brothers; for we are hoping the day is not far distant when we will be free, and can call you really brothers of one family—a smiling, free, and happy people.

Receive our fraternal greeting.

GIACOMO SGORBATI, *President.*

His Excellency ANDREW JOHNSON,
President of the United States of America.

[Translation.]

PROVINCE OF THE LEVANT,
City of Spezia, May 2, 1865.

SIR: The common council of this city, during its sitting of yesterday, agreeing to the proposition made by the members, Mr. Lorenzo Chiappeti, Mr. Paul Crezza, and Mr. Cesare De Negro, and having draped in mourning their national flag, now floating from this building during the sitting of the council, have voted to the government of the United States of America, and in particular to the present consul, William T. Rice, as also to the United States naval storekeeper, Colonel William L. Long, who both so worthily possess the esteem and the kindest regard of all our citizens, an address expressing their sincere sympathy at the mournful event which deprived that nation of the great restorer of her liberty.

The undersigned, therefore, beg to express to the representative of the American nation in this city their feelings of sympathy and of grief, in which all members of this council unite, at the loss of this great man.

In conclusion the writer begs to forward to you, sir, this present communication, trusting that you will accept and forward to your government, so ably represented by yourself and by the much esteemed Colonel Long, the assurance of the sincere sympathy and feelings of condolence which the undersigned, in the name of the municipal corps, now present to you.

MARQUIS F. CASTAGUOLA, *Mayor.*

The Honorable W. T. Rice,
  United States Consul, Spezia.

[Translation

THE SOCIETY OF THE WORKMEN OF SPEZIA.

May 4, 1865.

Citizen : The Society of the Workmen of Spezia are powerfully affected by the news of the infamous assassination committed on the honored person of President Lincoln, and on that of his worthy minister, Seward. This information, which, with reason, has saddened all humanity, and which has given birth to a feeling of horror towards the assassin and his accomplices, could not otherwise than find a painful echo in the hearts of the working classes in this city.

Representative citizen, Lincoln also was a workman—workman for all humanity ; his aim, the abolition of slavery, the fraternizing of races—liberty !

The memory of the great citizen cannot die ; and the memory of this second Washington will remain sadly everlasting, not only in the New, but also in the Old World.

The workmen, members of this society, who have draped their flag in mourning in consideration of this great affliction, address you, sir, expressing to you and to your fellow-countrymen the feelings of their grief. At the same time that they express these sentiments, coming from their very hearts, they make the warmest wishes for the triumph of the great principle of emancipation from slavery, the Union of America, and the prosperity of her glorious people.

From the hall of the working classes at Spezia.

For the society :

LUIGI URBINI, *President.*
G. SISMONDI, *Secretary.*

The Honorable Representative Citizen
  of the People of the United States of America, City of Spezia.

[Translation.]

MUNICIPAL COUNCIL OF SALZA IRPINA.

The entire municipality of Salza Irpina, full of horror for the assassination consummated upon the person of the illustrious President, Abraham Lincoln, deliberated unanimously to express their sentiments of grief for that horrible event; also, of the sentiment of sympathy which this population feel for the people of America, and for the sacred cause courageously fought for by the martyrs who are now pitied by all Europe; and the municipality begs the mayor to send a copy of this act to the American consul at Naples.

CAVALIER MICHELE CAPOZZI, *Mayor*.

FELICIANO PASQUALE, *Assessor*.

CARMINE DE PAISOLE, *Secretary*.

[Translation.]

*Letter of condolence from the common council of Somma Vesuviana, near Naples,
on the death of President Lincoln.*

SOMMA VESUVIANA, *May* 29, 1865.

SIR: The common council of Somma Vesuviana, at the ordinary session of the 25th instant, on motion of Counsellor Giova Errico, unanimously adopted the following resolution, which you will please bring to the knowledge of your government:

The municipality of Somma Vesuviana, horrified by the detestable misdeed that deprived the great American nation of its magnanimous President, ABRAHAM LINCOLN, desires to express to his successor, as a worthy representative of that generous people, the profound sorrow it felt at the announcement of the great misfortune, and hopes that the noble cause to which that life was consecrated, and to which it was sacrificed, may soon regain its former glory with the greatest triumph of civilization.

Accept the protests of my most profound esteem.

CAVALIER MICHELE PELLEGRINO.

The UNITED STATES CONSUL *in Naples*.

[Translation.]

MUTUAL HELP ASSOCIATION OF SASSARI, ISLAND OF SARDINIA.

The assassination of ABRAHAM LINCOLN has awakened a feeling of horror and indignation in every honest mind. The head of a generous and illustrious nation, which with noble perseverance he was laboring to restore to concord and power, his death marks a memorable epoch in the history of the United States, that in which the unfortunate African race was emancipated from the cruel hands of slave power. The death of a great man is certainly an immense misfortune ; but LINCOLN has left behind him in America a great people, who share his generous ideas and maintain the holy cause of humanity ; and though deplorable blindness, low interests, or fanaticism, have feloniously removed the glorious head of the American republic, there remain men educated in his political ideas, a whole people trained under wise institutions, and the flag of the Union will be respected and feared from the Mexican Gulf to Canada, from the Atlantic to the Pacific.

The Mutual Help Association of Sassari believes that it would fail in its duties to the solidarity of peoples if, in the sorrows of a brother people in America, it failed to protest against the abominable crime which has quenched a life spent in the service of the most sacred human interests, and to express its deep mourning for this calamitous event.

Sons of a nation which but recently vindicated its liberties and independence against foreign and domestic oppressors, and which suddenly lost a great man who, more than any other, contributed to our national enfranchisement, the Italians, above every other people, can appreciate and share the grief of the Americans.

Be pleased, Signor consul, to report these sentiments to your government, and be assured of the respect with which, in the name of the Mutual Help Association of Sassari, I have the honor to sign myself your most obedient servant,

S. SOLINAS, President.

The UNITED STATES CONSUL, Genoa.

[Translation.]

The common council of Torre del Greco to the United States consul in Naples.

TORRE DEL GRECO, May 6, 1865.

All those who have human hearts, and desire the improvement of the human race, have been moved by the news of the assassination of that illustrious patriot, ABRAHAM LINCOLN. The announcement of the unfortunate incident spread feelings of horror throughout Europe, and excited our deepest indignation.

The common council, as interpreter of the feelings of the inhabitants of this town, in its session of the 30th of April last, resolved to send the enclosed address of condolence to the American Congress. I have the honor to send it to you, Mr. Consul, requesting you to forward it to its place of destination.

ANTONIO A. BRANCACCIO, Mayor.

[Translation.]

Extract from the minutes of the common council of Torre del Greco, in the province of Naples.

APRIL 30, A. D. 1865

The common council met in its hall, the seventh ordinary meeting, in presence of the mayor, Antonio Agostino Brancaccio, the following councilmen being present : Rafaele d'Amato, Stapino Brancaccio, Silvestro Costabile, Giuliano Dedilectis, Luigi Dolce, Antonio d'Istria, Roberto Lullo, Agnello Lullo, Biondo Palomba, Antonio di Bartolomeo Palomba, Francesco Rajola, Vincenzo Scognamiglio, Francesco Maria Sorrentino, Stefano Sorrentino, Cavalier Andrea Vitelli, Michele Villano, making a quorum of seventeen out of the thirty members of the council, excluding the mayor and secretary.

On motion of Biondo Palomba, in regular order, the council unanimously adopted the following address of condolence for the cruel death of ABRAHAM LINCOLN, President of the republic of the United States of America, and ordered it to be sent to the American Congress, through the United States consul in Naples :

" He who, like LINCOLN, constitutes himself the redeemer of humanity, has a right to the love and gratitude of all succeeding generations. Such a person is immortal, and the whole world mourns his death. If the grief is great when such a man dies a natural death, how much greater it must be when he is hastened to an untimely tomb by the hand of an assassin ! Such a crime is scarcely comprehensible to a reasonable mind, and the being who commits it can scarcely be reckoned as a human being.

" The policy advocated by Mr. LINCOLN is victorious, and will endure forever. His successor, inspired by the glorious example, can easily remove any obstacles that might arise to impede his progress.

" The common council of Torre del Greco, in condoling with the American people for the assassination of LINCOLN, is sure his plan will be carried out by Mr. Johnson."

The above is a correct copy of the minutes adopted by the council, after hearing it read : and signed by the mayor, as president, by Cavalier Andrea Vitelli, the oldest member present, and by me, the secretary.

ANTONIO AGOSTINO BRANCACCIO,
President.

ANDREA VITELLI.
FRANCESCO PERLA, *Secretary.*

{ VICTOR EMANUEL, }
{ King of Italy. }

{ COMMON COUNCIL }
{ of Torre del Greco. }

[Translation.]

To the Congress of the United States of America:

While the recent victories of the federal army were announcing to the world the prompt termination of that gigantic struggle by which the principles of true liberty would be established in America, the terrible news of the assassination of ABRAHAM LINCOLN cast a shade of consternation and mourning over the spirits of all lovers of liberty and civil progress. Like all those who had such principles at heart, the Juvenile Association of Torre del Greco was struck with profound indignation and grief.

In uniting with the many voices that are heard in every part of the world proclaiming their horror for a crime that should not be recorded in history, for respect to humanity, and their sympathy for the great and free nation of which Mr. LINCOLN was the worthy chief, our society is assured that in him society has lost the bravest champion of its rights, and will welcome his idea, to which, like so many other great men, he was the illustrious and honored victim.

RAFAELLO PALOMBA,
BENIAMINO SAVARESE,
ILARIO SONEN,
DOMENICO ASCIONE,
ANGELO MINICACCI,
RAFAELE VITELLI,
The Society Committee.

Luigi Siné, *Secretary.*

Mr. Marsh to Mr. Hunter.

[Extract.]

No. 118.]　　　　　　　　LEGATION OF THE UNITED STATES,
　　　　　　　　　　　　　　Turin, April 29, 1865.

Sir: Two days since a telegraphic message, forwarded to this city for transmission to Constantinople, brought us the first announcement of the fearful crime to which the Chief Magistrate of the Union has fallen a victim. The want of direct intelligence and the brevity of the telegram led many to suspect that it was a false rumor, invented for purposes of speculation, but it was confirmed by later messages, and the post of this morning brings us many of the details of the assassination, as well as a notice of your appointment as Acting Secretary of State.

Upon the reception of the first message members of the Italian senate and chamber of deputies, which were then there in session, called at my house for information as to the truth of the report. This, in consequence of the accidental failure of telegrams to and from Mr. Adams, I was unable to give; but knowing, as I do, the character of the enemies with whom the late President had to contend, and remembering the threats of which he was often the object, I have long thought such an event probable, and did not hesitate to say that I so considered it.

You will receive from nearer sources abundant evidence of the reprobation and horror which this enormous offence against humanity has excited throughout Europe; and I am happy to say that the most eminent friends of Italian liberty are not behind the foremost in condemnation of the crime, and in regret for the sudden removal of a public officer who, at the moment of his death, enjoyed the reverence of the civilized world in a higher degree than any other man of our times.

The minister of foreign affairs has requested me to assure my government of the special regret and sympathy of the King of Italy, and of the present administration of the kingdom, and most of the foreign ministers at this court have expressed to me similar sentiments. The senate and the chamber of deputies have passed appropriate resolutions on the occasion, but as these will be officially communicated to the government, through the Italian minister at Washington, I forbear to transmit them.   *   *   *   *   *   *

Great interest is naturally felt and expressed respecting the probable policy of Mr. LINCOLN's successor, and the effect of the President's death on the political interests of the United States. It has been a great satisfaction to me to be able to testify, from personal acquaintance with the present incumbent of the presidential office, to the purity and elevation of his character, and to his soundness, ability, and integrity as a statesman, and at the same time to profess a confidence in the stability of our institutions which excludes all fear, either of a dangerous shock to them or of a temporary derangement of their normal function from even so calamitous an event as this.

It would be ungracious at this moment to inquire jealously into the sincerity of the official expressions of European regret, or into the probable effects of Mr. LINCOLN's death on the policy of foreign powers towards us. Happily the progress of our arms has secured us from all visible danger of European intervention; and if there are governments which, in earlier stages of the rebellion, might have availed themselves of such a conjuncture as this for evil ends, it is now too late to make it an occasion of successful wrong-doing by any European state to the people of the United States.

We are yet without definite information as to the condition of the Secretary of State, and of his son and assistant, but the telegraphic intelligence seems favorable to the life and complete restoration of both of them.

The great wisdom and ability with which Mr. Seward has conducted the foreign relations of the United States are universally acknowledged, and are, indeed, so deeply felt that his decease at this moment would be regarded by Europe as a loss to his country hardly less than that of the President himself, and I most earnestly trust both that his life may be saved, and that he may be spared the heavy affliction of the loss of a distinguished son.

I am, sir, with high respect, your obedient servant,

GEORGE P. MARSH.

Hon. WILLIAM HUNTER,
    Acting Secretary of State.

[Translation.]

The Italian Society of United Mechanics of Turin, to citizen George Perkins Marsh, Envoy, &c., &c., &c.

The Italian Society of United Mechanics of Turin, which is proud to have Giuseppe Garibaldi as honorary president, the man who contended in Italy for the triumph of that same principle for which ABRAHAM LINCOLN was assassinated, cannot remain silent on this great occasion.

Impressed with profound sorrow for the misfortunes of the United States of America, the officers of our society beg you to act as our interpreter to your countrymen, to express to them our high regard, particulary for one mechanic like us, who was born in Kentucky, and whose genius elevated him to the highest rank in the nation that trusted its destiny to his care; who served his country so well that the enemies of all good were forced to arm the hand of a hired assassin to take his precious life.

May free America find a successor worthy of ABRAHAM LINCOLN, and may the Monroe doctrine prevail for the good of the country.

Given in Turin, in the Society hall, the 30th of April, 1865.

[SEAL.]   ANDREA BONA, *President.*
           GIOVANNI GIROMPINI, *Vice-President.*
           GIACOMO SALZA, *Consul.*
           ENRICO SAPPIANI, *Secretary.*
           CARLO BENEDETTO,
           DOMENICI MARLI,
           PIETRO GIORGIO,
           GIUSEPPE MUSATTO,
                     Members.

[Translation.]

A∴ G∴ D∴ G∴ A∴ D∴ U∴

GRAND ORIENT OF MASONRY IN ITALY.

The G∴ M∴ regent of Masonry in Italy to the most honorable citizen G. Marsh, representative of the government of the United States in Italy.

TURIN, *April* 28, 1865.

The great man who has just disappeared in consequence of a horrid crime, ABRAHAM LINCOLN, was the powerful cause by which the abolition of slavery has become a reality; ABRAHAM LINCOLN is, in this respect, not only a great citizen of your country, but one of the principal benefactors of humanity.

Masons in every part of the world owe him a tribute of gratitude, of respect, and of veneration.

Permit me, sir, to beg you, in the name of the one hundred and eleven masonic lodges of our communion, to have the kindness to transmit to the government and people of the United States the expression of our sorrow, and our most sincere wishes for the entire completion of the work so well begun by the illustrious deceased, through the effect of the power of your republican institutions.

Our masonic lodges have put on mourning for nine days.

Accept, Mr. Minister, the expression of my profound respect.

FRANCOIS DE LUCA, 33.

[SEAL.]   *The Grand Chancellor,*

M. MACCHI, 33.

[Translation.]

TURIN, *May* 4, 1865.

DEAR SIR: The undersigned, representatives of the Italian emigrants, Venetians, Trentines and Istrians, exiles from their homes, are mourning for their mother country, and praying for a LINCOLN to sever the chains of foreign slavery, while they place this expression of indignation at the assassination of the President of the United States, a martyr of duty, in your hands, offering their most sincere condolence and fervent vows for the free prosperity of the glorious nation where the acts of its supreme magistrate demonstrate that government is made for the people, and not the people for the government.

Accept this testimony of our profound respect and admiration.

FILIPPO DE BONI,
President of the Council of Representatives,

AND THIRTEEN OTHERS.

Hon. GEO. P. MARSH,
United States Minister to Italy, Turin.

[Translation.]

TURIN, *May* 16, 1865.

HONORED SIR : The terrible catastrophe that has plunged your country into the deepest mourning has been echoed throughout the world, attaining the proportions of an universal calamity. The loyal and generous hearts of all true men have paid the tribute of regret at the tomb of the great man who deserved their esteem and admiration. The Polish emigrants in Turin, joining in the general grief, beg you to accept this expression of their sorrow and condolence, and offer their humble wreath to decorate the monument of the American martyr.

ABRAHAM LINCOLN had no equal; born in the ranks of the people, his merit elevated him to the highest position. He had not the help of fortune to secure his second election to the chief magistracy of a great nation. The corruption and intrigue of opponents did no harm to his cause; the independence and firmness of his character were his defence. He was indispensable to his country in the crisis it was suffering; his patriotism was increased by obstacles; new difficulties only served to develop new qualities in him, brought out by his devotion to the people's welfare. He marched forward, unterrified by the clamors of egotism and envy, uninfluenced by mean considerations. His appeal to arms to sustain the rights of humanity was greatly applauded on this side of the Atlantic. Stimulated by his example, the Poles, eternal pioneers of independence, recommenced their struggle against oppression and tyranny; they were incensed that the Old World should enslave whites, when America had just freed her blacks; but alone, weak and unsupplied, they had to yield, unconquered. The hour of justice had not come for them. They sought peace in exile, hoping that the sacred principles of ABRAHAM LINCOLN—the emancipation of oppressed humanity—would soon prevail throughout the world.

VALDIMIR COUNT SZOLDOSKI,

AND SIXTY-TWO OTHER POLISH SIGNATURES.

The UNITED STATES MINISTER, *in Turin.*

[Translation.]

MERCHANTS' ASSOCIATION OF VERCELLI.

VERCELLI, *May* 14, 1865.

HONORED SIR : The sad and horrible assassination of ABRAHAM LINCOLN, while it astounded all free and civilized nations, profoundly afflicted the great mass of merchants and artisans, who saw in the great President of the North American republic the noble principles of true democracy, the great redeemer of the slave, the magnanimous benefactor of humanity, who, from a man of the people, elevated himself by his genius and his virtue to the highest office in the gift of the nation.

The committee of the Merchants' Association of Vercelli, acting as interpreter for the society, expresses its horror at the abominable deed that has thrown the civilized world into mourning and consternation, and cherishes the most sincere hopes for the glorious and cheerful future of America, which, now that slavery is abolished, may be reunited in peace and harmony.

Long may America flourish! Glory to the memory of the immortal LINCOLN, whose name will be recorded in the eternal pages of history, as the greatest ever honored by humanity.

The same horror is felt at the iniquitous attack upon the illustrious minister, Seward, who was providentially preserved from the vile assassin's dagger for the good of the American people.

In discharging this sad duty, the committee begs you to accept the expression of its highest consideration and esteem.

GLIELLE GIUSEPPE, *President.*

GIUSEPPE GUGLIELMONJ, *Secretary.*

Hon. GEO. PERKINS MARSH,
  United States Minister to Italy, at Turin.

JAPAN.

Mr. Portman to Mr. Seward.

No. 40.]   LEGATION OF THE UNITED STATES IN JAPAN,
             Yedo, July 5, 1865.

SIR : Late in the evening of the 3d instant, the day of the arrival of the mail at Kanagawa, I received a message from the Gorogio to the effect that several officers of rank wished to visit me on this day. I was accordingly waited on by the governors for foreign affairs with a numerous suite, who, in the name of his Majesty the Tycoon, and his government, came to request me to convey to the President and yourself the sentiments of profound pain with which they had learned the assassination of Mr. LINCOLN and the attack on yourself, and also their sincerest wishes for your speedy recovery. I assured these officers that I should not fail to comply with this request at the earliest opportunity.

I have the honor to be, sir, very respectfully, your most obedient servant,

A. L. C. PORTMAN,
Chargé d'Affaires ad interim.

Hon. WILLIAM H. SEWARD,
Secretary of State, Washington.

Mr. Winchester to Mr. Portman.

YOKOHAMA, *June* 9, 1865.

SIR: It is with unusual emotion that I propose to discharge the duty of expressing the sentiments of profound pain and regret which the confirmation of the intelligence of Mr. LINCOLN's atrocious assassination has caused me, in common with all her Majesty's subjects in this country.

That such a deed should have been perpetrated by one of our common race is in itself sufficient reason for the profound indignation which this great crime has excited in the hearts of Englishmen. And I can only express my sincere hope that Providence, in permitting the removal of so good a man, under circumstances so awful, from the task of composing the difficulties necessarily following civil warfare, will raise up other instruments for carrying it out in the humane spirit of the deceased President.

I have the honor to be, sir, your most obedient, humble servant,

CHARLES A. WINCHESTER,
H. B. M. Chargé d'Affaires in Japan.

A. L. C. PORTMAN, Esq.,
Chargé d'Affaires ad interim of the United States in Japan.

LIBERIA.

Whereas the honorable ABRAHAM LINCOLN, late President of the United States of America, a ruler ordained of Heaven, has, by the ruthless hand of the assassin, been removed from his sphere of usefulness in this life; and

Whereas in the death of that great chief the American nation has sustained a severe loss, in which the interests of nations, as well as those of mankind generally, have participated; and

Whereas the government and people of the republic of Liberia, which is legitimately an offspring of the great American republic, fostered during the period of its colonial growth by a society of American citizens, and recently greatly favored and sustained by the United States government, recognized in the late President of the United States one who utterly abhorred slavery—a friend of the negro race and a promoter of the interests of Liberia ; and

Whereas, by the sudden and lamentable death of this great ruler, not only has a nation been deprived of its head, but a home and a hearth are desolate, and kindred hearts are broken, and tears of grief are shedding by those who, by reason of a foul murder, have been deprived of a companion, a father, a friend : Therefore,

Resolved by the President of the Republic of Liberia and his cabinet in council, That it is with sincere regret and pain, as well as with feelings of horror and indignation, the government of Liberia has heard of the foul assassination of the honorable ABRAHAM LINCOLN, late President of the United States of America.

Resolved, That the government and people of Liberia deeply sympathize with the government and people of the United States in the sad loss they have sustained by the death of so wise, so just, so efficient, so vigorous, and yet so merciful a ruler.

Resolved, That while with due sorrow the government and people of Liberia weep with those that mourn the loss of so great and good a chief, they are, nevertheless, mindful of the loss they themselves have experienced in the death of the great philanthropist whose virtues can never cease to be told so long as the republic of Liberia shall endure ; so long as there survives a member of the negro race to tell of the chains that have been broken ; of the griefs that have been allayed ; of the broken hearts that have been bound up by him who, as it were a new creation, breathed life into four millions of that race whom he found oppressed and degraded.

Resolved, That our prayers are also on behalf of him who has been called so suddenly to assume the reins of government, the honorable Andrew Johnson, President of the United States of America ; that we trust that the God who controls the destinies of nations will endue him with all wisdom necessary to rule so great a people, and continue to guide the nation in its rapid progress to the consummation of its greatness and glory

Resolved, That we express, moreover, our sympathy for the efficient statesman, the profound diplomatist, the honorable William H Seward, Secretary of State of the United States, who, with the Assistant Secretary of State, had nigh fallen a prey to that horrible conspiracy which has robbed the American nation of its brightest jewel.

Resolved, That while we are reluctant to invade the sacred precincts of domestic sorrow, we cannot refrain from expressing here our sympathy for Mrs. Lincoln, the estimable widow of the late President, exhorting her to receive to her consolation the words of Holy Writ, " Whom the Lord loveth He chasteneth," and to be sustained by the promises of Almighty God, who will be a husband and a father to the widow and orphans of him who, in his lifetime, was not only a ruler of his own people, but a father to millions of a race stricken and oppressed. That, while wicked men have desolated her home by the perpetration of a crime too horrible to be uttered, the renowned chief, the beloved companion, the tender father, has died to redeem a nation, a race ; and, dying in the performance of so noble a work, he has left behind a monument more lasting than brass, and generations yet unborn shall call him the mighty ruler, the great emancipator, the noble philanthropist.

Resolved, That copies of these resolutions be presented to the United States consul general in Monrovia, with a request that he forward a copy to the proper authority at Washington, and also one to Mrs. Lincoln.

By order of the President :

H. B. W. JOHNSON,
Secretary of State.

EXECUTIVE MANSION,
Monrovia, July 4, 1865.

SIR : I congratulate you upon your succession to the presidency of the United States of America, recently made vacant by the death of your illustrious predecessor, President ABRAHAM LINCOLN.

The distinguished position places you at the head of a great people, a nation whose exhibitions of valor, might, and power in war, during the four years just past, have struck the world with wonder and astonishment. They have astonished even the nation itself making them.

Identified as are the people of the republic of Liberia, over whose national affairs I am, in the providence of God, at present presiding, with millions of their race in America, and being so sensibly and gratefully impressed with a knowledge of the numerous favors directly and indirectly received from the United States government, first in their struggle to gain these shores from oppression, and then in their efforts to establish here a home and build up a negro nationality this side of the waters for themselves and their children after them, it were impossible for them to be indifferent to the grave events now taking place in that country.

They have been looking, and continue to look, with intense anxiety and concern upon those events. They have been duly impressed with just views of the great contest now going on in America between truth and error, between liberty and oppression, and have longed to see the contest cease, and a bright day of peace dawn upon that land, scattering far and wide the dark cloud which has for many years been hanging so portentously over it. They have ardently wished that both the originating cause of the unhappy civil discord now distracting a great people, and every circumstance contributing fuel to keep it at such heat and proportions as the world has witnessed and heartily lamented, could be forever done away.

These were some of their sincere desires and cherished hopes; and they were consoling themselves in the belief that they should soon realize them.

But when they received the distressing intelligence of the death of President LINCOLN, that able Chief Magistrate, who had for four long, consecutive years, and under the severest mental anguish, been defending the cause of liberty and endeavoring to open " the prison to them that are bound," that the prisoners might go free, their hearts were saddened, and they could not suppress the deep sorrow they felt at so mournful and sad an event, and now more than ever before they sympathize with the American nation in the deep troubles it is at this time experiencing. They record their deep grief at the loss it has sustained in the death of so indulgent, kind, liberal, and fatherly a chief as it found in President LINCOLN, and I feel that I can assure you, sir, of the sympathy of these people of Liberia for yourself, and of their unfeigned hope that you will be fully sustained by the great God of nations in the execution of the mighty duties devolving upon you, and in the prosecution of the great undertaking now before you.

May you be greatly prospered by Him by whom " kings reign and princes decree righteousness," and finally be crowned with honor in heaven which fadeth not away.

I am, sir, very respectfully yours,

D. B. WARNER.

His Excellency ANDREW JOHNSON,
President of the United States of America.

Mr. Pinney to Mr. Hunter.

LIBERIAN LEGATION,
New York, April 17, 1865.

SIR: With deepest personal sorrow over the sad intelligence, I have the honor to acknowledge your communication of Saturday.

The assassination of President LINCOLN and the attempt upon the life of the Secretary of State have made us a nation of mourners, and all loyal hearts are agonized by the dreadful tragedy.

The republic of Liberia will deeply sympathize with us, as in the sudden death of our President she suffers an irreparable loss. What we have done and proposed in her behalf will ever be gratefully remembered.

Much of that great flood of tears shed over this great sorrow will flow from the children of Africa, who looked to him especially as their deliverer.

The telegraphic news which we to-day received, as to the decided improvement of Secretary Seward and his son, greatly alleviates the prevalent sadness, and the hope is universal that they may speedily recover.

With distinguished consideration, I am truly yours,

J. B. PINNEY,
Chargé d'Affaires

Hon. W. HUNTER,
   Acting Secretary of State.

MONROVIA, AFRICA, *July* 19, 1865.

Whereas the sad and most affecting intelligence of the assassination of his Excellency ABRAHAM LINCOLN, President of the United States of North America, has reached this body; and whereas the loss of so great, good, and wise a man must be most keenly felt by the American people, over whom he was called to rule, as well as by humanity everywhere; and whereas we feel that our race, in common with all others, has sustained a loss in the death of this most excellent man, which possibly time will not repair; and whereas, through this most flagrant act of violence, sorrow and mourning have been made to enter the precincts of a once quiet, happy, peaceful home: Therefore,

Resolved by the mayor and city councilmen of the city of Monrovia in council assembled, That this body has learned with feelings of profound regret of the assassination of his Excellency ABRAHAM LINCOLN, President of the United States of North America, and that we regard with utter horror and detestation the crime by which a great people have been bereft of a great man.

Resolved, further, That we do hereby express our sincere and profound sympathy with the American people in the loss they have sustained by the sudden and untimely taking from among them their Chief Executive, by the ruthless hand of the assassin, in the month of April last.

Resolved, further, That in the person of the late President of the United States of North America, his Excellency ABRAHAM LINCOLN, no less as a private individual than as a public ruler, the negro race have lost a valuable and inestimable friend, who, while living, not less by his actions than by his words, exerted himself for the amelioration of the condition of that part of our race who have so long been in chains and slavery; and that we highly appreciate the many good acts that mark his life; and that we regard with high esteem his sense of justice and righteous acknowledgment of the right of all men to that boon of Heaven, equal freedom of life, limb, and thought.

Resolved, further, That our heartfelt sympathy is with Mrs. Lincoln, the most estimable widow of the late President, and with the present ruler, who has been so suddenly called to preside over so great a people.

Resolved, finally, That a copy of these resolutions be forwarded to the United States commissioner and consul general in Monrovia, with a request that he will forward them to the proper persons in Washington.

A true copy from the original:

W. FISK BURNS,
Clerk of Common Council of Monrovia.

Mr. Hanson to Mr. Seward.

[Extract.]

No. 38.]

LEGATION OF THE UNITED STATES,
Monrovia, July 5, 1865.

SIR: On the 30th ultimo the very melancholy tidings reached us of the sad loss which our nation has sustained by the death of our honored President, and also of the murderous attempt made upon your valuable life and that of your beloved son.

I assure you my grief at this great national calamity is profound, and my sympathy with you, in your sore affliction, deep and sincere.

It is my daily and earnest prayer that you and yours may be speedily restored to health, and that God may continue to guide and support you in your arduous duties, and that our President, Andrew Johnson, may be endowed with wisdom from on high.

The universal sympathy of the people of Liberia is accorded to us in our deep distress. Flags at half-mast have been floating daily from all the principal residences, &c., and expressions of condolence come to me from every quarter.

It is gratifying to my feelings to forward to you, herein, a proof of the interest felt in our affairs by the President of Liberia and his cabinet. At 12 m. yesterday a deputation, comprising all the members of the cabinet, called upon me at the legation for the purpose of presenting a preamble and certain resolutions adopted at a full meeting of the President and his cabinet, with a request that I would forward them to their proper destination. I left my bed of sickness to entertain them.

The honorable H. B. W. Johnson, secretary of state of the republic, on presenting the documents, made some very tender and eloquent remarks, to which. I endeavored to make a suitable reply; but I am fearful that they will all have passed from my memory before I shall have strength to pen them down. However, you can well conceive what they should be.

*   *   *   *   *   *   *   *

I have the honor to remain, sir, with deep sympathy and profound respect, your very obedient servant,

ABRAHAM HANSON.

Hon. WILLIAM H. SEWARD,
    Secretary of State.

MEXICO.

[Circular.—Translation.]

DEPARTMENT OF FOREIGN RELATIONS AND GOVERNMENT, DEPARTMENT OF GOV-
ERNMENT—FIRST BUREAU.

The official confirmation has been received that the President of the United States of America, ABRAHAM LINCOLN, died at Washington, at seven o'clock and twenty-two minutes, on the morning of the 15th day of April last, in consequence of the wound inflicted upon him by an assassin at half past nine o'clock on the previous night. The deplorable end of President LINCOLN is a cause of great regret to the government of the Mexican republic, and to all its good citizens, by reason of his eminent personal qualities, and because, during his administration, the government of the United States has continued in the most friendly relations with that of the Mexican republic in the difficult state of the affairs thereof.

With the view that the manifestations of the public sorrow for that sad event may be adopted, the citizen President directs that the national flag be hoisted at half-mast upon all the public buildings and at all the military stations during the day subsequent to the reception of this circular, and that all the authorities, functionaries, and employés, both civil and military, clothe themselves in mourning during nine days.

Independence and liberty!
CHIHUAHUA, *May* 16, 1865.

LERDO DE TEJADA.

The Citizen GOVERNOR OF THE STATE OF ———.

President Juarez to Mr. Romero.

[Translation.—Extract.]

CHIHUAHUA, *May* 11, 1865.

MY DEAR FRIEND :   *   *   *   We also received the day before yesterday the news of the total defeat of the confederate army on the 9th of April. The great pleasure this news afforded us was marred by the very sad impression which the shocking intelligence of President LINCOLN's assassination produced upon us. That great misfortune has profoundly impressed me, as Mr. LINCOLN, who worked with so much earnestness and abnegation for the cause of nationality and freedom, was worthy of a better fate than the poniard of a coward assassin. I do most earnestly hope that Mr. Seward's wounds will not be mortal, and that his son, too, may have been saved. I beg of you to pay a private visit to Mr. Seward in my name, expressing to him my grief for the misfortunes befallen upon him, and my best wishes for his speedy and complete recovery.   •

  *   *   *   *   *   *   *   *   *

BENITO JUAREZ.

Señor Don MATIAS ROMERO.

Mr. Romero to Mr. Hunter.

[Translation.]

MEXICAN LEGATION IN THE UNITED STATES OF AMERICA,
Washington, April 15, 1865.

MR. SECRETARY AD INTERIM : The grief I felt this morning, on hearing of the death of the President of the United States from a wound received last night in a theatre of this city, and of the serious wounds of the Secretary and Assistant Secretary of State, has not been less than yours expressed in the note of this date informing me of those unpleasant events, and which I have just received.

Your note also informs me that, according to the Constitution of the United States, the honorable Andrew Johnson, Vice-President of the United States, formally assumed the functions of President to-day, and authorized you to discharge the duties of Secretary of State *ad interim* till further orders.

Though the occasion is a sad one, I embrace it to renew to you, sir, the assurances of my distinguished consideration.

M. ROMERO.

Hon. WILLIAM HUNTER,
  Acting Secretary of State.

Governor Gibert to Mr. Elmer.

[Translation.]

LA PAZ, *May* 1, 1865

MY DEAR SIR: I have received your note of April 29, in which you advise me of the sudden death of the Chief Magistrate of the United States, who was assassinated during a period of great national rejoicing.

Entertaining the same sentiments as yourself, this government cannot do less than express its sincere sorrow for the unfortunate event.

I have the honor to repeat my assurances of respect, &c., &c.

F. GIBERT, *Governor, La Paz.*

Señor Don F. B. ELMER,
United States Consul.

[Translation.]

AT PROVIDENCIA, *May* 3, 1865.

MY DEAR SIR: The Golden City, arriving in your port on the 29th ultimo with her flag at half-mast, announced with this sign of mourning, even before coming to her moorings, one of the most treacherous murders that history will record. So it was, indeed. The periodicals received come to announce to us, with their columns clad in mourning, the assassination of the President of the United States, ABRAHAM LINCOLN, and the dangerous wounds of the honorable Secretary of State, Mr. William H. Seward.

Suffering under the terrible impression which this calamity has produced upon the inhabitants of this State, and to myself, I address you these lines as the sincere expression of my deep sorrow for the great loss the people of the United States have sustained in the person of their First Magistrate.

With distinguished appreciation, I am, very respectfully, your obedient servant,

D. ALVAREZ, *Governor.*

Mr. GILBERT M. COLE,
United States Consul at Acapulco.

[Translation.]

MEXICAN REPUBLIC—POLITICAL AND MILITARY GOVERNMENT OF THE STATE OF TOBASCO.

Mr. CONSUL: The kindred people of this continent, united in the lovely bonds of democracy, ought to share mutually in its joys and its sorrows. For this reason Mexico will ever deplore the unfortunate event of the 14th of April last, the death of the illustrious champion of liberty in the city of Washington. For this reason will Mexico forget her past misfortunes, in the midst of her present trials, and congratulate the great and heroic people of the United States on this day of glorious memory.

Accept, then, Mr. Consul, on this day—the anniversary of that auspicious day when your ancestors proclaimed their independence in the city of Philadelphia—my sincere congratulations, as a private individual, and as the representative of this State, of whose sympathies I believe myself, on this occasion, the most faithful interpreter.

Accept also, in the name of your government, the demonstrations of esteem and good will from the garrison of this place, who have kindred sentiments, and trust that Mexico in general, and Tabasco in particular, will be worthy members of the great democratic family that people the world of Columbus, in spite of the mean strategy now used to divide us.

I make vows to Providence for the happiness of the United States, and pray that the peace the great republic has just conquered at such a great sacrifice may last long, for the good of humanity.

You will please accept, on this account, the assurances of my personal esteem and consideration.

Republic and liberty .

San Juan Bautista, *July* 4, 1865.

G. MENDEZ.

Leon Alejo Torre, *First Officer.*

B. N. Sanders,
　　Consul of the United States at this port, Present.

MOROCCO.

Mr. McMath to Mr. Hunter.

No. 26.]　　Consulate of the United States of America
for the Empire of Morocco,
Tangier, May 4, 1865.

Sir : The lamentable news of the assassination of his Excellency Abraham Lincoln, President of the United States, reached this consulate by telegraph *via* Madrid, on the 28th ultimo. This intelligence has produced the most intense feeling of sorrow in the minds of all our population, native and foreign.

The event is so astounding that it is with difficulty I can bring myself to realize its occurrence or estimate its consequences. The blow is sudden, horrible, and irretrievable. Never has a murder been committed more momentous in its bearing upon the time. A nation mourns the inestimable loss of one of the greatest and purest statesmen that ever lived. He dies surrounded with the brightest halo of glory that has ever crowned the labor of a statesman, and his work will survive him, and the greatest victory of liberty and humanity will not have been won in vain. I am as yet without details which can give me the slightest idea of the cause of so grave an event. However, it seems difficult to suppose that a crime committed on the President had not been dictated by a political motive; and I may say this crime is not only odious but useless, for Providence will not fail to raise up worthy successors of him who has fallen a martyr to liberty, humanity, and constitutional government. To my bleeding and grief-stricken country I offer my sincere sympathy and condolence.

This consulate has gone into mourning for thirty days.

Immediately upon the receipt of this distressing news, I informed my colleagues that, as a mark of respect to the illustrious and unfortunate deceased President LINCOLN, the flag of the United States would be displayed at half-mast for a period of three days at this consulate, and stated that on this mournful occasion I would be pleased to see my flag accompanied with those of their respective nations. To this each of my colleagues assented, and at the same time expressed their sincere sympathy and condolence for the great national loss sustained in the untimely death of his Excellency President LINCOLN. I have also communicated this sad intelligence to my vice-consuls on the coast, and have requested them to display their flags at half-mast for three days and request their colleagues to accompany it with those of their respective nations.

The melancholy news of the attempted assassination of the honorable Secretary of State, and his son, the Assistant Secretary, reached me one day later than the former. Since then I have been advised by the latest news from London that there is a probability that both may recover from the wounds inflicted upon them. I sincerely hope and pray to Almighty God that both may be speedily restored to our common country, and to each my sincere sympathy is offered.

In profound grief for the events which have taken place, I have the honor to be, very respectfully, your obedient servant,

JESSIE H. McMATH.

Hon. WILLIAM HUNTER,
Acting Secretary of State, Washington, D. C.

THE NETHERLANDS.

Mr. Van Limburg to Mr. Hunter.

[Translation.]

NEW YORK, *May* 16, 1865.

SIR: In the Netherlands, as everywhere else, the news of the assassination of President LINCOLN, and of the attempt on the life of the Secretary of State, has caused a universal shock and deep indignation.

On the part of the royal government, the minister of foreign affairs would have wished to request Mr. Pike to be so good as to transmit to Washington the assurances of the sorrowful impression caused throughout the Netherlands by this double crime, but the temporary absence of the minister resident of the United States not putting that in my power, it is in virtue of the King's order, and in accordance with a resolution adopted by a council of ministers, that I am charged to present, without delay, to the American government the assurance of lively sympathy in the loss and profound indignation at the crime, in which all the Netherlands partake with the King.

I am charged to express, sir, at the same time, the wishes of his Majesty and of the royal government that Divine Providence may preserve the life of Mr. Seward, so precious to the people of the United States.

In acquitting myself of this duty, sir, I have the honor to repeat to you the assurances of my high consideration.

ROEST VAN LIMBURG.

Hon. WILLIAM HUNTER,
Acting Secretary of State, Washington, D. C.

Mr. Van Limburg to Mr. Hunter.

[Translation.]

DETROIT, *May* 25, 1865.

SIR: The minister of the King for foreign affairs has just given in charge to me, to communicate to you, a resolution passed on the 2d instant by the Second Chamber of the States General, tending to invite the royal government to make known to the government of the United States the sorrow and indignation the Chamber has felt on learning the perfidious and base outrage of which President ABRAHAM LINCOLN has been the victim.

On the occasion of this resolution, its mover, Mr. de Zuylen de Nywelt, remarked that in the Netherlands it was caused, more perhaps than any like resolution could be elsewhere, not alone by the ties of friendship and of alliance which for a long period have existed between the two countries, but moreover by the circumstance that a great many old families of Holland have established themselves in the United States, and that our country, at a period already remote, contributed much to the sowing of the seed from which the great American nation has sprung forth at a later day.

The minister of foreign affairs, fully adopting this principle, expresses anew the general indignation at the horrible crimes by which the President of the United States was snatched away from his great task at the moment when achieving the object of his efforts, and by which the lives of the Secretary and Assistant Secretary of State were put in peril.

It was in the nature of things, said Mr. Cremers, that the assassination of a man whose character bore so great a resemblance to that of the noble founder of our liberties should make a profound impression. Here, where the name of Balthazar Gerard (the assassin of William of Orange) is, even now, never pronounced without a horror, a crime resembling his must excite extraordinary sympathy and indignation.

I take pride, sir, in being again instructed to express to you similar sentiments; they cannot but convince you, as well as the President and people of the United States, of the lively and sincere friendship which attaches the Netherlands to the United States of America.

Please accept, sir, the fresh assurance of my very high consideration.

ROEST VAN LIMBURG.

Hon. WILLIAM HUNTER,
    Acting Secretary of State, &c., &c., &c.

Mr. Pike to Mr. Hunter.

[Extract.]

No. 164.]
                    UNITED STATES LEGATION,
                        The Hague, May 3, 1865.

SIR: *   *   *   *   *   *   *

The announcement of the assassination of the President, the news of which reached here last week, fills me with profound emotion. The dreadful suspense we were in, for many days, in regard to the Secretary of State and the Assistant Secretary, is happily removed by this mail. The tenor of our first advices was such that we had not dared to hope for the recovery of Mr. Seward, while we had taken for granted that the Assistant Secretary was no longer among the living. It is an inexpressible relief to receive the assurance that the lives of both are saved.

I have forwarded to the department a copy of Galignani's Messenger, containing one day's summary of the public commentary upon the hideous crimes committed by the assassins, which is but one of a series of the same character. By this record you may, in some measure, judge of the violent shock these monstrous assassinations have given to the European public. It would be difficult for me to exaggerate it by any description I could give.

I have been called upon by numerous gentlemen of high political distinction, among them the ministers of foreign affairs, who have desired to manifest their sympathy with the government in its distress; to bear their testimony to the pure and lofty character of the deceased President, and to express the universal horror and indignation at the foul deeds which have at once robbed the nation of its head and daringly put in imminent peril the life of his first cabinet officer.

I have the honor to be, with great respect, your most obedient servant,

JAMES S. PIKE.

Hon. W. HUNTER,
Acting Secretary of State, Washington.

Mr. Pike to Mr. Hunter.

No. 165.]
UNITED STATES LEGATION,
The Hague, May 4, 1865.

SIR: Yesterday the second chamber of the national legislature, the only branch now in session, passed resolutions instructing the ministers of foreign affairs to communicate to the cabinet at Washington their sense of the great loss sustained by the United States in the death of the President, to tender to them the sympathy of the chamber, and to express their horror and detestation of the foul crimes by which the President's life has been terminated and that of the Secretary of State endangered.

These resolutions were supported in debate by the minister of foreign affairs on the part of the government, and by M. Van Zuylen on the part of the opposition, and were unanimously carried.

To-day the minister of foreign affairs has called and communicated to me this action on the part of the second chamber, and requested me to transmit it to the government at Washington, and to add that nowhere in Europe has there been a profounder emotion felt than in Holland over the awful tragedy enacted in the United States, and nowhere can its condemnation be more heart-felt and unanimous.

I have the honor to be, with great respect, your most obedient servant,

JAMES S. PIKE.

Hon. W. HUNTER,
Acting Secretary of State, Washington.

NICARAGUA.

[Translation.]

GOVERNMENT HOUSE,
Leon, May 18, 1865.

MR. MINISTER: His Excellency the captain general, President, has been made acquainted with your despatch of the 17th instant, in which he is notified through me of the unfortunate events which occurred in Washington on the 14th of April last, the assassination of his Excellency the President of the United States of North America, Mr. ABRAHAM LINCOLN, and the serious wounds inflicted by the hand of another assassin on the person of the very illustrious Secretary of State, Mr. William H. Seward. I am also notified in the same communication of the elevation to the presidency, by virtue of the laws, of his Excellency the Vice-President, Mr. Andrew Johnson, and to the ministry temporarily of the chief clerk, Mr. Hunter, until the recovery of Mr. Seward, which now seems probable.

The government and people of Nicaragua are not nor could they be indifferent to an event which has so great effect on all classes of society, as well on account of the welfare of the country which Mr. LINCOLN governed so worthily, as because of such excesses. In a republic, too, like the United States—model of civilization and of grandeur—it seems impossible to conceive the existence of a man that, even by the means of the most exalted imagination, could conceive the design of applying his treacherous hand against the life of him who, by the general choice of the people, had been called for a fixed period to the presidential chair.

But the deed is done, sir, however extraordinary it may seem to those who know its magnitude; and while it meets solely with universal condemnation, let us indulge the grateful hope that his principles may be securely preserved for the United States of North America under the presidency of a successor worthy of the immortal LINCOLN, for which we trust in the co-operation of Mr. Seward, that veteran Secretary, whom Providence has so marvellously preserved for the benefit of his country.

These are the sentiments of his Excellency the President of Nicaragua, and in transmitting them to your excellency, with the expression of my sincerest sympathy, I have the honor to subscribe myself once again, your affectionate servant,

BASILIO SALINAS.

His Excellency A. B. DICKENSON,
Minister Resident of the United States, &c., &c., &c.

[Translation.]

GOVERNMENT HOUSE,
Leon, June 19, 1865.

SIR: Although this government has already paid its due compliments through the minister resident of the United States, I have to say, in answer to your esteemed despatch of the 18th April, ultimo, and the mournful news it contains, that the assassination of the illustrious President of the United States, ABRAHAM LINCOLN, and the barbarous assault on the persons of the honorable Secretary and Assistant Secretary of State, Mr. Seward and his son, martyrs of the glorious cause in which they were happily winning victory, have been in Nicaragua, as well as in all Central America and over the whole civilized world, the source of a general feeling of horror and sadness. Sympathy for the administration of Mr. LINCOLN, for the cause he maintained of freedom of the human kind, and with the impulse this same doleful event imparted to the triumphant opinion, cause this government religiously to cherish the glorious memory of the illustrious dead, to heartily hail the providential salvation of the honorable Mr. Seward and his son, whom we duly honor, and to behold with the highest esteem, respect, and our best wishes the heroic decision with which Mr. LINCOLN's worthy successor comes forward ready to perfect the sublime but unfinished work which falls to his lot.

The President trusts you have, in anticipation of the desire and well-known feelings of his administration, interpreted them with your usual faithfulness, near the government of the United States; and directs me to authorize you to leave a copy of this despatch with the honorable Secretary of State.

I am, sir, your obedient servant,

PEDRO ZELEDON.

His Excellency Don LUIS MOLINA,
  Envoy Extraordinary and Minister Plenipotentiary
    of Nicaragua, Washington.

Mr. Dickenson to Mr. Hunter.

[Extract.]

No. 101.]   LEGATION OF THE UNITED STATES,
          Leon de Nicaragua, May 19, 1865.

SIR: Your despatch No. 69, dated April 17, conveying the painful intelligence of the assassination of President LINCOLN and the murderous assault upon the Secretary and Assistant Secretary of State, has been received and read with a mixture of indignation, horror, and grief altogether beyond the power of words to express.

That even the rebellion itself, black and terrible as are its crimes, could be guilty of murdering our honored President, who was well known to harbor the kindliest feelings and the most forgiving spirit, even towards his enemies, and so cowardly assaulting with murderous intent his chief adviser and supporter, while in a helpless state on a sick-bed, for the purpose of robbing the nation of two of its ablest defenders, was beyond belief, until the fiendish acts themselves, with their surroundings, proved to be a part of its atrocious work.

It would seem also that the avenging arm of the stern patriot who is now our President was justly feared by the infamous traitors, and that he also was to be stricken down with the other strong pillars of the state, in order that the whole national fabric might thus be pulled down, Samson-like, and crushed together with the rebellion.

But even while we mourn for the long list of illustrious dead, headed by our honored chief, we can still thank God that our country survives their loss, to be held only the more precious and sacred hereafter because of the blood which has been shed in its defence.

*　　*　　*　　*　　*　　*　　*　　*　　*

Since the receipt of the melancholy news I have had the flags kept at half-mast and the legation draped in mourning. I also take due note of the order to wear crape on the left arm.

I am, sir, your obedient servant,

A. B. DICKENSON.

W. Hunter, Esq., *Acting Secretary of State.*

PRUSSIA.

Count Bismarck to Mr. Judd.

[Translation.]

Berlin, *April* 27, 1865.

The royal government is profoundly moved by the intelligence which reached here yesterday of the assassination of President Lincoln, and the simultaneous attempt on the life of the Secretary of State, Mr. Seward.

In view of the so happily existing friendly relations between Prussia and the United States, the undersigned cannot forbear to express to their government the sincere sympathy of the royal government with the great loss that this crime has inflicted upon them. He therefore requests the envoy extraordinary and minister plenipotentiary of the United States of America, Mr. Judd, that he will convey the expression of these sentiments to his government, and he avails himself of this occasion to renew to Mr. Judd the assurances of his distinguished consideration.

BISMARCK.

Mr. N. B. Judd, &c., &c., &c.

[Translation.]

Address of the members of the Prussian House of Deputies.

SIR: We, the undersigned members of the Prussian House of Deputies, beg you to accept the expression of our profoundest sympathy in the severe loss the government and people of the United States have suffered in the death of President LINCOLN, and alike the expression of our deepest horror at the shocking crime to which he fell a victim.

We are the more deeply moved by this public calamity inasmuch as it occurred at a moment when we were rejoicing at the triumph of the United States, and as the simultaneous attempt upon the life of the faithful partner of the President, Mr. Seward, who, with the wisdom and resolution of true statesmanship, supported him in the fulfilment of his arduous task, betrays the object of the horrible crime to have been, by the death of these great and good men, to deprive the people of the United States of the fruits of their protracted struggle and patriotic, self-sacrificing devotion, at the very moment when the triumph of right and law promises to bring back the blessings of a long-desired peace.

Sir, living among us, you are a witness of the heart-felt sympathy which the people have ever preserved for the people of the United States during this long and severe conflict. You are aware that Germany has looked with pride and joy on the thousands of her sons who in this struggle have placed themselves so resolutely on the side of law and right. You have seen with what joy the victories of the Union have been hailed, and how confident the faith in the final triumph of the great cause and the restoration of the Union in all its greatness has ever been, even in the midst of adversity.

This great work of the restoration of the Union will, we confidently hope, not be hindered or interrupted by this terrible crime. The blood of the great and wise chieftain will only cement the more firmly the Union for which he has died. This the inviolable respect for law and love of liberty which the people of the United States have ever evinced in the very midst of the prodigious struggles of their great war abundantly guarantees.

We request your good offices for giving expression with your government to our sincere condolences and our sympathies with the government and people of the United States, and proffer to yourself, sir, the assurances of our distinguished consideration.

DR. FRESE.	VON KATHEN.
R. FRŒNING.	DR. KALAN VON DER HOFE.
HAEGER ZIEGLER.	VIESEN.
BARON VON VAERST.	KNUPFEL.
VON CARLEWIG.	

AND TWO HUNDRED AND FIFTY OTHERS.

[Translation.]

Remarks of Deputy Dr. William Loewe in the Prussian House of Deputies.

GENTLEMEN: I have ventured to request the president to permit me to make a communication, for which I claim your sympathy. That which I wish to request of you does not, indeed, belong to the immediate field of our labors, but it goes so far beyond the narrow circle of private life that, in union with a number of our colleagues, I have ventured to call your attention to it. A considerable number of our colleagues feel the need, under the dismay produced by the shocking news of the unhappy death of President LINCOLN, to give expression to their feelings in regard to his fate, and their sympathy with the nation from whom he has been snatched away. ABRAHAM LINCOLN has fallen by the hand of an assassin, in the moment of triumph of the cause which he had conducted, and while he was in hopes of being able to give to his people the peace so long desired.

Our colleagues wish in an address to express the sympathy not of this house—this I say in order to remove all apprehension of a violation of the rules of the house—but the sympathy of the individual members of the house in this great and unhappy event. This address we desire to present to the minister of the United States.

Gentlemen, I will lay the address on the table, and I beg those of my colleagues who share with me the feeling of warm and heartfelt sympathy in the lot of a nation which is united by so many bonds with our own people, to give expression to those feelings by appending their signature to the address. These sympathies I regard as all the more justified, as the United States have won a new and splendid triumph for mankind through the great struggle which they have been carrying on for the cause of true humanity, and which, as I confidently hope, in spite of this murder of their chief, they will conduct to a successful termination. In expressing our feelings of pain, we desire, at the same time, to prove our hearty sympathy with the American nation, and those of our brothers who have taken part in the struggle for their cause. The man, gentlemen, who has fallen by the murderer's hand, and whom I seem to see with his simple, honest countenance—the man who accomplished such great deeds from the simple desire conscientiously to perform his duty—the man who never wished to be more nor less than the most conscientious and most faithful servant of his people—this man will find his own glorious place in the pages of history. In the deepest reverence I bow my head before this modest greatness, and I think it is especially agreeable to the spirit of our own nation, with its deep inner life and admiration of self-sacrificing devotion and effort after the ideal, to pay the tribute of veneration to such greatness, exalted as it is by its simplicity and modesty. I beg of you, gentlemen, accordingly to join in this expression of veneration for the great dead, which, without distinction of party, we offer to him as a true servant of his state, and of the cause of pure humanity.

[Translation.]

The Polish members of the Chamber of Deputies of Prussia, at this moment present in Berlin, join their German colleagues in expressing all the grief and indignation they have experinced on learning of the abominable crime to which the illustrious President LINCOLN has fallen a victim, a martyr of the great cause of the abolition of slavery.

AUGUSTE MIEZKOWSKI.	STANISLAU MOTLEY.
DR. LIBETT.	LEON WEGNER.
BOGUSTAVE LUBIENSKI.	JOSEPH POTUTICKI.
LYZBOWSKI PILASKI.	KADIMIRZ CHIAPOWSKI.
THOBAVSKI.	F. RESPAZDEK.
ZYCHLINSKI.	JOSEPH BOLEWSKI.
DAMILEWSKI.	CASIMIR KANTAK.

[Translation.]

PRUSSIAN LEGATION IN WASHINGTON,
April 16, 1865.

The undersigned, envoy extraordinary and minister plenipotentiary of his Majesty the King of Prussia, has been honored by a note from Mr. William Hunter, Acting Secretary of State of the United States, informing him of the assassination of the President of the United States, and the atrocious attempt upon the lives of the Hon. William H. Seward, Secretary of State, and his son Frederick W. Seward, Assistant Secretary, on the night of the 14th of this month. The attack resulted in the death of the Chief Magistrate of the republic, and the critical situation of the Secretary of State and his assistant from the serious wounds given by the assassin's hand.

The undersigned promptly expresses to Mr. Hunter his profound sorrow and indignation at the unheard-of act of cruelty and political fanaticism of which the President, ABRAHAM LINCOLN, was the victim, at a time when his devotion and constancy in efforts to re-establish the Constitution and the laws were crowned with success, and gave hopes of returning peace.

The undersigned is also informed by Mr. Hunter that Mr. Andrew Johnson, Vice-President of the United States, has entered upon the duties of President of the United States, in conformity to the Constitution, and that Mr. William Hunter is charged with the affairs of the Secretary of State till further orders.

The undersigned embraces the occasion of renewing to Mr. Hunter the assurances of his most distinguished consideration.

BARON GEROLT.

Hon. WILLIAM HUNTER,
Acting Secretary of State.

Mr. Judd to Mrs. Lincoln.

UNITED STATES LEGATION,
Berlin, May 1, 1865.

HONORED MADAM: I have the honor to inform you that to-day Captain Von Lucadon, personal aide-de-camp of his Royal Highness the Crown Prince of Prussia, called at this legation, by command of his Royal Highness, charged to convey to you, madam, through me, the sympathy that their Royal Highnesses, the Prince and the Princess Royal feel for your deep affliction, in the death of your worthy and honored husband, and their anxious desire for your health and well-being.

In executing that request, permit me to add, on my own behalf, the sincere sympathy I feel for your loss, and the deep grief that overwhelmed me at the death of one to whom I was bound by the strongest ties of friendship and love.

I am, madam, your obedient servant and friend,

N. B. JUDD,
United States Minister, Prussia.

Mrs. ABRAHAM LINCOLN.

[Translation.]

AIX-LA-CHAPELLE, *May* 5, 1865.

The undersigned, mayor and members of the municipality of the city of Aix-la-Chapelle, allow themselves to express to you, much honored Mr. Consul, representative of the United States for the Rhenish provinces and Westphalia, their sympathy for the great and irretrievable loss which your country has suffered by the atrocious murder of your highly gifted and noble President LINCOLN.

The horrible and abominable crime which deprived a country of its chief, in the very moment when his presence was most needed to heal the wounds and secure the results of a war of several years in defence of the noblest cause, has filled all Europe, and especially Germany, with abhorrence and dismay. We are more especially penetrated with these sentiments as our city has been in relations, for so many years, with your native land, and has the satisfaction of being the seat of the consulate for the Rhenish provinces and Westphalia.

We beg you, honored sir, as the worthy incumbent of the consulate, to bring the present resolutions to the knowledge of the government of your country, and to accept the assurance of our highest esteem.

C. E. DAHMEN.	RUMPEN.
E. VAN GULPEN.	FR'D NACKEN.
F. ERASMUS.	COMEL VAN GUAITA.
ED. KEPELKAUL.	SOMMER.
COUTZEN.	TH. ESSER.
N. BOCHLEN.	D. RODERBURG.
COUNT NELLESSEN.	D. HAHN.
VRANAUX.	V. MONHEIM.
VON PRAUGHE.	HOYER
D. MULLER.	FRED. CAYIN.
W. ZURHELLE.	JUNGBLUTH.
A. STARTZ.	

M. VESEY, *Consul of the United States*
        for the Rhenish Provinces and Westphalia.

Mr. Judd to Mr. Seward.

No. 93.]   UNITED STATES LEGATION,
                            Berlin, April 27, 1865.

SIR: Intelligence of the assassination of President LINCOLN, and of the murderous attack upon yourself and many members of your household, reached Berlin at about two p. m. yesterday. The statement had such an aspect of horror that I did not believe it. At the Exchange, where it was first received, it was pronounced a stock-jobbing report. I telegraphed immediately to Mr. Adams, and his reply was a confirmation of the dreadful tidings. Your condition, as reported, gives occasion for the most intense anxiety, and no words can express the feelings with which I await further despatches. The report states that your son, Frederick W. Seward, was killed in defending the life of his invalid father. A noble death for one so young and promising, though sad and mournful to surviving relatives and friends, to know that he died by the hand of an assassin. The terrible and tragic death of Mr. LINCOLN, and the calamities that befell your household in that fearful night, are heavy blows for one enfeebled by previous illness. May He who saved your life amidst all its horrors give healing to your wounds, and restore you again to health and usefulness.

I cannot realize that Mr. LINCOLN has been assassinated. He was saved from the Baltimore demons, when on his way to Washington, to be slain now in the midst of friends, and just at the moment when public affairs have assumed their brightest aspect, and peace and order are about to return to the country he loved so well.

All the afternoon and evening yesterday the legation was thronged with anxious and inquiring friends, and many tears fell from the eyes of strong men. Berlin talks of nothing else to-day. Expressions of horror and indignation at the foul murder of our great and good President, and of deep sympathy and condolence for our stricken people, mingled with fervent wishes that you may recover and survive the terrible affliction, are on the lips of all; on the lips of foreigners and strangers, who see in you the trusted friend and counsellor of our martyr President, and the man who for four years, so fraught with dangers and trials, has preserved peace with Europe.

The legation is draped in black, and the passing world beholds that this is a house of mourning.

I am, sir, your obedient servant,

N. B. JUDD.

Hon. WILLIAM H. SEWARD,
 Secretary of State, Washington.

Mr. Judd to Mr. Seward.

[Extract.]

No. 94.]   UNITED STATES LEGATION,
           Berlin, April 28, 1865.

SIR: I have to-day received a communication from the minister president and minister of foreign affairs, Herr von Bismarck Schoenhausen, expressing the deep sympathy of his Majesty's government with the government of the United States at the death of Mr. LINCOLN, and the attempt on your life, and desiring me to convey the expression of their sympathy to my government. Herr von Thile, under-secretary of state for foreign affairs, was charged with delivering the note in person, and came to the legation with it. In doing so, he expressed, in the warmest terms, for himself and his government, the deep feeling the sad occurrences have occasioned.

   *   *   *   *   *   *   *   *

My colleagues of the diplomatic corps are all calling to express their sympathy with us in this affliction, and their abhorrence of the foul deed.

I am, sir, your obedient servant,

N. B. JUDD.

Hon. WILLIAM H SEWARD,
 Secretary of State, Washington.

Mr. Judd to Mr. Seward.

No. 95.]
                                        UNITED STATES LEGATION,
Berlin, April 29, 1865

SIR: Telegraphic advices from the United States, by a later steamer, reached here at noon to-day, and it affords me sincere pleasure to learn that the first report of the death of Mr. Frederick W. Seward has been erroneous, and that, although in a critical condition, he still lives, and that notwithstanding the cruel and savage wounds inflicted on you by a cowardly assassin, in addition to the severe injuries sustained by your late accident, your condition was considered hopeful.

All of the members of the diplomatic corps have paid me their visits of regard and condolence. So have the King's chiefest officials, and many of the distinguished men of science and letters.

As the details of the horrible crime become known, the interest and excitement in every circle and among every class of men increases. It is the one theme of conversation and discussion. The public journals here and elsewhere are entirely filled with it. One intense and spontaneous burst of sorrow and indignation is ringing throughout Germany, and every one, high and low, great and humble, is eager to bear testimony of his admiration and grief for a great and good man departed.

Yesterday the subject was brought before the House of Deputies by one of its most distinguished members, Dr. William Loewe, well known among our German citizens in the United States, from his long residence in New York as a political exile from his fatherland. In eloquent and feeling terms he paid a warm tribute to President LINCOLN, and at the close of his remarks called upon the house to unite with him in an address appropriate to the occasion, to be presented to the American minister here. Nearly the whole house rose in token of concurrence, and the address, as drawn up by the speaker, is receiving numerous signatures. It is to be presented to me by a deputation of members, headed by the president and the two vice-presidents of the house. Dr. Loewe has conferred with me, and it is arranged that the address is to be presented on the afternoon of Monday next.

At my invitation the Americans at present in Berlin have met at the legation, and it has been decided to have divine services in memory of the late President on Tuesday next, May 2, at 4½ o'clock p. m., in the Dorothea church, the use of which for that purpose has been kindly granted us by the city authorities and the pastors of the church. President H. P. Tappan, formerly of Michigan University, will conduct the services for us

        I am, sir, your obedient servant,

                                      N. B. JUDD.

Hon. WILLIAM H. SEWARD,
    Secretary of State, Washington

Mr. Judd to Mr. Seward.

No. 96.]　　　　　　　　　　　UNITED STATES LEGATION,
Berlin, May 1, 1865.

SIR: This forenoon Captain von Lucadon, personal aide-de-camp of his Royal Highness the Crown Prince of Prussia, presented himself at the legation and informed me that he was charged by their Royal Highnesses the Prince and Princess Royal of Prussia to request me to transmit, on their behalf, to the government of the United States, their condolence at the sad event that had transpired, and desiring me also to convey to Mrs. Lincoln their kind sympathies in her affliction.

I am, sir, your obedient servant,

N. B. JUDD.

Hon. WILLIAM H. SEWARD,
Secretary of State, Washington.

Mr. Judd to Mr. Seward.

No. 97.]　　　　　　　　　　　UNITED STATES LEGATION,
Berlin, May 2, 1865.

SIR: In my despatch No. 95 you were informed that I had named Monday, the first day of May, as the time to receive from the members of the Prussian House of Deputies their address of condolence on account of the death of President LINCOLN, and the attempt to assassinate yourself. A note received in the morning of that day appointed five o'clock p. m. as the hour at which the deputation would be at the legation for that purpose.

I had concluded, from some casual remark of a member, that the deputation would be composed of some six or eight members; but to my pleasurable surprise on its arrival, I found it numbered twenty-six of the most talented, celebrated, and influential men of the Chamber, headed by the venerable President Graybow first vice-president, Herr von Unruh, and second vice-president Herr von Backum Dolffs. The additional names of the members of the committee were as follows:

Deputies.

Dr William Loewe; Prof. Dr. Virchow; Baron von Vaerst; Stavenhagen; Dr. Jur. Waldeck; Parrisius; Von Bonin, (ex-minister;) Bassenge; Schrœder; Dr. Ziegert; Duncker; Lent; Baron von Zedlitz and Kurzbach; Riebold; Schneider; Dr. Johann Jacoby; Raffauf; Von Saucken; Tarputschen; Dr. Siemens; Dahlmann; Dr. Krebs; Dr. von Bunsen.

The title of doctor repeatedly recurring indicates a university degree, and not that of a physician, as used in our country. Dr. Loewe, who had the honor of your personal acquaintance when he resided in New York, (the political troubles of 1848 and 1849 having caused his temporary absence from Prussia,) as stated in a former despatch, presented the address with a few remarks in German expressive of the deep feeling in all Germany at the death of Mr. LINCOLN, and your narrow escape from the same fate, at the hand of an assassin, which he followed by reciting the address in full. After apologizing in German for my imperfect use of that language, and asking to be allowed to respond in English, I expressed the thanks of the government and the people of the United States for this sympathetic manifestation of interest in our affliction, assuring them that the latest advices happily stated your improving condition, although the danger had not yet fully passed. That they might rest under the certain conviction that the object sought to be accomplished by the conspirators in these horrible and murderous attacks would not succeed. The government would not be paralyzed, but move stoutly and firmly forward in the political and social regeneration of the communities in rebellion. That the experience of the last four years has demonstrated, beyond question, the power of a people, under a republican form of government, to resist and overcome interior commotion and rebellion. That the administration of public affairs has passed to a new President, habituated to public life and to deal with national questions, and whose talents and firmness of purpose would speedily bring into submission what little remained of the rebellious spirit. That revenge was no part of our national character, but security for the future was the essential element that would control and guide the conduct of public affairs. That the people of the United States appreciated the sympathy of the German people during this terrible rebellion, and that the soldiers of German birth, many of whom, not even citizens, would be held in lasting remembrance by a grateful people, and that their memory would be bound with the laurel common to all who had fought this battle of freedom, without distinction as to nativity or color. One member of the committee, Mr. Schneider Sagan, was then in mourning for an only son killed at Petersburg, Virginia, and another, Deputy Raffauf, has now a son serving in the army of the United States. The German heart has been more moved by these awful occurrences than by any event in their own history since the year 1813. In the minds of the great mass of German readers, Mr. LINCOLN had come to symbolize the republic in all its attributes of the liberty and equality of all men, and their aspirations and hopes turned to him with admiration and affection. They feel that in him all humanity has lost a pure and noble champion.

After the close of my remarks some time was spent in friendly conversation with the various members of the committee, and I parted with them at last, deeply gratified and consoled by this mark of generous and noble sympathy with our people and our cause.

I enclose herewith the original address, with an English translation thereof by the secretary of this legation, Mr. Kreismann, who was present during the interview. It is signed by two hundred and thirty-eight members of the Chamber, and I feel persuaded that a fit place will be assigned by you for this interesting document in the archives of the State Department.

Your old acquaintance and friend, Professor Tellkampf, a member of the upper house, sought and obtained leave to add his signature. You will readily find his, to you, familiar handwriting.

.   I am, sir, your obedient servant,

N. B. JUDD.

Hon. WILLIAM H. SEWARD,
        Secretary of State, Washington.

Mr. Judd to Mr. Seward.

No. 98.]   UNITED STATES LEGATION,
                                            Berlin, May 2, 1865.

SIR: To-day, at one o'clock, a deputation, composed of Count Joseph Potulreki and Mr. St. Motty, both members of the Prussian Chamber of Deputies, presented to me an address, on the subject of the late terrible calamity to our nation, signed by the Polish members of the Prussian Chamber of Deputies, with a request to have the same laid before the government and people of the United States. I assured them of our full appreciation of this act of sympathy, and that I would not fail to immediately forward the address to my government.

I am, sir, your obedient servant,

N. B. JUDD.

Hon. WILLIAM H. SEWARD,
        Secretary of State, Washington, D. C.

Mr. Judd to Mr. Hunter.

No. 99]   UNITED STATES LEGATION,
                                            Berlin, May 4 1865.

SIR: Your official circular, dated April 17, is received. The intelligence of the assassination of President LINCOLN, and the attempt upon Mr. Seward, accompanied by the wounding of Mr. F. W. Seward, official notice of which is contained in your circular, reached Berlin on the 26th of April. I need not repeat again the grief and horror felt on receiving the tidings of the sad event.

The Americans in Berlin met at this legation, and resolved to hold appropriate divine services in memory of the lamented President. The original intention of meeting in the little chapel ordinarily used by us for religious worship had to be abandoned, on account of the almost universal desire of men of all classes here to afford them an opportunity of participating in the services, and mingling their grief with ours, in paying a last tribute to the great and good man departed. We therefore sought and readily obtained of the Berlin city authorities the use of the Dorothea church, one of the most spacious buildings of public worship here. It was arranged that the Reverend H. P. Tappan, D. D., of New York, now temporarily in Berlin, should conduct the services and deliver an address, and the German part of the exercises was intrusted to the very distinguished author and divine, Rev. Dr. Krummacher, chaplain to his Prussian Majesty at Potsdam, who kindly had consented to officiate on the occasion. We also obtained the services of the choir of the royal cathedral; the church was draped in black, and the American flag hung in mourning.

The services were among the most significant and solemn ever held in Berlin. The attendance was so large that many persons were unable to obtain admission, and remained standing outside in the churchyard. His Majesty the King was represented by Major General von Boyen, his aide-de-camp. The president of the minister of state, and minister of foreign affairs, Herr von Bismarck, was also present. So were the members of the diplomatic corps in full, a large number of the Prussian House of Deputies, and very many of the distinguished men of science, letters, and art. It was indeed a noble tribute to our martyr President and the cause in which he had died. I beg leave to enclose the order of exercises as printed for the occasion.

The addresses by Dr. Tappan and Dr. Krummacher were eloquent and feeling tributes to the public and private virtues of the deceased, and to the genius of our institutions in developing character, as illustrated in the life of Mr. LINCOLN. Throughout the whole of the exercises, the audience remained absorbed and profoundly touched by the simple solemnity and impressiveness of the scene, which will be long remembered by the people of Berlin.

There is no abatement as yet of the intense excitement and heartfelt sympathy in all classes of society, here and elsewhere, in Germany, over the sad event, and the possible and probable consequences thereof. All are moved, and seeking words and modes to show us their deep emotion and genuine sympathy.

The first feeling of many here and elsewhere, on learning of the assassination of President LINCOLN, was one of alarm and apprehension lest his death might be followed by anarchy and confusion, and our government be paralyzed. The quiet and undisturbed assumption of office by President Johnson, his speeches at his inauguration and on other occasions, have now removed all fear, and convinced all persons that the people and not dynasties rule in the United States; that our government and our institutions do not depend upon any man's

life, however great and good that man may be.   The American people stand
forth greater than ever in the eyes of Germany and Europe.

Whatever may have been done in the United States, Mr. LINCOLN is being
canonized in Europe   A like unanimity of eulogy by sovereigns, parliaments,
corporate bodies, by the people, and by all public journals, was never before
witnessed on this continent.   The most truthful and eloquent testimonials are
now given by some of those that belied him most while living.

I am, sir, your obedient servant,

N. B. JUDD.

Hon. WILLIAM HUNTER,
Acting Secretary of State, Washington.

[Translation.]

Address to the American people by the Berlin Workingmen's Club.

BERLIN, *May* 4, 1865.

Mr. MINISTER : With liveliest interest we have watched the giant struggle
for the rights of free labor which the United States of America have entered
upon, and have so .nobly maintained during four years.   With great joy we
beheld the star-spangled banner issuing triumphantly from this battle for freedom and civilization, for we fully understood the vast import and bearing of the
results thereby achieved.

In the midst of the rejoicings over these victories we are filled with horror
at the tidings of the cowardly assassination of President ABRAHAM LINCOLN.

Struck down by a murderous hand in the very fulfilment of his historical
mission, and when jubilant voices announced the triumph of freedom, it was not
vouchsafed him to enjoy the fruits of the victories which his kind and noble
heart prompted him, in the most conciliatory spirit, to employ only for the final
ending of the long war, and the restoration of a speedy peace.

ABRAHAM LINCOLN has finished his course and accomplished his work.
He has reached the highest step of the virtue of a citizen.   The son of a laboring man, and himself a laborer, he took up the fight for the rights of free labor
and carried it to a triumphant termination.

As a wise legislator, an energetic statesman, a loyal citizen, and a good man,
being a shining example for present generations and posterity, his memory will
be held sacred, not only by his fellow-citizens, but by all mankind, and the
greater the horror with which the intelligence of his murder is received, the
more brilliantly in immortal splendor will it cause the name and memory of
ABRAHAM LINCOLN to shine.

We fully share the sincere grief and deep abhorrence which this odious
crime against the President of the United States of America has inspired in the

minds of all right-thinking men. But in giving expression of our deep sympathy in the death of ABRAHAM LINCOLN, we feel compelled at the same time to give utterance of our hopes and wishes to the effect that the freedom which has thus been sealed with the blood of one of the noblest men will only the more fully prevail, and that the star-spangled banner may wave in triumph wherever it is unfurled, in battling for the cause of freedom and civilization.

We ask you, sir, to be pleased to bring this expression of our sympathies to the knowledge of the government of the United States.

"The Berlin Workingmen's Club:"

A. HORIG.	ROBT. NOUVEL.
L. HOFF.	ELEHMANN.
R. KREBS.	J. MÜLLER.

AND TEN OTHERS.

[Translation.]

Address of the Berlin Artisans' and Mechanic Union.

BERLIN, *May* 21, 1865.

Mr. PRESIDENT: The undersigned, a committee chosen in the meeting of the Berlin Altgesellen-Verein, held on the 9th instant, are charged to express to you, the representative of the great American republic, our profound horror and indignation at the assassination of the noble and faithful citizen, President ABRAHAM LINCOLN. Not merely the societies in Berlin, but the working-men in all Europe—we affirm it with pride—have ever frankly stood on the side of the Union in that giant struggle which the people of the United States—it is true, not without great sacrifices—have carried to a triumphant end; a struggle of labor truly free against slavery—of free labor such as we here, too, are striving for, and which in your country, in full possession of political rights, enjoys that respect which is due to it, as the source of all national wealth.

In renewing, therefore, the expressions of our sympathy for the cause of the Union, and our admiration for the noble and faithful citizen, President LINCOLN, permit us, Mr. President, to utter our conviction that you, a true son of the people, will be able to achieve the fullest recognition of the principles of human rights, so that your enemies, who are ours likewise, will hereafter be deprived of all their noxious influence and power.

By direction of the Altgesellen-Verein:

SCHLEY.	P. RANTY.
STENTY.	RIRMANN.
WELEY.	

Mr. ANDREW JOHNSON,
    President of the United States

[Translation.]

BERLIN, *May* 11, 1865.

To the President of the United States, Mr. Andrew Johnson :

Mr. PRESIDENT : In accordance with the resolution unanimously passed May 1, instant, in the Berlin section of the Allgemeiner Deutsche Arbeiter-Verein, we herewith express to you, as the representative of the great American commonwealth, our deep horror at the monstrous deed which robbed your country and the world of the good citizen and man, ABRAHAM LINCOLN, and assure you of our warmest sympathy with the cause whose martyr he has become.

Members of the working class, we need not affirm to you the sincerity of these our sympathies; for with pride we can point to the fact, that, while the aristocracy of the Old World took openly the part of the southern slaveholder, and while the middle class was divided in its opinions, the working-men in all countries of Europe have unanimously and firmly stood on the side of the Union. And how could it have been otherwise? as the gigantic battle which the people of the United States have fought so valiantly and gained so gloriously was the battle of *free labor* against slavery, of *truly* free labor—that is, in the full possession of its political rights, and therefore enjoys that respect which is due to the mother of all social wealth, and all political liberty, but which in Europe is unfortunately yet denied to labor, because here it has not yet conquered its political rights. The state of Franklin and LINCOLN, the state whose first citizen is now again a son of toil, has indeed vindicated the rights of labor; and the example it gives shall not be lost upon us.

Before concluding, we express once more our admiration for ABRAHAM LINCOLN, one of the purest and noblest among the pure and noble martyrs of liberty. He has done his duty. And happy the land which, after such a terrible war, after such an enormous crime, could, without the slightest disturbance of the State, make an Andrew Johnson the successor of an ABRAHAM LINCOLN.

In the name of the Berlin section of the Allgemeiner Deutsche Arbeiter-Verein :

> W. LIEBKNECHT.
> A. VOGT.
> C. SCHILLING.

PORTUGAL.

Mr. de Figaniere to Mr. Hunter.

[Translation.]

HIS MOST FAITHFUL MAJESTY'S LEGATION IN THE UNITED STATES,
Charlestown, Maryland, April 17, 1865.

SIR: Your note of the 15th instant, with the sad information of the awful events of the previous night, resulting in the unexpected death of President LINCOLN, was received by me this day with great regret.

Sincerely sympathizing with the government and people of the United States for the loss they have sustained, I trust that the honorable Secretary of State and his son, Mr. Frederick Seward, may recover from the injuries inflicted upon them.

I am also advised by your said note that, pursuant to the provision of the Constitution of the United States, Andrew Johnson, the Vice-President, has formally assumed the functions of President, and that you have by him been authorized to perform the duties of Secretary of State until otherwise ordered.

I take this occasion to offer to you, sir, the assurance of my great consideration.

DE FIGANIERE É MORAO.

Hon. WILLIAM HUNTER,
Acting Secretary of State of the United States, Washington.

[Translation.]

HOUSE OF PEERS.—SESSION OF MAY 5, 1865.

Mr. REBELLO DA SILVA. Mr. Speaker: I desire to bring forward some considerations on an affair which I deem of importance. My object is to present my reasons for the motion which I shall presently introduce.

The house is aware, by official documents published in the foreign papers, that a criminal event has plunged in grief and mourning a great nation on the other side of the Atlantic, the powerful republic of the United States.

The COUNT D'AVILA. I desire to speak on this incident on the part of the government.

Mr. R. DA SILVA. President ABRAHAM LINCOLN has been assassinated in the theatre, almost in the very arms of his wife!

The perpetration of this cruel act has caused profound pain in America and in every court of Europe. Every cabinet and every parliament have given vent to their deep feelings on such a painful event. It behooves all civilized societies, it becomes almost the duty of all constituted political bodies, to cause their manifestations to be accompanied by the sincere expression of horror and profound pain with which they deplore acts so grave and criminal. [Hear, hear.]

It very often happens, apparently through fatality or through the sublime disposition or unfathomable mysteries of Providence, which is the most Christian historic law, that in the life of nations, as in that of individuals, after attaining the highest position, after consummating the most eventful destiny, and even having reached the very highest steps in the scale of human greatness, when the road appears suddenly easy and smooth, when all clouds disappear from the horizon, and the brightest light enlivens every object around—it is then that an invisible hand raises itself up from darkness; that an occult and inexorable force arms itself in silence; and, brandishing the poniard of a Brutus, pointing the cannon of a Wellington, or presenting the poisoned cup of the Asiatic kings, dashes down from the heights the triumphant and laurelled victor, and casts him at the foot of Pompey's statue like Cæsar, at the feet of exhausted Fortune like Napoleon, at the feet of the Roman Colossus like Hannibal.

The mission of all great men, of all heroes, who are looked upon almost as demi-gods, while receiving as they do, from above, that short-lived omnipotence which revolutionizes society and transforms nations, passes away like the tempest's blast in its fiery car, and moments afterwards dashes itself against the eternal barriers of impossibility—those barriers which none can go beyond, and where all the pride of their ephemeral power is humbled and reduced to dust. God alone is immutable and great!

Death strikes the blow, or ruin attains them in the height of their power, as an evidence to all princes, conquerors, and nations, that their hour is but one and short, that their work becomes weak, as all human work, from the moment that the luminous column which guided them is extinguished, and darkness overtakes them on their way. The new roads which they have carved out, and whereby they expect to proceed undaunted and secure, have turned into abysses where they have fallen and perished, from the moment that the Most High numbered the days of their empire and their ambition. [Hear, hear.]

This has been witnessed as a terrible example, as an admirable lesson, in the catastrophes which have overtaken the most conspicuous men in history. And thus do we see this day the recent pages of the annals of the powerful republic of the United States spotted with the illustrious blood of one of its most remarkable citizens.

At the close of the first four years of a government, during which war became his motto, the President of the republic is suddenly struck down at the moment of his triumph, and his now inanimate and paralyzed hands let fall those reins of administration which the force and energy of his will, the co-operation of his countrymen, the prestige and sublimity of the grand idea which he personified and defended, have immortalized, with the accumulations of millions of arms on the battle-fields, and of voices in the popular elections. Re-elected, carried a second time on the popular bucklers to the supreme administration of affairs, at the moment when the ardor of a civil contest was subsiding, when the union of that immense dilacerated body seemed to foreshadow the healing up of the wounds whence had gushed forth for so many months, and in such torrents, the generous blood of the free, almost in the arms of victory, in the midst of that populace who loved him most, in the centre of his popular court, he suddenly meets with death, and the bullet of an obscure fanatic closes and seals up the golden volume of his destiny at the very hour when success promised a new life and was welcoming peace with joyful acclamations.

This is no king who disappears in the darkness of the tomb, burying with himself, like unto Henry IV, the realization of great hopes. He is the chief of a glorious people, leaving a successor in every citizen who shared his ideas, and who sympathized with his noble and well-founded aspirations. It is not a purple-covered throne which has been covered with crape—it is the heart of a great empire which has been cast into mourning. That cause of which he was the strenuous champion has not ceased to exist, but all weep at his loss, in horror at the crime and occasion, and for the expectations which his pure and generous intentions had inspired.

LINCOLN, a martyr to the prolific principle which he represented in power and in strife, now belongs to history and to posterity. Like unto the name of Washington, whose example and principles he followed, his own name shall be allied with the memorable era to which he belonged and which he appreciated.

As the champion of freedom in America, LINCOLN drew, without hesitation, the sword of the republic, and with the point thereof erased from the code of a free people that antisocial stigma, that blasphemy against human nature, the sad, shameful, infamous codicil of antiquated societies, the dark and repugnant abuse of slavery, which Jesus Christ was the first to condemn from the height of the cross when he proclaimed the equality of men before God, and which nineteen centuries of civilization, enlightened by the gospel, has proscribed and condemned as the opprobrium of these our present times. [Hear, hear.]

At the moment that he cast away the chains of an unfortunate race of men, and when he contemplated millions of future citizens in the millions of emancipated men—at the very moment that the echo of Grant's victorious cannon proclaimed the emancipation of the soul, of conscience, and of labor, when the lash was about to drop from the hand of the taskmaster, when the former hut of the slave was about to be converted into a home—at the moment that the stars of the Union, bright and resplendent with the gladdening light of liberty, waved triumphant over the fallen ramparts of Petersburg and Richmond—it was then that the grave opened its jaws, and the strong and the powerful falls to rise no more. In the midst of triumphs and acclamations, a spectre appeared unto him, and, like that of Cæsar in the ides of March, said, Thou hast lived!

Far be it from me to enter into the appreciation of the civil questions which have disturbed the brotherhood of the same family in America. I am neither their judge nor their censor. I bow down to a principle, that of liberty, wherever I see it respected and upheld; but at the same time I have learned to love and cherish another, not less sacred and glorious—the principle of independence. May the force of progress in our days bind again those who have been separated by differences of opinion, and may it reconcile the ideas which exist in the heart, the aspirations, and in the desire of all generous-minded men.

In this warfare, the proportions of which have exceeded everything that has ever been seen or heard of in Europe, the vanquished of to-day are worthy of the great race from which they descend. Grant and Lee are two giants whom history will in future respect in an inseparable manner. But the hour of peace was, perhaps, about to strike, and LINCOLN desired it as the reward of his pains, as the great result of so many sacrifices. After the exhibition of strength comes toleration. After the bloody fury of battles comes the fraternal embrace of citizens!

Such were his manifested intentions—these were the last and noble wishes which he had formed. And at this very instant, perhaps the only one in which a noble man is so powerful in doing good, and when the soul rises above whole legions as a pacificator, the hand of the assassin rises up in treachery and cuts off such mighty and noble purposes. [Hear, hear.]

Were not the American nation a people grown old in the painful strifes and experience of government, who is there that could foresee the fatal consequences of this sudden blow? Who knows but that, in such a case, the fiery torch of civil war, in all its horrible pomp and terror, would spread itself to the furthermost States of the federation? But, happily, no such calamity is to be apprehended. At the time that the press and public opinion have, with justice and severity, condemned this event, and given expression to their horror at the fatal crime—sentiments and feelings which are common to the whole of Europe—they pay homage to the ideas of peace and conciliation just as if the great man who first invoked them had not disappeared from the great scene of the world. And I purposely repeat the expression, *great man*, because, in truth, great is that man who, confiding alone in his own merits, rises from profound obscurity to the greatest heights, like Napoleon, like Washington, like LINCOLN; who elevate themselves to the heights of power and of greatness, not in virtue of the chances of birth or of a noble descent, but by the prestige of his own actions, by that nobility which begins and ends in themselves, and which is solely the work of their own hands. [Cheers. Hear, hear.]

The man who makes himself great and famous by his own acts and by his own genius is more to be envied than he who was born among inherited escutcheons of nobility. LINCOLN belongs to that privileged race—to that aristocracy. In infancy his energetic soul was tempered in poverty. In youth labor inspired him with the love of liberty and respect for the rights of men. Up to the age of twenty-two educated in adversity, with his hands hardened by honorable labor; while resting from the fatigues of daily toil, drinking in from the inspired pages of the Bible the lessons of the gospel; and in the ephemeral leaves of the public journals, which the morning brings forth and the evening disperses, the first rudiments of that instruction which is subsequently ripened by solitary meditation. Light gradually and gently illuminated that soul. The wings with which it took its flight then expanded and strengthened; the chrysalis felt one bright day the rays of the sun which called it into life; it broke through its bonds, and rose up from its humble condition to those luminous spheres where a higher destiny was awaiting its approach. The farmer, the laborer, the shepherd, like Cincinnatus, abandoned his plough half-buried in the earth, and, as a legislator in his native State, and subsequently in the national Congress, he prepared in the public tribunal to become one day the popular chief of many millions of people—the defender of the holy principle which Wilberforce inaugurated. What strifes, what agitated scenes, what a series of herculean works and incalculable sacrifices are involved and represented by their glorious results in these four years of warfare and government.

Armies in the field, such as ancient history speaks not of! Immense battles, during which the sun rises and sets two and three times before victory declares itself on either side! Heavy marches, where thousands of victims, whole legions covered with their dead every foot of conquered ground! Invasions, the daring and dangers whereof far surpass the records of Attila and the Huns! What awful obsequies for the scourge of slavery! What a terrible and salutary lesson has this people, still rich and vigorous in youth, given to the timid scruples of ancient Europe, now the battle-field of principles likewise sacred! These were the beacons, the landmarks, which guided his grand career. If the sword was the instrument in his hands, yet liberty, inspiration, and the courage which were the outgrowth of his principles were equally effective. Trampling down the thorns on his path, guiding his steps amidst the tears and the blood of so many holocausts, he still lived to see the promised land! He was not permitted to plant on that soil the auspicious olive-branch of peace and concord. When he was about to reunite the loosened bond of the Union; when he was about to infuse into the body of his country the vivifying spirit of free institutions, after collecting and reuniting its dispersed and bloody members; when the standard of the republic, its funeral dirges ended, its agonies of pride and defeat silenced and subsided, was about to rise again and to spread its glorious folds over a reconciled people, purified and cleansed from the stain of slavery—the great athlete stepped in the ring and fell, thus proving that, after all, he was but mortal! [Hear, hear, hear. Applause.]

I think this brief and hurried sketch is quite sufficient for the occasion. The Chamber being by its nature, by duty and by organization, not only the conservator but the faithful warden of traditions and principle, will not hesitate to take part in the demonstration which the elective Chamber has already adopted, thus following the example of all the enlightened parliaments of Europe. Silence in the presence of such criminal attempts can only be maintained by such senates as are dumb and void of elevated sentiments and aspirations. [Hear, hear.]

By voting the present motion the Chamber of Peers takes a part in the feelings of pain now experienced by all civilized nations. The crime which has closed the career of LINCOLN—a martyr to the noble principles of which this epoch has reason to be proud—is almost, is essentially a regicide, and a monarchical country cannot but abhor and condemn it. The descendants of those men who were the first in the sixteenth century to reveal to Europe the new road which, across stormy and unknown seas, opened the gates of the eastern world, must not be the last to bow down before the grave of a great citizen and a great magistrate, who himself piloted his people through terrible tempests and succeeded in leading them in triumph over the fallen ramparts of slavery's stronghold. Let each people and each era have its task and its share of glory. Let each illustrious citizen have his crown of laurel or his civic crown. [Hear, hear. Applause.]

The Minister of Foreign Affairs, COUNT D'AVILA. As a peer of the realm he takes part in this noble manifestation; as minister of the Crown he had already done as much in his own name at first, when mere rumors are circulated that the crime had been committed, and again after having received the order of his Majesty, as soon as no doubt unfortunately existed on the subject, in order to show what were the sentiments of the Portugese government.

Mr. REBELLO DA SILVA. Mr. Speaker: I am rejoiced to hear the words of the minister of finance and of foreign affairs. They give evidence that the government has acted in this affair with that propriety and promptitude which its duty indicated, and which are inspired by noble feelings. I shall now lay on the table my motion of order, as follows:

"The Chamber of Peers deplores, with the most sincere feelings of pain, the criminal act which has just thrown into mourning the sons of a great nation, by the death of the President of the United States of America, Mr. LINCOLN, who died a martyr to his duty.

"L. A. REBELLO DA SILVA."

The SPEAKER. The Chamber has heard the reading of this motion; I do not consider it necessary to have it again read from the table, as it would not have a better effect than when read by its author. [Hear, hear.]

Mr. REBELLO DA SILVA. The Count d'Avila has likewise signed the motion.

The SPEAKER. All the worthy peers who approve of the motion will be pleased to indicate as much.

It was unanimously approved.

The COUNT D'AVILA. I request that it be recorded in the minutes that the voting was unanimous. [Hear, hear.]

[Translation.]

HOUSE OF DEPUTIES.—SESSION OF MAY 3, 1865.

The PRESIDENT. The proposal just placed on the table by the deputy, Mr. Medeiros, will now be read. It is as follows:

"*Proposal.*—I move that the House do insert in its minutes a significant expression of the profound emotion with which it received the news of the barbarous assassination committed on the person of Mr. LINCOLN, the President of the United States of America, and that the worthy representative of that republic at this court be respectfully informed of the deliberation of the House on this subject.

"The Deputy HENRIQUE FERREIRA DE PAULA MEDEIROS.

"HOUSE OF SESSIONS, *May* 3, 1865."

The Minister of Public Works, Mr. CARLOS BENTO. I do not know whether the motion is admitted, but it appears to me that, from its very nature, it is of an urgent and unexceptional character. On my part I do not hesitate, in the name of the government, in sharing such a noble and feeling manifestation as the one contained in the proposal.

We are all unanimous in common with the civilized nations of Europe in condemning an act which has excited the indignation of the whole people without respect to party distinctions. All and every individual reprobates the fatal deed which has taken place in the United States.

I willingly take part in the expression of the vote contained in the proposal. I feel convinced that the Portuguese Parliament will not hesitate one moment in adopting the manifestation of such becoming sentiments. [Hear, hear.]

Mr. SANT'ANNA E VASCONCELLOS. I thank the illustrious deputy, the author of the motion, for having brought it forward, and I do so from my whole heart.

Mr. PAULA MEDEIROS. I thank the noble deputy for his expressions.

Mr. SANT'ANNA E VASCONCELLOS. If the disastrous war which has existed in America during the last three or four years has a justification, it is to be found in the one grand and noble motive which has dominated throughout, the abolition of slavery. The man who has just fallen a victim to the assassination which we all deplore maintained that noble and sublime idea. In view of the fact, which is in itself so much to be deplored, and in presence of the great and persistent idea of that great citizen, we cannot refrain from being unanimous in voting the motion.

The MINISTER OF PUBLIC WORKS. I spoke in the name of the government, and I can assure the house that the government has already tendered those manifestations which its duty and its feelings clearly indicated. I congratulate myself on the fact that the Parliament was allowed the opportunity, by a spontaneous initiative, of manifesting its sentiments.

On putting the motion to the vote, it was carried unanimously.

Count d' Avila to Mr. Harvey.

[Translation.]

DEPARTMENT OF STATE FOR FOREIGN AFFAIRS,
May 6, 1865.

I have the honor of handing you copies enclosed of a communication addressed to me by the secretary of the Chamber of Deputies, under yesterday's date, and of the motion referred to in said communication, which was presented in the session of the 3d instant, and voted unanimously, manifesting the sentiments of said Chamber in regard to the horrible deed committed on the person of Mr. ABRAHAM LINCOLN, late President of the United States of America.

While requesting you to bring these documents before your government, it is my duty to inform you that his Majesty's government, immediately that it was informed of an event which has saddened a nation whose destinies had been confided to so illustrious a magistrate, issued the needful instructions to his Majesty's minister at the United States, with a view to express to the American government the profound regret with which his Majesty the King and his government received the news of that event.

I avail of this opportunity to reiterate the assurances of my most distinguished consideration.

CONDÉ D'AVILA.

Count d' Avila to Mr. Harvey

[Translation.]

DEPARTMENT OF STATE FOR FOREIGN AFFAIRS,
May 12, 1865.

In addition to my note, dated 6th instant, I have the honor to hand you enclosed a copy of the communication which, under date of 9th instant, was sent to me by the vice-president of the Chamber of the Peers of the realm, as well as of the document, a copy of which accompanied it, containing the motion made in the session of the 5th instant, by the worthy Peer Luis Augusto Rebello da Silva—a motion in which I took part as a peer of the realm, and which was carried unanimously, to the effect of having it recorded .in the minutes— how deep was the pain experienced at the news of the horrible crime perpetrated on the person of Mr. LINCOLN, President of the United States. ·

In the aforesaid document you will find that part of the minutes which refers to the subject; and I have to request that you will be pleased to make known to your government the manifestations of said Chamber on an event which all so deeply deplore.

I avail of this opportunity to renew the assurances of my most distinguished consideration.

COUNT D'AVILA.

JAMES E. HARVEY, Esq., *&c., &c., &c.*

[Translation.]

CHAMBER OF WORTHY PEERS OF THE REALM.

MOST EXCELLENT SIR: The Chamber of Peers of the realm having unanimously resolved, in its session of the 5th instant, and on motion of the worthy Peer Luis Augusto Rebello da Silva, in which the worthy Peer Count d'Avila took part, to record in its minutes the expression of great pain which the Chamber felt at the news of the horrible crime committed in the United States of America on the person of Mr. LINCOLN, their illustrious President, I have now the honor of handing your excellency the enclosed copy, containing the aforesaid motion, and that part of the minutes which relates to the subject, in order that your excellency may, through such channel as may be deemed most appropriate, cause the same to be made known to the government of the United States.

My God preserve your excellency!

COUNT DE CASTRO, *Vice-President.*

PALACE OF THE CORTES, *May* 9, 1865.

His Excellency the COUNT D'AVILA,
Minister and Secretary of State for Foreign Affairs

DEPARTMENT OF STATE FOR FOREIGN AFFAIRS,
May 12, 1865.

True copy:

EMILIO ACHILLES MONTEVERDE.

Count d'Avila to Mr. Harvey.

[Translation.]

DEPARTMENT OF STATE FOR FOREIGN AFFAIRS,
May 16, 1865.

I have the honor of handing you, for your information, the enclosed copy of a despatch which the secretary of the Chamber of Deputies, now dissolved, addressed to me under date of the 13th instant, and likewise of the motion which accompanied the same, made by one of its members, and unanimously voted, on the occasion of communicating to the said Chamber the note which you addressed to the house on the 10th instant.

I avail of this opportunity to renew the assurances of my most distinguished consideration.

COUNT D'AVILA.

JAMES E. HARVEY, Esq., *&c., &c., &c.*

[Translation.]

BUREAU OF THE SECRETARY OF THE CHAMBER OF DEPUTIES,
Palace of the Cortes, May 13, 1865.

MOST EXCELLENT SIR: I have the honor of transmitting to your excellency, for your information, the enclosed copy of the motion, presented in this Chamber by one of its members, and voted unanimously, on the occasion of communicating to the house the note from the legation of the United States of America at this court, in reply to the manifestation of feeling and regret addressed to said legation on the atrocious assassination of the President of that republic.

May God preserve your excellency.

JOAQUIN XAVIER PINTO DA SILVA,
Deputy and Secretary.

His Excellency the MINISTER AND SECRETARY
OF STATE FOR FOREIGN AFFAIRS.

DEPARTMENT OF STATE FOR FOREIGN AFFAIRS,
May 16, 1865.

True copy:

EMILIO ACHILLES MONTEVERDE.

I move that it be recorded in the minutes that the Chamber has heard, with every demonstration of true respect and profound sympathy, the note which has just been read at the table and addressed to the house by the minister resident of the United States of America at this court.

I further move that the government be informed of this deliberation, in order to communicate the same to the distinguished minister.

JACINTHO AUGUSTO DE SANT'ANNA E VASCONCELLOS.

BUREAU OF THE SECRETARY OF THE CHAMBER OF DEPUTIES,
May 13, 1865.

Correct copy:

POSSIDONIO A. P. PICALUGA.

DEPARTMENT OF STATE FOR FOREIGN AFFAIRS,
May 16, 1865.

True copy:

EMILIO ACHILLES MONTEVERDE.

[Translation.]

DEPARTMENT OF STATE FOR FOREIGN AFFAIRS,
May 1, 1865.

The government of his Majesty has been informed of the horrible crime of which, unhappily, President LINCOLN and his Secretary of State, Mr. Seward, have been victims.

So sad an event, clothing in mourning a nation over whose destinies that distinguished magistrate presided, could not but be profoundly felt by the Portuguese nation, connected as it ever has been in the closest ties of friendship and good understanding with the United States.

The part which his Majesty's government takes in the grief which, with reason, oppresses the American nation, and the indignation which that crime has given cause for, have led me to direct you, by order of his Majesty the King, to make known, without loss of time and in the most express terms, to the government of the United States the feelings of true sorrow with which our sovereign lord and his government are penetrated by so fatal an occurrence.

God save your excellency!

CONDÉ D'AVILA.

Señor JOAQUIN CESAR DE FIGANIERE E MORAO.

[Translation.]

DEPARTMENT OF STATE FOR FOREIGN AFFAIRS,
May 8, 1865.

In addition to my despatch of the 1st instant, I send you the enclosed copies, as well of the despatch which the secretary of the Chamber of Deputies sent to me under date of the 5th, as of the resolution to which said despatch refers, presented at the sittings on the 3d, unanimously adopted, tending to manifest the regret of said Chamber at the horrible crime committed on the person of the President of the United States, Mr. ABRAHAM LINCOLN. Of these documents you will please to give knowledge to that government, stating that they were communicated to Mr. Harvey on the 6th of this month.

Their Majesties and highnesses are going on happily without change in their important health.

God, &c.!

CONDÉ D'AVILA.

Señor JOAQUIN CESAR DE FIGANIERE E MORAO.

[Translation.]

SECRETARIAT OF THE CHAMBER OF DEPUTIES,
Palace of the Cortes, May 5, 1865.

MOST EXCELLENT SIR: There having been represented by the Señor Deputy Henrique Ferreira de Paula Medeiros, at the session of this Chamber on the 3d instant, a resolution tending to give a manifestation of feeling in regard to the wicked assassination of the worthy President of the United States of America, I have the honor to send you a copy of the said resolution, to the end that you may cause it to reach the knowledge of the representative of that government at this court, with the declaration, that it may have its full effect, that it was unanimously approved by the Chamber.

God save your excellency!

JOAQUIN XAVIER PINTO DA SILVA,
Deputy Secretary.

His Excellency the MINISTER AND SECRETARY
OF STATE FOR FOREIGN AFFAIRS.

Mr. Harvey to Mr. Seward.

No. 336.]   LEGATION OF THE UNITED STATES,
Lisbon, April 28, 1865.

SIR : Mr. Adams telegraphed me last night from London the terrible news of the assassination of President LINCOLN, and of an atrocious attempt upon the life of Mr. Seward on the same evening, the result of which is not yet known here, by the hand of another assassin. These events have excited the profoundest emotion in all the circles of Lisbon, and have called out general and particular expressions of sympathy and respect from the government, the diplomatic body and the community.

I do not trust myself to speak of this great crime at a moment of mingled sorrow and prostration ; but I may be allowed to say, that after the grief natural to such an occasion, the sense of humiliation at the thought that an atrocity so awful could by possibility be perpetrated in a country like ours is that which most masters and overwhelms me.

Christian charity may, with the blessing of God, teach us to bow down before this stern trial, but the stain which it inflicts cannot soon be wiped out from a name heretofore untarnished by any such act of infamy.

If there was anything wanting to complete the fame of Mr. LINCOLN, it may be found in the crown of martyrdom with which an eventful career, in a most eventful epoch, has been closed, to the regret of a whole people, who shared his convictions, honored his virtues, and lament his "taking off."

I have the honor to be, sir, your obedient servant,

JAMES E. HARVEY.

Hon. WILLIAM H. SEWARD;
Secretary of State

Mr. Harvey to Mr. Seward.

No. 338.]   LEGATION OF THE UNITED STATES
Lisbon, May 11, 1865.

SIR : The papers will bring to your view the proceedings of the Cortes in regard to the recent melancholy event which has so much shocked the civilized world.

The note of the minister of foreign affairs only communicates the action of the Chamber of Deputies, because the motion in that body specially required it to be done, while that in the Peers did not do so. I have thought it best, however, to send a translated copy of the full proceedings in both branches of the Cortes, in order that their spirit may be the better appreciated. The tardy publication of the official journal does not permit at this time (on the eve of the departure of the mails) such a translation as I desired to furnish, but the general tone of the speeches is fairly reported. That of Mr. Rebello da Silva, in the Peers, was remarkably eloquent and touching, and has received very imperfect justice at the hands of the translator. In the pressure of the moment it has been found impracticable to translate one of the addresses, which is communicated in the original.

It seemed to me only becoming to make an acknowledgment of the note of the Chamber of Deputies.

Every manifestation of respect to the memory of the late President LIN-COLN which could be expected or desired has been made by this government and people, both in an official and in a private manner. His Majesty the King, immediately upon being informed of the sad event, sent me the kindest words of sympathy and regret. Every member of the government called in person to express similar sentiments, and when our ships of war, the Niagara and Kearsarge, exhibited the customary signs of mourning, on Sunday, Monday, and Tuesday last, the Portuguese national ships not only united in a similar observance, but Castle Belem also responded to all the salutes, by order of the authorities, and without any notice or request on our part.

While upon this subject I may be permitted to remark, as quite worthy of notice, that the popular legislative bodies of the different states of Europe have taken the initiative in nearly all the expressions of public sympathy. Such a tribute was not only fitting in itself towards our lamented President, but the fact is significant of a mighty change and progress in ideas and usages, as it is of a coming time, in the near future, when the peoples of Europe will claim the right to assert those great principles of political and personal liberty which ABRAHAM LINCOLN illustrated so well, and for which he may be said to have even made a sacrifice of his life.

I have the honor to be, sir, your obedient servant,

JAMES E. HARVEY.

Hon. WILLIAM H. SEWARD,
    Secretary of State.

[Translation from the Commercio da Lisboa.]

An address was delivered to-day to the minister of the United States at this court, expressing the deep feelings of pain and regret with which the news of the death of citizen ABRAHAM LINCOLN, late President of the United States, was received at Lisbon.

This address, which received its inspiration from Mr. José de Seabra Pessoa, was proposed at the association (centro) by the member Costa Pereira, and signed by the members J. Pessoa, Costa Pereira, E. Coetho, Brito Aranha, Vieira da Silva, and Gouveia.

At 11.30 the minister received the deputation, composed of Messieurs Vieira da Silva, Gonzalves, Costa Pereira, and José Seabra Pessoa. His excellency, in returning thanks for this spontaneous manifestation, addressed the committee in most agreeable and very flattering terms.

[Translation from the Jornal da Lisboa.]

A deputation from the "Association for Promoting the Improvement of the Laboring Classes" delivered to-day, about 11 o'clock, into the hands of the minister of the United States, an address of condolence voted at a meeting of the members, on the death of Mr. ABRAHAM LINCOLN, late President of that republic.

The minister received the deputation with every mark of consideration, declaring that he would immediately transmit the autograph message to his government; and he thanked the association for this proof of good feeling and fraternity between the people of the two nations.

[Translation.]

SIR: All the civilized countries, all the liberal men, are at present under the most affecting impression. The crime that struck with horror an illustrious people, worthy of universal consideration, was condemned by all those for whom the word liberty is the strongest chain than can unite them. From all quarters eloquent words were heard condemning the monstrous attempt by which the United States of America were deprived of the most useful citizen that in modern times has been elevated by that country to the high dignity of President of the United States. To these eloquent words of empires and nations, of people and states, are joined the humble homage of the Centro Promotor dos Methoramentos das Classes Laboriosas de Lisboa, that under the deepest grief shows his feelings when acquainted that LINCOLN, the emancipator of the slaves, fell a victim to the stroke of a cowardly assassin.

The Centro Promotor could not do otherwise than to partake the general feelings, for his ideas were offended with the crime by which America was deprived of such an illustrious man, mankind of a devotional friend, and the noble and magnanimous enterprise of the emancipation of the slaves of a strong and generous arm. The endeavor in which LINCOLN was engaged as a representative of his people's ideas, which he sustained for so long a time with the most heroic deeds, meant the extinction of the most reluctant stain with which the banners of some states are yet overshadowed; it means the abolishment of slavery, the emancipation of the black race, the transformation of the slave labor into free labor. To this sacred idea the Centro should render his most respectful homage, because in peaceful struggles he incessantly works to destroy the few vestiges of slavery that may yet press upon the laborious classes. The Centro, resolute defender of those who labor, does not see in the black race but men who ought to be protected by free labor, and elevated to that rank which cannot be contested before God by any race. ABRAHAM LINCOLN was the representative of these ideas. Providence designated him as a brilliant light for guiding the noble American people to the conquest of this victory of civilization. It was he that as an instrument of divine justice made the utmost efforts to extinguish upon earth the last traces which divide men from men, and which do not permit that its fruits may be only the share of work, and not of a privileged race. How could the Centro forget this unlucky event that covered with mourning a whole people, with whom the world condole in such painful suffering? The conquest was made. The slave was free. It was not without blood that this holocaust was consummated. But never liberty nor social rights were acquired without a great and immense martyrdom. The Roman slave deserved the most precious blood that has been spread upon earth. This is the history of all the conquests of liberty. It approached the time when, under the protection of peace, should be proved the value that has for the propriety and advancement of nations the liberty of labor upon the work of the slave. LINCOLN could not enjoy the result of his efforts, and show to his country where his enterprising character could arrive. Those who suffered with America this irreparable loss must have resignation, and let it be a lenitive to our grief; the well-founded hope that LINCOLN's work does not stop, and that among that free people shall appear as many statesmen as are required for this noble cause to complete its triumph.

These are, sir, the vows of the Centro; this is the manifestation of his feelings, by the fatal death of ABRAHAM LINCOLN, the President of the United States, the devoted friend to his people, the faithful follower of the honorable and liberal traditions of the country where Washington and Franklin lived.

Centro Promotor dos Methoramentos das Classes Laboriosas Office, June 11, 1865

The President,
FRANCISCO VIERRA DA SILVA.

The Secretaries,
MIGUEL JUSTINIANO CORREA É SILVA.
ALFREDO AUGUSTO CORREA.

Governor Amarol to Mr. Jones.

[Translation.]

No. 72.] EXPEDIENT OF FOREIGN AFFAIRS,
Macao, June 23, 1865.

SIR: I have the honor to acknowledge the receipt of your official letters, with date of yesterday, communicating to me, in one, your receipt of official confirmation from your government of the death of his Excellency ABRAHAM LINCOLN, President of the United States, and, in the other, notifying me that the sloop-of-war of your nation anchored in this port desires to make the usual funeral demonstrations for such a sad event to-morrow, the 24th, current.

At the first intelligence of this disgraceful event I expressed immediately to you the profound grief of which I was possessed. Repeating now this manifestation, I am sure that you will receive the same as a sincere expression of the good and cordial friendship existing between the peoples of the United States and Portugal, and no less as witness of my personal and lively sympathy toward your noble nation.

That was a doubly deplorable attempt which deprived a great country of its worthy chief just at the time when he had achieved the end of a civil war which had for so long a period ravaged it.

This fatal occurrence will serve, however, to render still more grateful and cherished the memory of his Excellency ABRAHAM LINCOLN to his countrymen for the eminent services which he bestowed, even to the sacrifice of his own life.

Furthermore, expressing my sorrow that his excellency the Secretary of State, Mr. Seward, and his son, Frederick Seward, should have been made victims of this attempt, I congratulate with you over the comforting intelligence that they are thought to be beyond peril of life.

It remains for me to say to you that to-morrow the forts of the city and the lorcha of war Amazona will have their ensigns at half-mast, and the Guia fort will accompany this demonstration of grief with discharges of cannon, a gun every half-hour.

God preserve you.

J. M. COELHO DO AMAROL,
Governor of Macao.

W. E. JONES, Esq.,
Consul dos Estados Unidos em Macao.

PERU.

[Translation.]

MINISTRY OF FOREIGN RELATIONS,
Lima, May 19, 1865.

The undersigned, minister of foreign relations of Peru, has been impressed with the most profound grief by the note of his excellency the envoy extraordinary and minister plenipotentiary of the United States of North America, concerning the painful death of the President of that republic, caused by a pistol-shot discharged upon him by an assassin.

The deed in itself and by the circumstances which surrounded it will be branded in the history of these times with the anathema of a universal reprobation.

Assuring his excellency, Mr. Robinson, that the government of Peru fully sympathizes with the afflicting sorrow which his excellency expresses for so unhappy an event, I have the honor to reiterate to him the professions of his very high consideration.

PEDRO JOSÉ CALDERON.
The ENVOY EXTRAORDINARY AND MINISTER PLENIPOTENTIARY
of the United States of North America.

[Translation.]

DEPARTMENT OF FOREIGN RELATIONS IN PERU.

Juan Antonio Pezet, constitutional President of the republic of Peru, to his Excellency the President of the United States of North America.

SIR: I comply with a necessity of my heart and with the most sacred duty in testifying to your Excellency the lively and intense grief which I experienced through the unhappy event which, on the 14th day of April last, put an end to the existence of his Excellency the President of your republic, ABRAHAM LINCOLN.

The very high qualities which adorned the illustrious dead, and among those which were surpassing, his judgment as a mandatory, his valor displayed during the heroic strife sustained in your country for the space of four years, and his magnanimity towards the offspring of that great people, had won for him throughout the world, and particularly in this republic, the purest sympathy and admiration; and the deplorable circumstances of his death have produced in a palpable manner among all my fellow-citizens a sentiment of profound grief, which will with difficulty be obliterated. In the midst of my sorrow I am consoled by the well-grounded hope which I cherish that you, inspired by the most ardent zeal and most intense love of your country, will reorganize very shortly, for whose preservation, progress, and prosperity I form the most cordial and sincere wishes.

Given at government house, Lima, on the 28th day of the month of May, in the year of our Lord 1865.

JUAN ANTONIO PEZET

PEDRO JOSÉ CALDERON,

[Translation.]

NEW YORK, September 25, 1865.

SIR: A delay as noticeable as inexplicable, which has happened to one of the mails despatched from Peru for this republic, has been the cause that only on the 23d of this month a despatch has reached me from my government, in which it orders me to transmit to his Excellency the President of the United States, through your excellency as the respected organ, the cabinet letter which the President of Peru addresses to him, expressing the sentiments which inspired the Peruvian people and government on the unhappy death of the eminent citizen, ABRAHAM LINCOLN.

I have the honor to send with this note, in original, an authentic copy of the said cabinet letter, and to ask your excellency to cause it to reach its high destination. I comply with an ardent wish of my heart in expressing to you once more the bitter and deep sorrow with which I have deplored the crime of which the Chief Magistrate of this republic was the victim, and the veneration in which he will live in my memory, as well as in that of almost all my countrymen, the memory of the illustrious martyr to freedom, civilization, and humanity.

I have the satisfaction to present myself to you with all respect.

JOSÉ ANTONIO G. GARCIA.

The SECRETARY OF STATE, Washington.

Manifestation of the citizens of the United States of North America in Arequipa, Peru.

AREQUIPA, June 3, 1865.

We, in accordance with the sincere and profound sympathy which actuates our patriotic hearts, have met together on this occasion to express condolence for the sad calamity which has befallen our country in the death of the much honored and beloved late President, ABRAHAM LINCOLN.

Therefore we, with great sorrow for the irreparable loss with which the

United States have so recently been afflicted, by the fiendish and horrible assassination of the late President, ABRAHAM LINCOLN——

Resolved, That in this awful calamity our country not only feels the vacancy of her first magistrate, but the loss of the most illustrious and distinguished of men in the cause of the Union and that of humanity.

Resolved, That we deeply sympathize with the family of the lamented late President in their affliction and bereavement.

Resolved, That we deeply sympathize with the sufferings of our eminent Secretary of State, the Hon. William H. Seward, and of his sons, caused by the hand of a desperate and inhuman assassin; and may Divine Providence preserve their lives to their families and their country.

Resolved, That copies of this expression of our heartfelt sympathies be forwarded to the families of the late President and the honorable Secretary of State; and that the same be published in the papers of Panama, New York, and Washington.

> EDMUND MOLLER.
> GEORGE CAREY.
> S. K. G. NELLIS.
> S. P. ALZAMORA.

Mr. Robinson to Mr. Seward.

No. 305.]   LEGATION OF THE UNITED STATES,
Lima, May 25, 1865

SIR: The steamer of the 18th instant brought to us the astounding intelligence of the assassination of President LINCOLN, so much honored and beloved by all the American people, and respected and esteemed wherever justice, humanity, and civilization have their advocates and defenders.

The announcement of this horrid tragedy was made by the telegraph from Callao immediately upon the arrival of the steamer of the English mail line, which entered the port with the American flag at the main at half-mast. The intelligence spread with electric rapidity, but its savage cruelty and horrid barbarism staggered belief, until the arrival of passengers in Lima with copies of the United States newspapers containing the particulars of the awful tragedy convinced us of its truth.

The feeling of indignation which the bloody and cowardly act excited was unanimous, pervading all classes, as was also the regret, that in this, the hour of their triumph over the wicked and atrocious rebellion, the people of the United States should lose their honored and revered chief, and civilization, justice, and religion a true sincere, and devoted friend.

Thus has passed away, by the sullen and vindictive shot of the assassin. a statesman whose honest purposes and sincere devotion to his constitutional duties had triumphed over the dark and bloody conspiracies of treason, and had secured the re-establishment of law, order, and security.   A martyr to the cause of humanity, he still, though dead, speaks to the hearts and affections of the American people in language more eloquent than words.

I received no official information of this deplorable event, but on the 19th instant I communicated to the minister of foreign relations the melancholy . intelligence in an official note.   On the same day I received a response from his excellency, expressing detestation of the crime, and the warmest sympathies of the Peruvian government with the American people for the loss they have sustained by this afflictive event.

On Saturday, the 20th, a committee of the Chilian citizens resident in this city waited upon me with a letter of condolence at this mournful occurrence and sympathy for the loss which the government of the United States and the cause of freedom had sustained.   The letter was numerously signed, and contained earnest and honest expressions of grief.

I expressed to the committee my gratitude for the noble and generous sentiments of fraternal feeling contained in their note.

On the 23d I received from the president of the municipality of this city, General Antonio G. de la Fuente, a letter expressing the utter detestation of the members of that honorable corporation at the crime, and their profound grief for the loss sustained by the United States and the cause of freedom throughout the world.

In fact, all classes of individuals hastened to express to me their sympathies for our loss, and their utter abhorrence of the crime and the assassin.   In Lima all the flags on the government houses. foreign legations, and consulates, were displayed at half-mast for three days following the arrival of the news, and no token or manifestation of mourning was lacking to show that these expressions of grief were sincere, not only for us as a people, but for the cause, the most decided champion of which had become a martyr to his devotion to duty.

At Callao were the same manifestations of grief and sympathy.   Immediately that the news became known in that city, although the steamer arrived late in the afternoon, the flags upon the government houses, the Peruvian and foreign ships of war, English and Spanish, were dropped at half-mast, and on the next day at noon the usual funeral salutes were fired from the United States steamer St. Mary's, accompanied by the sad responses from the Peruvian, English, and Spanish ships of war then in port, and from the fort of the castle on shore.

I cannot conclude this despatch without tendering my own sympathy and that of the citizens of the United States resident here and in Callao, to the honorable Secretary of State, and expressing their horror at the crime attempted upon him and his son, and the earnest hope for a speedy recovery from their wounds.

The assassination of the President, and the attempted one of the head of the Department of State, exhibit a conspiracy at which civilization stands aghast, and which for the results it intended, as well as for its atrocity, cruelty, barbarism, and infamy, stands unapproached and unapproachable in the annals of history.

I am, sir, your obedient servant,

CHRISTOPHER ROBINSON.

Hon. WILLIAM H. SEWARD, &c., &c., &c.

Mr. Robinson to Mr. Seward.

No. 306.]   LEGATION OF THE UNITED STATES,
Lima, May 26, 1865.

SIR: Believing that the American citizens resident in this capital and vicinity wished to have an opportunity to testify their sorrow for the great calamity that has fallen upon our nation in the lamentable death of President LINCOLN, and their horror and detestation of the crime of which he was the victim, I invited them to assemble at this legation on the 22d instant for that purpose.

On the day designated a large number of them assembled and passed the resolutions. A profound sadness and grief pervaded all present. This solemnity of feeling made it manifest that the nation had suffered a terrible misfortune in his death, while the mode in which it was perpetrated produced sad suspicions and gloomy forebodings that others might become victims to this expiring effort of treason; but none expressed a doubt in the ultimate triumph of our cause.

I am, sir, your obedient servant,

CHRISTOPHER ROBINSON.

Hon. WILLIAM H. SEWARD,
  Secretary of State, &c., &c., &c.

Mr. Robinson to Mr. Hunter.

No. 311.]   LEGATION OF THE UNITED STATES,
Lima, June 11, 1865.

SIR: Your despatch No. 159, communicating the sad intelligence of the assassination of President LINCOLN, at Ford's theatre, on the evening of the 14th of April last, and of the horrible attempt that was made about the same time to assassinate the Secretary of State in his own house, when an invalid in bed, suffering from injuries he had previously received from the dangerous accident which lately happened to him, and of the assault on Mr. F. W. Seward, was received by the steamer of the 2d instant.

The same intelligence was received, communicated in the columns of the United States papers and private letters by the mail of the 18th of May. Though I received no official intelligence by that mail, I communicated the notice of the President's death to the minister of foreign relations, as related in my despatch No. 305, of the date of the 28th of May. The same despatch gives also a narrative of the proceedings at Lima upon this melancholy event.

I can only add that language has no words sufficiently significant to express the abhorrence and detestation entertained by American citizens here, and all other persons, of the crime and its perpetrator; and their regret that he whose policy, integrity of purpose, and unwearied devotion to duty had been so successful in suppressing this gigantic rebellion should not have lived to witness the final and conclusive triumph. We feel that we have lost a friend as well as a statesman, who in the darkest hour of our bloody struggle never deviated from the glorious purpose of sustaining the Constitution and the government against the designs of heartless traitors who attempted their destruction.

The legation is draped in mourning for thirty days, and all our citizens will wear crape upon the left arm for the same space of time.

Your order to all officers and others subject to the orders of the Secretary of State, that the same should be worn by them for six months, has been received, and will be complied with by the members of this legation.

I have the honor to be, sir, your obedient servant,

CHRISTOPHER ROBINSON.

Hon. WILLIAM HUNTER,
Acting Secretary of State.

[Translation.]

ALCALDIA MUNICIPAL OF LIMA,
Lima, May 22, 1865.

MOST EXCELLENT SIR: The honorable municipality over which I have the honor to preside has been profoundly affected at the painful catastrophe which, in the person of his Excellency ABRAHAM LINCOLN, has deprived the world of an honest man, the United States of an unblemished ruler, and liberty of its most decided champion.

There is not a single heart that has remained indifferent in presence of so heinous a crime, and the municipality of Lima would think itself wanting in one of its most precious duties—gratitude to the great men who recognize and sustain the true rights of humanity—if it did not hasten to manifest to your excellency the indignation which the crime has caused to it, and the profound grief which its consummation has deserved from it. LINCOLN is dead, sir, but he will eternally live in the hearts of the good patriots and of the honest men of the earth. His name will be written in letters of gold, in order to record the value of virtue in rulers, while that of his assassin will be pronounced with horror so long as morality exists in the world.

Will your excellency deign to accept this sincere manifestation of the sentiments which animate the municipality, and my own private ones, although it is very painful to improve so sad an opportunity to subscribe myself your attentive servant.

ANTO. G. DE LA FUENTE.

His Excellency the MINISTER PLENIPOTENTIARY
of the United States of North America.

[Translation.]

SOCIETY OF THE FOUNDERS OF THE INDEPENDENCE OF PERU.

Liberty—Equality—Fraternity.

LIMA, May 23, 1865,

And the 44th year of the Independence and the 41st of the Republic,

SIR: The deplorable event which has moved the entire continent, drawing from it a cry of sincere grief, could not fail to be felt also by the " Society of the Founders of the Independence of Peru," over which I have the honor to preside, covering with mourning the heart of each one of its members. In the midst of the terrible allusions which have passed over our age-whitened heads it was a pleasing consolation that in the front of the American Union there existed so indefatigable a champion of liberty, ABRAHAM LINCOLN, whom entire humanity has seen during four years sustaining the most noble and sacred of causes. So energetic a chief would have been already sufficiently great by the excellent endowments of his heart, by the magnanimity and firmness of his republican principles, and by the elevation of the sacred cause of liberty which Providence confided to his inspirations; but it was necessary that so elevated a figure should shine through ages with the lustre of martyrdom, and destiny has been employed in realizing this mysterious work, snatching him suddenly from the arms of his family and his people.

Death has been able to carry off an apostle and a genius, but his teaching will survive, because it is the law of good causes to triumph and exist with an immortal life. Unfortunate he who so obtuse as not to see that the cause of liberty is made now more firm than ever since the illustrious blood of the most generous of martyrs has made it fertile.

We hope, then, full of faith that, for the good of these people and of entire humanity, there will be fulfilled the immortal destinies of that great and opulent nation on which the world looks with astonishment; meanwhile, sharing in the grief which oppresses all Americans, with the sincerity with which apostles of the same doctrine and relatives of the same family ought to do, we pray to God not to extinguish that faith, and that by it He will give to the illustrious victim the reward of his virtues on the majestic throne of his glory. The cause of liberty will have in heaven one who pleads for it, after having valorously sustained it before an astonished world.

The society charges me with transmitting to your excellency the expression of these sentiments; and in doing it, adding the proposition presented by one of its worthy members and unanimously approved, and as a fraternal resolution, it is pleasing to me to offer to your excellency the personal assurances of my greatest respect and consideration, as your obedient, attentive, and true servant.

ESTANISLAO CORREA Y GARAY.

His Excellency Señor CHRISTOPHER ROBINSON,
Envoy Extraordinary and Minister Plenipotentiary
of the United States of North America, &c., &c., &c.

[Translation.]

SOCIETY OF THE FOUNDERS OF THE INDEPENDENCE OF PERU.

At the session which the permanent junta held on Monday, the 22d instant, the worthy vocal of the said junta, C. D. José Antonio Alvarado, presented the following proposition, which was unanimously approved of:

Proposition.—The unhappy intelligence having arrived by the last steamer from Panama of the tragic death of the illustrious and virtuous President of the great North American republic, ABRAHAM LINCOLN, which took place on Saturday, the 15th of April last, and which has struck with horror the entire continent, on account of the irreparable loss of the eminent patriot, of the idol of republicanism, of the worthy successor of the immortal Washington, of the missionary of liberty, the friend of humanity, and the unwearied defender of the emancipation of the slave, the Society of the Founders of the Independence of Peru, composed of the last remains of the great liberating army which, with its blood and sacrifices, had the high glory of founding this nation free and independent of all foreign power, sustaining with valor and constancy that heroic struggle, imitating the example of that colossal republic, perform the sacred duty of manifesting, in a solemn manner, the bitter grief which animates them on account of the misfortune of that prominent citizen, the idol of the great

American family, and upon whom the greatest encomium would be too short to exalt his merit and virtues. And if a parricidal ball, fired by an American monster, cut the thread of his precious and interesting existence, that same ball has transpierced the hearts of the founders of the independence of Peru, leaving them overwhelmed in bitter weeping; and to manifest their profound grief, have resolved:

1st. That the members of the society wear mourning for eight consecutive days.

2d. That a committee wait upon his excellency the minister of the United States resident in this capital, placing in his hands a respectful note, expressing the sentiments of the society, requesting him to transmit it to his excellency the minister of foreign relations of that great republic, for the knowledge of his government and of all the sons of that afflicted nation, who are our brothers, and whom we accompany in the grief and affliction which they suffer at the death of their affectionate father.

3d. That the society invite the celebration of a funeral service to the memory of the illustrious martyr of liberty.

4th. That the act which the session of the permanent junta of the society has had with so laudable an end be published in the journals of the capital, as also the note directed to the minister of foreign relations, and which documents shall be published, as well as translated into the North American idiom, in order that all may be acquainted with the pure, just, and patriotic manifestation which the few founders of the independence who still remain make, out of respect to the noble victim immolated in defence of liberty.

Let note be given and exemption from the usual proceedings of rule.
LIMA, *May* 22, 1865.

JOSÉ ANTONIO ALVARADO.

Approved of unanimously:

CORREA,

J. JULIAN UGARTE,
Secretario Cesante.

LIMA, *May* 22, 1865.

In pursuance of the call made by the minister of the United States, a large and highly respectable meeting of the citizens of that country, resident in Lima and vicinity, assembled at the legation of the United States at 12 o'clock to-day, the 22d instant, for the purpose of expressing their sorrow at the untimely and lamented death of the late President, ABRAHAM LINCOLN.

The meeting was called to order by the honorable Christopher Robinson, envoy extraordinary and minister plenipotentiary of the United States to Peru, who, in eloquent and affecting language, spoke of the cause which had convened them, the virtues of the late President, the barbarity of his assassination, and his confidence in the future under the administration of President Johnson. During the speech of the minister, his audience gave tokens of their sympathy and sorrow by their most fixed attention and emotion.

At the conclusion of his remarks, the meeting was organized by the election of the minister as chairman; and Thomas J. Pope, secretary of the United States legation, was appointed secretary. On motion, a committee was appointed by the chairman to report a series of resolutions expressive of the sense of the meeting. Messrs. Thomas R. Eldridge, Hobson, Church, Moore, Davis, and Sartori were the committee, who in a short time returned and reported the following preamble and resolutions:

Whereas the honored, respected, and magnanimous Chief Magistrate of our nation, ABRAHAM LINCOLN, has been cruelly slain by the hand of a foul assassin; cut off in the fulness of his years, the maturity of his intellect, and the zenith of his usefulness and fame; slain in the presence of his family and friends, at a time when the nation of which he was the constitutional head was about to emerge from the horrors of a protracted and ruthless civil war, through a baptism of blood, to the glorious consummation of permanent reunion, and a new existence of universal liberty and justice; and whereas, under this last terrible stroke, this appalling tragedy, and wicked deed of a hydra-headed treason, unparalleled either in the base ingratitude of the act, committed so close upon the generous policy announced by the noble-hearted President to the people of the South, or in the ominous consequences, fraught as they may be with the welfare of millions of our fellow-countrymen, it becomes the duty of every citizen of our republic abroad, as well as at home, to express their heartfelt sorrow for the untimely loss of our great and good President, ABRAHAM LINCOLN; their cordial sympathy with his afflicted family; their horror at the deed, and most profound detestation of the means by which it has been consummated: we, the citizens of the United States of America, resident in Lima and vicinity, recognizing our loyalty to our beloved country, and, although at a distance from it, actuated by the same spirit of patriotism as our brethren at home, would place on record our firm and unshaken faith in its glorious destiny. Be it, therefore,

Resolved, That we have heard with the deepest sorrow and indignation of the death of President LINCOLN by the assassin's hand; that at this time, when the eyes of the nation were turned to him for the display of great practical wisdom and executive ability, for magnanimity and forbearance, blended with a firm and unalterable adherence to the principles of free government and liberty, his death is a most grievous national calamity.

Resolved, That while we recognize and deeply lament the terrible nature of the calamity which has befallen our nation, still, placing our trust in that Supreme Being who has so signally blessed our people hitherto, we do not despair of the ultimate success of our cause, to the sustaining of which, under the policy of the late President, we give our earnest support and countenance.

Resolved, That we will ever cherish the memory of ABRAHAM LINCOLN as the honest, fearless, patriotic, and noble defender of that Constitution which was originally cemented under the auspices of the immortal Washington, as the bulwark of universal freedom and civil liberty.

Resolved. That we tender the expression of our most profound sympathies to the consort and family of our late revered President, with our condolence for their irreparable bereavement, trusting that strength may be given to them to bear up under their great affliction.

Resolved, That as citizens of the United States we are profoundly grateful for the general, cordial, and generous sympathy manifested towards our nation by the government and people of Peru, as well as by the representatives and residents of other nations, in our great misfortune; that we extend to them all, individually and collectively, the assurance of our warmest acknowledgments for the honors paid and the respect shown to the memory of our late President·

Resolved, That to the press of Lima and Callao we offer our especial recognition of the able, eloquent, and cordial tributes of eulogy and sympathy on this event.

Resolved, That we offer to the honorable William H. Seward, Secretary of State of the United States, and to F. W. Seward, esq., Assistant Secretary of State, our unfeigned and profound sympathy in the hour of their affliction, caused by the hand of an infamous assassin; that we rejoice at their providential escape from death, and hopes of recovery, and trust that they may long be spared to do eminent service in the cause of our country.

Resolved, That copies of these resolutions be forwarded to the President of the United States, to the family of our late President, and to the honorable Secretary of State, and that they be published in the Comercio of this city, and the Washington Chronicle.

Resolved, That the legation of the United States in this city be draped in mourning for the space of thirty days, and that a committee be appointed to carry the same into effect.

Messrs. Barnes, Pope, and Ells were appointed on this committee

Mr. Robinson having addressed a few appropriate remarks to the meeting in reply to a vote of thanks which was given to him for his able conduct in the chair, the meeting was, on motion, adjourned.

CHRISTOPHER ROBINSON,
Chairman.

THOMAS J. POPE,
Secretary.

RUSSIA.

Prince Gortchacow to Mr. de Stoeckl.

[Translation.]

St. Petersburg, *April* 16–28, 1865.

Sir: The telegraph has brought us the news of the double crime of which the President of the United States has fallen a victim and Mr. Seward barely escaped.

The blow which has struck Mr. Lincoln, at the very moment when he seemed about to harvest the fruits of his energy and perseverance, has been deeply felt in Russia.

Because of the absence of the Emperor I am not in a position to receive and transmit to you the expression of the sentiments of his Imperial Majesty. Being acquainted, nevertheless, with those which our august master entertains toward the United States of America, it is easy for me to realize in advance the impression which the news of this odious crime will cause his Imperial Majesty to experience.

I have hastened to testify to General Clay the earnest and cordial sympathy of the imperial cabinet with the federal government.

Please to express this in the warmest terms to President Johnson, adding thereto our most sincere wishes that this new and grievous trial may not impede the onward march of the American people toward the re-establishment of the Union, and of that concord which is the source of its power and of its prosperity.

Receive, sir, the assurance of my very distinguished consideration.

GORTCHACOW.

His Excellency Mr. Stoeckl, &c., &c., &c.

Prince Gortchacow to Mr. Clay.

[Translation.]

St. Petersburg, *April* 16–28, 1865.

Sir: Although the absence of his Majesty the Emperor makes it impossible for me to obtain and communicate to you the expression of the sentiments which my august master would have felt at the news of the foul crime to which the President of the United States has just fallen a victim, and which Mr. Seward has barely escaped, I did not wish to delay in testifying to you the lively and profound sympathy of the imperial cabinet for the federal government in this new trial which Providence has reserved for it. I have asked our minister at Washington to communicate it to the Vice-President, Mr. Johnson. Will your excellency transmit it to him, together with our sincere wishes that this abominable crime will not hinder the progress of the American nation towards the establishment of the Union and of peace, which are the pledges of its power and its prosperity ?

Will your excellency be pleased to accept the assurance of my most distinguished consideration ?

GORTCHACOW.

C. M. CLAY, Esq., *&c., &c., &c.*

Prince Gortchacow to Mr. Clay.

[Translation.]

ST. PETERSBURG, *May* 16, 1865.

Mr. MINISTER: In informing you, in the name of the imperial cabinet, of the profound indignation excited by the assassination of the President of the United States, and the heartfelt sympathy which the American government and people have met with among us in this their national grief, I was certain of having expressed the sentiments of his Majesty the Emperor.

Scarcely has my august master returned to his dominions when he orders me to testify to you his grief at this painful event. Tried himself by a woful loss, which is also a cause of national mourning for Russia, the Emperor joins in the unanimous regrets which encircle the memory of the eminent statesman snatched away so suddenly, and in so terrible manner, from his noble career.

His Imperial Majesty requests us, your excellency, to transmit to you, in his name, the assurance of his living and deep sympathy with the family of the late Mr. LINCOLN, and with his Excellency President Johnson.

I also fulfilled the orders of my august master by informing you how much his Imperial Majesty has been touched by the spontaneous testimonials of respect which the federal officers have shown to the memory of his dearly beloved son during the passage of the squadron bearing to Russia his mortal remains.

I have already communicated to the federal government the thanks of his Imperial Majesty through his representative at Washington. He asks of you the favor to reiterate them.

Be assured, your excellency, of my very distinguished consideration.

GORTCHACOW.

General CLAY, *&c., &c., &c.*

Mr. Clay to Mr. Seward.

No. 79.] LEGATION OF THE UNITED STATES,
St. Petersburg, Russia, May 4, 1865.

SIR: I know not how to express my grief for the loss of our great and good President LINCOLN, and my indignation at the crime of which he is a victim.

I thank God that you are spared to us, and I trust that our country and the nations will still continue to reap the fruit of your patriotic labors and pacific sentiments. The ambassadors of France and England called in person, and those who did not do so wrote letters full of admiration for the virtues of the late President, and horror at the crime of his assassination. His Imperial Highness the Grand Duke Constantine sent his aide-de-camp, General Greigg; her Imperial Highness the Grand Duchess Helen sent Baron Rosen; and his Imperial Highness the Prince d'Oldenburg called in person, all to utter sentiments of sorrow and sympathy with the American government and people. A great many distinguished Russians also expressed their grief at our loss in words and through the press. Her Imperial Highness the Grand Duchess Helen, who is well versed in the politics and history of our country, has invited me to call upon her, informally, on Saturday, with a view of giving us further evidence of her kind feelings for our nation and its progressive cause, of which she is an admirer.

These sentiments of esteem and sadness are gratifying to me, and such as lead me to the hope that the martyrdom of our noble friend will, at home and abroad, consecrate in the hearts of all men the principles of liberty and self-government for which LINCOLN lived and died.

President Johnson enters upon the duties of his office under great difficulties. I like the words of humility and calm devotion which characterize the partial revelation of his views at his accession to office.

That which won for Mr. LINCOLN most admiration in Europe was his moderation in expression and firmness in action.

The new President, we are told, proposes to retain the old cabinet, and, we trust, the old policy of peace with foreign nations and magnanimity in all things at home consistent with the *destruction of slavery* and the *restoration of the Union.*

The prayers of the good of all the world follow him in his responsible task.

I beg you will lay this paper before the President.

Hoping to hear of you and your son Frederick Seward's speedy recovery, I remain your most obedient servant,

C. M. CLAY.

Hon. WILLIAM H. SEWARD,
Secretary of State, Washington, D. C.

Sir Andrew Buchanan to Mr. Clay.

HER BRITANNIC MAJESTY'S EMBASSY,
St. Petersburg, April 28, 1865.

Sir Andrew Buchanan, her Britannic Majesty's ambassador, has had the honor to receive the note by which his excellency General C. M. Clay, the minister of the United States, has acquainted him with the assassination of Mr. LINCOLN, the President of the United States, and with the attempt which was made at the same time to murder Mr. William H. Seward, the Secretary of State; and further informing him that, in consequence of the former of these distressing events, Mr. Andrew Johnson has succeeded to the presidency of the Union.

In thanking General Clay for this communication, Sir Andrew Buchanan begs leave to express his sympathy with his excellency, and the people of the United States, on the great national calamity which they have sustained, while he participates in the abhorrence of its authors, which their atrocious crime must excite throughout America and the civilized world.

Sir Andrew Buchanan avails himself of this opportunity to offer to General Clay the assurance of his high consideration.

The Minister of Italy to Mr. Clay.

[Translation.]

ST. PETERSBURG, *April* 29, 1865.

MY DEAR COLLEAGUE : I had desired to offer you in person my heartfelt sympathy, but on account of indisposition I am obliged to defer my visit.

In the meanwhile, I know not how I can better interpret the sentiments of my government than in joining in the sorrow with which your country has been so cruelly stricken, by the loss of her greatest citizen and most eminent statesman.

The blood of a martyr in so noble a cause will strengthen the American Union, whose power and prosperity have every good wish of Italy. In renewing to you, my colleague, my expressions of sorrowful sympathy, and in thanking you for your communication, I have the honor to tender you the assurance of my high consideration.

LAUNAY.

The Minister of Belgium to Mr. Clay.

[Translation.]

St. Petersburg, *April* 28, 1865.

The minister of Belgium has had the honor of receiving the note which his excellency the minister of the United States has had the kindness to address to him, in order to inform him of the death of the President of the United States, ABRAHAM LINCOLN, who was assassinated in his box at the theatre in Washington, on the 14th instant, as well as of the dangerous wound which menaces the life of the Secretary of State, Mr. William H. Seward.

It is with an unmingled feeling of horror that the undersigned has heard of these cowardly and foul attacks, which will cause an outburst of sorrow not only in America, but in Europe, and the whole world; and he joins in the grief which cannot fail to be caused by the loss of an eminent statesman, called by his fellow-citizens to direct the destinies of his country.

JONGHE D'ARDOYE.

The Minister of Sweden and Norway to Mr. Clay.

[Translation.]

St. Petersburg, *April* 28, 1865.

YOUR EXCELLENCY: In hastening to acknowledge the sad communication, by which your excellency has just informed me of the assassination of Mr. LINCOLN, President of the United States of America, I beg you to accept my most profound expressions of sympathy, and also of horror, for the foul deed which has deprived your country and your government of their worthy and illustrious chief.

I seize the present occasion to offer to your excellency repeated assurances of my high consideration.

WEDEL JARLSBERG,
Minister of Sweden and Norway.

Mr. C. M. CLAY,
Minister of the United States of America.

ROME.

Mr. King to Mr. Hunter.

No. 37.]   LEGATION OF THE UNITED STATES AT ROME,
April 29, 1865.

SIR: The appalling intelligence of the assassination of President LINCOLN, and the attempt upon the lives of the Secretary and the Assistant Secretary of State, which reached Rome on the morning of the 27th instant, excited the most profound and universal sentiment of horror and indignation among men of every class, condition, and nation. The first account represented that the Assistant Secretary of State had also fallen a victim to the assassin's knife, and that the life of the Secretary was despaired of; but we are at least spared this aggravation of horrors, the latest despatch reporting that "Secretary Seward is out of danger," and that his son, though in imminent peril, is still alive. As the tidings spread the Americans in Rome gathered together at the rooms of the United States legation and held a meeting to give utterance to the feelings which the news had excited in every loyal breast. The resolutions adopted but feebly express the intense emotions which the dastardly crime of the southern conspirators has everywhere aroused. Nor is this confined only to our own countrymen. From the cardinal secretary of state, the ambassadors of France, Spain, and Austria, the representatives of Russia and Brazil, and other members of the diplomatic corps, and from some of the principal Roman nobility and citizens, I have received assurances of the utter detestation with which they regard the crime, and of their profound sympathy with the government and people of the United States in the hour of terrible trial and affliction. May Almighty God safely guard and guide our country through the surging waves of trouble into the calm sunshine of peace and public order.

In token of respect for the memory of the great and good man who died as he had lived, faithful to his trust and at the post of duty, I have caused the rooms of the United States legation to be draped in mourning. The loyal Americans in Rome have all assumed the usual badges of mourning, as a slight manifestation of their sorrow for the lamented death of our President and of regard for his memory.

I need scarcely add that we await with trembling anxiety further news from America, and that it is the devout prayer of all true-hearted Americans in Rome that the lives of the Secretary and Assistant Secretary may be spared to their country.

I am, sir, with great respect, your obedient servant,

RUFUS KING.

Hon. WILLIAM HUNTER,
Acting Secretary of State, &c., &c., &c.

Mr. King to Mr. Hunter.

[Extract.]

No. 38.]　　　　　LEGATION OF THE UNITED STATES AT ROME,
May 6, 1865.

SIR: The terrible catastrophe of the 14th of April at Washington still occupies all thoughts and tongues on this side of the water, and has called forth from the courts and people of Europe an expression of heart-felt sympathy and sincere sorrow unparalleled in history. Appropriate religious services were held in the United States legation rooms here, which were largely attended by Americans and others.   *   *   *   *   Our latest advices from home, to the 22d of April, encourage the belief that both the Secretary and Assistant Secretary of State have escaped the fate designed for them by their brutal and cowardly assailant, and still live to serve their country. I need not say with what unfeigned gratitude and joy this news has been received, not only by the Americans, but by men of all nations in Rome.

I had an official interview with Cardinal Antonelli a day or two since. His Eminence embraced the opportunity to express to me, for himself and for the Holy Father, the horror with which they regarded the bloody act which had struck down the head of the American republic, and aimed a like blow at the life of the chief counsellor, and of their earnest sympathy for the American government and people in this hour of trial and affliction. His Eminence further begged that I would make known these sentiments to the authorities at Washington.   *   *   *   *   *   *   *   *

I have the honor to be, with great respect, your obedient servant,

RUFUS KING.

Hon. WILLIAM HUNTER,
　　Acting Secretary of State, &c., &c.

Mr. King to Mr. Hunter.

[Extract.]

No. 39.]　　　　　LEGATION OF THE UNITED STATES AT ROME,
May 13, 1865.

SIR: I duly received a copy of the circular from the State Department, under date of April 17, directing all officers and others subject to its orders to wear crape upon the left arm for the period of six months, in honor to the memory of our late illustrious Chief Magistrate. Anticipating in this respect the wishes of the department, I had already caused the United States legation rooms here to be suitably draped, and in common with all loyal Americans now in Rome, had assumed the customary badge of mourning, which will be worn during the time prescribed. It is a melancholy satisfaction to know that the grief we feel at the bereavement the republic has sustained meets with general and earnest sympathy in all parts of the Old World ; and that in Europe, as in America, enlightened public opinion has already inscribed among the most illustrious names on the roll of fame that of our martyred President.

*   *   *   *   *   *   *   *

I have the honor to be, with great respect, your obedient servant,

RUFUS KING.

Hon. WILLIAM HUNTER,
    Acting Secretary of State.

Mr Parish to the American citizens in Rome.   Read at the American chapel.

ROME, *April* 29, 1865.

LADIES AND GENTLEMEN, BRETHREN AND SISTERS IN CHRIST: With the kind permission of your excellent representatives, and as having enjoyed as a diplomatic guest the hospitality of the United States during four years more than forty years ago, I hope I may not be thought presumptuous in mingling with your sacred grief an expression from the old country, the land of our grandsires, being myself wholly unconnected with politics.

If my fellow-countrymen at Rome are not present with you this day to manifest their horror at the event which has deprived you of the Chief Magistrate of your choice, of that conscientious spirit who lived and toiled and died that all his fellow-citizens might be united in peace, be assured that the motives of their absence must be reluctance to intrude, uninvited, into the grave of your domestic affections. The profound sympathy of our own sovereign and of her royal family, so often bursting forth in the days of your heavy trials, must guarantee to you the love at such a moment of the many millions who, within so many horizons, own her sway. But while we are all here in spirit to denounce the most odious of crimes, let us acknowledge how hopeful is the dawn of your future life, when he who now rules in the shrine of the pious Washington has given the impress of his power and of the happiness of every transatlantic soul in his first inaugural words, " I am in the hands of God." Thus may we be all " of one accord " in every place, united in Christ, one in God and God in us.

HENRY HEADLEY PARISH.

SPAIN.

[Translation.]

DEPARTMENT OF STATE, PALACE,
April 27, 1865.

SIR: I have the honor to inform you that I have received your note of this date, in which, unhappily, I find confirmed the sad news of the horrible crimes committed on the persons of his Excellency the President of the United States, ABRAHAM LINCOLN, and of the distinguished Secretary of State, Mr. Seward.

Knowing as you do the sentiments of sincere friendship and good intelligence which animated the government of the Queen, my lady, with respect to the United States, you will easily comprehend the horror with which we have learned the treacherous murder of the Chief Magistrate of that great nation which you so worthily represent, and how much we deplore also the villianous attack upon Mr. Seward, for whose recovery we make the most fervent vows.

I beg you to be pleased to make known to his Excellency the President of the republic the sentiments of profound indignation which the sad events you announce have produced in the mind of her Majesty the Queen, and in that of her government; and I thus renew to you the assurance of my distinguished consideration.

L. ARRAZOLA.

The CHARGÉ D'AFFAIRES OF THE UNITED STATES.

[Translation.]

DEPARTMENT OF STATE, BUREAU OF POLITICAL AFFAIRS,
Madrid, May 9, 1865.

MOST EXCELLENT SIR: The president of the council of ministers, on the 5th instant, directed this department as follows:

By her Majesty's orders, and for the instruction of the department under your charge, I transmit to your excellency copies of the resolutions passed by the Senate and House of Representatives, sympathizing with the United States, and deploring the abominable crime committed upon the person of your worthy President, Mr. ABRAHAM LINCOLN. Communicated by royal order, through the minister of state, I transmit them to you, with the said copies, that you may send them to your government.

God grant you many years.

UNDER SECRETARY MIGUEL BANUELOS.

[Translation.]

PALACE OF THE SENATE, *May* 3, 1865.

President of the Council of Ministers, Senate Chamber:

The Senate in session this day has unanimously resolved that it sympathizes with the United States in the profound grief caused by the death of its worthy President, ABRAHAM LINCOLN.

God grant you many years.

JUAN DE SEVILLA,
Secretary of the Senate.

HILARION DEL REY,
Secretary of the Senate, President of the Council of Ministers.

A signed copy:

M. BANUELOS.

[Translation.]

PALACE OF CONGRESS, *May* 2, 1865.

President of the Council of Ministers, Chamber of Deputies:

The House of Deputies in session yesterday unanimously resolved that it sympathizes with the United States in the profound grief caused by the death of its worthy President, ABRAHAM LINCOLN.

This we communicate to you for the information of her Majesty's government and subsequent action.

God grant you many years.

RAFAEL CHACON *D. S.*

COUNT OF CAMPOMANES, D. S.,
President of the Council of Ministers.

This copy has a rubric:

M. BANUELOS.

The Duke of Valencia to Mr. Perry.

[Translation.]

PRESIDENCY OF THE CABINET OF MINISTERS,
Madrid, May 5, 1865.

SIR: The horrible crimes committed on the persons of the President and Secretary of State of the United States have caused a painful and profound sensation in the Spanish nation, which is united to that great republic by the ties of a true friendship and a cordial sympathy.

Although at the first moment this sad news reached us I hastened to make known to you, personally, the profound grief of her Majesty the Queen, my august sovereign, and of her government, at that immense misfortune, I have the honor to-day to transmit to you the annexed copies of the declarations made by the Senate and the Congress of Deputies, associating themselves to the great sorrow of that generous nation for the abominable crime perpetrated upon the person of its illustrious and respected President.

The affliction which the death of that eminent statesman has produced to the government of her Majesty is in part relieved by the welcome news that the life of the Secretary of State for foreign affairs is happily not in great danger, but, on the contrary, that there are well-founded hopes he may obtain a prompt and complete recovery. Please God it may be so, for the good and prosperity of that noble country, of which you are the most worthy representative!

I avail myself of this occasion to renew to you the assurance of my most distinguished consideration.

The DUKE OF VALENCIA.

The CHARGÉ D'AFFAIRES OF THE UNITED STATES.

[Translation.]

PRESIDENCY OF THE CABINET OF MINISTERS—SENATE.

PALACE OF THE SENATE, May 3, 1865.

To the President of the Cabinet of Ministers:

EXCELLENCY: The Senate in session of to-day has unanimously declared that it associates itself to the profound grief produced in the United States by the horrible crime committed on the person of their worthy President, ABRAHAM LINCOLN.

God guard your excellency many years.

JUAN DE SEVILLA,
Senator Secretary.
HILARION DEL REY,
Senator Secretary.

It is a true copy:

VALENCIA.

[Translation.]

PRESIDENCY OF THE CABINET OF MINISTERS—CONGRESS OF DEPUTIES.

PALACE OF THE DEPUTIES, *May* 2, 1865.

To the President of the Cabinet of Ministers:

EXCELLENCY: The Congress of Deputies in the session of yesterday has declared unanimously that it associates itself to the profound sorrow of the United States for the abominable murder of their worthy President, ABRAHAM LINCOLN.

The which we communicate to your excellency for the information of her Majesty's government and the consequent effects.

God guard your excellency many years.

THE COUNT OF CAMPOMANES,
Deputy Secretary.

RAFAEL CHACON,
Deputy Secretary.

It is a true copy:

VALENCIA.

[Translated from the original as it stands on the official journal of the Senate.]

DEBATE IN THE SPANISH SENATE, MAY 3, 1865.

The COUNT OF VISTAHERMOSA said:

SENATORS: The circumstance that this body has not been in session till to-day since the unwelcome news reached Madrid of the infamous assassination committed on the person of the worthy President of the United States, Mr. LINCOLN, has prevented me from addressing the Senate as I do at this moment, in the persuasion that it will know how to associate its sentiments of grief and indignation to those produced in the whole civilized world by the crime which has snatched from life a person so illustrious and so distinguished for his eminent services.

When all peoples in both hemispheres rise with one voice to condemn the cowardly assassins who have blackened the brilliant pages of that wonderful war just when the country already saw peace on the horizon, and when, undoubtedly, that peace is owing to the efforts, the constancy, and the skill with which the lamented Mr. LINCOLN has directed those events, it seems just that the Senate should manifest expressly and spontaneously its profound sorrow and regret at an event as terrible as it has been unexpected—an event which has left on the minds of senators, as upon those of all the civilized world, a deep furrow of execration.

If I shall not have interpreted the sentiments of the Senate in a manner worthy of its elevated character, let it supply my shortcomings, and address to the government of that republic a manifestation such as our president considers fit, informing the Queen's government of this manifestation, and making it extensive to the illustrious widow who has seen snatched away so prematurely the companion of her life, so that the world may know that if the Spanish Senate cares for the rights and immunities of people, it watches no less carefully over the rights of the kings and heads of government who rule the destinies of other nations.

I therefore call upon the government of her Majesty to give the proper explanation of what has been done in this important question.

The President of the Cabinet of Ministers, the Duke of VALENCIA, said : The government of her Majesty records with much pleasure the motion made by the senator, Count of Vistahermosa. As soon as the government learned officially the horrible crime committed in the United States, we went to her Majesty's presence to inform her of it, so that she might give me such orders as she thought fit. Her Majesty ordered me to go and visit the representative of the United States at Madrid, and to express to him the grief and the indignation which her Majesty had felt at a crime so horrible, as well as all the interest which her Majesty felt for the leaders of the republic and for the people of the United States.

In fulfilment of the royal precept, I went to the house of the representative of the United States, and made to him, in the name of her Majesty and of the government, that manifestation, which he gratefully acknowledged ; and I requested him to transmit the same to his government, so that the latter—with which Spain maintains and seeks to maintain such good relations, and he also labors to maintain them for the good of both nations—should be made aware of the sentiments which animate the Queen and her government.

At the same time an official communication, signed by the minister of state was sent to Señor Tassara, her Majesty's minister plenipotentiary at Washington, making known to him the same manifestation. This is what her Majesty's government can say in reply to the senator.

The COUNT OF VISTAHERMOSA said : I thought I was already aware, from what had been said in the Congress of Deputies, that this had been the course of her Majesty's ministers. I thought it right to make this motion, so that the whole Senate, in whose sentiments I trust I am not mistaken, might have an opportunity to join in this profound sorrow for the unmerited misfortune which has fallen upon the people of the United States, and I request the Chair, for this purpose, to consult the opinion of this House.

The President of the Senate, the Marquis of DUERO, then said from the chair : I am certain that the Senate authorizes me at this moment, and, with the Senate, all Spaniards of the provinces beyond seas and of the peninsula, to declare that the impression produced by the horrible crime committed against the President of the republic of the United States has been unanimous, and that we join ourselves to the manifestations which the civilized world is now making on account of this sad event, desiring solemnly to make known the sincere wishes of Spain for the prosperity and peace of the American republic.

The question will now be put whether the Senate approves this declaration.

The secretary of the Senate, SEVILLA, having put the question, it was resolved affirmatively by a unanimous vote.

[Translated from the original as it stands on the official journal of the congress.]

DEBATE IN THE SPANISH CONGRESS OF DEPUTIES, MAY 1, 1865.

The deputy Señor LASALA (opposition) said: Public attention has been occupied in these days by the events which have given rise to inevitable discussion in the Senate and in this house, and by another, also a bloody event, occurring in a foreign land, to which I beg now to call the attention of the congress.

When other governments and parliaments are making manifestations on account of this horrible event, it seems natural that in the Spanish Parliament, in the Parliament of the nation which, by Cuba and Porto Rico, is neighbor to the United States, something should be said, and that the initiative should be taken by the liberal opposition of the government of her Majesty. That country which had been great in peace has not been less great in war. In that war, perhaps the most gigantic which history records, it seems indeed that, in order so immense a pyramid of corpses should be grandly crowned, it was necessary that the body of the President of the United States should fall by the ball of an assassin.

The government of her Majesty—I wish to do it justice—I suppose, will have manifested its sentiments, but I desire to know in what form; because, if it should not have been in some solemn form expressing adequately these sentiments of the whole country, I shall feel obliged to make use of my right as a deputy, and put this manifestation into some other form.

The President of the Cabinet of Ministers, Duke of VALENCIA, said: Her Majesty's government, some days since, by extraordinary and unofficial channels, learned the crime which had been committed in the United States, but did not wish to take any official steps while the information it had received should not be confirmed; but as soon as it was known officially, the government made haste to lay this intelligence before her Majesty.

On taking the orders of the Queen, I received the charge from her Majesty to go and visit the chargé d'affaires of the United States in Madrid, and to express to him the profound sorrow, the immense affliction, which the Queen and the government had experienced by the horrible crimes committed on the person of the President of that republic, on that of the minister for foreign affairs, and on that of the son of the latter.

At the same time an official communication was sent to him by the department of state in similar terms, and a copy of the same was also sent to her Majesty's minister in Washington, so that he should communicate the same sentiments to the new President of the republic.

We have not laid these papers before the House, because it was not customary to do so. We wished that the initiative should be taken by the deputies themselves, and it is immaterial whether this comes from the benches of the opposition or from this side, because in this case there can be but one general and unanimous sentiment in the whole House, as there is in the whole nation; for the whole nation cannot do otherwise than lament a horrible crime—an assassination perpetrated in this way on the person of the chief of a friendly nation, united to Spain in the best relations, and which, throughout the whole time of the war, has been giving and is now giving us the most positive proofs of the good sentiments which animate it in respect to all questions and all the interests of Spain.

The government, therefore, associates itself to the motion made by the deputy, and would wish that the whole House and all Spain should manifest these same sentiments, not only because this is just, but also on account of the reciprocity of sentiments which ought to exist between that nation and Spain.

The Deputy Señor CLAROS (ministerial) said: The president of the cabinet of ministers has very properly undertaken to express, not only in the name of the government of the Queen, but in that of the majority of this House, the perfect identity of sentiment which animates all of us with respect to the proposition made by the honorable deputy who has just spoken. In this point, as the president of the cabinet has well said, there can be no diversity of opinion whatsoever among any of the deputies who sit in this Chamber. The abominable crime of which the illustrious personage who presided over the American Union has been the victim, is a thing which must wound painfully the fibres of all who have any sentiments of morality, and profoundly all those who have any political instinct.

It is evident that this poison which corrodes the entrails of European societies has infiltered itself beyond the Atlantic, and that it reaches all peoples. Consequently, if in the past we are afflicted by the crimes committed in Europe against crowned heads, on this occasion the future ought to afflict us still more, seeing that we discover the disease to have extended to all humanity. We who glory in being partisans of the principle of authority, we ought to feel this more than any. In fact, we believe that the principle of authority is a species of reflex of the divine power—understanding this phrase in its right sense—in the sense in which it seems to me it cannot be denied by anybody, considering the public power in its august social manifestations, not precisely in kings, as is vulgarly believed, but in whomsoever represents it socially and legitimately, is sacred.

This principle, then, is for us incarnate in the person of the President of a republic, as it is in that of our own august sovereign, or in that of any crowned head of Europe. We, therefore, join ourselves to this worthy, opportune and most fitting manifestation, and I think in so saying I interpret faithfully the sentiments of the majority—(by many deputies: Yes, yes,)—and I may say we are perfectly agreed to what has been said by the Deputy Lasala, and by the president of the cabinet. To us it is most grateful, seeing that we are divided on other questions in which our opinions differ, to be perfectly united on this point, which is of great interest, for the question is the condemnation, present and future, of those sacrilegeous attacks against a principle alike sacred to every member of this house.

The President of the Cabinet of Ministers said: I omitted to state to the Congress that the latest information of the government is that the Secretary of State for Foreign Affairs, who has been wounded most seriously, as well as his son, it is hoped may both recover from the sad condition to which they were reduced, and that the assassin is arrested.

The Deputy Señor LASALA: Both times the president of the cabinet has risen he has satisfied me completely. This is what I hoped for from the government of her Majesty on this occasion, and without entering now into any considerations upon the origin of power, it seems to me that in point of fact the house is now ready to make the manifestation which the president of the cabinet has indicated. I, personally, ought not to propose it. And, although there are here many persons more competent, better authorized, and more conspicuous than I am on these benches, and on the other side of the house, they would not have authority sufficient to make this manifestation. But there is in this chamber one person who can make it, (the orator is interrupted by the president of the congress,) and at this moment he is interrupting me to say that he will make it.

The President of the Congress of Deputies, from his chair, said: Gentlemen Deputies—I consider it my privilege as well as duty to interpret on this occasion the sentiments of you all, of the whole congress and of the nation, declaring that this house associates itself to the profound affliction which has fallen upon the United States in the horrible crime committed upon the person of the President of that republic, and which has just occupied the attention of this house.

The question being then put whether the House adheres to the declaration made by its president, it was agreed to without a dissenting voice; and, on motion of Deputy Jove y Hevia, it was ordered to be entered on the records, with the adhesion of the House by a unanimous vote

---

[Translation.]

SPANISH LEGATION IN WASHINGTON,
New York, June 9, 1865.

The undersigned, minister plenipotentiary of her Catholic Majesty, has the honor to address the honorable Acting Secretary of State, informing him, in the name of his government, of the profound horror and indignation felt by the Crown, the representatives, and the Spanish people, at the news of the assassination of the late President of the United States, ABRAHAM LINCOLN, and the attack upon the person of the honorable Secretary of State, Mr. William H Seward.

The following accompanying documents are evidence of this sentiment: No. 1 is a copy of a communication, dated May 1, from her Majesty's first secretary of state, transmitting to the undersigned a note of the 21st of April, in reply to one from the United States chargé d'affaires of the same date announcing that sad event; No. 2 is a copy of another communication of the 9th of May, containing two resolutions on the same sad subject, adopted unanimously by the Cortes.

As the honorable Acting Secretary will see, the undersigned presents himself personally to the Chief Magistrate of the republic to express these sentiments.

The undersigned regrets that indisposition has retained him in New York, and thus prevented him from presenting these documents sooner, though they might have been delivered to the Department of State in another way.

It is scarcely necessary to add that the undersigned sympathizes deeply with the government and people of the United States under these distressing circumstances, and hopes the honorable Acting Secretary of State will give him an opportunity to fulfil the charge of his government towards the President of this republic.

The undersigned embraces this occasion of renewing to the honorable Acting Secretary of State the assurances of his most distinguished consideration.

GABRIEL G. Y TASSARA.

Hon. ACTING SECRETARY OF STATE
of the United States.

Mr. Arrazola to Mr. Tassara.

[Translation.]

MADRID, *May* 1, 1865.

MOST EXCELLENT SIR: I transmit, by royal order, to your excellency a copy of the note I sent to the United States chargé d'affaires in reply to one from him, informing me of Mr. LINCOLN's assassination, who was President of the republic, and of the attempt on the life of Mr. Seward, Secretary of State. Struck with the greatest indignation at such atrocious and horrid crimes, her Majesty's government hastens to express to the representative of the United States at this court the profound sorrow produced upon the mind of the Queen and her ministers by the death of the distinguished statesman that has filled the whole country with mourning.

I hope Mr. Perry will not delay to communicate the mentioned note to his government; and, besides this, her Majesty desires you to approach Mr. LINCOLN's successor in person, and confirm the sentiments expressed in the note, assuring him that the Spanish government cherishes the hope that the sad event, the subject of this despatch, may not produce a change of the friendly relations now existing between Spain and your republic.

May God grant you many years.

LORENZO ARRAZOLA.

[Translation.]

LEGATION OF SPAIN AT WASHINGTON,
Washington, May 10, 1865.

The undersigned, minister plenipotentiary of her Catholic Majesty, has received from the captain general of Cuba a communication, in which, referring to the horrible assassination of President LINCOLN, and to the attempt committed on the persons of the honorable Secretary and Assistant Secretary of State, Mr. William H. Seward and Mr. Frederick W. Seward, he says to me what follows: "I ask you to please to express to Mr. Seward my sorrow, as governor of this island and as an individual, for these calamities, and the vows I address to the Almighty for the prompt recovery of himself and son, informing him at the same time of the general indignation which has been caused by the outrage on the President of the republic and himself, and that I await with anxiety news of his recovery."

The undersigned has the honor to bring this to the knowledge of the honorable Secretary of State *ad interim*, asking that on his part he will please inform Mr. Seward of it, with similar expressions on the part of the undersigned.

The undersigned avails of the occasion to reiterate to the honorable Acting Secretary of State the assurances of his highest consideration.

GABRIEL G. Y TASSARA.

Hon. WILLIAM HUNTER,
    Acting Secretary of State.

Manuel Mayol to Mr. Giro.

[Translation.]

JEREZ, *May* 9, 1865.

CITIZEN CONSUL: Identified with the cause of your country, which is the cause of liberty throughout the world, and at the same time impressed with sadness on account of the horrid assassination just committed upon the person of the illustrious republican LINCOLN, various friends and political co-religionists of this city have decided to send a congratulation for the happy termination of your war, in which we at the same time express our sorrow for the crime that has just taken place. Wishing it may quickly arrive at its address, we have concluded to ask you, (provided there is no objection,) if we may send it immediately to your consulate, so that you can forward it directly and thus give us the assurance that it will not be lost.

Send your answer, if you please, to Armas street, No. 2, infants' public school, where it will be anxiously expected by your very humble servant,

MANUEL MAYOL.

Manuel Mayol to Mr. Giro.

[Translation.]

JEREZ, *May* 12, 1865.

CITIZEN CONSUL: Availing ourselves of the generous offer you made to us in your letter of the 10th instant, I take the liberty to trouble you with the annexed manifesto, that you may send it, as you politely offered to do, to the minister of your nation in Madrid, who will send it with safety and despatch to its place of destination.

Although it has but six signatures, it is none the less certain that it is the will of the democracy of this town, whose signatures we have not taken the trouble to collect, because it would make the document too large.

    With that intent, I have the honor to be, &c., &c.,

MANUEL MAYOL.

[Translation.]

SPAIN, ANDALUSIA,
Jerez de la Frontera, May 2, 1865.

CITIZEN VICE-PRESIDENT: As soon as the insidious and treacherous hand of the southern planters put an end to the existence of the illustrious republican, LINCOLN, a sentiment of horror and indignation seized our minds, a sentiment that springs from the bottom of the hearts of the freemen of Old Europe, and, mingling with that of our brothers of Young America, fills all tyrants with fear and dread.

    The happy termination of your war—the first in the world from the greatness of the cause you were defending—was not enough to extinguish the malevolent and cruel instincts of the unworthy merchants of human flesh, in presence of the sacred fire of the idea you were sustaining—an idea that fills the minds of modern generations, and is the banner that will lead us on to victory, amid the shouts of justice and liberty.

    Remember, Mr. Vice-President, that Providence has placed the cause of humanity in your hands; that the fulfilment of sacred duties weighs upon your conscience; and do not forget either that, as the emancipation of the slave is a glorious page to be recorded in the history of free nations, and is now welcomed by the world with admiration and enthusiasm, Europe and the world expect that the consequences of the great social revolution, of which you are the representative, will soon be felt.

    Courage, Mr. Vice-President, and remember that if the great nation in whose font still burns the sacred flame of the Revolution has comprehended the greatness of its mission in choosing you to direct its destiny, you have upon your conscience the future of the people that have been intrusted to your care, and not only them, but the oppressed of the whole world. One more step in the way that your great nation has opened, and the cause of humanity and liberty is safe.

    Permit us, however, citizen Vice-President, with the frankness and loyalty of good liberals, to reveal a symptom of pain on remembering the hesitation of the great republic at the beginning of the war, and the excuses after victory was gained. Justice is tarnished by shadows, though they be cast by convenience; slavery is the negative of manhood; and if at first there was a moment of hesitation, be resolute, quick, and firm at last. Human rights are worth more than riches; let there be no more slaves for a single day, although great but passing calamities might be the result.

Receive our most loyal congratulations upon the triumph you have gained, and in it you will find a tear of each one of the workers who wish you well; deposit it in the tomb that covers the remains of the immortal LINCOLN.

> MANUEL MAYOL.
> MIGUEL PARADOS.
> CARLOS REISLE.
> RAMON DE CALA.
> JOSÉ HUERTAS.
> PEDRO SCHMIDT.
> SIMON CARO.

Mr. Perry to Mr. Seward.

[Extract.]

No. 193.] LEGATION OF THE UNITED STATES,
Madrid, April 29, 1865.

SIR: Thank God, we are permitted still to address you. A telegram from Queenstown informs me at this moment "that Mr. Seward and his son are likely to recover."

It is a relief from the suspense which has kept my hand bound since the evening of the 26th, when Mr. Adams's telegram informed me of the tragedy in Washington.

Pray accept for yourself, dear sir, the expression of my horror and my grief at the foul crime of which you have been the victim; and say also to the Assistant Secretary of State that I associate myself with him in sympathy for all his sufferings.

The death of President LINCOLN by the hand of an assassin at the moment when the great work with which his name is indissolubly connected for all time touched the term of success when the greatest insurrection known in history, striking for human slavery and at the life of the republic, succumbs at last to the valor of our democratic armies, and the persistent virtue of our people, led by the President of their own choice twice elected, and set up before friends and foes as their executive. The death of this Chief Magistrate, elevated by force of great events to a place in history not less than that of every other human name which the annals of the race record, and filling that broad place worthily, occurring at such a moment and in such a way, has sent a shock of horror through Europe.

The Spanish people have been thunderstruck. I have heard ordinary men, ignorant that an American was listening, offer to lose a right hand if only this news might not be true. Men were rushing into this office until one o'clock at night, unwilling to believe, unable to control the emotion this news had stirred, and an unfeigned grief got the better of all form and etiquette in the manifestation of the sympathy of this generous-hearted people for the loss of President Lincoln.

Your name, sir, was also on every lip; but men hoped against hope, and God has permitted this yearning of the universal heart of men to plead for you.

I felt it would be so; I cannot tell you how or why, but in spite of the desolating sweep of the first telegrams, something stirred within me with the consciousness that Mr. Seward still lived and would live. Heavy as the pall of grief closed over the loss of Lincoln, we have refused to mourn for you, and now we know that your work was not yet finished.

How should it be, if it is now, precisely when the military triumph is gained, and the political and diplomatic questions generated by the war are up for settlement, that the sage counsel, the long-experienced and the steady hand of William H. Seward is needed in America and relied upon in Europe?

We mourn for our President. But after all let an American speak, for whom the 3,000 miles of distance which separate him from the turmoil and distraction of that scene serve, perhaps something as the lapse of time will serve to his countrymen at home, to enable him to see events in their general form and purport as they will stand in history.

The triumph of the American democracy in saving the second great republic attacked by a slaveholding oligarchy stands parallel in the world's record with the triumph of the Roman democracy when they destroyed the first great republic, attacking that slaveholding oligarchy.

Abraham Lincoln and Julius Cæsar are names which henceforth personify the throes of men for liberty in two supreme epochs of history, which can be compared only the one with the other. An emperor was the result of the efforts of the Roman democracy, as it has since been of other people.

A citizen President, equally triumphant over the slaveholding patrician element, but himself obedient to law, is the result of our people's virtue and his own. The singular parity of incident which closed the career of these two men, when the triumph was assured, will grave eternally on the memory of the generations the contrast of the result established, the immense advance of humanity since Cæsar fell.

God's instrument in a work which makes his name immortal, Lincoln died at a glorious moment; success was assured, and if he had been ambitious he could not have chosen another death. His work was done! We call out for his tenacity in doing right, his steady honesty in executing justice tempered with mercy; but these are qualities of our northern people, and he was great only as he typified these. The people remain, and I doubt not will find their representative.

Meantime, what do we know of the divine purposes to be served by this crowning crime, which sets the everlasting seal on the forehead of this rebellion?

What is the position to-day of those men who rose against the republic for the perpetuation of human slavery?

Speaking from Europe, I may say: already that assassin blow has done more to finish up the sympathies of men for the defenders of slavery and oligarchy than all that has happened before or since the war began. Though the military power of the rebels is broken, men still paid their tribute of respect to the valor of their soldiery, the skill of their generals, and the political decision of their leaders; and these sentiments have great sway over the minds of men, and impede them from discerning the deformity of the principles for which those armies and those leaders fought.

But the night of April 14, 1865, has dispelled forever the mistaken sympathies which the audacity of April 13, 1861, generated, and has left the enemies of human progress naked before the world, with only such moral support henceforth as those decidedly of their own kind can give them.

This in Europe. I ought to forbear from speculating upon its effects in America, but I will say that I do not suppose the men who have made their names illustrious in a bad cause had any personal connection with a deed so foul; their errors have not clouded the moral faculties of the leaders of the rebellion to such an extent as this, nor are the southern people generally to be charged with immediate complicity in this infamy.

It is precisely because I do not believe this that I wait to see a reaction in the South itself against the cause which can prepare such instruments, and give rise, even incidentally, to such a deed. God's hand shall work in the hearts of the South itself through the martyrdom of LINCOLN and the steadfast magnanimity of that great people whose principles he represented, and which I do not look to see belied even under this last provocation. Thus I do not doubt the moral death of the rebellion in the South itself will date from the day LINCOLN was murdered. And I shall be greatly mistaken if the political work of pacification and reconstruction of the great democratic republic, homogeneous and united as never before, shall not be found to be notably facilitated by the very events which might seem at first to disturb its course. Such is my faith; pardon its expression.

I have not waited instructions to order mourning in this legation, and recommend the same in all our consulates in this jurisdiction for thirty days.

*   *   *   *   *   *   *   *

The popular newspapers appeared in mourning yesterday. The members of the foreign diplomatic corps and many eminent men have called to express their sympathy.

No manifestation has yet been received from the Queen's government, nor the Chambers now in session.

The interior condition of affairs in Spain is at a point so critical that hardly anything else can be expected to be thought of by this government.

The minister of state is ill, and retires from Madrid. His substitute *ad interim*, the minister of grace and justice, is also ill and confined to his chamber.

Once more, sir, I grasp your hand in respectful sympathy.

Your obedient servant,

HORATIO J. PERRY.

Hon. WILLIAM H. SEWARD,
　Secretary of State, Washington.

Mr. Perry to Mr. Seward.

No. 194.]　　　　　　　　LEGATION OF THE UNITED STATES,
　　　　　　　　　　　　　　Madrid, May 1, 1865.

SIR: After my despatch No. 193 was written, on the 29th ultimo, I received an official visit from the Duke of Valencia, president of the cabinet of ministers, attended by his aids, who came to say to me, in the name and by special order of the Queen, how great was the horror and the grief with which her Majesty had learned the news of the assassination of President LINCOLN, and her Majesty begged me to be pleased to make known to President Johnson her profound and sincere sympathy with him and the American nation for the loss we had sustained in the person of our late most worthy and illustrious President.

I thanked the duke, and begged him to convey provisionally to her Majesty the expression of my own gratitude for her Majesty's warm manifestation of sympathy in the grief of my government and nation, which I would not fail to transmit immediately to Washington.

Yesterday I received the official note from the minister of state *ad interim*, Sr. Arrazola, dated on the 27th instant, and which the Duke of Valencia had also announced, in his visit on the 29th instant, was being prepared to be sent to me. Sr. Arrazola is ill and confined to his chamber, and Sr. Banuelos, assistant secretary of state, informed me this was the only paper he had signed for a number of days past.

The duke also informed me that Mr. Tassara, Spanish minister at Washington, would be instructed to make a similar manifestation to you personally in Washington.

To-day the congress of deputies, now in session, has also taken action upon the same subject. The Deputy Lasala, of the opposition, inquired of the government if anything had been done to manifest the sentiment of this nation at the horrible events in Washington.

The Duke of Valencia, in the name of the government, recited to the Chamber the steps taken by the Queen and by the ministers.

The Deputy Claros, ministerial, also made a remarkable speech, which was saluted by the whole house with marks of applause.

Then the president of the congress, from his chair, said :

" SENORES DEPUTIES : I consider it my privilege as well as duty to interpret on this occasion the sentiments of you all, of the whole congress, and of the nation, declaring that this house associates itself to the profound affliction which has fallen upon the United States, in the horrible crime committed upon the person of the President of that republic, and which has occupied the attention of the house at this moment."

The question being then put, whether the house adheres to the declaration just made by the president, it was voted without a dissenting voice, and, on motion of Deputy Jove y Hevia, it was ordered to be entered on the record with the adhesion of the house by a unanimous vote.

This debate is worthy to be transmitted to you entire, and I shall send it, translated from the official journal of the Chamber, as soon as it can be prepared.

With sentiments of the highest respect, sir, your obedient servant,

HORATIO J. PERRY.

Hon. WILLIAM H. SEWARD,
    Secretary of State, Washington.

[Translation.]

MADRID, *May* 31, 1865.

HONORED SIR : Our personal experience has taught us that true grief is a friend of silence, and we feel that which overwhelms you and us is to be more poignant because we have been silent.

For that reason we have restrained the impulses of our souls till now, and have suppressed the expression of the strong emotions that have agitated our lives. But now that our sincere sorrow has become calm, and reason has resumed her sway, we are going to fulfil a sacred duty—sacred to every generous mind, and most sacred to us because we are young men and Americans.

Sons of the two islands, only separated from you by a narrow sea, strictly connected with the great republic by the interchange of produce and of ideas. whatever relates to her is of interest to us, inasmuch as we have silently sympathized with her in her recent days of glory, and now condole with her in her hour of mourning.

As men we weep for LINCOLN; the perfidy that deprived him of his earthly existence is repugnant to the heart of every man; enemies to that social infamy which, under the name of slavery, is a disgrace to the land of liberty, as it is a reproach to the beloved country of our birth, we felt, with LINCOLN, the holy emotions that he felt when he saw his great task done; we Cubans and Porto-ricans, borne by providential destiny towards the future of America, shuddered with the last convulsion of the great man; we spirits, lovers of goodness and of liberty, which is its political expression, would have lamented the eternal absence of that strong mind that gave us the consolation of seeing liberty guaranteed, at least in the land he made greater by his greatness, if we did not know that death kills the body and not the soul; that LINCOLN's body was killed, but his spirit was the soul of the giant nation that he knew how to govern.

After Washington there came other Washingtons; after LINCOLN there will come, there has already come, another Lincoln. This hope, this assurance, calms our grief, and it is scarcely a condolence that we send you, but a prayer that you may be worthy of America.

> NARCISO URDANEBIO.
> JOSÉ FERNANDEZ.
> TRISTAN MEDINA.
> CALISTO R. LOIRA.
> FEDERICO FERNANDEZ DE LA REGUERA.
> ANTONIO GONZALES Y HERRERA.
> RAMON P. TRUJILLO.
> ALBERTO ABRISQUETA Y EBRENTZ.
> FRANCISCO JAVIER CASERO.
> FRANCO. PUENTO.
> AND TWENTY-THREE OTHER NAMES.

His Excellency ANDREW JOHNSON,
> *President of the United States of America.*

[Translation.]

SINEU, *May* 14, 1865.

To the President of the United States:

The Committee of Progress of the town of Sineu, in Majorca, regarding with the deepest feeling of indignation the horrible crime which the liberator from slavery—the man of high principle, the great patriot, LINCOLN, has been the victim—LINCOLN, the man whose vigorous soul never wavered in view of the terrible trials reserved for his government, and for whom history, gathering the last testimonial of his lofty wisdom, valor, and patriotism, will reserve the highest place among the most illustrious citizens of the earth—sympathizes heartily with you in the deep regret which pervades the great republic of which you are the worthy President; congratulating you at the same time that, if Providence, in its inscrutable designs, has permitted that he should be stricken down in order to finish the immense work of the reorganization of the Union, peace has crowned his colossal efforts, and that from this moment the fratricidal war which, for a time, desolated a country so beautiful and prosperous, may be considered as at an end.

God preserve your valuable life.

> DOMINGO PUNTORT, *President.*
> ANTO. BAVEOLO.
> SEBASTIAN FERRA.
> MIGUEL OLIVEZ.
> PEDRO RAY'DA REAL.
> FRANCISCO GUECAS, *Secretary.*

SWEDEN AND NORWAY.

Count Manderström to Mr. Campbell.

[Translation.]

MY DEAR SIR: It is with the utmost dismay I find in the evening papers a telegram from New York of the 15th instant, to the following purport:

"President LINCOLN has been shot by an assassin. He died to-day. A murderous attempt has been directed against Mr. Seward. His recovery is doubtful."

This news is from Hamburg. I have received nothing to confirm it up to this hour. I hope it is an untrue, or at least exaggerated report; of course I will communicate to you what I receive.

You cannot doubt, my dear sir, the general sentiments of horror and indignation by which this awful news will be received in my country, and I beg to express to you the feelings of my most cordial sympathy.

I remain, my dear sir, with great truth and regard, yours, very truly,

> MANDERSTRÖM.

WEDNESDAY EVENING.

Count Manderström to Mr. Campbell.

[Translation.]

APRIL 27, 1865.

MY DEAR SIR: I hasten to communicate to you the following details, transmitted from London yesterday evening, but which reached me only this morning:

It appears that President LINCOLN was murdered in his box at the theatre; the assassin, whose name is Booth, jumped down from the box on the scene and effectually escaped. He went directly to Baltimore, and was apprehended there. It was an accomplice of Booth who made the attack upon Mr. Seward, in his sick-room, and wounded him dangerously. His son, Mr. Frederick Seward, hastening to help his father, was murdered on the spot.

General Grant was to have been present at the play, but was prevented by official business; this being mentioned, I suppose there was some plan laid against him.

Such a shocking series of atrocious crimes, up to this date never witnessed in your country, cannot fail to impress the minds of all good citizens and make them rally round the banner of order.

I reserve myself to answer officially to your note, but thought it my duty not to lose time in giving you all the details I have received.

I am, my dear sir, your very obedient servant,

MANDERSTRÖM.

Count Manderström to Mr. Campbell.

[Translation.]

STOCKHOLM, *April* 27, 1865.

SIR: I have received the official communication by which you have confirmed this morning the melancholy intelligence, already in circulation yesterday evening, of the odious outrage to which the President of the United States fell a victim on the evening of the 14th of this month.

I have thought it my duty to bring this overwhelming news immediately to the knowledge of my august sovereign, and it is by his express order that I hasten to convey to you, sir, all the horror and profound regret with which it has inspired him. Not only the old and excellent relations which existed between the two governments, but the high esteem and the sincere consideration professed by the King for the noble character and eminent qualities of the illustrious President, who has been torn from a country to the welfare of which he was devoted, by the most atrocious crime, may easily explain the sentiments of just grief and sad sympathy with which the King is penetrated, and the reprobation with which his Majesty stamps a shameful assassination, directed by a parricidal hand against that good man,

The crime is aggravated by the infamous attack made upon the distinguished statesman confined to his bed of suffering, and who, wounded also in his most cherished affections, seems to leave us little hope of seeing him recover from his physical and mental anguish.

The King has charged me to beg you, sir, to testify to your government the sentiments entertained by him, and which, be assured, are shared by the two peoples united under his sceptre.

In giving utterance to the most sincere wishes that this frightful misfortune does not injure the United States of America, the government of the King expresses the hope of continuing with President Johnson the same relations of confidence and amity which have been maintained under the government of the illustrious President whose loss we so bitterly deplore.

In begging you, sir, to accept the expression of my most profound personal regret, I permit myself to add the assurances of my most distinguished consideration. MANDERSTRÖM.

Mr. CAMPBELL,
    Minister resident of the United States of America.

Baron de Wetterstedt to Mr. Hunter.

[Translation.]

LEGATION OF SWEDEN AND NORWAY,
Washington, April 16, 1865.

SIR: The lamentable events of which you did me the honor to inform me by your note of yesterday had already come to my knowledge through the public reports, and filled my heart with feelings of gloom and indignation. His Majesty's government takes too sincere an interest in the welfare of this commonwealth not to learn with profound regret the sudden and violent death of the President of the United States, in a moment when his wisdom and experience were so well needed, and when the turn of events seemed to promise to himself some reward for the trials of the past.

May the lives of those noble victims who have not yet succumbed under the blows of the assassin be spared, by God's mercy, to their country and their sorrow-stricken families.

I thank you for bringing to my notice that the Vice-President of the United States has assumed the functions of President, and that you have been authorized, sir, to perform the duties of Secretary of State until otherwise ordered.

I avail myself of this opportunity to offer to you the assurance of my high consideration.

N. W. DE WETTERSTEDT.

Hon. W. HUNTER,
    Acting Secretary of State, Washington.

[Extract.—Translation.]

NEW YORK, *May* 17, 1865.

DEAR SIR: Allow me to transmit to you, unofficially, a copy of a despatch which I have just received from Count Manderström, his Majesty's minister for foreign affairs, giving account of the deep impression produced on the Swedish government by the news of the horrible murder of the late President, of which despatch I would have taken the liberty to make lecture to you had I been present in Washington. I enclose likewise a copy of the accompanying note from Count Manderström to your minister at Stockholm, for the possible event that you should not yet have received the same from Mr. Campbell. You will easily perceive that these letters were written down on the first incorrect information of the deed transmitted by the telegraph.

The Swedish newspapers that have reached me give ample evidence of the horror and indignation provoked in the whole country by the news of the murder. They are filled with articles speaking in the warmest terms of the event. In no country in Europe, I venture to say—and it has certainly not escaped your attention—has the sympathy for the cause of the Union been more deep and unanimous, and the eminent qualities of the late President been better appreciated than in my native land. Immediately on the receipt of the painful tidings, the flags on the public buildings in Stockholm and Gothemburg and on the vessels in the harbors of these cities were hoisted on half-mast; a public feast which was to take place at Gothemburg in honor of the fall of Richmond was inhibited, as a token of respect for the memory of the lamented victim.

* * * * * * * *

I am, sir, with high consideration, your obedient servant,

N. W. DE WETTERSTEDT.

Hon. W. HUNTER,
    Acting Secretary of State, Washington.

[Translation.]

STOCKHOLM, *April* 27, 1865.

MONSIEUR LE BARON: We are astonished by the horrible news that has just reached us from Washington. A telegram from Hamburg yesterday gave us the intelligence of the attacks on the President and Mr. Seward. I wrote immediately to Mr. Campbell, asking him if the report was confirmed, hoping it might be untrue or exaggerated. A telegram from London that night gave the particulars, with the names of the assassins, and reported the death of Mr. Seward, junior. Early this morning Mr. Campbell showed me a despatch from Mr. Adams, in London, in which the report is officially confirmed. Thereupon I sent the enclosed note to Mr. Campbell, expressing the sentiments of the King and his subjects in regard to the affair.

The odious crime, unheard of till now in the annals of the United States, inspires general horror and evokes universal condemnation, but it is the great and irreparable loss to the country that causes the greatest regret.

Mr. LINCOLN's firm and resolute character, his good common sense, and his associations, acquired general esteem for him in Europe, and I fear it will be hard to find his equal at the time of a crisis like that which prevailed at the moment of his death. And it is still more distressing to the United States to lose at the same time the eminent statesman at the head of its foreign affairs, and whose demise I am sure will be most earnestly felt. We wait impatiently to hear from you, though we cannot hope for an authentic report under a week.

We hear that the murderer Booth has been arrested, but the report is hardly correct, as it comes on the same day with the other rumors.

No words can express the horror felt here at the announcement of the execrable crime.

Accept my regards, &c., &c., &c.

MANDERSTRÖM.

Mr. Campbell to Mr. Seward.

[Extract.]

No. 17.]
LEGATION OF THE UNITED STATES,
Stockholm, April 30, 1865.

SIR: On the evening of the 26th of April a telegram from the embassy of the United States in London was received at this legation, announcing the death, by assassination, of ABRAHAM LINCOLN, President of the United States; also an attack upon the life of the Secretary of State, resulting in injuries so severe as to render his recovery doubtful.

Overwhelmed with horror by these woeful news, which were already in circulation in Stockholm, inspiring grave misgivings and vague fears in the minds of many friends of the republic who but imperfectly understood her organization, I deemed proper on the following morning to announce to the department of state and of foreign affairs of Sweden and Norway the facts of the death of the President of the United States of America, and the installation of his constitutional successor in executive office. At the same time I communicated to Count Manderström the afflicting intelligence of the condition to which you, sir, had been reduced by a murderous attack.

The prompt and sympathetic response of his excellency displays a warmth of emotion unusual in official papers, and is in harmony with the reprobation and horror felt by all classes of Swedish people.

These sentiments have sought expression at this legation in such varied forms as have deeply touched my heart, and caused me to feel that the blow dealt my beloved country by an assassin's hand is resented by all Christendom.

I have the honor to report the direct and marked action of the King, who commissioned the Count Axel Cronheilm, an officer of the royal staff, to visit the legation of the United States with messages of condolence, coupled with the strongest possible terms of detestation for the parricide, and assurances of the admiration entertained by him for the personal character and attributes of our lamented Chief Magistrate. These sentiments of sympathy for a mourning people, and reprobation for the crime by which they have been bereaved, were expressed in such feeling and earnest words as were worthy of the noble heart of his Majesty, and must prove acceptable to the nation in whose behalf they were uttered. It was also the desire of the King that I would convey to him the earliest intelligence of your health, sir, as his Majesty felt the deepest interest in the preservation of a life so eminent and valuable.

In addition to the official communication from the department of state of Sweden and Norway, that most excellent gentleman, Count Manderström, in a personal visit and private notes, evinced such feelings as commands my gratitude.

In some of the ports the flags were at half-mast for the death of the President; the public journals spoke with appreciation of his life and death; while one paper, in the deepest mourning, contained an article very acceptable to the American heart. The Swedish court has worn mourning for several members of royal houses in Europe during the past winter, but in no instance have I observed a popular tribute comparable with this. The members of the diplomatic corps in Stockholm have been instant in their tokens of sympathy, and the American residents here have sought at the legation such comfort and information as might soothe their grief and allay their fears. The Baron Feysack and Lieutenant Anderson, gallant officers of Sweden, whose swords have been drawn in the service of the United States, came to offer their condolences to the country they had defended, as did also the Count Piper, formerly minister resident at Washington, and other distinguished Swedes. If the transmission of these details appear unnecessary, I find my excuse in the conviction that such tokens of sympathy in a remote land for their national grief must be as acceptable to the American people as they have been to their representatives.

I may be suffered here to give utterance to my own emotions upon the dire calamity which has visited my country. The hand raised against the life of the President has inflicted a grievous wound upon every American heart; and in common with millions bereaved of their chief, I deeply feel the outrage perpetrated upon sacred national rights. With regard to ABRAHAM LINCOLN, whom I knew, and loved as a personal friend, I recognize with awe that God's instrument has been laid away in heaven's armory. Remembering how, in the raging of political tornadoes, he bore himself with the passionless calm of some grand abstraction, and, divested of prejudice or favor, devoted himself to the large ends of human freedom and national life, I feel that his death was the seal to the deeds of his life, and he closed his eyes on great purposes achieved to open them upon the immortal crown. To his country he leaves the rich legacy of a beneficent government preserved; the American idea of liberty attained; and the noble record of the Christian life he lived, the patriot's end he wrought, and the martyr's death he died, to embellish her story.

Allow me to tender you, sir, my respectful sympathy for the mental and physical suffering you have sustained, and express most fervid thanksgiving to God, who in His mercy has spared a life so valuable to our country.

Praying for your speedy restoration to health, and usefulness,

I have the honor to be your obedient servant,

JAMES H. CAMPBELL.

Hon. WILLIAM H. SEWARD,
Secretary of State, &c., &c., &c.

Letter of Fredrika Bremer.

[Translation.]

THURSDAY, *April* 27, 1865.

DEAR * * *: Can it be true, what a telegram from New York reported last night? Mr. LINCOLN murdered! dead! I hope it is not true; I cannot, will not believe it. Can you tell me how it is? If it should be so it is not for him or the cause I grieve. His work is done, the cause is gained, the war at an end, but woe to the South! It has killed its best protector during this awful moment. Oh, if Mr. Campbell and you could tell me that it is not true.

Yours, faithfully,

FR. BREMER.

[Translation from a Stockholm paper of April 27, 1865.]

ABRAHAM LINCOLN.

During the whole time civil war was raging in the United States we had been accustomed to receive information of the most varied and changeable description. It was seldom the friends of liberty here received any good tidings without having them followed by others most painful in their character; but surely, after the last week's glorious bulletins, bringing news of victory upon victory, nobody expected to receive a message so painful and full of grief as the telegram brought us last evening. In the moment of his triumph, when the rebellion was nearly crushed and everybody again was thinking sincerely of the regeneration of the Union, ABRAHAM LINCOLN was struck by the assassin's bullet—he to whom, during the war, the whole world was looking up as the true symbol of that great idea, the abolition of slavery, the established fact of universal freedom, and that free labor is honorable; he should be sacrificed when these sublime thoughts were almost realized. It is a beautiful death; the martyr's wreath of freedom has to engrave on its leaves the name of a new victim for its holy cause, and LINCOLN will be forever surrounded by an imperishable glory of honor. But the victim has, in this instance, as has happened many times before, when the blood of heroes for liberty was spilt, fallen by the assassin's hand, which will brand with eternal infamy all those protectors of slavery who, rising under the plea of defending the rights of the single state, properly only fought for the preservation of their feodal institutions, thereby being able to live by the sweat of the brow of slavery. It may seem hard and strange to throw the blame on those persons before knowing something more particular about this most painful event; but it has too much of probability in itself not to suppose at once that the whole plan had its origin from that very source.

We remember still quite distinctly how LINCOLN, on his way to Washington to be inaugurated as President of the United States on the 4th of March, 1861, was compelled against his own will, but by the pressing entreaties of all his friends, to make his journey through Maryland on by-roads and during the darkness of night to avoid these protectors of slavery who there laid in ambuscade for him. Already then did those wretches aspire after his life, believing in their shortsightedness that their cause could be saved by the death of one of their fellow-beings. Rumors have afterwards been busy about conspiracy against his life. No one would believe it at the time; but now, when we have seen that the parties never tired before they gained the end they sought for, it looks very probable. Yes; they have gained it, but their cause shall not gain anything by it A party which uses such miserable means has pronounced its own sentence, and even their friends in Europe must surely take part in the general outcry of indignation which now sounds through the whole civilized world, and perhaps be compelled to turn their backs on their cause, if they do not desire to be counted as accomplices in the deed. In the North this outcry will have serious consequences for those who have been the cause of it. Immediately after the last great victory of Grant, several of the most prominent men, and almost all the principal papers in the United States, advised LINCOLN and his cabinet to issue a general amnesty for the rebels, only on the condition that the seceded States should submit and again join the Union. Slavery was already considered abolished. Does any one now believe that the same spirit of reconciliation will exist? Does any one doubt that this crime will not cry out for vengeance? If so, we must acknowledge we have been entirely mistaken in the Yankees. The original good-natured humor in these men makes it very easy for them to offer the hand of reconciliation, knowing themselves to be the victors. But should their passions be roused once more before they hardly have had time to be calmed, they will, of course, be furious against all who stand behind this infamous deed and are its nearest accomplices. We observed already, a few days ago, that this war, as far as the North is concerned, does not show a single death-sentence for political offences, which, at least, if we make any comparison with what we have been used to see under similar circumstances in our old Europe, will grant them an everlasting honor. The war has been one of the most spirited and hottest-fought party wars, and in the north treachery has often raised its head so high that the most severe punishment could with justice have been applied. Shall we still be so fortunate as to see that same moderation continued? We do wish it for the sake of liberty; but who would dare to reproach those republicans now, if at the height of this excitement they should exercise retaliation? What we at least now are sure in saying is, that peace now will cost the southern States a great deal more than otherwise would have been the case. (Here follows a sketch of Mr. LINCOLN's life.)

To write the history of ABRAHAM LINCOLN during the time he was President, even as brief as possible, would be the same as to write the history of the Union during the whole important period from 1860 to 1865, when the future of the republic was in the balance. Room for that is not in a short sketch like this, and the time to do it in with impartiality will not be reached for many years. Many have reproached LINCOLN for irresolution as a statesman, and accused him of being without determination to meet the issue of the day. This is said more specially with regard to his position on the slavery question when the rebellion first commenced. Nothing was more natural than an accusation of this kind upon a time when the different political parties were arraigned against each other in fierce combat; but the future will give him credit for his strength and determination—that, surrounded as he was by that turmoil of wild passions, he was yet able to control himself and preserve that firmness of purpose which the leader of the destinies of a great people so much needs, but which we do not always find in them.

He often resisted the impetuous patience of his own party, which, without consideration or forethought, declared slavery abolished without paying the slightest attention to the words of the Constitution. Being cognizant of that fact, he tried in the beginning a conciliatory mode, and would accede to the rebellious States the right to govern themselves. He appointed afterwards a certain time at the expiration of which they had to submit or to lose their privileges. He also procured a consent of Congress to recompense those States who by their own consent abolished slavery, and to give them a limited compensation for their "living" property. First, when every effort failed, and not only a party, but the whole people of the North—of course we do not include that party called "peace democrats"—had arrived at the conclusion that nothing could be done in that way; first then took ABRAHAM LINCOLN the reins in his own hands and procured the consent of Congress to abolish slavery unconditionally. If we can judge from his actions and by their effects, does it not seem as if it had been his plan from the beginning to make that the opinion of the whole people which had hitherto only been the opinion of a few, and under these circumstances can he not with justice be called a far-seeing statesman? He was, besides all this, the type of the so-called Yankee people, of that pure northern Anglo-Saxon race, persevering and determined to obtain the object he had in view. In this way he had gradually become a man of the people, who knew how to select the very moment when to speak, and also to choose the best practical way fit for the occasion. He was a good citizen, and to every American and to every friend of the progress of liberty his name will through centuries shine beside that of Washington. Peace to his ashes, and may they bring forth blessed fruit to the cause of everything that is good. The telegram informs us that the assassins have not been contented with one victim. Grant seems only to have an accident to thank for the preservation of his life, and the Secretary of State, Mr. Seward—the right hand of the President—though on his sick-bed at the time, was not spared by the hands of the murderer. His fate is not decided, but his brave son has fallen, trying to defend the life of a father.

SAXE-MEININGEN.

[Translation.]

Most Honorable Mr. Consul: His Highness the Duke, my most gracious liege, has received with pain the news of the great loss which the United States of North America have suffered by the death of President Abraham Lincoln.

Sincerely admiring the noble qualities of his heart and intellect, and the greatness of mind with which he achieved the grand object of restoring the Union, his Highness has been most deeply moved by the atrocious crime to which the illustrious representative of the United States has been sacrificed, and the Duke cannot omit to express his most mournful sympathy, and through me to request your honor to convey to the government of the United States these expressions of his sentiments; expressing at the same time the wish of the Duke, that the peril in which the life of Mr. Secretary Seward has been pending may, by the favorable improvement of his condition, be considered as passed, and that he may very soon be restored to health.

I embrace the occasion to express, &c., &c.

VON UTTENHOVEN,
Provisional President of the Ducal Council of State.

S. Hirshbach,
United States Consul, Sonneberg.

SWITZERLAND.

[Translation.]

BERNE, *April* 28, 1865.

The Federal Council have been apprised by the public papers of the horrible crime, the victims of which are two of the most worthy and most noble citizens and statesmen of the United States.

One cry of horror and indignation at this act, inspired by the most brutal passion and the most heinous fanaticism, has resounded through the whole civilized world, and particularly through Switzerland, a country whose analogous institutions unite it so closely with its great sister republic.

The Federal Council hasten to address their most sincere condolence to the honorable minister resident of the United States in Switzerland, by expressing to him their profound grief over this shocking event and the strong sympathy which they feel at this great calamity.

Free Switzerland, with similar institutions, will not cease to devote all her sympathies to free America and to her tendencies inspired by truth and humanity—sympathies deriving new strength from this catastrophe.

The Federal Council cannot conclude without expressing the consoling hope that the new Union, reconstituted under the auspices of fraternity and reconciliation, will follow with increased energy the path which Providence has traced out for her, and erect before the eyes of the world the most sublime monument to the glory of the illustrious victim.

With these sentiments the Federal Council have the honor to renew to Mr. Fogg the assurances of their high consideration.

In the name of the Federal Council:

SCHENK,
President of the Confederation.
SCHIESS,
Chancellor of the Confederation.

[Translation.]

No. 57.]

The Swiss Federal Council to the Swiss Consulate General in Washington.

MR. CONSUL GENERAL: Through the public journals the but too certain intelligence reaches us of the terrible deed which deprives the Union of two of her noblest and purest citizens and statesmen.

A thrill of horror and deep indignation over this consummation of infuriated passion and fanaticism pervades the entire civilized world, and more particularly

Switzerland, considering herself united by the most cordial and nearest ties to her great sister republic.

We invite you, therefore, to express to the present President of the United States, in the name of the Swiss Federal Council, our most sincere and heartfelt condolence. You will please assure the President of the renewed and sincere sympathies which free Switzerland, with kindred institutions, entertains for the efforts of the American government in the cause of truth and humanity. These sympathies have received new impulse by the last terrible calamity which has befallen the people of the United States.

You will, finally, not fail to express our sincere hope that the American Union, reunited in love and conciliation, now mightier than ever, will, with renewed energy, strive to accomplish the great destiny which Providence has assigned her, and thus present to the world herself as the grandest monument reared in commemoration of the great dead.

Accept the assurances of our distinguished consideration, in the name of the Swiss Federal Council.

> SCHENK, *President.*
> SCHIESS,
> *Chancellor of the Confederation.*

Mr. Hitz to Mr. Seward.

CONSULATE GENERAL OF SWITZERLAND,
Washington, April 15, 1865.

SIR: The national calamity which has just befallen the United States is, in all its bearings, one of such stupendous magnitude that Switzerland, in the person of her representatives, stands appalled at the enormity of the deed which deprived a republic of a Chief Magistrate who not only was first in establishing universal freedom throughout the land, foremost in offering the hand of conciliation to a misguided enemy of traitors, devotedly beloved by his countrymen, but was also respected abroad, and looked up to with confidence in every clime where freemen draw breath. When, therefore, the representative of the time-honored republic of Switzerland expresses, in her behalf, sincere sympathy for the irreparable loss sustained, just in an hour of triumph, by her great sister republic the United States, I pray it may be accepted as the heartfelt emotion of a national heart which has ever beat in unison with that of the United States, and with those great principles of free government whereof his excellency, your late esteemed President, ABRAHAM LINCOLN, appeared to be the embodiment.

Switzerland joins in the universal bereavement of freemen, and while tendering her humble offering of sympathy at the shrine of an afflicted nation, seeks to convey consolation in the assurance given, that "He whom the Lord loveth he chasteneth;" wherefore these trials which Almighty God has, in the province of divine wisdom, seen proper to visit upon a free people are but an evidence of His love, and, it is prayed, harbingers of blessings evermore.

And now, sir, with feelings of inmost sympathy for your own personal and family afflictions, and gratitude to the Lord for the preservation of your invaluable life and services to a mighty yet sorely stricken nation in a most momentous epoch of its history,

I remain, with sentiments sincere, though unspoken,

JOHN HITZ,
The Consul General of Switzerland.

Hon. WILLIAM H. SEWARD,
Secretary of State.

[Translation.]

To the Editor of the Bund, in Berne:

The Mutual Aid Society of the north part of the Canton of Aargau, at a meeting held on the 21st instant, (seventy-six members being present,) unanimously resolved to approve of the address of sympathy and condolence of the Swiss Confederation to the North American sister republic beyond the ocean.

While making this communication, we ask you to accept the sincere expression of our high esteem.

FERD. AFFOLSTER, *President.*

N. DINKELMANN, *Secretary.*

[Translation.]

Council of the Canton of Uri to the Bundesrath, in Berne.

ALTORF, *May* 8, 1865.

GENTLEMEN: Willingly following the example of other cantons, we have the honor to inform you that in our session of this day we have unanimously resolved to assent to the general address of sympathy and condolence of the Swiss Confederation to the North American Union, on account of the assassination of its excellent President, ABRAHAM LINCOLN. We have no doubt but this sympathy is universal, and we send you this declaration that you may take due notice of it and forward it to its place of destination. In the mean time, we give our best wishes for your prosperity, and recommend you to the protection of Divine Providence.

In the name of the council:

K. E. MULLER, *President.*

GISLER, *Secretary.*

[Translation.]

AARAU, *April* 28, 1865.

HONORED SIR: The government counsellor of the canton of Aargau has just heard of the great misfortune that has overtaken our sister republic beyond the ocean, on the 14th of April, by the hand of the assassin, and feels the greatest sympathy and indignation the event can impart. The general sorrow is the more intense, as it fell like a thunderbolt upon the joy and hope with which the civilized world was congratulating the victorious star-spangled banner upon the heroic days of Richmond and Petersburg. We have therefore unanimously resolved, in our session of this day, to express our deepest sympathy for the government of the United States, upon the horrid death of their great President LINCOLN, and we request the honorable minister resident of that country to communicate it to his government.

May God preserve the United States, bestow more great and unblemished victories upon their flag in contests for freedom and the holy rights of man, and soon crown the sublime sacrifice and heroic deeds of their arms with all the blessings of a glorious peace.

Accept, dear sir, with the above sympathy, the expression of our most distinguished consideration.

In the name of the government counsellor of the canton of Aargau:

The Landammann President,
A. TELLER.
The Secretary of State,
KINGIER.

Hon. Mr. FOGG,
Minister Resident of the United States of North America, in Berne.

[Translation.]

AARAU, *April* 28, 1865.

DEAR SIR: It is my desire to contribute to the great address of sympathy to the American nation, and I therefore request you to add the enclosed sheet to it. Be kind enough also to have a copy of it sent to the federal committee in Berne, and oblige your very humble servant,

Professor DR. TROXLER.

The undersigned, as a free citizen of a free country, considers himself supremely happy in having this opportunity to express his grateful feelings for a country that has at last succeeded in the emancipation of all its people of every race and color. So many years have passed since we had the struggle for our liberties that we have almost forgotten our troubles at that time, and our reasons for contentment would not be appreciated now were it not for the existence of some oppressed and suffering people in Europe not very far from our own borders, on either side of us.

The people of the United States of North America can now congratulate themselves that they are one, that all cause of dissension is removed, and that they have no Russia or Austria near them to disturb their peace. Let all animosities be buried; let the people of the same flesh and blood, though dwelling in different sections of the land, forget that they were ever mortal enemies, and all may yet be well. They have the Bible and religion among them, and let them rejoice that it is so. Religion and morality are the indispensable props of public welfare. Let them cultivate these and do unto their neighbors as they would be done by, and they will never come to harm.

TROXLER.

AARMADT, *April* 28, 1865.

[Translation.]

Chief justice and council of the canton of Appenzell, of the Inner Rhodes, to Dr. John Wyttenbach, of the grand council in Berne.

APPENZELL, *May* 5, 1865.

SIR: In a letter of the 1st instant, the committee for the address of sympathy and condolence to the American Union invited us to participate with him in it, as many of the Swiss cantons have already done.

The sympathy of the people of the Inner Rhodes for the Americans in their four years of civil war for freedom and Union, and their sorrow for the sad misfortune of the death of President LINCOLN, the noblest citizen of that glorious land, induce us, in the name of the inhabitants of our canton, to join in the address to our fellow-citizens of that bereaved country.

With great respect, in the name of the chief justice and council,

BROGER, *Justice.*

SONDEREGGER, *Secretary.*

[Translation.]

ARWANGEN, *April* 30, 1865.

To the Editor of the Bund, in Berne:

I hereby empower and request you to add my name as a signer to the general address of sympathy and condolence from the Swiss Confederation to the government in Washington. You will also have the kindness to communicate the following resolution of a public meeting held in this place yesterday on the same occasion.

With much regard,

DR. FRIEDRICH CAMPE.

THE RESOLUTION.

The citizens of Arwangen rejoice at the great victories of the North, while they sincerely deplore the loss of the great man who perished by the assassin's hand. They assembled to the number of three hundred and two, and unanimously give this expression of their feelings, hoping the document may be conveyed to its proper destination.

In the name of the meeting, the special committee :

J. H. EGGER, *President.*

J. MORGENTHALER, *Secretary.*

S. L. ERNST, *Treasurer.*

Hundreds of signatures might have been obtained in this neighborhood for the address, had our time not been so limited.

[Translation.]

AARMUHLE, May 27, 1865.

Mr. PRESIDENT : At a public meeting of the citizens of Aarmuhle, district of Interlachen, it was unanimously resolved to ratify the Swiss address of gratulation and sympathy to the people of the North American Union.

Respectfully,

M. WYDER, *President.*

P. VORTER, *Secretary.*

The Hon. BUNDESRATH
of the Swiss Confederation in Berne.

[Translation.]

AARBERG, June 2, 1865.

To the Bund, in Berne :

The teachers in the district of Aarberg have watched the events of the American war with much interest, and were exceedingly rejoiced when the news of Union victories resounded in our land. As our joy was profound, so was our grief, when, a few days later, news saddened us with the sombre fact that the great republican citizen, LINCOLN, had fallen by the hand of an assassin.

Thirty members of the district synod of Aarberg, in their session of the 29th of May, unanimously resolved to approve of the address of sympathy and condolence to the American Union.

Requesting you to give notice of this fact, we remain, &c.,

MATTI, Secretary.

Mr. Fogg to Mr. Hunter.

No. 87.]
UNITED STATES LEGATION,
Berne, May 3, 1865.

SIR: Your despatch of April 17, apprising me of the assassination of President LINCOLN, is just received. The shocking intelligence had already been flashed by telegraph all over Europe, several days earlier, as had also the scarcely less astounding news of the probable fatal attempt upon the lives of Secretary and Assistant Secretary Seward.

No words can convey any sort of idea of the excitement produced among all classes, rulers and people, on this side of the Atlantic. At first no one was willing to believe it. The news was too terrible for belief. But soon a despatch from Mr. Adams in London put an end to all doubts. The deed, terrible as it was, had been done, and the "foremost man of all the world" in the hearts of millions on both sides of the Atlantic lay stretched in death by the dastardly hand of an assassin.

The millions in America who loved Mr. LINCOLN as a father and revered him as the purest and greatest of patriotic statesmen, could scarcely have mourned him more profoundly than did the masses in Europe. Especially dear was he to the citizens of this little republic of Switzerland, where, from the beginning of our great struggle, his firm, true hand has ever been upheld by the warm sympathies and prayers of a free and gallant people, who had themselves not long since been called to strangle a somewhat similar though far less iniquitous and sanguinary conspiracy against their nation's life.

You will have seen how all Europe is moved. I am able to do nothing but receive visits and letters of condolence from citizens, foreign ministers, and members of the government. These last—some of them at least—I will send you with my next despatch.

Of my own personal grief over this great calamity this is, perhaps, not the place to speak, but I cannot forbear. Few men, out of his own family and neighborhood, were so circumstanced as to know Mr. LINCOLN better than myself, up to the time of my leaving for my present post. He was kind to me, and I loved him as a father. I mourn him now as my dearest earthly friend.

I pray God that the blow of the assassin may not have proved fatal to Mr. Seward and his son.

Asking you to express to them, if living, my most profound and heartfelt sympathy in their and our country's great suffering, I have the honor to be your obedient servant,

GEORGE G. FOGG.

Hon. W. HUNTER,
Acting Secretary of State of the United States of America.

Mr. Fogg to Mr. Hunter.

[Extract.]

No. 88.]   UNITED STATES LEGATION,
                                                Berne, May 4, 1865.

SIR: *   *   *   *   Letters of condolence are being prepared and forwarded to me from nearly all the cantonal governments and from
the citizens of every portion of Switzerland.   The mourning and regret for the
death of our President are universal from the old men to the boys in the schools.
I am convinced that no other man in any part of the world held such a place
in so many millions of hearts.

Later I will forward to the State Department copies of the originals of
the addresses now coming into the legations from the cantons, cities, and communes, near and remote, of Swizerland.

I herewith append also a copy of my note to the Federal Council in
acknowledgment of theirs.

With the highest respect, your obedient servant,
                                            GEORGE G. FOGG.

Hon. WILLIAM HUNTER,
        Acting Secretary of State of the United States of America.

Mr. Fogg to Mr. Seward.

No. 93.]   UNITED STATES LEGATION,
                                                Berne, June 20, 1865.

SIR: I have the honor to forward herewith to the State Department, by
the hand of Henry A. Smythe, esquire, of New York, appointed bearer of
despatches to Washington, two bound volumes* containing over 300 original
addresses of congratulation, sympathy, and condolence from the various cantonal
governments, municipalities, communes, associations, schools, and leading citizens of Switzerland, expressive of the universal joy occasioned by the triumphant suppression of the rebellion in the United States, the destruction of
slavery, and the re-establishment of the American Union, and of the quite as
universal sorrow over the assassination of the late President LINCOLN, the events
of whose life, and the moment and manner of whose death, will enshrine him
in the pantheon of history as the most illustrious character of modern times.

The volumes contain official addresses from the governments of twenty-
one cantons, (all save one, Fribourg,) something more than 20,000 original

---

* The addresses referred to in this despatch are published in an alphabetical arrangement
based upon the names of the towns from which they emanated.

autographs, comprising all the members of the Federal Council, members of the cantonal governments, magistrates, clergymen, and military officers. In truth, they comprise the aggregate and congregate voice of all Switzerland, whose heart, hopes, and prayers have been with our government in all the long, bloody, and sometimes apparently doubtful struggle through which we have passed.

As these various addresses have been sent or brought to me by delegations or committees, I have been obliged to make many brief speeches and write many letters, returning thanks, in behalf of the government and people of the United States, for a sympathy as sincere and deep as it was universal.

Trusting that these addresses and memorials will be sacredly preserved in the archives of the State Department, as evidence of the solidarity of sentiments and aspirations between the people of Switzerland and those of the United States.

I have the honor to be your obedient servant,

GEORGE G. FOGG.

Hon. WILLIAM H. SEWARD,
Secretary of State of the United States of America.

[Translation.]

Council of the canton of Berne to the Bundesrath

BERNE, *May* 8, 1865.

GENTLEMEN: We respectfully request you on our part, by diplomatic means, to communicate to the government of the United States of North America our congratulations on the recent Union victories, together with the expression of our sympathies for their misfortunes, and our horror at the assassination of President LINCOLN, and the attempt on the life of Secretary Seward.

These Union victories will serve to realize and strengthen the principles of the free republic, will fix its fate, and form the most remarkable epoch in the pages of modern history. For these principles the great citizen and renowned statesman offered himself as a sacrifice, and was immolated as a martyr!

But we are firmly persuaded that the cowardly assassination of its great leader will not impede the progress of the republic in the way of liberty, virtue, and intelligence, and his successor may be urged on to complete the task begun in the good cause by his predecessor.

Accept the assurance of our distinguished consideration.

F. SCHERZ, *President.*

DR. TRÄCHSEL, *Secretary.*

[Translation.]

To the honorable George G. Fogg, Minister Resident of the United States, Berne:

To the hands of his Excellency ANDREW JOHNSON,
President of the United States, at Washington:

BERNE, *May* 12, 1865.

The undersigned has the honor herewith to transmit to you the address of sympathy and condolence to the American Union voted by a meeting of Swiss citizens at Berne, and accompanied by the declarations of accession sent in from all parts of the whole Swiss Confederation.

It required but the slight impulsion of this address to arouse in Switzerland a lively and most universal movement of sympathy for the American sister republic. After the members of the high Federal Council and of the grand council of the canton of Berne had opened the list of signatures, the governments of Argovy and Soleure gave the signal for the accession also of the cantonal governments, most of whom have, upon the immediate invitation of the address committee, not hesitated to comply either by letters to the Federal Council, or by direct individual signature, and in the names of their cantons.

In Geneva a meeting of 4,000, and in Chaux-de-fond one of 2,000 persons was held in order to vote a separate address. The grand councils of Vaud and Picino also have voted separate manifestations of sympathy. Besides a number of the most prominent citizens of the country, a great many communal authorities and private citizens, particularly from the cantons of Berne, Basle-Town, Neufchatel, Aargan, Zurich, (town of Winterthur,) Fribourg, (town of Murten,) Basle, Campagne, &c., have acceded to our address. The aggregate number of signatures, which at this moment cannot be given quite accurately, may be estimated for the accompanying address alone at about 10,000, if the number can add anything to the value of the testimonials of sympathy from all classes and professions, authorities, and private individuals.

The greatest act of sympathy, however, was the resolution of the Landsgememde of Glaris, an assembly of from 5,000 to 6,000 voters of a Swiss canton of 30,000 inhabitants, who in the open air make the laws of their country, and of which occasion they availed themselves, at the suggestion of their Landammann, unanimously to rise, and with uncovered heads to manifest their sympathy with the American Union.

· In accordance with this manifestation, the government of another democratic canton, namely, Grisons, has submitted the question of a demonstration of sympathy and condolence by the people of Grisons, to all the thirty-nine district assemblies, which in that canton are equal to the Landsgememde; and there is no doubt that on Sunday, the 14th May, the voters of a canton of 90,000 inhabitants will also unanimously proclaim their sympathy for the United States.

In view of these tokens it may well be asserted that it is the whole Swiss people who, in this moment, offer to the American people their greeting of brotherly sentiment. Our sole wish is, that it may be received in the same spirit by the citizens of the American Union.

With the highest consideration, in the name of the address committee,

F. GENGEL,

Editor of the Bund.

P. S.—It will hardly be necessary to explain that the term "democracy" in the address is not synonymous with the party denomination in America. The address of condolence also is directed to Mr. Vice-President Johnson, because it was drawn up before his (known) inauguration as President. And in regard finally to the external appearance of the signatures, the apology may be given that though much may be left to be desired, they are not the less sincere.

[Translation.]

To his Excellency ABRAHAM LINCOLN,

President of the United States of America:

HONORED SIR: We, the undersigned citizens of Switzerland, avail ourselves of the occasion of the news of the termination of the American war to congratulate you from the bottom of our hearts upon the reconstruction of the Union.

One hundred years have not yet elapsed since the American nation, by her first war of independence, laid the foundation of her democratic and republican liberty. The fruit of her victory was the winning of a whole continent for the republic, and the proclamation of the great sentiment of human rights, which soon spread itself over all Europe. By the victorious termination of her second war the people of America have also practically restored to life the rights of man, and established by their acts that man shall be neither lord nor slave, but *that all men are born to be free.*

But not only this: while destroying slavery and restoring to the oppressed black race their rights, the American people have also saved the white race. They have destroyed the fundamental elements of a rising aristocracy, which attempted to propagate the principle of oppression upon both sides of the ocean, and which would have substituted privilege for popular self-government, and despotism for democracy. The triumph of the Union has shown that democracy is not a vain idea, but a real truth, and that the *nations also are born to be free.*

Of all the nations of the globe none is more entitled or more qualified to recognize this than the Swiss. Switzerland is the oldest existing republic in the civilized world, and liberty and equality of all her citizens her vital air. Well might the monarchists and aristocrats of Europe, even those professing to be liberal, have doubted the triumph of the North, and even secretly wished its defeat. Free Switzerland was aware that the struggle there going on was for the cause of free labor and of the democratic republic, and that their champion, the North, must finally triumph.

Of all the nations, also, none has more occasion for rejoicing at the triumph of the North. Surrounded from all sides by great monarchies, where liberal ideas are undergoing a doubtful struggle, Switzerland is like an oasis, and without friendly sympathizers in Europe. She is strong enough, it is true, to defend herself, and by her example to encourage others; but she is too weak to guide the fortunes of Europe upon the republican track.

Across the ocean, however, now stands, new-born, a powerful, great republic, superior to any enemies. By their own inherent power the American people have themselves overcome the evil of which all the glorious republics of old have perished, and which threatened her also with destruction. Recovered, there she now stands forever an example and a rock of liberty. The republic has established herself forever in the history of the world. Who will now deny that a republic can maintain herself with great nations?

This triumph is a historical fact—a fact for all mankind; for there can be no doubt that this truth will not fail to send its lustre over to us. As the deliverance of the Union from a foreign yoke has driven its waves towards our continent with irresistible sway, so will also the surge of her regeneration reach the European shores.

All those who are in favor of despotism and slavery have received the news of the fall of Richmond with a secret feeling of alarm; while all free hearts beat stronger in the heightened hope that the cause of liberty must triumph also in Europe. Of all, however, Switzerland rejoices the most; for to her the triumph of the North is a pledge that the republic will never perish, but take deeper root.

This is the reason for our lending a most emphatic expression to the sympathy which we have invariably cherished for the feeling. No feeling of hatred towards the succumbed tarnishes our congratulation; while we are convinced that the government will follow up its triumph by firmness in matters of principle and magnanimity towards the subdued, to the complete political reconstruction of the Union. We declare our full, emphatic sympathy with the principles of democratic self-government and free labor, which have gained new ground in the Union; with the men who have, in the true spirit of these principles, led her stars; with the genuine democratic statesman, ABRAHAM LINCOLN, so dear to Switzerland; with the brave federal army and her excellent leaders, and, finally, with the noble American people, who have triumphed over their enemies and over themselves.

The motto between the two sister republics shall be, forever: "The cause of democracy and of the republic must triumph!"

[Translation.]

To his Excellency ANDREW JOHNSON,
    Vice-President of the United States, Washington:

HONORED SIR: We just receive the appalling news of the assassination of the President of the United States, Mr. ABRAHAM LINCOLN. We are also aware that our address cannot reach the excellent man who has now fallen, as it were, a victor on the field of battle, a victim of his republican honesty, uprightness, and conciliatory mind.

Permit us to express our most profound sympathy and grief over this event. The Swiss people abhor from the bottom of their hearts such a mode of warfare determined on—but, we would gladly believe, not with the consent of the people—by the partisans of the South. Switzerland, however, is fully confident that even if this new vicissitude should again disturb the hopes of a speedy peace, the triumph of the cause of the North, and of the democratic republic, will be the more complete.

[Translation.]

BERNE, *May* 5, 1865.

To the Editor of the Bund:

HONORED SIR: As an opponent to the old and new Sonderbund, I respectfully request you to add my name to the address of sympathy and condolence of the Swiss people to the government and people of the North American Union.

                                    JUSTUS SCHALLER.

[Translation.]

BERNE, *May* 5, 1865.

To the Editor of the Bund, in Berne: ·

SIR: We have the honor to inform you that the local section of the Commercial and Manufacturing Association in Berne has unanimously resolved to join you in the general address of sympathy and condolence to the American Union.

We hereby transmit a list of the signatures of our members, (88 in number,) and remain your obedient servants.

In the name of the committee:

C. WILHELMUS GRAFFENRIED, *President.*

ALBERT YERSIN, *Secretary.*

[Then come the 88 names of the members.]

[Translation.]

Signatures of the members of the Helvetia Student's Union to the address of sympathy for the United States of America.

GOTTFRIED FLENTISSEN, JR., *President.*

ADOLPHE FRENE, *Law Student.*

JOHANN RITSCHARD, *Juris Student.*

FRIEDRICH MATHYS, *Theological Student.*

ALEX. IMMER, *Theological Student.*

AND FIFTEEN OTHER NAMES.

[Translation.]

BERNE, *May* 3, 1865.

The students of the Concordia Society, nineteen members, have this day resolved to unite in the address of sympathy and condolence to the American Union.

In the name of the Concordia:

A. SCHEURER, *President, Law Student.*

BERGER, *Secretary.*

[Translation.]

BERNE, *May* 7, 1865.

Mr. EDITOR: The Berne Typographia hereby announce their assent to the address of sympathy and condolence to the government of the North American free States.

For the society:

KARL KÖNIG, *President.*

S. MAYER, *Secretary.*

[Translation.]

BERNE, *May* 6, 1865.

The undersigned society, at a full meeting this day, unanimously passed the following resolutions:

1. We cordially approve of the address of sympathy and condolence to the American Union now circulating in this city.

2. We order that every member of the society sign his name to this paper, and that it be properly executed.

In the name of the Frohsinn Männerchor, of Berne:

J. HUBER, *President.*

T. BUCHERT, *Secretary.*

[Eighty-four signatures follow.]

[Translation.]

THE MENNER TURNVEREIN (MEN'S GYMNASTIC UNION) OF THE CITY OF BERNE.

Resolved, At a meeting on the 5th of May, 1865, to approve of the address of sympathy and condolence to the United States of America, on account of the suppression of the rebellion and assassination of President LINCOLN, in the name of all their members, forty-four in number.

For the Turnverein:

GO. STRELIN, *President.*

A. FRANTOCHI, *Secretary.*

[Translation.]

BURGDORF, *May* 6, 1865.

DEAR SIR: In honor to the memory of the great man beyond the sea, who, with so much courage, strength and patience, wisdom and moderation, directed the destinies of his country through a long and bloody war, and was at last struck down by the merciless hand of a cruel assassin, I desire that my name be added to the address of the Swiss Confederation to the American nation. I made inquiries about a meeting to be held in this place; but I find there is no one here who takes sufficient interest in such things to get it up; I therefore take this means of making my wishes known to you.

Yours, with great esteem,

F. WELCHLI.

Mr. TSCHARNER,
     Editor of the Bund, in Berne.

[Translation.]

BLEIENBAH, NEAR SOLEURE,
May 7, 1865.

SIR: Since our government seems to have forgotten the address of sympathy and condolence to the government of the United States, and nobody here thinks any more about it since it was first presented, and as I had not the good fortune to see it, being absent at the time, I respectfully request you to add my name to the list of signers to the expression of joy and sorrow for our republican brethren beyond the ocean.

With great esteem,

N. T. MOLLET,
Supreme Judge.

[Translation.]

BOLLINGEN, *May* 7, 1865.

Mr. EDITOR: The Bollingen Reading Society, consisting of twenty members, at an ordinary meeting last evening, resolved to join in the address of sympathy and condolence to the United States of North America on account of the assassination of their excellent President, ABRAHAM LINCOLN, and to rejoice with them in their victories for the triumph of humanity by the abolition of slavery.

Respectfully, in the name of the society,

SOLOMON FLUKIGER,
President.

JOHN MUHLETHALER,
Actuary.

[Translation.]

BREMGARTEN, NEAR BERNE,
June 9, 1865.

The common council and Choral Union of Bremgarten declare that they cordially join in the Swiss address of sympathy to the American Union, which originated in Berne.

We hereby most sincerely wish the greatest prosperity to the American

Union in its restoration after great victories, and express our most cordial sympathy for its bereavement by the death of its excellent President, LINCOLN.

> "The star-spangled banner,
> O long may it wave
> O'er the land of the free
> And the home of the brave!"

SCHELLENBERG GONDRATH.
President of the Council.

FRIEDRICH AESCHER, *Secretary.*

In the name of the Choral Union:

FRIEDRICH AESCHER, *Director.*

JOHANNES WUETHRICHT, *Secretary.*

[Twelve members of the council, and fourteen members of the Choral Union.]

[Translation.]

BIENNE, *May* 7, 1865.

DEAR SIR: I hereby enclose you the signatures of the members of various societies, assembled by order of the district authorities, to express their approbation of the address of sympathy and condolence of the inhabitants of little Switzerland to the great sister republic of the United States.

What man, what true Swiss, did not feel the warm blood run swifter in his veins and his heart pulsate audibly at the news of the great events in America, the perpetual abolition of slavery!

I remain, with much esteem, the old interventioner,

ALEX. SCHÖNI.

BIEL, *(Bienne.)*

In the name of about 800 persons assembled, on the 25th of April, to celebrate the victories and the abolition of slavery in the United States.

ALEX. SCHÖNI,
For the Standing Committee.

JOHN SESSLER, *Secretary*

Dr. JOHN WITTENBACH,
of the Grand Council in Berne.

[Translation.]

BIENNE, *May* 21, 1865.

SIR: Deign to accept the most profound condolence for the cruel death of the man most dear to all republican hearts, from a true Swiss republican, whose son fought against the southern rebels as chief of a company of light artillery, in the first Virginia regiment.

The delay of this expression of sympathy from me is owing to my removal from Morat to this place. When I left Morat the address had not been circulated there, and when I got here it had been sent to Berne.

Yet I hope it is not too late to join a friend in sending congratulations to our friends beyond the sea, with wishes for their prosperity and that of their new noble representative.

Accept our sympathy and our most sincere wishes for the future prosperity of the Union.

Respectfully,

JEAN JENK, SR.,
at Bonjean, near Bienne.

I take pleasure in joining in the above condolence and good wishes.

R. MÜLLER,
Brother of a surgeon in the army of the Union.

His Excellency the MINISTER RESIDENT
of the United States of America in Switzerland.

[Translation.]

BRUNNEN, *May* 6, 1865.

To the Bund:

As the pious hearts of Switzerland have always throbbed in sympathy with the good people of America, now grieving for their noble President LINCOLN, we cordially join in the address of condolence prepared for them by the people of the Swiss Confederation.

We hope you will convey this expression to its proper address.

A. NIDÉRAST.
P. BENL.

[Translation.]

Mayor and council of the canton of Basel-Stadt to the Bundesrath, in Berne.

BASEL, *May* 6, 1865.

GENTLEMEN: We learn from the public papers that your supreme authorities have voted an address of sympathy and condolence to the United States, on account of the death of their worthy President, at a time when long-desired peace was just taking the place of a terrible war.

We presume the address is in the name of all the cantons, and we are thankful for the opportunity of adding our names to it. But if we are mistaken, we suggest that a circular be promulged for the purpose that each canton may know what to do.

We commend you to the protection of Divine Providence, and subscribe ourselves,

C. STCHLIN, *Mayor.*

DR. BISCONOFF, *Secretary.*

[Translation.]

At a public meeting held in the Lutheran church, in Balgach, at half-past ten o'clock in the forenoon of the 7th of May, 1865, on a motion made by C. Vulker, after the close of the polls for the district election, the following resolution was unanimously adopted :

"The citizens of Balgach, at a meeting held on the 7th of May, 1865, unanimously resolved to ratify the address of sympathy and condolence from the Swiss Confederation to the American Union, and requested the authorities of the canton of St. Gall to make it known to the proper persons."

Adopted unanimously. The above abstract is correct.

S. OESCH, *President.*

NÜNSCH, *Notary.*

T. U. SONDEREGGER,

EDWARD WALTZLER,

Vote Counters.

[Translation.]

BULLE, CANTON OF FRIBOURG,

May 12, 1865.

To the Bund, Berne :

As no one seems to have courage to get up a particular demonstration of sympathy for the cause of the northern States of America in this place, we resident Germans, have thought proper to call a meeting and declare our approval of the general Swiss address, and to express our pleasure at the northern victories, and our grief for the murder of President LINCOLN.

In thanking the Berne committee for having taken the initiative in this affair, the undersigned beg leave to express their high esteem for the promoters of the good cause.

CARL BÜCHNER,
Druggist, of Darmstadt.

ADAM HENRICH,
Gardener, of Hesse-Darmstadt.

CLEMENT NARGELE,
Apothecary, from the Grand Duchy of Baden.

VALENTIN ROTHGEB,
Knife-maker, from Rhenish Bavaria.

JOHN MAYER,
Grand Duchy of Baden.

REINHARD MEYER,
Weaver, of Grand Duchy of Baden.

H. ZECH, *Merchant, same place.*

GUSTAV KAMMER,
Wood-seller, Hesse-Darmstadt.

MAURICE ANDREÆ,
Gardener, Saxony.

JOHN HENRY GÄRTNER,
Grand Duchy of Hesse-Darmstadt.

CARL MEYER,
Blacksmith, Grand Duchy of Baden.

PETER KRANTZ,
Shoemaker, from Maehenheim, Hesse-Darmstadt.

[Translation.]

Meeting of the inhabitants of Brittnau, in church, Sunday afternoon, May 14, 1865.

The number of qualified voters over twenty years of age, 385.

On motion of Parson Bauman, seconded by other persons present, it was unanimously resolved to approve of the Swiss national address to the people of the United States of North America:

1st. In view of congratulations on the happy conclusion of the four years' war, which has produced the greatest of blessings to the country, namely, the institution of the rights of man, the enjoyment of personal liberty and freedom, without regard to the accidental differences of complexion, corporeal circumstances or descent, in opposition to the execrable evil of negro slavery in the southern States; and

2d. In consideration of the expression of condolence for the death of that most excellent man, ABRAHAM LINCOLN, President of the United States.

The above is a true copy of the original:

MAT. WÄLCHLI, *President.*
A. WÄLCHLI, *Clerk.*
JACOB BRAK,
J. ZIMMERLIK,
Vote Counters.

[Translation.]

The Agricultural Society of the district of Baden to President Johnson.

BADEN, IN AARGAU, *May* 21, 1865.

As members of an agricultural society, and as citizens of a free country, we feel bound to join in the chorus that solemnly swells in the praise of the holy cause of humanity, freedom, and equality to all men as brothers, and that precious blessing of a republic, unbroken unity. Therefore have we followed with intense interest the banner of our sister republic beyond the ocean, which waved for the holy blessing, and watched the changes of events as closely as if they had been in our own land—now with joy, and then with fear and trembling. Great was our exultation when the good cause triumphed; but a terrible blow struck down our joy. Close upon the news of victory came the tidings of the death of LINCOLN, the noble, unmoved champion of freedom and the Union.

Permit us, therefore, to express to you our most sincere congratulation on the triumph of the good cause, and to tell our deep sorrow for the death of President LINCOLN, the noble martyr of liberty.

Permit us, as kindred people, to extend the friendly hand of brotherhood, and crown his head with laurel in his last sleep, and plant the mourning cypress over his untimely grave.

May his martyrdom produce the rich fruit that the true martyrs of humanity have always yielded.

In the name of the society:

KETTIGER, *President.*

JOHN MULLER, *Secretary.*

[Translation.]

BÜREN, *June* 4, 1865.

SIR: We learn through the central state functionary here that you are authorized to receive the addresses of sympathy which societies and Swiss people desire to make to the government of the United States. We therefore send you the address of the teachers of Büren, that you may attend to the proper disposal of it.

With esteem,

J. PFISTER, *Assistant Teacher.*

The COMMANDER OF THE HUNTER CORPS *of the Canton of Berne.*

[Translation.]

Expression of adhesion to the address of sympathy to the North American Union by the people of Switzerland.

BÜREN, IN THE CANTON OF BERNE, *June* 5, 1865.

The great rejoicing on account of the recent great victories of the American Union has found an echo in our hearts, as that country has always been friendly to us, and friendly to freedom throughout the world.

"Freedom to man, though he be born in chains," says our great poet, Schiller, in his ideal enthusiasm for freedom and the dignity of manhood. Whoever considers these words, and understands them properly, cannot help feeling how superior a man who believes in and practices them is to one who is governed by the demon of servitude and oppression. Whoever has a heart that beats warm for the greatest blessings of humanity, must join the general gratulation of the friends of freedom everywhere on the triumph of the glorious cause for human rights on American soil.

ABRAHAM LINCOLN, the mighty leader of these great events, the manly model of civic virtue, of pure and noble humanity, will be held holy in the memory of the inhabitants of his native land, and be worshipped by the world. May this idea console the country that is destined to live on in prosperity for his cruel death. May this view in the history of nations, and of our country in particular, teach us that it is the will of Providence for all religious, social, or political reforms to be accomplished by a baptism of blood.

May God keep the people of the North American Union ever hereafter in freedom, peace, and unity.

In the name of the synod:

JOHANN PFISTER, *Assistant Teacher.*

[Translation.]

CHAUX DE FOND, SWITZERLAND, *May* 7, 1865.

The radical electors of Chaux de Fond, republic and canton of Neufchatel, in Switzerland, assembled this day, to the number of two thousand, for the purpose of exercising their civil rights, and adopted unanimously the following address to the government of the United States:

The news of the triumph of the northern cause has filled the hearts of all the radicals of Neufchatel with joy, and has delighted their brothers of all the Swiss cantons. Yours is the cause of true republicans in every country. Like you, the Swiss radicals desire the emancipation of all men; the triumph of the cause of progress, with its happy consequences, the reign of order.

That abominable crime, the murder of President LINCOLN has received no greater reprobation in any part of the world than with us. We will ever keep his illustrious name in our memories; but we comfort ourselves with the thought that the cause of the North did not die with one of its best citizens, but will live to triumph in the hands of his successor and his able generals.

It was also voted to have this resolution sent to the United States minister at Berne.

This is a certified copy:

[SEAL.]   A. RIBAUX, *Justice of the Peace,*
                  President of the Radical Committee.

[Translation.]

CHAUX DE FOND, *May* 4, 1865.

The undersigned give their most perfect adhesion to the address sent by the Federal Council of Switzerland to the government of the United States of America, both as regards the triumph of the northern cause and the memory of the eminent and lamented President LINCOLN.

A. RIBAUX.	LEON INREY.
PAUL VUILLE.	JULES LAMBERCIER.
E. ROUILEN.	JULES DUBOIS.
ALEXANDRE HESS.	J. A. WILEIMRIER.
H. F. GERRIT.	AUG. BARBEY.
ARNOLD NICOND.	L. C. DELLENBACH.
EDOUARD ROBERT.	PAUL CALAME.
DUBOIS CALAME.	T'S ARMAND TISSOT.
ALB. DUCOMMUN.	LUCIEN HUMBERT.
ED. BEGUELIN.	ENG. JUNOD.
ROBERT BORNAND.	NUMA DIOZ.
GUSTAVE LUPOLD.	H. GRANJEAN PERRENON.
ULYSSE PERRETT.	ZINGO BERTON.

LOUIS BORNET.

AND ABOUT 2,300 NAMES FROM CHAUX DE FOND.

[Translation.]

CHUR, *May* 24, 1865.

The undersigned most cordially approves of the Swiss address of sympathy to the United States, and requests to contribute his signature to its columns of subscribers in our native land.

DR. CARL HILTON,
Lawyer in Chur.

[Translation.]

The minor council of the canton of the Grisons (Graubünden) to Mr. Florian Gengee, editor of the Bund, in Berne.

CHUR, *May* 8, 1865.

SIR: Thanking you for your estimable letter of the 29th instant, we assure you that our chief authorities, as well as the people in general, feel the most profound sympathy for the American Union; and we are confident that similar sentiments prevail throughout all Switzerland, on account of the calamitous event that has overwhelmed that country.

Now as to the best manner of expressing this sympathy, it seems to us that an official publication of the state council, as representatives, and in the name of the whole confederation, and in the proper form, should be addressed to the government of the United States.

However, in case the address of sympathy and condolence is sent to us, we are ready to assent to it with our signatures.

With much esteem,

H. P. BELLI, *President.*

In the name of the state council, the chancery director,

J. B. TSCHARNER.

[Translation.]

The minor council of the canton of Grisons to the honorable state council.

CHUR, *May* 10, 1865.

LOYAL FELLOW-CITIZENS: The recent important news from America, the glorious Union victories over the seceded States, the horrid murder of the well-deserving President LINCOLN, have called up feelings of the deepest sympathy in all Switzerland.

The minor council, convinced that the people participate in this sentiment, have not hesitated so to express it; but as they intend to call a meeting for that purpose on the 14th instant, we will leave the more perfect expression of their feelings to the promised official report of the popular assembly.

We therefore invite the presidents of the different circles to meet here on Sunday, the 14th instant, to consider whether it accords with the feelings and wishes of the authorities of the canton of Grisons to congratulate the United States on their victories, and offer condolence for the death of their excellent President, ABRAHAM LINCOLN.

Not doubting but the people of Grisons will joyously accept the opportunity to express their republican sentiments and cordial sympathy for the American Union, we respectfully request the different presidents to answer the above question without delay.

We commend you, brethren, to the protection of Divine Providence.

H. P. BEELI, President.

J. P. TSCHARNER, Secretary.

[Translation.]

The minor council of the canton of Grisons to the Hon. Swiss Bundesrath, in Berne.

CHUR, June 1, 1865.

GENTLEMEN: The latest important news from our sister republic beyond the ocean—the great conflict between the States of the North American Union, the signal victories of the loyal citizens and all their liberty-loving friends over those who would have severed the bonds of Union, and the death of the Union President LINCOLN, the worthy, estimable, unmoved representative of the good cause, who fell a sacrifice to the desire of accomplishing his holy commission—all these events are felt and appreciated or deplored, not only in the valleys of our canton, but over all Switzerland.

The information that reaches us through the public papers of the glorious victories of the nation and the tragic death of its President has awakened the most lively feelings of gratulation on the one part, and the deepest sentiments of sorrow in our bosoms on the other, towards a country that has always been our friend.

The sincerity of this sympathy is the less doubtful, as many of our people's kindred were the warriors in that holy crusade for freedom and right, and many more are still living free and happy under that star-spangled banner for which they have victoriously fought.

With this intention, we thought proper to make out an address and send it to the thirty-nine districts of this canton on the 14th ultimo, when the district elections were to take place, to have the vote taken upon it. On the 10th a special proclamation was issued, a copy of which has been sent you for your consideration, and circulated throughout the canton, putting this interrogatory to the voters: Whether it accords with the feelings and wishes of the authorities of the canton of Grisons to congratulate the United States on their victories, and offer condolence for the death of their excellent President, ABRAHAM LINCOLN. The result of the votes in the thirty-nine districts has reached us, after much delay, and we are happy to report it as unanimous in favor of the interrogatory, and at every precinct especial expressions of sympathy were made by many of the voters. It is now our wish and desire that this perfect expression of the sympathy of our people be sent to the government of the United States, through the proper channel. In the mean time we embrace the opportunity to send our respects and feelings of distinguished consideration.

H. P. BEELI, *President.*

J. B. TSCHARNER, *Secretary.*

[Translation.]

The Chancery of Grisons to the Bund.

CHUR, *May* 19, 1865.

Mr. EDITOR: As the report of the votes of this canton was late coming to hand, we have not been able hitherto to inform you of the result In answer to yours of the 15th instant, we have the honor to say that the address of sympathy and condolence from the citizens of the Swiss Confederation to the American Union is fully approved of, as far as we can learn. Official reports from several places have not yet been received, but we have no doubt they will accord with the sentiments expressed in the Berne address.

Respectfully,

G. MARCHION, *Chancellor.*

THE MANNERCHOR AND MUSICAL UNION OF DIEGTEN, CANTON OF BASELLAND.

Fifty-four signatures and this motto:

> Es blinken der Sterne so viele
> In's dunkel des Lebens hinein;
> Es dringen die Vœlker zum Ziele,
> Bei ihrem helleuchtenden Schein.

[Translation.]

> Many stars twinkle
> In life's weary way,
> Leading us onward
> To heavenly day.

[Translation.]

To the President of the Central Union of Glorus.

EINSIEDELN, *May* 10, 1865.

By order of the Workingmen's Union of Einsiedeln, I herewith send you a list of signatures to the address of sympathy to the American people. Other lists from this canton must have been sent you already. Hoping you will have the kindness to comply with the request, I remain, in the name of the Workingmen's Union of Einsiedeln,

Your obedient servant,

MARTIN FUCHS, *Actuary.*

[Translation.]

To the government and free people of the United States of North America.

The Swiss laborers and Workingmen's Union have hereby resolved to approve of the address of sympathy and devotion to the free people of the United States of North America, on account of their recent great victories and advantages, both in a political and social regard, and the undersigned citizens of Einsiedeln, in the canton of Schwyz, and the members of the Workingmen's Union of the same place, send their cordial congratulations for triumphs, and their heartfelt sorrows for the atrocious murder of the noblest and greatest citizen of the Union, President ABRAHAM LINCOLN.

CARL HENSLER,
President of the Workingmen's Union.
E. SCHADER,
Vice-President.
AND NINETY-SEVEN NAMES.

[Translation.]

The Democratic Circle of Estavayer, animated by similar sentiments to those announced at the Fribourg popular meeting of the 14th of May instant, and anxious to show their brothers beyond the sea their sympathy for the victories over the South, thus restoring peace to the American Union by the triumph of the liberal cause, and also to express their indignation and sorrow at the ruthless and savage act of the monster Booth, who deprived them of the most worthy and pure of republicans, their illustrious President LINCOLN, declare that they approve of the resolntion passed at the public meeting at Fribourg, and join in the address to the republicans of the United States.

A. MOURET, *Attorney at Law.*
JOSEPH BRUNO VOLLERY.
A. BUCHS PROUVREUX.
NICHOLAS SANSONNENS.
P. N. COLLAND.
ANTOINE MARMY.
JAQUES SANSONNENS, *Teacher.*
C. A. L. DAFFLON.

AND THIRTY-ONE OTHER NAMES.

[Translation.]

DISTRICT OF FRANCHES MONTAGNES.

Signatures to the Berne address of sympathy to the people of the American Union, congratulating them on the victorious restoration of their government, and condoling with them on the loss of ABRAHAM LINCOLN, their savior.

KATMANN, *Prefect.*
E. BROSSARD, *Judge.*
GENERAL QUELAIN.
LIEUTENANT HUSSBAUMER.
CAPTAIN HENNIN.
CAPTAIN GIRARD.

AND FORTY-TWO OTHERS.

[Translation.]

FRIBOURG, *May* 24, 1865.

SIR: I have the honor to transmit you the following documents:

1. An address, voted by a popular assembly at Fribourg, on Saturday, the 13th of May, with 411 signatures.

2. A supplementary address, signed by 106 citizens of Gruyere,* most of them from the industrious and liberal little city of Bulle.

3. A second declaration of assent to the address voted by the Democratic Circle of the city of Estavayer,† with 39 signatures, 556 signatures in all, which the people of Fribourg beg you to accept and transmit to your American

---

* For this enclosure see Gruyere.
† For this enclosure see Estavayer.

countrymen, as a token of friendship, republican confraternity and very sincere sympathy.

Receive the assurance of our very distinguished consideration.

AUG. MAJEUX.

Mr. G. G. FOGG,
Minister Resident of the United States, at Berne.

[Translation.]

FRIBOURG, *May* 13, 1865.

To the Republicans of the United States:

All free nations, and those waiting for their freedom, hail the final triumph of your arms with sentiments of happiness and hope, as the cause of justice, liberty, humanity, and civilization were sheltered by your banners.

Without hate for your wayward brothers, the Swiss people shout with joy at the news of your success, for it assures the immortal principles of democracy, and restores peace, concord, and prosperity to your great and wonderful republic, which we are proud to call our sister and to love as such.

How great was our consternation, how sincere our lamentations, when we heard of the tragic death of your great citizen LINCOLN, a victim of the most atrocious crime known to the world, at the moment when we expected to see him crowned with the purest glory, and worshipped with veneration by all good people, as the fruits of four years of perseverance and gigantic struggles.

Why was not the assassin's hand disarmed at the last moment by so much republican virtue, so much nobility and magnanimity?

Republicans of the United States, who are weeping over the tomb of the most illustrious of your children, allow your brethren of Helvetia's hills and dales to join in your mourning, and lay upon the tomb in their turn the wreaths of regret and fraternal sympathy.

Republicans of America, republicans of Switzerland and old Europe, let us remain ever united, in days of misfortune as in times of prosperity.

May God give you consolation and courage, and always protect your beautiful country and free institutions.

AUG. MAJEUX,	CHARLES FONDLEY.
Editor of the Fribourg Journal.	JOSEPH GENDRE.
Z. CASTELLA.	PHILIPPE TECHTERMANN.
DR. C. HUYDUC.	CHRISTIAN BLANC.
T. THACSEN.	PIERRE WICHT.
DR. JOSEPH SCHNYDER, SR.	AUG. MOHR PFULGER.
CHARLES SCHWAB.	LUCIEN BIELMANN.

AND THREE HUNDRED AND NINETY-EIGHT OTHER SIGNATURES.

[Translation.]

The president and council of the canton of Thurgau to the Bundesrath, in Berne.

FRAUENFELD, *May* 3, 1865.

GENTLEMEN: By a circular from the Berne committee for the address of sympathy and condolence to the American Union, we are invited to join in its approval, together with the governments of Aargau, Ticino, and Soleure.

We have thought it would be better for each canton to draw up an address, through its chief authorities, and have it presented at meetings of the inhabitants for their approval, and then send it to the general government to be forwarded through the minister to the foreign government.

But if our views of the subject are not correct, we willingly indorse your address, in the name of the inhabitants of Thurgau, as our people rejoice at the victories for the holy rights of man, and highly condemn the atrocious crime that attempted to destroy their effect, wishing the greatest prosperity and peace to our sister republic beyond the ocean.

Requesting you to report this declaration to the proper authorities, we remain your attentive and serving fellow-countrymen,

EILOFF, *President.*
RUKSTUHT, *Chancellor.*

[Translation.]

Telegram from Frauenfeld to Berne, (received May 8, 1865.

To the Editor of the Bund, in Berne:

The Thurgan Mutual Aid Society, at a special meeting this day, has unanimously declared its adhesion to the Swiss address of sympathy and condolence to the people of the United States.

MANN, *Actuary.*

STRAHEN, *Telegraph Agent.*

[Translation.]

The district synod of teachers in the civil district of Fraubrunn, canton of Berne, to the American legation in Berne.

The synod of teachers in the civil district of Fraubrunn hereby unanimously declare its full approval of and solemn adhesion to the address of sympathy from the honorable Union Council of Switzerland to the government of the American Union for the glorious preservation of its integrity, and offers its sincere sympathy for the decease of President ABRAHAM LINCOLN, and horror at the misdeed that deprived him of existence.

Accept this act as a sincere, though feeble, demonstration of its good wishes for the prosperity of our glorious sister republic of America.

With devotion and esteem,

K. LAUENBERGER, *President.*

ULRICH CHRISTENEN, *Secretary.*

[Translation.]

GRUTLI SOCIETY OF GENEVA.

GENEVA, *May* 13, 1865.

To the Bund, in Berne:

Mr. EDITOR: I respectfully request you, by these few lines, to hand the enclosed paper to the central address committee in Berne.

Accept my thanks for the invitation to join in the expression of sympathy for our sister republic beyond the ocean, and believe me your humble and obedient servant,

C. ROTH. *President.*

[Translation.]

The Geneva Grutli Union Society to the committee on the address of sympathy and condolence to the American Union, in Berne.

GENEVA, *May* 13, 1865.

DEAR SIR: Our society, in its session of to-day, unanimously voted to approve of the address of sympathy and condolence of the Swiss Confederation to the government of the North American Union. The number of members voting is 235.

Accept the assurance of our high esteem and consideration.

C. ROTH, *President.*

[Translation.]

The state council of the republic and canton of Geneva to the honorable minister resident of the United States at Berne.

GENEVA, *May* 5, 1865.

SIR: Impressed with the sentiments that animated the people of Geneva on hearing of the crime committed upon the person of the honorable ABRAHAM LINCOLN, the state council of the canton of Geneva wish to express, through your mediation, to the great American republic the sorrow it feels at that deplorable event.

Our country participates in the mourning that is spread among your people, and if words of sympathy can afford any consolation to them in their deep sorrow, we beg you to be our interpreter in presenting to the government of your country the expression of the profound regret of the people of Geneva, and their wishes for the future prosperity of the American Union.

The state council:

> MOÏSE VAUTIER, *President.*
> CHAS. RICHARD, *Vice-President.*
> T. FLOT.
> S. VENAY.
> S. MOÏSE PIQUET.
> ELIE DUCOMMUN, *State Chancellor.*

[Post tenebras lux.]

[Translation.]

The state council of the republic and canton of Geneva to the minister resident of the United States of America near the Swiss Confederation, in Berne.

GENEVA, *May* 15, 1865.

SIR: We have the honor to enclose you herewith an extract of the deliberations of the grand council of our canton, which you will please remit to the government of the United States of America, as a new evidence of the sentiments that animate the republic of Geneva towards her sister of the New World.

Accept the assurance of our most distinguished consideration.

In the name of the state council:

> ELIE DUCOMMUN, *Chancellor.*

[Translation.]

Extract from the records of the grand council of the republic and canton of Geneva, of the 15th of May, 1865.

DECREE OF THE GRAND COUNCIL.

The grand council, on motion of one of its members, unanimously resolved to join in the pledge of sympathy sent by the state council, in the name of the people of Geneva, to the United States minister on the occasion of the crime committed upon the person of President LINCOLN, and to thank the state council for offering its medium for the sentiments of sorrow the deplorable event has excited in the bosoms of the entire population of Geneva.

Made and given in Geneva on the 15th of May, 1865, under the seal of the republic, and with the signatures of the president and secretary of the grand council.

ED. AUBERT,
President of the Council.

HENRI SUBIT, *Secretary.*

Examined for authentication of the signatures of Mr. Edward Aubert, president of the grand council of the canton of Geneva, and of Mr. Henri Subit, secretary of the same corps.

[SEAL.]

ELIE DUCOMMUN,
State Chancellor.

GENEVA, *May* 15, 1865.

[Translation.]

The people of Geneva to the people of the United States of America.

GENEVA, *May* 3, 1865.

Brothers on the other side of the ocean :

The energetic defender of the integrity of his country, the valorous champion of the abolition of slavery, the great citizen, LINCOLN, has fallen a victim of the most cowardly crime. His death is a loss for humanity and for liberty in both hemispheres. It is not the people of the United States alone, but all free peoples with them, who have to mourn for this upright patriot. LINCOLN was the type of those disinterested characters, of those valiant and humble hearts which democracies.must count in great numbers to maintain their rights inviolate, and to assure their continual march towards progress. In the midst of the terrible trials which the American Union has encountered, in all the exigencies of civil war, this upright patriot had but one purpose in view, to respect his oath of fidelity to the Constitution, to prevent the dismemberment of the great republic, to efface the only stain upon its flag, slavery. This is what President LINCOLN has realized; he has accomplished this gigantic task without harm to the liberty of the people, with probity and energy in the choice of means, with moderation and generosity towards the vanquished; and for these eminent qualities, for this disinterestedness, he has been basely assassinated.

This was more than a crime against the inviolability of human life. It was a crime of treason to republics. In a country where the people alone is sovereign; in democracies, where laws, freely discussed and agreed to, are the basis of society, magistrates have a sacred character; to strike them down is to insult the whole people—is to commit the most abominable of high crimes.

Geneva comes solemnly to associate her sorrow and regret with the great grief which this terrible blow has caused the United States. In the darkest days, when the starry flag was held in check by a rebellion whose real purpose was to consolidate the institution of slavery, and to extend it to territories destined to form new States, the people of Geneva met to send a testimony of sympathy and words of encouragement to the American Union. Her wishes have been realized. The United States emerge from civil war free and more powerful than ever. The little republic of Europe sees with profound satisfaction the result of the trials which the American people have undergone for four years; she breathes a prayer that this power may never be employed to weaken popular liberty and sovereignty, to violate oaths, and satisfy ambitious projects of conquest.

The civil war of the United States will have the same effect for them, we trust, as the Sundenbund, which in 1847 drenched Switzerland with blood. It is from this period that Helvetia dates the closest union between all the cantons, without distinction of language, without consideration of local interests. Let the conduct of President Lincoln serve as an example, and the same homogeneity will be realized in the United States. The only cause of division is slavery; may this be scattered forever, even to its smallest roots, and the great republic will have no more internal dangers. The maintenance of its integrity is of the last importance for the future of the republics of the New World. Events have shown this: like a train of powder, no sooner did civil war break out in the Union, than American democracies were in danger. St. Domingo, Paraguay, Mexico, are the plain proofs of this. These facts speak—they speak loudly, and need no commentary. If any one could still doubt the necessity of maintaining the great republic in its integrity, such facts should dispel all uncertainty.

Liberty and power compel, says liberal Europe, while fixing her eyes upon the American Union. It is for you, strong and free people, to give an example for other people; you have done it nobly up to this time; you will do it still—you will do it even to the end; you will utterly abolish slavery, and you will stretch a tutelar hand to the liberties of all peoples. We earnestly desire this, and have confidence that it will be; for you have numerous citizens whose only ambition is to follow in the footsteps of the Washingtons, Franklins, and Lincolns. It is with this conviction that the people of Geneva, assembled in meeting, say to you, brothers on the other side of the ocean: Long live the republic of the United States of America! Long live liberty!

Done in meeting, the 3d day of May, at the Electoral building, and unanimously adopted by the four thousand persons present.

MOISE VANTIER,
President du Consul d'Etat.

AD. CATALAN,
LOMBARD, *M.*,
CHS. PFEFFER,
A. CARTERET, *Deputié*,
AMBERY, *Avocat.*
H. FAZY,
G. KLAPHA, *General.*
FEHR. OTH,
CH. VOGT,
J. DIDAY,
G. ZARLINDEN,
The Committee.

[Translation.]

The Polish refugees in Switzerland to the great nation the republic of the United States.

Fraternal greeting and profound sympathy!

Republican Citizens:

After a fatal struggle of twenty months for the independence and liberty of our country, after countless losses, we, exiles from our homes, under the ægis of the free Swiss nation, the only oasis of liberty in Europe, contemplate with hearts palpitating with emotion your gigantic struggle, supported by rights the most sacred to humanity. The news of your heroic and glorious exploits filled us with admiration, and your triumphs made us poor Poles forget our own misfortunes on beholding the great champions of liberty.

Republican citizens: Now, when the most despotic governments of old Europe are hastening to send you expressions of their sympathy, on the occasion of the horrible crime that has deprived you and all friends of liberty of its greatest defender, your President elect, ABRAHAM LINCOLN, we beg you to accept the feeble vote of sincere sympathy and profound sorrow from a few people—a handful of exiles.

Our whole nation cannot express its sentiments for you, because its people are scattered over the face of the earth; but you can accept our good wishes as the feeble echo of a friendly people.

Fraternal greeting and sympathy?

In the name of the Polish Mutual Aid Society of Geneva:

> STRYIENSKI.
> J. STELLA.
> ANTOINE SZCZESNOWICZ.
> JOSEPH CWIERORALUKWICZ.
> FRANZ KASPERO.

In the name of the Polish Mutual Aid Society of St. Gallen:

> The Polish abbot, E. SZCZENIOWSKI.
> JOSAPHAT OKNIOSKI.
> TOMAS RUSZLEJKO.
> JAN BORACZYNSKI.
> LUDWIH FRJHICH.

[Translation.]

The undersigned, citizens of Grueyere, join their fellow-countrymen of Fribourg in the address to the republicans of the United States.

> J. GIENOZ.
> JULES GLASSON.
> CHAS. BRASCHAUD.
> F. DEIRONE.
> TH. BAYS.
> F. DEEROUX.
> F. DALER.
> GIETENHOFF TOBIE.
> JOSEPH DUBOIS.
> FREDERIC LAMDRY.
> AND NINETY-SIX OTHER NAMES.

[Translation.]

The state committee of the canton of Glarus to the honorable union council in Berne.

GLARUS, *May* 7, 1865.

Mr. President and Gentlemen of the Council:

In its meeting of this day the common council, through its presiding officer, proposed an expression of its sentiments on account of recent events in America

The oldest and smallest republic in Europe will not let this favored opportunity pass to call a meeting of its citizens under the free azure of God's heaven, and express to the youngest and largest republic in the world its warmest sympathy for its sufferings—its sorrow for the assassination of the good citizen ABRAHAM LINCOLN, and its best wishes for the restoration of the American Union and its continued prosperity.

We beg you to make this known to the American legation, and receive our commendations of you to Providence for our mutual welfare.

In the name of the land committee:

DR. T. HEER, *Chief Justice.*
T. CHAM, *Council Clerk.*

[Translation.]

GLARUS, *June* 4, 1865.

To the Editor of the Bund, in Berne:

The undersigned has the honor to enclose you herewith lists of the autograph signatures of the Swiss work-unions, in the different sections of this canton, to be appended to the address of sympathy and condolence to be sent to the people of North America, with the request that you deliver it to the proper authorities for that purpose.   If I am not mistaken, there are 515 signatures in all.   I am very sorry I could not send it sooner; but it is not my fault.   I also have to regret that the lists are in no better order.

In the name of the Swiss Central Union:

L. GRIST, *President.*

[Here follow 515 names.]

[Translation.]

HERZOGENBUSCHSEE, *May* 20, 1865.

To the Bund, Berne:

SIR: I herewith enclose you the address of the Mannerchor of this place, together with the declaration of assent of the Waugen Trade Union, with many signatures.

Circumstances prevented me from sending it sooner, but I hope it is not too late to reach its destination through your kindness.

Accept the assurance of my perfect esteem and devotion.

By order:

JOHN SPAHR.

[Translation.]

*Assenting declaration of the Herzogenbuschsee Mannerchor to the Swiss address
of sympathy to the American Union.*

The members of the Herzogenbuschsee Mannerchor declare their assent
to the address of sympathy to the American Union as follows, inviting all neighboring unions and citizens partial to the cause to join them in it.

The feeling of cordial friendship and warm sympathy which the Swiss
express in every rank for the American people, in their varied fortunes, has
also penetrated our circle and awakened the deepest sentiments among us.

We join in the general jubilee of all persons who are friendly to freedom
at the great victory of the North American Union over Richmond. We hail
with joy the end of the four years' civil war, the end of frightful sacrifices and
untold sufferings; and we rejoice at the triumph of freedom and humanity over
the infamous system of oppression that ruled the nation so long.

We join our American brethren in their jubilation that the great and holy
principles of our constitutions show that the democratic republic depends upon
the sovereignty of the people, and the future is in their hands.

We feel that, by this victory, not only Americans, but all who have been
aroused to consciousness must see the great advances made towards the time
when the rights of man must prevail, when no other crown than that of merit
can be worn, and no title of nobility but that of virtue and fitness.

We turn again with wonder and affection to the starry banner of our sister
republic that has blotted out its only stain in this baptism of blood, and around
which so many heroes have assembled, to show the world how powerful is
Divine Providence in the choice of its instruments to prove the simple majesty
of manhood.

The beautiful personification of all these virtues, in our opinion, was
ABRAHAM LINCOLN, "the man with the brow of iron and the heart of gold."

As we joined in the song of victory, the reward of the great citizen's labor,
so did the news of his assassination strike our hearts with terror.

As we shudder at such events of history, we must remember, "that it is
man's destiny to make the greatest sacrifices for the greatest good, buy the best
blessings with the dearest gifts, and remember that he must labor not only for
the passing comforts of to-day, but for the lasting blessings of hereafter."

In this belief, we can understand why Providence often uses means, incom-
prehensible to us, to heal the wounds of humanity, by offering its champions as
victims to martyrdom.

The angel of peace and freedom will now come from the vault of Springfield to breathe the breath of resurrection and regeneration over the land; and
when men in after years shall commemorate Good Friday as the death-day of
their holy Redeemer, they will remember it as the day of martyrdom for his

truest disciple, the liberator of millions of slaves, the noble paragon of virtue and humanity, ABRAHAM LINCOLN.

In conclusion, we express our steadfast hope in the future fate of our great sister republic, and our confidence in its manly rulers; and cordially join in the address of sympathy of our countrymen, wishing the welfare of the Union in the words of the great Franklin, "May it live forever."

Members of the Mannerchor:

A. FRIEDRICH BORN, *President.*

J. G. WEGST, *Director*

G. F. EBERBACH, *Secretary.*

AND ONE HUNDRED AND FORTY NAMES.

[Translation.]

The state council of the canton of Lucerne to the honorable Swiss Union Council in Berne.

LUCERNE, *May* 4, 1865.

Mr. President and Gentlemen of the Council:

You have resolved to send the expression of your sympathies for the loss of the President of the United States of North America, by assassination, to the legation of that country near the Swiss Confederation.

We participate in your feelings of detestation and horror at that awful deed, but as your officers are the constitutional organs of communicating with foreign powers, we have refrained from sending our letter of condolence to that legation, and we now thank you for proposing the signing of the circular sent to us in the name of the Confederation, to which we most cordially assent.

At the same time we embrace the occasion to express our distinguished consideration.

In the name of the government council:

T. WEISS, *Chief Justice.*

DR. WILLI, *State Secretary.*

[Translation.]

LUCERNE, *May* 6, 1865.

DEAR SIR: The sad news lately come across the ocean that ABRAHAM LINCOLN, President of the North American Union, and now regarded as one of the greatest men who ever lived upon this earth, was ruthlessly struck down by the bloody hand of an assassin, has filled the whole world with indignation and grief.

England's proud Queen condescended to give her cordial sympathy, in a writing of her own hand, to the afflicted widow of the worthy republican; and the governments of the highest monarchs of the world sent their sympathies and solemn well-wishes to the democratic land. It is very natural, then, that the message of sad news from America should have been felt in free Switzerland, and caused our patriotic hearts to beat in sympathy with those of a sister republic, bound to us by the closest ties of warmest friendship and similarity of institutions. America and Helvetia, may they ever bear the same relations to each other as now. We have seen the glorious American colors floating at a glorious festival in our land, (the feast of Freeshooters at Luzerne, the 7th day of July, 1853;) we know the beauty of the stars and stripes, and let us wish them success wherever they may wave, in whatever battle they may be tried.

When the first news of the horrible assassination of the greatest man in America reached us, we were overwhelmed, and felt as if the country was ruined; but when we reflected it might be the inscrutable orders of Divine Providence to give us a lasting monument of a free country, we felt resigned to fate.

I have not thought proper to wait till a public meeting should be called in Lucerne, but I have given expression to my feelings now, and send you the sheet that you may insert it in the Bund, and add my name to the address when it is brought up.

Accept the assurances of my distinguished consideration.

JOHN KILCHMAN.

Mr. F. GENGEL,
    Editor of the Bund, in Berne.

[Translation.]

To the Editor of the Bund, in Berne:

HONORED SIR: As the undersigned had not the good fortune to see the address of sympathy and condolence to the American Union, being absent from his place of residence while it was circulating, he respectfully requests you to add his name to the list of signers to that patriotic document.

I remain yours, with much esteem,

KASIMIR PFYFFER.

[Translation.]

Council of the canton of Basel-Landschaft to the Swiss Bundesrath, in Berne.

LIESTHAL, *June 5,* 1865.

We hereby communicate to you, for the information of the authorities of the American Union, that a vote was taken in this canton, on the 28th of

May last, when 6,040 legal voters approved of the address of sympathy and condolence, which was drawn up at the Cassino, in Berne, the 25th of April, congratulating the people of the North on the happy delivery of the country from rebel rule, and condoling with them on the loss of their excellent and worthy President by a murderer's hand.

Some few precincts of our canton remain to be heard from, and we thought it well to wait for the entire vote; but as we are confident that ours are the sentiments of all the Swiss people, we conclude to send this as it is.

Commending you to the protection of Divine Providence, we accept the occasion to express the assurance of our distinguished consideration.

F. BRODBEETZ, President.

B. BANGA, Secretary.

[Translation.]

SWISS CONFEDERATION.

State council of the canton of Ticino to Dr. John Wyttenbach, member of the grand council in Berne.

LUGANO, May 4, 1865.

SIR: We have received Mr. F. Gengel's letter of the 1st, inviting us to join in the address of sympathy an condolence of the central committee of the capital to the American Union, on account of the assassination of President LINCOLN.

This is the text of the resolutions passed by our state government: The grand council of the republic and canton of Ticino—

1. In the name of the people, expresses its profound sorrow for the horrid assassination of ABRAHAM LINCOLN, the illustrious President of the United States.

2. The flag of the Ticino parliament shall be draped in mourning for three days.

The council of this state fully accedes to the above resolution of the grand council of state and the republic.

We hereby communicate it to the federal council, and also to you, according to Mr. Gengel's directions, and avail ourselves of the occasion to express our greatest esteem and consideration.

By the state council:

C. MOROFINI, President.

L. PRIODA, Secretary of State.

[Translation.]

LAUSANNE, *May* 6, 1865.

SIR: In reply to your circular of the 1st instant, we are instructed to inform you that the grand council of this canton, on the proposal of the state council, had voted an address to the Congress of the United States of North America, to express the sentiments of profound regret it feels at the news of the assassination of the President of the United States, and at the same time to give to the Congress and people of the United States a public pledge of sympathy for the cause of liberty, defended with so much patriotism, courage perseverance and moderation by the noble victim whose loss we now deplore.,

Accept the assurance of our distinguished consideration.

In the name of the chancery of the state and canton of Vaud:

THE CHANCELLOR, CAREY.

Mr. F. GENGEL,
 President of the Committee for the Address
  to the Government of the United States, at Berne.

[Translation.]

State council of the canton of Vaud to the Swiss Federal Council in Berne.

LAUSANNE, *May* 8, 1865.

Mr. PRESIDENT AND COLLEAGUES: We have the honor to transmit you a resolution passed by the grand council of the canton of Vaud, at its session of the 3d instant, enclosing an address to the Congress of the United States, on the occasion of the assassination of President LINCOLN.

The resolution is accompanied by a letter addressed to the President of the United States.

We respectfully request you, Mr. President and gentlemen of the council, to have these documents sent to their place of destination through the United States minister resident in Berne.

We accept this opportunity to repeat the assurance of our high consideration, and to recommend you to Divine protection.

In the name of the state council:

JOLY, *President.*

CAREY, *Chancellor.*